STANDARD 3: Observing, Documenting, and Assessing to Support Young Children and Families

NAEYC STANDARDS AND OUTCOMES	CHAPTER AND TOPIC	ADDITIONAL FEATURES
3a. Understanding the goals, benefits, and uses of assessment. 3b. Knowing about assessment partnerships with families and with professional colleagues. 3c. Knowing about and using observation, documentation, and other appropriate assessment tools and approaches. 3d. Understanding and practicing responsible assessment to promote positive outcomes for each child.	CHAPTER 1 Arnold Gesell, 25 • The Child Study Movement, 27 CHAPTER 2 Assessing Program Quality, 56 • The Process of Assessing Programs, 58 • Why Program Assessment Is Important, 58 • Essential Steps Before You Begin, 59 CHAPTER 4 Albert Bandura, 99 • Jean Piaget, 102 • Arnold Gesell, 114 CHAPTER 5 Record Keeping, 145 • Purposes for an Annual Performance Review, 158 • Components of an Effective Assessment, 159 • Self-Evaluation, 159 • Types of Assessments, 161 CHAPTER 6 Key Elements and Purposes of Observation, 168 • Contexts for Understanding Observations, 173 • Common Types of Observation Systems, 176 • Goals and Tools of Child Assessment, 188 • Authentic Assessment: The Portfolio, 197 CHAPTER 7 Actively Observe, 222 CHAPTER 12 Integrating Technology into Learning, 377 CHAPTER 13 Language and Literacy Skills, 402 CHAPTER 15 Program Quality, 470 • Child Abuse and Neglect, 475	CHAPTER 4 Diversity Box: Male/Female Concepts in Girls and Boys, 124 CHAPTER 5 DAP Box: Portfolio-Based Assessment, 162 CHAPTER 6 Diversity Box: Do You Have a "Diversity Bias"?, 172 • Brain Research Says: Observation: Capture the Brain at Work or Overload, 186 • Teaching With Intention: From Observation to Intention and Action, 194 • TeachSource Video: Progress Monitoring: Using Transitional Time in an Early Childhood Classroom, 204 CHAPTER 13 Diversity Box: Speaking with a Stutter, 403

STANDARD 4: Using Developmentally Effective Approaches to Connect with Children and Families

NAEYC STANDARDS AND OUTCOMES	CHAPTER AND TOPIC	ADDITIONAL FEATURES
4a. Understanding positive relationships and supportive interactions as the foundation of their work with children. 4b. Knowing and understanding effective strategies and tools for early education. 4c. Using a broad repertoire of developmentally appropriate teaching/learning approaches. 4d. Reflecting on their own practice to promote positive outcomes for each child.	CHAPTER 1 Mid-century Developments, 22 • Sputnik and the War on Poverty: Head Start, 23 • T. Berry Brazelton, 26 • Importance of Childhood , 31 • Transmitting Values, 31 CHAPTER 2 DAP in Action, 41 • What DAP Looks Like, 42 • Mixed-Age Groupings, 44 • Looping: Continuity of Care, 44 CHAPTER 3 Applying Word Pictures to Teaching Strategies, 70 • Culture, Race, and Ethnic Considerations, 70 • The Inclusive Classroom, 85 • Dealing with Bias and Stereotypes, 86 CHAPTER 4 Play, 119 • Brain Development, 126 CHAPTER 5 Engage in Reflective Teaching, 154 CHAPTER 6 Communicate with Families, 196 • Testing and Screening, 201 • Concerns about Assessment, 203 CHAPTER 7 Guidance, Discipline, and Punishment: What Works, 216 • What Is Guidance?, 216 • Inductive Guidance, 216 • What Is Discipline?, 217 • What Is Punishment?, 217 • Toward Self-Discipline, 218 • The Language of Guidance and Discipline, 218 • Behavior Models, 221 • Preventing Misbehavior, 222 • Indirect Guidance, 223 • Ten Effective Strategies: The Guidance Ladder, 223 • Giving Children Choices, 226 • Setting Limits, 226 • Active Problem Solving, 227 • Time Out, 229 • Physical Intervention, 229 • Behavior That Is Challenging, 229 CHAPTER 9 Developmentally Appropriate Learning Environments, 256 • Three Core Aspects of DAP Environments, 258 • Developmentally Appropriate Schedules, 285 • Defining Interpersonal Elements, 287 CHAPTER 10 Fostering Collaboration and Mutual Learning, 302 • The Teacher's Role in Learning Through Play, 308 • Setting the Stage for Play, 310 • Ways to Foster Skills, Knowledge, and Learning, 311 • Culturally Responsive Teaching, 312 • Teacher-Directed Learning, 317 • The Project Approach, 324 CHAPTER 12 The Internet, 377 CHAPTER 13 A Rich Literary Environment, 396 • Effective Approaches for Curriculum, 404 • Special Topic: Supporting Dual Language Learners, 411 CHAPTER 14 Emotional Skills, 423 • Social Skills, 439 • Creative Skills, 453 • Special Topic: Nurturing Emotional Intelligence, 461 CHAPTER 15 Multicultural Education, 482 • Bilingual Education, 484	CHAPTER 3 Teaching With Intention: Using Word Pictures, 70 CHAPTER 4 DAP Box: Take Piaget with You, 108 • TeachSource Video Case: Young Children's Stages of Play, 120 CHAPTER 7 Teaching With Intention: Inductive Guidance and the Firefighter Rules, 218 • TeachSource Video Case: Elementary Classroom Management: Basic Strategies, 218 • DAP Box: Fostering Developmentally Appropriate Guidance, 221 • Brain Research Says: Do Rewards Work?, 225 • TeachSource Video Case: Guidance for Young Children: Teaching Techniques for Encouraging Positive Behavior, 227 CHAPTER 8 Teaching With Intention: Saying Good-Bye, 248 CHAPTER 9 Diversity Box: A Place at the Table, 261 • Teaching With Intention: Noise and Busy-ness, 288 CHAPTER 10 Teaching With Intention: A Balancing Act: Child-Directed and Teacher-Directed Experiences, 318 • Brain Research Says: The Brainy Teacher, 328 CHAPTER 12 DAP Box: A Teaching Style for Intellectual Development, 359 • TeachSource Video Case: Exploring Math Concepts through Creative Activities, 365 CHAPTER 13 Teaching With Intention: Contribute to Communication Competence, 406 • DAP Box: Set up a Literacy Yard, 408 • TeachSource Video Case: English Language Learners: Partnering with Parents, 413 CHAPTER 14 Diversity Box: Feelings: What If the Messages Are Different?, 427 • Teaching with Intention: Do I *Have* to Share?, 448 CHAPTER 15 Teaching With Intention: Helping Children Cope with Stress, 475

Continued in back

Beginnings and Beyond

Foundations in Early Childhood Education

**NINTH
EDITION**

Beginnings
and Beyond

Foundations in Early Childhood Education

Ann Miles Gordon

Kathryn Williams Browne
Skyline College

WADSWORTH
CENGAGE Learning·

Australia • Brazil • Japan • Korea • Mexico • Singapore • Spain • United Kingdom • United States

Beginnings and Beyond: Foundations in Early Childhood Education, Ninth Edition
Ann Miles Gordon and Kathryn Williams Browne

Editor-in-Chief: Linda Ganster

Executive Editor: Mark Kerr

Managing Development Editor: Lisa Mafrici

Editorial Assistant: Greta Lindquist

Media Editor: Elizabeth Momb

Brand Manager: Melissa Larmon

Senior Market Development Manager: Kara Kindstrom

Content Project Manager: Samen Iqbal

Art Director: Jennifer Wahi

Manufacturing Planner: Doug Bertke

Rights Acquisitions Specialist: Tom McDonough

Production and Composition: Graphic World Inc.

Photo Researcher: Megan Lessard

Text Researcher: Pablo D'Stair

Copy Editor: Graphic World Inc.

Text Designer: Lisa Buckley

Cover Designer: CMB Design

Cover Image: iStock_000015933195 © Anaimd

For product information and technology assistance, contact us at
**Cengage Learning Customer & Sales Support,
1-800-354-9706.**
For permission to use material from this text or product,
submit all requests online at
www.cengage.com/permissions.
Further permissions questions can be e-mailed to
permissionrequest@cengage.com.

The Standards and Key Elements are from NAEYC, "NAEYC Standards for Early Childhood Professional Preparation." Position Statement. Washington, DC: NAEYC. Reprinted with permission from the National Association for the Education of Young Children (NAEYC). Copyright © 2009 by NAEYC. Full text of all NAEYC position statements is available at www.naeyc.org/positionstatements. These correlations are suggested by the authors.

Library of Congress Control Number: 2012942037

Student Edition:

ISBN-13: 978-1-133-93696-1

ISBN-10: 1-133-93696-2

Loose-leaf Edition:

ISBN-13: 978-1-133-94054-8

ISBN-10: 1-133-94054-4

Wadsworth
20 Davis Drive
Belmont, CA 94002-3098
USA

Cengage Learning is a leading provider of customized learning solutions with office locations around the globe, including Singapore, the United Kingdom, Australia, Mexico, Brazil, and Japan. Locate your local office at **www.cengage.com/global.**

Cengage Learning products are represented in Canada by Nelson Education, Ltd.

To learn more about Wadsworth, visit **www.cengage.com/wadsworth**

Purchase any of our products at your local college store or at our preferred online store **www.CengageBrain.com.**

Printed in the United States of America
3 4 5 6 7 16 15 14

Dedication

To the women who share this regenerative stage
of life with me, with grateful thanks for their abundant
spirits and generous hearts: Puddin Nix, Sally Zimmerman,
and Jan Moore.
— AMG

To the students and colleagues of Skyline
College—a most inspiring mix of professionals
and fellow learners on the path of higher education.
And to Julia and Campbell, once again: my inspiration
as children and now as wonderful adults.
— KWB

Contents

SECTION 2
Who Is the Young Child?   65

CHAPTER 3
Defining the Young Child   66

CHAPTER 4
Developmental and Learning Theories   90

SECTION 3
Who Are the Teachers?   139

CHAPTER 5
Teaching: A Professional Commitment   140

SECTION 4
What Is Being Taught?   295

CHAPTER 10
Curriculum: Creating a Context for Learning and Play   296

CHAPTER 11
Planning for the Body: Physical/Motor Development in Action   336

SECTION 5
How Do We Teach for Tomorrow?   467

Preface

Our Viewpoint

The early childhood field is a dynamic profession full of many challenges and great rewards. Teachers being trained today have the opportunity to respond to and affect the critical issues facing early childhood educators now and in the future. Students confront the challenge of teaching a diverse group of learners differentiated by their abilities, ethnic and cultural backgrounds, family support, values, and beliefs. They learn to navigate the tension between standards and assessments and developmentally appropriate principles and practice. Through field experiences, students experience the everyday commitment to children's growth and learning. They learn the meaning of professionalism and how their personal development fosters their professional life. In order to accomplish this daunting but exciting task, students need a text that is current, comprehensive, and able to connect knowledge and theory to the classroom—one that has a variety of models and that deepens their understanding of themselves as members of a lively and fulfilling profession. *Beginnings and Beyond: Foundations in Early Childhood Education* accomplishes that goal.

The purpose of *Beginnings and Beyond* is to promote the competence and effectiveness of new teachers through a presentation of basic knowledge, skills, attitudes, and philosophies based on the premise that new teachers must have opportunities to learn fundamental skills as they begin their teaching experience. The text expresses a viewpoint about quality early education and what practices ensure excellence. In the area of cultural sensitivity and multicultural relationships, we promote a "both/and" attitude, following the National Association for the Education of Young Children (NAEYC) guidelines for developmentally appropriate practices. The "both/and" thinking provides a flexible, nonpolarizing approach to the complexities of early childhood practices. Readers will find the "both/and" influence throughout the text but especially in the areas of early literacy, spiritual development, discipline, diversity, and anti-bias strategies. The point of "both/and" is particularly emphasized in school and family relationships where cultural differences and distinctions are always at play.

Culturally Appropriate Practice and Developmentally Appropriate Practice

Culturally appropriate practice and developmentally appropriate practice continue to be subthemes of this text. We emphasize the importance of creating programs and building curricula based on an understanding of the nature of the child and the factors affecting a child's growth and development. We believe it is important that students realize the deep and crucial contributions that children's family, culture, and language make to development. NAEYC's years of experience in the definition and application of developmentally appropriate practice have given us further insights, which are reflected throughout the book.

Demographic issues drive the direction of early childhood programs, and the text reflects that fact. *Beginnings and Beyond* maintains the emphasis that every child and family is unique and that they deserve the respect and affirmation of their cultural identity. This edition, therefore, weaves a strong multicultural perspective and consciousness throughout the text to help prospective teachers and caregivers increase their sensitivity to different cultural practices and values. This feature has become one of the book's strongest points.

How Do We Meet the Needs of Today's Learners?

Beginnings and Beyond is intended for college students who are interested in young children, beginning teachers who plan to engage in early care and education, practitioners in direct service to children and families, and professionals in the workforce who are enlarging their knowledge base. Through our comprehensive chapter coverage and unique pedagogical features, we provide a resource that meets the needs of today's early child educators.

Chapter Organization

The overall organization of the book takes the student from the history of early childhood education to current issues and future trends. Four key themes emphasized in the beginning and ending chapters weave the past and present together as students learn about (1) social reform, (2) the importance of childhood, (3) transmitting values, and (4) professionalism.

Five basic questions set the tone for each section by asking the reader to reflect on the wide-ranging nature of early childhood education. The book's flexibility allows instructors to begin with any section that seems appropriate to meet the needs of their classes. The five sections and chapter descriptions are as follows:

- **What Is the Field of Early Childhood Education?** In Section 1, descriptions of early childhood history and the types of programs provide a basis for understanding the complexity of the field.

  Chapter 1 describes the origin of early education through history, which forms the theory on which students base their teaching, and then students learn about events that have shaped the field. Students meet the many contributors to early childhood education, such as the famous (Rousseau, Dewey, and Hill), the ancient (the Greeks), and contemporary influences (Reggio Emilia). New ideas about building a personal philosophy of teaching and neuroscience challenge students to apply historical ideas to present-day practices.

  Chapter 2 moves the student directly into the importance of developmentally appropriate practice (DAP) in creating good programs for young children. The principles of DAP are matched with examples of DAP in action so that students see a direct correlation between the DAP criteria and classroom application. A discussion of early childhood core programs leads into variations of programs for different ages. The section on the relationship between assessment and high-quality programs helps students understand the various issues that affect quality.

- **Who Is the Young Child?** Section 2 begins with a discussion of the young child's growth, followed by an overview of the developmental and learning theories that form the cornerstone of our knowledge about children.

  Chapter 3 provides students with an understanding of the nature of the children they teach and their common characteristics, wide individual differences, and those with special needs. Word Pictures, which are age-level descriptions, are a popular feature with students who have used this text because they enable students to anticipate children's needs and plan appropriate experiences that are inclusive of all children.

  Chapter 4 gives the student a concise description of universal and life span theories and other developmental topics on which sound teaching principles and practices are based. Play, as a cornerstone of learning, and updated information on gender stereotyping and neuroscience research put the theories to use.

- **Who Are the Teachers?** Section 3 defines the aggregate of influences that act as teachers in the early childhood setting. Each chapter enlarges the student's view of what makes up a professional teacher.

  Chapter 5 describes the roles and responsibilities of an early childhood teacher as "professionalism in action" and introduces students to a broader definition of teaching. Examples of everyday ethical dilemmas provide opportunities for students to discuss their values and beliefs in response to the NAEYC Code of Ethical Conduct. The chapter also explores team-teaching situations, the importance of teacher evaluations, and the key elements for successful field experiences.

  Chapter 6 enhances the student's ability to observe and record the behavior of young children. Along with a comprehensive description of observational tools and effective techniques, there are updated segments about child evaluation, early learning standards, and concerns about testing and screening.

  Chapter 7 demonstrates how guidance and behavior are critical factors in the life of a classroom teacher through vignettes that help the student understand how and why young children behave as they do. Problem solving, conflict resolution, and a wide range of guidance techniques give students the necessary tools to guide young children's behavior.

Chapter 8 offers the student a perspective on the all-important collaboration of families and teachers in creating the best possible learning environment for young children. Discussions of the definition of a family, today's family structures, and challenges facing parents bring a relevancy to students' experiences.

Chapter 9 defines the characteristics of high-quality environments that include elements of health, safety, and nutrition, as well as approaches that emphasize anti-bias, self-help, and the inclusion of children with varying abilities. Key dimensions of the physical, temporal, and interpersonal environments help students understand how the intentional use of the environment serves as a teaching strategy for positive behavior and engaged learning.

■ **What Is Being Taught?** Section 4 is a composite answer to the all-important question, "What are we teaching our children?" The first chapter in the section discusses the role of the curriculum and is followed by four chapters that address curriculum for the major developmental domains.

Chapter 10 is based on the premise that a play-based curriculum is the foundation for early childhood learning, and the chapter provides students with examples and models of developmentally and culturally appropriate approaches to a play-based curriculum. Students learn the importance of play, how to develop emergent and integrated curricula, and how to create projects. They understand how different learning styles can be applied to curriculum development and look at five popular curriculum models.

Chapter 11 explores the physical and motor skills of young children, the importance of learning through movement, and basic skills children need to learn. This chapter helps the student plan appropriate experiences and curriculum that strengthen children's physical growth.

Chapter 12 translates cognitive research, such as developmental psychology, multiple intelligences, and neuroscience, into curriculum practices, along with the special topic of computers in a program.

Chapter 13 addresses the development of language and literacy, the many ways teachers provide skill experiences for children, and the special topic of supporting dual language learners.

Chapter 14 offers conceptual information about the psychosocial domain (emotional, social, creative, and spiritual dimensions), and effective curriculum

approaches for feelings, sharing, music and movement, and a special topic of emotional intelligence.

■ **How Do We Teach for Tomorrow?** Section 5, which encompasses Chapter 15, helps the student take a broad look at issues facing the early childhood field today. It also serves as a bookend to the first chapter, repeating the four basic themes of the text in light of current needs.

1. "Ethic of Social Reform" reflects current issues such as affordable child care, universal preschools, and the influence of national legislation.
2. "The Importance of Childhood" explores childhood stress, abuse and neglect, poverty, and divorce and their effects on children.
3. "Transmitting Values" includes the media culture, the effect of violence and disasters, and class differences.
4. In the "Professionalism" section, standards are discussed, as are wages and work conditions and child advocacy.

In each of these sections, the students learn about the reality of children's lives and how early childhood professionals can help them prepare for the challenges and responsibilities of adult life.

Special Features and Pedagogy

We offer numerous learning aids and engaging features to enrich the learning experience of students and to connect theory to practice. These include:

■ **NEW—Learning Objectives** at the beginning of the chapter match the main chapter headings to provide students with a clear road map to the topics they will encounter in each chapter. The end-of-chapter Summary, Review Questions, and Observe and Apply activities are also linked to the Learning Objectives.

■ **NEW—The NAEYC Standards for Initial and Advanced Early Childhood Professional Preparation** that apply to each chapter are

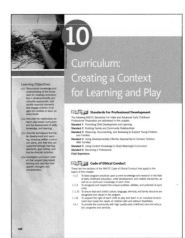

noted at the beginning of the chapter to help students focus on relevant chapter content.

■ **The NAEYC Code of Ethical Conduct,** which highlights core values, ideals, and principles that apply to the chapter content, is featured at the beginning of each chapter. This feature provides opportunities for students to become familiar with the Code of Ethical Conduct and see its direct application to the teaching experience.

■ **NEW—Brain Research Says . . .** is a new feature in each chapter that highlights some of the most important aspects of brain research and development today. The research is linked to classroom use and teacher application through questions that invite students to reflect on how this relates to their teaching.

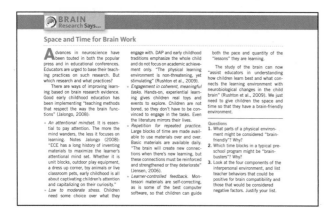

■ **NEW—Teaching With Intention** is a highlighted section in each chapter that discusses a concrete example related to the chapter content of how intentional teaching is practiced in early childhood programs. The questions at the end promote reflective teaching on the part of the student.

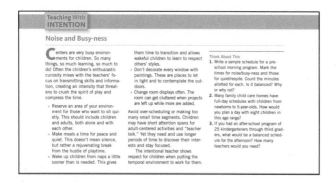

■ **TeachSource Video** features allow students and instructors to relate important chapter content to real-life scenarios in early child care settings. The

videos provide students with an opportunity to hear from real educators who are doing the work that they are preparing to do. The Video Cases and other engaging video clips provided on the Education CourseMate website offer critical thinking questions and give students ample opportunities for reflection and discussion.

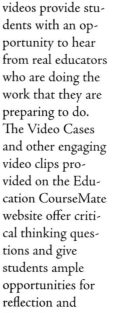

■ **NEW—Developmentally Appropriate Practice (DAP) boxes** are included in each chapter to emphasize material that represents a DAP. This feature gives the student reader a concrete example of DAP in action.

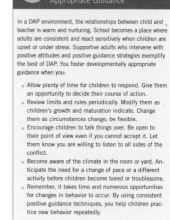

■ **NEW—Diversity feature boxes** in every chapter bring attention to a relevant aspect of diversity (e.g., gender, language, inclusion, culture) as an integral part of the teaching experience and expand the student's understanding of what diversity means in the early childhood setting.

■ **The Word Pictures special section** in Chapter 3 describes the major characteristics of children from infancy through 8 years of age. This popular feature helps students become familiar with expected behaviors in young children as a frame of reference for creating programs and planning curriculum that responds to the children's interests as well as their abilities and needs.

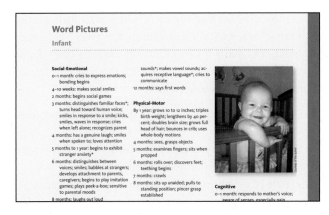

Word Pictures

Infant

Social-Emotional
0–1 month: cries to express emotions; bonding begins
4–10 weeks: makes social smiles
2 months: begins social games
3 months: distinguishes familiar faces*; turns head toward human voice; smiles in response to a smile; kicks, smiles, waves in response; cries when left alone; recognizes parent
4 months: has a genuine laugh; smiles when spoken to; loves attention
5 months to 1 year: begins to exhibit stranger anxiety*
6 months: distinguishes between voices; smiles; babbles at strangers; develops attachment to parents, caregivers; begins to play imitation games; plays peek-a-boo; sensitive to parental moods
8 months: laughs out loud

sounds*; makes vowel sounds; acquires receptive language*; cries to communicate
12 months: says first words

Physical-Motor
By 1 year: grows 10 to 12 inches; triples birth weight; lengthens by 40 percent; doubles brain size; grows full head of hair; bounces in crib; uses whole-body motions
4 months: sees, grasps objects
5 months: examines fingers; sits when propped
6 months: rolls over; discovers feet; teething begins
7 months: crawls
8 months: sits up unaided; pulls to standing position; pincer grasp established

Cognitive
0–1 month: responds to mother's voice; aware of senses, especially pain

- **New and improved end-of-chapter aids** provide the student with an overall review of the material within the chapter. The Summary, Review Questions, and Observe and Apply features are linked to the Learning Objectives at the beginning of the chapter and to the main chapter headings and suggest practical ways to integrate knowledge, theory, and experience. Key terms remind students of the most important concepts and the Helpful Websites and References provide added resources for students to expand their knowledge.

- **A correlation chart to the latest NAEYC Standards for Initial and Advanced Early Childhood Professional Preparation** is found on the inside covers of this book. The handy chart makes it easier for students to see where the key standards in the field are addressed in specific chapters and topics throughout the text.

What's New in This Edition

The ninth edition of *Beginnings and Beyond* represents a completely updated work, both in the content and presentation. Some highlights of the new coverage and features include:

- **Every chapter has been honed to improve readability,** allowing students to readily grasp the material through features that challenge them to think about their desire to teach, inform them of best practices, and reinforce the content.

- Students will find **information that is presented in a truly accessible manner,** from the all-new chapter opening pedagogy and learning aids (such as the new Learning Objectives keyed to chapter headings and the addition of relevant NAEYC Standards for Early Childhood Professional Preparation) to the comprehensive study and review materials at the end

of the chapter (Summary, Review Questions, and Observe and Apply activities). In addition, we streamlined and reorganized several key chapters for better comprehension.

- New special boxed features on **neuroscience/brain research and development** called "Brain Research Says . . ." draw out connections to brain research in relation to specific chapter content and conclude with critical thinking questions.

- **Developmentally Appropriate Practice (DAP)** discussions are highlighted in each chapter as a separate feature and references are found throughout the text.

- **Diversity** continues to be integrated and emphasized throughout the text, but it is also highlighted with a new Diversity boxed feature in each chapter.

- The topic of **intentional teaching** is highlighted with a boxed feature "Teaching With Intention" in each chapter that offers a specific, content-related example and reflection questions.

- **Updated and increased coverage of standards and accountability** are noted at the beginning of each chapter, as well as on the inside covers. NAEYC Standards for Professional Preparation links are added to the beginning of each chapter, as are relevant Code of Ethical Conduct references. An NAEYC Standards Correlation Chart is found on the inside covers of the book for quick references to relevant chapters.

- **Expanded coverage of key areas,** including play-based learning, children with special needs, behavior that is challenging, team teaching, diversity, emergent curriculum, brain-based learning, technology and digital media use, professionalism, school-age children, and current issues and trends in the field.

- **Expanded TeachSource Video features** are integrated into each chapter to illustrate topics and best practices, accompanied by questions for reflection.

- **A completely new and improved design** strengthens our presentation and improves students' comprehension.

Accompanying Teaching and Learning Resources

The ninth edition of *Beginnings and Beyond* offers many ancillary materials that can support and enhance the text experience and an instructor's presentation of the course. From planning to presentation to testing, materials are available to provide students with an engaging and relevant exposure to the broad scope of topics in early childhood education.

Instructor's Manual and Test Bank

The updated instructor's manual provides a chapter-by-chapter plan for organizing a course using *Beginnings and Beyond*. In addition to chapter overviews, outlines, key terms, resource lists, discussion topics, and teaching tips, this manual also includes a test bank with true/false, multiple-choice, matching, and short answer questions for each chapter.

Microsoft PowerPoint® Lectures

Vibrant PowerPoint® lecture slides for each chapter assist you with your lecture by providing concept coverage using images, figures, and tables directly from the textbook.

Education CourseMate Website

Cengage Learning's Education CourseMate website brings course concepts to life with interactive learning, study, and exam preparation tools that support the printed textbook. CourseMate includes an integrated eBook, quizzes, flashcards, TeachSource Videos with associated questions, and more, including EngagementTracker, a first-of-its-kind tool that monitors student engagement in the course. The accompanying instructor website offers access to password-protected resources such as an electronic version of the instructor's manual, test bank, and PowerPoint slides. To access the instructor website, please visit **www.cengage.com/login.** Students should visit www.cengagbrain.com to register their code or purchase access.

WebTutor™ with eBook for Blackboard and WebCT

Jump-start your course with customizable, rich, text-specific content within your Course Management System. Whether you want to web-enable your class or put an entire course online, WebTutor delivers. WebTutor offers a wide array of resources, including access to the eBook, quizzes, flashcards, TeachSource Videos with associated questions, and more.

Professional Enhancement Series

An additional supplement to accompany the ninth edition is the Introduction to Early Childhood Education Professional Enhancement resource for students. This resource, which is part of Wadsworth Cengage Learning's Early Childhood Education Professional Enhancement Series, focuses on key topics of interest to future early childhood teachers, directors, and caregivers. This supplement, and other "primers" on key areas in early childhood education, can be bundled with this text on request. Some of the tools provided are:

- Tips for getting off to a great start in your new environment.
- Suggestions for materials that promote development for children from infancy through primary grades.
- Tools to assist in observing children and in gathering data to help set appropriate goals for individual children.
- Case studies of relevant, realistic situations and best practices for successfully navigating them.
- Insights into issues and trends facing early childhood educators today.

About the Authors

Ann Miles Gordon has been an early childhood professional for more than 45 years as a teacher of young children, a teacher of parents, and a teacher of college students. She has taught in laboratory schools, church-related centers, and private and public preschool and kindergarten programs. Ann taught at the Bing Nursery School, the laboratory school for Stanford University's Department of Psychology, where she was a head teacher and lecturer in the Psychology Department. Ann also served as an adjunct faculty member in several community colleges, teaching the full gamut of early

Courtesy of the auth

childhood courses. Ann served for 14 years as executive director of the National Association of Episcopal Schools, where more than 1,100 early childhood programs were a part of her network. Ann is semi-retired and a hands-on grandmother of two, through which she brings an enhanced perspective on infants and toddlers to *Beginnings and Beyond*, as well as up-to-date experience with center-based child care.

Kathryn Williams Browne has been teaching children, families, and students for more than 30 years. First a teacher of young children—nursery school, parent cooperative, full-day child care, prekindergarten, bilingual preschool, kindergarten, and first grade—she later moved to Stanford University's lab school, where she served as head teacher and psychology lecturer. Coauthoring *Beginnings and Beyond* with Ann was enhanced by Kate's role as a parent: her two children were born during the first two editions, so the book grew along with them. Her consultant and school board experience offered perspectives into public policy and reform. Kate teaches in the California Community College system, coordinating the Early Childhood Department and the Early Childhood Mentor program, which offer the richness of a diverse student population coupled with the challenges of access and privilege that parallel those in the early education field itself. Special assignments include the State Faculty Association, Academic Senate, and Educator Competencies integration, which add special challenges of diversity and professionalism of early childhood education.

Ann and Kate are also coauthors of *Beginning Essentials in Early Childhood Education* (Wadsworth Cengage Learning, 2013), *Early Childhood Field Experiences: Learning to Teach Well* (Pearson, 2014), and *Guiding Young Children in a Diverse Society* (Pearson, in revision).

Acknowledgments

At Cengage Learning, we would like to thank Lisa Mafrici, managing development editor, for her skillful guidance, constant encouragement, and patience; Mark Kerr for his wry humor and enthusiasm for our project; and to the rest of the team at Cengage Learning for their professionalism and support.

Our reviewers, whose valuable gift of time and energy enhances the book's usefulness, have been superb with their insights and suggestions. We want to thank:

Nurun Begum	East Stroudsburg University
Josephine Fritts	Ozarks Technical Community College
Jeanne Helm	Richland Community College
Miranda Lin	Illinois State University
Linda Mahoney	Mississippi University for Women
Barb Tengesdal	University of Mary
Valerie Valentine	University of Rio Grande/Rio Grande Community College
Richard Wagner	Front Range Community College
Eileen Yantz	Gaston College

Beginnings and Beyond

Foundations in Early Childhood Education

What Is the Field of Early Childhood Education?

SECTION 1

1

History of Early Childhood Education

Learning Objectives

LO1 List the major historical contributions from outside the United States that influence modern early childhood education.

LO2 Describe the primary influences within the United States on early childhood education.

LO3 Identify the three professions that closely connect to the field and their major contributions to early childhood education.

LO4 Define the four major themes that shape practices and policies of early childhood education.

naeyc Standards For Professional Development

The following NAEYC Standards for early childhood professional development are addressed in this chapter:

Standard 1 Promoting Child Development and Learning
Standard 2 Building Family and Community Relationships
Standard 5 Using Content Knowledge to Build Meaningful Curriculum
Standard 6 Becoming a Professional

naeyc Code of Ethical Conduct

These are the sections of the NAEYC Code of Ethical Conduct that apply to the topics of this chapter:

Core Values: We have committed ourselves to appreciating childhood as a unique and valuable stage of the human life cycle.
Section I. Childhood is a unique and valuable stage of the human life cycle.
Section I I-1.3. To recognize and respect the uniqueness and the potential of each child.
Section III I-3B.2. To do nothing that diminishes the reputation of the program in which we work unless it is violating laws and regulations designed to protect children of the provisions of this Code.

Please refer to Figure 1-2, *An Abbreviated Timeline for Early Childhood Education,* and online at the Education ⓔ CourseMate for an expanded timeline as you read this chapter.

Introduction

Early childhood education has a rich and exciting history. The stories of our field chronicle courageous people who took steps toward improving children's lives. Critical events have had a hand in shaping the history of early childhood education. As the conditions of childhood and early education have changed through the centuries, its educators have also adapted to those challenges.

While reading this chapter, imagine yourself as a time traveler. As you go back in time, you span the centuries and meet the people whose vision helped to shape our profession. You learn how Froebel's own unhappy childhood inspired a new way of teaching called the kindergarten. You see the passion and struggle of Montessori as she convinces the world that "slum children" can learn and succeed. In the 1960s, you witness the dedication of America to create a program for preschoolers known as "Head Start." You see early childhood teaching become a profession that includes infants and toddlers, as well as kindergarten and early primary grades.

There is more than one right way to educate young children. Every culture has the task of socializing and educating their young. The historical record may document several educational philosophies, but there is no single monopoly on ideas about children. People inside the United States and across the world have influenced our ideas about children and their education. Other disciplines (medicine, education, and psychology) inform early childhood teaching. Current issues always influence what is happening for young children and their teachers. What emerge are some consistent themes over time.

All professions have a canon of beliefs and practices. As you acquire this knowledge, you begin to develop your own *philosophy of teaching* (based, in part, on information gathered in this chapter). As you do, be sure to constantly rethink your practices. See "Teaching With Intention" to delve into why knowing the history of early childhood education is important.

All professionals should re-examine themselves on a regular basis because although understanding historical records makes sense for **professional** development, recognizing that they are a reflection of certain cultural norms is also crucial. For example, mainstream educational philosophy claims the following

areas are "universal," but cross-cultural research has shown them not to be:

- Early attainment of individuality and independence.
- The necessity of early and free exploration.
- The critical importance of the early stimulation of intellect and language.

The first reflects a priority of many Western European cultures, but it is not a common practice in societies that promote group harmony and interdependence. Second, many indigenous groups hold their very young children close, carrying them along while they work; there is no data that indicate these children develop poorly. Third, although American educational systems of the early 21st century are building on increasing academic and intellectual standards, there is no universal mandate for an exclusive focus on this developmental domain in the early years. Figure 1-1 offers other traditional educational practices, their historical context, and alternatives to consider as you create your own educational philosophy. Perhaps some of the mistakes of the past can be avoided if history is remembered.

Defining the Terms

The term **early childhood education** refers to group settings deliberately intended to affect developmental changes in children from birth to 8 years of age. In school terms, it includes group settings for infants through the primary years of elementary school, kindergarten through 3rd grade in the United States. In programmatic terms, the education of young children includes formal and informal group settings regardless of their initial purpose. For instance, after-school programs for elementary ages are included, as are their formal academic sessions.

Early childhood educators thus build bridges between a child's two worlds: school (or group experience) and home. It is during these years that the foundation for future learning is set; these are the **building block years**, during which a child learns to walk, talk, establish an identity, print, and count. In later years, that same child builds on these skills to be able to climb mountains, speak a second language, learn to express and negotiate, write in cursive, and understand multiplication.

Influences from Abroad

When did early childhood education first begin? Refer to Figure 1-2, *An Abbreviated Timeline for Early Childhood Education,* and to the expanded timeline on the

Why Does History Help?

Most early childhood education students and many educators know little about the origins of their chosen profession. To better build your philosophy of teaching, note the links between the past to *your* present:

Support: Learning the works of others gives us validation of our ideas. The philosophies of Froebel, Montessori, and Dewey are part of the foundation of our educational practices. Traditional early childhood practices reflect European values and beliefs, and looking beyond the dominant culture to writings of Africa, Asia, and South America broadens your viewpoint.

Inspiration: Knowing our deep roots helps develop professional expression. Ideas of past educators offer you more methods of teaching. An historical overview clarifies how children and learning are viewed based on the religious, political, and economic pressures.

Identity and Commitment: Accepting the mission of our field commits you to enhancing the education, development, and well-being of young children. Such identity brings with it an awareness of the diversity in cultural norms. Be cautious of theories or opinions claiming to be "universal." For instance, history notes that schools of the past were overwhelmingly created for boys; this gender bias of past practices adds to the underdevelopment of girls and prevails today in parts of the world.

Add your voice to those crusaders for education as you create your personal philosophy of education. Include an element of reform in making the work of teaching into a legitimate profession. Listen to their voices, so you can develop your own.

Think About This

1. If you didn't know anything about the history of the field, what mistakes would you likely make in your first year of teaching?
2. Which historical figures interest you in developing a personal philosophy of teaching?
3. What are the strongest ideas that draw you into this work? Why would finding historical roots for your professional identity help you in your career?

---

accompanying Education CourseMate as you read this chapter. Getting a visual sense of when and where things happened can help you make sense of the various threads in our tapestry of early childhood educational history.

Looking at the timeline lets you see how impressive the accomplishments really are. For instance, there are many anniversaries to celebrate at this time (Fanjul, 2011):

- Forty-five years ago: Congress passed bills that authorized both Head Start and Elementary and Secondary Education Act/Title 1.
- Twenty-five years ago: NAEYC's accreditation for programs serving young children was launched.
- Twenty years ago: The Child Care and Development Block Grant was created to help working families afford child care.

In addition, the timeline helps us see that it is impossible to pinpoint the origins of humankind. There are few records from millions of years ago. Some preparation for adult life was done informally, mostly through imitation. As language developed, communication occurred. Children learned dances, rituals, and ceremonies, and both boys and girls were taught skills for their respective roles in the tribe. Ancient historical documents seem to indicate that child-rearing practices were somewhat crude;

DeMause (1974) even suggests that the further one goes back in history, the more likely the case of abandonment and brutality.

European Roots

The definition of childhood has varied greatly throughout history. For example, in ancient times children were considered adults by age 7. A society's definition of childhood influences how it educates its children.

In Ancient Times

Many of our own practices are founded on those developed in Greece and Rome. Greek education—and virtually all classical European schooling—was provided for the boys of wealthy families, while girls and working-class children received training for domestic work or a trade.

Education began by age 6 or 7, although Plato and Aristotle both spoke of the need to educate the younger child. Some ancient Romans felt that education should begin at home as soon as a child began to talk, and they highlighted the use of rewards and the ineffectiveness of corporal punishment (Hewes, 1993).

Probably the first education in schools outside the home or homelike apprenticeship was in ancient Greek

Reflecting on Practices: Building Your Philosophy of Teaching

Educational Practice	Historical Context and ECE Trend/Practice	Think Again . . .
Same-age grouping	K–12 schools in the United States since 1850s target curriculum goals.	■ Learning takes place with "guided collaboration," which often occurs with an older "expert." ■ Children learn when challenged to accommodate to higher level thinking, likely to occur with a mixed-age range. ■ Developing values of caring and responsibility happen best when children practice helping and protecting younger children. ■ Reduced family size indicates that multi-age experiences should happen in schooling. ■ Diversity (gender, culture, exceptionality, etc.) makes strict target goals unrealistic.
Daily schedules	Routines are the framework for programs, offering security and predictability.	■ Children's sense of time is unlike that of adults, so rigid schedules do not correspond to their development. ■ Brain research indicates a need for stimulation, change, and challenge rather than the same structure constantly.
Curriculum is at the center of good programs.	A plan for learning should be driven by specific outcomes in order to be assured that children are learning.	■ Not following an adult-planned and driven curriculum worked well for geniuses such as Einstein, Erikson, and Bill Gates. ■ Educators as diverse as Dewey and Steiner promoted curricula based on children's interests or innate spirit. ■ Children appear to learn well through a curriculum that emerges, following their interests and timetable.

© Cengage Learning 2011

FIGURE 1-1 As you develop a philosophy of teaching, be sure to examine common beliefs and practices of the profession.

and Roman times. Plato (427 BC), Aristotle (384–323 BC), Cicero (143–106 BC), and Polybius (222–204 BC) founded schools, with the model of small-group tutoring, teaching wealthy boys thinking skills, governing, military strategy, and managing commerce. Our word *educate* comes from a Latin verb *educare*, through a French verb *educere*, to draw forth or to lead.

As the Roman Empire deteriorated and society fell apart (400–1200 AD), childhood lasted barely beyond infancy. Although education was the responsibility of

parents, most were busy fighting for survival. Childhood was not seen as a separate time of life, and children were used in the labor force. People left villages and towns for the safety of a local baron or king, and schools ceased to exist. Few members of the ruling class could read or write their names, and the monastery schools were for priests and religious instruction only.

The education of children was fairly simple before the 15th century; there was no educational system, and the way of life was uncomplicated as well. The

An Abbreviated Timeline for Early Childhood Education

Authors' Note: A debt of gratitude is owed to D. Keith Osborn for his outstanding historical research and to James L. Hymes, Jr., for his generous time and perspective.

5th–3rd centuries BC to AD 1400s Few records exist concerning child-rearing practices; the development of cities gives rise to schooling on a larger scale.

1423 & 1439 The invention of printing and movable type allows knowledge to spread rapidly; ideas and techniques become available to large numbers of people; printing is credited with bringing about the end of the Middle Ages and the beginning of the Renaissance.

1657 *Orbis Pictus,* by Comenius, is the first children's book with pictures.

1690 John Locke published his essay, which postulated that children are born with a tabula rasa, or clean slate, on which all experiences are written.

1740–1860s Sabbath Schools and Clandestine Schools are established as facilities to educate African Americans in the United States.

1762 *Emile,* by Rousseau, proclaims the child's natural goodness.

1801 *How Gertrude Teaches Her Children,* by Pestalozzi, emphasizes home education.

1826 *Education of Man,* by Froebel, describes the first system of kindergarten education as a "child's garden," with activities known as "gifts from God."

1837 Froebel opens the first kindergarten in Blankenburgh, Germany.

1860 Elizabeth Peabody opens the first English-speaking kindergarten in Boston.

1861 Robert Owen sets up infant school in New Lanark, England, as an instrument of social reform for children of parent workers in his mills.

1871 The first public kindergarten in North America opens in Ontario, Canada. (First public American kindergarten: 1873).

1873 The Butler School at Hampton Institute is opened as a free school for black children, including kindergarten curriculum for five-year-olds.

1880 First teacher-training program for kindergartners, Oshkosh Normal School, Pennsylvania.

1892 International Kindergarten Union founded; becomes the Association for Childhood Education in 1930, increasing its scope to include elementary education.

1896 John Dewey establishes a laboratory school at the University of Chicago and develops a pragmatic approach to education, becoming the father of the Progressive Movement in American education.

1897 *My Pedagogic Creed* is published, detailing the opposition to rote learning and the philosophy of educating "the whole child."

1903 The Committee of Nineteen, a splinter group of the International Kindergarten Union, forms to report various philosophical concepts. Members include Patty Smith Hill, Lucy Wheelock, and Susan Blow.

1907 Casa di Bambini (Children's House) is opened by Maria Montessori in a slum district in Rome, Italy. She later develops an educational philosophy and program to guide children's growth through the senses and practical life experiences.

1909 First White House Conference on Children is held by Theodore Roosevelt, leading to the establishment of the Children's Bureau in 1912.

1911 Deptford School, an open-air school in the slums of London, is opened by Margaret McMillan. The school emphasizes health and play, thus coining the phrase "nursery school."

1915 First U.S. Montessori school opens in New York City.

1916 The Bureau of Educational Experiments, which becomes Bank Street College of Education (and laboratory school) in 1922, is founded by L. S. Mitchell, who is a leading proponent of progressive education at the early childhood level.

FIGURE 1-2 An abbreviated timeline for early childhood education (see the Education CourseMate for an expanded version).

1916 First Cooperative Nursery School opens at the University of Chicago.

1918 First public nursery schools are opened in England.

1921 A. S. Neill founds Summerhill school in England, which becomes a model for the "free school" movement (the book entitled *Summerhill* is published in 1960).

1922 Abigail Eliot opens Ruggles Street Nursery School and Training Center.

1925–1926 The National Committee on Nursery Schools is founded by Patty Smith Hill; it becomes NANE and eventually NAEYC.

1926 Gesell establishes the Clinic of Child Development at Yale University and studies norms of child growth and behavior.

1926–1927 Research facilities are founded at several American universities and colleges (e.g., Smith College, Vassar College, Yale University, and Mills College).

1927 Dorothy Howard establishes the first Black Nursery School in Washington, DC, and operates it for over 50 years.

1929 Lois Meeks Stolz names the first President of the National Association for Nursery Education (later to become National Association for the Education of Young Children), and joins the Teachers College (Columbia University) faculty to start the laboratory school and Child Development Institute. Stolz later becomes the Director of the Kaiser Child Service Centers during World War II.

1929 Susan Isaacs publishes *The Nursery Years*, which contradicts the more scientific psychological view of behavior shaping and emphasizes the child's viewpoint and the value of play.

1929–1931 Hampton Institute, Spellman College, and Bennett College open Black laboratory nursery schools, emphasizing child development principles as in other lab schools and serving as training centers.

1933 WPA (Works Projects Association) opens emergency nurseries for Depression relief of unemployed teachers.

1935 First toy lending library, Toy Loan, begins in Los Angeles.

1936 The first commercial telecast is shown in New York City, starring Felix the Cat.

1943–1945 Kaiser Shipyard Child Care Center, run by Lois Meeks Stolz, James Hymes, and Edith Dowley, operates 24-hour care in Portland, Oregon.

1944 *Young Children* is first published by NAEYC.

1946 Dr. Spock's *Baby and Child Care* is published. It advocates a more permissive attitude toward children's behavior and encourages exploratory behavior.

1946 Loris Malguzzi starts school of Reggio Emilia, Italy, emphasizing the child's individual creative expression.

1948 USNC OMEP, the United States National Committee of the World Organization for Early Childhood Education, is founded to promote the education of children internationally and begins to consult with UNICEF and UNESCO in the United Nations. It starts publishing a journal, *The International Journal of Early Childhood*, in 1969.

1954 U.S. Supreme Court ruled in *Brown v Board of Education* that in public education the doctrine of "separate but equal" has no place.

1956 La Leche League is established to provide mothers with information on breast-feeding, childbirth, infants, and child care.

1960 Katherine Whiteside Taylor founds the American Council of Parent Cooperatives, which later becomes the Parent Cooperative Pre-schools International.

1960 Nancy McCormick Rambusch founds the American Montessori movement.

1962 Perry Preschool Project, directed by David Weikart, opens in Ypsilanti, Michigan, and conducts longitudinal study to measure the effects of preschool education on later school and life.

1964–1965 The Economic Opportunity Act of 1964 passes, becoming the foundation of Head Start Programs in the United States, as part of a federal "War on Poverty."

1966 The Bureau of Education for the Handicapped is established.

1966 NANE becomes National Association for the Education of Young Children (NAEYC).

1969 Pediatrician T. Berry Brazelton publishes *Infants and Mothers*, along with several other books and numerous articles advocating a sensible and intimate relationship between parents and children.

(continues)

1969 The Ford Foundation, Carnegie Corporation, and the Department of Health, Education, and Welfare subsidize the Children's Television Workshop, which develops *Sesame Street.*

1971 Stride-Rite Corporation of Boston opens a children's program on site, becoming a vanguard for employer-supported child care.

1972 The Child Development Associate Consortium is started by Edward Ziegler to develop a professional teacher training program (now known as CDA).

1975 PL 94-142, the Education for All Handicapped Children bill, passes, mandating appropriate education for special needs children in the "least restrictive environment" possible, thus defining the concepts of "mainstreaming" and "full inclusion."

1979 The United Nations declares an International Year of the Child.

1982 Marion Wright Edelman establishes the Children's Defense Fund, a Washington-based lobby on behalf of children, and particularly children of poverty and color.

1983 *A Nation at Risk* is published, which concluded "If an unfriendly foreign power had attempted to impose on America the mediocre educational performance that exists today, we might well have viewed it as an act of war."

1984 NAEYC publishes a report entitled "Develomentally Appropriate Practices," which outlines what is meant by "quality" work with young children from infancy through age 8.

1985 NAEYC establishes a National Academy and a voluntary Accreditation system for centers, in an effort to improve the quality of children's lives, and confers its first accreditation the next year.

1986 U.S. Department of Education declares the Year of the Elementary School. PL. 99-457, amending 94-142, establishes a national policy on early intervention for children as young as infants.

1990 The Child Care Development Block Grant is established to improve the quality, availability, and affordability of child care programs.

1990 U.N. Children's World Summit includes the following goals to be reached by the year 2000: (1) to reduce child mortality below age 5 by one third; (2) to provide universal access to basic education; and (3) to protect children in dangerous situations.

1990 The Americans with Disabilities Act (ADA) is passed, requiring programs of all sizes to care for and accommodate the needs of children with disabilities whenever they are reasonably able to do so.

1991 "Ready to Learn/America 2000," part of the U.S. government's educational strategy for reforming American public schools, is published.

1991 The first Worthy Wage Day, organized by the Child Care Employee Project, is held on April 9, drawing attention to the inadequate compensation of early childhood workers and how this affects the retention of a skilled and stable work force.

1993 The Family and Medical Leave Act (FMLA) passes, providing new parents with 12 weeks of unpaid, job-protected leave.

1996 The first "Stand for Children" demonstration is held in Washington, DC, drawing 200,000 participants.
Rethinking the Brain, published by the Family and Work Institute, summarizes the new research on children's brain development.

1997 The Child Development Permit Matrix is adopted by the California Commission on Teacher Credentialing, introducing the career ladder concept into early childhood public education.

1998 The 100,000th CDA Credential is awarded by Carol Brunson Phillips, Executive Director of the Council for Early Childhood Professionals.

2002 In the U.S., the "Leave No Child Behind" legislation is passed.

2003 Universal preschool is considered as a next step in providing equal access to quality early educational experiences for all children under 5 years of age.

2007 State-funded preschools rose in per-child funding, expanded access, and moved toward higher quality standards.

2008 12 states in the US still provide no state preschool for their children.

2010 Common core state standards for grades K-12 in English language arts and mathematics is published.

FIGURE 1-2 *(continued)*

church control of school in the medieval period meant that education projected a view of children as basically evil in their natural state. The value of education was in preparation for an afterlife. Children learned mostly through their parents or by apprenticeship outside the family. The child was expected and encouraged to move into adulthood as fast as possible. Survival was the primary goal in life. Because the common religious belief was that people were naturally evil, children had to be directed, punished, and corrected constantly.

What little we know of systematic learning developed during the Dark Ages through the policies of Charlemagne—who proclaimed that the nobility should know their letters—and from monastery schools that maintained libraries. A new social class in the form of craft guilds began to grow as apprenticeships expanded. Although education was sparse, the seeds of learning were planted, including the introduction of the concepts of equality and brotherhood, a continuing concern of educators today.

In the Renaissance and Reformation

The European Renaissance and Reformation (1400–1600) brought more ease and freedom for the common person. Children were seen as pure and good. The printing press, invented by Johannes Gutenberg in 1439, made books more available to the common person rather than exclusively to the domain of monks and church-sponsored schools. Martin Luther (1482–1546) urged parents to educate their children by teaching them morals and catechism.

The first humanist educators began to advocate a basic education for all children, including girls and the poor. The call for a *universal education* and *literacy* are two fundamental effects of this period on education as we know it today. Concern for the common man was on the rise, as skilled craftsmen formed a kind of middle class. By the 1500s, schools that taught subjects such as reading, writing, arithmetic, and bookkeeping were fairly common throughout Europe.

The German school system was established at this time and would influence education in all parts of Europe. People changed the way they looked at children and their education. Towns grew and expanded, and there was an opportunity to move to new lands. Living conditions improved and infant mortality waned. Children were living longer. The acquisition of knowledge and skills at an earlier age became important. If educated, children could be expected to help their family improve its situation. Parents found they needed help in teaching their children.

	Cornix cornicatur,	à à	A a
	The *Crow* crieth.		
	Agnus balat,	b è è è	B b
	The *Lamb* blaiteth.		
	Cicàda stridet,	cì cì	C c
	The *Grasshopper* chirpeth.		
	Upupa dicit,	du du	D d
	The *Whooppoo* saith.		
	Infans ejulat,	è è è	E e
	The *Infant* crieth.		
	Ventus flat,	fi fi	F f
	The *Wind* bloweth.		
	Anser gingrit,	ga ga	G g
	The *Goose* gagleth.		
	Os halat,	hà'h hà'h	H h
	The *Mouth* breatheth out.		
	Mus mintrit,	ì ì ì	I i
	The *Mouse* chirpeth.		
	Anas tetrinnit,	kha, kha	K k
	The *Duck* quaketh.		
	Lupus ululat,	lu ulu	L
	The *Wolf* howleth.		
		[mum	
	Ursus murmurat,	mum-	M m
	The *Bear* grumbleth.		

Orbis. Pictus, by Johann Comenius

Orbis Pictus, by Johann Comenius, is considered the first picture book written for children.

Into Modern Times

Johann Amos Comenius Comenius (1592–1670), a Czech educator, wrote the first picture book for children. Called *Orbis Pictus* (*The World of Pictures*, 1658), it was a guide for teachers that included training of the senses and the study of nature. Comenius fostered the belief that education should follow the natural order of things. His ideas included the "school of the mother's lap," in which children's development follows a timetable of its own and their education should reflect that fact. Comenius advocated approaching learning based on the principles of nature. He believed that "in all the operations of nature, development is from within," so children should be allowed to learn at their own pace. He also proposed that teachers should work with children's own inclinations, for "what is natural takes place without compulsion" (Gianoutsos, 2011). Teachers must observe and work with this natural order—the timetable—to ensure successful learning. This idea was later reflected in Montessori's sensitive periods and Piaget's stages of development. Today it is recognized as the issue of school **readiness.**

Comenius also stressed a basic concept that is now taken for granted: learning by doing. He encouraged parents to let their children play with other children of the same age. Rather than pushing a standard curriculum, Comenius said that "the desire to know and to learn should be excited . . . in every possible manner" (Keatinge, 1896). He also reflected the growing social reform that would educate the poor, as well as the rich.

In summary, probably the three most significant contributions of Comenius are *books with illustrations,* an emphasis on *education with the senses,* and the *social reform* potential of education.

John Locke An English philosopher of the 1600s, Locke (1632–1714) is considered to be the founder of modern educational philosophy. He based his theory of education on the scientific method and the study of the mind and learning. Locke theorized the concept of **tabula rasa,** the belief that the child is born neutral, rather than evil, and is a "clean slate" on which the experiences of parents, society, education, and the world are written. He based his theory on the scientific method and approached a child as a doctor would examine a patient. He was one of the first European educators to discuss the idea of individual differences gleaned from observing one child rather than simply teaching a group. Education needed to take the individual learner into account.

The purpose of education, he claimed, is to make man a reasoning creature. A working knowledge of the Bible and a counting ability sufficient to conduct business was the fundamental education required of adults, so children were taught those basics. Locke suggested that such instruction should be pleasant, with playful activities, as well as drills. Locke's influence on education was not felt strongly at the time. Later, however, his best ideas, such as the notion that the teacher must work through the senses to help children reach understanding, were popularized by Rousseau. Today, teachers still emphasize a sensory approach to learning.

In summary, Locke's contribution is felt most in our acceptance of *individual differences,* in *giving children reasons* as the basis for helping children to learn, and in his *theory of a "clean slate"* that points to the effect of the environment on learning.

Jean-Jacques Rousseau After Comenius, new thoughts were everywhere in Europe. Locke offered some educational

HultonArchive/iStockphoto

Rousseau advocated that children were naturally good and should have a flexible and less restrained school atmosphere.

challenges, and Darwin brought a change to science. The time was ripe for new ideas about childhood. Rousseau (1712–1778), a writer and philosopher, proposed that children were not inherently evil, but naturally good. He is best known for his book *Emile* (1761) in which he raised a hypothetical child to adulthood. He reasoned that education should reflect this goodness and allow spontaneous interests and activities of the children. "Let us lay it down as an incontrovertible rule that the first impulses of nature are always right; there is no original sin in the human heart . . . the only natural passion is self-love or selfishness taken in a wider sense."

Rousseau's ideas on education in and of themselves were nothing short of revolutionary for the times. Making what might be considered the first comprehensive attempt to describe a system of education according to nature, his concern for the learner led him to the idea that children learn from firsthand information and their views are different from those of adults. Moreover, a child's mind develops in distinct phases and teachers should adjust their instruction accordingly.

Although he was not an educator, Rousseau suggested that school atmosphere should be less restrained and more flexible to meet the needs of the children. He insisted on using **concrete** teaching materials, leaving the abstract and symbolism for later years. His call to *naturalism* transformed education in such a way that led educators to eventually focus more on the early years. For instance, he encouraged others to "sacrifice a little time in early childhood, and it will be repaid to you with usury when your scholar is older" (*Emile*, 1761). Pestalozzi, Froebel, and Montessori were greatly influenced by him. The theories of developmental stages, such as of Jean Piaget and Arnold Gesell (see Chapter 4), support Rousseau's idea of natural development. In Europe, his ideas had a ripple effect that sent waves across the Atlantic Ocean.

Rousseau's ideas are still followed today in early childhood classes. *Free play* is based on Rousseau's belief in *children's inherent goodness* and ability to choose what they need to learn. Environments that stress autonomy and self-regulation have their roots in Rousseau's philosophy. Using *concrete rather than abstract materials* for young children is still one of the cornerstones of developmentally appropriate curriculum in the early years.

Johann Heinrich Pestalozzi Pestalozzi (1746–1827) was a Swiss educator whose theories on education and caring have formed the basis of many common teaching practices of early childhood education. Like Rousseau, he used nature study as part of the curriculum and believed that good education meant the development of the senses. Rather than simply glorify nature, however, Pestalozzi became more pragmatic, including principles on how to teach basic skills and the idea of "caring" as well as "educating" the child. Pestalozzi stressed the idea of the **integrated curriculum** that would develop the whole child. He wanted education to be of the hand, the head, and the heart of the child. Teachers were to guide self-activity through intuition, exercise, and the senses. Along with intellectual content, he proposed that practical skills be taught in the schools. He differed from Rousseau in that he proposed teaching children in groups rather than using a tutor with an individual child. Pestalozzi's works, *How Gertrude Teaches Her Children* and *Book for Mothers*, detail some procedures for mothers to use at home with their children. Probably his greatest contribution is the blending of Rousseau's strong romantic ideals with his own egalitarian attitude: "I wish to wrest education from the outworn order of doddering old teaching hacks as well as from the new-fangled order of cheap, artificial teaching tricks, and entrust it to the eternal powers of nature herself" (in Silber, 1965).

In summary, Pestalozzi's contributions are strongest around the *integration of the curriculum* and *group*

teaching. He initiated *sensory education* and blended both *freedom* and *limits* into working with children.

Friedrich Wilhelm Froebel Froebel (1782–1852) is one of the major contributors to early childhood education, particularly in his organization of educational thought and ideas about learning, curriculum, and teacher training. He is known to us as the "Father of the Kindergarten," not only for giving it a name, but for devoting his life to the development of a system of education for young children. The German word **kindergarten** means "**children's garden**," and that is what Froebel felt best expressed what he wanted for children less than 6 years of age. Because his own childhood had been unhappy, he resolved that early education should be pleasant. He attended a training institute run by Pestalozzi and left to promote children's right to play, to have toys, and to be with trained teachers by founding a Play and Activity Institute. Early childhood historian Dorothy Hewes (1993) notes:

> Froebel started his kindergarten in 1836, for children aged about two to six, after he had studied with Pestalozzi in Switzerland and had read the philosophy promoted by Comenius two hundred years earlier. His system was centered around self-activity and the development of children's self-esteem and self-confidence. In his *Education of Man*, he wrote that "Play is the highest phase of child development—the representation of the inner necessity and impulse." He had the radical idea that both men and women should teach young children and that they should be friendly facilitators rather than stern disciplinarians.

More than 100 years ago, Froebel's kindergartens included blocks, pets, and finger plays. Froebel observed children and came to understand how they learned and what they liked to do. He developed the first educational

FroebelUSA.com

A Froebelian kindergarten at the end of the nineteenth century.

toys, which he termed "gifts" (*gaben* in German), as seen in Figure 1-3.

Angeline Brooks (1886), a teacher in an American Froebelian kindergarten in the late 1800s, described the gifts this way:

> Froebel regarded the whole of life as a school, and the whole world as a school-room for the education of the [human] race. The external things of nature he regarded as a means to making the race acquainted with the invisible things of the minds, as God's *gifts* for use in accomplishing the purpose of this temporal life. Regarding the child as the race in miniature, he selected a few objects which should epitomize the world of matter in its most salient attributes and arranged them in an order which should assist the child's development at successive stages of growth. "Froebel wanted teachers to see how children developed as they manipulated specific objects (gifts and occupations he designed for their education), such as blocks for design construction, parquetry shapes for picture creation, and drawing forms" (Reifel, 2011).

Some of his theories about children and their education later influenced Montessori and were reflected in the educational materials she developed, as well as modern kindergarten (Brosterman, 1997).

Every day, teachers in centers and homes across the country practice the Froebelian belief that one's first educational experiences should be a *child's garden:* full of pleasant discoveries and delightful adventure, where the adults' role is to plant ideas and materials for children to use as they grow at their own pace.

Maria Montessori designed materials, classrooms, and learning methods for young children.

Froebelian Gifts

When the children are just making friends with the teacher and with each other, it is very interesting and profitable for them to formulate their mite of knowledge into a sentence, each one holding his ball high in the air with the right hand and saying:

My ball is red like a cherry.
My ball is yellow like a lemon.
My ball is blue like the sky.
My ball is orange like a marigold.
My ball is green like the grass.
My ball is violet like a plum.

FIGURE 1-3 When introducing the gifts, the teacher in Froebelian settings would teach children rhymes and finger plays.

Maria Montessori   At the turn of the century, Montessori (1870–1952) became the first female physician in Italy. She worked in the slums of Rome with poor children and with mentally retarded children. Sensing that what they lacked was proper motivation and environment, she opened a preschool, *Casa di Bambini,* in 1907. Her first class was 50 children from 2 to 5 years of age. The children were at the center all day while their parents worked. They were fed two meals a day, given a bath, and provided with medical attention. Montessori designed materials, classrooms, and a teaching procedure that proved her point to the astonishment of people all over Europe and America.

Before her, no one with medical or psychiatric training had articulated so clearly the needs of the growing child. Her medical background added credibility to her findings and helped her ideas gain recognition in this country. The Montessori concept is both a philosophy of child development and a plan for guiding growth, believing that education begins at birth and the early years are of the utmost importance. During this time, children pass through "sensitive periods," in which their curiosity makes them ready for acquiring certain skills and knowledge.

Montessori was an especially observant person and used her observations to develop her program and philosophy. For instance, the manipulative materials she used were expensive, so they were always kept in a locked cabinet. One day the cabinet was left unlocked, and the children took out the materials themselves and worked with them quietly and carefully. Afterward, Montessori removed the cabinet and replaced it with low open shelves. She noticed that children liked to sit on the floor so she bought little rugs to define the work areas. In analyzing how children learn, she concluded that they build themselves from what they find in their environment, so she designed the school around the size of the children. Because of her enlightenment, a carefully prepared environment with child-sized furniture and materials are common features of early educational classrooms.

By focusing on the *sequential steps of learning*, Montessori developed a set of learning materials still used widely today. One of her most valuable contributions was a theory of how children learn: children teach themselves if only we will dedicate ourselves to the self-creating process of the child. She believed that any task could be reduced to a series of small steps. By using this process, children could learn to sweep a floor, dress themselves, or multiply numbers.

After Montessori was introduced in the United States in 1909, her methods received poor reception and were often misunderstood. Chattin-McNichols (1993) notes that "adaptation of her methods in a variety of ways, a focus on academics by demanding middle-class parents, and a flood of 'trainers' and authors eager to capitalize on Montessori contributed to a rapid downfall of Montessori schools in the United States by 1925 or so." A second American Montessori movement began in the late 1950s and early 1960s. Differences between European and American society and education generated the American Montessori Society, founded by Dr. Nancy McCormick Rambusch. According to Chattin-McNichols (1993):

> Today with a much wider range of children than ever before, the majority of Montessori schools are private preschools and child care centers, serving 3- to 6-year-old children. But there are many which also serve elementary students and a small (but growing) number of programs for infants, toddlers, and middle-school students. . . . The word *Montessori*, however, remains in the public domain, so that Montessori in the name of a school or teacher education program does not guarantee any adherence to Montessori's original ideas.

To summarize, Montessori's contributions were substantial to all we do in early childhood programs today. A *prepared environment*, **self-correcting** and *sequential materials*, teaching based on *observation*, and a trust in *children's innate drive to learn* all stem from her work. (Montessori education as a curriculum model is discussed in Chapter 10.)

Rudolf Steiner Steiner (1861–1925) was an Austrian philosopher, scientist, and artist whose lectures for the German factories of Waldorf-Astoria led to the establishment of schools now known as Waldorf Schools. This system has influenced mainstream education in Europe, and its international reputation is felt in North America today. A growing independent school movement, Waldorf schools number more than 1,000 worldwide (www.waldorfanswers.org, 2004).

Steiner theorized that childhood is a phase of life important in its own right, and the environment must be carefully planned to protect and nurture the child (see Figure 1-4). His philosophy, known as *anthroposophical spiritual science*, emphasized the children's spiritual development, imagination, and creative gifts. As did Froebel and Montessori, Steiner emphasized the whole child and

Steiner's Ages of Childhood			
Age	Span	Child Learns by...	Emphasis
The Will	0-7	Imitation	Role models and beautiful environment
The Heart	7-14	Authority	Consistency with enthusiasm and feeling
The Head	14+	Challenge	Intellectual study for real mastery

© Cengage Learning 2011

FIGURE 1-4 Rudolf Steiner created a system of education in the early 1900s that was based on educational goals for the whole child and the transformation of the spirit/soul.

believed that different areas of development and learning were connected into a kind of unity. The role of the teacher is that of a mother figure, and her goal is to allow the child's innate self-motivation to predominate. The teacher is to understand the temperament of each child, and to go with it; thus, play has a large place in Waldorf classrooms.

Self-discipline emerges from the child's natural willingness to learn and initiate, and the classroom needs to support this self-regulation process. Yet, although the child's inner life is deeply valued by Steiner, experiences in early childhood must be carefully selected. For instance, fairy stories help children acquire time-honored wisdom; modern Waldorf followers insist that television be eliminated.

In summary, for Steiner, the people with whom the child interacts are of central importance. (Waldorf schools are addressed with curriculum models in Chapter 10.)

Nontraditional Perspectives

You can likely notice how traditional early childhood educational practices reinforce European-American values and beliefs. Education is often built from the knowledge base of its teachers; curriculum usually draws from the system—cultural, economic, or political—that is most familiar. If teachers are trained on European writings and the ideas of university-educated Americans, then their own teachings would likely reflect those philosophies.

But there have always been other influences on our child-rearing and educational practices, especially those of our upbringing or of the communities whose children and families we teach. We know that there is more than one "right way" to care for and educate children.

What nontraditional perspectives influenced early childhood education? As mentioned before, information about non-Western early childhood history is not easily accessible (see "Additional Resources" for a reading list). Gonzalez-Mena (2001) summarizes some of these perspectives in this way:

> Historically, attitudes toward childhood in China and Japan were influenced by Confucius' writings (551–479 B.C.), which stressed harmony. Children were seen as good and worthy of respect, a view not held in Europe until more recently.
>
> Native-American writings show close ties and interconnectedness, not only among families and within tribes but also between people and nature. Teaching children about relationships and interconnectedness are historical themes of early education among many indigenous peoples. Strong kinship networks are themes among both Africans and African

Americans; people bond together and pool resources for the common good. Whether these contemporary tendencies come from ancient roots, historic, and modern oppression, or all three, remains unclear.

> Latin American and Hispanic cultures value children highly and emphasize the importance of cooperation and sensitivity to authority figures. Families from the Pacific Islands stress the connection to family, as well as the importance of respecting one's elders.

Early education practices have been influenced by many of these perspectives. For instance, understanding and accepting each child's family and cultural perspectives includes a working knowledge of the variations in attitudes and child-rearing practices. Learning about nontraditional cultures and behaviors has become critical for professional teachers to honor diversity both in the classroom and in the larger societal context (see Chapters 3 and 9–15).

Whether or not an activity or program is developmentally suited to a particular age or individual was put into more modern context in the mid-1980s when specific descriptions were required to support NAEYC's efforts to accredit early education programs. Defining what is appropriate now includes as much about the family and culture of a child as the age and even the individual characteristics. Developmentally appropriate practices (DAP) are defined and expanded in the next chapter. The dynamic nature of "DAP" allows for both basic principles and variation. This means that it can reflect the best, most current thinking of the field, and it requires periodic evaluation and revision. Personal application of nontraditional perspectives is part of your professional identity (see the Diversity, "Finding Your Place at the Table").

American Influences

Significant moments in American history have served as turning points in education in general, as well as for early childhood education in particular. As you will read, the American educational system has been dynamic, from its onset in Colonial America to developmentally appropriate practices and common core standards of today.

Colonial Days

When thinking of Colonial America, people often envision the one-room schoolhouse. Indeed, this was the mainstay of education in the New England colonies. Although home-teaching of the Bible was common, children of elementary

DIVERSITY

Finding Your Place at the Table

"The field of Early Child Education eagerly awaits, with hopeful expectation, your special contribution. 'What could I possibly have to offer?' you ask. Your history, or life story, is your greatest asset. Tucked away in your early years are special experiences that can shape the lives of small children" (Williams, 2011).

The challenges from your childhood can enhance your work with children as you add your own sensitivity and perspective. In that way, you make your place at the table of early childhood education, in whatever workplace it may be, both your own and an opening for children. Drawing on the stories and memories may require you to check with your family and others who knew you then. Again, Williams prompts you to consider:

1. What expectations does your culture have for young children? (Consider what messages society sends to families about the activities in which these children should participate.)

2. In which activities did you participate as a child younger than 8 years old? (Remember the toys with which you played or activities your family said you liked.)

3. Did you participate in preschool? If so, what was the setting? Was it in your home, the home of others, a neighborhood childcare facility, or a larger group center? (You might consider how it was physically organized and the people involved.)

4. Were your contacts with others ethnically diverse or localized to one cultural group? (Cultural identity can be defined in many ways such as geographical, religious, racial, and so forth. Many of our identities include many cultures; that is, they are multicultural.)

5. What did you gain from those early years that will help you as an early childhood educator? (Look for a way this can be passed to others.)

6. Describe one way you would like to improve the early childhood education you received. (By rethinking what you did not receive, you can change this in the lives of those you are involved with.)

Finding your own personal diversity helps you find uniqueness within the diverse experiences of your life, which brings richness to your work and treasures to share with the children, families, and professionals that you serve.

---

age were sent to school primarily for religious reasons. Everyone needed to be able to read the Bible, the Puritan fathers reasoned. All children were sent to study, though historically boys were educated before girls. Not only was the Bible used in school, however; new materials like the *New England Primer* and the *Horn Book* were also used.

Early life in the New England colonies was difficult, and estimates run as high as 60 percent to 70 percent of children younger than age 4 dying in colonial towns during the "starving season." Discipline was harsh, and children were expected to obey immediately and without question. Parents may have loved their children, but Puritan families showed little overt affection. Children were important as economic tools, and they worked the land and were apprenticed into trades early.

In the South, it was a different story. Plantation owners imported tutors from England or opened small private schools to teach just their sons to read and write. Although the reasons were different from those in New England, the results were similar: a very high percentage of adult readers. From these came the leaders of the American Revolution and the new nation. History can provide us with reminders of the strides that have been made in American history and

Time Life Pictures /Contributor/Time & Life Pictures/Getty Images

The *Horn Book* was a common reading primer in colonial American schools.

that the challenge of overcoming bias and unequal access continues.

The Revolutionary War brought the establishment of both the Union and religious freedom. By affirming fundamental principles of democratic liberty, the Founding Fathers paved the way for a system of free, common, public school systems, the first the world had seen (Cubberly, 1920). However, after the Revolutionary War, there were no significant advances in education until the late 1800s. Leaders such as Thomas Jefferson felt that knowledge ought to be available to all, but that opinion was not widely shared. Most of the post-Revolutionary period focused on growing crops and pioneering the frontier, not teaching and educating children. Even by the 1820s, education for the common man was not readily available. Industrialization in both the North and South did little to encourage reading and writing skills. Manual labor and machine-operating skills were more important. Although public schools were accepted in principle, in reality, no tax basis was established to support them.

Children in Enslavement

The first African Americans were not slaves but indentured servants, whose debts repaid by their labor would buy them their freedom. However, by 1620, Africans were brought to the New World as slaves. In many states, children of slaves were not valued as human beings but rather as property of the owner. During the Revolutionary War, many Americans turned against slavery because of the principles of the natural rights of the individual, as embodied in the Declaration of Independence and, later, in the United States Constitution. By the early 1800s, most northern owners had freed their slaves, although living conditions for them were generally poor.

Because of the high economic value of children as future laborers, there was a certain level of care given to pregnant women and babies. Osborn (1991) tells of a nursery on a South Carolina plantation around 1850 in which

> . . . infants and small children were left in a small cabin while the mothers worked in the fields nearby. An older woman was left in charge and assisted by several girls 8–10 years of age. The infants, for the most part, lay on the cabin floor or the porch—and once or twice daily, the mother would come in from the field to nurse the baby. Children of toddler age played on the porch or in the yard and, at times, the older girls might lead the group in singing and dancing.

Before the Civil War, education was severely limited for African Americans. Many southern states prohibited literacy instruction for enslaved Africans, so female African American teachers helped establish Clandestine Schools, also known as midnight schools, because plantation owners banned teaching (Jones-Wilson, 1996). After the Civil War, most education came through the establishment of Sabbath schools because literacy training was considered part of religious instruction. Because of its necessary secretive existence, few records are available, although it is reasonable to conclude that the curriculum was similar in both types of schools.

After the Civil War, private and public schools were opened for African Americans. Major colleges and universities were founded by the end of the 1800s. Booker T. Washington, born into slavery, founded the Tuskegee Normal & Industrial Institute in Alabama in 1881 and emphasized practical education and intercultural understanding between the two races as a path to liberation. Many former slaves and graduates established schools for younger children. Of integrated schools, Osborn (1991) reports:

> Generally, however, if the schools accepted Blacks at all, it was on a strictly quota basis. . . . Blacks were often excluded from kindergartens. Thus as the early childhood education movement began to grow and expand in the years following the Civil War, it grew along separate color lines.

Hampton Institute of Virginia established a laboratory kindergarten for African Americans in 1873, and by 1893 the Institute offered a kindergarten training school and courses in child care. The graduates of Hampton Institute became the teachers at the laboratory school because, in the words of its principal, "[the] students know the children and the influences surrounding them. . . . Their people are proud to see them teaching. They furnish what has always been a missing link between me and the parents" (Pleasant, 1992). It would be worth investigating whether all laboratory schools for African Americans copied European models, as did those of most American universities, or if they reflected some African influences.

A Progressive Era

By the end of the 1800s, however, a nationwide reform movement had begun. The Progressive Movement of the late 1800s and first half of the 20th century changed the course of education in both elementary and nursery schools in America. Coinciding with the political progressivism in this country, this philosophy emphasized a **child-centered approach** that gained

Music time at Hampton Institute kindergarten.

Courtesy of Hampton University Archives

advocates from both the scientific viewpoint (Dewey, Hall) and those of a psychoanalytic bent (Hill, Isaacs). Some of the major features of the educational progressive philosophy were:

1. We must recognize individual needs and individual differences in children.
2. Teachers [must be] more attentive to the needs of children.
3. Children learn best when they are highly motivated and have a genuine interest in the material.
4. Learning via rote memory is useless to children.
5. The teacher should be aware of the child's total development—social, physical, intellectual, and emotional.
6. Children learn best when they have direct contact with the material (Osborn, 1991).

These beliefs were instrumental in changing the old traditional schools from a strict and subject-based curriculum to one that centered on children's interests as the foundation for curriculum development. Progressives wanted educators to work on "how a school could become a cooperative community while developing in individuals their own capacities and satisfying their own needs" (Dewey, 1916). Although Dewey (1858–1952) and others did not reject the teaching of basic skills, the shift was away from such subject matter education.

John Dewey

Dewey was the first real American influence on American education. Raised in Vermont, he became a professor of philosophy at both the University of Chicago and Columbia University. In the years that followed, Dewey was responsible for one of the greatest impacts on American education of all time.

Dewey believed that children were valuable and that childhood was an important part of their lives. Like Froebel, he felt that education should be integrated with life and should provide a training ground for cooperative living. As did Pestalozzi and Rousseau, Dewey felt that schools should focus on the nature of the child. Until this time, children were considered of little consequence. Childhood was rushed. Children as young as 7 were a regular part of the work force—on the farms, in the mines, and in the factories. Dewey's beliefs about children and learning are summarized in Figure 1-5.

Dewey's ideas of schooling emerged from his own childhood and his family life as a parent. Jane Dewey, his sixth child, offered that "his own schooling had bored John; he'd disliked the rigid, passive way of learning forced on children by the pervasive lecture-recitation method of that time" (Walker, 1997). Furthermore, the Dewey's parenting style caused a stir among friends and neighbors; the children were allowed to play actively in

---

Dewey's Pedagogic Creed

My Pedagogic Creed—John Dewey	What It Means Today
1. "…I believe that only true education comes through the stimulation of the child's powers by the demands of the social situations in which he finds himself."	This tells us that children learn to manage themselves in groups, to make and share friendship, to solve problems, and to cooperate.
2. "…The child's own instinct and powers furnish the material and give the starting point for all education."	We need to create a place that is child-centered, a place that values the skills and interests of each child and each group.
3. "…I believe that education, therefore, is a process of living and not a preparation for future living."	Prepare children for what is to come by enriching and interpreting the present to them. Find educational implications in everyday experiences.
4. "…I believe that … the school life should grow gradually out of the home life … it is the business of the school to deepen and extend … the child's sense of the values bound up in his home life."	This sets the rationale for a relationship between teachers and parents. Values established and created in the home should be enhanced by teaching in the schools.
5. "…I believe, finally, that the teacher is engaged, not simply in the training of individuals, but in the formation of a proper social life. I believe that every teacher should realize the dignity of his calling."	This says that the work teachers do is important and valuable. They teach more than academic content; they teach how to live.

FIGURE 1-5 John Dewey expressed his ideas about education in an important document entitled "My Pedagogic Creed." (Washington, D.C.: The Progressive Education Association, 1897.)

---

the same room as adult guests, to ignore wearing shoes and stockings, and even to "stand by during the birth [of brother Morris] while Mrs. Dewey explained the process" (Walker, 1997). His passionate belief in the innate goodness of children, in the principle of mind-body unity, and in the encouragement of experimentation shaped John Dewey's ideals.

A new kind of school emerged from these ideals. Even the buildings began to take on a different look. Movable furniture replaced rows of benches. Children's projects, some still under construction, were found everywhere. The curriculum of the school began to focus on all of the basics, not just on a few of the academics. If a group of 6-year-olds decided to make a woodworking table, they would first have to learn to read to understand the directions. After calculating the cost, they would purchase the materials. In building the table, geometry, physics, and math were learned along the way. This was a group effort that encouraged children to work together in teams, so school became a society in miniature. Children's social skills were developed along with reading, science, and math. The teacher's role in the process was one of ongoing support, involvement, and encouragement.

The contribution of John Dewey to American education cannot be underestimated. Dewey's ideas are part of today's classrooms in several ways. His child-oriented schools are a model of child care centers and family child care homes, as learning and living are inseparable. The teacher's role served as a model for current *intentional teaching* methods (see Teaching With Intention feature in every chapter). As the following sections on kindergarten and nursery schools illustrate, John Dewey had a vision that is still alive today.

The Field Expands: Kindergarten

The word **kindergarten**—German for "children's garden"—is a delightful term. It brings to mind the image of young seedlings on the verge of blossoming. The similarity between caring for young plants and young children is not accidental. Froebel, the man who coined the word *kindergarten*, meant for that association to be made. As a flower opens from a bud, so too does a child go through a natural unfolding process. This idea—and ideal—are part of the kindergarten story.

The first kindergarten was a German school started by Froebel in 1837. Nearly 20 years later, in 1856, Margaretha Schurz, a student of Froebel, opened the first kindergarten in the United States. It was for German-speaking children and held in her home in Wisconsin.

John Dewey's lab school involved children in activities of a practical, real-life nature, such as weaving small rugs to use in the classroom.

Schurz inspired Elizabeth Peabody (1804–1894) of Boston, who opened the first English-speaking kindergarten there in 1860. Peabody, in turn, after studying kindergartens in Germany, influenced William Harris, superintendent of schools in St. Louis, Missouri. In 1873, Harris allowed Susan Blow (1843–1916) to open the first kindergarten in the United States that was associated with the public schools. By the 1880s, kindergarten teachers such as Eudora Hailmann were hard at work inventing wooden beads, paper weaving mats, and songbooks to use with active 5-year-old children.

Look at kindergarten in a historical perspective to trace the various purposes of this specialized educational experience. At first, Froebel's philosophy (see section on Froebel earlier in this chapter) was the mainstay of kindergarten education. At the same time, kindergartens began to become an instrument of social reform. Many of the kindergartens started in the late 1800s were established by churches and other agencies that worked with the poor and were called charity kindergartens. For instance, "in the early kindergartens, teachers conducted a morning class for about 15 children and made social calls on families during the afternoon. The children were taught to address the teachers as 'Auntie' to emphasize her sisterly relationship with their mothers" (Hewes, 1993).

Moreover, by early 1900, traditional kindergarten ideas had come under the scrutiny of G. Stanley Hall

and others who were interested in a scientific approach to education. Dewey advocated a community-like (rather than garden-style) classroom. A classic clash of ideals developed between followers of Froebel (conservatives) and those of Dewey's new educational viewpoint (progressives). For those who saw kindergartens as a social service in an era of rising social conscience, the reasons for helping the less fortunate were similar to the rationale that led to the creation of Head Start 60 years later.

The emphasis in a Froebelian kindergarten was on teacher-directed learning. Dewey's followers preferred a more child-centered approach, with teachers serving as facilitators of children's learning. This is the same tension that exists today between the "back to basics" movement and the supporters of child-centered education. The progressives found fault with the "gifts" of Froebel's curriculum. Those who followed Dewey believed that "real objects and real situations within the child's own social setting" should be used (Read & Patterson, 1980). Froebel was viewed as too structured and too symbolic; Dewey was perceived as child-oriented and child-involved. Even the processes they used were different. Froebel believed in allowing the unfolding of the child's mind and learning, whereas Dewey stressed adult intervention in social interaction.

The reform of kindergarten education led to the creation of the modern American kindergarten. By the 1970s, the trend was to focus on the intellectual development of the child; thus there was an emphasis on academic goals for 5-year-olds. By the late 1990s, the concept of developmentally appropriate practices advocated a shift toward more holistic, broad planning for kindergarten. (Today's kindergarten programs are discussed in Chapter 2.)

Patty Smith Hill

Hill (1868–1946) of Teacher's College, Columbia University, was an outstanding innovator of the time and one of the Progressive Movement's most able leaders. It was she who wrote the song "Happy Birthday," created sets of large blocks (known as "Patty Hill blocks," now known as hollow and unit blocks) and founded the National Association for Nursery Education (NANE). The largest association of early childhood educators, it is known today as the National Association for the Education of Young Children (NAEYC). Trained originally in the Froebelian tradition, she worked closely with G. Stanley Hall and later with John Dewey. Thus her philosophy of classroom teaching was a blended one. She believed strongly in basing curricula and programs on the nature and needs of the children, and she was one of the major education experimenters of her day. She was:

> . . . guided by principles of democracy and respect for individuals. She argued for freedom and initiative for children, as well as a curriculum relevant to children's lives. It was she who originated large-muscle equipment and materials suitable for climbing and construction, a departure from the prescribed small-muscle activities of the Froebelians. Patty Hill also urged unification of kindergarten and first-grade work, but her objective was not to start 5-year-olds on first grade work, as we today might readily assume. Rather, emphasis was on giving six-year-olds the opportunity for independent, creative activities before embarking on the three R's. (Cohen & Randolph, 1977)

These ideas became the backbone of kindergarten practice. Moreover, Hill did not work for kindergarten alone. In fact, during the 1920s, Hill rekindled Froebel's early ideas to promote nursery schools for children too young to attend kindergarten. Regardless of controversy within, kindergartens were still on the fringes of the educational establishments as a whole. In fact, Hill (1941) herself commented that "adjustment to public-school conditions came slowly . . . [and] until this happy adjustment took place, the promotion of the self-active kindergarten children into the grades has made it possible for the poorest and most formal first-grade teacher to criticize and condemn the work of the best kindergarten teacher as well as the kindergarten cause, because of the wide gap that existed between kindergarten and primary ideals at that time."

As Hill and others prevailed and made continual improvements in teaching methods, materials, guidance, and curriculum, the interests of kindergarten and primary education could be seen as more unified.

Nursery Schools

The very phrase "nursery school" conjures up images of a child's nursery, of a carefully tended garden, and of a gentle place of play and growing. In fact, the name was coined to describe a place where children were nurtured (see the section later in this chapter on the McMillan sisters). Nursery schools have always been a place of care, for the physical needs, the intellectual stimulation, and the socio-emotional aspects of young children's lives.

Establishment in America

Early childhood educators took Dewey's philosophy to heart. Their schools reflected the principles of a child-centered approach, active learning, and social cooperation. By the 1920s and 1930s, early childhood education had reached a professional status in the United States. Nursery schools and day nurseries went beyond **custodial** health care. They fostered the child's total development. The children were enrolled from middle- and upper-class homes, as well as from working families. However, until the 1960s, nursery schools served few poor families.

Parent education was acknowledged as a vital function of the school and led to the establishment of **parent cooperative schools**. Brook Farm, a utopian cooperative community in the 1840s, had "the equivalent of an on-site child care center 'for the use of parents doing industrial work' or for mothers to use 'as a kindly relief to themselves when fatigued by the care of children'" (Hewes, 1993). The first of these parent participation schools was developed in 1915 at the University of Chicago, where a group of faculty wives started the Chicago Cooperative Nursery

Traditional nursery and kindergarten included circle time.

Golden Gate Kindergarten Association

School. Research centers and child development laboratories were started in many colleges and universities from about 1915 to 1930. These laboratory schools were active in expanding knowledge of the importance of a child's early years. As Stolz (1978) describes it, "the [preschool] movement from the beginning was integrated with the movement for child development research. The purpose . . . was to improve nursery schools, and, therefore, we brought in the people who were studying children, who were learning more about them, so we could do a better job." It is noteworthy that professionals such as Hill, Stolz, Dowley, and others encouraged researchers to share their findings with classroom teachers to integrate these discoveries into the daily programs of children.

These schools followed one of two basic models. One model, patterned after the first psychological laboratory in Leipzig, Germany, in 1879, was formed to train psychologists in the systematic training of child study. This model adopted a scientific approach to the study of human beings, as the field of psychology itself attempted to become more like the biologic sciences. The second approach, like the Butler School of Hampton Institute and later Spelman College, was established primarily for training teachers. The latter model took its influence almost exclusively from educational leaders. The nursery school laboratory schools attempted a multidisciplinary approach, blending the voices from psychology and education with those of home economics, nursing, social work, and medicine. By 1950, when Katherine Read Baker first published *The Nursery School: A Human Relationships Laboratory* (now in seven languages), the emphasis of the nursery school was on understanding human behavior and then building programs, guidance techniques, and relationships accordingly. In her estimate,

> . . . the nursery school is a place where young children learn as they play and as they share experiences with other children. . . . It is also a place where adults learn about child development and human relationships as they observe and participate in the program of the school. . . . Anyone working in an educational program for children, even the most experienced person, needs to be learning as well as teaching. The two processes, learning and teaching, are inseparable.

Lucy Sprague Mitchell

Early childhood education in the United States grew out of John Dewey's progressive movement largely because of Lucy Sprague Mitchell (1878–1967) and her contemporaries. Raised in an environment of educational and social reform, Mitchell developed the idea of schools as community centers, as well as places for children to learn to think. As Greenberg (1987) explained, Mitchell gathered together, in a democratic, cooperative venture, many talented people to brainstorm, mastermind, and sponsor:

- A remarkable Bureau of Educational Experiments
- A school to implement and experiment with these principles
- A laboratory to record and analyze how and why they function as she knew they did (and as we know they do!)
- A teachers' college to promote them
- A workshop for writers of children's literature (a new genre—a number of currently famous authors of juvenile books attended)
- A bulletin to disseminate it all, as well as to disseminate what a plethora of progressive educators were up to elsewhere, *beginning* in 1916!

Strongly influenced by John Dewey, she became a major contributor to the idea of "educational experiments," that is, trying to plan with teachers the curriculum experiences that would then be observed and analyzed "for children's reactions to the various learning situations [and] the new teaching techniques" (Mitchell, 1951). For instance, Mitchell suggested that teachers expand on what they knew of children's "here-and-now" thinking by making

> . . . trips with kindergarteners to see how work was done—work that was closely tied up with their personal lives . . . the growth in thinking and attitudes of the teachers had moved far . . . toward the conception of their role as a guide as differentiated from a dispenser of information.

By establishing Bank Street College of Education (and its laboratory school), Lucy Sprague Mitchell emphasized the link between theory and practice—namely, that the education of young children and the study of how children learn are intrinsically tied together.

Abigail Eliot

The nursery school movement was pioneered by Eliot (1892–1992). A graduate of Radcliffe College and Harvard University, Eliot had worked with the McMillan sisters (see section in this chapter) in the slums of London. A social worker by training, she became interested in children and their relationships with their parents. Eliot had a lively and clear view of what good schools for children could be. She is generally credited with bringing the nursery school movement to the United States. She founded the Ruggles Street Nursery

School in the Roxbury section of Boston, teaching children and providing teacher training, and served as its director from 1922 to 1952, when it was incorporated into Tufts University. Today, it is known as the Eliot-Pearson Department of Child Study.

Eliot became the first woman to receive a doctoral degree from Harvard University's Graduate School of Education and, after retiring from Tufts, moved to California where she helped establish Pacific Oaks College. In all her work, she integrated Froebel's gifts, Montessori's equipment, and the McMillans' fresh air, as well as her own ideas. As she put it (Hymes, 1978):

> . . . the new idea—was program. I had visited many day nurseries in Boston as a social worker. I can remember them even now: dull green walls, no light colors, nothing pretty—spotlessly clean places, with rows of white-faced listless little children sitting, doing nothing. In the new nursery school, the children were active, alive, choosing.

Mid-century Developments

Even as the economic crisis of the Depression and the political turmoil of World War II diverted attention from children's needs, both gave focus to adult needs for work. Out of this necessity came the Works Progress Administration (WPA) nurseries of the 1930s and the Lanham Act nurseries of the 1940s. The most renowned

Celebrating a birthday in a WPA (Works Progress Administration) nursery program, provided by the Lanham Act for women in the workforce during World War II.

Courtesy of WPA (Works Progress Administration)

program of the mid-century was the Kaiser Child Care Centers.

Kaiser Child Care Centers

During World War II, funds were provided to deal with the common situation of mothers working in war-related industries. Further support came from industry during World War II. An excellent model for child care operated from 1943 to 1945 in Portland, Oregon. It was the Kaiser Child Care Centers. Kaiser became the world's largest such center and functioned "'round the clock" all year long. A number of services were made available on-site. An infirmary was located nearby for both mothers and children. Hot meals were made available for mothers to take home when they picked up their children. Lois Meek Stolz was the director of the centers, and James L. Hymes, Jr. was the manager. He describes the centers this way:

> . . . The centers were to have three distinctive qualities. One, they were to be located not out in the community but right at the entrance to the two shipyards, convenient to mothers on their way to and from work. They were to be industry-based, not neighborhood-centered. Two, the centers were to be operated by the shipyards, not by the public schools and not by community agencies. They were to be industrial child care centers, with the cost borne by the Kaiser Company and by parents using the service. Three, they were to be large centers, big enough to meet the need. In the original plan, each center was to serve a thousand preschool children on three shifts. (Hymes, 1978)

These centers served 3,811 children. As Hymes points out, they provided 249,268 child care days and freed 1,931,827 woman work-hours.

Once the war had ended, though, the workers left. Child care was no longer needed, and the centers closed. The Kaiser experience has never been equaled, either in the universal quality of care or in the variety of services. However, it left us a legacy, which Hymes has stressed ever since (in Dickerson, 1992): "It is no great trick to have an excellent child care program. It only requires a lot of money with most of it spent on *trained* staff."

The model Kaiser Child Care Centers provided for child care remains exemplary.

Civil Rights

As early as the beginning of the 20th century, the United States Supreme Court upheld laws concerning "the core of the Jim Crow system, the public schools in which white and black children first experienced the reality of

Genevieve Naylor/CORBIS

Kaiser Shipyard operated a model child care center during World War II.

segregation . . . Jim Crow schools—which taught their students only those skills needed for agricultural work and domestic service—fit the needs of the whole economy and society" (Irons, 2004). The term itself comes from a character in a late 1880s minstrel show and refers to the complete system of segregation.

World War I played an important role in moving large numbers of blacks from the rural South to the cities of the North and West, beginning what has been called the Great Migration. By 1930, the reported literacy rate for blacks had doubled from 1900 to just more than 80 percent, but "the educational status of blacks in the Jim Crow states remained abysmally low in 1950" (Irons, 2004). The Depression was a particularly difficult time for African Americans, as the living standards for those Americans in poverty plummeted. President Franklin Roosevelt's administration and the emerging industrial union movement gave impetus to blacks looking for both employment and political change. World War II continued the process of transformation for many adults, but for children, the situation was still bleak.

The stage for another legal challenge to segregation was set. As Weinberg (1977) states, "Midcentury marked a turning point in the history of black America. The movement for equality came under black leadership, embraced unprecedented numbers of Negroes, and became national in scope. A persistent black initiative forced a reformulation of public policies in education." Children were starting to be considered citizens with rights.

The attack against the segregation system had begun. As seen in the historic cases of *McLaurin v Oklahoma* (1950) and *Brown v Board of Education of Topeka* (1954) the concept of "separate but equal" was overturned. Furthermore, the Civil Rights Act of 1964 continued to address the struggle for equality of opportunity and education, one that persists today in our schools and society (see "Ethic of Social Reform" later in this Chapter).

The Free School

A. S. Neill (1883–1973) was the most famous proponent of the "free/natural school" movement of the midcentury. His book *Summerhill* describes 40 years of that educational program, of which he was headmaster. Neill claimed that most education was defective because it arose from the model of original sin. Assuming children were inherently evil caused educators to force children into doing what was contrary to their nature. Neill shared Rousseau's belief in noninterference, as he states, "I believe that a child is innately wise and realistic. If left to himself without adult suggestion of any kind, he will develop as far as he is capable of developing" (1960).

Neill's belief in freedom was practiced in his school, where children governed themselves and worked toward equal rights with adults. The benefits from such liberties were touted as highly therapeutic and natural, an escape from repression and guilt. Several influences are clear in these educational programs: Rousseau's belief in the *child's innate goodness*, Freud's idea of the *dangerous effects of guilt*, and some of the *social idealism* of Dewey and the Progressives.

Sputnik and the War on Poverty: Head Start

After World War II, few innovations took place until a small piece of metal made its worldwide debut. Sputnik, the Soviet satellite, was successfully launched in 1957 and caused an upheaval in educational circles. Two questions were uppermost in the minds of most Americans: Why were we not first in space? What is wrong with our schools? The emphasis in education quickly settled on engineering, science, and math in the hope of catching up with Soviet technology.

The Civil Rights struggle in the early 1960s soon followed. In pointing out the plight of the poor, education was highlighted as a major stumbling block toward equality of all people. It was time to act, to declare a "war on poverty" that robbed America of its pre-eminent position in the world.

Project Head Start was conceived as education's place to fight the "war on poverty." The same goals of Froebel and Montessori formed the basis of Head Start: helping disadvantaged preschool children. This was a revolution in American education, not seen since the short-lived child care programs during World War II. This project was the first large-scale effort by the government to focus on children of poverty.

Head Start began in 1965 as a demonstration program aimed at providing educational, social, medical, dental, nutritional, and mental health services to preschool children from a diverse population of low-income families. In 1972, it was transformed into a predominantly part-day, full-year program. Key features included offering health services, small groups, parent-teacher collaboration, and the thrill of communities getting involved with children in new ways. Osborn (1965) tells us:

> I wish I knew how to tell this part of the story . . . the bus driver in West Virginia who took time off from his regular job and went to the Center to have juice and crackers with "his" children because they asked him to. . . . The farmer who lived near an Indian Reservation and who each morning saddled his horse, forded a river and picked up an Indian child—who would not have attended a Center otherwise . . . they represent the true flavor of Head Start.

Over the years, Head Start has provided comprehensive developmental services to more than 10 million children and their families.

This was an exciting time, a national recognition of the needs of young children and a hope for a better quality of life. Head Start was an attempt to make amends, to compensate poor children by preparing them for school and educational experiences. Parents, who were required to participate at all levels, were educated along with their children. The purpose of the community-based governing boards was to allow the program to reflect local values and concerns. Concurrently, underprivileged, poor people were being encouraged to take part in solving some of their own problems.

The spirit of Head Start was infectious. As a result of community interest in Head Start, there was a burst of enthusiasm for many programs for the young child. Thanks to Head Start, there is national attention to the need for providing good care and educational experiences for young children. The Head Start program is recognized as an effective means of providing comprehensive services to children and families, serving as a model for the development of the ABC Child Care Act. (The program is discussed in Chapter 2.)

Infant-Toddler Care

Some people say we are in the midst of a second child care revolution for young children, as two parents, single parents, and step-parents all leave the home to work in greater numbers than ever before. Parents must rely on educators to teach their children from a very young age, including infants. While many European industrialized nations have addressed these issues, the United States has not completely faced this reality or risen to the challenge.

The roots of infant-toddler care stem from the women's movement of the 1920s, which brought attention to deeply held beliefs about child-rearing and early education practices. When America was mobilized around World War II, children's care was addressed so as to enable mothers to work while fathers were in the armed forces. With the advent of 1960s, women once again soared into the workplace, and both parents once again focused on work outside the home. Care for children by extended family, family child care homes, and centers is on the rise.

The American public is unclear about what is the best way to raise our very young children, especially those younger than age 2. Women, by and large, are working outside of the home and are not available around the clock to care for infants and toddlers; men are not, by and large, electing to stay home or raise their children full time. There are not nearly enough properly funded centers or family child care homes for very small children, and the patchwork system of parents, extended family, and neighborhood adults fragments the care. As we learn more about the critical time period of 0–2 years of age for brain development, we need to look carefully at quality child care for infants and toddlers.

More Recent Developments

In the late 20th and into this century, three practices are serving as turning points for contemporary early education.

- **DAP.** Developmentally Appropriate Practices (DAP, 1997, 2003, 2007) articulated early education's

National Archives

Head Start is the largest publicly funded education program for young children in the United States.

principles of standard teaching practices that enhanced the growth of the whole child and included age, family, and individual elements. Look for the DAP box in each chapter.

- **NCLB.** The No Child Left Behind Act (NCLB, 2001) reauthorized the Elementary and Secondary Education Act, calling for extensive implementation of state educational standards. Chapter 15 discusses educational reform.
- **Common Core Standards.** Common Core State Standards (CCS, 2010) call for new standards in English language arts and mathematics for grades K-12. These may be as significant as *Brown v Board of Education* in changing the direction of education for years to come (Weber, 2011). Learn more about these standards in the curriculum in Chapter 10 and 15.

Interdisciplinary Influences

Several professions enrich the heritage of early childhood. This diversity was apparent from the beginning as the first nursery schools drew from six different professions: social work, home economics, nursing, psychology, education, and medicine. Three of the most consistent and influential of those disciplines were medicine, education, and child psychology.

Medicine

The medical field has contributed to the study of child growth through the work of several physicians. These doctors became interested in child development and extended their knowledge to the areas of child rearing and education.

Maria Montessori

Maria Montessori (1870–1952) was the first woman in Italy ever granted a medical degree. She began studying children's diseases and, through her work with mentally defective children, found education more appealing. Her philosophy is discussed earlier in this chapter and is part of the Chapter 10 curriculum models.

Sigmund Freud

Sigmund Freud (1856–1939) made important contributions to all modern thinking. The father of personality theory, he drastically changed how we look at childhood. Freud reinforced two specific ideas: 1) a person is influenced by his early life in fundamental and dramatic ways, and 2) early experiences shape the way people live and behave as adults. Thus psychoanalytic theory is mostly about personality development and emotional problems. Freud's work set into motion one of the three major strands of psychological theory that influence the developmental and learning theories of early childhood today. Though he was not involved directly in education, Freud and psychoanalytic theory influenced education greatly. Chapter 4 expands on the theory and its application in early childhood education.

Arnold Gesell

Arnold Gesell (1880–1961) was a physician who was concerned with growth from a medical point of view. Gesell began studying child development when he was a student of G. Stanley Hall, an early advocate of child study. He later established the Clinic of Child Development at Yale University, where the data he collected with his colleagues became the basis of the recognized norms of how children grow and develop. He was also instrumental in encouraging Abigail Eliot to study with the McMillan sisters in England.

Gesell's greatest contribution was in the area of child growth. He saw maturation as an innate and powerful force in development. "The total plan of growth," he said, "is beyond your control. It is too complex and mysterious to be altogether entrusted to human hands. So nature takes over most of the task, and simply invites your assistance" (Gesell, Ames, & Ilg, 1977).

Through the Gesell Institute, guides were published using this theory. With such experts as Dr. Frances Ilg and Dr. Louise Bates Ames, Gesell wrote articles that realistically portrayed the child's growth from birth to adolescence. These guides have sharp critics regarding their overuse and inappropriate application to children of cultures other than those studied. Moreover, their approach can be limiting, particularly as we think of developmentally appropriate practices and the importance of both individual variation and family and cultural diversity (Copple & Bredekamp, 2010). Chapter 3 uses Gesell's "ages and stages" material to develop the word pictures used widely as a yardstick of normal development, and Gesell's maturation theory is discussed in Chapter 4.

Benjamin Spock

Benjamin Spock's book *Baby and Child Care* was a mainstay for parents in the 1940s and 1950s. In a detailed "how-to" format, Dr. Spock (1903–1998) preached a common-sense approach that helped shape the childhood of many of today's adults. By his death in 1998, the book had sold almost 50 million copies around the world and had been translated into 42 languages.

Medical doctors such as Benjamin Spock have contributed to early care and education in significant ways.

Spock saw himself as giving practical application to the theories of John Dewey (see this chapter) and Sigmund Freud (see this chapter and chapter 4), particularly in the ideas that children can learn to direct themselves, rather than needing to be constantly disciplined.

Spock suggested that mothers use the playpen less and allow children freedom to explore the world first-hand. To that end, he asked parents to "child proof" their homes—a radical thought at the time. The word *permissiveness*, as it relates to child-rearing, became associated with Dr. Spock's methods, although Spock himself described his advice as relaxed and sensible, while still advocating for firm parental leadership.

Dr. Spock became an outspoken advocate for causes that extended his ideas. He was an active critic of those forces—economic, social, or political—that destroy healthy development. Dr. Spock noted:

> Child care and home care, if well done, can be more creative, make a greater contribution to the world, [and] bring more pleasure to family members, than 9 out of 10 outside jobs. It is only our mixed-up, materialistic values that make so many of us think the other way around (1976).

T. Berry Brazelton

Dr. T. Berry Brazelton (1918–) is a well-known pediatrician who supports and understands the development of infants and toddlers. He developed an evaluation tool called the Neonatal Behavioral Assessment Scale (the NBAS is also known as "the Brazelton") to assess newborns. Co-founder of the Children's Hospital Unit in Boston, professor emeritus of pediatrics at Harvard Medical School, and a former president of the Society for Research in Child Development, he is also a well-known author. His pediatric guides for parents deal with both physical and emotional growth. His writings speak to the parents' role in child-raising, such as setting limits, listening to what children say, and observing what they do, as in the following discussion:

> I think many working parents have a very tough time thinking about limits. They find it difficult to say no, to set behavior standards. . . . Parents tell me, "I can't stand to be away all day and then come home and be the disciplinarian." We have to realize how hard it is for parents to discipline these days. They need a lot of reinforcement to understand how important reasonable discipline is to the child. Teachers can be very important here, helping parents see the need to expect more adequate behavior (2001).

Brazelton advocates a national parental leave standard and is involved in a federal lobbying group known as "Parent Action." He hosted the nationally syndicated show *What Every Baby Knows*; is co-founder of *Touchpoints*, an educational training center focusing on teacher/parent communication about early development; and writes about key areas of need for children to develop well (Brazelton & Greenspan, 2001).

Education

Early childhood is one part of the larger professional field known as education. This includes elementary, secondary, and college or postsecondary schools. Along with Rudolf Steiner, John Dewey, and Abigail Eliot, several other influences from this field bear attention.

The McMillan Sisters

In the first three decades of this century, these two sisters pioneered in early education. Nursery schools in Britain and America probably were developed because of the drive and dedication of the McMillan sisters.

Both women had broad international backgrounds. They grew up in North America and Scotland. Margaret studied music and language in Europe. She was well read in philosophy, politics, and medicine. Rachel studied to become a health inspector in England.

Health studies of 1908 to 1910 showed that 80 percent of children were born in good health, but by the time they entered school, only 20 percent could be classified that way. Noticing the deplorable conditions for children younger than age 5, the McMillan sisters began a crusade for the slum children in England.

Queen Mary (left) with some of the children from the nursery school attached to the Rachel McMillan Training College in Deptford (1930).

Their concern extended beyond education to medical and dental care for young children. In 1910, they set up a clinic in Deptford, a London slum area, which became an open-air nursery a year later. The McMillans called it a "nurture school." Later, a training college nearby was named for Rachel. With no private financial resources, these two women faced tremendous hardships in keeping their school open. It is to their credit that Deptford still exists today.

The McMillans' theory of fresh air, sleep, and bathing proved successful. "When over seven hundred children between one and five died of measles, there was not one fatal case at Deptford School" (Deasey, 1978). From the school's inception, a primary function was to research the effects of poverty on children.

Of the two sisters, Margaret had the greatest influence at the school at Deptford. After Rachel died in 1917, Margaret continued to champion early education issues beyond Deptford. "Her clinics, night camps, camp school, baby camp, open-air nursery school, and training college all reflected her conviction that health was the hand-maiden of education" (Bradburn, 2000). Abigail Eliot writes of her:

> Miss McMillan invented the name [nursery school]. She paid great attention to health: a daily inspection, the outdoor program, play, good food—what she called "nurture." But she saw that an educational problem was also involved and she set to work to establish her own method of education for young children. This was why she called it a "school" (Hymes, 1978).

Susan Isaacs

Susan Isaacs (1885–1948) was an educator of the early 20th century whose influence on nursery and progressive schools of the day was substantial. In 1929, she published *The Nursery Years*, which emphasized a different point of view than that of the behaviorist psychologists of the times. She interpreted Freudian theory for teachers and provided guidance for how schools could apply this new knowledge of the unconscious to the education of children. She proposed:

> . . . the opportunity for free unhindered imaginative play not only as a means to discover the world but also as a way to reach the psychic equilibrium, in working through wishes, fears, and fantasies so as to integrate them into a living personality (Biber, 1984).

The teacher's role was different from that of a therapist, she asserted, in that teachers were to encourage play as a bridge in a child's emotional and intellectual development.

Isaacs's influence is felt today in schools whose philosophy emphasizes the child's point of view and the notion of play as the child's work.

The Child Study Movement

A survey of education influences is incomplete without mentioning the Child Study Movement in the United States beginning in the 1920s. It was through this movement that education and psychology began to have a common focus on children. Besides the Gesell Institute, many research centers and child development laboratories were established at colleges and universities around the country. The Merrill-Palmer Institute, for example, began in 1920 as a school to serve Detroit, Michigan's, urban children and later served as a model for the Head Start Program; in addition, it sponsored research and training about children and families. Schools of psychology looked for children to observe and study; schools of education wanted demonstration schools for their teachers-in-training and for student-teacher placement. Schools of home economics wanted their students to have firsthand experiences with children. Schools of education hoped to develop leadership from among its teaching and research staff. These on-campus schools provided a place to gather information about child development, psychology, and educational innovation (Harms & Tracy, 2006).

This period of educational experiments and child study led to an impressive collection of normative data by which we still measure ranges of ordinary development. The Child Study Movement was the impetus that began the search for the most appropriate means of educating young children. Laboratory schools reflect the interest of several disciplines in the growth of the young child.

© Cengage Learning

On campus schools have a legacy from the Child Study Movement of early- to mid-20th century where students can learn in a laboratory setting.

The British Infant Schools

Developed by Robert Owen in the early 19th century, the British infant schools had a strong commitment to social reform. Owen was a self-made businessman whose philosophy extended to the creation of an ideal community. Like Rousseau, he believed that people were naturally good but were corrupted by harsh environment and poor treatment. He took his ideas to the British House of Commons, speaking against the common practice of child labor. He then was invited to take over the building of a school in New Lanark, a 2,000-person community near several textile mills. Once there, he stopped employment of children younger than 10 years, sent younger children to nursery and infant schools he built, and required the mills to allow secondary-age children to reduce their labor time to go to school. His son and a daughter immigrated to the United States and founded the community of New Harmony. Both utopian communities were built on Owen's ideas of a new social order built on experimentation and reform.

In England, the term *infant school* refers to the kindergarten and primary grades. In 1967, the Plowden Report proposed a series of reforms for the schools. These changes paralleled those of Owen and mainstream American early education. Three aspects of this **open school** style that received the most attention were:

1. *Vertical (or mixed age) groupings.* Children from 5 to 8 years of age are placed in the same classroom. Several teachers may combine their classes and work together in teaching teams. Children may be taught by the same teachers for two or three years.
2. *Integrated day.* The classroom is organized into various centers for math, science, and the arts. The teacher moves from one child or center to another as needed. Play is often the central activity, with an emphasis on follow-through with children's ideas and interests as they arise.
3. *Thinking over facts.* There is an underlying concept that the process of thinking takes precedence over the accumulation of facts. Learning how to think rather than stockpiling data is encouraged. How to identify and solve problems is valued more than having a finished product. Teachers focus on the child's current learning rather than on the future.

The Infant School model of mixed age range is used widely in early learning centers and school-age programs in the United States, while elementary schools still hold primarily to the one-year/one-grade model.

Reggio Emilia

In the last part of the 20th century into the present time, another educator and educational system have influenced early childhood thinking. Loris Malaguzzi (1920–1994) developed his theory of early childhood education from his work with infants, toddlers, and preschoolers while working as the founder and Director of Early Education in the town of Reggio Emilia, Italy. His philosophy includes creating "an amiable school" (Malaguzzi, 1993) that welcomes families and the community and invites relationships among teachers, children, and parents to intensify and deepen to strengthen a child's sense of identity. Malaguzzi continually asked teachers to question their own practices and listen to the children, as we can hear in his letter (Gandini, 1994) excerpted below:

> My thesis is that if we do not learn to listen to children, it will be difficult to learn the art of staying and conversing with them. . . . It will also be difficult, perhaps impossible, to understand how and why children think and speak; to understand what they do, ask, plan, theorize or desire. . . . Furthermore, what are the consequences of not listening? . . . We adults lose the capacity to marvel, to be surprised, to reflect, to be merry, and to take pleasure in children's words and actions.

Reggio Emilia has attracted the attention and interest of American educators because of its respect for children's work and creativity, its project approach, and its total community support. Its focus on child self-expression and the emergent curriculum model are discussed in Chapter 10.

Psychology

The roots of early childhood education are wonderfully diverse, but one taproot is especially deep: the connection with the field of psychology. In this century particularly, the study of people and their behavior is linked with the study of children and their growth.

Initially, child development was mostly confined to the study of trends and descriptions of changes. Then, the scope and definition of child development began to change. Psychodynamic theories of Freud and Erikson were contrasted by behaviorist theories of Watson and Skinner and by the cognitive theories of Piaget and Vygotsky. Bowlby and Ainsworth studied attachment, Kohlberg and Eisenberg moral development, and Maccoby and Gilligan gender differences.

Developmental psychologists now study the processes associated with those changes. Specifically, child development focuses on language acquisition, the effect of early experiences on intellectual development, and the process of attachment to others, and how neuroscience discoveries reveal developmental processes. Such is the world of early childhood—it is no wonder that we are so closely tied to the world of psychology, as discussed in depth in Chapter 4.

Themes in Early Childhood Education

When we review the colorful and rich history of early childhood education, four major themes emerge. Each is reflected in the many influences on early childhood education.

Ethic of Social Reform

The first theme, the ethic of social reform, expects that schooling for young children leads to social change and improvement. Maria Montessori, Robert Owen, the McMillans, Patty Smith Hill, Abigail Eliot, and the Head Start program all tried to improve children's health and physical well-being by attending first to the physical and social welfare aspects of children's lives. Other more recent examples, including Marian Wright Edelman, Louise Derman Sparks, Robert Coles, and Jonathan Kozol, illustrate how important this theme is to our work.

Marian Wright Edelman is an outstanding children's advocate. A graduate of Spelman College and Yale Law School, Edelman began her career as a civil rights lawyer. (She was the first black woman to be admitted to the Mississippi state bar.) By the 1960s she had dedicated

herself to the battle against poverty, moving to Washington, D.C., and founding a public interest law firm that eventually became the Children's Defense Fund (CDF). CDF has become the United States' strongest voice for children and families (see Figure 1-6).

The author of several books, including *Families in Peril, The Measure of Our Success*, and *The Sea Is So Wide and My Boat Is So Small*, Edelman advocates for equity in social reform:

> [We] seek to ensure that no child is left behind and that every child has a Healthy Start, a Head Start, a Fair Start, a Safe Start, and a Moral Start in life with the support of caring families and communities (Edelman, 2006).

CDF: Child Advocacy as Social Reform

1975	Assisted in passing the Education for All Handicapped Children Act
1979	Blocked attempts to eliminate $200 million for Social Services
1980	Supported Adoption Assistance & Child Welfare Act
1982	Helped forward the Children's Mental Health Program
1990	Supported Act for Better Child Care (Child Care & Development Block Grant)
1994	Reauthorized Head Start with Quality Improvements
1997	Promoted Children's Health Insurance Program (CHIP)
2001	Expanded Child Care Tax Credit
2002	Food Stamp provisions preserved
2003	Preserved CHIP funding to all states
2007	Evaluation of the CDF freedom schools, summer enrichment programs, find that children score higher on standardized reading achievement tests.
2008	Published its annual State of America's Children, reporting that it lags behind nearly all industrialized nations in key child indicators.
2010	Established its online research library, using data from a wide range of sources, primarily federal data systems such as the Bureaus of the Census and of Labor Statistics, and from nonprofit and educational entities such as the Kaiser Family Foundations and National Association of Child Care Resource and Referral Agencies.

© Cengage Learning 2014

FIGURE 1-6 Children's Defense Fund, led by Marian Wright Edelman, has successfully advocated for children with research and persistence for more than three decades.

BRAIN
Research Says...

What Is Neuroscience and Why Should We Care?

When the field of psychology began to develop in the 1800s, new questions began to surface about the brain and the mind. Freud's ideas about the subconscious mind, Piaget's concepts of the thinking mind, and behaviorists' work on changing thoughts and attitudes via shaping behavior all led to the emergence of cognitive science in the late 1980s. A landmark report by the National Academy of Sciences entitled *From Neurons to Neighborhoods: The Science of Early Childhood Development* (Shonkoff & Phillips, 2000) joined early childhood education with neuroscience. Since then, the development and availability of brain-imaging techniques provide glimpses of brain activity as an individual thinks and feels.

We are now in what might be called the "century of the brain." If the human brain is like the hardware of a computer, the mind may be seen as the software. Further, this software changes as it is used; people assign different meaning to the inputs and outputs of things. Brain structures can now be mapped on a matrix. The work of cognitive neuropsychologists allows us to link specific regions of the brain with specific cognitive processes such as verbal and memory skills, attention, emotional responding, and motor coordination. Experimental techniques used on animals (that could not be ethically used with humans) have revealed the brain regions that connect with psychological processes. Combining computed tomography (CT) and magnetic resonance imaging (MRI) developed during the late 20th century with the more recent functional magnetic resonance imaging (fMRI) and positron emission topography (PET) allows us to determine the location of tumors or lesions as well as study the genetic basis of differences (Byrnes, 2001).

The new frontier of neuroscience is showing us the remarkable plasticity of the brain, as well as the critical nature of the early years. "Early experiences determine whether a child's developing brain architecture provides a strong or weak foundation for all future learning, behavior and health" (CDC/Harvard, 2007). Neuroscience, hand-in-hand with child development research, can address questions about why you—and society—must invest in young children.

Questions

1. If this is the "century of the brain," what do you think will change in educational practices?
2. What do you think parents should know about brain development in the first five years of a child's life?
3. What would "investing in young children" look like in your community? In your state?

This reform work is being carried on by her son, Jonah, who now organizes the annual Washington, D.C., rally "Stand for Children."

Louise, in collaboration with Betty Jones and the Anti-Bias Task Force of Pacific Oaks and Julia Olsen Edwards of Cabrillo College, has published several books and countless articles about anti-bias education. These works outline several areas in which children's behavior is influenced by biases in our society and suggests a host of ways that teachers (and parents) can begin addressing these issues. These professionals have added an important dimension to the notion of social reform, for they focus attention on ourselves, the school environment, children's interactions, and the community of parents and colleagues in educational settings.

Finally, social reform in contemporary times has been championed by educators and citizens beyond early childhood education. Robert Coles, a psychiatrist and educator, has written and lectured extensively about his observations and work with children of poverty and is best known for *Children of Crisis: A Study of Courage and Fear* (1971). Jonathan Kozol has spoken extensively about segregation in the schools, most notably in his books *Letters to a Young Teacher* (2007) and *Savage Inequalities: Children in America's Schools* (1991), in which he writes:

> Surely there is enough for everyone in this country. It is a tragedy that these good things are not more widely shared. All our children ought to be allowed a stake in the enormous richness of America. Whether they were born to poor white Appalachians or to wealthy Texans, to poor black people in the Bronx or to rich people in Manhasset or Winnetka, they are all quite wonderful and innocent when they are small. We soil them needlessly.

A challenge of our profession is to create funding mechanisms to provide early educational experience for *all* children regardless of family income. Founded in 1948, the Annie E. Casey Foundation, one of the largest private foundations in the United States, is based on helping vulnerable kids and families succeed. Educators today still assert that tired, undernourished children are not ready to learn or to be educated. Social reform can go further as described in Chapter 15.

Importance of Childhood

The second theme is **the importance and uniqueness of childhood.** In fact, the entire concept of the child as a special part of human existence and, therefore, a valuable part of the life cycle rests on this theme.

The saying "As the twig is bent, so grows the tree" could apply to all children and their early childhood learning experiences, as well as to an individual child. When people accepted the importance of childhood, they began to take responsibility for a quality life for children. From Comenius, Rousseau, and Froebel of earlier centuries to Neill, Russell, and the Child Study Movement of the 1900s, society began to provide for the health and physical welfare of children and come to understand the necessity to care for their minds. Reflecting on public thinking about childhood over the past four centuries reveals these patterns (Mintz, 2004):

- Premodern childhood (through 17th century)—children as adults in training
- Modern childhood (18th–20th centuries)—children as innocent and fragile creatures

Childhood is a special time of life.

© Cengage Learning

- Postmodern childhood (late 20th to 21st centuries)—children as participants/consumers of culture and the common life

We believe the early years form the foundation for later development, physically, intellectually, socially, and emotionally. This viewpoint takes a holistic approach; that is, all developmental areas of a child matter and blend together to form a complete child. Even as we teachers outline the separate developmental domains, we must take into account the whole child, for each part influences the whole. Current trends that support this theme are developmentally appropriate practices (DAP) and the contexts of culture and family that we are becoming familiar with in our global community (see Diversity feature in every chapter). Children come to us with a genetic history and from families that identify with a range of racial, ethnic, cultural, language, and socioeconomic groups.

Moreover, early childhood educators believe that play is essential to children's development. Of increasing concern to childhood advocates is the pushing of children toward adulthood too fast and away from childhood too quickly. Spurred by the advent of technology and social media and the rush to academic content, young children are pushed unnecessarily out of a relaxed childhood by a fast-paced society whose pressure to succeed puts children of all ages at risk. The classic comments of Dr. David Elkind (1982) ring true today:

> We should appreciate the value of childhood with its special joys, sorrows, worries, and concerns. Valuing childhood does not mean seeing it as a happy, innocent period but rather as an important period of life to which children are entitled. They have a right to be children, to enjoy the pleasures and to suffer the trials of childhood that are infringed upon by hurrying. Childhood is the most basic human right of children.

Children need special attention during these years. Childhood is fundamentally different from adulthood; it needs to be understood and respected as such. Children's styles of learning, of letting the child "learn by doing" and "learn by discovery," are part of the essential respect for children and childhood. Public recognition of that need has created a wealth of programs for the young not dreamed of at any other time in history.

Transmitting Values

The third recurrent theme in our educational heritage is that of **transmitting values.** What children should ultimately *do* and *be* is at the core of all child-rearing practices, whether in the home or the school. Values—whether social, cultural, moral, or religious—have been the essence of education for centuries.

- Puritan fathers valued biblical theology, so schools of their time taught children to read the Bible.
- Rousseau and Froebel valued childhood, so they created special places for children to express their innate goodness and uniqueness.
- The works of Montessori, Dewey, and Steiner reflected a belief in the worth and dignity of childhood.
- Ed Ziegler of Head Start and Derman-Sparks of the Anti-Bias Curriculum realized that the child's self-worth would be enhanced by valuing one's culture or origin.

These educators all transmitted their values into the educational practices we have inherited.

Many issues clamor for our attention. Information overload threatens to drive us to distraction and inertia. "People are so overwhelmed," wrote Brazelton and Greenspan (2001). "While they're whirling around, they don't have time to stop and think, 'What are my values? Do my children really come first? Am I making time for them in my life?'" Many young families today are aware of this situation and are looking for spiritual and moral direction for themselves and their children.

Children learn what they live. Valuing and connecting home cultural knowledge with an early childhood program is challenging. Successful teaching practices must reflect teaching practices at home in substantial ways; blending basic life skills, ethics, culture, and traditions builds substance in our children and in our society. This teamwork is possible if (and this is a big *if*) adults can find a way to honor diversity and still form a cohesive culture. "An ability to reach unity in diversity will be

the beauty and test of our civilization," said Mahatma Gandhi. It is our ethical responsibility to articulate our values as educators and to include those of the families we teach.

Teaching children to live in a democratic society has always been valued in the United States. In the curriculum from early education through college, this belief is reflected as we educate our children for citizenship. Being an early childhood educator provides you with the opportunity to be an agent for social change—to actually translate the values of democracy into practice. Successful teaching practices include the process of defining our values and working on how we teach them; both are the critical issues in education.

Professionalism

The fourth recurrent theme is **professionalism**. "If you are thinking about working with young children as a career, perhaps you are wondering how early childhood education compares in prestige and importance with elementary or secondary education," wrote Stanford's Edith Dowley (1985). As one of the original Head Teachers of the Kaiser Child Care Centers, Dowley had seen many changes in her nearly half-century in the field: "Is it truly a profession for growth and change? Can a student preparing to work with young children today look forward to a challenging, intellectually stimulating, and rewarding future in an early childhood profession?"

If you have read this chapter, then you already know the answer. The early years are a special time of life, and those who work with young children can openly declare their calling. There are four aspects of this sense of professionalism:

- *Sense of identity*. Early childhood professionals see themselves as caregivers who strive to educate the

Early educational experiences transmit society's values to children.

TeachSource Video

Watch the TeachSource Video entitled "Teaching as a Profession: An Early Childhood Teacher's Responsibilities and Development." After you study the video clip, view the artifacts, and read the teacher interviews and text, reflect on the following questions:

1. How does preschool teacher Samantha Brade show her sense of the importance of early childhood education, and what values is she trying to transmit?

2. How does Samantha demonstrate professionalism, and why should this inform one's teaching?

whole child, taking into consideration the body, the mind, and the heart and soul (see Chapter 3).

- *Purpose to engage in developmentally appropriate practices* (DAP). What constitutes quality care and education calls for blending three knowledge bases:

  1. Child development and learning.
  2. The strengths, interests, and needs of each child.
  3. The social and cultural contexts in which children live.

  (See the DAP Box in each chapter.)

- *Commitment to ethical teaching and to child advocacy.* Being a professional means behaving with a child's best interests in mind, keeping confidentiality when discussing issues in the classroom and about families, upholding a code of ethics, and taking one's self and work seriously. (See Chapter 5 and connections to the Code of Ethical Conduct in all chapters.)

- *Participation in the work as a legitimate livelihood.* Early childhood education is more than glorified babysitting; the people who provide care and education to young children deserve wages and working conditions that are worthy of their efforts. The Center for the Study of Child Care Employment, led by Marcy Whitebook and others, is attempting to both define and highlight the issues of labor and employment of early childhood workers as a profession (see Chapter 15).

"In the last decade and a half, the boundaries of the profession have changed rather dramatically for teachers. As we have become a more complex and diverse society, the roles traditionally ascribed to teachers have taken new meaning and significance. In the case of teachers of young children, their role has expanded to encompass many, heretofore, duties and responsibilities that were often considered to be part of the home" (Cruz, 2008). The challenges we face in meeting our professional obligations are considerable. Cruz continues:

Aside from the traditional roles that teachers have assumed, they are now expected to serve as curriculum specialists, diagnosticians, health care providers, family counselors, adult educators, program managers, child development experts, child advocates, mental health specialists, nutrition specialists, and many others too numerous to list. At the same

---

 Making Good Teaching a Professional Enterprise

As you look to making teaching your profession, you need to be familiar with developmentally appropriate practice (DAP). The foundation of good teaching for young children is based in engaging in practices, regardless of the setting, that are appropriate to the children in front of you. A blend of the familiar and the novel, with the challenges of meaningful and relevant experiences that are full of play and focus, helps all children grow and learn.

At the same time, making this a profession includes articulating what DAP is and ensuring that the public understands and endorses these priorities. The *Save Our Schools March* on Washington, D.C., on July 30, 2011, was an event that did just that. Luminaries such as Jonathan Kozol, Diane Ravitch, and Matt Damon spoke out on behalf of teachers. "Teachers are my heroes," stated Kozol. "I always feel safe in a group of teachers." Ravitch added, "We join together—parents, students, school leaders, teachers—to insist that the public schools are the public trust. . . . [E]ducation is a right, not a race. . . . Our goal is to prepare all children to be winners in their own lives."

To inspire is part of a teacher's commitment to DAP, as Damon's comments point out (www.washingtonpost.com [2011]):

I was raised by a teacher. My mother is a professor of early childhood education. And from the time I went to kindergarten through my senior year in high school, I went to public schools. I wouldn't trade that education and experience for anything.

I had incredible teachers. As I look at my life today, the things I value most about myself—my imagination, my love of acting, my passion for writing, my love of learning, my curiosity—all come from how I was parented and taught. . . .

But it's more than that. My teachers were EMPOWERED to teach me. Their time wasn't taken up with a bunch of test prep—this silly drill and kill nonsense that any serious person knows doesn't promote real learning. No, my teachers were free to approach me and every other kid in that classroom like an individual puzzle. They took so much care in figuring out who we were and how to best make the lessons resonate with each of us. They were empowered to unlock our potential. They were allowed to be teachers.

Making good teaching a professional enterprise asks you to speak out about what YOU know is good for children.

time, the teaching profession is confronting new notions of pedagogy and more intense scrutiny by professional groups. With the focus on standards, readiness initiatives, assessment, and other forms of accountability, the field of early education is truly being reinvented.

So where do we go from here? We have professional organizations to guide us (see Figure 1-7). These organizations have made improvements in the status of children, and they have begun to outline standards and practices for the people who call themselves "early childhood professionals."

The four themes—an ethic of social reform, the importance of childhood, the transmission of values, and professionalism of the field—have been at the center of early education for centuries. Occasionally one theme dominates, as it did in the 1960s when the desire for social reform led to the creation of Head Start. At other times, they seem indistinguishable from one another. Together, they have shaped the direction of early childhood education as we know it today. As we learn more about children, society, and ourselves, the 21st century will be a time to reconsider and redefine our aims and directions. It is a formidable challenge—and one for us to meet in flexible, innovative ways.

Guides to the Early Childhood Profession

Document	Goal	Source/Access
Code of Ethical Conduct	Provide a moral compass for early childhood educators	Feeney & Freeman (1999), Feeney (2011), Gordon & Browne, Appendix A
Developmentally Appropriate Practices	Provide guidance about current understandings, values, and goals for working with children in group settings	Copple & Bredekamp (2010), Gordon & Browne, Chapters 2 and 9
Program Accreditation Criteria & Procedures	Establish recommended standards for practice, serving as benchmarks	NAEYC Academy (2006) Gordon & Browne, Chapters 2 and 15
Early Childhood Professional Preparation	Guidelines for teacher education	NAEYC Standards for Professional Preparation Programs (2009), CA ECE Competencies (2011), Gordon & Browne, Chapters 5-8

FIGURE 1-7 Documents that promote professionalism in early childhood education.

SUMMARY

LO 1 Major contributions to the field of early childhood education have come from Europe. Since the mid-1700s, philosophers such as Comenius, Locke, Rousseau, and Pestalozzi wrote about children and their education. From the 1800s, educators such as Froebel, Montessori, and Steiner opened schools based on their interpretations and innovations. Other perspectives from China, Japan, Native Americans, and Africa have added to the educational thinking of our time.

LO 2 American influences began in the days of colonialism and slavery. The Progressive era of the late 1800s and early 1900s expanded the field with the work of Dewey, Hill, Mitchell, and Eliot. Parent cooperatives and the Child Study Movement expanded the types of schooling for young children, as did child care centers at the Kaiser Shipyards and Head Start for low-income families. Recent developments in the United States include developmentally appropriate practices, No Child Left Behind, and common core standards.

LO 3 The disciplines of medicine, education, and psychology have made profound influences on the field. Theories of doctors like Montessori, Freud, and Gesell established a base on which Spock and Brazelton built. The MacMillan sisters and Isaacs helped spur the inclusion of health and play into early childhood settings, and the multi-age range of the British Infant Schools and creativity of Reggio Emilia today adds important educational components. Psychology has a rich history (elaborated in Chapter 4), which today includes work with neuroscience.

LO 4 Four themes emerge in early childhood education throughout history. They are the ethic of social reform, the importance of childhood, the transmission of values, and professionalism. These themes make good teaching a professional enterprise that is worthy of advocacy and dedication. The contributions of many pioneers leave us dreams for the young children of our society. This can give meaning to our lives as teachers as we continue to create a climate for the child who will make history tomorrow.

Key Terms

professional
early childhood education
building block years
readiness
tabula rasa
concrete
integrated curriculum

kindergarten/children's garden
self-correcting
child-centered approach
kindergarten
custodial
parent cooperative schools
open school

vertical groupings (mixed age)
integrated day
ethic of social reform
importance and uniqueness of childhood
transmitting values
professionalism

Review Questions

1. Match the name with the appropriate phrase. Put them in the order that best matches your own theory of early childhood education. State your reasons.

   Rousseau "prepared environment"
   Montessori "nurture" school
   Froebel children are naturally good
   Malaguzzi father of kindergarten
   Dewey common-sense approach
   Spock first picture book for children
   McMillan sisters Progressive Movement
   Comenius Reggio Emilia

2. Read the following list of some nontraditional and mainstream perspectives as described in the chapter. After each, trace its original root and put at least one example of how this perspective could be practiced in an early childhood classroom today.

Perspective	Roots in Early Childhood Practice
Harmony	
Kinship networks	
Close ties to nature	
Respect for elders	
Cooperative work	
Expressiveness	

3. Maria Montessori made several contributions to education. What are some of her theories, and how did she adapt them for classroom use? How are Montessori materials or teaching methods used in your classroom?

4. Name the four themes that have guided early childhood education throughout its history. Include a person and a concept for each theme and explain why they match the theme.

Observe and Apply

1. Choose a school or center near you, and interview the director or lead teacher. What philosophies are important? What were some of the social, economic, and political issues of the times when it was founded? Ask to look at any old photos, handbooks, or newspaper clippings. Why would documenting the history of a program be useful?
2. Identify and describe five key people who influenced the field of early childhood education. With whom would you like to have studied or worked? Why? Ask your professor, a teacher, and a principal/director and compare your findings with your own.
3. Write your own pedagogic creed. List what you consider to be the most important beliefs you hold about educating young children. How do you see those beliefs expressed in school today?
4. Make a list of the values you think are important to teach children. In an adjoining column, add the ways in which you would help children learn those values. In other words, list the materials and curriculum you would use.

Helpful Websites

American Federation of Teachers Educational Foundation **www.aft.org**

Annie E. Casey Foundation   **www.aecf.org**

Association for Childhood Education International **www.acei.org**

British Infant School **www.sparatcus.schoolnet.co.uk**

Center for the Study of the Child Care Workforce **www.irle.berkeley.edu/cscce**

The Children's Defense Fund **www.childrensdefense.org**

National Association for the Education of Young Children **www.naeyc.org**

National Center for Children and Poverty **www.nccp.org**

National Institute for Early Education Research **www.nieer.org**

North American Reggio Emilia Alliance **www.reggioalliance.org**

Society for Research in Child Development **www.srcd.org**

Waldorf Schools   **www.waldorfanswers.org**

The Education CourseMate website for this text offers many helpful resources and interactive study tools. Go to CengageBrain.com to access the TeachSource Videos, flashcards, tutorial quizzes, direct links to all of the websites mentioned in the chapter, downloadable forms, and more.

References

Aries, P. (1962). *Centuries of childhood.* New York: Knopf.

Baker, K. R. (1950). *The nursery school: A human relationships laboratory.* New York: Saunders.

Biber, B. (1984). *Early education and psychological development.* New Haven, CT: Yale University Press.

Bradburn, E. (2000). Margaret MacMillan: 1860-1933. In A. Gordon & K. W Browne (Eds.), *Beginnings and beyond* (5th Ed.). Clifton Park, NY: Thomson Delmar Learning.

Brazelton, T. B., & Greenspan, S. (2001). *The irreducible needs of young children: what every child must have to grow, learn and flourish.* Cambridge, MA: DaCapo Press.

Brooks, A. (1886). *Four active workers.* Springfield, MA: Milton Bradley.

Brosterman, N. (1997). *Inventing Kindergarten.* New York: Harry N. Abrams.

Byrnes, J. P. (2001). *Minds, brains, and learning.* New York: Guilford Press.

Center on the Developing Child at Harvard University. (2007). *A science-based framework for early childhood policy: Using evidence to improve outcomes in learning, behavior and health for vulnerable children.* http://www.developingchild.harvard.edu.

Chattin-McNichols, J. (1993). In A. Gordon & K. W Browne (Eds.), *Beginnings and beyond* (3rd Ed.). Clifton Park, NY: Thomson Delmar Learning.

Cohen, D. H., & Randolph, M. (1977). *Kindergarten and early schooling.* Englewood Cliffs, NJ: Prentice-Hall.

Coles, R. (1971). *Children of crisis: A study of courage and fear.* New York, NY: Houghton Mifflin.

Comenius. (1658). *Orbis Pictus* (The World of Pictures). Pressburg, Bratislava.

Copple, C. C., and Bredekamp, S. (Eds.). (2010). *Developmentally appropriate practice in early childhood programs serving children birth through age eight.* (3rd Ed.). Washington, D.C.: NAEYC.

Cottrol, R.J., Diamond, R. T., & Ware, L. B. (2004, Summer). The Decline of the Idea of Caste: Setting the Stage for *Brown v. Board of Education.* American Educator, AFT.

Cubberly, E. P. (1920). *A brief history of education.* Boston: Houghton Mifflin.

Damon, M., Kozol, J., and Ravitch, D. (July 30, 2011). "Save Our Schools: March & Rally on Washington, D.C.-*Washington Post.* http://www.washington post.com.

Deasey, D. (1978). *Education under six.* New York: St. Martin's Press.

DeMause, L. (1974). *The history of childhood.* New York: Psychohistory Press.

Derman-Sparks, L. (1988). *The anti-bias curriculum: Tools for empowering young children.* Washington, D.C.: NAEYC.

Derman-Sparks, L. & Olsen Edwards, J. (2010) *Antibias education for young children and ourselves.* Washington, D.C.: NAEYC.

Dewey, J. (1897, 1916). *My pedagogic creed.* Washington, D.C.: The Progressive Education Association and Democracy and Education.

Dickerson, M. (1992, Spring). James L. Hymes, Jr.: Advocate for young children. *Childhood Education.*

Dowley, E. (1985). Early childhood education in the shipyards. In A. Gordon & K. W Browne, *Beginnings and beyond* (1st Ed.). Clifton Park, NY: Thomson Delmar Learning.

DuBois, W E. B. (1995). *The talented tenth.* Published in The Negro Problem (1903), excerpted in F. Schultz (Ed.), *Sources: Notable selection in education.* Guilford, CT: Dushkin.

Edelman, M. W (2006). *The state of America's children.* Washington, D.C.: Children's Defense Fund.

Elkind, D. (1982). *The hurried child.* Reading, MA: Addison-Wesley.

Fanjul, S. (2011, January). Many anniversaries. *Young Children,* 66(1).

Feeney, S. (2011). *Professionals in early childhood education: Doing our best for young children.* Upper Saddle River, NJ: Pearson.

Feeney, S., & Freeman, N. K. (1999). *Ethics and the early childhood educator: Using the NAEYC Code.* Washington, D.C.: NAEYC.

Froebel, F. (1887). *The education of man* (M. W. Hailman, Trans.). New York: D. Appleton.

Gandini, L. (1994, July). Tribute to Loris Malaguzzi. *Young Children,* 49(5).

Gesell, A. L., Ames, L. A., & Ilg, F L. (1977). *The child from five to ten.* New York: Harper & Row.

Gianoutsos, J. (2011). Locke and Rousseau: Early Childhood Education. *The Pulse,* 4(1). http//:www.baylor.edu./pulse.

Gonzalez-Mena, J. (2001). *Foundations: Early childhood education in a diverse society.* Mountain View, CA: Mayfield.

Greenberg, P. (1987, July). Lucy Sprague Mitchell: A major missing link between early childhood education in the 1980s and progressive education in the 1890s-1930s. *Young Children,* 42(5).

Harms, T. & Tracy, R. (2006, July). University laboratory schools in early childhood education. *Young Children,* 61(4).

Hewes, D. (1993). On doing history. In A. Gordon & K. W Browne (Eds.), *Beginnings and beyond* (3rd Ed.). Clifton Park, NY: Thomson Delmar Learning.

Hill, P. S. (1996). Kindergarten. From the American Educator Encyclopedia (1941). In Paciorek & Munro. *Sources: Notable selections in early childhood education.* Guildford, CT: Dushkin.

Hilliard, A. G., III. (1997, September). Teacher education from an African American perspective. In

J. Irvine (Ed.), *Critical knowledge for diverse teachers and learners.* Washington, D.C.: AACTE.

Hymes, J. L., Jr. (1978-79). *Living history interviews (Books 1-3).* Carmel, CA: Hacienda Press.

Hyson, M. (Ed.) (2003). *Preparing early childhood professionals: NAEYC's standards for programs.* Washington, D.C.: NAEYC.

Irons, P. (2004, Summer). Jim Crow's Schools. *American Educator,* AFT.

Jones-Wilson, F. C. (1996). Westport, CT: Greenwood Press. *Encyclopedia of African-American Education.*

Keatinge, M. W. (1896). *The great didactic of John Amos Comenius* (Trans. and with introductions). London: Adams and Charles Black.

Kozol, J. (1991). *Savage inequalities: Children in America's schools.* New York: Crown Publishers.

Malaguzzi, L. (1993, November). For an education based on relationships. *Young Children.*

McMillan, M. (1919). *The nursery school.* London and Toronto: J. M. Dent & Sons; New York: E. P. Dutton.

Mintz, S. (2004). *Huck's raft: A history of American childhood.* Cambridge, MA: Belknap Press of Harvard University.

Mitchell, L. S. (1951). *Our children and our schools.* New York: Simon & Schuster.

Montessori, M. (1967). *The Montessori method* (Trans. A. E. George). Cambridge, MA.

National Academy. (2006). *Accreditation criteria & procedures (Revised).* Washington, D.C.: NAEYC.

Neill, A. S. (1960). *Summerhill: A radical approach to child rearing.* New York: Hart.

Osborn, D. K. (1991). *Early childhood education in historical perspective* (3rd Ed.). Athens, GA: Education Associates.

Pleasant, M. B. B. (1992). *Hampton University: Our home by the sea.* Virginia Beach, VA: Donning.

Read, K., & Patterson, J. (1980). *The nursery school & kindergarten: Relationships and learning* (7th Ed.). New York: Holt, Rinehart, & Winston.

Reifel, S. (2011, March). Our proud heritage: Observation and early childhood teaching—evolving fundamentals. *Young Children,* 6(1).

Rousseau, J. J. (1761). *Emile* (Trans. by B. Foxley). London and Toronto: J. M. Dent & Sons..

Shonkoff, J. P., and Phillips, D. A. (Eds.). (2000). *From neurons to neighborhoods: The science of early childhood development.* Washington, D.C.: National Academies Press.

Silber, K. (1965). *Pestalozzi: The man and his works.* (2nd Ed.). London: Routledge and Kegan Paul.

Spock, B. (1947). *The common sense book of baby and child care.* New York: Duell, Sloan & Pierce.

Spock, B. (1976, April). Taking care of a child and a home: An honorable profession for men and women. *Redbook Magazine.*

Steiner, R. (1926). *The essentials of education.* London: Anthroposophical Publishing.

Stolz, L. M. (1978). In J. Hymes. *Living history interviews.* Carmel, CA: Hacienda Press.

Walker, L. R. (1997, Fall). John Dewey at Michigan. *Michigan Today.*

Weber, S. (September 5, 2011). ASCD edge in brief: Turning points. http://edge.ascd.org/_Turning Points/blog/4976758/127586.html.

Weinberg, M. (1977). *A chance to learn: The history of race and education in the United States.* Cambridge, MA: Cambridge University Press.

Williams, S. M. (2011). Insights from the field: A delightful story. *Beginnings & beyond.* (8th Ed.). Belmont, CA: Wadsworth Cengage Learning.

Types of Programs

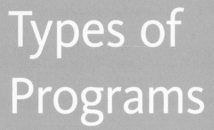 **Standards For Professional Development**

The following NAEYC standards for initial and advanced early childhood professional preparation are addressed in this chapter:

Standard 1 Promoting child development and learning

Standard 2 Building family and community relationships

Standard 3 Observing, documenting, and assessing to support young children and families

Standard 4 Using developmentally effective approaches to connect with children and families

Standard 5 Using content knowledge to build meaningful curriculum

Standard 6 Becoming a professional

Field Experience

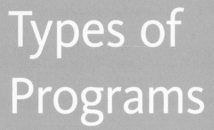 **Code of Ethical Conduct**

These are the sections of the NAEYC Code of Ethical Conduct that apply to the topics of this chapter:

Section I:

I-1.2   To base program practices upon current knowledge and research in the field of early childhood education, child development and related disciplines as well as on particular knowledge of each child.

P-1.7   We shall strive to build individual relationships with each child: make individual adaptations in teaching strategies, learning environment, and curricula; and consult with the family so that each child benefits from the program.

Section II:

I-2.8   To help family members enhance their understanding of their children, as staff are enhancing their understanding of each child through communications with families, and support family members in the continuing development of their skills as parents.

P-2.2   We shall inform families of program philosophy, policies, curriculum, assessment system, cultural practices, and personnel qualifications, and explain why we teach as we do—which should be in accordance with our ethical responsibilities to children.

Section IV:

I.4.1   To provide the community with high quality early childhood care and education programs and services.

P.4-6   We shall be familiar with laws and regulations that serve to protect the children in our programs and be vigilant in ensuring that these laws and regulations are followed.

Learning Objectives

LO1 Examine the underlying theoretical principles of developmentally appropriate practices applied to a variety of early childhood programs.

LO2 Describe the core programs of early childhood education, program types, and their differing philosophies.

LO3 Identify the variation of program options and range of delivery systems that impact the lives of children and their families.

LO4 Assess early childhood programs utilizing indicators of quality early childhood practices that support all children including those with diverse characteristics.

Developmentally Appropriate Practice in Early Childhood Programs

Throughout this text and whenever NAEYC principles are discussed, we use the term *developmentally appropriate practice*. What exactly is **developmentally appropriate practice**, or **DAP**, as it is more familiarly known?

More than 20 years ago, NAEYC published a position paper, which articulated standards for high quality care and education for young children. The guidelines were a response to the need for a set of unified standards for accreditation through NAEYC's newly established National Academy of Early Childhood, and gave a necessary antidote to the more teacher-directed, academic preparation and skills-teaching methods that were encroaching on many early childhood programs.

The DAP approach stressed the need for activity-based learning environments based on what we know about children through years of child development research and what we observe of their interests, abilities, and needs. The position paper was revised over the years to be more inclusive by moving from an "either/or" point of view to that of "both/and." In other words, there are many right ways to apply DAP principles.

Three Core Components of DAP

The position statement of "Developmentally Appropriate Practice in Early Childhood Programs Serving Children from Birth through Age 8" (NAEYC, 2009) cites three core considerations on which teachers and caregivers should base their decisions about young children's growth and development:

1. *What is known about child development and learning*—knowledge of age-related characteristics that permit general predictions about what experiences are likely to best promote children's learning and development. This is the core around which the idea of *developmentally appropriate* is built.
2. *What is known about each child as an individual*—what practitioners learn about each child that has implications for how best to adapt and be responsive to individual variations.
3. *What is known about the social and cultural contexts in which children live*—the values, expectations, and behavioral and linguistic conventions that shape children's lives at home and in their communities that practitioners must strive to understand in order to ensure that learning experiences in the program

or school are meaningful, relevant, and respectful for each child and family. Figure 2-1 shows how these three core principles work together.

The following scenario shows how these core considerations are applied when planning a developmentally appropriate program for toddlers:

1. *What does child development tell us about toddlers?* We know that toddlers express their need to do everything by themselves, usually more than they can actually achieve. They like to feel independent and learn quickly if given a little help and then encouraged to do what they can for themselves (see Chapters 3 and 4 for more detail).
2. *What do we know about each child as an individual?* Many of these toddlers rely on their parents to help them put on their clothes, feed them, or put their toys away. Others are being taught these tasks at home. Most of the children come to the teachers for assistance and a few ask for help. One toddler will persist at a dressing task for nearly five minutes while another will throw shoes across the floor if they do not fit the first time.
3. *What do we know about the social and cultural context in each child's life?* Most of the children in this group come from homes in which help is readily available from siblings and extended family members. The group's dominant cultural values and child-rearing practices reinforce dependence and community, although there is a smaller group of families that want their children to become independent as soon as possible.

By looking at all three core considerations together, we have some decisions to make about setting goals toward greater independence for the toddlers. Respecting cultural and social contexts means we begin by talking to families,

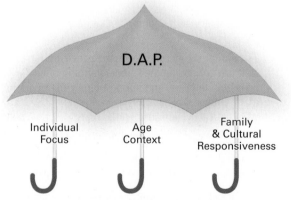

FIGURE 2-1 There are a variety of early childhood programs to fit the needs of children and their families.

A developmentally appropriate program takes into consideration this child's age, individual abilities, and the culture of her home and family.

perhaps at a parent meeting, in which families are invited to share their child-rearing practices from their cultural viewpoint. Once we have an understanding of what families expect and want, we have an opportunity to work together to negotiate a solution that will be beneficial both for the toddlers and for the families. When developmentally appropriate elements are taken into consideration, the bonds between families and teachers are strengthened and the best interests of the children prevail.

Guidelines for DAP

DAP provides the context for learning environments in which children's abilities are matched to the developmental tasks they need to learn. DAP is based on what we know about how children learn and what we know about individual children and their families. This collective knowledge is applied to each decision that is made about the program. Copple and Bredekamp (2009) suggest five key areas of practice that guide the decision-making process.

1. *Creating a Caring Community of Learners* begins with programs that support and value all children, regardless of age, ability, gender, or racial and ethnic background and where respectful, cooperative, and positive relationships create optimum learning conditions. The learning environment has a positive emotional climate that supports the enjoyment of learning and fosters each member's well-being.
2. *Teaching to Enhance Development and Learning* includes a balance of teacher-directed and child-initiated learning, time for in-depth exploration, integrated curriculum, and scaffolded learning.
3. *Planning Curriculum to Achieve Important Goals* reflects the knowledge of how children learn, what they learn, and when they learn it. Articulated goals include standards to be met. Curriculum relates to children's interests and needs and includes all developmental domains.
4. *Assessing Children's Development and Learning* is ongoing and monitors each child's progress in meeting program goals. Assessment methods include observations and work samples and the results are used to plan curriculum that further the effectiveness of classroom experiences.
5. *Establishing Reciprocal Relationships with Families* means developing collaborative relationships with families that promote a sense of partnership based on mutual need, understanding, and negotiation.

Each chapter of this text, individually and collectively, supports and demonstrates these five guidelines for developmentally appropriate practices in developmentally appropriate programs.

DAP in Action

Developmentally appropriate principles reflect the many intentional decisions teachers make based on their knowledge of how children learn and grow. Developmentally appropriate principles benefit children in many ways:

1. In constructing their own understanding of concepts and from instruction by more competent peers and adults.
2. Through opportunities to see connections across disciplines through integration of curriculum and engaging in in-depth study.
3. With a predictable structure and routine in the learning environment and from the teacher's flexibility and spontaneity in responding to children's emerging ideas, needs, and interests.
4. By making meaningful choices about what children will do.
5. From situations that challenge children to work at the edge of their capacities and from ample opportunities to practice newly acquired skills.

Courtesy of the author

What DAP Looks Like

- Programs and curriculum respond to the children's interests as well as their needs.

  While digging in the sand pit, four children uncover water. Others rush to see it. The teacher sees their interest and asks them about the bridges and tunnels they are starting to build.

- Children are actively involved in their own learning, choosing from a variety of materials and equipment.

  Some children search the yard for materials that will bridge the water. Others go inside to find the big book on bridges. Still others dig in other areas of the sandpit to find more water and to try building tunnels for the water. One child finds a walnut shell and floats it on the water. The teacher encourages and supports each child's involvement.

- Play is the primary context in which young children learn and grow.

  Each day, the children rush outside to see their bridges and tunnels. The teacher has helped them find materials that will act as a cover over the bridge. Inside, several children are making dolls from twigs and fabric scraps to use in the project.

- Teachers apply what they know about each child and use a variety of strategies, materials, and learning experiences to be responsive to individual children.

  Josephina is drawing a picture of the bridge and is having trouble with the arches. Knowing that Josephina is somewhat shy and uneasy in large groups, the teacher asks Aldo (who is easygoing and loves to draw) to look at Josephina's picture to see if he might help her. The two children focus on the drawing, each making observations that help Josephina take the next step in her artwork.

- Teachers consider widely held expectations about each age group and temper that with challenging yet achievable learning goals.

  In preparation for a field trip to see two bridges that are near the school, the teacher sets out her expectations (walk with a buddy, stay together, stay on the sidewalk, do not run, etc.). Because this is their first field trip of the school year, the teacher rehearses the children for several days prior to the trip. Music and rhythm accompany them as they practice walking with a friend and play number games of "two-by-two" during group times.

- Teachers understand that any activity has the potential for different children to realize different learning from the same experience.

  After the field trip, Josephina draws a different type of arch for her bridges. Selena, Gracie, and Sam take over the block corner to build bridges and tunnels; three others join them. Maddie finds a book on flowers; they look like some of the flowers she saw on the way to the bridges. Reilly wants to play London Bridge at group time.

- All aspects of development—physical, social-emotional, cognitive, and language—are integrated in the activities and opportunities of the program.

  The bridge project promotes physical (walking, digging), cognitive (learning how bridges and tunnels are built, researching in books), language (construction terms, such as piers, spans, suspension), social-emotional (pairing up two-by-two), and creative (drawing a bridge, adding flowers, trying tunnels).

Each of these examples shows how to meet the needs of all children, no matter their abilities and background. Keep in mind that while each principle defines one particular factor, all of the principles are interrelated and that cultural and social differences, for instance, are a factor in all of the principles.

Early Childhood Core Programs

From the types available, to the numbers of children who attend these schools, the name of the game in early childhood programs is diversity. The range can encompass a morning nursery school for toddlers, a primary school classroom, an infant-parent stimulation program, or a full child care service for 3- to 6-year-olds. Some programs

TeachSource Video

Watch the TeachSource Video Case entitled "Curriculum Planning: Implementing Developmentally Appropriate Practice in an Early Childhood Program." After you study the video clip, view the artifacts, and read the teacher interviews and text, reflect on the following questions:

1. What examples of developmentally appropriate practices did you see or hear mentioned by preschool teacher Ke Nguyen and her colleagues? Compare and contrast your observations with the text.

2. How would you judge the quality of this program? What are some of the criteria you would use?

DIVERSITY

Developmentally and Culturally Appropriate Practice (DCAP)

"One of the most profound aspects of education in the United States today is its cultural complexity" (Hyun, 2007). The need for consistency between a child's home culture and school, what Hyun calls "culturally congruent learning," challenges today's teachers to be culturally responsive in all areas of teaching. Culturally appropriate practice is the ability to go beyond one's own sociocultural background to ensure equal and fair teaching and learning experiences for all. This concept, developed by Hyun (1998, 2007), expands DAP to address cultural complexities that emphasize the adult's ability to reflect more than a single perspective or knowledge. Preparing teachers and caregivers for multiculturalism is not just about becoming sensitive to race, gender, ethnicity,

religion, socioeconomic status, or sexual orientation, according to Hyun. It is also related to an understanding of the way individual histories, families of origin, and ethnic family cultures make us similar to and yet different from others. Through such insights, teachers are able to help all children develop a sense of their own self-identity as they respond to the emerging identities of others.

Teachers support a more culturally congruent atmosphere when they address the social and cultural context in which children live by asking themselves:

1. Do the activities and materials help children see the relationship between what happens in school and the lives of their home and community?

2. Does their learning create new possibilities for multicultural understandings?
3. Is the inclusion of cultural knowledge and materials done without demeaning or devaluing a child's heritage?
4. Do the activities and materials support one culture's domination over others?

There are many ways to meet the third core component of DAP that highlight the importance of connecting a child's sense of cultural continuity between home, school, and community. Interview a teacher of an early childhood program about how their program promotes cultural congruity. Would you add any questions to the previous list?

---

run for only a half-day; others are open from 6:00 AM until 7:00 PM. Still other centers, such as hospitals, accept children on a drop-in basis or for 24-hour care. Child care arrangements can range from informal home-based care to more formal school or center settings. Religious institutions, school districts, community-action groups, parents, governments, private social agencies, and businesses may run schools.

Factors That Determine Types of Programs

Programs in early childhood settings are defined by many factors, and each is an integral part of the mission of the program. Any given program is a combination of these factors and each has an impact on the quality and type of learning that takes place. Some of the factors that influence programs are:

1. Ages of the children who are being served
2. Philosophical, theoretical, or theological ideals
3. Goals of the program
4. Purpose for which the program was established
5. Requirements of sponsoring agency
6. Quality and training of teaching staff

Individual attention and warm relationships are essential components of every program.

7. Shape, size, and location of physical environment
8. Cultural, ethnic, economic, and social make-up of the community
9. Financial stability

Programs for young children also exist to serve a number of needs, which impact programs goals and mission. Some of these are:

- Caring for children while parents work (e.g., family child care homes or child care centers)
- Enrichment programs for children (e.g., half-day nursery school or laboratory school)
- Educational programs for parent and child (e.g., parent cooperatives, parent–child public school programs, or high school parent classes)
- An activity arena for children (e.g., most early childhood programs)
- Academic or readiness instruction (e.g., primary grades and many pre-kindergarten programs)
- Culturally or religiously specific programs (e.g., a school setting with a definitive ethnic focus or a church-related school that teaches religious dogma)

These programs generally reflect the needs of society as a whole. Millions of mothers of children younger than age 6 are in the labor force. Early childhood programs provide a wide range of services for children to meet the demands of working parents. In 2008, 78 percent of mothers with children from ages 6 to 17 were in the labor force, compared with 64 percent of mothers with children younger than the age of 6 (U.S. Bureau of Labor Statistics, 2011).

Special Program Features

A program usually has any number of goals or missions. One mission may be to encourage children to learn from one another. This philosophy has two important features that are reflected in many early childhood programs. The following two sections describe how mixed-age groupings and looping contribute to the goals of the program.

Mixed-Age Groupings

Placing children of several age levels into the same classroom is called **mixed-age grouping**. In these classes, younger children learn from older children and older children learn by teaching younger children. This practice is often referred to as family, heterogeneous, vertical, or ungraded grouping and has been around for many years. The one-room schoolhouse, the schools of Reggio Emilia, Waldorf schools, and Montessori programs reflect mixed-age groupings. The age range among children in mixed-age groups varies, and there is usually a difference from 2 to 4 years.

There are many advantages to mixed-age groups:

- The program is geared toward the needs of each child's developmental level and pace, allowing children to advance as they are ready.
- A sense of family and community is fostered through caring and a sense of responsibility toward one another. Siblings may be in the same class.
- Social skills are enhanced as children learn from and model interactions with children of different ages.
- A wide range of behaviors, learning styles, and temperaments are valued and accepted. Older children learn patience as they help younger children problem solve. Younger children are challenged by older peers who teach them more complex activities.
- Cooperative learning is encouraged.
- Teachers come to know and understand children in greater depth that allows them to build programs and curriculum well-suited to each child's strengths and challenges.

There are challenges associated with mixed-age groupings. The potential for older children to take over and/or overwhelm the younger ones is real, as is the possibility that younger children will pester the older children. This requires monitoring by the teaching staff, and the Reggio Emilia schools offer a good model of this process. In these Italian programs, older children have the responsibility to work with the younger children, explaining things and helping them find appropriate roles to take in their projects.

The academic and social advantages of mixed-age grouping cannot occur without a variety of activities from which children may freely choose and the opportunity for small groups of children to work together. Teachers must be intentional about encouraging children to work with others who have skills and knowledge they do not yet possess, and teachers need adequate preparation to succeed with a mixed-age group.

It is easy to see how mixed-age groupings reflect the principles of Dewey, Piaget, Gardner, and Vygotsky, whose "zone of proximal development" is made more available through the interactions of peers as well as adults. The practice of mixed-age grouping has much to commend it and must be seriously addressed as an issue in programs for young children.

Looping: Continuity of Care

The practice of keeping a teacher and the same group of children together in the same class for at least two years is called **looping**. As with mixed-aged grouping, it is an old idea revisited to provide greater continuity of care and education. Today, looping is customary in the Waldorf schools, Reggio Emilia programs, and Montessori, and it has emerged in other programs for a number of reasons. Proponents of looping suggest that it:

- Offers stability and emotional security to children and allows them to grow at their own rate.
- Gives teachers a greater opportunity to get to know children and therefore be able to individualize the program for them.
- Fosters better social interactions among children and strong relationships between teachers and families.
- Allows children to experience being both the youngest and the oldest in the class as students move on and new students join the group.
- Enhances a sense of family and community within the classroom.

In the schools in Reggio Emilia, infants and toddlers are kept in the same class with the same teachers for three years to provide a family-like environment. Looping is often paired with multi-aged classrooms, which further extends the natural, family-like atmosphere.

Critics of looping cite the need for experienced teachers who enjoy teaching across the age levels and who can work with the same children over an extended period of time. Looping does not fit all teachers and all children, and it could be offered as an option for parents and teachers to meet the needs of those who believe its advantages are worthwhile.

Any of the following early childhood programs may include mixed-age groups and looping. The educational and philosophical goals of the program determine what features to include.

The Core of Programs of Early Childhood Education

The following sections explore the different types of programs available to families. Each has unique characteristics, emphases, and challenges.

Traditional Nursery School/Preschool

The **traditional nursery school**/preschool exemplifies a developmental approach to learning in which children actively explore materials and in which activity or learning centers are organized to meet the developing skills and interests of the child. Most of these programs serve children from 2½ to 5 years of age.

The philosophy of these schools is best described by Katherine Read Baker in her now classic book *The Nursery School: A Human Relationships Laboratory* (1950). First published more than sixty years ago, this book serves as an encyclopedia of the traditional nursery school, its methods, and its philosophy, reflecting the influence of Comenius, Locke, Rousseau, Pestalozzi, Froebel, and Montessori.

The idea of a school as a place of human activity mirrors the thoughts of Dewey, Piaget, Erikson, and others. Baker develops this philosophy fully with an educational model that emphasizes the human needs, growth patterns, and relationships in a young child's life.

Developmentally, a traditional nursery school focuses on social competence and emotional well-being. The curriculum encourages self-expression through language, creativity, intellectual skill, and physical activity. The basic underlying belief is the importance of interpersonal connections children make with themselves, each other, and adults.

The daily schedule (see Figure 2-2) reflects these beliefs. Large blocks of time are devoted to free play, a time when children are free to initiate their own activities and become deeply involved without interruptions, emphasizing the importance of play. In this way, children learn to make choices, select playmates, and work on their interests and issues at their own rate. A dominant belief is that children learn best in an atmosphere free from excessive restraint and direction.

Typically, there is a balance of activities (indoors and out, free choice, and teacher-directed times) and a wide variety of activities (large- and small-muscle games, intellectual choices, creative arts, and social play opportunities).

A nursery school is often a half-day program, but many offer extended hours.

The Role of the Teacher The role of the teacher and methods of teaching are important factors in a traditional nursery school. They assume that young children need individual attention and should have personal, warm relationships with important adults. Therefore, the groups of children are generally small, often fewer than 20 in a class.

Half-Day Schedule	
9:00	Children arrive at school
9:00–9:45	Free play (indoors)
9:45	Cleanup
10:00	Singing time (large group)
10:15–10:30	Toileting/snack time (small group)
10:30–11:30	Free play (outdoors)
11:30	Cleanup
11:45	Story time
12:00	Children leave for home

© Cengage Learning 2011

FIGURE 2-2 A sample schedule for traditional half-day nursery schools is the core of early education programs.

The teacher–child ratio is low, as few as 6 to 10 children for each teacher. Teachers learn about children's development and needs by observation and direct interaction, rather than from formalized testing. They work with children individually and in small groups and often teach through conversation and materials. Teachers encourage children to express themselves, their feelings, and their thinking. Such rapport between teacher and pupil fosters self-confidence, security, and belonging. Proponents of the traditional nursery school believe that these feelings promote positive self-image, healthy relationships, and an encouraging learning environment.

Universal Preschools Increasing numbers of school districts offer pre-kindergarten programs for 4-year-olds, although some include 3-year-olds as well. Depending on their goal, these programs fall somewhere between traditional nursery schools and not quite full-day care. For some, the focus is to promote school readiness; others give priority to children at risk for school failure, children who come from families in which English is not spoken, or low-income families. Universal preschools for 3- and 4-year-olds could meet the growing demand for child care in families where both parents work outside the home. In states in which early education has achieved a level of support, all 4-year-olds are eligible for enrollment, regardless of income. The concept for universal preschools is and will be a continuing issue (see Chapter 15 for further discussion).

Child Care Centers

By definition, a **child care center** is a place for children who need care for a greater portion of the day than what the traditional nursery school offers. The school schedule is extended to fit the hours of working parents. A longer day means that ordinary routines such as meals and naps are woven into the program. These full-day options are also educational settings, echoing but extending the curriculum of a half-day program.

Child care needs are met in many ways, from center-based care to family settings. Child care centers can include preschools, employer-sponsored care, Head Start, for-profit and nonprofit institutions, religious institutions, colleges, YMCAs, public schools, social service agencies, and family child care.

Full-day child care is not a modern phenomenon. Some of the first nursery schools in England operated from 8:00 AM until 4:00 or 5:00 PM. (as noted in Chapter 1). Child care centers often serve infants and toddlers, as well as 2½- to 5-year-olds. Many offer kindergarten, before- and after-school options, and summer programs.

Routines, such as eating, provide a balance to an active and busy day at the child care center.

Scheduling Compare the nursery school schedule (Figure 2-2) with the child care schedule (Figure 2-3). The morning starts slowly. Children arrive early because their parents must go to work or school. The center may supply breakfast, midmorning and midafternoon snacks, and a noon lunch. A nap period for one to two hours for all the children gives a needed rest and balances their active, social day with quiet, solitary time. The program also includes extended experiences outside the school—field trips, library story hour, or swimming lessons—because children spend the major portion of their waking hours on-site. As the day draws to a close, children gather together quietly, with less energy and activity.

Full-Day Schedule

7:00–8:30	Arrival/breakfast; limited indoor play
8:30	Large group meeting
8:45–9:45	Free play (inside)
9:45	Cleanup/toileting
10:00	Snack time (small groups)
10:15–11:30	Free play (outside)
11:30	Cleanup/hand-washing
12:00	Lunch
12:30	Toothbrushing/toileting
1:00–2:00	Nap time
2:00–3:00	Free play (outside)
3:00	Group time
3:15	Snack time (small groups)
3:30–5:00	Inside and outside free play/library hour
5:00	Cleanup
5:15–5:30	Departure

FIGURE 2-3 A typical full-day care schedule. Most child care programs combine education and caring for basic needs.

Licensing Licensing is the process of fulfilling the legal requirements, standards, and regulations for operating child care facilities. There are no national standards or policies regarding licensing of child care facilities in the United States. Many local and state governments require licensing of child care centers and family child care homes, but there is no central licensing agency in every state. Depending on the state, a license may be issued by the Department of Health, Department of Education, or Department of Social Welfare.

Children spend long hours in child care, and many programs are sponsored by a variety of agencies such as churches, public schools, and private for-profit firms. With this diverse mix, a universal set of standards for licensing is imperative to ensure the best possible care for all children who need these services.

Staffing The staff in a full-day setting is often called on to deal with the parenting side of teaching. Children in full-day care may need more nurturing and clearer consistency in behavioral limits. At the same time, they need individual flexibility, understanding, and regular private time with caring adults.

Parents' needs also may be greater and require more of the teachers' time. Child care parents may require extra effort; they have full-time jobs as well as child-rearing responsibilities draining their energies. It takes a strong team effort on the part of the teacher and the parent to make sure the lines of communication stay open and that families and schools are mutually supported.

The teaching staff has staggered schedules, a morning and an afternoon shift. Administration of this type of program is therefore more complex. An effort must be made to ensure that all teachers get together on a regular basis to share the information and details about the children in their care. Both shifts must be aware of what happens when they are not on-site to run the program consistently. (See Chapter 15 for further discussion on child care issues.)

Family Child Care

In **family child care**, the provider takes care of a small number of children in a family residence. The group size can range from two to twelve, but most homes keep a low adult–child ratio, enrolling fewer than six children. It is reminiscent of an extended family grouping.

More than 1.7 million children are in family child care arrangements (NACCRRA, 2010). The home setting, sometimes right within the child's own neighborhood, offers an intimate, flexible, and convenient service for working parents. Children in a family child care home can range from infants to school-age children who are cared for after regular school hours.

The developmental ranges that family child care providers must meet may range from infancy up to 12 years, which poses a challenge to develop experiences and activities for a mixed-age group of children. Family child care providers work and live in the same environment posing logistical problems of storage, space definition, and activity space. Often, family child care providers care for their own children within their programs, leading to problems with separation and autonomy of their children and providing enough time to the child as a parent. Family child care providers are administrators and managers, as well as teachers and caregivers, faced with budgets and fee collections.

Advantages Family child care is good for children who do well in small groups or whose parents prefer to place them in a family-style setting. This is especially true for infants and toddlers. Family child care homes often schedule flexible hours to meet the needs of parents who work. The wide age range can be advantageous as well. Consistency and stability from a single caregiver throughout the child's early years and a family grouping of children provide a homelike atmosphere that is especially appropriate for infants and toddlers.

Family child care providers own and operate a small business in their homes. Providing child care is a way for women who want to remain at home with their children to contribute to the family income. Meeting the requirements for licensing; fulfilling all the administrative tasks of a business and an educational program; and keeping current with the local, state, and federal tax requirements are part of the professionalism required for this type of child care arrangement.

Challenges Many homes are unregulated; that is, they are not under any sponsorship or agency that enforces quality care, and many are exempt from state licensing. Family child care providers often lack knowledge of child development and early education and are not required to take courses. The National Association for Family Child Care has established an accreditation system and promotes high-quality family child care through professional development, public education, and policy initiatives (NAFCC, 2011).

Family child care providers can feel isolated from others in the child care field. A hopeful sign, however, is that more articles on family child care are being included in professional publications, and early childhood conferences and workshops are now including issues related to the family child care provider. This type of care could be a star in the galaxy of child care options. Small and personalized, it offers parents an appealing choice of home-based care. It

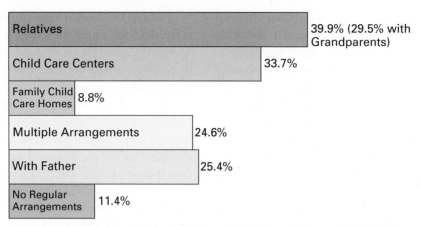

Relatives	39.9% (29.5% with Grandparents)
Child Care Centers	33.7%
Family Child Care Homes	8.8%
Multiple Arrangements	24.6%
With Father	25.4%
No Regular Arrangements	11.4%

FIGURE 2-4 Child care options. (Data from: U.S. Bureau of Census. *"Who's Minding the Kids?"* Childcare Arrangements, Spring, 2005. Survey of Income and Program Participation. Retrieved August 2011.)

is obvious, though, that further regulation of standards, availability of training for providers, and an awareness of the advantages of family child care need to be addressed. For those who need child care, this should be a viable alternative; for those who want to work at home, this type of career should be given serious consideration.

The options for child care are many. In Figure 2-4 the choices that parents make when looking for child care are addressed.

Variations of Core Programs

There are many variations of the core programs that provide care and education for young children. These programs differ primarily due to the sponsoring agencies, the children they serve, their underlying mission, and whether or not they are nonprofit or for-profit organizations.

Head Start: An Early Intervention Model

In 1965, the federal government created the largest publicly funded education program for young children ever. Head Start began as part of this country's social action in the "war on poverty," and the implications of the program were clear: If at-risk poverty-stricken children could be exposed to a program that enhanced their schooling, their intellectual functions might increase, and these gains would help break the poverty cycle.

Over the past 40-plus-year history, Head Start has served more than 27 million children and their families

(Head Start, 2011). The success of Head Start can be attributed to its guiding objectives and principles, most expressed through:

- *Its comprehensive nature.* The child is seen as a whole, requiring medical, dental, and nutritional assessment, as well as intellectual growth. Extensive health, education, and social services are offered to children and their families.
- *Parent participation and involvement.* Head Start expects parents to serve as active participants and get involved in the program at all levels: in the classroom as teacher aides, on governing boards making decisions about the program, and as bus drivers and cooks.
- *Services to families.* Many of the **comprehensive** services offered to children are extended to parents as well to assist them in their fight against poverty. Paid jobs in the program, continuing education, job training, and health care are some of the support services families received.
- *Community collaboration.* Interest and support from the local community help Head Start respond to the needs of the children and families it serves. Public schools, religious institutions, libraries, service clubs, and local industry and businesses help to foster responsible attitudes toward society and provide opportunities for the poor to work with members of the community in solving problems.
- *Multicultural/multiracial education.* Since its inception, Head Start has sought to provide a curriculum that reflects the culture, language, and values of the children in the program. Head Start efforts in this regard have been the models for other early childhood programs.

• *Inclusion of children with special needs.* Since 1972, Head Start has pioneered the inclusion of children with disabilities in its classrooms. By 2009, 11.5 percent of Head Start enrollment consisted of children with disabilities (Head Start, 2010).

• *Ecology of the family.* Head Start programs look at children within the context of the family in which they live and view the family in the context of the neighborhood and community. This concept of taking the many forces that work against low-income families and viewing them as interrelated is a key factor in Head Start's success (see also Chapters 1 and 15).

The success of Head Start led to the creation of three specific programs that furthered the goals of Head Start: Parent & Child Centers, which serve infants and toddlers and their families; the Child and Family Resource Programs, which provide family support services; and the Child Development Associate credential, which provides early childhood training and education for Head Start teachers.

It should be noted that, at the beginning, one aim of Head Start was to change the language and behavior patterns of the low-income children served, many of whom came from minority groups, and to resocialize them into cultural patterns and values of the mainstream, middle class. Head Start was a "compensatory" program, and the implications were that children from poor or minority families were unprepared for the demands of school in terms of language and cognitive skills, achievement, and motivation. This widely held perspective of the 1960s was known as the "cultural disadvantage" model, which suggests that any language, cognitive, or relational style that differs from the Anglo, mainstream, middle-class style is necessarily detrimental to rather than supportive of the educational process.

Contrast this view with the more recent, pluralistic perspective, called the "cultural difference" model, which affirms that no one way of "behaving and believing" should be required for successful participation in school or society. Figure 2-5 summarizes today's Head Start programs.

Early Head Start

Early Head Start was established in 1994 as part of the Head Start Reauthorization Act. This program serves low-income families with infants and toddlers and pregnant women and is based on Head Start's four cornerstones: child development, family development, staff development, and community building.

Nine principles guide the efforts of Early Head Start: 1) high quality; 2) prevention of developmental concerns and promotion of healthy child development; 3) positive relationships and continuity in care-giving; 4) parent involvement; 5) inclusion; 6) culture; 7) comprehensiveness, flexibility, responsiveness and intensity to respond to families needs; 8) smooth transitions into Head Start programs; and 9) collaboration with local communities to maximize resources available to families.

Evaluating Early Intervention Effectiveness

The High/Scope Perry Preschool Project was not a Head Start program but had an enormous impact on policy makers and government officials and affected Head Start funding in significant ways.

There are similarities among all programs, but the relationship among parents, children, and caregiver is the universal consideration.

A Picture of Head Start	
Enrollment	
904,153 children	
Ages Enrolled	
5-year-olds:	3%
4-year-olds:	51%
3-year-olds:	36%
Under 3:	10%
Race/Ethnic Population	
Native American/Alaskan Native:	4%
Hispanic/Latino:	35.9%
Black/African American:	30%
White:	39.9%
Asian/Pacific Islander:	2.3%
Biracial/Multiracial:	7.8%
Other:	16.7%

FIGURE 2-5 Head Start continues to be a vital program that serves the needs of a diverse population. This information is for the fiscal year 2010. (U.S. Department of Health and Human Services, the Office of Head Start, 2011.)

The High/Scope Perry Preschool Study. This project presented the most convincing evidence to date of the effectiveness of early intervention programs for low-income children. Started in the 1960s, it is the first longitudinal study to measure the effects of preschool education and to track the children from preschool years through age 27.

Children from one randomly assigned group were placed in high quality early childhood programs at age 3; the other group did not attend preschool. The results showed great differences between the children who had the advantage of a high quality program and those who did not. Low-income children who had attended preschool significantly outperformed those who had not.

The children attending the preschool program were better educated, spent fewer than half as many years in special education programs, had higher earnings, were less likely to receive welfare, and were five times less likely to be arrested. Gender differences were also noted. Preschool program girls had a significantly higher rate of graduation than did the girls who did not attend preschool, whereas, in comparison, preschool program boys completed slightly less schooling than nonpreschool boys (Weikart, n.d.).

Not only did this study underscore the need for high quality preschool programs for children who live in poverty, but it also demonstrated the potential impact that Head Start had on the country's future. It is the first study of its kind to suggest the economic impact of early intervention. Because most of the children in the high quality early childhood program required less remedial education, had better earning prospects, and were less costly to the welfare and justice systems, early intervention in education was shown to be cost-effective.

Head Start Today

Head Start has had a rocky history, its contributions notwithstanding. Struggling against budget cuts and controversy over its effectiveness, Head Start has undergone program improvements and expansions.

The original vision of Head Start was improved and expanded for the 1990s as a model that challenges the effects of poverty and promotes physically and mentally healthy families. Head Start has a formidable challenge ahead as it protects the high quality of its original charter while expanding and increasing services. As the early childhood field has become more professionalized, so has Head Start. By 2013, all Head Start head teachers will be required to have a bachelors' degree, continuing its efforts as a model of effective early intervention, child care, and education.

Variety of Early Childhood Program Options

Early childhood programs take many forms and allow families to choose the best option to meet their needs. Variations of the core programs are outlined in Figure 2-6.

Infant/Toddler Programs

The inclusion of infants and toddlers in group care is the result of more mothers in the workforce. Infant/toddler programs may be full-day centers or they may be part-time. Most are a combination of physical care coupled with intellectual stimulation and development.

Parent relationships are an especially important part of any program for babies and toddlers. The general intention of these centers is to provide care that is supplemental to family life and that supports the child's family structure. To do that, the caregiver at an infant/toddler center:

- involves the parents in the everyday decisions about the care of their child,
- provides them with information about the child's day, and
- strengthens the child's sense of belonging to that particular family.

Philosophy of Infant/Toddler Care

Through the insights of Piaget and Erikson (see Chapter 4) and continuing research in brain development, we have come to view the infant as an involved person, one who experiences a wide range of intellectual and emotional abilities. Although they may appear to be helpless beings, babies are in fact persons with feelings, rights, and an individual nature.

Caregiving routines are at the heart of the infant/toddler program and are the curriculum foundation for this age group. The challenge is to find ways to use these daily routines to interact, develop trust and security, and provide educational opportunities. In many cases, the caregiver's role extends to helping parents use these same common occurrences to promote the optimal development of their child. Magda Gerber, a pioneer in infant care, coined the term **educaring** to describe the relationship between an infant and an adult. Observing, listening, and reading babies' cues are key elements in educaring.

Gerber's philosophy is based on the use of responsive and reciprocal interactions in which baby and caregiver learn about each other. Communicating through care giving routines (diapering, feeding) in one-to-one intense and focused interactions is a foundation of Gerber's approach to caring for infants and toddlers (Gerber, 1979).

More recently, The Program for Infant/Toddler Care (PITC) has gained attention for its philosophy of a

Chart of Variations of Early Childhood Programs

Type	Sponsor	Ages	Schedule	Key Characteristics	Settings
Parent cooperative	School districts, private owners	Preschoolers; often mixed-age groups	Full-day and/or half-day	Parents commit to teaching in the classroom on a regular basis; regular parent education meetings; time-consuming; lower costs	Community centers, privately owned buildings, churches, synagogues
Laboratory schools	College or university	Preschool, infant/toddlers	Full-day and/or half-day	Students and teachers often participate in teacher training and research activities; offer model programs	Located on or near campus
Employer sponsored	Individual business or corporation	Infant/toddlers, preschooler, school age	Full-day and/or half-day	Is an employee benefit option for parents; may be available as a voucher for any child care arrangement	Often on or near job site; hospitals, factories, and government agencies, as well as child care centers and family child care homes
For profit (proprietary)	Corporations and individuals	Infant/toddler, preschool, kindergarten, before-school and after-school ages	Full-day and/or half-day	May be part of a national/regional chain or individually owned; great variety of services and programs offered year-round; major purpose is to make a profit	Individual centers owned by franchise or corporation
Nonprofit centers	Community, churches, synagogues, government agencies	Infant/toddlers, preschool, school age	Full-day and/or half-day	Subsidized by sponsoring organization or government agency, which often provides low or free rent	Community buildings, government office buildings, churches, synagogues
Programs in religious institutions	Religious organization	Infant/toddler, preschool, school age	Full-day and/or half-day	May be a community outreach program where no religious dogma is taught or may be part of the ministry of the sponsor and include religious dogma in the curriculum; tends to be one of the largest providers of child care in the United States; tax exempt as a nonprofit; sharing space with congregational programs may be difficult	Churches, synagogues
Before-school and after-school care	Public schools, community organizations, YMCAs, YWCAs, churches, synagogues	Preschool and elementary school ages	Before and after school hours	Safe place for children during parent's working hours; may provide holiday, vacations, and summer programs	Schools, community centers, YMCAs, YWCAs, child care centers

© Cengage Learning 2014

FIGURE 2-6 There is a diverse array of programs that are considered variations on the core of early childhood education.

relationship-based curriculum. Caregivers get "in tune" with each infant and learn from the child what he or she needs, thinks, and feels. They design environments that offer appropriate developmental challenges and strengthen the child's family and cultural identity. Caregivers study the infants and reflect on and record what they observe for future learning encounters (The Program for Infant/Toddler Care, 2011).

Unique Characteristics

Infant and toddler programs differ from preschool programs in a number of ways. There is a greater need for security, exploration, and social-emotional growth. Infant and toddler programs reflect these needs by:

- Creating a stable environment with low staff turnover and low caregiver–child ratios.

- Providing more one-to-one physical care.
- Ensuring immediate response from adults.
- Following up with parents and families on a daily basis.
- Using ordinary routines as learning opportunities.
- Developing skills that go beyond teaching: mothering, being a playmate.
- Promoting intentional rather than discovery learning.
- Developing finely tuned interpretation skills to recognize need and distress signals in young children.
- Understanding the significance of cultural sensitivity as children gain a sense of their own identity.

An important consideration in infant care is the daily separation of parent and child. As you will learn in Chapter 4, **attachment** is the deep bond and personal relationship that connects infants to the important people in their lives, such as parents and caregivers. The more secure the attachment, the more positive effects it has on the child. Research on the influence of daily separation suggests that it is the *quality* of care that impacts attachment security. When the caregiver–infant ratio is low and the caregiver's interactions are warm, positive, and knowledgeable about child development, children's cognitive, social, and emotional development thrive (McCartney et al., 2007).

The distinction between programs for infants and those for toddlers is also important. Just as a scaled-down version of preschool is not a toddler program, neither is a scaled-down version of a good day for toddlers an appropriate model for infants. The mobility of the toddler, for instance, requires different amounts of space and time in the schedule than those required for infants. Routines are also the focus of the toddler's day but in a different way. Mealtimes and toileting provide daily opportunities for toddlers to explore and to express their emerging sense of self. Hand-washing—even eating—becomes a time to fill, to taste, to dump, and to pick up. Again, the curriculum emerges from a developmental need toddlers have of "Me! Mine!" To foster that independence, that wanting to "do it myself," routines that allow for experimentation, mistakes, and messes make a good toddler curriculum. Good programs for infants and toddlers, then, are distinctly arranged for their developmental needs and are not simply modified versions of what works well in a program for 3-year-olds.

Kindergarten

The kindergarten year is one of transition from early childhood programs into a more formal school setting and is considered the first year of formal teaching. Kindergarten programs abound throughout the United States. They are found in elementary public and private

Active involvement with people and objects helps infants and toddlers develop feelings of self-identity, curiosity, and creativity.

schools, religious institutions, and as part of preschool child care centers.

Length of Day

The length of kindergarten programs is under debate in many states and schools districts. A few states require a full-day kindergarten and nearly all states offer only half-day kindergarten. Some states do not offer kindergarten at all. Kindergarten may be mandatory for 5-year-olds in some states and not in others.

Too often the arguments regarding the costs of such programs overshadow a more basic question: What are the best and most appropriate kindergarten programs, teaching methods, and curricula, regardless of the length of day? The following should be considered in response to this question:

- *The purpose of the kindergarten program.* How will the kindergarten program foster the goals in appropriate curricula and adapt to the needs of children? The goal should begin with the child and build the program to fit the child's needs, skills, and developing abilities.
- *The effects of a full day on children.* Many children have already been in a child care setting for up to 10 hours a day and have shown they thrive in programs that are suited to their ages, development styles, and needs. There is no question that most children can handle a full-day kindergarten program, providing it is adapted to their age, interests, and abilities.
- *The needs and concerns of families.* Some families may want a full-day program because they work and need a safe and nurturing place for their children. Others who do not work outside the home may want to keep their children with them a while

longer. Families need to have a choice about the type of program that best suits their family.

- *The effect on teachers.* A full-day kindergarten means that class is extended for a longer period of time, providing opportunities to improve the quality of the program by individualizing the curriculum. Teachers in half-day kindergartens often teach one class in the morning and one in the afternoon. The negative effects on planning, continuity, parent relationships, and individualizing curriculum are obvious, not to mention the risk of teacher burnout.

- *The concerns of the administration.* The cost-effectiveness of extending a kindergarten program all day undoubtedly requires more staff, more supplies and equipment, and greater food-service costs. The policy makers in any school setting must take these into account along with the other issues, but one would hope they are not limited by them.

- *The nature and quality of the extended-day program.* Often, in programs in which children are in half-day kindergarten, the quality of the extended-care part of their day is not equal to their school experience. In many extended-day programs, the staff is untrained, has a high turnover rate, and does not reflect the same program goals for the **kindergartener.**

School Entry Age

Most states establish an arbitrary date (e.g., September 1) by which children must be a certain age to enter kindergarten. Lowering and raising the age for beginning kindergarten is debated frequently. Some parents hold children out of kindergarten for one year and enroll them when they are age 6, a practice called "redshirting" (Katz, 2000). Teachers retain many children each year in kindergarten; and administrators have created an array of kindergarten-substitute programs such as "developmental," "extra-year," or "transitional" kindergartens. By the time they finally reach kindergarten, children are now in class with late 4-year-olds and 5- and 6-year-olds—a vast developmental span under one roof. Research shows mixed results for these practices.

Some of the methods used to create more homogeneous kindergarten classrooms or to raise expectations for kindergarten admittance are:

- Inappropriate uses of screening and readiness tests.
- Discouragement and/or denial of entrance for eligible children.
- Creation of transitional classes for those who are considered not ready for kindergarten.
- An increasing use of retention (NAECS/ NAEYC, 2001).

The issue of **school readiness** has been a hot topic for years. Early childhood professionals agree that children should be able to enter kindergarten when they are of legal age and that schools should be prepared to meet the needs of children where they are in their development. Instead schools have developed a variety of methods noted earlier to create more homogeneous classes rather than address the variety of developmental stages of children of kindergarten age. There are many reasons children enter school without the resources and tools to succeed, such as poverty, language and cultural differences, access to high-quality early education programs, and lack of effective early intervention that includes comprehensive services. These are the necessary tools children need to be ready for school.

Curriculum: Developmental or Academic?

Critical issues such as school-entry age and length of school day are related to kindergarten curriculum issues. Kindergarten programs range from relatively traditional classes to highly structured, academically oriented classes. Over the past 20 years, the push to teach separate skills, such as reading, writing, and math, has created more and more academically focused kindergartens in which worksheets and teacher-directed lessons are the norm. As kindergartens have changed, there is greater pressure on teachers to accelerate children's learning. Hatch (2005) cites three specific changes that have altered the course of kindergarten programs:

1. Children today experience very different childhoods than even a decade ago.
2. Knowledge of how children learn and develop has expanded.
3. The standards-based reform movement has changed expectations for kindergarteners by imposing arbitrary standards of performance. This increases the academic expectations on them and the pressure on teachers to comply with regulations.

It is clear that Froebel's "children's garden" has wandered far from its child development roots. Curricula in which play is not respected as a vehicle for learning, reading is taught as a separate skill, and attempts are made to accelerate children's learning are at odds with kindergarten history. Revisit Chapter 1 and read again about Froebel, Dewey, Piaget, Patty Smith Hill, Susan Isaacs, and other pioneers and their approach to learning. Educating the whole child is very much in evidence in their work as is their basic connection to child development theory and research. (For further discussion on the negative effects of early academics, see Chapter 3 for developmental ranges and Word Pictures for appropriate expectations. In Chapter 6, the related questions of standardized

BRAIN
Research Says...

Redshirting and Readiness

Neuroscience has established the fact that the brain is constantly changing. This *plasticity* means that the brain is always adapting and reorganizing on a daily basis. New connections are being created by everyday experiences and learning is taking place. Brain plasticity persists into adulthood but is especially pronounced in the early stages of life. At the same time the brain is growing, it is *pruning* itself, getting rid of unused synapses in a "use it or lose it" function. If the brain is rewiring itself so extensively in the preschool and early elementary years, and requires meaningful, positive experiences to grow, it begs the question: "Why is redshirting, or keeping children back one year, still being practiced?" It would appear that redshirting is actually counterproductive because it deprives the child of a challenging and stimulating school environment. The best way to give children the greatest

opportunity to learn is to put them in their age-appropriate classroom setting as soon as possible where their brains are immersed in growing, learning, and changing.

The issue of school readiness has been a hot topic for years. Early childhood professionals agree that children should be able to enter kindergarten when they are of legal age and that schools should be prepared to meet the needs of children where they are in their development. This is supported by recent brain development research that stresses stimulation and challenges as a way to foster brain growth and learning. Instead, schools have developed a variety of methods noted earlier to create more homogeneous classes rather than address the variety of developmental stages of children of kindergarten age. (See further discussion of school readiness in Chapter 15.)

There are many reasons children enter school without the resources and tools to succeed, such as poverty, language and cultural differences, access to high-quality early education programs, and lack of effective early intervention that includes comprehensive services.

Readiness has been defined as ready children, ready families, ready communities, ready early care and education, and ready schools (Rhode Island KIDS COUNT, 2005). All of these are necessary if we want all children to be ready for successful school experiences that use their brain potential to greatest advantage.

Questions
1. When might it be appropriate to delay a child's entry into school?
2. Why do disadvantaged children have the most to lose from delayed entry into school?

---

testing and screening are discussed. In Chapters 10 and 15, related issues are explored.)

Kagan and Kauerz (Gullo, 2006) provide four reflections on what kindergartens can and should be in the future. They integrate concerns about the developmentally appropriate integrity of kindergartens and the domination of imposed standards and testing:

1. Kindergarten must remain "special," that unique year in which play is a legitimate medium for establishing children's learning patterns, and in which curriculum, standards, and assessments are in sync with preschool and first grade.
2. Kindergarten must keep the child front and center, even with the new emphasis on content. Curriculum must address the full range of developmental domains (social, emotional, cognitive, and physical) to prepare children for more formally taught content. Children's curiosity, enthusiasm, initiative, and willingness to learn must be nurtured to enhance their overall ability to learn.
3. Kindergarten must acknowledge and support differences in the needs of children and their families.

Different learning styles in children must be addressed as well as family needs for flexibility in the structure, such as full- or half-day sessions.
4. Kindergarten must foster positive relationships between the children and their teachers, between families and the school, and between the school and the community. The success of these relationships can help establish trust and respect that last throughout the child's school years.

Kindergarten is a significant transition in the lives of children and families and a critical year in a child's growth and development. It should be made available and accessible to all children in the United States.

Early Elementary/Primary Grades

Early childhood is defined as children from birth through age 8. Often overlooked as part of a comprehensive view of young children are first through third grades, serving children from ages 6- to 8-years-old. These grades focus on the basic academic skills of reading, writing, math, science, social studies, art and drama, health and safety, and physical

Kindergarteners are able to enjoy close friendships.

education. Although these subjects are usually taught separately, the curriculum should be integrated so that children learn subject matter through a variety of activities.

Unique Characteristics

Dramatic changes are taking place in the primary-age child. Children this age are eager to learn and are developing logic and reasoning skills as they move from Piaget's preoperational stage to one of concrete operations (see Chapter 4). Their learning tasks are more difficult than in kindergarten and require greater persistence and effort. Starting at about age 6, children begin to plan out and think through their actions and take others' views into consideration. As they grow more independent in their learning, primary-age children like choosing their own tasks, working cooperatively in small groups with their classmates, and participating in planning each day's work. Group discussions and planning projects address the child's needs to be part of the planning process. Enhancing the child's enthusiasm for learning is a primary task for the teachers of this age group.

Play for the primary-age child now revolves around rules that accompany organized games, board games, and cards. Learning still takes place through independent exploration and manipulation of materials, so classroom centers are an important part of the environment. The classroom itself may be more structured but it is important that developmentally appropriate early childhood principles, practices, and environments are applied through third grade.

The Challenge of Academic Standards

Teaching in the primary grades presents challenges due to the pressure of local, state, or national standards that dictate what children need to learn at this age and grade level. All states now have these standards for each grade level and each subject matter. As a result, teachers may have little or no control over what they teach and the unfortunate result may be a curriculum that "teaches to the test"; that is, one that stresses only the subject matter on which the child is tested. The best curriculum for the primary-age child is one that is in **alignment** with the standards so that the subject matter matches what the standards say children should know and do at this grade and subject level. Accountability through learning standards continues to have a strong impact on the early elementary years. (Further discussion of early learning standards and their effect on teaching and learning is discussed in many of the following chapters.

School-Age Child Care

Before-school and after-school programs are designed for children before they start or after they finish their regular academic day. This type of care is usually available for children from ages 5 to 12. There are 8.4 million children participating in after-school programs, and that number continues to grow (America After 3PM, 2011).

Staff for after-school programs comes from a variety of backgrounds, most of which include some experience with children, such as teachers, recreation specialists, or specialists within the arts. As with most child care programs, however, high turnover and low wages affect the quality of the service. Finding qualified staff is the major challenge facing school-age providers, along with finding space and funding (Neugebauer, 2007).

Two national organizations, the National School-Age Care Alliance and the National Institute on Out-of-School Time created an accreditation system for after-school care. Their goals are to set professional standards, accredit high quality programs, and support program improvement.

There is a critical need for safe, recreational programs for after-school care. *America After 3 PM* reports that more than 25 percent of America's school children are on their own in the afternoons. These **self-care** children are a young and vulnerable population. Children need the safety, the creative opportunity, and the emotionally supportive relationships that out-of-school care can provide. These programs are natural extensions of responsible child care and are essential services to children and their families.

Homeschooling

The homeschool movement began in the 1950s as an alternative to public education. Today, approximately 1.5 million students are homeschooled, nearly 3 percent of the school age population. The majority (84 percent) of homeschooled children receive all of their education

Teaching With
INTENTION

A Thoughtful Beginning

As a beginning kindergarten teacher Shawndra wants to establish appropriate and positive relationships with her students. Before school starts, she interviews two experienced teachers to see what experience has taught them. Mac, a long-time second grade teacher, tells her to earn children's respect by having fair, clear, and consistent classroom rules. Mattie, who has taught kindergarten for three years tells Shawndra that being well prepared but flexible are the keys to good relationships with students.

These conversations prompt Shawndra to reflect on her own life as a student and look at her former teachers and how they created a respectful and supportive classroom atmosphere. One teacher stands out in her mind, her preschool teacher when Shawndra was 5-years-old. Mrs. Olivera's classroom was fun and fascinating (Ah, Mattie's point about preparation and flexibility!) and classroom rules were at a minimum (Mac is right: consistency is important). Most of all, Shawndra felt involved in the life of the classroom.

During the first week of school, Shawndra and her students had several brainstorming sessions about classroom behaviors and what kind of a climate they would like to create. By the end of the second week, the students unanimously agreed to a short list of rules they felt were important. What Shawndra succeeded in doing, by asking the class for their opinions and taking ownership of the rules, was to let students know she respected them and believed in their innate abilities to work together and got them involved.

Think About This
1. Do you think Shawndra's solution worked? Why? Why not?
2. What do you think were the most important suggestions that formed Shawndra's decision?
3. How can Shawndra's experience help you plan for creating successful relationships with children in your class?

---

at home, whereas some attend school part of the time (National Center for Educational Statistics, 2011).

Three reasons why parents select homeschooling are for the school environment, to provide religious instruction, and dissatisfaction with the academic instruction available elsewhere. From 2003 to 2007, the percentage of students whose parents reported that religious instruction was the most important factor increased from 73 to 83 percent (National Center for Education Statistics, 2011).

The educational philosophies and methods used in homeschooling are widely diverse and range from pre-packaged curriculum that parents buy to "relaxed homeschooling" and "unschooling" (Cloud & Morse, 2001). The "relaxed" or "natural" homeschooling method involves real-life projects as teaching opportunities, such as taking care of the farm animals or building a table. "Unschooling" uses no curriculum plans, and children pursue their own interests. If some of this seems familiar, you might want to look back at Chapter 1 and review the various educational philosophies on which early childhood programs are based.

Some concerns expressed by educators regarding homeschool educational programs include: 1) lack of quality control due to varying regulations; 2) lack of socialization opportunities for students; 3) lack of sports opportunities; 4) the extreme time commitment demanded of parents; 5) lack of accountability, regulations, and policies surrounding homeschooling; and 6) the loss of revenue for public education.

Assessing Program Quality

Each week, more than 12 million children younger than the age of 5 are in some type of child care arrangement (U.S. Census Bureau, 2010) and each of these early childhood settings differs in the level of quality they provide. What does it mean to have a "high quality" program that benefits children and their families?

Indicators of Quality

Early childhood programs vary greatly in their educational goals and practices, their methods of instruction, and even in the kind of social "mood" or atmosphere they create.

Yet the quality of these programs is based on three essential factors:

1. The teacher–child ratio; that is, the number of children cared for by each staff member
2. The total size of the group or class
3. The education, experience, and training of the staff

The importance of these three factors cannot be underestimated, and they underscore each of the criteria in the DAP box "High-Quality Programs = DAP." The following 10 criteria are found in every chapter throughout this text.

DAP High-Quality Programs = DAP

The National Association for the Education of Young Children (NAEYC) has established a list of criteria for high-quality early childhood programs. These criteria are used for accreditation of programs by NAEYC and are based on a consensus of thousands of early childhood professionals (NAEYC, 2005).

1. **Relationships.** Positive relationships help children develop personal responsibility, self-regulation, constructive interactions, and academic mastery. Warm sensitive relationships help children feel secure and develop a positive sense of self, respect for others, and the ability to cooperate.

2. **Curriculum.** The curriculum draws on research for concepts, skills, and methodology that fosters children's learning and maximizes learning through time and materials as well as provides learning opportunities for children individually and in groups.

3. **Teaching.** Developmentally, linguistically, and culturally appropriate teaching practices enhance children's learning, as does multiple instructional methods, including teacher-directed, child-directed, and structured and unstructured learning opportunities. Teachers reflect the children's backgrounds, needs, interests, and capabilities in their instructional approaches. When more than one teacher is in the classroom, a team teaching approach is used.

4. **Assessment of Child Progress.** Appropriate and systematic assessment measures, which are culturally sensitive, inform needs. Assessments aid in identifying children who need additional instruction and/or intervention and further assessment.

5. **Health and Safety.** A healthy state of well-being enhances a child's ability to learn. Adults help protect children from illness and injury and help them make healthy choices for themselves.

6. **Teachers.** The teaching staff is educationally qualified, knowledgeable, and professionally committed to supporting children's learning and development, as well as families' diverse needs and interests. The teachers who have specific preparation in child development and early childhood education are more likely to have warm, positive interactions with children, promote richer language experiences, and create a higher quality

learning environment. Ongoing professional development ensures that teachers reflect current research and best practices.

7. **Families.** Good family relationships are collaborations between home and school and reflect family composition, language, and culture. They are based on mutual trust and respect in recognition of the primacy of the family in the life of the child.

8. **Community Relationships.** The program establishes relationships with and uses the resources of the community to realize program goals. By helping to connect families with a variety of resources, the children's health and development is enhanced.

9. **Physical Environment.** A safe, healthy, and accessible environment and well-maintained indoor and outdoor areas foster learning, health, and safety for young children. The design of the facilities and the activities support a high-quality program.

10. **Leadership and Management.** The program effectively administers policies, procedures, and systems that support a stable staff and strong personnel, fiscal, and program management. Effective governance and structure, program accountability, positive community relations, and a supportive workplace create a high-quality environment for all.

Visit an NAEYC accredited early childhood site and a nonaccredited program. Use these 10 criteria to assess the overall quality of the program. How do these programs compare? What issues seem to be the most challenging in meeting the standards for high-quality in both settings? Do you think accreditation based on these criteria is useful in creating high-quality? In promoting DAP? Why? Why not?

Quality early care and education contribute to the healthy cognitive, social, and emotional development of all children but particularly those from low-income families. The cost of child care is disproportionately high for poor families, so those who might benefit the most have the most difficult time affording quality care. Good, affordable, accessible child care that meets the increasing needs of American families is one of today's most crucial issues. Observation tools that measure quality in early childhood programs is discussed later in the chapter under "How to Evaluate a Program."

Research Studies on Quality

Every day, scores of parents search for affordable programs and reliable providers. A study by the National Association of Child Care Resource and Referral Agencies (NACCRRA, 2008) polled more than 1,000 parents nationwide to find out what parents want in child care. Quality was mentioned more than any other issue.

Issues That Affect Quality

The focus of the child care issues centers on a few core problems that threaten the *quality* of child care throughout the country:

- The annual turnover rate for child care staff is more than 30 percent (Whitebook & Sakai, 2004). Minimal benefits, lack of health care, and low wages account for this high rate of turnover.

- Twenty percent of child care center teachers have a high school diploma or less and 43 percent of assistant teachers have a high school diploma or less. Forty-four percent of family child care providers have only a high school diploma (NCCRRA, 2010).
- Average earnings of child care workers are $9.70 per hour or $20,350 annually. Preschool teachers earn $12.80 per hour or $26,610 per year (NCCRRA, 2010).

The triple threats to child care—quality, cost, and compensation—are discussed further in Chapter 15.

Highlights from three long-range research projects support the premise that high-quality child care programs have lasting impact on children's lives:

1. The Abecedarian Project, conducted by the Frank Porter Graham Child Development Center at the University of North Carolina, is the first study to track participants from infancy to age 21. The children were considered at risk for potential school failure.

    Important factors in determining quality were in place to ensure success: staff experience and education, little or no staff turnover, small teacher–student ratios, group size, and parent participation. Significant benefits for the children enrolled in the program for five years included the likelihood of attending a four-year college and delaying parenthood until after high school. Moreover, by age 15, twice as many of the children who did not receive intervention services had been placed in special education programs than those who had been in child care. By age 21, most subjects were either gainfully employed or in college. Only 30 percent of the child care children had to repeat a grade in school compared with 56 percent of the others.

2. The Children of the Cost, Quality, and Outcomes Study Go to School (Whitebook, Sakai, Gerber & Howes, 2001), tracked children from child care years through second grade. The findings noted that:

    - Children who receive good, quality child care had better social and cognitive skills in kindergarten and beyond.
    - Children who were at risk gained the most from positive child care experiences and sustained these gains through second grade.
    - Children who had closer relationships with their child care teachers had better behavior and social skills through second grade.

3. A 25-year federally funded study at the Child-Parent Centers in Chicago is the longest follow-up ever of an established large-scale early childhood program. According to Reynolds, Temple, Ou, Arteaga, and White (2011), the participants showed higher levels of education, socioeconomic status, and better jobs, as well as lower rates of substance abuse, grade retention, drop-out rates, arrest, and incarceration than those who did not attend an early childhood program that offered comprehensive services to children and families.

All three of these studies show positive economic benefits of quality early childhood education.

The Process of Assessing Programs

As educators, we are constantly evaluating, judging, and rating areas such as:

- *Curriculum.* Will this language game help develop the listening skills of 3-year-olds?
- *Materials and equipment.* If we order the terrarium, will there be enough money for the math lab?
- *The environment.* Should the children begin school with free play or a group time? Where can we store the nap cots? Do the cubbies create a hazard out in the hallway?
- *Children's behavior.* Evan and Francie interrupt each other too much. Should they be placed in separate work groups?
- *Teacher effectiveness.* Yolanda still finds it difficult to lead a group time. How can she be supportively challenged?

As a process, an **assessment** involves making decisions, choices, and selections. In its simplest form, it is a process of appraisal. A good assessment encourages positive change. It is easy to continue the same program, the same teaching techniques, year after year when a school is operating smoothly. Sometimes it is not clear what—or how—improvements could be made. A regular assessment process keeps a system alive and growing and helps to give meaning and perspective to children, teachers, and programs. An assessment that helps clarify issues and ideas brings renewed dedication and inspiration.

Why Program Assessment is Important

There are four major reasons for making an annual assessment of a program for young children.

To Gain an Overview   Evaluating a program gives an overview of how all the various components function together. The fundamental questions are: Is this a good place for children? Would you want your child to be here? What is a high-quality program for young children? Looking at children, teachers, and the total environment, a program evaluation reveals the environment as an integrated whole. These assessments add an awareness of how one area is

Evaluations are part of everyday life in an early childhood setting. Observations highlight ways to improve the program.

related to another and how the parts mesh in a particular setting. Such evaluations, then, are the standards of quality and include:

- Children's progress
- Teacher performance
- Curriculum development
- The financial structure
- Family involvement
- The community at large
- The governing organization of the school

In program evaluations, each of these is assessed for how it functions alone and how each works in concert with the others.

To Establish Accountability A program evaluation establishes accountability. This refers to a program's ability to answer to a controlling group or agency, for instance, the school board or the government office or the parents and the community in which the program operates. These groups want to know how their funds are being spent and how their philosophy is being expressed through the overall program.

To Make Improvements Program evaluations are an opportunity to take an objective look at how the goals of the school are being met. A good evaluation supports the strengths of the existing program and suggests areas in which changes might improve overall effectiveness. An in-depth assessment increases the likelihood that program goals and visions are realized. The evaluation helps determine the direction the program may take in the future.

To Acquire Accreditation Evaluations are a necessary step for some schools that wish to be approved for certification or accreditation by various organizations or government agencies. Such groups require that a school meet certain evaluation standards before the necessary permits are issued or membership is granted. Agencies, such as a state department of social services or department of education, often license family child care homes, whereas private schools may need to follow certain criteria to be affiliated with a larger organization (such as the American Montessori Society).

The National Academy of Early Childhood Programs, a division of NAEYC, has established an accreditation system for improving the quality of life for young children and their families. The accreditation system articulates standards for physical, social, emotional, and cognitive development of children in group care. The academy established goals for accreditation on the basis of 10 criteria, which are outlined on page 57.

Essential Steps Before You Begin

To ensure the most productive assessment, take the following steps:

1. **Set goals.** Without evaluation, goals are meaningless. Evaluation helps shape a goal into a meaningful plan of action. To be useful, an evaluation must include suggestions for improving the performance or behavior. The assessment tool that only describes a situation is an unfinished evaluation; goals for improvement must be established.
2. **Define expectations.** In every early childhood setting, more than one set of expectations is at work. The director has job expectations of all the teachers. Teachers have standards of performance for themselves, the children, and parents. Parents have some expectations about what their children will do in school and about the role of the teachers. Children develop expectations regarding themselves, their parents, teachers, and the school. A good evaluation tool outlines clearly and specifically how expectations have been met in a system of mutual accountability. Evaluations provide information by which to rate performance, define areas of difficulty, look for possible solutions, and plan for the future.
3. **Be inclusive.** A good evaluation instrument should be culturally appropriate and recognize the many ways that a program can be multicultural and anti-biased in its operations. In Chapter 9, you will learn about anti-bias and inclusive environments. (See Figure 9-4 for a checklist for creating an inclusive setting.)
4. **Define the objectives.** A program evaluation begins with a definition of the program's objectives. Knowing why a program is to be evaluated indicates how to tailor the procedure to the needs and characteristics

Checklist for Program Evaluation

The Physical Environment

_____ Are the facilities clean, comfortable, safe?

_____ Are room arrangements orderly and attractive?

_____ Are materials and equipment in good repair and maintained?

_____ Is there a variety of materials, appropriate to age levels?

_____ Are activity areas well-defined?

_____ Are cleanup and room restoration a part of the daily schedule?

_____ Are samples of children's work on display?

_____ Is play space adequate, both inside and out?

_____ Is personal space (e.g., cubby) provided for each child?

The Staff

_____ Are there enough teachers for the number of children?

_____ How is this determined?

_____ Are the teachers qualified? What criteria are used?

_____ Is the staff evaluated periodically? By whom and how?

_____ Does the school provide/encourage in-service training and continuing education?

_____ Do the teachers encourage the children to be independent and self-sufficient?

_____ Are the teachers genuinely interested in children?

_____ Are teachers aware of children's individual abilities and limitations?

_____ What guidance and disciplinary techniques are used?

_____ Do teachers observe, record, and write reports on children's progress?

_____ Are teachers skilled in working with individual children, small groups, and large groups?

_____ Does the teaching staff give the children a feeling of stability and belonging?

_____ Do teachers provide curriculum that is age-appropriate and challenging?

_____ How would you describe the teachers' relationships with other adults in the setting? Who does this include, and how?

_____ Can the teaching staff articulate good early education principles and relate them to their teaching?

Parent Relationships

_____ How does the classroom include parents?

_____ Are parents welcome to observe, discuss policies, make suggestions, help in the class?

_____ Are different needs of parents taken into account?

_____ Where and how do parents have a voice in the school?

_____ Are parent-teacher conferences scheduled?

_____ Does the school attempt to use community resources and social service agencies in meeting parents' needs?

The Organization and Administration

_____ Does the school maintain and keep records?

_____ Are scholarships or subsidies available?

_____ What socioeconomic, cultural, and religious groups does the school serve?

_____ What is the funding agency, and what role does it play?

_____ Is there a school board, and how is it chosen?

_____ Does the school serve children with special needs or handicaps?

_____ Is the classroom group homo- or heterogeneous?

_____ What hours is the school open?

_____ What age range is served?

_____ Are there both full- and part-day options?

_____ Is after-school care available?

_____ Does the school conduct research or train teachers?

_____ What is the teacher-child ratio?

The Overall Program

_____ Does the school have a written, stated educational philosophy?

_____ Are there developmental goals for the children's physical, social, intellectual, and emotional growth?

_____ Are the children evaluated periodically?

_____ Is the program capable of being individualized to fit the needs of all the children?

_____ Does the program include time for a variety of free, spontaneous activities?

_____ Is the curriculum varied to include music, art, science, nature, math, language, social studies, motor skills, etc.?

_____ Are there ample opportunities to learn through a variety of media and types of equipment and materials?

_____ Is there ample outdoor activity?

_____ Is there a daily provision for routines: eating, sleeping, toileting, play?

_____ Is the major emphasis in activities on concrete experiences?

_____ Are the materials and equipment capable of stimulating and sustaining interest?

_____ Are field trips offered?

_____ Do children have a chance to be alone? In small groups? In large groups?

Cultural Responsiveness

_____ Are multicultural perspectives already incorporated throughout the school, classroom curriculum, and classroom environment?

_____ Do my attitudes (and those of all staff) indicate a willingness to accept and respect cultural diversity? How is this demonstrated?

_____ Do classroom materials recognize the value of cultural diversity, gender, and social class equity?

_____ Do curricular activities and methods provide children opportunities to work and play together cooperatively? In mixed groups of their choice or at teacher direction?

_____ Do schoolwide activities reflect cultural diversity? How is this noticed?

_____ Does the program planning reflect the reality (views and opinions) of families and the community?

_____ Does the curriculum include planning for language diversity? For full inclusion? (Adapted from Baruth and Manning, 1992, and de Melendez and Ostertag, 1997.)

© Cengage Learning 2011

FIGURE 2-7 Checklist for areas of program evaluation.

⊡ This checklist can be downloaded from the Education CourseMate website.

of an individual school. With the objectives defined, the choice of evaluation instrument becomes clear. If, for example, a program objective is to provide a healthy environment for children, the evaluation tool used must address the issues of health, safety, and nutrition.

5. *Choose an evaluation instrument.* Evaluation instruments vary with the purpose of the program evaluation. NAEYC's accreditation guidelines are effective (described as 10 essentials for high quality programs on pages 57), as are four rating scales developed by the Frank Porter Graham Child Development Institute at the University of North Carolina at Chapel Hill. Each focuses on a specific early childhood setting:

   - Infant/Toddler Environment Rating Scale (ITERS-R), which is designed to assess programs for children from birth to 21 years of age
   - Early Childhood Environment Rating Scale (ECERS-R) for preschool through kindergarten programs serving children from 5 to 21 years of age
   - Family Child Care Environment Rating Scale (FCCERS-R) for use in homes that serve infants through school-age
   - School-Age Care Environment Rating Scale (SACERS) assesses group care programs for children from 5 to 12 years of age

See Chapter 9 for details of how these elements are used in planning environments. Figure 2-6 is a checklist that includes the program areas to include in an evaluation.

Implement the Findings

The evaluation process is complete when the results are tabulated and goals are set to meet the recommendations of the evaluation. Program administrators meet with the teaching staff to discuss the challenges highlighted by the evaluation. A process is put into place for addressing the issues, a calendar is established to create a timeline for improvement, the appropriate staff members are assigned the responsibility for making the changes, and the process begins anew. Evaluations are only as useful as the implementation plan. They can help identify specific concerns, determine the areas of growth and potential development, and be a blueprint for the future.

Summary

LO 1 High-quality early childhood programs reflect the core elements of developmentally appropriate practices (DAP) by basing the program on what is known about child development and learning, what is known about each individual child, and what is known about the child's social and cultural context. By following DAP guidelines, early childhood programs maximize the benefits children gain from attending an early education program. Following the guidelines for developmentally and culturally appropriate practice (DCAP) ensures equal and fair teaching and learning experiences for all students.

LO 2 The traditional nursery school and its sister programs of child care centers and family child care form the core of early childhood programs. Each has unique characteristics, scheduling, hours of operation, licensing requirements, and a combination of child care and education. The teacher's role in each setting differs according to the length of day that children attend, the number of caregivers, and the needs of parents and families.

LO 3 Early childhood programs reach a broad population and parents have a range of delivery systems from which to choose. An array of programs in parent cooperatives, laboratory schools, faith-based settings, and before/after school are available and serve children from infancy through elementary school. These programs are under the sponsorship of public and private schools; community organizations; churches; synagogues; local, state, or federal governments; corporations; and colleges and universities.

LO 4 A good assessment process evaluates quality according to established professional criteria that serves as a reference for making changes that improve the teaching and learning in that setting. The assessment includes a clear purpose, knowing who and what will be evaluated, and what use will be made of the results. Teachers, children, and the program must be assessed individually and then evaluated as a whole. Each supports and depends upon the other. An evaluation is a way to look at how these relationships are working. The result is a better prepared staff and a program of greater quality.

Key Terms

developmentally appropriate practice (DAP)	licensing	school readiness
mixed-age grouping	family child care	alignment
looping	comprehensive	self-care
traditional nursery school	educaring	assessment
child care center	attachment	accountability
	kindergarteners	

Review Questions

1. What are the three core considerations of developmentally appropriate practices? How do they contribute to children's learning?
2. What are the core programs of early childhood education? How are they similar? How are they different?
3. What are the variations of the core programs and who do they serve?
4. What are three factors that affect the quality of early childhood programs? How do they influence program assessment?

Observe and Apply

1. Choose one program and describe why you would like to teach in it. What are the most attractive elements of the program? What are some of the challenges you would have working in such a program?
2. Visit a family child care home. Look at the home as if you were a prospective parent. What did you like most? Least? Is the home licensed? If so, for how many children? After talking with the family child care provider, what do you think are the challenges of this type of program? What do you think are possible solutions to these problems?
3. Visit a Head Start program and a local kindergarten. Compare their programs in terms of appropriate or inappropriate curriculum. What are the major concerns of the teaching staff in each type of setting? What are the controversies about each of these programs in your community?
4. As you reflect on the various options for teaching in an early childhood program, what are the most important factors a program must have for you to teach in that setting?
5. What aspect of an assessment process gives you the greatest concern? How do you think you will handle criticism?

Helpful Websites

Bureau of Labor Statistics,   **www.stats.bls.gov**

U.S. Department of Education,   **www.ed.gov**

Families and Work Institute,   **www.familiesandwork.org**

National Institute on Out-of-School Time,   **www.niost.org**

National Network for Child Care,   **www.nncc.org**

National Association for Family Child Care,   **www.nafcc.org**

Child Care Information Exchange,   **www.ccie.com**

National Center for Education Statistics,   **www.nces.ed.gov**

Culturally and Linguistically Appropriate Services,   **www.clas.uiuc.edu**

Center for Child Care Workforce,   **www.ccw.org**

International Nanny's Association,   **www.nanny.org**

Head Start/Early Head Start,   **www.acf.hhs.gov/programs/ohs**

ChildStats, www.childstats.gov

U.S. Census Bureau, www.census.gov

Children's Defense Fund,
www.childrensdefense.org

About Homeschooling,
www.homeschooling.about.com

National Association for the Education of Young
Children, www.naeyc.org

🔵 The Education CourseMate website for this text offers many helpful resources and interactive study tools. Go to CengageBrain.com to access the TeachSource Videos, flashcards, tutorial quizzes, direct links to all of the websites mentioned in the chapter, downloadable forms, and more.

References

Afterschool Alliance. (2010). *America After 3 PM: Key findings.* (2010). http://www.afterschoolalliance.org. Retrieved August 5, 2011.

Baker, K. R. (1950). *The nursery school: A human relationships laboratory.* Philadelphia, PA: Saunders.

Bureau of Labor Statistics. Frequently asked questions, 2010. http://www.bls.gov. Retrieved August 2011.

(The) Carolina Abecedarian Project. (1999). The Frank Porter Graham Child Development Institute. The University of North Carolina at Chapel Hill: Author.

Cloud, J., & Morse, J. (August 27, 2001). Home sweet school. *Time,* pp. 47–54.

Copple, C., & Bredekamp, S. (2009). *Developmentally appropriate practice in early childhood programs serving children from birth through age 8.* Washington, D.C.: National Association for the Education of Young Children.

Cost, Quality, and Child Outcomes Study Team. (1995). *Cost, quality and child outcomes in child care centers.* Denver, CO: Department of Economics, University of Colorado at Denver.

Gerber, M. (1979). Respecting infants: The Loczy model of infant care. In E. Jones (Ed.), *Supporting the growth of infants, toddlers, and parents.* Pasadena, CA: Pacific Oaks.

Harms, T., Clifford, R. M., & Cryer, D. (1998). *Early Childhood Environmental Rating Scale* (Rev. Ed.). New York: Teachers College Press.

Hatch, J. A. (2005). *Teaching in the new kindergarten.* Clifton Park, NY: Thomson Delmar Learning.

Head Start. (2010). *2010 Head Start fact sheet.* Washington, D.C.: Head Start Bureau, Department of Health and Human Services.

Hyun, E. (2007). Cultural complexity in early childhood: Images of contemporary young children from a critical perspective. *Childhood Education,* 85(5), pp. 261–266.

Hyun, E. (1998). *Making sense of developmentally and culturally appropriate practice (DCAP) in early childhood education.* New York: Peter Lang.

Kagan. S. L., & Kauerz, K. (2006). Making the most of kindergarten: Trends and policy issues. In D. F. Gullo (Ed.) *Teaching and learning in the kindergarten year.* Washington, D.C.: National Association for the Education of Young Children.

McCartney, K., Dearing, E., Taylor, B., & Bub, K. (2007). Quality childcare supports the achievement of low-income children: Direct and indirect pathways through caregiving and the home environment. *Journal of Applied Developmental Psychology,* 28, pp. 411–426.

National Association of Child Care Resources and Referral Agencies (NACCRRA). (2010). Leaving children to chance: 2010 update. Retrieved July 2011. www.naccrra.org.

National Association for Family Child Care. (2011). *NAFCC accreditation and information.* Salt Lake City, UT: Author.

National Association for the Education of Young Children Position Statement. (2009). Developmentally appropriate practice in early childhood programs serving children from birth through age 8. In Copple, C. & Bredekamp, S. (Eds.), *Developmentally appropriate practice in early childhood programs.* Washington, D.C.: Author.

National Association for the Education of Young Children. (2005). *NAEYC early childhood program standards & accreditation criteria.* Washington, D.C.: National Association for the Education of Young Children.

National Association of Early Childhood Specialists in State Departments of Education and the National Association of Education for Young Children. (2001, September). Still unacceptable trends in kindergarten entry and placement. *Young Children,* pp. 59–62.

National Center for Education Statistics. (2011). *Fast facts: homeschooling.* Washington, D.C.: Author. Retrieved July 9, 2011. www.nec=es.ed/gov/fastfacts.

National Coalition for the Homeless. (2007). *How many people experience homelessness?* NCH Fact Sheet #2. National Coalition for the Homeless, June, 2008.

Neugebauer, R., Wilson, M., & Ballas, T. (2007, September/October) School-age child care trend, part II. *Child Care Information Exchange,* pp. 28–39.

Program for Infant/Toddler Care (PITC). (2011). http://www.pitc.org. Retrieved August 5, 2011.

Reynolds, A. J., Temple, J. A., Ou, S. R., Arteaga, I. A., and White, R. A. B. (June 9, 2011). School-based early childhood education and age-28 well-being:

Effects by timing, dosage, and subgroups. *Science.* http://www.sciencedaily.com. Retrieved August 5, 2011.

Rhode Island KIDS COUNT. (2005). Getting ready: Findings from the National School Readiness Indicators Initiative: A 17 State Partnership. http://www.gettingready.org. Retrieved August 5, 2011.

U.S. Bureau of Labor Statistics. (2011). *Labor force statistics from the Current Population Survey: Women in the Labor Force: a Databook (2009 Edition).* Washington, D.C.: U.S. Bureau of Labor: Author. Retrieved August 7, 2011.

United States Census Bureau. (2007). *Who's minding the kids? Child care arrangements: Spring, 2005.* Survey of Income and Program Participation (SIPP). Internet release date February 2008. Washington, D.C.: Author.

Schweinhart, L. J. (n.d.). *The High/Scope Perry Preschool Study Through Age 40.* Ypsilanti, MI: High/Scope Educational Research Foundation.

Whitebook, M., Sakai, L., Gerber, E., & Howes, C. (2001). *Then and now: Changes in child care staffing, 1994–2000.* Washington, D.C.: Center for the Child Care Workforce.

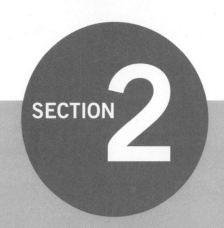

Who Is the Young Child?

© Cengage Learning

© Cengage Learning

3

Defining the Young Child

Learning Objectives

LO1 Describe what is meant by the whole child and define the major domains of development.

LO2 Demonstrate an awareness of developmental ages and stages using Word Pictures to recognize the major developmental milestones.

LO3 Recognize the characteristics of typical and atypical development and describe adaptations needed to support children with diverse abilities.

naeyc Standards For Professional Development

The NAEYC Standards for Initial and Advanced Early Childhood Professional Preparation addressed in this chapter are:

Standard 1 Promoting Child Development and Learning

Standard 2 Building Family and Community Relationships

Standard 3 Observing, Documenting, and Assessing to Support Young Children and Families

Standard 4 Using Developmentally Effective Approaches to Connect with Children and Families

Standard 5 Using Content Knowledge to Build Meaningful Curriculum

Standard 6 Becoming a Professional

naeyc Code of Ethical Conduct

These are the sections from the NAEYC Code of Ethical Conduct that apply to the topics in this chapter:

Ideals:

I-1.1　To be familiar with the knowledge base of early childhood care and education and to stay informed through continuing education and training.

I-1.2　To base program practices upon current knowledge and research in the field of early childhood education, child development, and related disciplines, as well as on particular knowledge of each child.

I-1.3　To recognize and respect the unique qualities, abilities, and potential of each child.

I-1.8　To support the right of each child to play and learn in an inclusive environment that meets the needs of children with and without disabilities.

I-1.9　To advocate for and ensure that all children, including those with special needs, have access to the support services needed to be successful.

Principles:

P-1.3.　We shall not participate in practices that discriminate against children by denying benefits, giving special advantages, or excluding them from programs or activities on the basis of their race, national origin, immigration status, preferred home language, religious beliefs, medical condition, disability or the marital status/family structure, sexual orientation, or religious beliefs or other affiliations of their families.

The Whole Child

The concept of "the whole child" is based on the accepted principle that all areas of human growth and development are integrated. It is only for the purpose of studying one area or another in depth that categories are created. In reality, all areas of growth are knitted together in a mutually supportive network creating the uniqueness of each child.

Teachers quickly learn what makes each child special, what they look like when they move their bodies, change expressions, or assume a posture. We can tell when Sonja is hurt, happy, or harried by the way she moves and looks. Rodrigo's face mirrors his distress or his delight. The observant teacher reads children through the ways they express the "whole child."

Developmental Domains

We use six **developmental domains** to define the "whole child" and express how children grow and develop:

1. *Social-emotional development*: includes a child's relationship with herself and others, self-concept, self-esteem, and the ability to express feelings.
2. *Physical–motor development*: includes gross motor, fine motor, and perceptual motor activity.
3. *Cognitive development*: includes curiosity, the ability to perceive and think, memory, attention span, general knowledge, problem solving, analytical thinking, beginning reading, and computing skills.
4. *Language development*: includes children's utterances, pronunciation, vocabulary, sentence length, and the ability to express ideas, needs, and feelings. It includes receptive language (do they understand what they hear?) and verbal ability (what do they say?).

   The interaction among the developmental domains is a key element to understanding the "whole" child. Figure 3-1 shows the connection of each developmental domain in relation to the others.
5. *Cultural identity development.* This suggests the interconnections between developmental stages and a growing awareness of one's attitudes toward others. Various cultural milestones appear in each age group which, when appropriately fostered, can increase a child's sensitivity to differences. The Word Pictures on pages 71–78 indicate cultural identity growth in the early years and are highlighted by an asterisk.
6. *Creative development.* This includes the usual creative activities such as movement, dance, music, and painting, as well as originality, imagination, divergent thinking, and problem solving.

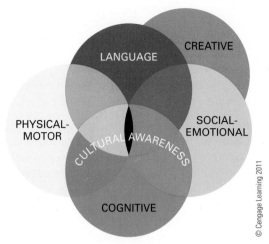

FIGURE 3-1 How areas of growth are interrelated: Each area of growth is affected by and influences every other area of development.

Children: alike, yet different.

Developmental Ages and Stages: Major Milestones

Descriptions of children's common characteristics date back to a classic collection of research by Gesell and Ilg. (See Chapters 1 and 4 for related discussions.) Age alone does not determine a child's capabilities, but it does provide a guideline for establishing appropriate expectations. Despite the wide range of individual differences at all ages, common behaviors lend a perspective to help teachers prescribe programs, plan activities, and create curricula.

One area of development affects the other. Figure 3-1 helps us to visualize the interrelationship of the whole child. Think how each area might affect or interact with the others:

- Physical development affects how children feel about themselves. Children who appreciate their body and its power feel confident in what they can do (social-emotional).
- Intellectual skills interact with language development and creativity. When children have mastered their primary language, they can then clarify some of their thought processes.
- The kindergartner who masters using scissors (physical) is ready to try printing. The fine-motor skills enhance the cognitive task of learning the alphabet.
- A child with a hearing loss is likely to have language delay as well; thus the physical development affects the language part of growth.
- The child who has trouble making friends (social) is likely to exhibit his unhappiness (emotional) in the school yard (physical) and in the math period (intellectual).

Observe a classroom during free play or activity time. What interactions do you see between developmental domains? How does this affect the child's ability to learn? Describe yourself at this age, commenting on what developmental domains were your strengths.

The Value of Word Pictures

Each developmental phase has characteristics traits. These are described in the following pages as **Word Pictures**. Word Pictures are designed to help classroom teachers plan learning experiences for a group of children. Word Pictures are a valuable teaching tool because they help teachers know what to expect and when to expect it. The developmental and learning theories in Chapter 4 and their classroom applications help you understand the basis from which these Word Pictures are drawn. See "Teaching With Intention" box later on in this chapter for specific ways to use the Word Pictures. (Chapter 10 has more practical applications and examples for planning curriculum.)

In Behavior and Guidance

We use guidance and discipline strategies based on the expected behaviors common to a given age range. Many so-called problem behaviors are normal behaviors of the age at which they occur: 2-year-olds are easily frustrated as they grow increasingly independent. Four-year-olds test limits and are resistant to controls. The knowledgeable teacher accepts these characteristics and guides each child accordingly.

Word Pictures of a child, taken from age-level charts, help teachers know what to expect and when to expect it. By using the charts as a reference, teachers lessen the risk of expecting too much or too little of children at any given age. **Age-level characteristics** give a frame of reference for handling daily situations and a basis for planning appropriate guidance measures. When using Word Pictures, ask yourself which ones:

Are most common to the ages of the children in the class
Are appropriate for children in group settings
Suggest guidance and disciplinary measures
Have implications for planning a developmentally
    appropriate curriculum
Are culture milestones, *which are highlighted by an asterisk*, to suggest the interaction of children's development and their awareness of attitudes toward race and culture

In Curriculum

Word Pictures can be used to tailor curriculum planning to an individual child or a particular class or group on the basis of known developmental standards. A group cooking experience, for instance, allows children to choose their level of comfort and involvement. As an early reader at age 4, Darragh loves to read the recipe to others. Lourdes's favorite activity is to mix the ingredients together, refining her small motor skills. Von, who loves to play with mud and clay, spreads the cookie sheet with oil while Felicity helps the teacher adjust the oven temperature. Cooking is always a fun activity but serves a greater purpose when planned with individual children in mind. The skills and abilities of the specific age group helps to determine the

Adults see children through many filters. What is it like to look through children's eyes?

BRAIN
Research Says...

The Architecture of the Brain

Block play is one of the most popular activities in preschool programs. When young children first encounter blocks, they make piles, stack them, or lay them out in a row. As they have more experiences with blocks, more complex building emerges as children build walls and floors, bridges, and enclosures. At first, playing with blocks is an end in itself but with more experience, blocks are used in a larger architectural plan. "I need to put these blocks on top of each other to build a second story to my garage," says 5-year-old Gian-Francesco. It is almost as if the first year of block building was a practice period to lay the foundation for more complex work.

So it is with how the young child's brain develops. Foundational concepts of brain development (National Scientific Council on the Developing Child, 2010) help us understand three basic blocks on which brain development is based. (See the video series, "Three Core Concepts in Early Development," available at www.developingchild .harvard.edu/resources/multimedia/ video/three_core_concepts/.)

Concept 1: Experiences build brain architecture. Through daily activities and experiences the brain cells (neurons) shape the neurological networks that create the foundation for emotions, logic, memory, motor skills, social-emotional behaviors, and vision. Each neuron creates an axon (which sends signals) and dendrites (which receive signals). Axons and dendrites join to form synapses. Simple circuits form the basis for more complex brain circuits. Electrical activity is triggered by sensory experiences and fine-tunes the brain's architecture. As you supervise block play, notice all the architecture there, and remember that the brain is being built as well.

Concept 2: "Serve and return" shapes the brain's architecture. If you have ever played tennis or ping-pong, you have participated in "serve and return." Your partner serves the ball to you and you hit it back, returning the serve. Now think of the image of new parents cooing, babbling, and smiling at their baby. That, too, is a "serve and return" activity and is key to forming strong brain architecture. The back and forth interactions between children and adults form the foundation of brain architecture on which all future development will be built. "Serve and return" interactions help create the neural connections between all the different areas of the brain, and they build the child's emotional and cognitive skills. The best advice for teachers and parents is to create "serve and return" interactions to enhance the child's growing brain.

Concept 3: Toxic **stress** hinders healthy brain development. Persistent adversity in young children, such as poverty, neglect, abuse, family violence, parental substance abuse, and severe maternal depression cause toxic stress. The body's stress management system is activated and sends the stress hormone cortisol into the body. The body's reaction to stress includes rapid increase of heart rate and a rise in blood pressure. These responses help the body deal with stress and then return to normal when the brain perceives that the stress is past. However, when stress is prolonged and the child is without supportive adult help, the stress level persists and affects the brain's architecture. The neural connections become reduced by stress overload at a time when they should be growing new ones. High levels of cortisol can disrupt the learning process by inhibiting reasoning abilities, which can lead to emotional and cognitive problems. These early experiences of deprivation and stress become hardwired into the brain.

Questions

1. Aside from block play, what other experiences in an early childhood program helps to build the brain's architecture? List those that are appropriate for infants and toddlers, for preschoolers, and for school-age children.
2. How would you "serve and return" with a 3-year-old? A school-age child?
3. What is our role as early childhood educators in reducing persistent stress in children's lives?

kind of activities at which children can succeed while still taking the next steps in their development. See the next section for guidelines on using the Word Pictures as tools for planning. Chapters 10 through 14 have more practical applications and examples for planning curricula.

In Cultural Awareness

Derman-Sparks and Edwards (2010) point out that children become aware of and form attitudes about racial and cultural differences at a very early age. Their experiences with their bodies, social environment, and cognitive development combine to help them form their own identity and attitudes. As they develop cognitively, children become aware of differences and similarities in people. These cultural milestones are included in the Word Pictures to indicate how, as children come to a sense of themselves as individuals, their attitudes and behaviors toward others can be influenced.

Teaching With INTENTION

Using Word Pictures

Setting goals for individual children and for the group is an important part of a teacher's role. We intentionally observe all developmental domains—physical-motor, cognitive-language, social-emotional, creative—so that we have a picture of the whole child. To plan effectively, we reflect on what we know about each child, what we need to know, and what we know about the group. Assessing children's development and measuring their progress provides the information needed to create appropriate teaching strategies and curriculum. It tells us what children know and what they can do. Use the Word Pictures to find the baseline, the place where each child starts from, and that will be used at a later date to determine growth over time by measuring the child's progress against the original assessment. The following six guidelines will help you get started:

1. Balance your impression of the Word Pictures with your experiences of children. *Example: Toddlers are always on the move and prefer standing and squatting to sitting in a chair. Observe a toddler story time to see how many children are sitting on the floor, how many are standing, and how many are squatting on their haunches.*
2. Make a profile of the whole child to balance your impression of the whole child. *Example: At 3½-years-old, Chad's language skills were those of a 7-year-old. He tended to talk in long and convoluted sentences and other*

children had difficulty relating to him. After looking over Chad's profile, the teachers focused on his social development and worked with Chad's parents on finding him a friend. In class, the teachers modeled more appropriate ways to engage other children in conversation and play.

3. Get perspective on the range of developmental norms a child exhibits over time. *Example: Children have varying levels of development at any point in time. Look at the Word Pictures for the group just older and younger than the age level of the child you are observing. A typical child may have the physical development of a 3-year-old, the language skills of a 4-year-old, and the social coping skills of a 2-year-old. Children exhibit some of the behaviors appropriate in a two- to three-year range.*
4. Remember that these norms of development refer to average or typical behavior, and they should not be applied too literally. *Example: Use these examples with discretion. If Dixon and Emma are the only two children in the class reading at the next grade level, do not expect the rest of the class to achieve the same success. The Word Pictures are norms and will help you track Dixon and Emma's progress in developmental domains as well as cognitive-language. The Word Pictures are not intended for comparing children's abilities, but rather to provide a*

compilation of information on individual children.

5. Keep in mind that children go through most of the stages described and in the same sequence, but they do so at their own rates of growth. *Example: Individual differences occur as development follows its orderly and predictable path as children acquire the abilities and skills that are necessary to succeed in the next stages. Elaina may not yet have the writing skills of her peers, but with appropriate experiences and teaching strategies, we can help her progress over a period of time.*
6. Focus on what the children can do rather than on what they cannot do. Use the characteristics to compare the child's rate of growth. *Example: In observing Dwayne, it is important to assess where he is in relation to other 4-year-olds, but it is more important to know where he is six months from now, a year from now, and what he was like a year ago. From this, a clear picture of his rate of growth emerges.*

Think About This

1. How do Word Pictures help you understand the concept of the "whole child"?
2. How do Word Pictures help you work with parents and families?
3. What other use can you find for Word Pictures?

Applying Word Pictures to Teaching Strategies

The Word Pictures focus on the critical issues that teachers address when planning for a group of children. We have included six basic developmental areas to give a more complete picture of each age group. In Chapter 4, you will come to appreciate the importance of research and significant theories from which these Word Pictures are drawn.

Culture, Race, and Ethnic Considerations

The answer to "Who is the young child?" takes on new meaning as we look at the ethnic mix of American life. A multicultural explosion has swept across the nation, filling early childhood programs with children from many different cultural backgrounds. There are more students in the classroom who are culturally and linguistically different

(text continued on page 79)

Word Pictures

Infant

Social-Emotional

0–1 month: cries to express emotions; bonding begins

4–10 weeks: makes social smiles

2 months: begins social games

3 months: distinguishes familiar faces*; turns head toward human voice; smiles in response to a smile; kicks, smiles, waves in response; cries when left alone; recognizes parent

4 months: has a genuine laugh; smiles when spoken to; loves attention

5 months to 1 year: begins to exhibit stranger anxiety*

6 months: distinguishes between voices; smiles; babbles at strangers; develops attachment to parents, caregivers; begins to play imitation games; plays peek-a-boo; sensitive to parental moods

8 months: laughs out loud

9 months: screams to get own way

Play is activity only for present moment

Fears unfamiliar: people, places, things*

Beginning sense of separate self*

Language

0–1 month: turns head in response to voices; cries to express needs

6–8 weeks: coos; gestures to communicate: pushes objects away; squirms; reaches out to people*; pouts; smacks lips; shrieks; points

2 months: makes voluntary vocal sounds

3 months: babbles

6–12 months: plays imitation sound games; responds to variety of sounds*; makes vowel sounds; acquires receptive language*; cries to communicate

12 months: says first words

Physical-Motor

By 1 year: grows 10 to 12 inches; triples birth weight; lengthens by 40 percent; doubles brain size; grows full head of hair; bounces in crib; uses whole-body motions

4 months: sees, grasps objects

5 months: examines fingers; sits when propped

6 months: rolls over; discovers feet; teething begins

7 months: crawls

8 months: sits up unaided; pulls to standing position; pincer grasp established

9 months: creeps

10 months: feeds self with spoon

11 months: stands alone; cruises

12 months: takes first steps

Late infancy: can move hands in rotation to turn knobs

Newborn motor activity is mostly reflexes

Creative

Discovers and explores hands and feet

Expresses and discovers emotion

Talks by babbling, cooing, and gurgling

Plays peek-a-boo

Responds to facial expressions

Courtesy of the author

Cognitive

0–1 month: responds to mother's voice; aware of senses, especially pain, touch*

10 weeks: memory is evident*

4 months: makes smiles of recognition

7–10 months: solves simple problems (knocks over box to get toy)

8 months: begins to believe in permanence of objects; follows a simple instruction

8–12 months: becoming intentional in behavior

11 months: begins trial-error experimentation

12 months: plays drop/retrieve games, pat-a-cake

Explores with hands and fingers

Smiles, vocalizes at image in mirror*

*Key characteristics of cultural awareness or identity.

Toddler

Social-Emotional

Almost totally egocentric

Likes to be noticed; loves an audience

Lacks inhibitions

Insists on own way, assertive

Likes doing things by self

Independent, has self-identity*

Adapts easily

Refers to self by name

Laughs loudly at peek-at-boo

Cries when left alone

Curious*

Relates to adults better than children

Active, eager

Talks mostly to self

Usually friendly

Strong sense of ownership

Mimics adult behavior*

Experiences and shows shame*

Language

Some two-word phrases

Enjoys vocalizing to self

Babbles in own jargon

Uses "eh-eh" or "uh-uh" with gestures

Names closest relatives*

Repeats adults' words*

Points to communicate needs, wants

Shakes head "no" to respond*

Responds to directions to fetch, point

Obeys verbal requests

Asks "What's that?" or "Whassat?"*

Understands simple phrases

Uses five to 50 words

Physical-Motor

Awkward coordination; chubby body

Tottering stance

Creeps when in a hurry

Walks with increasing confidence

Walks with feet wide apart, arms out, head forward

Finds it difficult to turn corners

Goes up and down stairs holding on

Backs into chair to sit down

Can squat for long periods of time

In constant motion

Loves to pull/push objects

Runs with stiff, flat gait

Uses whole-arm movements

Carry and dump becomes a favorite activity

Scribbles

Turns pages two or three at a time

Zips/unzips large zipper

Likes holding objects in both hands

Creative

Responds to mood of music

Freely examines every object

Sings phrases of nursery rhymes

Loves to finger-paint and explore texture

Stares; takes it all in

"The age of exploration"

Makes up nonsense syllables

Cognitive

Points to objects in a book

Matches similar objects

Fits round block in round hole

Loves opposites: up/down, yes/no*

Imitates simple tasks

Interest shifts quickly

Short attention span

Follows one direction

Gives up easily but easily engaged*

Conclusions are important: closes doors, shuts books

Thinks with feet; action-oriented

Builds tower of three or four small blocks

*Key characteristics of cultural awareness or identity.

Two-Year-Old

© Cengage Learning

Social-Emotional

Self-centered

Unable to share, possessive

Clings to familiar; resistant to change*

Ritualistic; insists on routines*

Dependent

Likes one adult at a time*

Quits readily; easily frustrated

Goes to extremes

Impulsive; shifts activities suddenly

Easily distracted

Pushes, shoves

Finicky, fussy eater; some food jags

Refers to self by given name*

Treats people as inanimate objects*

Dawdles; slow-geared

Plays parallel to other children

Watches others*

Likes people*

Excited about own capabilities

Language

Uses two- or three-word sentences

Telegraphic sentences: "Throw ball"

Has difficulty in pronunciation

"Me," "Mine" most prominent
   pronouns*

Spontaneous language; rhythmic,
   repetitive

Constant talking; interested in sound

Sings phrases of song, not on pitch

Cannot articulate feelings

Frustrated when not understood

May stutter

Asks "Whassat?" about pictures*

Can match words with objects

Repeats words and phrases

Uses 50 to 300 words

Physical-Motor

Uses whole-body action: pushes, pulls,
   pokes

Climbs into things

Leans forward while running

Climbs stairs one by one

Dependent on adults for dressing

Can help dress/undress

Has reached one-half potential height

Bladder/bowel control begins

Feeds self

Thumb-forefinger opposition complete

Grasps cup with two hands

Awkward with small objects

Lugs, tumbles, topples; unsteady

Alternates hands; hand preference is
   developing

Can rotate to fit objects

Expresses emotions bodily*

Sensory-oriented

Cuts last teeth

Has difficulty relaxing

Creative

Imitates other children

Combines parallel play and fantasy
   play

Plays with sounds; repeats syllables
   over and over

Enjoys simple finger plays

Can follow simple melodies

Learns to scribble

Uses art for sensory pleasure

Cognitive

Recognizes, explores physical characteristics of objects*

Investigates with touch and taste

Intrigued by water, washing

Likes to fill and empty things

Has limited attention span

Lives in present

Understands familiar concepts*

Can tell difference between black
   and white*

Needs own name used

Likes simple make-believe

Does one thing at a time

Remembers orders of routines

Recalls where toys are left

Classifies people by gender*

Names familiar objects in books

*Key characteristics of cultural awareness or identity.

Social-Emotional

Highly imitative of adults*

Wants to please adults; conforms*

Responds to verbal suggestions

Easily prompted, redirected

Can be bargained with, reasoned with

Begins to share, take turns, wait

Avid "me-too"-er*

Exuberant, talkative, humorous

Has an imaginary companion

Has nightmares, animal phobias

Plays consciously, cooperatively with others*

Plays spontaneously in groups

Demonstrates fears

Goes after desires; fights for them

Asserts independence often

Often stymied, frustrated, jealous

Sympathizes*

Strong sex-role stereotypes*

Language

Talkative with or without a listener

Can listen to learn*

Likes new words*

Increases use of pronouns, prepositions

Uses "s" to indicate plural nouns

Uses "ed" to indicate past tense

Uses sentences of three or more words

Says "Is that all right?" a lot

Talks about nonpresent situations

Puts words into action

Moves and talks at the same time

Substitutes letters in speech: "w" for "r"

Intrigued by whispering

Uses 300 to 1,000 words

© Cengage Learning

Physical-Motor

Has well-balanced body lines

Walks erect; nimble on feet

Gallops in wide, high steps

Alternates feet in stair climbing

Suddenly starts, stops

Turns corners rapidly

Swings arms when walking

Jumps up and down with ease

Uses toilet alone

Loses baby fat

Achieves bladder control

Rides a tricycle

Puts on, takes off wraps with help

Unbuttons buttons

Has some finger control with small objects

Grasps with thumb and index finger

Holds cup in one hand

Pours easily from small pitcher

Washes hands unassisted

Can carry liquids

Has activity with drive and purpose

Can balance on one foot

Creative

Dramatizes play

Enjoys slap-stick humor

Laughs at the ridiculous

Experiments with silly language

Imaginary companion may appear

Tricycle becomes many objects in dramatic play

Acts out own version of favorite story

Enjoys simple poems

Learns color concepts

Cognitive

Matches people according to physical characteristics*

Estimates "how many"

Enjoys making simple choices

Alert, excited, curious

Asks "why?" constantly*

Understands "It's time to . . ."

Understands "Let's pretend . . ."

Enjoys guessing games, riddles

Has lively imagination*

Often over generalizes*

Carries out two to four directions in sequence

Often colors pages one color

Can't combine two activities

Names and matches simple colors

Has number concept of one and two

Sees vague cause-and-effect relationships*

Can recognize simple melodies

Distinguishes between night and day

Understands size and shape comparisons

*Key characteristics of cultural awareness or identity.

Four-Year-Old

Social-Emotional

Mood changes rapidly

Tries out feelings of power

Dominates; can be bossy, boastful, belligerent

Assertive, argumentative

Shows off; is cocky, noisy

Can fight own battles

Hits, grabs, insists on desires

Explosive, destructive

Easily over stimulated; excitable

Impatient in large groups*

Cooperates in groups of two or three*

Develops "special" friends* but shifts loyalties often

May exclude others from play*

Resistant; tests limits

Exaggerates, tells tall tales

Alibis frequently

Teases, outwits; has terrific humor

May have scary dreams

Tattles frequently

Has food jags, food strikes

Language

Has more words than knowledge

A great talker, questioner

Likes words, plays with them

Has high interest in poetry

Able to talk to solve conflicts*

Responds to verbal directions

Enjoys taking turns to sing along

Interested in dramatizing songs, stories

Exaggerates, practices words

Uses voice control, pitch, rhythm

Asks "when?" "why?" "how?"*

Joins sentences together

Loves being read to

Physical-Motor

Longer, leaner body build

Vigorous, dynamic, acrobatic

Active until exhausted

"Works": builds, drives, pilots

Can jump own height and land upright

Hops, skips

Throws large ball, kicks accurately

Hops and stands on one foot

Jumps over objects

Walks in a straight line

Races up and down stairs

Turns somersaults

Walks backward toe-heel

Accurate, rash body movements

Copies shapes such as a cross, square

Can draw a stick figure

Holds paint brush in adult manner, pencil in fisted grasp

Can lace shoes

Dresses self except back buttons, ties

Has sureness and control in finger activities

Alternates feet going down stairs

Creative

Is adventurous

Shows vivid imagination

Displays great interest in violence in imaginary play

Loves anything new

Demonstrates more elaborate dramatic play

Makes up new words, sounds, and stories

Enjoys complexity in book illustrations

Exaggerates and goes to extreme

Likes funny poetry

Tells spontaneous story with artwork

© Cengage Learning

Can put on elaborate plays with puppets

Finds ways to solve problems

Combines words and ideas

Cognitive

Does some naming and representative art

Gives art products personal value

Can work for a goal*

Questions constantly*

Interested in how things work

Interested in life-death concepts

Has an extended attention span

Can do two things at once

Dramatic play is closer to reality*

Judges which of two objects is larger

Has concept of three; can name more

Has accurate sense of time

Full of ideas

Begins to generalize; often faulty*

Likes a variety of materials

Calls people names*

Has dynamic intellectual drive*

Has imaginary playmates

Recognizes several printed words

*Key characteristics of cultural awareness or identity.

Five-Year-Old

© Cengage Learning

Spells out simple words

Takes turn in conversation

Has clear ideas and articulates them*

Insists "I already know that"

Asks questions to learn answers*

Makes up songs

Enjoys dictating stories

Uses 1,500 words

Tells a familiar story

Defines simple words

Answers telephone, takes a message

Thinks out loud*

Social-Emotional

Poised, self-confident, self-contained

Sensitive to ridicule*

Has to be right; persistent

Has sense of self-identity*

May get silly, high, wild

Enjoys pointless riddles, jokes

Enjoys group play, competitive games*

Aware of rules, defines them for others*

Chooses own friends; is sociable*

Gets involved with group decisions*

Insists on fair play*

Likes adult companionship*

Accepts, respects authority*

Asks permission

Remains calm in emergencies

Language

Uses big words and complete
sentences

Can define some words

Physical-Motor

Completely coordinated

Has adult-like posture

Has tremendous physical drive

Likes to use fine-motor skills

Has accuracy, skill with simple tools

Draws a recognizable person*

Handedness is evident

Dresses self completely

Cuts on a line with scissors

Begins to color within the lines

Catches ball from three feet away

Skips using alternate feet

Enjoys jumping, running, doing stunts

Rides a two-wheeler

Balances on a balance beam

Jumps rope, skips

Runs lightly on toes

Likes to dance; is graceful, rhythmic

Sometimes roughhouses, fights

Creative

Explores variety of art processes

Becomes engrossed in details of painting, blocks

Fantasy is more active, less verbal

Thinks out loud

Has ideas; loves to talk about them

Can learn simple dance routine

Enjoys making patterns, designs

Puts on simple plays

Has idea of what to draw—wants to
make something recognizable

Cognitive

Curious about everything*

Wants to know "how?" and "why?"*

Likes to display new knowledge, skills

Somewhat conscious of own
ignorance*

Knows tomorrow, yesterday

Can count 10 objects, rote counts to 20

Sorts objects by single characteristic*

Knows own name, address, town

Makes a plan, follows it, centers on task

Sorts objects by color, shape

Concepts of smallest, less than, one-half

May tell time accurately, on the hour

Knows what a calendar is used for

Seldom sees things from another's
point of view

*Key characteristics of cultural awareness or identity.

Six- and Seven-Year-Olds

Social-Emotional

Six-year-old

Likes to work, yet often does so in spurts

Does not show persistence

Tends to be a know-it-all

Free with opinions and advice

Brings home evidence of good school-work

Observes family rules*

Gender-role stereotypes are rigid*

Friends easily gained, easily lost*

Tests and measures self against peers*

Makes social connections through play*

Friends are of same sex*

Believes in rules except for self*

Active, outgoing

Charming

Proud of accomplishments

Shows aggression through insults, name-calling*

Seven-year-old

More serious

Sensitive to others' reactions*

Eager for home responsibilities

Complaining, pensive, impatient

Shame is common emotion*

Leaves rather than face criticism, ridicule, disapproval*

Complains of unfair treatment, not being liked*

Shows politeness and consideration for adults*

Enjoys solitary activities

First peer pressure: needs to be "in"*

Wants to be one of the gang*

Relates physical competence to self-concept*

Self-absorbed; self-conscious

Language

Six- and seven-year-olds

Enjoy putting language skill to paper

Talk with adults rather than to them*

Chatter incessantly

Dominate conversations

Speech irregularities still common

Learning to print/write

Acquisition of new words tapers off

Bilingual capacities nearly complete* if English is second language

Ability to learn new language still present*

Physical-Motor

Six- and seven-year-olds

Basic skills need refinement

Like to test limits of own body

Value physical competence*

Work at self-imposed tasks

Need daily legitimate channels for high energy

Learn to ride two-wheeler, skate, ski

Use motor skills as a tool for socializing

Boisterous, enjoy stunts and rough-housing

Susceptible to fatigue

Visual acuity reaches normal

Hungry at short intervals, like sweets

Chew pencils, fingernails, hair

Creative

Six-year-old

Tries out artistic exploration seriously for the first time

Industrious

Greater interest in process, not product

Eager, curious, enthusiastic

Loves jokes and guessing games

Loves to color, paint

Understands cause and effect

Likes cooperative projects, activities, tasks

Interested in skill and technique

© Cengage Learning

Seven-year-old

Likes to be alone listening to music

Wants work to look good

The age for starting music lessons

Driven by curiosity, desire to discover and invent

Intensely interested in how things work; takes apart, puts back together

Uses symbols in both writing and drawing

Interested in all sorts of codes

Likes to select and sort objects

Cognitive

Six- and seven-year-olds

Work in spurts, not persistent

Letter and word reversal common

Learn to read, beginning math skills

Can consider others' points of view*

Use logic, systematic thinking*

Can plan ahead

Enjoy collecting: sorting, classifying

Can sequence events and retell stories

Concepts of winning and losing are difficult*

Like games with simple rules*

May cheat or change rules*

Want "real" things: watches and cameras that work

Sift and sort information*

Can conceptualize situations*

Enjoy exploring culture of classmates*

*Key characteristics of cultural awareness or identity.

Eight-Year-Old

Social-Emotional

Outgoing, enthusiastic

Enormously curious about people and things*

Socially expansive*

Judgmental and critical of self and others*

Ambivalent about growing up

Often hostile but attracted to opposite sex

Growing self-confidence

Learns about self through others: peers, parents*

Is aware of and sensitive to differences from other children*

Begins to evaluate self and others through clothing, physical attraction, social status*

Likes to meet new people, go new places*

Has emerging sensitivity to personality traits of others*

Eager for peer approval and acceptance*

Growing sense of moral responsibility

Joins clubs

Chooses same-sex playmates

Struggles with feelings of inferiority

Likes to work cooperatively

Responds to studies of other cultures*

Has growing interest in fairness and justice issues*

Language

Talks with adults

Attentive and responsive to adult communication*

© Cengage Learning

Teases members of opposite sex

Talks about "self"*

Talkative, exaggerates

Likes to explain ideas

Imitates language of peers

Enjoys storytelling and writing short stories

Physical-Motor

Beginning to engage in team sports*

Often a growth-spurt year

Speedy, works fast

Restless, energetic, needs physical release

Plays hard, exhausts self

Eye-hand coordination matures; learning cursive handwriting

Enjoys competitive sports*

Hearty appetite, few food dislikes

Repeatedly practices new skills to perfect them

Creative

Has great imagination

Enjoys riddles, limericks, knock-knock jokes

Likes to explain ideas

Visual acuity and fine-motor skills come together

Is most productive in groups

Shows interest in process and product

Cognitive

Criticizes abilities in all academic areas

Seeks new experiences*

Likes to barter, bargain, trade

Enjoys creating collections of things

Interested in how children from other countries live*

Thinks beyond the here-and-now boundaries of time and space

Enjoys role-playing character parts*

Tests out parents to learn more about them

Needs direction, focus

Enjoys all types of humor

Full of ideas, plans

Gaining competence in basic skills

Industrious, but overestimates abilities

Interested in process as well as product of schoolwork

Growing interest in logic and the way things work

Takes responsibility seriously*

*Key characteristics of cultural awareness or identity.

from the teaching staff and from each other. Unless teachers are informed and educated about these differences, they may misinterpret a child's abilities, learning, and needs. Too often, language barriers between a teacher and a child lead to the conclusion that the child is a slow learner or has a disability.

Many families are unfamiliar with school culture in the United States and the expectations schools have about family involvement and participation. Some parents are illiterate in their own language. An informed and supportive teacher can help children succeed under these circumstances.

A lack of understanding about the culture, history, beliefs, and values of the children is harmful to a child's self-concept (see Derman-Sparks and Edwards, 2010, and other references in this book). When there are no assessment tools or instructional materials in the language of the children or that depict their native heritage, children are placed at a distinct disadvantage and often eliminated from programs and services that could help them succeed.

Children of Mixed Heritage

One group of children and families who have often been neglected in the discussion of race are those who are biracial or interracial. **Biracial** children have parents who are of different races, for instance, a child of a Native American and a white person. All combinations of races can produce a biracial child, such as a Korean/African American child, or a Chinese American/Japanese American child. **Interracial** children have parents who represent more than two racial or ethnic backgrounds. These terms also apply to children who are adopted by parents of a different race.

Kelly (2009), a black woman married to a white man, writes about her newborn son, reflecting some of the emotion tied to children of mixed heritage: "I was worried that our son would be so light-skinned as to appear Caucasian, and I wanted him to look Black. . . . I wanted to claim [him] for "my" side—in league with [me] against small minds, casual racism, and discrimination. . . . at seven months after his birth, [my son] is the exact shade you'd get if you mixed his father and me up in a paint can—a color I call golden."

The election of Barack Obama, who is biracial, as President of the United States has evoked needed conversations that bring to light many of the issues facing children and families who are interracial.

Culturally Sensitive Teaching

It is important to help interracial children gain a positive self-concept and identity at an early age. Classroom environments and curricula should intentionally reflect images of interracial children and families to help children recognize and connect with people who share their heritages so that they learn to see and understand themselves.

Educators need to encourage open discussions of racial identification and give children some positive experiences in talking about their heritage. Consult with families about how they handle their mixed heritage and how they identify themselves and their children. Focus on their needs as a family to help them nurture their child in an interracial context.

Cultural sensitivity means that each child's heritage is honored, that it is understood as unique from other cultures, and that it is respected. It means that teachers must become familiar with the cultural norms of the children in their classes and build bridges for children and their families into the more dominant culture.

The culturally sensitive teacher gets to know each of the families as a separate entity and becomes familiar with their individual expressions of culture and values. Today's teacher recognizes that one family does not represent the totality of the culture (which would be stereotyping) and is careful not to overgeneralize from one example. The effective teacher is called on to integrate these insights into curriculum planning, as well as in their relationships with the children's families, in order to serve the best interests of the young child.

Children with Diverse Abilities

Watching and working with children exposes a range of diversity among the group. Megan is challenged by eye-hand coordination, Ariel has difficulty attending to tasks, and Hans stutters when he is excited. What accounts for these developmental differences?

Factors That Influence Developmental Differences

There are several factors that influence the way children grow and develop.

Genetic Makeup

Each child has a unique combination of **genes** that determine eye and hair color, height, body shape, personality traits, and intelligence. Certain diseases, such as Tay-Sachs, cystic fibrosis, and sickle cell anemia, are linked through heredity (Berk, 2009).

Environment

From conception, the brain is affected by environmental conditions. An individual child's rate and sequence of development reflects the interactions among the brain, the body, and the environment. The attitudes with which children are raised, their culture, socioeconomic status, the kinds of caregiving they experience, and their community combine in countless ways to affect growth. Nutrition, safety, play space, adult relationships, neighborhood, and family stability affect individual development. Whether a child lives in relative poverty or riches, environmental factors interact with genes to create a single, individual person.

Gender and Race Differences

Girls and boys differ in both the rate and the pattern of growth, especially during adolescence. Ethnic variations in growth are common. African American and Asian American children seem to mature faster than do North American Caucasian children (Berk, 2009). Growth "norms" should be used with caution and with respect to ethnic differences.

Learning Styles

Children exhibit a number of different approaches to learning that must be accounted for when planning programs. Some are quiet; others move around and talk, while others seem never to listen. While on a field trip to the farm, these children demonstrate three common learning styles:

- Lorenzo watches, looks around, and visually absorbs the environment. He calls to others, "See the goat!" and "Look at that." Lorenzo is a **visual learner.**
- Olivia chatters away to her friends as they enter the barnyard. "Listen to all the noise the sheep are making." "Hear the horses?" While she enjoys listening to what others have to say, Olivia has difficulty waiting for her turn to talk. Olivia is an **auditory learner.**
- As she runs ahead of the other children, Anna calls out, "Get over here so we can touch them!" Looking up at the teacher, she begs, "Take me closer. I want to see what sheep feel like." Anna is a **tactile learner.**

Each of the children responds to the experience in a way that reflects an individual learning style. Lorenzo interprets the field trip in pictures, by drawing or painting what he saw. Olivia repeats stories from her experience over and over again as she integrates her experience at the farm. Anna plays out her farm experience by making clay animals or dancing an "animal dance." (In Chapters 4 and 10, learning styles are further discussed in terms of Gardner's Multiple Intelligences.)

In our diverse world, teachers should be sensitive to the influence of sex, race, and individual patterns of development.

The implication for teachers is that programs are planned to meet the needs and challenges of the whole group. Individual differences are incorporated into the planning. Activities are selected to allow for a variety of responses from children at different stages of development and learning styles.

Planning for Diverse Abilities

When teachers are aware of the range of developmental differences and learning styles of the children in the class, they incorporate those variations into the planning process. Figure 3-2 suggests some strategies for how to plan for these types of variations.

Collaborating with Families

Families are usually the first to notice that their child is not developing according to the norms. They may ask the child's teacher to watch for signs of hearing impairments, lack of necessary motor skills, or language imperfections. Because early diagnosis and intervention are important, teachers assess the child's overall skills. If both the family and the teachers feel there is a potential

Planning for Developmental Differences and Learning Styles

The learning environment can be arranged so that children of every skill level can work and play together when you:

- Make sure the materials and activities are in a variety of formats. Art can be expressed in paints, crayons, markers, clay, wood, and paper.
- Address the variations of development within a one-year span. A selection of books would include wordless books, easy-reader books, picture books, short story books, Braille books, and alphabet and number books.
- Plan around the known similarities within the group and allow for the needs and interests of all the children. There is great interest in the 3-year-old class for three new baby siblings. Add more dolls, carriages, beds, and doll clothes to the dramatic play area.
- Small groups may help some children with a new learning experience. In preparation for an upcoming field trip to the fire station, hold small group discussion so that each child is able to listen, ask questions, and participate in the planning. Rehearse rules for walking with a buddy, staying with the group, and expected behavior while at the fire station.
- Modify materials and activities to make them accessible to all children. Make sure that all surfaces, indoor and out, are wide enough, stable, and safe for wheelchairs. Have multiples of popular items (shovels, telephones, dolls). Use a small tray for puzzle pieces or Legos to contain the activity and define the work space.
- Every classroom can be adapted for children with special needs. Consult with each child's family to explore together ways to enhance learning.

© Cengage Learning 2014

FIGURE 3-2 An inclusive classroom provides a way for every child—regardless of ability—to experience growth and learning.

problem, further resources and services are explored through social service agencies and public health offices. The early childhood professional is not an expert in diagnosing learning exceptionalities but can be effective in helping family's secure proper referrals and treatment.

State and federal laws require that when a child from 3 to 21 years of age is identified with having a disability, an **individualized education program (IEP)** is developed by a team composed of the child's parents, a special education teacher, a regular classroom teacher, a representative of the local education agency, and other specialists. They base the IEP on the strengths of the child and present level of functioning as well the goals and concerns of the family. The team establishes long-term goals and short-term objectives to meet those goals. Special education and related services are determined as well as where and when the inclusive programs take place.

For infants and toddlers younger than 3 years of age who receive early intervention services, an **individualized family service plan (IFSP)** is put in place. A significant difference between this plan and the IEP is the focus is on the whole family, who determine the goals. Family-centered as well as child-centered services are made available to enhance family functioning.

The IEP and the IFSP are part of IDEA, the Individuals with Disabilities Education Improvement Act, which stems from the Education for All Handicapped Children Act of 1986. The Diversity Box, "The Right to Be Included," outlines the important legislation that led to the creation of these programs.

Children With Special Needs

The term special needs includes many conditions that may or may not be noticeable. To be designated as having special needs, a child's normal growth and development is: 1) delayed; 2) distorted, atypical, or abnormal; or 3) severely or negatively affected (Allen & Cowdery, 2012). This definition includes the physical, mental, emotional, and social areas of development. The terms "exceptionality" and "**disability**" are both used to define atypical development.

Two types of children come under the category of children with special needs: 1) children who have some sort of exceptionality and 2) children who are gifted. They extend the definition of "Who is the child?" and are discussed separately in this section.

There are children who have some obvious characteristics that qualify them for special-needs status:

- Five-year-old Pete, blind from birth, has been in nursery school for three years.
- Chrissy, a 4-year-old with multiple **exceptionalities**, has her daily program in a special school supplemented by attending the child care center three afternoons each week.
- Travis is a child with Down syndrome, and this is his first experience in a school not restricted to atypical children.

Other children with less apparent exceptionalities are defined as children with special needs.

In the course of normal development, any one area of a child's growth is affected by the development of the whole child, and this holds true for children who do not develop according to the norms. Any single exceptionality may lead to other multi-handicapping conditions:

- A child with a profound hearing loss is often delayed in speech production or language abilities and suffers social isolation due to the inability to hear and speak with peers.
- A child with a speech impairment or cleft palate may have the intellectual capacity to put simple puzzles together but may not yet have the language to engage verbally in songs and finger play.
- A child with **Down syndrome** may have congenital heart defects, intellectual impairments, eye abnormalities, or poor physical coordination.
- Children who have cerebral palsy, a central nervous system disorder, often have other exceptionalities, such as intellectual delays, epilepsy, and hearing, visual, and speech problems (Kiernan, et al., n.d.).

Figure 3-3 lists a number of exceptionalities, from mild to severe, that teachers of young children may encounter.

Learning Disabilities

Children with learning disabilities are found in almost every classroom; they have no discernable condition but, nevertheless, are having problems with one or more basic skills or learning disabilities that keep them from storing, processing, and producing information. These conditions may include:

- Poor memory skills; difficulty in following directions; eye–hand coordination problems; and trouble discriminating between letters, numbers, and sounds.
- Dyslexia, the most common specific learning disability, causes children to reverse letters (such as *d* and *b*) or words (such as *was* and *saw*), although many children do this who are not dyslexic.
- A strength in another area, such as math, and yet have a learning difficulty with language. Learning difficulties are usually not a singular dysfunction. Children who exhibit problems with reading and writing often have difficulties with spatial relationships and body coordination.

Observations of these behaviors can give teachers some of the first warning signs of learning disorders.

A learning disability does not mean that a child is intellectually impaired or delayed. A child with a learning disability usually has a normal or above normal IQ (Allen & Cowdery, 2012) and tends to develop normally, but the task of reading seems to highlight several areas of difficulty: problems of visual perception, inability to integrate visual and auditory information, impaired memory, problems with language, and difficulty distinguishing the separate sounds in words. This wide range of symptoms, the number of potential causes, and the varying degrees to which children exhibit the symptoms make learning exceptionalities difficult to diagnose.

Teachers of Young Children May Encounter a Variety of Disabilities

- *Speech and language:* hearing impairment, stuttering, articulation problems, cleft palate, chronic voice disorders, learning disabilities.
- *Physical-motor:* visual impairment, blindness, perceptual motor deficits, orthopedic disabilities such as cerebral palsy, spina bifida, loss of limbs, muscular dystrophy.
- *Intellectual:* cognitive delays, brain injury, brain dysfunction, dyslexia, and learning disabilities.
- *Social-emotional:* self-destructive behavior, severe withdrawal, dangerous aggression toward self and others, noncommunicativeness, moodiness, tantrums, attention-deficit/hyperactivity disorder, severe anxiety, depression, phobias, psychosis, autism.
- *Health impairments:* severe asthma, epilepsy, hemophilia, congenital heart defects, severe anemia, malnutrition, diabetes, tuberculosis, cystic fibrosis, Down's syndrome, sickle cell anemia, Tay-Sachs disease, AIDS.
- *Specific learning disabilities:* difficulties with language use and acquisition, spoken and written language affected, perceptual handicaps, brain injury, minimal brain dysfunction, dyslexia, developmental aphasia.

© Cengage Learning 2011

FIGURE 3-3 These disorders may range from mild to severe, and children exhibit a variety of abilities and needs even if they are diagnosed with the same condition. For further information concerning a specific condition, the student should consult a special education textbook.

Use caution against early diagnosis of a young child as "learning disabled" because young children differ in their individual rates of growth, and many differences and delays are within the range of normal development.

Attention-Deficit/Hyperactivity Disorder (ADHD)

Do you know a child who never sits still—one who is constantly on the move, talks excessively, and disrupts classroom activities? This behavior is typical of children with a condition known as **attention-deficit/hyperactivity disorder (ADHD)**, which, according to Berk (2009), affects up to 3 to 5 percent of all school-age children, more often boys than girls. The median age at onset of ADHD is 7 years (National Institutes of Health, 2012).

The National Resource Center on ADHD (2011) notes three subtypes of ADHD that are common today:

1. ADHD predominately inattentive type (ADHD-1)
   - Makes careless mistakes
   - Does not pay close attention to details
   - Easily distracted; hard to maintain attention
   - Does not appear to listen; seems forgetful
   - Has trouble with follow-through
   - Loses things; has difficulty with organization
   - Might avoid tasks that take prolonged intellectual effort
2. ADHD predominately hyperactive-impulsive (ADHD-HI)
   - Fidgets, squirms
   - Has trouble staying seated, runs about

- Talks excessively; difficulty with being quiet during activities
- Blurts out answers; interrupts; intrudes on others
- Has difficulty waiting to take turns
3. ADHD combined type (ADHD-C)
   - Child or adult meets criteria from both categories listed previously.

Children with ADHD can be difficult to manage both at home and in the classroom. Their constellation of behaviors may apply at some level to many children, but teachers must be cautious about labeling the normally active, somewhat disruptive child as having ADHD. The child with ADHD exhibits these behaviors in extreme, usually before age 7 (Berk, 2009).

Medication is a common treatment for children with ADHD, but because its effects are short term and its side effects can be serious, it is controversial. The most effective approach appears to be a combination of medication and individual behavior management strategies (Allen & Cowdery, 2009; Berk, 2009). There is no easy solution for dealing with children who have ADHD; further research into the cause of this disability and development of safe effective treatments are clearly needed. Figure 3-4 suggests guidance techniques that help children with ADHD.

Autism Spectrum Disorder

Autism spectrum disorder (ASD) is a neurological condition that includes autism, Asperger syndrome, and nonspecified pervasive developmental disorders (PDD). ASD is characterized by impaired language

Effective Guidance Strategies for Children with ADHD

Strategy	Example
Maintain regular and consistent routines and rules.	"Remember, Sitara, always wash your hands before eating lunch."
Have realistic expectations.	"I know it is hard for you to wait. Why don't you go over to the math lab and work until I am ready."
Make eye contact when giving directions, using clear and simple explanations.	"Look at me Toby, so I know that you are listening. Good. Now let's go over the assignment together."
Allow time for transitions by giving a plan for the next step.	"In three minutes it will be time to have small groups, so please finish your snacks."
Select jobs in which the child will be successful.	"Richy, please get enough rulers for everyone at this table."
Recognize accomplishments.	"Good job. You counted out enough for each of us."

© Cengage Learning 2014

FIGURE 3-4 These examples help children with ADHD modify their behavior.

and communication skills as well as repetitious behaviors. The symptoms are evident by age 3 and may appear as early as 18 months of age. ASD is more common in boys than girls and in siblings of a child with ASD (National Institutes of Health, 2012).

Children with ASD commonly have problems with 1) verbal and nonverbal communications, making eye contact, holding conversations, and smiling; 2) social skills, such as sharing emotion and grasping how others think and feel; and 3) repetitive routines and behaviors, repeating words and phrases over and over, and obsessively following schedules (National Institutes of Health, 2012).

Some ASD symptoms are severe and cause a child to appear very differently from other children; other children may exhibit only mild forms of ASD symptoms and not be noticeably different. Every child with ASD is different from every other child with ASD, depending on the severity of the symptoms.

There is no cure or single treatment for children with ASD. Some of the solutions that help to manage the symptoms so that children may learn are behavior management therapy (see Chapter 7), speech and language therapy, and physical and occupational therapy. There are no medications to treat ASD, but some medications can treat some of the symptoms. As noted in the Diversity Box on page 86 the law requires free public education from age 3 to 21 for children with special needs, such as ASD. A team composed of parents, teachers, caregivers, school psychologists, and other child development specialists collaborate to create an IEP best suited to each child (National Institutes of Health, 2012).

As of this writing, the American Psychiatric Association is redefining ASD. The new guidelines may eliminate some of those who are currently getting special education services. Check the National Institutes of Health at www.nichd.nih.gov/health/topics/asd.cfm for updates.

Many children with ASD attend schools with normally developing children. The following strategies are useful in guiding children with ASD:

- Use simple, direct, and short statements.
- Demonstrate actions: show the child the puzzle and where it goes in the shelf.
- Encourage social interactions with other children.
- Foster interactions with adults by encouraging the child to use simple words when he or she wants something.
- Maintain an environment with a predictable schedule and minimal distractions.
- Establish frequent communication with the family.

TeachSource Video

Watch the TeachSource Video entitled, "Programs for Children with Autism." After you study the video clip, reflect on the following questions:

1. Why do you think there is such a low child/adult ratio? In what ways was it successful? Unsuccessful?

2. Would you like to teach children with ASD? Why or why not? What would be the most challenging aspect of teaching young children with ASD?

Children Who Are Gifted and Talented

The U.S. Department of Education's time-tested definition of **gifted and talented children** is: "children and youth with outstanding talent who perform or show the potential for performing at remarkably high levels of accomplishment when compared with others of their age, experience, or environment. Outstanding talents are present in all cultural groups . . . and across all economic strata" (USDE, 1993). The National Association for Gifted Children (2011) identifies six areas of giftedness. A child may be gifted in more than one but not in all six areas:

Creative thinking: Independent and original thinker in speech and writing, creates and invents, improvises, challenged by problem solving and creative tasks, has sense of humor, and does not mind being different from the crowd.

General intellectual ability: Observant and inquisitive, hypothesizes, formulates abstractions and processes information in complex ways, excited about new ideas, learns rapidly, uses a large vocabulary, and is a self-starter.

Specific academic ability: High ability in memorization and comprehension, acquires basic skill knowledge quickly, widely read and high academic success in special interest area, pursues special interest with enthusiasm and vigor.

Leadership: Fluent and concise in self-expression, self-confident, well-liked by peers and has high expectations for self and others, assumes responsibility and is well organized, has good judgment and foresees consequences and implications of decisions.

Psychomotor: Enjoys participation in various athletic opportunities, well coordinated, good manipulative and motor skills, high energy level, exhibits precision in movement, and challenged by difficult athletic activities.

Visual/Performing Arts: Unusual ability to express self, feelings, and mood through dance, drama, and music; outstanding sense of spatial relationships; a high level of creative expression; observant; and likes to produce rather than copy.

Ford et al. (2002) have long promoted the view that the percentage of blacks and Hispanics are underrepresented in identification as gifted and that this oversight is linked to standardized tests that are often culturally and linguistically inappropriate for many students. They further note that the inclusion of the word "potential" in the definition of gifted is a critical factor that will enhance the inclusion of children who are ethnically and culturally in the minority, children with special needs, and children of poverty. It serves as a reminder that giftedness is a trait that cuts across all socioeconomic and cultural groups.

Early childhood teachers should be aware of some traits children who are gifted display so that they can recognize potentially gifted children in their care. Further, because the majority of children in the early years are too young for IQ or standardized tests, teachers are likely to have unidentified gifted children in their programs.

The Teacher's Role

The teacher's role with children who are gifted is that of providing challenge and stimulation. Children who are gifted may need scaffolding strategies to support their learning. In early elementary grades, children who are gifted may be advanced to an older group, or spend part of the day in special classes where they can interact with like-minded peers. A more common approach in early childhood has been in the area of curriculum enrichment. In this way, the child remains with age-level peers to develop social skills. Children who are gifted often feel isolated from their nongifted peers and may have social and emotional difficulties. These factors must also be considered in planning programs.

Curriculum areas are developed in more complex ways. The child who is gifted needs a learning environment that supports intellectual risk-taking, the use of logic and abstract concepts, and curiosity and enhances their specific talents. All the children in the classroom benefit from this enrichment; each responds according to his or her abilities and a rich curriculum benefits the whole class.

Families of children who are gifted need support and encouragement as well as guidance in dealing with their child's exceptionality. Together, teachers and parents can explore what best suits each individual child so that this giftedness may be nurtured and challenged at home and at school.

The Inclusive Classroom

In the past, children with special needs were integrated into classrooms only after they had met certain standards and expectations. Often they were assigned to separate special education classes. When ready, they were mainstreamed into classrooms with typically developing children. Inclusion means that a child with special needs is a full-time member of a regular classroom, a more natural environment, with children who do, as well as those who do not, have special needs.

More than a word definition is at stake, however. Inclusion is the right to belong, to have worth, and be accepted as a valuable part of society. Teachers are a key factor in the successful integration of children with exceptionalities. Their attitude is critical; they must be committed to teaching all children with equal caring and concern, regardless of their intelligence or skill levels. Some strategies to enhance inclusion in the classroom are:

- Support social encounters between children who have special needs and those who do not by encouraging them to get involved in a wide variety of activities together. Some children with special needs require assistance and modeling for successful social play and interactions.
- Build a play-based curriculum on the strengths of each child—those who have disabilities and those who do not—that include materials and activities that challenge their capabilities. Work with individual families to integrate each child's IEP into the overall plan.
- Teachers who work with children who have special needs should have specific training and guidance to ensure that each child is challenged developmentally.

Inclusion is a critical concept for all children. For typically developing children, it is an opportunity to learn to

All children, regardless of abilities, learn and grow through play.

DIVERSITY

The Right to Be Included

During the past 50 years there has been significant public recognition of and funding for education programs for persons with special needs. Previously, pubic and private attitudes were ones of shame and segregation. Past generations hid adults and children with special needs in their homes or secluded them in institutions. Keeping special populations out of sight gave way to providing separate opportunities for them. Public consciousness is now sufficient to understand that not all people with special needs are necessarily mentally impaired. The current practice of integrating children with varying exceptionalities into ongoing programs in schools—and into the mainstream of American life—is a more humane practice. Significant legislation and practices that fostered the practice of inclusion are:

1972: Head Start required that a minimum of 10 percent of its enrollment be reserved for children with disabilities and led the way toward large-scale inclusion.

1975: **Public Law 94-142**, the Education for All Handicapped Children Act—the so-called Bill of Rights for the Handicapped was passed and guarantees free public education to disabled persons from three to 21 years of age "in the least restrictive" environment. Parents of children with special needs are an integral part of the development of their child's individualized education plan (IEP) in which the strengths and needs of the family are taken into consideration.

1986: **Public Law 99-457**, the Education of the Handicapped Amendments provides funding for children who were not included in the previous law: infants, toddlers, and 3- to 5-year-olds. This law also allows for the inclusion of "developmentally delayed" youngsters and leaves local agencies the opportunity to include the "at-risk" child in that definition.

1990: Congress reauthorized Public Law 94-142 and renamed it the Individuals with Disabilities Education Act (IDEA) (Public Law 101-576). The law covered two new categories: autism and traumatic brain injury.

1990: Public Law 101-336, the Americans with Disabilities Act (ADA), makes it unlawful to discriminate against people with disabilities and requires that they have equal access to public and private services, as well as reasonable accommodations.

Each step taken during the past 50 years has given thousands of children the right to be included and promotes the dignity and worth of all individuals.

accept differences in people. For the child with special needs, typically developing children serve as age-appropriate behavior models. Some children with special needs may not have an opportunity to hear the language of their normal peer group. They may not know how to play with another child or how to communicate in socially acceptable ways. In the inclusive classroom, with sensitive and knowledgeable teachers, children with exceptionalities are helped to realize their potential as growing and learning children.

Dealing with Bias and Stereotypes

One of the most important issues for a child with special needs is to be accepted. Young children are known for their forthrightness in commenting on and asking questions about what confuses or frightens them. Children without special needs may be anxious about what another child's exceptionality may mean to them. Although this is a common reaction and age appropriate, we cannot allow an individual to be rejected on the basis of his or her abilities. Derman-Sparks and Edwards (2010) suggests the following strategies:

- The rejection must be handled immediately with support and assurance given to the child who was rejected that this type of behavior is not permitted.
  Example: "No, Rachel. You cannot tell Gina that she can't play because she is in a wheelchair. Let's look at ways you can include her in your play."
- It is important to help children recognize how they are different and how they are alike.
  Example: "Gina is very good at writing stories, just like you, Rachel. Perhaps you could write a story together."

Mitch Kezar/Stone/Getty Images

Educators must help all children develop a pride in their cultural heritage.

- Children need to have their fears about other children's abilities and exceptionalities taken seriously and to have adults understand their concerns.

   Example: "I'm glad you told me that Emma frightened you because she is blind. You don't have to be afraid that you, too, will be blind. Emily was born without sight and when you were born, you were able to see. You could use your eyes to help Emily walk to the playground."

- Questions must be answered promptly, truthfully, and simply. Use the children's own curiosity, and let the child with special needs answer questions, whenever possible.

   Example: "Yes, Emily, Janice has some questions about being blind. Would you like to tell her how you are able to read with Braille?"

All children benefit when adults are willing to confront bias and deal with children's **prejudice** and misconceptions. When we provide opportunities for children to interact with people who look and act differently than they do, we actively foster acceptance and respect for the individual. (More gender diversity issues are found in Chapter 15.)

Summary

LO 1 The concept of the whole child means that you include all developmental dimensions: the physical, cognitive, social, emotional, and linguistic areas of growth. Although they may be discussed separately, each area of growth is affected by and affects every other development area.

LO 2 Word Pictures describe the common behaviors and characteristics typical to an age group that helps teachers look at specific areas of a child's development to plan appropriate experiences for the group as well as the individual child. Changing demographics bring more culturally and linguistically diverse children into early childhood classrooms who call for culturally sensitive teaching and efforts to work with parents from a multicultural perspective.

LO 3 Children may share many typical characteristics while displaying wide individual differences. Atypical development includes a variety of exceptionalities, such as learning disabilities, dyslexia, Attention deficit/hyperactivity disorder (ADHD), autism spectrum disorder (ASD), and children who are gifted and talented. In an inclusive classroom, the environment and the curriculum are adapted to fit the needs of each student who has an exceptionality. All children require a learning environment that supports their unique needs. Federally mandated programs for children from birth through age 21 offer early intervention services for children diagnosed with a disability.

Key Terms

Word Pictures	tactile learner	individualized education program (IEP)
developmental domains	disability	individualized family service plan (IFSP)
age-level characteristics	exceptionalities	special needs
stress	Down syndrome	inclusion
biracial	attention-deficit/hyperactivity disorder (ADHD)	mainstreaming
interracial	gifted and talented children	prejudice
genes	Public Law 94-142	
visual learner	Public Law 99-457	
auditory learner		

Review Questions

1. What are some of the reasons for using the concept of the whole child in early education? How is each child unique?
2. How can Word Pictures be a valuable tool for planning programs for young children? What role does cultural considerations play when discussing developmental stages?
3. Who are the children with special needs? Why is it important for teachers to know about the variety of special needs? What are some of the difficulties that must be overcome for successful inclusion of children with special needs?
4. What do educators need to consider when teaching children who are gifted and/or talented?

Observe and Apply

1. Select two children who are approximately the same age. Using the Word Pictures, compare their physical, cognitive, language, creative, and social development. How are they alike? How are they different? What conclusions do you draw about their developmental level?
2. Observe a class of children with special needs in an inclusive classroom. What would you do to foster interactions between the children who have exceptionalities and the children who do not? What verbalizations are used about a child's exceptional condition, and do other children seem to understand how their friends are similar to them as well as different?
3. Survey a classroom for its cultural, racial, and ethnic mix. How do the classroom and the curriculum reflect the various heritages of each child? What suggestions would you make to enhance cultural sensitivity in this class? How do you think this information affects your teaching?
4. Have you ever experienced feeling "different"? In what context? How does this inform your work with children? With families?
5. What would do you if a child made racial slurs against another child in the class? How did it make you feel? What can you do to affirm the feelings of the child who was called names?

Helpful Websites

National Resource Center on AD/HD
www.help4adhd.org

National Society for the Gifted and Talented
www.nsgt.org

National Institute of Neurological Disorders and Strokes **www.ninds.nih.gov**

Individuals with Disabilities Education Act
www.idea.ed.gov

The Division of Early Childhood for Exceptional Children **www.dec-sped.org**

The ARC (formerly National Association of Retarded Citizens) **www.thearc.org**

The Center for the Study of Biracial Children **csbchome.org**

The Education Course Mate website for this text offers many helpful resources and interactive study tools. Go to CengageBrain.com to access the TeachSource Videos, flashcards, tutorial quizzes, direct links to all of the websites mentioned in the chapter, downloadable forms, and more.

References

Allen, K. E., & Cowdery, G. (2012). *The exceptional child: Inclusion in early childhood education.* Belmont, CA: Wadsworth Cengage Learning.

Berk, L. E. (2009). *Child development.* Boston: Allyn & Bacon.

Derman-Sparks, L., & Olsen Edwards, J. (2010). *Anti-bias education for young children and ourselves.* Washington, D.C.: NAEYC.

Ford, D.Y., Harris III, J. J., Tyson, C.A., & Frazier Trotman, M. (2002, revised). *Theory into practice: Providing access for culturally diverse gifted students: from deficit to dynamic thinking.* Columbus: The Ohio State University, on behalf of its College of Education (2003).

Hirsch, E. (Ed.) (1974). *The block book.* Washington, D.C.: National Association for the Education of the Young Child.

Kelly, R. Beyond just black and white. (February 2, 2009). *Newsweek,* Volume CLIII, 41.

Kiernan, S., et al. (not dated). *Mainstreaming preschoolers: Children with orthopedic handicaps.* Washington, D.C.: U.S. Department of Health, Education, and Welfare.

National Association for Gifted and Talented. (2011). Giftedness defined: What is gifted and talented? http://www.nsgt.org. Retrieved August 11, 2011.

National Institutes of Health. Autism spectrum disorders (ASDs). http://www.nichd.nih.gov/health. Retrieved January 23, 2012.

National Resource Center on ADHD. (2011). About ADHD: Statistical prevalence. http://www.help4adhd.org. Retrieved August 13, 2011.

National Scientific Council on the Developing Child (2). Video Series. *Three core concepts in early development.* http:developingchild.harvard.edu/activitiescouncil/

United States Department of Education website. The Jacob K. Javits Gifted and Talented Student Education Act of 2001, Section 5464. Retrieved July 31, 2011. www.2.ed.gov/javits/index.html

Ann Miles Gordon & Kathryn Williams Browne–Authors

4

Developmental and Learning Theories

Learning Objectives

LO1 Compare and contrast the eight major theoretical perspectives that relate to child development.

LO2 Examine central developmental topics of cultural diversity, attachment, play, gender, moral development, and brain-based research as vehicles for creating developmentally appropriate practices.

LO3 Articulate how developmental and learning theories explain children's growth and development.

naeyc Standards For Professional Development

The following NAEYC Standards for early childhood professional development are addressed in this chapter:

Standard 1 Promoting Child Development and Learning
Standard 2 Building Family and Community Relationships
Standard 5 Using Content Knowledge to Build Meaningful Curriculum
Standard 6 Becoming a Professional

naeyc Code of Ethical Conduct

These are the sections of the NAEYC Code of Ethical Conduct that apply to the topics of this chapter:

Section I. We are committeed to supporting children's development and learning.

Ideals:
I-1.1   To be familiar with the knowledge base of early childhood care and education and to stay informed through continuing education and training.
I-1.2   To base program practices upon current knowledge and research in the field of early childhood education, child development and related disciplines, as well as on particular knowledge of each child.

Introduction

While taking a routine report at an elementary school, a police officer was interrupted by a girl of about 6 years old. Looking the officer up and down, she asked, "Are you a cop?" "Yes," said the woman, and continued writing the report. "My mother said if I ever needed help I should ask the police. Is that right?" "Yes, again," replied the officer. "Well, then," she said as she extended her foot forward, "would you please tie my shoe?"

What was this child thinking? Can you see how she took in information from her mother and then applied it to her own life? How do children do that? What is the process of listening, thinking, and then doing?

While working for an organization that delivers lunches to elderly shut-ins, a mother used to take her preschool son on the afternoon rounds. He was always intrigued by the various appliances there, particularly the canes, walkers, and wheelchairs. One day, she saw him staring at a pair of false teeth soaking in a glass. He turned to her and whispered, "The tooth fairy will never believe this!"

Look how this child applied his fantasy world to what he encountered. During the years from birth to middle childhood, how do young children come to understand the world? How do they make sense of what they see, touch, and experience?

The father of 6-month-old Michiko puts one end of a toy monkey in his mouth and dangles it in front of her. Michiko gazes intently, getting still and wide-eyed, finally reaching up tentatively to touch the doll. Yet, when Keith's nanny tries the same thing with him, the 9-month-old smiles and laughs as he grabs it and tries to shove it back into her mouth.

How is it that two children can respond so differently? Is this simply a few months' age difference? Is it because of their gender or ethnic differences? Or has one child played this game before and not the other?

Major Theories

So many remarkable transformations take place in the early years. Development, the orderly set of changes in the life span, occurs as individuals move from conception to death. Those of us curious about children want to know the nature of these changes and the reasons why things happen.

A developmental theory is a "systematic statement of principles and generalizations that provides a coherent framework for understanding how and why people change as they grow older" (Berger, 2012). A learning theory attempts to explain how learning takes place. By observing children, theorists try to make sense out of what they see, looking for patterns and variations to make a kind of story that explains the reasons or causes of the details. Research allows us to look at many children or a group of children over time, even one child with intense scrutiny, to seek these explanations.

Early childhood education draws from several fields of study. Much of what we know about children today comes from child development and child psychology research that tries to answer these questions:

- How do children develop?
- What do they learn and in what order?
- What do children need to be ready to learn?
- What affects learning?
- Do all children develop in the same ways?
- What are the similarities and differences in growth and development?

To begin to answer these questions, we need some way to look for information and then choose and organize the facts so that we can understand what we see. In other words, we need a **theory**. Theories are especially useful in providing a broad and consistent view of the complexity of human development (Berger, 2012).

- Theories produce hypotheses. They allow us to make an educated guess (called a **hypothesis**) about children's behavior and development.
- Theories generate discoveries. Because these theories are based on experience, teachers can check their validity as they observe children every day.
- Theories offer practical guidance. The theories you read form the foundation of developmentally appropriate practice (DAP) that is a guide for teachers at all levels of early education.

The basic quest for sound theories about development and knowledge and for systematic statements about behavior and development has given educators much to consider in forming their own ideas about children.

Early childhood teachers should know how children develop and how they learn. Knowing how children develop is critical in making the daily decisions about curriculum, the classroom setting, and children. To be effective with children, teachers need a thoughtful philosophy and approach that is based on what we know about how children develop and what works to help them learn and understand. The teacher who is well-versed in theory has invaluable tools to work with parents, advise the family of the range of typical behavior, and talk to parents about concerns that are beyond the norms. Therefore, it is important to have a background in both developmental psychology and learning theories.

The Nature of Development

A child is a blend of many parts that interrelate in different ways and change with growth over time. Such complexity and dynamic change call for ways to organize our thinking through identifying developmental domains and posing major questions.

Developmental Domains

The study of human development requires insight and information from many disciplines because each person develops simultaneously in body, mind, and spirit; thus, we usually divide development into three domains to make it easier to study. We try to consider separately the three aspects that make up the whole of development (Figure 4-1). We can then better understand the major processes of development that parallel these developmental areas:

- Biological processes describe changes in the body.
- Cognitive processes are those changes in one's thought, intelligence, and language.
- Socio-emotional processes reflect changes in an individual's relationships with other people, emotions, and personality.

Questions about Development

Major issues are raised in the study of development. The science of development seeks to understand why and how people change or remain the same over time; as a science, it depends on theories, research methods, and critical analyses to understand the what, how, and why of development. Because of this, all kinds of children—younger and older, rich and poor, of various ethnicities, backgrounds, culture and experience—must be studied. Three major questions drive research and practice:

1. *Is children's development due more to maturation or experience?* The changes we see in children over time may be due to internal or external influences. Some theories claim children change because of innate, biologic, or genetic patterns built into the human being; others claim that they are shaped by the environment and experiences (such as parents, materials, TV, school, and so on) of life. This argument is often referred to as the **nature/nurture controversy**, also known as the problem of heredity versus environment. As you remember from Chapter 1, this issue has been discussed for centuries. On the "nature" side, Rousseau argued that the child is born with natural, or innate, goodness. Locke, however, asserted that it

© Cengage Learning 2014

FIGURE 4-1 The various domains of child growth and development are interrelated and interdependent.

was "nurture" that mattered. He contended that children entered the world with a *tabula rasa*, or clean slate, on which all experience and learning was then written. Today, most psychologists and educators agree that the patterns of development and learning are complex and not so simply explained. The eight theories discussed here focus on variations that emphasize one or the other (Figure 4-2).

2. *Is growth smooth and continuous or more stage-like?* Some theories emphasize a gradual, cumulative kind of growth, more like "from an acorn, a giant oak will grow." The seedling becomes more oak-like gradually over time. This continuity of development is usually the viewpoint of theories that emphasize experience (nurture). Other theories depict children's growth as a sequence of stages that are clearly marked by distinct changes, more like "caterpillar into butterfly." In the cocoon, the chrysalis does not become more caterpillar-like, but, instead, becomes

a different kind of organism. This viewpoint emphasizes the innate conditions of development (nature).

3. *What can theory and research do for early childhood educators?* Science has opened our eyes to the amazing complexity of the mind and the wondrous path of growth in the body. This was not always so.

- In previous generations, little scientific information was available by which parents (and teachers) could assess the validity of theories. Many beliefs were espoused by adults about children, such as "You'll spoil the baby if you respond to his demands too quickly," or "Children who suffer early neglect and deprivation will not realize their normal potential." These statements can be powerful, particularly as they are passed on to you by your family and culture. However, some ideas are rooted in myth rather than reality.

- The study of child development was mostly confined to the study of trends and descriptions of age

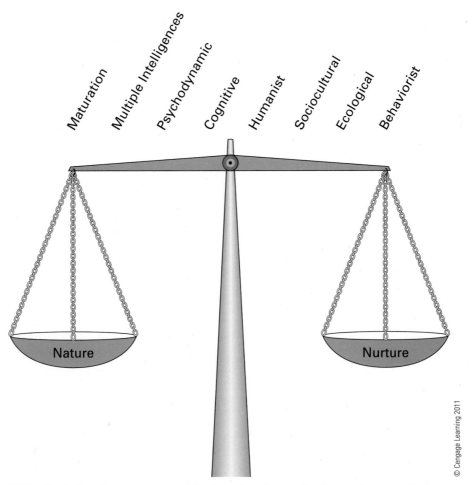

© Cengage Learning 2011

FIGURE 4-2 Development is a combination of the forces of nature and nurture. Each theory offers its own emphasis on heredity/prenatal conditions and environmental/life experiences.

changes. As the 20th century progressed, the scope and definition of child development changed radically. Developmental psychologists studied how psychological processes begin, change, and develop. Child development focused on language acquisition, various early effects on later intellectual development, and the process of attachment to others. Now, developmentalists are taking a life-span approach to development, taking into considerations the many directions and contexts of development, understanding the power of culture and the resilience and plasticity of individual growth, and using new tools of technology to unlock the secrets of the brain.

Child development researchers and theorists have accumulated a rich store of knowledge, based on scientific hypothesis that is then tested with evidence. They can help sort fact from fiction.

The Most Excellent Eight

No one set of principles encompasses all developmental and learning theories. We have chosen eight theories. Some are grand theories that describe either universal processes or the entire span of development (psychodynamic, behaviorist, cognitive). Others are mini-theories that explain just a part of development (multiple intelligences, maturation, humanistic). A few are emergent theories (sociocultural, ecological) that are relatively new. They are commonly known as 1) psychodynamic theory, 2) behaviorist theory, 3) cognitive theory, 4) sociocultural theory, 5) ecological theory, 6) multiple intelligences theory, 7) maturation theory, and 8) humanistic theory.

While writing this chapter, we were reminded of this children's incident:

> While playing "school" in the dramatic play area, Noemi insisted on wearing pretend glasses, as her favorite teacher did. "No!" cried Venecia. "They will make you mad and crabby!" (In fact, her teacher only wore the glasses when she was too tired to wear contact lenses.) "Yes, I will," replied Noemi. "She wears them cuz they makes her smarty-pants." (This is another viewpoint and a kind of myth about intelligence and eyewear.) "You're both wrong," called out Charly. "Everybody knows you have to wear glasses and hoop earrings to be a teacher." (As a matter of fact, the teacher did look like this.) Everyone looked puzzled, and then the play resumed.

Just like these children, not all the experts agree or even think alike. Because the field of child development is broad, encompassing a wide variety of opinion and fact, there is no one theory that describes everything.

Moreover, these theories arose at different time periods, in various countries. Each theory describes children and their processes in different ways. It is up to you, the educator, to decide which ones best describe children and their growth. Read carefully, and then compare your experiences with the theories and concepts you read here. As a teacher, you have a diversity of theories from which to establish a professional philosophy.

Psychodynamic Theory

Psychodynamic theory is about personality development and emotional problems. **Psychodynamic** theories look at development in terms of internal drives that are often **unconscious**, or hidden from our awareness. These motives are the underlying forces that influence human thinking and behavior and provide the foundation for universal stages of development. In psychoanalytic terms, children's behavior can be interpreted by knowing the various stages and tasks within those stages.

Sigmund Freud

Sigmund Freud began his career as a medical doctor and became interested in the irrational side of human behavior as he treated "hysterics." His technique, asking people to recline on a couch and talk about everything, was ridiculed by the medical establishment as the "talking cure." Then, as patients revealed their thoughts, fantasies, and problems, he began to see patterns.

Psychoanalytic Theory

According to Freud, people possess three basic drives: the sexual drive, survival instincts, and a drive for destructiveness. Of the first, childhood sexuality, Freud outlined development in terms of psychosexual stages, each characterized by a particular part of the body (Figure 4-3). In each stage, the sensual satisfaction associated with each body part is linked to major challenges of that age. For instance, the toddler issues of biting and thumb sucking, the preschool interest in "doctor play," and the school-age focus on gender identification can be seen in a psychosexual context. Each stage also has its own conflicts between child and parent, and how the child experiences those conflicts determines basic personality and behavior patterns.

Freud (1920) put forth this theory, and his ideas were expanded on by Anna Freud (his daughter), Carl Jung, Karen Horney, and others. Although Freud's interest was abnormal adult behavior and its causes, his conclusions have had a major effect on our conception of childhood and its place in the life span.

Freudian Stages of Childhood Psychosexual Development

Stage	Age	Description/Major Area
Oral	Birth to 2	Mouth (sucking, biting) source of pleasure
		Eating and teething
Anal	2–3	Bowel movements source of pleasure
		Toilet learning
Phallic	3–6	Genitals source of pleasure
		Sex role identification and conscience development
Latency	6–12	Sexual forces dormant
		Energy put into schoolwork and sports
Genital	12–18	Genitals source of pleasure

© Cengage Learning 2011

FIGURE 4-3 Freud's psychoanalytic theory of childhood development. Psychoanalytic theory contends that each stage has its own area of pleasure and crisis between the child and parent of society.

To Freud, the personality was the most important aspect of development, more central to human growth than language, perception, or cognition. Personality was defined by three structures:

1. Id—the instinctive part that drives a person to seek satisfaction
2. Ego—the rational structure that forms a person's sense of self
3. Superego—the moral side that informs the person of right and wrong

He thought that the personality developed in a fixed pattern of stages that emerged as the body matured naturally. How children were treated while going through those stages determined whether they developed healthy or abnormal personalities. In particular, the mother–child relationship was important in each stage. Thus, the interaction between the child's wishes and needs and how these were treated (by the mother or other adults) was a focal point for proper development.

All psychoanalytic explanations of human development emphasize the critical importance of relationships with people and the sequence, or stages, of personality development. The psychoanalyst Erik Erikson expanded and refined Freud's theory of development. It is Erikson whose ideas have most affected early childhood education.

Erik Erikson

Erik Homberg Erikson is perhaps the most influential psychoanalyst of the modern era and certainly a key figure in the study of children and development. His interests in children and education included a teaching background in progressive and Montessori schools in Europe.

After clinical training in psychoanalysis, he remained interested in the connections between psychotherapy and education. His books, *Childhood and Society* (1950) about his version of Freud's theory, and Pulitzer Prize–winning *Gandhi's Truth* (1969), helped him become well known in the United States. Erikson became the first child analyst in the Boston area and worked for both University of California at Berkeley and Stanford University.

Psychosocial Theory

Erikson's theory of human development, like those of Freud and Piaget, states that life is a series of stages through which each person passes, with each stage growing from the previous ones. He proposes eight stages of **psychosocial** development, each representing a critical period for the development of an important strength. Positive growth allows the individual to integrate his or her physical and biologic development with the challenges that the social institutions and culture present. Each stage is characterized by an emotional challenge.

A key point of Erikson's theory is how the stages build from previous experience. A stage is a period during which certain changes occur. What one achieves in each stage is based on the developments of the previous stages, and each stage presents the child with certain kinds of problems to be solved. When children succeed, they go on to attack new problems and grow through solving them. Erikson gave us the term **identity crisis** to describe how people struggle with a pair of competing urges at each stage as they try to answer, "Who am I?" (Figure 4-4).

A second key point of Erikson's theory is balance. In Erikson's framework, balancing a child's wishes and the demands of the environment with a mentally healthy dose of each emotion is essential for personality strength. Everyone

© Cengage Learning 2011

FIGURE 4-4 Eriksonian crisis in a young child's life. Psychosocial theory claims that conflicts are opportunities to balance competing urges. The child who takes initiative (grabbing a toy) can also feel guilt (returning it).

has certain biologic, social, and psychological needs that must be satisfied to grow in a healthy manner. Medicine and neuroscience have learned much about physical needs—diet, rest, and exercise. Basic intellectual, social, and emotional needs also must be met for an organism to be healthy. Eriksonian theory speaks to these needs. Whether these needs are met or left unfulfilled affects development.

Erikson differed from Freud in some fundamental ways. First, he emphasized the drive for identity and meaning in a social context rather than the Freudian notion of sexual and aggressive drives. Second, development occurs throughout the life span, in contrast with the notion that personality is shaped only in childhood. Finally, the developmental struggles that occur during one's life can be overcome later. You can go back; while it is true that the first four stages play a key role in developing ego identity, problems of childhood can be dealt with in later stages so that the adult can achieve vitality.

The following text elaborates on the first four stages in the early childhood period because of their importance to the field of early childhood education. (See Figure 4-5 for all eight stages.)

Stage 1: Trust versus Mistrust (Birth to 1 Year)

Erikson's first stage is roughly the first year of life and parallels Freud's oral-sensory stage. Attitudes important to development are the capacity to trust—or mistrust—inner and outer experiences. By providing consistent care, parents help an infant develop a basic sense of trust in self and an ability to trust other people. They give affection and emotional security as well as provide for physical needs. Inconsistent or inadequate care creates mistrust. In extreme cases, as shown by Spitz's classic studies on infant deprivation, lack of care actually led to infant death (Spitz & Wolf, 1946). A less extreme case might form isolation or distrust of others. Given a solid base in early trust, though, the typical infant develops the virtue, or strength, of hope.

Babies must learn trust at two levels: first, a belief that significant adults will be present to meet their needs, and, second, a belief in their own power to make changes and cope. As adults engage with infants, they encourage attachment by holding babies close when feeding them and responding right away to their distress when they cry. When working with infants and toddlers, teachers must take special care to provide a predictable environment and consistent caregiving. Babies are totally dependent on adults to meet their needs; they are particularly vulnerable to difficulties because they have few skills for coping with discomfort and stress. Therefore, it is critical that they be cared for by warm, positive adults who are sensitive and respond affectionately to an infant's needs as soon as they arise. The topic of attachment discussed in this chapter and Chapter 8 reinforces the critical role of collaboration

Psychosocial Stages of Erikson's Theory

Stage	Description	Challenge	Strength
Stage One	Newborns	Trust vs. Mistrust	Hope
Stage Two	Toddlers	Autonomy vs. Shame and Doubt	Willpower
Stage Three	Childhood	Initiative vs. Guilt	Purpose
Stage Four	School	Competence (or industry) vs. Inferiority	Competence
Stage Five	Adolescence	Search for identity vs. Role confusion	Fidelity
Stage Six	Young adulthood	Intimacy (love and friendship) vs. Isolation (loneliness)	Love
Stage Seven	Grown-ups	Generativity (caring for the next generation) vs. Stagnation	Care
Stage Eight	Old age	Integrity vs. Despair	Wisdom

© Cengage Learning 2011

FIGURE 4-5 Erikson's theory of psychosocial development. Centering on basic crises at each stage of development, the theory proposes that these conflicts are part of the life process and that successful handling of these issues can give a person the "ego strength" to face life positively.

with families and teachers. In this way, the very young develop the key strength of trust.

Stage 2: Autonomy versus Doubt (2 to 3 Years)

The second stage, corresponding to the second and third years of life, parallels the muscular-anal period in Freudian theory. The child learns to manage and control impulses and to use both motor and mental skills. To help a child develop a healthy balance between **autonomy** and doubt, parents should consider how to handle their toddlers' toilet learning and growing curiosity to explore. Restrictive or compulsive parents may give the child a feeling of shame and doubt, causing a sense of insecurity. Successful growth in this stage gives children strength of will. "This stage, therefore, becomes decisive for the ratio of love and hate, cooperation and willfulness, freedom of self-expression and its suppression. From a sense of self-control without loss of self-esteem comes a lasting sense of good will and pride; from a sense of loss of self-control and of foreign over-control comes a lasting propensity for doubt and shame" (Erikson, 1963).

Encouraging a sense of autonomy while teaching limits without shaming is a delicate balance. Budding curiosity means high energy, so the daily schedule should include plenty of time for active movement and flexibility to deal with fluctuating energy and mood. Toileting is a learned behavior just as dressing, painting, and singing are; a relaxed attitude about this area helps the child gain mastery without shame. The key strength of positive identity can be developed. Chapter 7 elaborates on how to help guide children using positive discipline.

Stage 3: Initiative versus Guilt (3 to 5 or 6 Years)

The third stage of Eriksonian theory corresponds to the preschool and kindergarten years and parallels Freud's phallic stage of development. The developmental task is to develop a sense of purpose. Out of autonomy comes initiative, and from healthy doubt can come a conscience. For example, a preschooler grabs another's toy; he may run and hide when the crying begins. The teacher gently leads the child to give it back and allows the regret to be expressed through making amends. A group of kindergarten girls have a great idea to put on a play but are disorganized about planning, so the teacher guides them to choose a title, name the various roles, and make a "to do" list so that they can execute in constructive and cooperative ways. Adult interaction matters: An overly restrictive adult may end up with a child who is easily discouraged and inhibited. On the other hand, parents or teachers signaling no restraints give the child no clear idea of what is socially acceptable and what is not.

Teaching children of this age is both exhilarating and exasperating. Many find this stage easier physically than the previous two but more challenging socially. It is a time when children move in two opposing directions: accomplishment or destruction. To support children's development of initiative with reasonable expectations, teachers can:

- Encourage children to be as independent as possible.
- Focus on gains and attempts rather than on mistakes.
- Set expectations aligned with a child's individual abilities.
- Focus curriculum on real things and on doing instead of simply listening.

The key strength that grows out of this stage is purpose. Chapters 9 and 10 concentrate on environmental and curricular issues.

Stage 4: Industry versus Inferiority (6 to 12 Years)

Erikson's fourth stage, beginning with the primary school years and ending with puberty, parallels Freud's latency period. The major theme in this stage is mastery of life, primarily by adapting to laws of society (people, laws and rules, relationships) and objects (tools, machines, the physical world). This is the child's most enthusiastic time for learning. The stage is "the end of early childhood's period of expansive imagination. The danger in the elementary school years is the development of a sense of inferiority—of feeling incompetent and unproductive" (Santrock, 2009). It is also a time of great adventure. Children begin to think of being big and to identify with people whose work or whose personality they can understand and admire.

- *Find a place in my own school*: Be the line leader on the way to the cafeteria, the goalie on the soccer field, scribe at a scout meeting.
- *Applying myself to something new*: Try organizing and serving snacks at the after-school center.
- *Handling the "tools of the tribe"*: Learn to use colored pencils, to read aloud, to fill out forms, to check out balls and bats.

Problems arise if the child feels inadequate and inferior to such tasks. A parent or teacher who overemphasizes children's mistakes could make them despair of ever learning, for instance, the multiplication tables or cursive handwriting. This is particularly sensitive for the child with special needs and for those who are learning a second language. Adults should "mildly but firmly coerce children into the adventure of finding out that one can learn to accomplish things which one would never have thought possible by oneself" (Erikson, 1963). Parents must not let their children restrict their own horizons by doing only what they already know. Particularly in social situations, it is essential for children to learn to do things with others, as difficult and unfair as this may sometimes be. The key strength that can develop is mastery. Chapters 11 to 14 address curriculum for all domains.

Applying Psychosocial Theory to Work with Children

First, Erikson has a clear message about the importance of play. Second, the theory offers guidelines for the role of adults in children's lives.

Play is a critical part of children's total development. Most schools for children younger than age 6 have periods of time allotted for play called "choice time" or "free play." Erikson supports these ideas explicitly by stating that the senses of autonomy and of initiative are developed mainly through social and fantasy play. He suggests that child's play is "the infantile form of the human ability to deal with experiences by creating model situations and to master reality by experiment and planning. . . . To 'play it out' in play is the most natural self-healing measure childhood affords" (Erikson, 1964). (See the Developmental Topic on "Play" later in this chapter.)

The adult is primarily an emotional base and a social mediator for the child. Teachers become interpreters of feelings, actions, reasons, and solutions. We help children understand situations and motives so that they can solve their own problems. Look at each child's emotional makeup and monitor his or her progress through developmental crises; each crisis is a turning point of increased vulnerability and also enhanced potential. Allow the child, in Erikson's words:

> . . . to experience over and over again that he is a person who is permitted to make choices. He has to have the right to choose, for example, whether to sit or whether to stand, whether to approach a visitor or to lean against his mother's knee . . . whether to use the toilet or to wet his pants. At the same time he must learn some of the boundaries of self-determination. He inevitably finds that there are some walls he cannot climb, that there are objects out of reach, that above all, there are innumerable commands enforced by powerful adults (1969).

In infant/toddler programs, adults foster independence in toddlers by giving children simple choices ("Juice or milk?") and not false ones ("Do you want your diaper changed?"). In preschool and kindergarten, a teacher allows

In Erikson's theory, the adult serves as a social mediator for the child.

children to take initiative and does not interfere with the results of those actions. Still, adults help children learn reasonable limits and results. The third-graders at a birthday party are laughing and shouting in the bedroom, when suddenly the birthday girl emerges in tears with several others in tow trying to tell what happened. The adult who helps them lets them take turns in the telling and declares how scary it was when someone fell off the bouncing bed and bumped her head helps the children acknowledge real feelings and learn to interact around social challenges.

The issues of early childhood, from Erikson's theory, are really human issues. The remnants of these stages stay with us all our lives, and teachers who are aware of their own processes can fully appreciate the struggles of children.

Behaviorist Theory

Behaviorism is the most pragmatic and functional of the modern psychological ideologies. Behaviorist theories describe both development and learning. Initiated during the 1920s and continually modified today, behaviorism is considered the most distinctly American theory because 20th century psychology in the United States expanded its concepts in research and application so widely. To summarize the **behaviorist theory**, we have chosen five theorists: Ivan Pavlov, John Watson, Edward Thorndike, B.F. Skinner, and Albert Bandura.

The Behaviorists

What is known today as "behaviorism" begins with the notion that a child is born with a "clean slate," a *tabula rasa* in Locke's words, on which events are written throughout life. The conditions of those events cause all important human behavior. Behaviorists often insist that only what can actually be observed is accepted as fact. Only behavior can be treated, they say, not feelings or internal states. This contrasts to the psychodynamic approach, which insists that behavior is just an indirect clue to the "real" self, that of inner feelings and thoughts.

Ivan Pavlov, a Russian physiologist, was working in a laboratory, studying how animals digest food. He noticed that the dogs in his laboratory would anticipate their meals when they heard or saw their attendants making preparations. Instead of starting to salivate just when food was set in front of them, the dogs would salivate to a number of stimuli associated with food. He identified this simple form of learning as respondent conditioning. The association of involuntary reflexes with other environmental conditions became known as classical conditioning, a cornerstone of behaviorist theory.

John B. Watson was an American theorist who studied Pavlov's experiments, then translated those ideas of conditioning into human terms. In the first quarter of the 20th century, Watson made sweeping claims about the powers of this classical conditioning. He declared that he could shape a person's entire life by controlling exactly the events of an infant's first year. One of his ideas was to discourage emotional ties between parents and children because they interfered with the child's direct learning from the environment (though he later modified this). Nonetheless, he gave scientific validity to the idea that teachers should set conditions for learning and reward proper responses.

Edward L. Thorndike also studied the conditions of learning. Known as the "godfather of standardized testing," Thorndike helped develop scales to measure student achievement and usher in the era of standardized educational testing (see Chapter 6). He set forth the famous **stimulus–response** technique. A stimulus recalls a response in a person; this forms learned habits. Therefore, it is wise to pay close attention to the consequences of behavior and to the various kinds of **reinforcement**.

B.F. Skinner took the idea of *tabula rasa* one step further to create the doctrine of the "empty organism." That is, a person is like a vessel to be filled by carefully designed experiences. All behavior is under the control of one or more aspects of the environment. Furthermore,

Skinner maintained that there is no behavior that cannot be modified. Some people argue that Skinnerian concepts tend to depersonalize the learning process and treat people as puppets. Others say that behaviorist psychology has made us develop new ways to help people learn and cope effectively with the world.

Albert Bandura refined behaviorism beyond conditioning into a social learning theory. **Socialization** is the process of learning to conform to social rules. Social learning theorists watch how children learn these rules and use them in groups. They study the patterns of reinforcement and reward in socially appropriate and unacceptable behavior and how children learn. Children acquire most of their social concepts—the rules by which they live—from models. They observe parents, teachers, and peers in the course of daily life. **Social learning theory** implies that the models children are most likely to imitate are those who are warm, rewarding, and affectionate. Attachment is also part of the process. The most significant models are people to whom the child is emotionally tied.

From this arose a new concept known as **modeling**. This is what used to be known as learning and teaching by example. For instance, children who see their parents smoking will likely smoke themselves, and those who witness kindness to others are likely to imitate it. In fact, Bandura's studies provided "strong evidence that exposure to filmed aggression heightens aggressive reactions in children. Subjects who viewed the aggressive human and cartoon models on film exhibited nearly twice as much aggression than did subjects in the control group who were not exposed to the aggressive film content" (Bandura, 1963). This work suggests that pictorial mass media—television, video games, and computer activities—serve as important sources of social behavior. Any behavior can be learned by watching it, from language (listening to others talk) to fighting (watching violence on television).

Bandura's theory (2001) has expanded into a cognitive model of **self-efficacy**, theorizing that children think hard about what they see and feel. Children learn from observing and modeling others, but also from understanding and acting on their own behavior. This leads to self-regulated learning. As early as the preschool years, children are developing internal standards and reflective thinking that influences a child's behavior "from the inside out." Thus, personal and cognitive factors influence behavior, as does the environment, and, in turn, children's behavior can affect the environment around them. Adding the factors of modeling and reflective thinking to behaviorist theory links it to Erikson's psychosocial theory and to Piaget's cognitive theory (discussed next in this chapter).

Theory of Behaviorism and Social Learning

What is behavior, or learning, theory all about? Learning occurs when an organism interacts with the environment. Through experience, behavior is modified or changed. In the behaviorist's eyes, three types of learning occur: 1) classical conditioning; 2) operant conditioning; and 3) **observational learning** or modeling. The first two are based on the idea that learning is mostly the development of habit. What people learn is a series of associations, forming a connection between a stimulus and response that did not exist before. The third is based on a social approach. Figure 4-6 summarizes these three types of behaviorist learning processes.

Classical Conditioning

Classical conditioning can be explained by reviewing Pavlov's original experiments. A dog normally salivates at the sight of food but not when he hears a bell. When the sound of a bell is paired with the sight of food, the dog "learns" to salivate when he hears the bell, whether or not food is nearby. Thus, the dog has been conditioned to salivate (give the response) for both the food (unconditioned stimulus) and the bell (conditioned stimulus). Similarly, when the school bell rings in the afternoon, children begin to gather their papers into backpacks to go home. They have been conditioned to the sound of the bell; ask any teacher who has had to deal with a broken bell system how strong this conditioning is. Classical conditioning can also account for the development of **phobias**. Watson used a young boy in a laboratory to test this theory. He showed the boy a white rat, then sounded a loud noise. After only seven pairings, the boy would cringe at the sight of the rat without the bell sounding at all. Only a few painful visits to a childhood dentist can teach a lifetime fear of dental health professionals.

Operant Conditioning

Operant conditioning is slightly different from classical conditioning in that it focuses on the response rather than the stimulus. In operant conditioning, the process that makes it more likely that a behavior recurs is called reinforcement. A stimulus that increases the likelihood of repeated behavior is called a **reinforcer**. Most people are likely to increase what gives them pleasure (be it food or attention) and decrease what gives them displeasure (such as punishment, pain, or the withdrawal of food or attention). The behaviorist tries to influence the organism by controlling these kinds of reinforcement.

A positive reinforcer is something that the learner views as desirable:

"social reinforcers"	attention, praise, smiles, or hugs
"nonsocial reinforcers"	tokens, toys, food, stickers

For example, you would like Claire to begin to use a spoon instead of her hands to eat. Before conditioning, you talk to her whenever she eats. During the conditioning period, you can give attention each time she picks up a spoon during feeding times and ignore her when she uses her hands. Afterward, she is more likely to use a spoon and less often her hands. This is an example of a positive reinforcer, something that increases the likelihood of the desired response.

The reinforcers can be negative as well. A negative reinforcer is removal of an unpleasant stimulus as a result of some particular behavior. Circle time is Jimmy's favorite activity at school. Yet he has difficulty controlling his behavior and consistently disrupts the group. Before conditioning, he is told that if he talks to his neighbors and shouts responses at the teacher, he will be asked to leave the circle. During the conditioning period, Jimmy is praised whenever he pays attention, sings songs, and does not bother those around him (**positive reinforcement**). When he begins to shout, he is told to leave and return when he can sing without shouting (**negative reinforcement**). A negative reinforcer is used to stop children from behaving in a particular way by arranging for them to end a mildly aversive situation

Behaviorist Learning Processes

	Classical Conditioning	Operant Conditioning	Modeling
Kind of behavior	Reflexive	Voluntary	Voluntary
Type of learning	Learning through association	Learning through reinforcement	Learning through observation and intimation
Role of learner	Passive	Active or passive	Active

© Cengage Learning 2011

FIGURE 4-6 Behaviorist learning processes. Classical conditioning, operant conditioning, and modeling are three ways of learning, describing how behavior is learned and the role of the learner in each process.

immediately (in this case, the boy has to leave the group) by improving their behavior. Jimmy, by controlling his own behavior, could end his isolation from the group.

Punishment is different from negative reinforcement. Punishment is an unpleasant event that makes the behavior less likely to be repeated; that is, if Jimmy were spanked every time he shouted, then his shouting would be the punished behavior, and it is likely he would begin to shout less. However, when leaving the group is the reinforcer for shouting, he tries to stop shouting to increase the likelihood of being able to stay and not be taken away from the group. Negative reinforcement thus increases the likelihood that the desired behavior is repeated (staying in the group) and removes attention from the less desirable behavior (the shouting). The "time-out" chair, for instance, could be viewed as either a punishment or a negative reinforcer. If used as exclusion from the group or a withdrawal of playing privileges, a child would find the time out as a punishment. On the other hand, if a child could leave the time out more quickly by exhibiting certain behaviors (instead of the "bad" behavior), it might be seen as a negative reinforcer.

Reinforcement, both positive and negative, is a powerful tool. It is important for adults to realize that it can be misused. It is wise to be careful, particularly in the case of negative reinforcement. An adult may not be gentle with a negative reinforcer when angry with a child's inappropriate behavior. Educators and parents should be aware of the possibilities and check their own responses.

Modeling

Modeling is the third kind of conditioning and is also known as observational learning. Social behavior is particularly noteworthy to early childhood professionals, as most work with children in groups and thus witness social behavior constantly. Any behavior that involves more than one person can be considered social. One of the most negative social behaviors is aggression. It is this type that Albert Bandura researched, finding that much of it is learned by watching others.

Aggression is a complex issue, involving various definitions and behaviors. To illustrate social learning theory, Bandura defines aggression as behavior intended to inflict harm or discomfort to another person or object. Bandura showed a short film of aggressive behavior to young children. The original mid-1960s studies are summarized next.

Each child in Bandura's experiment viewed one of three films. In all three films, an adult hit, kicked, and verbally abused an inflated Bobo doll in ways that young children are unlikely to do spontaneously. The films differed in what happened to the model after the aggressive sequence. In one film, the model was lavishly rewarded with praise and foods that appealed to preschoolers, such as candy and caramel popcorn. In another film, the model

© Cengage Learning

Social reinforcers include attention and smiles as well as praise.

was punished in a dramatic way, including severe scolding and a spanking. The third film simply ended after the model's aggressive behavior, with no consequences following the aggression. After viewing one film, each child in the experiment was allowed to play in a room with a Bobo doll, all the toys used in the aggression film, and a variety of other toys.

The results are most impressive, especially to those working with young children. The level of aggression expressed by each child was directly related to what the children saw as the consequences in the film. When offered prizes, they imitated almost exactly what their model had done. Also, children appeared more likely to attack one another after viewing the attacks on the Bobo doll in film. Further studies have shown that children's levels of aggression are higher right after viewing the film but less so when shown it again six months later (Berger, 2011). Regardless of the controversy that may surround any study of children's aggression or the effects of watching filmed violence on youngsters, the social learning theory deserves serious consideration. The effect of television and media viewing on children is discussed in Chapter 15.

Can Rewards Actually Punish?

Alfie Kohn, a nationally known educator and author, is a strong critic of behaviorism. He cites research showing that rewards decrease motivation; in fact, the more rewards are used, the more they seem to be needed. Furthermore, punishment and negative reinforcement produce short-term compliance only and often disregard feelings, needs, and intentions. "Skinnerian thinking—caring only about behaviors— has narrowed our understanding of children and warped the way we deal with them.... In a nutshell, it's the child who engages in the behavior, not the behavior itself, who matters" (Kohn, 2006).

Teachers intentionally shape children's behavior, deliberately reinforcing what the want children to do, and attempting through behavior modification techniques to get children to move away and stop behavior that adults find unacceptable. These intentions must be implemented carefully, however, or unintended consequences may occur.

Think About This
1. Do you think children end up being "punished by rewards"?
2. How do you shape children's behavior?
3. How much of what we do with children can be explained by behaviorism?

Applying Behaviorist Theory to Work with Children

Behaviorist theories make a strong case for how the environment influences our behavior:

- *Physical environment:* A teacher arranges the room so that positive learning is enhanced.
- *Daily schedule:* Routines and sequence of events are planned to encourage habits.
- *Teacher/child interaction:* Teachers respond carefully to children to shape their behavior.

Adults are powerful reinforcers and models for children. A learning situation comprises many cues; it is up to adults to know what those cues are and how to control them. Teachers who use behavior modification techniques know both what children are to do and how they are reinforced for their behavior.

Each teacher and program must consider the impact of this theory and how to apply it to classroom and client.

What children learn is shaped by the circumstances surrounding the learning. Experiences that are enjoyable are reinforcing. From the peek-a-boo game with an infant to a 7-year-old's first ride on a skateboard, an experience is more likely to be repeated and learned if it is pleasant. Social learning is particularly powerful in the lives of young children. Adults must be mindful of their own behavior; watching children as young as 2 years old play "family" or "school" convinces the most skeptical critic that any behavior is learnable and can become part of children's behavioral repertoire.

Cognitive Theory

Adult: What does it mean to be alive?
Child: It means you can move about, play—that you can do all kinds of things.
Adult: Is a mountain alive?
Child: Yes, because it has grown by itself.
Adult: Is a cloud alive?
Child: Yes, because it sends water.
Adult: Is wind alive?
Child: Yes, because it pushes things.

How do children learn to think, and what do they think about? **Cognitive theory** describes the structure and development of human thought processes and how those processes affect the way a person understands and perceives the world. Piaget's theory of cognition forms a cornerstone of early childhood educational concepts about children; others have developed this theory further into a constructivist theory of learning.

Jean Piaget

Jean Piaget was one of the most exciting research theorists in child development. A major force in child psychology, he studied both thought processes and how they change with age. Piaget's ideas serve as our guide to cognitive theory because of the thoroughness of his work. He had great influence on child psychology, theories of learning, intellectual development, and even philosophy. He became the foremost expert on the development of knowledge from birth to adulthood.

How did Piaget find out about such matters? A short review of his life and ideas reveals a staggering volume of work and a wide scope of interests. Born at the turn of the century, Piaget built on his childhood curiosity in science and philosophy by working with Dr. Simon at the Binet Laboratory (Simon and Binet devised the first intelligence test). While recording children's abilities to answer questions correctly, he became fascinated with children's incorrect responses. He noticed that children tended to give similar kinds of wrong answers at certain ages.

Thus, Piaget launched into a lifelong study of intelligence. He believed that children think in fundamentally different ways from adults. He also developed a new method for studying thought processes. Rather than using a standardized test, he adapted the psychiatric method of question and response. Called the *methode clinique*, it is a technique in which adults ask questions and then adapt their teaching and further inquiries based on children's answers (see Chapter 6).

Piaget then began studying children's thought processes. With his wife, one of his former students, he observed his own children. He also began to look closely at how actively children engage in their development. Prolific his entire life, Piaget gave us a complex theory of intelligence and child development. He recorded, in a systematic way, how children learn, when they learn, and what they learn.

Theory of Cognitive Development

While others thought that the development of thinking was either intrinsic (nature) or extrinsic (nurture), Piaget thought that neither position offered a full explanation for a child's amazing and complex behaviors.

His theory relies on both maturational and environmental factors. It is called maturational because it sets out a sequence of cognitive (thinking) stages that is governed by heredity—how the body is structured biologically, with automatic (instinctive) behaviors such as an infant sucking at birth. It is called an environmental theory because the experiences children have directly influence how they develop and build their own knowledge rather than simply absorbing instruction (Piaget & Inhelder, 1972).

Theory Basics

The basic premise of cognitive theory is that thinking and learning are processes of interaction between a person and the environment. Piaget also believed that all species inherit a basic tendency to organize their lives and adapt to the world around them. This is known as a constructivist theory (see next section); that is, children actively construct knowledge on an ongoing basis. They are developing and constantly revising their own knowledge. All people use three basic processes to think: the adaptive processes of assimilation and accommodation and the balancing process of equilibration (see Figure 4-7).

As they experience the world, they take in new information and either absorb it into what they already know **assimilation** or create a new place for it **accommodation**, thus returning to a sense of balance **equilibration**. In doing so, children figure out what the world is all about and then work toward surviving in that world. Piaget believed children learn best when they are actually doing the work (or play) themselves, rather than being told, shown, or explained to, which were the dominant teaching methods of the day. Having studied Montessori methods, Piaget concluded that teachers could prepare a stimulating environment and also interact with the children to enhance their thinking.

Regardless of their age, all people develop **schemas**, or mental concepts, as a general way of thinking about, or interacting with, ideas and objects in the environment. Very young children learn perceptual schemas as they taste and feel; preschool children use language and pretend play to create their understanding; school-age children develop more abstract ideas, such as morality schemas, which help them determine how to act.

Piaget theorized that thinking develops in a certain general pattern in all human beings. These stages of thinking are the psychological structures that go along with adapting to the environment. Piaget identified four major stages of cognitive development:

Sensorimotor stage	0 to 2 years
Preoperational stage	2 to 6 or 7 years
Concrete operational stage	6 to 12 years
Formal operational stage	12 years to adulthood

TeachSource Video

Watch the three TeachSource Videos on "Piaget's Sensorimotor, Preoperational, and Concrete Operational Stages." After you study the video clips, reflect on the following questions:

1. How does children's thinking change over the early years, and how does this affect what is planned in early childhood education classrooms for the three age groups?

2. Why should teachers know developmental or learning theories before they create programs for young children?

Piaget's Three Processes of Cognitive Adaptation

Assimilation:

Taking new information and organizing it in such a way that it fits with what the person already knows.

Example: Juanita sees an airplane while walking outside with her father. She knows that birds fly. So, never having seen this flying thing before, she calls it a "bird (pájaro)." This is what we call *assimilation*. She is taking in this new information and making it fit into what she already knows. Children assimilate what they are taught into their own worlds when they play "school" by taking turns and "house" with their dolls and toys or other people.

Accommodation:

Taking new information and changing what is already thought to fit the new information.

Example: Aaron is at the grocery store with his mother and newborn baby. He calls the woman in the line ahead of them "pregnant" although she is simply overweight. After being corrected, he asks the next person he sees, "Are you pregnant or just fat?" This is what we call *accommodation*. Having learned that not all people with large bellies are pregnant, he changes his knowledge base to include new information. Children accommodate to the world as they are taught to use a spoon, the toilet, or a computer.

Equilibration:

A mental process to achieve a mental balance, whereby a person takes new information and continually attempts to make sense of the experiences and perceptions.

Example: Colby, age 7, gets two glasses from the cupboard for his friend Ajit and himself. After putting apple juice into his short, wide glass he decides he'd rather have milk, so he pours it into Ajit's tall, thin glass. "Look, now I have more than you!" says his friend. This puzzles Colby, who is distressed (in "disequilibrium"): How could it be more when he just poured it out of his glass? He thinks about the inconsistency (and pours the juice several times back and forth) and begins to get the notion that pouring liquid into different containers does not change the amount (the conservation of liquids). "No, it isn't," he says, "it's just a different shape!" Thus, Colby learns to make sense of it in a new way and achieve equilibrium in his thinking. Children do this whenever they get new information that asks them to change the actual schemas, making new ones to fit new experiences.

© Cengage Learning 2014

FIGURE 4-7 In Piagetian theory, the processes of assimilation, accommodation, and equilibration are basic to how people think (cognition) and learn.

Each person of normal intelligence goes through these stages in this order, although the rate depends on the individual and experience. Each stage of development has critical lessons for the child to learn in order to think and make sense of the world (Figure 4-8).

Piaget's theories revolutionized our thinking about children's thinking and challenged psychologists and educators to focus less on *what* children know than the *ways* they come to know. But was Piaget right? Researchers have been exploring and debating the ideas of cognitive theory for many years, often engaging in what Piaget himself called "the American question": Can you speed up the rate in which children pass through these intellectual stages of development?

There are two main criticisms of Piaget's theory: the age and the stage.

1. *The Age:* He seems to have been wrong about just how early many cognitive skills develop. For example, virtually all the achievements of the concrete operational period are present in at least rudimentary or fragmentary form in the preschool years.

This might simply mean that Piaget just had the ages wrong—that the concrete operations stage really begins at age 3 or 4.

2. *The Stage:* Research on expertise now shows that specific knowledge makes a huge difference. Children and adults who know a lot about some subject or some set of materials (dinosaurs, baseball cards, mathematics, etc.) not only categorize information in that topic area in more complex and hierarchical ways; they are also better at remembering new information on that topic and better at applying more advanced forms of logic to material in that area.

Developmental psychologists now believe that Piaget's theory of distinct stages is not correct, but the idea of a sequence in thinking is. Furthermore, neuroscience research has discovered that brain maturation seems to follow a sequence that parallels the various thinking stages of development (see later in this chapter). Children progress from one stage to the next, changing their thinking depending on their level of maturation and experience with the environment.

Stages of Early Childhood Cognitive Development

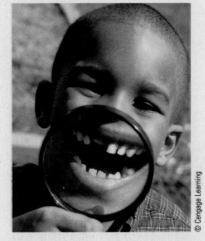

As a baby

Sensorimotor Period

Key concept

Object permanence

Definition

—the understanding that objects continue to exist even when they are out of sight

—essential to understanding the physical world

Explanation

—Birth to four months, infants respond to objects but stop tracking them if they are covered.

—Four to eight months, infants will reach for an object if it is partially covered.

—By eight to twelve months, infants will search for hidden objects randomly, anywhere.

—By 12 to 18 months, toddlers will search for an object where they last saw it.

—By—18 to 24 months, toddlers will search for hidden objects in systematic way.

As a preschooler

Preoperational

Key concept

Symbolic play and language

Definition

—the use of ideas, images, sounds, or symbols to stand for objects and events = symbolic play

—the use of an abstract, rule- governed system of symbols that can be combined to communicate information = language

—essential to developing the capacity to think

Explanation

—From 14 to 19 months, representational ability emerges.

—By 24 months, most can use substitute objects in pretend play.

—Nine to twelve months, infants begin to use conventional social gestures.

—Around one year, first words emerge.

—18 to 24 months, first sentences appear.

As a primary child

Concrete Operational

Key concept

Reasoning

Definition

—Actions can be carried out mentally.

—Logical reasoning replaces intuitive thinking in concrete situations.

—Classification skills develop.

—Essential to ability to think logically.

Explanation

—can coordinate several characteristics rather than a single property

—reversibility emerges; can see the same problem from several perspectives

—can divide things into sets and reason about their relationships

—Conservation skills emerge; an amount of liquid remains the same, no matter the container.

FIGURE 4-8 During each stage of cognitive development, children learn a key concept that enhances their thinking and reasoning.

Certain innate physical skills, such as fine motor coordination, determine how much a child is capable of doing. Certain environmental factors, such as the kinds of experiences the world and adults provide, influence the rate of growth. Throughout the process, as new information comes in, the child learns and grows (Ginsburg & Opper, 1987).

Applying Cognitive Theory to Work with Children

What can teachers learn from the complicated cognitive theory? Piaget's writings do not apply directly to classroom methods or subject matter per se, and therefore, careful interpretation is required. In fact, he never claimed to be an educator. However, Piaget's theories provide a framework, or philosophy, about children's thinking. A constructivist theory of education has arisen. Additionally, Piagetian theory has three implications for both environment and interactions.

Constructivist Theory

The constructivist theory of education changed the century-old **transmission model** of teaching, in which the teacher possesses the knowledge and transmits it directly to the children. In contrast, a new method based on Piaget's theory emerged. **Constructivism** is a theory of learning that states that individuals learn through adaptation. What they adapt to is directly influenced by the people, materials, and situations with which they come into contact.

This theory holds that people build on pre-existing knowledge, be it intellectual, social, or moral. One of its basic tenets is that children learn by creating their own knowledge by giving subjective meaning to what they experience. Another fundamental idea is that children learn by taking new ideas and integrating them into their existing knowledge base. This is exactly in line with Piaget's processes of assimilation and accommodation.

Based on ideas from Dewey and Piaget and supported by sociocultural theory, this **transactional model** of teaching actively engages a child in tasks designed to create personal meaning. Learning is an active process, based on the belief that knowledge is constructed by the learner rather than transferred from the teacher to the child. Although there may still be some direct instruction and demonstrations as there are in classes based on behaviorist views, a constructivist program promotes children's social, cognitive, and moral development more than do most teacher-centered programs. It is a theory used extensively in the emergent curriculum model (see Chapter 10).

Materials

Materials are used in a special way in applying Piaget's theory to early education. Children need many objects to explore so that they can later incorporate these into their symbolic thinking. Such materials need to be balanced among open-ended ones (such as sand and water activities, basic art and construction materials), guided ones (cooking with recipes, conducting experiments, classification and seriated materials), and self-correcting ones (puzzles, matching games, such as some of the Montessori materials). It is important to remember that young children need to be involved with concrete objects and to explore and use them in their own ways, which include both sensorimotor and beginning symbolic play.

Scheduling

Scheduling is giving children plenty of time to explore their reality, especially through the use of play. A Piagetian classroom is likely be noisy, with periods of time for children to "act out" their own ideas. Also, time is scheduled for imitation of adult-given ideas (songs, finger plays, and stories). Constructivist classrooms look diverse because the style and cultures of the teacher and children prevail. Children have choices and make decisions on significant parts of their learning. The teacher is a facilitator and co-constructor of the curriculum, does less talking while the learners do more, and provides more guidance and written observations rather than enforcing rules or giving tests.

Teachers

Teachers must have a particular developmental point of view. The teacher who knows the stages and levels of thinking of the children is one who can guide that class into new and challenging opportunities to learn and grow.

In working with children younger than the age 5, we must remember that, because they do not understand mental representations very well, they have trouble recognizing that another person may view or interpret things differently than they do. This **egocentric** viewpoint is both natural and normal but must be factored into teachers' thoughts as they work with children. For instance:

- You may be able to ask a 6- or 7-year-old: "How would you feel if you were in that situation?" For a younger child, the question is incomprehensible.
- The preschool child is likely to have trouble distinguishing how things seem or appear from how they really are (see Figure 4-9). If something *seems* dangerous (the scary-looking shadow in their bedroom), it *is* dangerous, and the friendly-acting strangers are safe because they look non-dangerous. Young children are gullible and trusting, in part because of their inadequate understanding that things may not be as they appear.

The teacher's role is to build an environment that is stimulating and conducive to the process of constructing meaning and knowledge. The preprimary schools of Reggio Emilia (see Chapters 9 and 10) encourage children to create their own material representations of their understanding by using many types of media (drawing, sculpture, stories, puppets, paper). At kindergarten and school-age levels, learning literacy and mathematics is considered a developmental process that the teacher facilitates by providing modeling, authentic experiences, mini-lessons on specific topics, and frequent opportunities for students to consult with and learn from each other. Many constructivist classrooms work on creating

FIGURE 4-9 Children's ideas, or mental representations, change with age. The older child recognizes that, although the contents of the box are only one thing out in the world, they can be represented in people's heads in more than one way—a possibility that escapes the younger child. (Special thanks to John Flavell for the example and the research. Reprinted by permission of John Flavell.)

community through rule-creating; in fact, teachers in those classrooms would tell us that "The only way to help students become ethical people, as opposed to people who merely do what they are told, is to have them construct moral meaning" (Kohn, 2005).

To encourage thinking and learning, teachers should refrain from telling children exactly how to solve a problem. Rather, the teacher should ask questions that encourage children to observe and pay attention to their own ideas. Teachers should:

- Use or create situations that are personally meaningful to children.
- Provide opportunities for them to make decisions.
- Provide opportunities for them to exchange viewpoints with their peers.

Perhaps more important is the awareness that all children have the capability to reason and be thinkers at their particular stage of development.

Teachers must remember that young children:

1. Think differently from adults.
2. Need many materials to explore and describe.
3. Think in a concrete manner and often cannot think out things in their heads.
4. Come to conclusions and decisions based on what they see, rather than on what is sensible and logical to an adult.

5. Need challenging questions and the time to make their own decisions and find their own answers.

The thoughts and ideas of Piaget are impressive, both in quantity and quality. The collective works of this man are extremely complex and often difficult to understand. Yet they have given us a valuable blueprint.

It is Piaget's genius for empathy with children, together with true intellectual genius, that has made him the outstanding child psychologist in the world today and one destined to stand beside Freud with respect to his contributions to psychology, education, and related disciplines. Just as Freud's discoveries of unconscious motivation, infantile sexuality, and the stages of psychosexual growth changed our ways of thinking about human personality, so Piaget's discoveries of children's implicit philosophies, the construction of reality by the infant, and the stages of mental development have altered our ways of thinking about human intelligence (Elkind, 1977).

Sociocultural Theory

An awareness of culture and family influences on development and an interest in the programs at Reggio Emilia, Italy, have led to a closer look at the works of Vygotsky. His sociocultural theory focuses on the child as a whole and incorporates ideas of culture and values

Take Piaget with You

Piaget's stages of cognitive development can be used to implement the first "umbrella handle" (see Figure 2-1) of developmentally appropriate practices. Read these examples, then answer the questions.

Age in years	Stage	Description	Activity
0–2	Sensorimotor	Thinking with their hands and feet, eyes and ears	Have toys near the crib so that young infants can bat and create movement (mastery of hands); cover an interesting toy with a blanket so that an older infant can look for it (object permanence); offer toddlers blocks to stack (coordination of schemes)
2–7	Preoperational	Exploring with activity & curiosity	Create water play with containers and play dough with rollers (centration); when in conflict, help children to articulate their wishes and views first, then listen to another's differing view; point out differences then find a common solution (egocentrism)
7–11	Concrete operational	Reasoning with beginning logic	Using water and clay, ask children to explain their reasons and see if they can follow transformation from beginning to end (reversibility); with chapter books, ask them to explain a character's reasoning for their actions, then to contrast it with their own (de-center)

into child development, particularly the areas of language and self-identity. In his view, children's development was more than just a response to personal experience. Rather, children are influenced in fundamental ways by their family, community, and socioeconomic status. Studies on cognitive and language patterns among young children in selected populations (Fouad & Arredondo, 2007) have confirmed the deep role of culture in learning.

Lev Vygotsky

Born in 1896 in Byelorussia, Lev Vygotsky graduated from Moscow University with a degree in literature in 1917. For the next six years, he taught literature and psychology and directed adult theater as well as founding a literary journal. In 1924, he began work at the Institute of Psychology in Moscow, where he focused on the problems of educational practice, particularly those of handicapped children. Toward that end, he gathered a group of young scientists during the late 1920s and early 1930s to look more closely at psychology and mental abnormality, including medical connections. Unfortunately, his career was cut short by tuberculosis; he died in 1934 at age 38. Yet in that short time, he studied the works of Freud, Piaget, and Montessori. His theory is also rooted in experimental psychology, the American philosopher William James, and contemporaries Pavlov and Watson (see the behaviorist theory section of this chapter).

Sociocultural Theory

Vygotsky's work is called **sociocultural** because it focuses on how values, beliefs, skills, and traditions are transmitted to the next generation (Vygotsky, 1978). There are similarities to several other theories:

- Like Erikson, Vygotsky believed in the connection between culture and development, particularly the interpersonal connection between the child and other important people.
- Like Maslow (see later in this chapter), he considered the child as a whole, taking a humanistic, more qualitative approach to studying children.

Like Piaget, Vygotsky asserted that much of children's learning takes place during play. This is because language and development build on each other, and the best way to develop competency is through interaction with others in a special way.

At the same time, sociocultural theory has unique perspectives that differ from other theories:

- *Behaviorist.* Though he understood the primary behaviorists of his day, he differed from them in that he emphasized family, social interaction, and play as primary influences in children's lives, rather than the stimulus-response and schedules of reinforcement that were becoming so popular in his day.
- *Piagetian.* Rather than moving through certain stages or sequences (as Piaget proposed), children's

mastery and interaction differ from culture to culture. Adults, Vygotsky noted, teach socially valued skills at a very early age; children's learning is, therefore, quite influenced by what is valued in their social world. Piaget insisted that, although children needed to interact with people and objects to learn, the stages of thinking were still bound by maturation. Vygotsky claimed that interaction and direct teaching were critical aspects of a child's cognitive development and that a child's level of thinking could be advanced by just such interaction.

Vygotsky believed that the child is embedded in the family and culture of his community and that much of a child's development is culturally specific. There are three ways culture is passed on: The first is imitative learning (like Bandura); the second by instructed learning (such as following directions); and the third by collaborative learning (working together with guided help or in play). Children learn through guided participation with others, especially in a kind of apprenticeship in which a tutor supports the novice not only by instruction but also by doing. Social interactions lead to continuous step-by-step changes in children's thoughts and behavior, so relationships between a teacher and a learner both impart skills and provide the context and cultural values of that skill, as well as teaching how to build relationships and use language: Engaging together matters (Berk, 2000).

Three concepts are key to understanding sociocultural theory.

1. *Zone of proximal development.* When a mentor senses that the learner is ready for a new challenge—or simply wants the learner to come along—he or she draws the novice into a **zone of proximal development** (ZPD), which is the range of learning that would be beyond what the novice could learn alone but could grasp with help. For example, Sergio can ride a tricycle alone and has hopped onto his sister's two-wheeler. Surely he will fall. But if his uncle runs alongside and helps him get balanced, he can do more. Of course, it takes many attempts, but with assistance, Sergio can increase his ZPD and eventually ride on his own.

   Who can help a child's ZPD? Initially, of course, it is the family. For instance, a young girl is carried even as a toddler to the open market with her mother. There, she watches and is guided toward learning how to touch cloth, smell herbs, taste food, and weigh and compare amounts. Is it any wonder she learns advanced math skills and the language of bargaining early? Second, the teacher is involved. For example, assisting a child complete a puzzle, put on mittens, or

resolve a conflict helps children learn problem solving skills. Third, other children—older ones who have more expertise or peers who may have superior skills or simply offer help—can help a child's learning. Cooperative learning, in which small groups of peers at varying levels of competence work toward a shared goal is common in a Vygotskian classroom.

2. *Scaffolding.* This concept describes the kind of **scaffolding**, or helpful structure, created to support the child in learning. Although not originally used by Vygotsky, the term helps define the most important components of tutoring. Just as a physical scaffold surrounds a building so that it might be worked on, so does the child get hints, advice, and structure in order to master a skill or an activity. This can be seen in children's developing speech, in guidance, and in ordinary tasks, as learning to ride a bike. Adults can arouse interest in a task, simplify it—scaffold it—so that it is within the child's ability and teach enthusiasm by helping the task get accomplished.

3. *Private speech.* Vygotsky believed that language, even in its earliest forms, was socially based and critical to how children internalize and learn. Rather than egocentric or immature, children's speech and language development during the ages of 3 to 7 years is merged with and tied to what children are thinking. During these transitional years, the child talks aloud to herself; after a while, this self-talk becomes internalized so that the child can act without talking aloud. Vygotsky contended that children speak to themselves for self-guidance and self-direction and that this private speech helps children think about their behavior and plan for action. With age, **private (inner) speech** (once called "egocentric speech"), which goes from out loud to whispers to lip movement, is critical to a child's self-regulation.

Applying Sociocultural Theory to Work with Children

Sociocultural theory has five implications for the classroom teacher.

1. Family and culture. *A child's family and culture need to be incorporated into a child's schooling.* Teachers must genuinely embrace (rather than give lip service) to the concept that the child's first teacher is the family. Each family may emphasize certain skills—vocabulary development, cooperation with siblings, self-care, and independence—that serve as the sociocultural context for learning. For instance, children of color in American society are socialized

In Vygotsky's sociocultural theory, children learn as other people create a kind of scaffolding to support the children.

to operate in two worlds and thus must achieve a kind of **bicognitive development** (along with bicultural and perhaps bilingual skills). Such work has led to a focus on "learning styles" (see Chapter 10). Research done with different cultural groups has reinforced the importance of looking at culture as part of the context in which the child lives and learns (Rogoff, 1990; York, 2005).

2. Teacher/child relationship. Teacher/child relationships are vital to learning. The teacher and learner adjust to one another; teachers use what they know about children to guide their teaching and plan their curriculum. Sociocultural theory supports both emergent curriculum (see Chapter 10) and spontaneous, teachable moments of the anti-bias curriculum (see Chapter 9). Of course, young children need adults to help create curriculum and set an environmental stage for learning. But they also need teachers to mediate social relationships and conflicts, to ask questions and know where a child is headed. Adults help children learn by seeing the challenge, giving assistance when needed, and noticing when the task is mastered and the child is ready for a new challenge.

3. Tools for learning. Pay close attention to the psychological and cultural "tools" used to teach. For example, some American children are taught to tie a string around their fingers as a memory device, whereas in Russia they tie a knot in their handkerchief. Tunes can aid learning (like the alphabet song); the higher mental functions need the help of a person who knows the tools of the society to learn.

4. Value of play. *Play is crucial for learning.* It is in play that the child practices operating the symbols and tools of the culture. Vygotsky (1978) puts it this way:

Action in the imaginative sphere, in an imaginary situation, the creation of voluntary intentions, the formation of real-life plans and volitional motives—all appear in play and make it the highest level of preschool development. The child moves forward essentially through play activity. Only in this sense can play be considered a leading activity that determines the child's development.

For instance, children might build a structure with blocks; the teacher encourages them to draw the building and then map the entire block corner as a village or neighborhood. The adult serves an important role as an intellectual mediator, continually shifting to another set of symbols to give children a different way of looking at the same thing.

5. Individual differences. *Individual differences still matter.* In a Vygotskian classroom activities are planned to encourage both assisted and cooperative learning. Teachers observe for opportunities to increase an individual's ZPD by planning experiences for extending the upper limit. Classrooms work best with multi-aged grouping, or at least with plenty of opportunity for older "buddies" to lead and younger ones to help.

Ecological Theory

The ecological theory is based on the premise that development is greatly influenced by forces outside the child. "No person can be understood in isolation, at just one moment in time. Urie Bronfenbrenner deserves credit for recognizing this fact" (Berger, 2011). Bronfenbrenner applied a general systems theory to human development in the 1970s, as the ecology movement began in America and Europe. Development is "a joint function of person and environment and human ecosystems include both physical factors—climate, space, home, and school—and the social environment—family, culture, and the larger society" (Bronfenbrenner, 2000).

Urie Bronfenbrenner

Born in the former Soviet Union, Bronfenbrenner immigrated to the United States at age 6, settling in New York. After studying psychology and music at Cornell University, he did graduate work in developmental psychology. He served as a clinical psychologist in the United States Army during World War II. When he returned to civilian life, he worked on the faculties of the University of Michigan and Cornell University, where he crafted this well-known theory (Bronfenbrenner, 1979).

Ecological Systems Theory

Bronfenbrenner's model describes four systems that influence human development, nested within each other like a circle of rings. With the child at the center, these four are the settings in which a child spends a significant period of time, the relationships of those settings, the societal structures, and then the larger contexts in which these systems operate (see Figure 4-10). The influences among these systems are critical to acknowledge: Just as in nature, activity in one part affects all the other parts. For example, a sudden income drop affects the family in many ways: The parents may be preoccupied and unavailable to the child, who may then need more attention

from the caregivers at school, who in turn may ask for more resources from the community for the family.

Applying Ecological Theory to Work with Children

The usefulness of this theory is in its combining of many methods—multidisciplinary, multicultural, and multidirectional—to understand the developing child. The values of the community (the exosystem) can influence social conditions (the macrosystem) and, in turn, be influenced by the individual family or program (microsystem). For example, think of an area where several families with young children move into the neighborhood. The community priorities shift to incorporate more family interests; parents get everyone involved in creating a neighborhood playground. In doing so, the city council lobbies the state legislature to adopt more "family-friendly" political policies. Many systems thus have a profound effect, both directly and indirectly, on children's development.

Imagine if the situation were reversed. Parents with very little voice in their community might have had a city council that was unresponsive to their needs. The playground would never have been built, the children would have little visibility in the neighborhood except to be

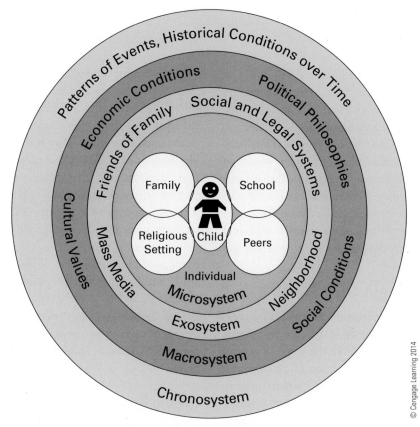

© Cengage Learning 2014

FIGURE 4-10 Ecological theory shows the various systems that influence in a child's development.

troublesome, and the families would feel like outsiders in the community. Thus, the dynamic nature of many systems is described well in ecological theory.

The ecological theory underscores the need for working partnerships between early childhood programs, the families they serve, and the societal structures children need to grow. The mesosytem, for instance, involves all the connections between the microsystems. Put the young child in the center (see Figure 4-10), and it includes all the communication processes between the child's family and teachers. Therefore, letters home, parent–teacher conferences, chats on arrival and departure, and phone calls would all contribute to the child's mesosystem. In this regard, the ecological theory possibly best encompasses most of the questions about the nature of development posed at the beginning of the chapter.

Multiple Intelligences Theory

There is a century-old argument about whether intelligence is a single, broad ability (as measured by an IQ test) or a set of specific abilities (more than one intelligence). Gardner's theory promotes the idea of many, or multiple, intelligences.

Howard Gardner

Howard Gardner, a professor of human development at the Harvard Graduate School of Education, has been very influential in the ongoing debate about the nature of intelligence. Born in Pennsylvania, he earned both bachelor and doctorate degrees at Harvard University and was fortunate to have Erikson as a tutor. Influenced by the works of Piaget and working with Jerome Bruner, Gardner became part of the Harvard's Project Zero research center for education where he wrote several seminal books on this theory (Gardner, 1983, 1993, 2000). Gardner currently teaches at Harvard in education and Boston University in neurology.

Theory of Multiple Intelligences

The theory of **multiple intelligences** asserts that there is strong evidence, both from the brain-based research (see discussion in this chapter) and from the study of genius, that there are at least nine basic different intelligences. Gardner's view of the mind claims that "human cognitive competence is better described in terms of sets of abilities, talents, or mental skills, which we call 'intelligences.' All normal individuals possess each of these skills to

some extent; individuals differ in the degree of skill and the nature of their combination" (1993). Multiple intelligences theory thus pluralizes the traditional concept of intelligence, which becomes the ability to solve a problem or to create a product (see Figure 4-11). First conceived as seven intelligences, Gardner revised his work to add naturalistic and then existential intelligences as useful constructs to describe the expanded definition.

Solving a problem includes the ability to do so in a particular cultural setting or community. The skill needed and developed depends very much on the context in which the child lives. For example, we know now that certain parts of the brain are designated for perception, bodily movement, language, or spatial processing. Everyone who has a functional brain is able to demonstrate some skill in these areas. But the child who has special "musical intelligence," for instance, hears a concert and insists on a violin (as did Yehudi Menuhin). Or the child whose culture depends on running for its daily living (as do some people of Kenya) is more likely to have children well developed in that area of intelligence. Gardner writes of Anne Sullivan, teacher of blind and deaf Helen Keller, as an example of interpersonal intelligence, for she could understand what Helen needed in a way no one else could.

Applying Multiple Intelligences Theory to Work with Children

Gardner's theory of multiple intelligences has had a big impact on schools, transforming curricula and teaching methods from preschool to high school (Gardner, 2000). Even *Sesame Street* has taken to applying the theory to developing its programs. Teachers in early childhood use the theory daily as they individualize their environments, curricula, and approaches. The child whose facility with puzzles exceeds that of his classmates is given a chance to try more complex ones. The children who thrive in dramatic play are offered a time to put on a puppet show for the class. The one whose mind works especially musically, logically, or interpersonally is encouraged to develop those special gifts.

At the same time, there is no one right way to implement multiple intelligences. Project Zero was founded to study and improve the design of performance-based assessments and to promote the use of multiple intelligences to achieve more personalized curriculum and instruction (Gardner et al., 1998). In a similar way to a constructivist classroom, a class with a multiple intelligences focus would have teachers developing their own strategies and developing curricula and assessment methods based on both their own and their children's culture and priorities and on the individual children's intelligences (see Chapters 10 and 12).

How Are You Smart?

Area	Definition	Example
Musical Intelligence	The capacity to think in music, to be able to hear patterns, recognize them, and then remember them.	Gardner cites the importance of music in cultures worldwide, as well as its role in Stone Age societies, as evidence of this.
Bodily-Kinesthetic Intelligence	The capacity to use parts or all of your body to solve a problem or make something.	We can see this in a person's ability in sport (to play a game), in dance (to express a feeling, music or rhythm), in acting, or in making a product.
Logical-Mathematical Intelligence 	The capacity to think in a logical, often linear, pattern and to understand principles of a system; most common intelligence tested with standard "IQ" tests.	Problem solving is often remarkably rapid (as in gifted children), and this thinking is often nonverbal (the familiar "Aha!" phenomenon).
Linguistic Intelligence	The capacity to use language to express thoughts, ideas, and feelings and the ability to understand other people and their words.	The gift of language is universal; spoken language is constant across cultures, and the development of graphic language is one of the hallmarks of human activity.
Spatial Intelligence 	The capacity to represent the world internally in spatial terms, as in problem navigation, in the use of maps, and in relying on drawings to build something.	Playing games such as chess and all the visual arts—painting, sculpting, drawing—use spatial intelligence, as do the sciences such as anatomy, architecture, and engineering.
Interpersonal Intelligence	The capacity to understand other people and focus on contrasts in moods, temperaments, motivations, and intentions.	Master players in school notice how others are playing before entering; some children seem to be born leaders; teachers, therapists, religious or political leaders, and many parents seem to have the capacity to notice distinctions among others.
Intrapersonal Intelligence	The capacity to understand yourself, knowing who you are, how you react, and the internal aspects of one's self.	Often having access to their own feeling life, they draw on a range of emotions as a means of understanding and guiding their own behavior. Children with an innate sense of what they can and cannot do and often know when they need help.
Naturalist Intelligence	The capacity to discriminate among living things (plants, animals), as well as a sensitivity to other features of the natural world (clouds, rock configurations).	This intelligence is valuable for hunters, gatherers, and farmers and is important to those who are botanists or chefs.
Existential Intelligence	The ability to contemplate questions beyond sensory input, such as considering the infinite or unexplained phenomena.	Individuals who are drawn to issues of life and death and questions of morality, and ponder the meaning of existence and other matters of the spirit, such as clergy, shaman, and spiritual leaders.

© Cengage Learning 2014

FIGURE 4-11 Gardner's multiple intelligences theory describes a new way of looking at intelligence.

Maturation Theory

In the 1940s and 1950s, Dr. Arnold Gesell established norms for several areas of growth and the behaviors that accompany such development. His theory of maturation underscores these norms (Gesell, 1940).

Arnold Gesell

As noted in Chapter 1, Arnold Gesell was a physician intrigued with the notion that children's internal clock seemed to govern their growth and behavior. The Gesell Institute, which fosters the work of Dr. Louise Bates Ames (1979) and others, continues to provide guidelines for how children mature from birth to puberty. The Word Pictures discussed in Chapter 3 are excellent examples of the information maturational theory and research have provided.

Theory of Maturation

Maturation, by definition, is the process of physical and mental growth that is determined by heredity. The maturation sequence occurs in relatively stable and orderly ways. **Maturation theory** holds that much growth is genetically determined from conception. This theory differs from behaviorism, which asserts that growth is determined by environmental conditions and experiences, and from cognitive theory, which states that growth and behavior are a reflection of both maturation and learning.

Maturation and growth are interrelated and occur together. Maturation describes the quality of growth; that is, while a child grows in inches and pounds, the nature (or quality) of that growth changes. Maturation is qualitative, describing the way a baby moves into walking, rather than simply the age at which the baby took the first step. Growth is *what* happens; maturation is *how* it happens.

Studies have established that the maturation sequence is the same for all children, regardless of culture, country of origin, or learning environment. But there are two vital points to remember:

- Although maturation determines the sequence of development, the precise age is *approximate*. The sequence of developmental stages may be universal, but the rate at which a child moves through the stages varies tremendously.
- Growth is *uneven*. Children grow in spurts. Motor development may be slow in some stages, fast in others. For instance, a baby may gain an ounce a day for two months, then only half a pound in an entire month. Usually there is a growth spurt at puberty, with some children at age 13 nearly their adult height, others not yet five feet tall. This unpredictability brings, again, much individual variation.

Applying Maturation Theory to Work with Children

Maturation theory is most useful in describing children's growth and typical behavior. In Chapter 3, these normative data were used to develop Word Pictures that describe common characteristics of children at different ages. Such charts help adults understand behavior better and keep them from expecting too much or too little.

At the same time, be cautious not to overgeneralize from the normative charts. Remember that there is great individual variation and uneven growth. Gesell's initial data were focused on a narrow portion of the population and were derived from American children only. Further work in the past three decades has adjusted the ranges with succeeding generations of children and an ever larger and more diverse population. Maturation theory has inspired developmental norms that help parents, teachers, and physicians alike determine whether a child's growth is *within* the normal range.

Humanistic Theory

As the field of psychology began to develop, various schools of thought emerged. The **humanist theory** has a place in early childhood education because it attempts to explain how people are motivated.

The Humanists

By the middle of the 20th century, two "camps" dominated the American psychological circles. The first (psychodynamic) included the Freudians and Eriksonians. The second (behaviorism) began with Watson and Thorndike and expanded with Skinner and Bandura. Abraham Maslow articulated another set of ideas. He called it the "third force" (or humanistic psychology), which focused on what motivated people to be well, successful, and mentally healthy (Goble, 1970).

Humanistic theory is centered on people's needs, goals, and successes. This was a change from the study of mental illness, as in psychotherapy, or the study of animal behavior, in the case of much behaviorist research. Instead, Dr. Maslow studied exceptionally mature and successful people. Others (Rogers, Perls, Watts, and Fromm) added to what was known about healthy personalities.

The humanists developed a comprehensive theory of human behavior based on mental health. Maslow's theory of human needs is clearly a "Western" philosophy, although it is often presented as a universal set of ideas. In fact, other cultures would see life differently. For instance, an African worldview might see the good of the community as the essential goal of being fully human. Scandinavian cultures with more of a "collective" orientation, rather than an emphasis on the individual or self, would see serving the family or group as the ultimate goal of humanity. Humanistic psychology can also be seen as being at odds with cultures and religions that seek ultimate reliance on a supreme deity, putting "God" rather than "self" at the top of the hierarchy. One must always question the underlying values of a theory, and humanist theory is no exception.

Theory of Human Needs

Maslow's theory of **self-actualization** is a set of ideas about what people need to become and stay healthy. He asserts that every human being is motivated by a number of basic needs, regardless of age, gender, race, culture, or geographic location. According to Maslow (1954), a basic need is something:

- Whose absence breeds illness.
- Whose presence prevents illness.
- Whose restoration cures illness.
- Preferred by the deprived person over other satisfactions, under certain conditions (such as very complex, free-choice instances).
- Found to be inactive, at low ebb, or functionally absent in the healthy person.

These needs, not to be denied, form a theory of human motivation. It is a hierarchy, or pyramid, because

The maturational sequence is the same for all children, although the precise age is approximate, so there is tremendous individual variation in children of a particular age.

there is a certain way these needs are interrelated, and because the most critical needs form the foundation from which the other needs can be met (see Figure 4-12).

Applying Humanistic Theory to Work with Children

The **basic needs** are sometimes called **deficiency needs** because they are critical for a person's survival, and a deficiency can cause a person to die. Until those are met, no other significant growth can take place. How well a teacher knows that a hungry child ignores a lesson or is simply unable to concentrate. A tired child often pushes aside learning materials and experiences until rested. The child who is deprived of basic physiologic needs may

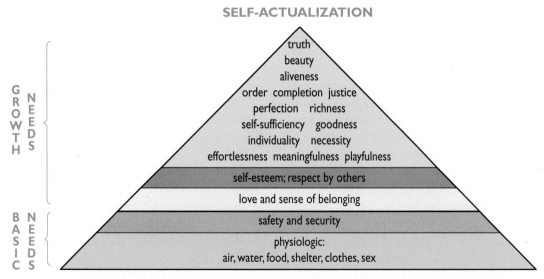

SELF-ACTUALIZATION

GROWTH NEEDS

truth
beauty
aliveness
order completion justice
perfection richness
self-sufficiency goodness
individuality necessity
effortlessness meaningfulness playfulness

self-esteem; respect by others

love and sense of belonging

BASIC NEEDS

safety and security

physiologic:
air, water, food, shelter, clothes, sex

FIGURE 4-12 Maslow studied healthy personalities and theorized that what people need for growth is a hierarchy of basic and growth needs. (Adapted from Maslow, 1954.)

be able to think of those needs only; in fact, "such a man can fairly be said to live by bread alone" (Maslow, 1954). The humanists would strongly advocate a school breakfast or lunch program and would support regular rest and nap times in programs with long hours.

Once the physiologic needs are satisfied, the need for safety and security emerges. Maslow points at insecure and neurotic people as examples of what happens when these needs are left unfulfilled. These people act as if a disaster is about to occur, as if a spanking is on the way. Given an unpredictable home or school, a child cannot find any sense of consistency and so is preoccupied with worrying and anxiety. Maslow would advise teachers to give freedom within limits, rather than either total neglect or permissiveness.

The **growth needs** can emerge when the basic needs have been met. Higher needs are dependent on those primary ones. They are what we strive for to become more satisfied and healthy people.

The *need for love and belonging* is often expressed directly and clearly by the young children in our care. A lack of love and sense of belonging stifles growth. To learn to give love later in life, one has to learn about love by receiving it as a child. This means learning early about the responsibilities of giving as well as receiving love.

The *need for esteem* can be divided into two categories: self-respect and esteem from others. Self-esteem includes such needs as a desire for mastery, for adequacy, for a sense of confidence that comes with competence and achievement, and feelings of independence and freedom. When one gets recognition and appreciation, one gets respect from others and feels a sense of status and reputation.

Self-actualization is what gives a person satisfaction in life. From the desire to know and understand the world and people around us comes a renewal of self-knowledge. For the early childhood educator, these needs are expressed in the enthusiasm, curiosity, and natural drive to learn and try. In meeting these needs, a person finds meaning for life, an eagerness to live, and a willingness to do so.

Children must have their basic physical and emotional needs met before higher cognitive learning can be fulfilled. Moreover, the child who seems stuck in a particular "needs area" likely stays there until that basic need is satisfied. A hungry, insecure, or hurt child is a poor learner. Teachers must continually advocate better physical and social conditions for all children.

Maslow's theory has important implications for child care. Children's basic needs are teachers' first concern: Teachers must ensure that children are properly clothed, fed, and rested as well as safe and secure. Only then are they ready to address curriculum and skill development.

Developmental Topics

There are several special issues that apply developmental and learning theories to work with children. Five topics most relevant to early childhood education are 1) cultural diversity, 2) attachment, 3) play, 4) gender, 5) moral development, and 6) brain-based research. The teacher well versed in these developmental topics is able to make better decisions concerning classrooms and curricula. Moreover, they are able to connect with families around those points and those people most important to them: the children.

Cultural Diversity

"Human nature is a cultural process. As a biological species, humans are defined in terms of our cultural participation. We are prepared by both our cultural and biological heritage to use language and other cultural tools and to learn from each other" (Rogoff, 2003). Development can be fully understood only when it is viewed in the larger cultural context. We can readily see the importance of culture in child rearing and family interaction, yet we often overlook its effect on education. We must know about children in their own setting, their own context, to understand them well enough to teach them. The ecology of a child's life must be acknowledged and brought into our work.

Global Examples

A quick international scan shows the influence of cultural orientation:

- England. The primary curricular emphasis is on children's social development until age 3, after which academic competence is emphasized.
- Norway and Sweden. Educators focus on developmental issues, particularly socio-emotional development, and families are encouraged to wait on formal academic teaching until primary school at age 6.
- Japan. In Asian countries where children's physical well-being and primary health care have improved to the point where they are no longer issues, the focus is on academic achievement and excellence.
- China. Model kindergartens in China include choices during playtime as well as structured outdoor exercises and whole-group instruction that includes child participation and questions.
- Eastern Europe. While academic achievement is not stressed in the Czech Republic or Hungary, young children are taught the importance of work and art, and they participate in cultural programs by the time they are 3.

Let us turn to the United States. "[I]nterpersonal episodes [are] absolutely saturated with cultural assumptions about the right way to think, feel, and behave. There are some real cultural differences about how to be a good parent and how to be a good child," states Stanford University's Hazel Markus (2005). For example:

- A mom leaned over a stroller, handed a silent 3-year-old a juice drink and announced, "It's hot. You must be thirsty."
- A 7-year-old ran up to his mother and grandmother and tried to get the younger woman's attention. She said, "I don't care how excited you are—don't interrupt your grandmother when she's speaking."
- A dad, sounding exasperated, told his 18-month-son, "Okay, now, you have a choice: either you wear this hat or we put on sunscreen. Which do you want?" The child replied, "I want juice."

These conversations reflect values—middle-class Euro-American, Latino, or East Asian. Ethnicity and cultural identity clearly play an important role in child development.

Three Key Issues

Teachers are challenged to work from an understanding of different patterns in culture and parenting and practices. Three issues are helpful to keep in mind.

1. *Watch for a culture gap.* Large numbers of children are members of a cultural group but are being taught by members of other cultural groups. Although this need not be catastrophic, research shows that four problems tend to develop (Lawrence-Lightfoot, 2004):

   There are problems when the *language* that is spoken by the child is not understood by caregivers from another culture.
   There are problems when caregivers have low *expectations* for children based largely on the children's membership in a low-status cultural group, rather than on the actual abilities of the children.
   There are problems when caregivers are unprepared to deal with children whose general behavioral *style* is different from that of the caregivers.
   There are problems when standard *testing* and *assessment* techniques are applied to certain cultural groups with insufficient recognition of, or respect for, the cultural patterns of the group.

2. *Update your theory.* Most early theories were based on observations of male or white subjects. This risks a skewed view of development. We encourage you to read studies of development that include other ethnic populations (Phinney, 2006). Ethnic minority children have been ignored in past research or viewed as variations from the norm. Often the group studied is given an ethnic label (such as Latino) that assumes the group is homogeneous and glosses over critical differences among the people in the group.

   Moreover, when ethnic groups are studied, often the focus is on children's problems. The range of existing differences makes more research—and also more teacher interest in individual family cultures—essential. Without such knowledge, teachers may misunderstand children with cultural patterns that are different from the mainstream and children and their families, in turn, may misunderstand the larger society or a school's practices and a teacher's behaviors.

3. *Theories have their limits.* Theories can foster a broad outlook about children in general, but these theories must be viewed in light of both cultural diversity and a respect for individuality.

If we wish to have more inclusive educational policies and practices—those that embrace the full variety of children and families residing on our communities—it is essential to have a theoretical interpretation of our common experiences as humans that can also help us to understand those ways in which we diverge from one another. While the field of psychology has done much to help us understand the individual mechanisms of behavior and development, . . . cultural psychology, . . . makes clear that what is highly valued and nurtured in one cultural setting may be considered improbable, if not inappropriate, from a cross-cultural perspective. (New & Beneke, in Feeney et al., 2009).

While children are forming their identity and self-worth, they often struggle with conflicting messages from home, media, school, and peers about who they are and what they are worth.

Knowing what child development information to use across cultures and what varies among cultures helps teachers apply theories (see Figure 4-13). Chapter 3 helps you identify these universals. While reading all these theories, try to look beyond any one model, and define a set of principles that are fundamental to good practice and that can information.

Attachment

Attachment is a term used particularly in the works of John Bowlby and Mary Ainsworth and a concept used in Burton White's descriptive work and Magda Gerber's Resources for Infant Educarers (RIE) programs for infants and toddlers. Attachment is the emotional connection, an "affectional tie that one person or animal forms

Children: All, Some, One

All children are alike . . .
- have the same needs and rights
- go through the same developmental stages
- have the same developmental goals

Some children are alike . . .
- similar cultural and social expectations will create commonalities
- rate of vocabulary increase is similar within groups with priority of language expression
- children show similar helping behaviors from families who value harmony

Each child is unique . . .
- genetic makeup
- temperament
- sensory sensitivity
- interests
- motivation

FIGURE 4-13 Make child development theories useful without overgeneralizing (patterned after Caldwell, 1983).

between himself and another specific one—a tie that binds them together in space and endures over time" (Ainsworth, 1979).

Expression and Types of Attachment

The child or adult who is attached to another uses that person as a "safe base" from which to venture out into the world, a source of comfort when distressed or stressed, and a support for encouragement. Attachment behaviors are anything that allows a person to get and stay attached, such as smiling, eye contact, talking, touching, and even clinging and crying.

"It is an essential part of the ground plan of the human species—as well as that of many other species—for an infant to become attached to a mother figure. This figure need not be the natural mother but can be anyone who plays the role of the principal caregiver" (Ainsworth, 1979).

Freud believed infants became attached to those who fed them. Erikson asserted that the first year of life was critical for attachment, in the stage of trust versus mistrust.

Research does show that human and animal babies do indeed send signals to their mothers very early. Infants begin the social smile at 6 weeks and positive reactions to familiar people by 3 months. The human infant's early signals include crying and gazing, both of which are powerful to adults, and a kind of rhythmic sucking that appears to keep the mother engaged. Soon after appears the synchrony, a coordinated interaction between an infant and caring adult that connects the two. Becoming more frequent and elaborate as time goes on, it helps the infant express feelings and the sensitive adult to respond.

Developmentally, children develop an initial bond and then proceed to develop real mutuality—that is, to learn and practice almost a "dance" between themselves and their favored loved one. Bowlby (1969, 1973) found that, although virtually all infants develop attachments, including to multiple caregivers, they differ in how secure they are in those attachments. Furthermore, attachment can be measured in the infant and toddler, as seen in children's response to a stranger both in and out of the parent's presence (see Figure 4-14).

An Alternative View

Not everyone believes that attachment is so important to later competence and identity. Infants are resilient, and children can grow positively within wide variations of parenting. Researchers have found cultural variations in attachment. German babies are more likely than American babies to be categorized as avoidant, but this might be because the culture encourages early independence. Japanese babies are more likely to be seen as avoidant, but this could also be a factor of the method used to record it, which calls for children to be left in a room without the mother, a situation that rarely occurs for most Japanese infants.

Some developmentalists claim the theory ignores the context and diversity of how children are socialized, and by whom. "I believe that European Americans are obsessed with attachment because we hold our babies less than almost any other cultural group in the world," writes a colleague (Saxton, 2001). "Attachment does not seem to be an issue, much less a concept, in cultures in which children are carried, held, or sleep with their parents for the better part of the first three years." Most children get attached to a primary caregiver. While in most cases it is the mother, it is who is part of the daily life that counts—it might be the father, grandparents, or other adults.

Researchers have found that most infants tested in the stranger situation demonstrated secure attachment. Still, when attachment fails, children are placed at

Patterns of Attachment

	Exploratory Behavior Before Separation	Behavior During Separation	Reunion Behavior	Behavior with Stranger
Secure	Separates to explore toys; shares play with mother; friendly toward stranger when mother is present, touches "home base" periodically.	May cry; play is subdued for a while; usually recovers and is able to play.	If distressed during separation, contact ends distress; if not distressed, greets mother warmly; initiates interaction.	Somewhat friendly; may play with stranger after initial distress reaction.
Anxious/ambivalent (resistant)	Has difficulty separating to explore toys even when mother is present; wary of novel situations and people; stays close to mother and away from stranger.	Very distressed; hysterical crying does not quickly diminish.	Seeks comfort and rejects it, continues to cry or fuss; may be passive—no greeting made.	Wary of stranger; rejects stranger's offers to play.
Anxious/avoidant	Readily separates to explore toys; does not share play with parent; shows little preference for parent versus stranger.	Does not show distress; continues to play; interacts with the stranger.	Ignores mother— turns or moves away; avoidance is more extreme at the second reunion.	No avoidance of stranger.

FIGURE 4-14 Patterns of attachment. (From Ainsworth, M. D. S., & Wittig, B. A., 1969. "Attachment and Exploratory Behavior of One-Year-Olds in a Strange Situation." In B. M. Foss, Ed. *Determinants of Infant Behavior* [Vol. 4] London: Methuen. From Understanding Children, by Judith Schickendanz, © 1993 by Mayfield Publishing Company. Reprinted with permission of McGraw-Hill Companies.)

tremendous risk (White, 1995). Failure of attachment can come from:

- Parents who did not have secure attachments as children
- Neglectful conditions, such as depression, abject poverty
- Abusive parents that discourage bonding
- Premature infants with underdeveloped systems
- Blind infants who cannot engage in gazing

Intervention can help unattached persons learn the skills to connect, teaching specific interactive techniques with ongoing supports such as crisis hotlines and personal counseling.

Careful questions should be asked about full-day care, particularly for infants, to ensure that children's attachment to their families is not undermined. We can conclude that children are not at any higher risk in high-quality child care. This highlights the need for such programs, as is addressed further in Chapter 15.

Play

Play! What a wonderful word! It calls up images from the past, those childhood years when playing was the focus of our waking hours. "Will you play with me?" is one of the most expressive, expectant questions known. It carries with it hope and anticipation about a world of fun and make-believe, a world of adventure and exploration, a world of the young child.

City streets, parks and fields, tenements, huts, empty rooms, and backyards are all settings for play. Play is a way of life for children; it is their natural response. It is what children do and it is serious business to them. Any activity children choose to engage in is play; it is never ending.

Play is the essence of creativity in children throughout the world. Play is universal and knows no national or cultural boundaries. Educators and psychologists have called play a reflection of the child's growth, the essence of the child's life, a window into the child's world (Frost, Wortham, & Reifel, 2011). It is a self-satisfying activity through which children gain control and come to understand life. Play teaches children about themselves; they learn how tall—or short—they are, what words to use to get a turn on the swing, and where to put their hands when climbing a ladder. Through play, children learn about the world: what the color purple is, how to make matzo balls, and how to be a friend. Play helps children define who they are.

Types of Play

Play takes many forms. Children play when they sing, dig in the mud, build a block tower, or dress up. Play can be purely physical (running, climbing, ball throwing) or highly intellectual (solving an intricate puzzle, remembering the words to a song). Play is creative when crayons and paint are used. Its emotional form is expressed when children pretend to be mommies, daddies, or babies. Skipping rope with a friend, playing tag, and sharing a book are examples of the social side of play.

There is a general sequence to the development of play (see Figure 4-15). Babies and toddlers have a clearly defined social self. Infant play begins with patterns established at birth: babies gaze, smile, and make sociable sounds in response to the quality and frequency of attention from a parent or caregiver. Socialization of infants occurs through interaction. By the end of their first year, infants smile at and touch one another and vocalize in a sociable effort. Toddlers play well on their own (*solitary play*) or with adults. They begin solitary pretend play around 1 year of age. They still watch others (*onlooker*). During the toddler years, as children become more aware of one another, they begin to play side by side, without interacting (*parallel play*). They are aware of and pleased about but not directly involved with the other person. It is during this year that toddlers begin some form of coordinated play, doing something with another child. The preschool years bring many changes for

children in relation to social development. The number and quality of relationships increase as does the ability to play with other children. At first, this is accomplished just by a child's presence in a group: playing at the water table with four other children or joining a circle for finger plays (*associative play*). When children join forces with one another in an active way, when they verbalize, plan, and carry out play, group play is established. It can be characterized as "Let's do it together," whether building a house for the farm animals or engaging in rough-and-tumble wrestling. *Cooperative play* is the most common type of peer interaction during the preschool years and into the school-age period.

Keep in mind that children's play always portrays their own social values and family ethnic practices. Developmentally and culturally appropriate practice would remind us that our understanding and knowledge about play have been based on Euro-American cultural patterns (Parten, 1932). Wise early childhood practitioners incorporate this perspective into their work with children.

Most play is unstructured and happens naturally when the curriculum is designed for play. **Spontaneous play** is the unplanned, self-selected activity in which children freely participate. Children's natural inclinations are toward play materials and experiences that are developmentally appropriate. Therefore, when they are allowed to make choices in a free play situation, children choose activities that express their individual interests, needs, and readiness levels.

Dramatic play—or imaginative or pretend play—is a common form of spontaneous play. Three- and four-year-olds are at the peak of their interest in this type of activity. In dramatic play, children assume the roles of different characters, both animate and inanimate. Children identify themselves with another person or thing, playing out situations that interest or frighten them. Dramatic play reveals children's attitudes and concepts toward people and things in their environment. Much of the play is wishful thinking, pretending great strength and deeds. This is the way children cope with their smallness or lack of strength and is considered important in psychodynamic theory.

Two types of dramatic play are noteworthy:

1. **Superhero** play is appealing to children because it so readily addresses their sense of helplessness and inferiority. Pretending to be Wonder Woman makes it easier to understand and accept the limitations of the real world. It helps children learn about power and friendship, allows them a way to test their physical limits and explore feelings, and answer the "big questions about the world, such as 'what is right and wrong, what is good and bad, what is fair and unfair,

Play Categories

Unoccupied Play

- May stand in one spot
- Looks around the area
- Performs random movements that have no apparent goal

Solitary Play

- Plays alone
- Plays independently of others

Onlooker Play

- May watch while others play
- May talk but does not enter play
- Shows active interest in the play

Parallel Play

- Plays alongside others
- Plays separately from others but with toys or actions that are similar to the others

Associative Play

- Play involves social interaction but little or no organization
- Interested in each other without an agreed-upon plan

Cooperative Play

- Socially interacts in a group with a sense of group identity
- Joins an organized activity, a prototype for games

FIGURE 4-15 Parten's play categories, developed by observing free play patterns in nursery school settings.

what is life and death, what is a boy and a girl, and what is real and fantasy'" (Hoffman, 2004).

At the same time, this kind of play makes many adults uncomfortable because the children's play is often loud, disruptive, filled with conflict and problems, and solved with violence. Children sometimes end up in stereotypical, repetitive play that seems to ignore other learning. (See Chapter 14 for strategies.)

2. Sociodramatic play happens when at least two children cooperate in dramatic play. Dramatic play provides the means for children to work out their difficulties by themselves. By doing so, they become free to pursue other tasks and more formal learning.

Both types of play involve two basic elements: imitation and make-believe.

Pretending to be a firefighter, Sherry grabs a piece of rope and runs toward the playhouse, saying "shhshhshshshshsh" while pretending to squirt water on the fire. She shouts to her playmates, "Over here! Come over here! The fire is on this side."

Sherry's make-believe scenario and her ability to follow the rules of behavior common to firefighters (grabbing hoses, calling for help) are the two critical factors from Vygotsky's point of view: That firefighting scene supports his theory that cognitive skills develop through social interactions. Sherry exemplifies a child moving from concrete to abstract thought because she did not require realistic objects (a hose and water) but imagined them with a rope and her ability to create the sound of water. This ability to separate thoughts from actions and objects will stand Sherry in good stead when she studies math concepts. Rules that children follow in make-believe play teach them to make choices, to think and plan about what they will do, and to show willingness toward self-restraint, as children learn to follow the social rules of pretend play. This is important preparation for real-life situations.

Value of Play

For the first half of the 20th century, interest in children's play focused on emotional causes and effects. The main theme was the emotional releases that play provided children. Psychodynamic theory recommended play as a suitable outlet for expressing negative feelings, hostility, and aggression. Clay can be pounded, balls can be kicked and thrown, and dolls can be spanked. Young children give free expression to a wide range of emotions, playing them out and releasing tension.

But play is more than an avenue for emotional release. Play is universal to childhood experiences because it is intrinsically motivated; that is, it is naturally satisfying to children. In addition,

- Play is relatively free of rules except for those children impose on themselves.
- Play is controlled and dominated by the children.
- Play is carried out as if the activity were real life.
- Play focuses on the activity—the doing—rather than on the end result or product.
- Play requires the interaction and involvement of the children.

Play promotes learning for the whole child, providing benefits for all developmental domains (American Academy of Pediatrics, 2007; Elkind in Washington & Andrews, 2010).

Play as the Cornerstone of Learning

Outside of child development circles, there has been little appreciation in the United States culture for the value and importance of play for young children. In times of rising expectations and academic standards, educators and families feel pressured to focus on activities related to school readiness. If children are just playing, how will they learn? Play is viewed by some as the opposite of work, not as a cornerstone of learning. Play is often trivialized by sayings like "That is mere child's play."

A growing body of research shows that every school success indicator is enhanced by play (Elkind, 2010).

© Cengage Learning

Learning through play takes many forms and happens naturally in unplanned, self-selected activities.

Moreover, young children learn by doing because they live in the world of action and feelings more than words. To reclaim play as a special activity crucial to children's development, we should look at play as the foundation from which children venture forth to investigate, to test out. Curriculum takes on expression through play; teachers plan curriculum that uses play as the medium for learning. As they mature, children integrate and assimilate their play experiences. What started out as play—the sheer fun of it—is transformed into learning experiences. Curiosity about magnets at age 5 nourishes a scientific attitude for the later years, as well as a foundation for studying gravity, planetary movements, and the like. Feeling free to sing out at group time at age 3 can prepare a child to be an active participant in the kindergarten classroom at age 6.

Teachers want children to learn about themselves, to learn about the world around them, and to learn how to solve problems. A childhood filled with play opportunities should culminate in these three types of learning:

1. *Learning about themselves* includes developing a positive self-image and a sense of competence. Children should know and feel good about themselves as learners. They should develop a sense of independence, a measure of self-discipline, and knowledge based on full use of their sensory skills.

Play is the cornerstone for learning.

2. *To learn about others and the world around them* means developing an awareness of other people. Teachers want children to perfect their communication and social skills so that they are more sensitive participants in the world in which they live. This means that children learn and appreciate the values of their parents, the community, and society at large. When children become aware of the demands of living in today's society, that awareness can help them become more responsible citizens. The emphasis on social interaction and group relationships in the early childhood setting underscores this goal.

3. *To learn to solve problems*, children need to be accomplished in observation and investigation. When exploring a puzzle, for example, children need to know how to manipulate it, take it apart, and put it back together, to see how other people solve puzzles, and to know how to get help when the pieces just do not seem to fit together. They should know how to predict and experiment. What will happen, wonders a kindergartner, when a glass is placed over a glowing candle? How will that change if the glass is large or small? What is the effect if the glass is left over the candle for a long time or for a second? Young children also need to learn how to negotiate, discuss, compromise, and stand their ground, particularly when they encounter and solve problems socially. "I want the red cart and someone already has it," thinks the preschooler. "Now what? How can I get it? What if the other person says no? Will the plan that works with my best friend work with someone else? When do I ask for help? Will crying make a difference?" To be effective problem solvers, children must know and experience themselves and others.

Play in the early years is a key to school success and solid development.

Gender

Are girls and boys different in terms of development and learning? What are these differences, and how do they occur? What differences are caused by "nature" and which ones by "nurture"? Should we treat our girls and boys the same or differently? The realities and the myths surrounding sex differences and their effect on behavior from infancy to adulthood is the subject of interest, controversy, and research.

Definitions

Sex differences are the biological differences between males and females; **gender differences** are culturally imposed distinctions in the roles and behaviors. While boys and girls are about the same size and shape in childhood, gender differences and adult distinctions are more significant.

There are two aspects of gender development that are particularly important in the early years: **gender identity** (the sense of being female or male, which most children acquire by age 3), and **gender role** (the set of expectations that define how a male or female should behave, think, and feel). Gender is important to some developmental and learning theories.

Theories and Research

Freud asserted that behavior was directly related to reproductive processes. His stages of psychosexual development reflect the belief that gender and sexual behavior are instinctual. Erikson also claimed that anatomy was destiny: Males were more intrusive because of genital structure, and females were more inclusive. He later modified his view, saying that women were overcoming their biological heritage. Erikson's identification theory came from the view that the preschool child finds the opposite-sex parent attractive but steers away from this by identifying with the same-sex parent.

Piaget and Bandura both emphasized that children learn through observation and imitation, and that through reinforcement, children learn gender-appropriate behavior. Proponents of this view point to how parents encourage girls and boys to engage in certain activities and types of play. Certainly the media communicates sexist messages; this theory would claim that such stereotyping influences the development of gender roles.

The works of Eleanor Maccoby (1974, 1998) have provided both hard data and an open forum for discussions about how people grow and the complex interaction

DIVERSITY

Male/Female Concepts in Girls and Boys

For all the current talk about gender differences, research about gender differences lagged at the end of the 1900s in favor of other topics. Some contemporary developmentalists have a new interpretation, known as gender-schema theory. Children develop mental ideas, or schema (a Piagetian concept) about gender on the basis of the behavior patterns they see (a behaviorist model). Gender-schema, then, is a cluster of concepts about male and female physical characteristics, behaviors, and personality traits. As soon as children understand labels of "girl" and "boy," they seek out information about each and then try to imitate those that match their identity. Thus children use sex as one way to organize their perceptions (schema) about the world. Boys show better memory for "masculine" toys, and girls for "feminine" ones (Martin & Ruble, 2006).

For instance, the "strength-weakness" dimension may be taught and shown to children such that strength is linked to maleness and weakness to female stereotype. Because children work toward gender-appropriate behavior, it is likely that most boys fight when in a conflict, in part because that is expected, and girls attempt gentleness or helplessness to build an identity in line with that gender-schema (Ruble et al., 2006).

---

between heredity and environment that makes child development so fascinating. These findings help teachers understand gender identity and its implications for education:

- By age 2, children name themselves as girl or boy and can identify adult strangers as daddies or mommies.
- By age 4, children label toys (dolls, trucks) and some roles (soldier, nurse) appropriate for one gender and not the other.
- Children develop gender stability (the understanding of staying the same sex throughout life) by age 4 and gender constancy (a person keeps the same gender regardless of appearance) by about 5 or 6.
- Sex-typed behavior begins to appear at age 2 or 3, when children tend to choose same-sex playmates and sex-typed toy preferences, and children become more selective and exclusive as they mature.
- By elementary school, the playground is like a "gender school," with children showing a clear preference for same-sex peers.

Developmental Differences

What are the real differences between girls and boys? Physically, males grow to be 10 percent taller than females, and girls are less likely to develop physical or mental disorders than are boys. Boys are also more active than girls and physically more aggressive overall. However, there are fewer differences in verbal aggression, although males do show less self-regulation than females (Eisenberg, Martin, & Fabes, 1996). There are no significant differences between girls and boys in intelligence or reasoning behavior. Some cognitive functioning and personality differences do exist, but overall the differences are small and there is no overall pattern.

Teachers and parents, as well as researchers, have observed that boys and girls seem to show distinct differences in their play choices, play behavior, and toy selection from an early age. Although biology certainly plays a part, it would seem that parents and society exert powerful influences. The toys parents and teachers choose (dolls for girls, trucks for boys), the predominance of females in early childhood settings, television shows and advertising, and toy store displays combine to communicate a very strong reinforcement of traditional sex-role expectations.

Gender Stereotyping

To break through the restrictiveness of gender stereotyping, teachers need to pay careful attention to the messages they give children. One challenge we face is the female culture of early childhood programs. Women dominate the early childhood education workforce, so children are often only exposed to women's interaction styles (Wardle, 2004). If boys struggle in our programs, we must be alert to the activities and schedules we establish, behaviors we may reward or punish, the "goodness of fit" for both boys and girls in our programs. In the environments we prepare for them, the materials they use, and the examples we model, children create their own ideas and learn behavior that works for them in the world.

Moral Development

People used to assume that young children needed to be taught exactly what was "right" and "wrong" and that was enough. In the past 30 years, research has shown that moral development is a more complex process with both a cognitive and an emotional side to it. Several theorists and researchers have proposed how to think about children's moral development. The theories of Jean Piaget, Lawrence Kohlberg, Nancy Eisenberg, and Carol Gilligan are discussed here.

Cognitive-Developmental Base

Piaget (1965) investigated children's moral reasoning by presenting children with pairs of stories and asking them which child was "naughtier." From this, he discovered that children younger than age 6 base their judgment on the amount of damage done, not the child's intentions. By middle childhood, children are beginning to take intent into account so that one can begin to see a shift in moral reasoning toward the end of the early childhood period from objective judgments based on physical results and concrete amounts to more subjective considerations (such as the purpose of the perpetrator or psychological factors). The connections to children's cognitive stage of development is interesting, and adults might consider that a child's protests over wrongdoing ("I didn't mean to do it!") may very well signal a new level of reasoning, with the realization that one's intentions do matter.

Kohlberg (1981) is best known as a theorist in social development, addressing educational practice and gender constancy as well. Building on Piagetian dimensions, Kohlberg's theory of moral development involves both social growth and intellectual reasoning. People move from stage to stage as a result of their own reasoning power, and they see for themselves the contradictions in their own beliefs. As with Erikson and Piaget, Kohlberg's stages are hierarchical—a person moves forward one by one, and no stage can be skipped. On the basis of children's responses to moral dilemmas similar to those of Piaget, Kohlberg identified three levels of moral development (Figure 4-16). For early childhood educators, research shows that preconventional reasoning (stages 1 and 2) is dominant into elementary school.

Kohlberg's theory has been criticized for placing too much emphasis on moral thought and not enough of moral behavior. Most of the stories, or dilemmas, that Piaget and Kohlberg used were about stealing, lying, disobeying rules, and the like. Further, many point out that his view is culturally biased and the stories asked are not applicable to all children. Western moral doctrine emphasizes individual rights; other cultures focus on a greater respect for traditional codes and practices.

Modern Revisions

Researcher and theorist Nancy Eisenberg (1983, 1992) has explored the kinds of reasoning children use to justify good (prosocial) behavior. She asks children what they would do in situations with a moral dilemma. One

---

Kohlberg's Stages of Moral Development

I. Preconventional Morality

Stage 1:   Punishment and obedience orientation
Might makes right; obey authority and avoid punishment.

Stage 2:   Individualism and relativist orientation
Look out for number one; be nice to others so they will be nice to you.

II. Conventional Morality

Stage 3:   Mutual interpersonal expectations
"Good girl, nice boy"; approval more important than any reward.

Stage 4:   Social system and conscience
"Law and order"; contributing to society's good is important.

III. Postconventional Morality

Stage 5:   Social contract
Rules are to benefit all, by mutual agreement; may be changed same way; the greatest good for the greatest number.

Stage 6:   Universal ethical principles
Values established by individual reflection, may contradict other laws.

© Cengage Learning 2011

FIGURE 4-16 Kohlberg's Stages of Moral Development. Cross-cultural data and extensive American research indicate a persuasive universality and a strong sequence of stage development in children's moral development.

of her stories involves a child on the way to a friend's birthday party. The child encounters someone who has fallen and is hurt. What should the child do: help the hurt child and miss cake and ice cream, or leave the child and go on to the party?

Such questions brought to light several levels of prosocial reasoning. In the early childhood years, children seem to be engaged in level one (*hedonistic reasoning*), in which the individual's own needs are put first. In the case mentioned earlier, the child would leave the hurt person and go to the party ("I won't help because I have to go to the party"). As children move through middle childhood, they tend to move to level two, in which the needs of another begin to be considered and to increase in importance. Answers to the story would begin to shift toward including others ("I'd help because they'd help me next time"). Eisenberg's stages roughly parallel Kohlberg's and help broaden these concepts without contradicting the fundamental arguments.

Carol Gilligan (1982, 2011) challenges Kohlberg's strong emphasis on justice and fairness and his omission of caring for others. Gilligan notes that because girls and boys are socialized differently, their moral judgments will be quite different. For instance, boys may be raised with the idea that justice and fairness are the key moral bases, whereas girls may be taught that caring and responsibility to others are central. Buzzelli (2002) has also worked extensively on young children's moral understanding and has applied recent research to children's development of peer relationships. Although this claim of different moral ideas based on gender differences has yet to be fully researched, it is an important thought to keep in mind, particularly when teaching and raising young children.

Moral development is often deleted from the curriculum in American schools. Further, one aspect of moral development that has been studied very little is that of children's spirituality and faith. Because of the separation of church and state in American public schools, many educators shy away from discussions of anything that might be considered "religious." In doing so, educational programs also find themselves staying out of anything that helps children understand who they are and the greater questions of life and its meaning. Yet even John Dewey called moral education the "hidden curriculum," conveyed through the atmosphere of every program. Elementary schools occasionally have some kind of teaching for "character education," or a values clarification class. In addition, most caregivers will tell you what children notice about life and death issues and about caring for others is part of everyday experiences.

Brain Development

We are aware of the importance of the first 5 years in the physical, social, and cognitive-language development of the child (Copple & Bredekamp, 2009). These same five years are the most critical with respect to the developing brain. Neuroscience research has developed sophisticated technologies, such as ultrasound; magnetic resonance imaging (MRI); positron emission tomography (PET); and effective, noninvasive ways to study brain chemistry (such as the steroid hormone cortisol). Brain scans and other technologies have made it possible to investigate the intricate circuitry of the brain. We now know the number of dendrite connections are estimated to be more than 100 billion (Miller & Cummings, 2007), and the implications are equally staggering.

Forming language, identifying cultural and social norms, and learning to distinguish right from wrong requires this intensive neurological growth to take place, thus strengthening the connections between neurons. This rapid growth in the minds of young children inspires them to explore, to discover, to play, and to make the natural connections between self, others, and their surrounding world.

No aspect of biological growth is more critical than the rapid growth of the brain. A newborn's skull is disproportionately large, because it must be big enough to hold the brain, which at birth is 25 percent of its adult weight. In contrast, the neonate's body is typically only 5 percent of adult weight. By age 2, the brain is almost 75 percent of adult brain weight; the child's body is only about 20 percent as big as it will be. During the prenatal and early childhood period, the brain develops faster than any other part of the body so that by age 7 it is almost fully grown (Berger, 2012).

We once believed that brains were entirely formed by genes and prenatal influences only. Certainly, by the sixth prenatal month, nearly all of the billions of neurons (nerve cells) that populate the mature brain have been created, with new neurons generated at an average rate of more than 25,000 per minute (Thompson, 2001). Today, neuroscientists believe in plasticity, the concept that growth changes throughout life for a variety of reasons. The timetable for brain development varies by region, and it is likely that brain development continues into adulthood. Still, early childhood is a critical time for brain development. The timing and quality of early experiences combine to shape brain architecture (Shonkoff et al., 2008; Galinsky, 2010).

What We Have Learned

At least three important conclusions can be made at this time:

1. *The brain operates on a "use it or lose it" principle.*
   Brain development begins at one month in utero

and proliferates the nerve cells. "Once neurons are formed, they quickly migrate to the brain region where they will function. Neurons become differentiated to assume specialized roles, and they form connections (**synapses**) with other neurons that enable them to communicate and store information" (Thompson, 2001).

Using a dual process of blooming and pruning, neurons first create more synapses than the brain retains, and then prunes back those that are not used. At birth, one has about 100 billion brain cells and 50 trillion connections among them. With use, these cells grow bases (axons) and branches (**dendrites**) that reach out to make connections with other cells. The brain thus adapts to the stimulation and experience the child receives. Newborns respond to universal sounds, but their speech perception over time becomes limited to that of the family (and child care) languages. The typical experiences of hearing and responding to language, for instance, contribute to brain growth.

2. *The brain is vulnerable in early childhood.* Chronic maternal stress during pregnancy and after birth can threaten healthy brain growth. As children move from infancy through preschool, their brain functions are developing according to what is received. "Neural development, stress hormones, and brain specialization are three areas of brain research that inform and support developmentally appropriate practices (DAP) in early childhood education" (Gallagher, 2005). When the brain perceives a threat or stress, the body reacts. Stress can trigger a flood of hormones, particularly **cortisol**, that may create an overreaction. Continuous overproduction of cortisol can create other problems with the endocrine system. In contrast, satisfying and responsive circumstances soothe and avoid such flooding. Teachers contribute to brain growth as they provide DAP educational experiences. Important, too, are prenatal and postnatal health care, and efforts to avoid malnourishment and keep stresses manageable at home.

3. *The quality of the environment is crucial.* The biological environment takes a huge role in brain development, so the level of nutrition and health care and protection from drugs and environmental toxins must be monitored. By age 2, most pruning of dendrites has already occurred. By age 7, the brain has grown to its adult size, and the basic areas of sensory and motor cortexes are functioning. **Myelination**, the fatty coating of dendrites and axons, speeds transmission of nerve impulses between neurons and enables children to think and react faster. Fast and complex communication can now occur.

The core of the environment is interpersonal: People matter. Positive adult–child interaction promotes brain development.

Most of the significant ways that caregivers promote healthy development occur quite naturally during the course of sensitive adult–child interactions. For instance, the "parent-ese" that facilitates early language, the caregiving routines that promote predictability and memory skills, the patient structuring of an activity to make it manageable for a child, and the protective nurturance that manages a baby's emotions show that when sensitive adults do what comes naturally, their behavior is optimally suited to promoting early cognitive, socio-emotional, and neurobiological growth (Thompson, 2001).

With impoverishments, you may lose the dendrites. Stressed, depressed, or absent parents or caregivers do not give children the environmental experiences they need for neurobiological growth. Established patterns of behavior are increasingly difficult to change as individuals get older; it is more effective and efficient to get things right the first time than to try and fix them later.

"One theme from the research on children and learning is that babies' brains appear to be wired to help them understand and know about the world in specific ways, and that this learning begins long before babies can be taught this kind of knowledge" (Galinsky, 2010). Moreover, after the sensory and motor areas of the brain develop, the prefrontal cortex development begins. This is the part of the brain that controls the executive functions of managing attention, emotions, and behavior; it begins in the preschool years and doesn't mature until young adulthood. It is this area of the brain that is needed for the person to acquire essential life skills: focus and self-control; perspective taking; communicating; making connections; critical thinking; taking on challenges; and self-directed, engaged learning (Galinsky, 2010).

Applications to Early Education

Applying brain research to early education programs is a challenge. It is easy to become overwhelmed with unfamiliar vocabulary and complex neurological processes. By becoming knowledgeable about the brain and well-versed in DAP, early childhood professionals can create healthy environments and engaging, meaningful experiences (see Figure 4-17). The study of the brain assists educators in understanding how children learn best and provides them with evidence for how to build optimal educational experiences.

How Brain-based Research Aligns with Developmentally Appropriate Practices

Brain-based Research (BBR) Suggests . . .	Developmentally Appropriate Practice (DAP) Asserts . . .	Early Childhood Education (ECE) in Action . . .
The human brain is constantly seeking information from outside stimuli and uses all senses.	Learning occurs in a setting that provides choices and variety in the environment.	A sensory table, a block corner, dress-up clothes, and painting are offered during activity time.
No intelligence or ability unfolds until or unless it is offered and/or modeled.	Development advances when children have opportunities to practice newly acquired skills both at and just beyond their present level of mastery.	Children have access to ongoing, familiar materials (play dough, sand, trikes) and challenging lessons (sink/float experiment, story dictation, obstacle course)
The brain processes on many paths, can deal with many inputs at once, and prefers multiprocessing	Development proceeds toward greater complexity and organization as children internalize experience.	Multisensory activities are offered and organized for both low and high order thinking, and connections are shown when introducing new information
A number of areas of the brain are simultaneously activated during a learning experience	Children are active learners, drawing on direct physical and social experience as well as culturally transmitted knowledge.	Field trips, activities, presentations from families, technology, and multicultural units are offered.
The brain changes physiologically as a result of experience, with new dendrites forming that hook new experiences to old ones.	Development occurs in a relatively orderly sequence, with later abilities and skills building on those already acquired.	Hands-on activities provide strong associations, and curriculum by theme or project aid in connected learning.
Each region of the brain is a sophisticated network of cells that interconnect one part of the brain to another.	Domains of children's development are closely related, with growth in one area influencing other domains.	Integrated curriculum allows for learning in many ways, and activities are presented using Gardner's multiple intelligences.
Each brain is unique, with differences from 2 to 3 year age span, and learning new knowledge or skills changes the gain structure.	Development proceeds at varying rates from child to child as well as unevenly within each child.	Choices allow children to select activities appropriate to their developmental level, mixed age groupings are encouraged, and individualized education plans are created.

FIGURE 4-17 Discoveries in neuroscience parallel the work described in developmentally appropriate practices and have clear application to early education activities. (Based on Rushton et al., 2009.)

Using Developmental and Learning Theories

As a teacher, you must think about what you believe about children, development, and learning. Theories, research, and key developmental topics are part of educational philosophy. Two critical questions arise: 1) How do I reconcile contradictions among the theories? and 2) How can I decide which is "right"?

To answer the first question, remember that each theory addresses a particular aspect of development. Psychodynamic theory focuses on the development of personality, behaviorist on the conditions of learning, cognitive on how children think and learn, maturation on how development progresses, and humanist on the

Connect the Dots: How Neuroscience Supports Theory and DAP

Neuroscience research is intertwined with basic principles of learning and appropriate practices of early childhood education. Rushton (2011) provides these four principles; we connect the dots to classroom practice, then ask you to do the same.

Principle #1: "Every brain is uniquely organized." . . . *Provide materials that match child skills at several levels.* For instance, alphabet awareness would call for writing materials in the art area, sandpaper letters in the library, sand trays with an alphabet chart in the sensory corner, and alphabet blocks in the block corner.

Principle #2: "The brain is continually growing, changing, and adapting to the environment." . . . *Provide a*

people-friendly environment. Children are welcomed with a smiling greeting, have familiar places for their belongings, are invited to help create classroom space, and have teachers who are responsive to their changing mood and energy.

Principle #3: "A brain-compatible classroom enables connection of learning to positive emotions." . . . *Give children reasonable choices.* Allowing children to make some decisions ("Do you want to brush you teeth first or set up your nap space?") and some choices ("What game shall we play at outside circle today?") leads to feelings of positive power and competence.

Principle #4: "Children's brains need to be immersed in real life,

hands-on, and meaningful learning experiences that are intertwined with a commonality and require some form of problem-solving." . . . *Set up time for small groups to get immersed in a topic without interruption.* If a child walks in with an interesting item, facilitate exploration and sharing instead of sending it to the cubby. Encourage children to elaborate—to you, to visitors, or anyone else who will listen—their explanations and critical thinking.

Questions
1. What play experiences encourage brain growth?
2. What hazards in a school day might be inappropriate to brain development?

conditions for overall health. Moreover, each topic has its avid proponents with a body of research that supports it. Because every theory and topic has its own focus and advocates, they are all rather subjective and somewhat narrow. In other words, no *one* theory tells us everything.

To address the second question, thoughtful teachers develop their own viewpoints. Begin to decide what you believe about children, learning, and education. Try to avoid the pitfall of taking sides. Instead, integrate theory into your teaching practices by comparing the major developmental and learning theories with your own daily experiences with young children.

Most early childhood educators are **eclectic** in their theoretical biases. That is, they have developed their own philosophies of education based on a little of each theory. Each teacher has an obligation to develop a clear set of ideas of how children grow and learn. We are fortunate to have choices (see Figure 4-18).

Basic Tenets

Most educators agree on some basic tenets based, in part, on theories of development and learning:

1. *Basic needs.* Children's basic physiologic needs and their needs for physical and psychological safety must be met satisfactorily before they can experience

and respond to "growth motives." [Humanist, Brain Development]

2. *Factors in development.* Children develop unevenly and not in a linear fashion as they grow toward psychosocial maturity and psychological well-being. A wide variety of factors in children's lives, as well as the manner in which they interpret their own experiences, has a bearing on the pattern and rate of progress toward greater social and emotional maturity. [Psychosocial, Behaviorist, Maturation, Ethnicity/Culture]

3. *Crises in Childhood.* Developmental crises that occur in the normal process of growing up may offer maximum opportunities for psychological growth, but these crises are also full of possibilities for regression or even negative adaptation. [Psychosocial, Cognitive, Ecological, Play, Moral Development]

4. *Striving for Mastery.* Children strive for mastery over their own private inner worlds as well as for mastery of the world outside of them. [Psychosocial, Cognitive, Multiple Intelligences, Play]

5. *Relationships and Interactions.* The child's interactions with significant persons in his life play a major part in his development. [Psychosocial, Behaviorist, Sociocultural, Humanist, Attachment, Gender Identity, Brain Development]

Summary of Major Theories

Theory	Major Theorists	Important Facts
Psychoanalytic	Sigmund Freud	Basic instinctual drives of sex, aggression, and destructiveness Stages of psychosexual development Personality structures of id, ego, and superego
Psychosocial	Erik Erikson	Maturational emphasis Stage theory of social and emotional development Crises at each level Teacher: Emotional base, social mediator
Behaviorist	John Watson Edward Thorndike B. F. Skinner Albert Bandura	Environmental emphasis Stimulus–response Conditioning (classical and operant) Reinforcement (positive and negative) Modeling Teacher: Arranger of environment and reinforcer of behavior
Cognitive	Jean Piaget	Maturational and environmental emphasis Assimilation and accommodation Stage theory of cognitive development Teacher: Provider of materials and time and supporter of children's unique ways of thinking
Sociocultural	Lev Vygotsky	Zone of proximal development Private speech Collaborative/assisted learning
Multiple intelligences	Howard Gardner	Many kinds of intelligence Problem-solving and product-creating
Maturation	Arnold Gesell	Emphasis on heredity Normative data Teacher: Guider of behavior based on what is typical and normal
Humanist	Abraham Maslow	Environmental emphasis Mental health model Hierarchy of human needs Teacher: Provider of basic and growth needs
Developmental topics	Mary Ainsworth John Bowlby Nancy Eisenberg Carol Gilligan Lawrence Kohlberg Eleanor Maccoby	Attachment and categories research Attachment theory Expands moral development to prosocial Questions categories of moral development Moral, cognitive, and sex-role development Sex differences research
Brain development	Bruce Perry Daniel Siegel Stephen Rushton Ellen Galinsky Ross Thompson	New insights into early development "Use it or lose it" principle DAP and brain-based research connections Life skills and brain development Parallels between all domains and brain growth

© Cengage Learning 2011

FIGURE 4-18 Major theories include the "most excellent eight" and several key developmental topics, including brain development.

Developmental Research Conclusions

Research, and the information it yields, must serve the needs of the practitioner to be useful. Teachers can combine researchers' systematic data with personal observations and experiences, including the significance of relationships, language and thinking, biologic factors, and special needs (see Chapter 6). To keep in mind the real child underneath all these theories, teachers apply developmental research to their own classroom settings. "Theories of child development can serve as guides for assessing the developmental levels of any children. They can help us know what children's

One of the conclusions of research and theory is that children's interactions with significant people in their lives play a major role in development.

competencies are and where we should begin instruction. Theories of development can serve as guides for planning instruction for individuals and for groups" (Charlesworth, 2011). Figure 4-19 consolidates what developmental research has found and how it can be put into practical use with young children.

There is so much information now about children and their development. It is easy to feel overwhelmed, and easier still to believe what we read. Santrock (2009) advises us:

- Be cautious about what is reported in the popular media.
- Do not assume that group research applies to an individual.
- Do not generalize about a small or clinical sample.
- Do not take a single study as the defining word.
- Do not accept causal conclusions from correlational studies.
- Always consider the source of the information and evaluate its credibility.

Conditions for Learning

Caring for children means providing for total growth, creating optimal conditions for learning in the best possible environment. Developmental theory helps define conditions that enhance learning and from which positive learning environments are created. Research on all theories extends the knowledge of children and learning. Coupled with practical application, both theory and research have helped all to recognize that:

1. *Learning must be real.* We teach about the children's bodies, their families, their neighborhoods, and their school. We start with who children are and expand this to include the world, in their terms. We give them the words, the ideas, and the ways to question and figure things out for themselves.

2. *Learning must be rewarding.* Practice makes better, but only if it is all right to practice and to stumble and try again. We include the time to do all this by providing an atmosphere of acceptance and of immediate feedback as to what was accomplished (even what boundary was just overstepped). Also, practice can make a good experience even better, as it reminds children in their terms of what they can do.

3. *Learning must build on children's lives.* We help connect the family to the child and the teacher. We realize that children learn about culture from family and knowledgeable members of the community, such as teachers, librarians, grocers, and the like. We know important family events and help the family support happenings at school. For children, learning goes on wherever they may be, awake and asleep. Parents can learn to value learning and help it happen for their child.

4. *Learning needs a good stage.* Healthy bodies make for alert minds, so good education means caring for children's health. This includes physical, emotional, and mental health. Psychological safety and well-being are theoretical terms for the insight, availability, and awareness teachers bring to their classrooms. On the lookout for each child's successes, we prevent distractions in the way furniture is arranged, how noisy it is, and how many strangers are around. Mental health is both emotional and intellectual. We try to have a variety of materials and experiences, and a flexible schedule when someone is pursuing an idea, building a project, or finishing a disagreement.

As long as we care for children, we will have our hands full. With the theoretical underpinnings presented here, we have the tools with which to make our own way into the world of children and of early childhood education.

Developmental Research Tells Us	Teachers Can
1. Growth occurs in a sequence.	Think about the steps children will take when planning projects. Know the sequence of growth in their children's age group.
2. Children in any age group will behave similarly in certain ways.	Plan for activities in relation to age range of children. Know the characteristics of their children's age group.
3. Children grow through certain stages.	Know the stages of growth in their class. Let family know of any behavior that is inconsistent with general stages of development.
4. Growth occurs in four interrelated areas.	Understand that work in one area can help in another.
5. Intellectual growth: Children learn through their senses. Children learn by doing and need concrete experiences.	Have activities in looking, smelling, tasting, hearing, and touching. Realize that talking is abstract; have children touch.
Cognitive growth happens in four areas: Perception (visual, auditory, etc.)	Provide materials and activities in matching, finding same/different, putting a picture with a sound, taste, or with a symbol. Provide opportunities to find and label things, talk with grown-ups, friends, tell what it "looks like," smells like, etc.
Language Memory	Know that memory is helped by seeing, holding objects, and people. Recognize that reasoning ability is just beginning, so children judge on what they see rather than what you may want them to realize.
Reasoning	Be sure adult explanations aid in understanding reasons. Practice finding "answers" to open-ended questions such as "How can you tell when you are tired?"
6. Social growth: The world is only from the child's viewpoint.	Expect that children will think of only their own ideas at first. Be aware that the rights of others are minimal to them.
Seeing is believing.	Remember that if they cannot see the situation, they may not be able to talk about it.
Group play is developing.	Provide free-play sessions, with places to play socially. Understand that group play in structured situations is difficult because of "self" orientation.
Independence increases as competence grows.	Know that children test to see how far they can go. Realize that children will vary from independent to dependent (both among the group and within one child).
People are born not knowing when it is safe to go on.	Understand that children will need to learn by trial and error.
Adult attention is very important. Young children are not born with an internal mechanism that says "slow down."	Know the children individually. Move into a situation before children lose control.
7. Emotional growth: Self-image is developing.	Be alert for each child's self-image that may be developing. Give praise to enhance good feelings about oneself. Know that giving children responsibilities helps self-image. Talk to children at eye level. Children learn by example. Model appropriate behavior by doing yourself what you want the children to do.
8. Physical growth: Muscle development is not complete. Muscles cannot stay still for long. Large muscles are better developed than small ones. Hand preference is being established.	Do not expect perfection, in either small- or large-muscle activity. Plan short times for children to sit. Give lots of chances to move about; be gentle with expectations for hand work. Watch to see how children decide their handedness. Let children trade hands in their play.
A skill must be done several times before it is internalized. Bowel and bladder control is not completely internalized.	Have materials available to be used often. Plan projects to use the same skill over and over. Be understanding of "accidents." If possible, have toilet facilities available always, and keep them attractive.

FIGURE 4-19 Developmental research tests theories of growth and learning to find out about children and childhood.

Put Those Theories to Work!

Decision making in teaching can be difficult. Can theory help us?

It is 10 AM at the infant-toddler center. Fifteen-month-olds Kenya and Peter are crying and fussy this morning. Neither has eaten since breakfast. They have been indoors all morning.

Theory: *Maturation theory.* Children's physical developmental needs affect their emotional states.

Plan: Schedule regular times for active movement. Be sure to offer food and watch for signs of hunger.

Mario and Therese, both in wheelchairs, joined the first grade last month, but their parents report that neither wants to come to school. Their academic work is at grade level, but they participate very little. They seem familiar with their teacher.

Theory: *Sociocultural theory.* Children need to feel part of the class culture in order to learn well.

Theory: *Psychosocial theory.* The children can identify with the teacher and become successful but may feel incompetent with unfriendly or indifferent classmates.

Theory: *Cognitive theory.* They can understand other points of view as long as it is in real situations.

Plan: Put each child in a small group to design and build wheel toys for pets. Building on the newcomers' expertise in a cooperative activity gives all the children the scaffolding needed to be successful and helps the new children become accepted into the class.

Preschoolers Jared and Panya have been arguing about who has brought the "best" toy to child care. Others have heard the ruckus and have stopped to watch the two start a fight.

Theory: *Cognitive theory.* Their egocentric thinking prevents them from seeing any view other than their own.

Also, they are unable to hold two ideas at the same time, so they cannot see that both toys are "good."

Theory: *Behaviorist theory.* The children can learn from watching others and applying other's example to their own behavior.

Plan: The teacher engages the children in a conflict resolution method that gets all children to express their own ideas, both about the problem and for some solutions, so they can practice hearing another's ideas while still holding their own. The teacher models praising each child's positive characteristics in the other's presence, showing other ways to behave appropriately and how the children and their toys can play together.

Think About This
1. How can theory illuminate what is going on with a child or in a center?
2. Which theories make the most sense to you—and why?

Summary

LO1 Developmental and learning theories form the cornerstone of our knowledge about children. The eight major theoretical perspectives that relate to child development and learning are psychodynamic, behaviorist, cognitive, sociocultural, ecological, multiple intelligences, maturation, and humanist.

LO2 The central developmental topics of ethnicity and culture, attachment, play, gender, moral development, and brain development are vehicles for creating developmentally appropriate practices. Each offers new vistas of possibility and better teaching and learning.

LO3 Developmental and learning theories explain much of children's growth and development. There are several basic tenets in early childhood education that connect with the theories and topics. Developmental research offers useful conclusions that outline conditions for learning. By consistently applying the insights from research and theory, we show our willingness to make a commitment to children.

Key Terms

theory	positive reinforcement	maturation
hypothesis	negative reinforcement	maturation theory
nature/nurture controversy	punishment	humanist theory
psychodynamic theory	cognitive theory	self-actualization
unconscious	assimilation	basic needs (deficiency needs)
psychosocial	accommodation	growth needs
identity crisis	equilibration	attachment
autonomy	schemas	spontaneous play
behaviorist theory	sensorimotor	superhero
stimulus–response	transmission model	sociodramatic play
reinforcement	constructivism	sex differences
socialization	transactional model	gender differences
social learning theory	egocentric	gender identity
modeling	sociocultural	gender role
self-efficacy	zone of proximal development	prosocial
observational learning	(ZPD)	synapses
classical conditioning	scaffolding	dendrites
phobia	private (inner) speech	cortisol
operant conditioning	bicognitive development	myelination
reinforcers	multiple intelligences	eclectic

Review Questions

1. Match the theorist with the appropriate description:

B.F. Skinner	Ecological theory
Abraham Maslow	Multiple intelligences
Jean Piaget	Sex differences
Albert Bandura	Attachment
Mary Ainsworth	Social learning
Eleanor Maccoby	Zone of proximal development
Erik Erikson	Psychosocial development
Arnold Gesell	Behaviorism
Lev Vygotsky	Developmental norms
Howard Gardner	Cognitive theory
Uric Bronfenbrenner	Self-actualization

2. Describe in a sentence each of the major developmental topics and its connection to early childhood education.
   Ethnicity and culture
   Attachment
   Play
   Gender
   Moral development
   Brain development

3. "Using developmental and learning theories, teachers create developmentally appropriate practice in their programs." Explain this concept and give three specific examples.

Observe and Apply

1. You are a teacher in a large urban child care center. Your preschool children arrive by 7:00 AM and usually stay until after 5:00 PM each day. What would you do first thing in the morning? Use Maslow's hierarchy of needs to justify your answer. What do you know about your group's development? Use Piaget's cognitive stages to build your answer. What assumptions, if any, can you make about their cultural background? How do you find out about what each child is ready to learn?

2. What do you think of the influence of television on children's behavior? Consider the typical cartoons that the children you know are watching. From a behaviorist perspective, what are they learning? With sociocultural theory in mind, what else would you have them watch or do?

3. Observe children in a center as they say good-bye and then start their day. What can your observations tell you about their attachment levels? What can teachers do to support attachment and also help children separate? What is the difference in play when 1) a teacher interacts with children in their play and 2) a teacher is not involved? What are your conclusions?

Helpful Websites

Alliance for Childhood
   www.allianceforchildhood.org

American Educational Research Association
   www.area.net

ERIC (Educational Resources Information Center)
   www.eric.ed.gov

Early Childhood Research Quarterly
   www.naeyc.org/publications/ecrq

Gesell Institute   **www.gesellinstitute.org**

National Association for the Education of Young
   Children   **www.naeyc.org**

National Institute for Early Education Research
   www.nieer.org

Society for Research in Child Development
   www.srcd.org

◎ The Education CourseMate website for this text offers many helpful resources and interactive study tools. Go to CengageBrain.com to access the TeachSource Videos, flashcards, tutorial quizzes, direct links to all of the websites mentioned in the chapter, downloadable forms, and more.

References

General Texts

Berger, K. S. (2012). *The developing person* (9th Ed). New York: Worth.

Berk, L. (2011). *Infants and children* (7th Ed). Boston: Allyn & Bacon.

Charlesworth, R. (2011). Developmental theory: The foundation of developmentally appropriate practice. In A. M. Gordon & K. M. Browne, *Beginnings & Beyond* (8th Ed). Belmont, CA: Wadsworth/Cengage.

Santrock, J. W. (2009). *Children* (11th Ed). Boston, MA: McGraw Hill.

Psychodynamic Theory

Erikson, E. H. (1963). *Childhood and society* (2nd Ed). New York: Norton.

Erikson, E. H. (1964). Toys and reasons. In M. R. Haworth (Ed.), *Child psychotherapy: Practice and theory*. New York: Basic Books.

Erikson, E. H. (1969). A healthy personality for every child. In P. H. Mussen, J. J. Conger, & J. Kagan (Eds.), *Child development and personality* (3rd Ed). New York: Harper & Row.

Erikson, E. H. (1969). *Gandhi's truth*. New York: W.W. Norton & Company.

Freud, S., & Hall, G. Stanley. (1920). *A general introduction to psychoanalysis*. New York: Boni & Liveright.

Spitz, R. A., & Wolf, K. M. (1946). Analytic depression: An inquiry into the genesis of psychiatric conditions in early childhood, II. In A. Freud, et al. (Eds.), *The psychoanalytic study of the child (Vol. II)*. New York: International Universities Press.

Behaviorist Theory

Bandura, A. (1963). Imitation of film-mediated aggressive models. *Journal of Abnormal and Social Psychology*.

Bandura, A., Barbaranelli, C., Vittorio Caprara, G., & Pastorelli, C. (2001). Self-efficacy beliefs as shapers of children's aspirations and career trajectories. *Child Development*, 72(1), pp. 187–206.

Kohn, A. (2006). *Unconditional Parenting: Moving from Rewards & Punishments to Love & Reason*. New York: Atria Books/Simon & Schuster.

Skinner, B. F. (1953). *Science and human behavior*. New York, NY: MacMillan Co.

Cognitive Theory

Elkind, D. (1977). Giant in the nursery school—Jean Piaget. In E. M. Hetherington & R. D. Parke (Eds.), *Contemporary readings in psychology*. New York: McGraw-Hill.

Elkind, D., & Flavell, J. (Eds.). (1996). *Essays in honor of Jean Piaget*. New York: Oxford University Press.

Ginsburg, H. & Opper, S. (1987). *Piaget's theory of intellectual development*. New York: Prentice Hall.

Kohn, A. (2006). *Unconditional parenting.* New York: Atria Books/Simon & Schuster.

Piaget, J., & Inhelder, B. (1972). *The psychology of the child* (2nd Ed). New York: Basic Books.

Sociocultural Theory

Berk, L. (2000). Vygotsky's sociocultural theory. In A. Gordon & K. W. Browne, *Beginnings and beyond* (5th Ed). Clifton Park, NY: Thomson Delmar Learning.

Fouad, N. A., & Arredondo, P. (Eds). (2007). *Becoming culturally oriented: Practical advice for psychologists and educators.* Washington, D.C.: American Psychological Association.

Rogoff, B. (1990). *Apprenticeship in thinking: Cognitive development in a social context.* New York: Oxford University Press.

Vygotsky, L. S. (1978). *Mind in society: The development of higher psychological processes.* Cambridge, MA: Harvard University Press.

York, S. (2005). *Roots and wings: Affirming culture in early childhood programs.* St. Paul, MN: Redleaf Press.

Ecological Theory

Berger, K. S. (2011). *The developing person* (9th Ed). New York: Worth.

Bronfenbrenner, U. (2000). Ecological system theory. In A. Kazdin (Ed.), *Encyclopedia of Psychology.* Washington, D.C.: American Psychological Association and Oxford Press.

Bronfenbrenner, U. (1979). *The ecology of human development: Experiments by nature and design.* Cambridge, MA: Harvard University Press.

Multiple Intelligences Theory

Gardner, H. (1983). *Frames of mind.* New York: Basic Books.

Gardner, H. (1993). *Multiple intelligences.* New York: Basic Books.

Gardner, H., Gridman, D. H., Krechevsky, M., & Chen J-Q. (1998). *Project Zero frameworks for early childhood education* (Vol. 1–3). New York: Teachers College Press.

Gardner, H. (2000). *Intelligence reframed: Multiple intelligences for the 21st century.* New York: Basic Books.

Maturation Theory

Ames, L. B., & Ilg, F. (1979). *The Gesell Institute's child from one to six; The Gesell Institute's child from five to ten; The infant in today's culture.* New York: Harper & Row.

Gesell, A. (1940). *The first five years of life.* New York: Harper & Row.

Humanist Theory

Goble, F. G. (1970). *The third force: The psychology of Abraham Maslow.* New York: Grossman.

Maslow, A. H. (1954). *Motivation and personality.* New York: Harper & Row.

Developmental Topics

Ethnicity and Cultural Diversity

Caldwell, B. (1983). *Child development and cultural diversity.* Geneva, Switzerland: OMEP World Assembly.

Lawrence-Lightfoot, S. (2004). *The essential connection: What parents and teachers can learn from each other.* New York: Ballantine Books.

Markus, H., in Vaughan, L. J. Culture as sculptor: Markus explores 'Models of Self.' Stanford University, *The Bing Times,* November, 2005.

New, R. R., & Beneke, M. (2009). Negotiating diversity in early childhood education: Rethinking notions of expertise. In Fenney, S., Galper, A., & Seefeldt, C. (Eds.) *Continuing issues in early childhood education* (3rd Ed). Columbus, OH: Merrill/Pearson.

Phinney, J. S. & Alipuria, L. I. (2006). Multiple social categorization and identity among multiracial, multiethnic, and multicultural individuals. In R. J. Crisp & M. Hewstone (Eds.), *Multiple social categorization: Process, models, and applications.* New York: Psychology Press.

Rogoff, B. (2003). *The cultural nature of human development.* New York: Oxford University Press.

Attachment

Ainsworth, M. (1979, October). Infant-mother attachment. *American Psychologist,* pp. 131–142.

Bowlby, J. (1969, 1973). *Attachment and loss (Vols. I and II).* New York: Basic Books.

Saxton, R. (2001). *Personal communication.*

White, Burton L. (1995). *The new first three years, revised.* NY: Fireside Publications.

Play

American Academy of Pediatrics: Ginsberg, K.R., Committee on Communications, and Committee on Psychosocial Aspects of Child & Family Health. (2007). Clinical report: The importance of play in promoting healthy child development. http://www.aap.org/pressroom/playFINAL.pdf.

Elkind, D. (2010). Play. In V. Washington & J. D. Andrews (Eds.). *Children of 2020: Creating a better tomorrow*. Washington, D.C: Council for Professional Recognition.

Frost, J. L., Wortham, S. C., & Reifel, S. (2011). *Play and child development* (4th Ed). Upper Saddle River, NJ: Prentice Hall.

Hoffman, E. (2004). *Magic capes, amazing powers: Transforming play in the classroom*. St. Paul, MN: Redleaf Press.

Parten, M. B. (1932). Social participation among preschool children. *Journal of Abnormal and Social Psychology*, 27, pp. 243–269.

Gender

Eisenberg, N., Martin, C. L., & Fabes, R. A. (1996). Gender development and gender effects. In D.C. Berliner & R.C. Calfee (Eds.), *Handbook of educational psychology*. New York: Macmillan.

Maccoby, E. E. (1998). *The two sexes*. Cambridge, MA: Harvard University Press.

Maccoby, E. E. & Jacklin, C. N. (1974). *The psychology of sex differences*. Stanford, CA: Stanford University Press.

Martin, C. L. & Ruble, D. (2006). Children's search for gender cues: Cognitive perspectives on gender development. *Current Directions in Psychological Science*, 13(2), pp. 67–70.

Ruble, D. N., Martin, C. I., & Berenbaum, S. A. (2006). Gender development. In N. Eisenberg, W. Damon, & R. M. Lerner (Eds.) *Handbook of child psychology, Vol 3. Social, emotional, and personality development*. Hoboken, NJ: Wiley.

Wardle, F. (2004). The challenge of boys in our early childhood programs. *Early Childhood News* (January-February, 2004).

Moral Development

Buzzelli, C. & Johnston, B. (2002). *The moral dimensions of teaching: Language, power, and culture in classroom interaction*. London: Routledge.

Eisenberg, N., Lenon, R., & Roth, K. (1983). Prosocial development in middle childhood: A longitudinal study. *Developmental Psychology*, 23, pp. 712–718.

Eisenberg, N. (1992). *The caring child*. Boston, MA: Harvard University Press.

Gilligan, C. (1982). *In a different voice*. Cambridge, MA: Harvard University Press.

Gilligan, C. (2011). *Joining the resistance*. Boston: Polity/Wiley & Sons.

Kohlberg, L. (1981). *The philosophy of moral development*. New York: Harper & Row.

Piaget, J. (1965). *The moral judgment of the child*. NY: Free Press.

Brain-Based Research

Copple, C., & Bredekamp, S. (Eds.) (2009). *Developmentally appropriate practice in early childhood programs serving children from birth through age 8* (3rd Ed). Washington, D.C.: National Association for the Education of Young Children.

Galinsky, E. (2010). *Mind in the making*. Washington, D.C.: National Association for the Education of Young Children.

Gallagher, K. (2005). Brain research and early childhood development: A primer for developmentally appropriate practices. *Young Children*, 60(4), pp. 12–20.

Miller, B. & Cummings, J. (Eds.) (2007). *The human frontal lobes*. New York: Guilford Press.

Rushton, S. (2011). Neuroscience, early childhood education and play: We are doing it right! *Early Childhood Education Journal*, 39, pp. 89–94.

Rushton, S., Joula-Rushton, A., & Larkin, E. (2010). Neuroscience, play and early childhood education: Connections, implications and assessment. *Early Childhood Education Journal*, 37, pp. 351–361.

Shonkoff, J. P., et al. (2008). The timing and quality of early experiences combine to shape brain architecture: working paper 5. Cambridge, MA: Harvard University Center on the Developing Child.

Thompson, R. A. (Spring-Summer 2001). Development in the first years of life. *The Future of Children, Vol. 11, No. 1, Caring for Infants and Toddlers*, pp. 20–33.

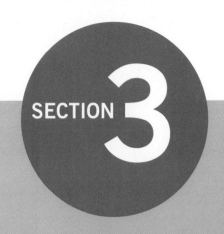

Who Are the Teachers?

© Cengage Learning

© Cengage Learning

5

Teaching: A Professional Commitment

Learning Objectives

LO1 Understand the roles and responsibilities of today's early childhood teachers with regard to diversity and personal attributes.

LO2 Define the essential attributes of becoming a professional teacher, including professional preparation standards and upholding ethical standards of behavior.

LO3 Demonstrate collaboration skills for team teaching interactions and proficiency in positive team relationships.

LO4 Understand how assessments relate to best teaching practices and professional development.

LO5 Demonstrate knowledge of the importance of field experience and articulate the value of supervised teaching.

naeyc Standards For Professional Development

The following NAEYC Standards for Initial and Advanced Early Childhood Professional Preparation are addressed in this chapter:

Standard 1 Promoting Child Development and Learning

Standard 2 Building Family and Community Relationships

Standard 3 Observing, Documenting, and Assessing to Support Young Children and Families

Standard 4 Using Developmentally Effective Approaches to Connect With Children and Families

Standard 5 Using Content Knowledge to Build Meaningful Curriculum

Standard 6 Becoming a Professional

Field Experience

naeyc Code of Ethical Conduct

These are the sections of the NAEYC Code of Ethical Conduct that apply to the topics of this chapter:

A. Responsibility to coworkers

Ideals:

I-3A.1 To establish and maintain relationships of respect, trust, confidentiality, collaboration, and cooperation with coworkers.

I-3A.2 To share resources with coworkers, collaborating to ensure that the best possible early childhood care and education program is provided.

I-3A.3 To support coworkers in meeting their professional needs and in their professional development.

I-3A.4 To accord coworkers due recognition of professional achievements.

B. Responsibilities to employers

Ideals:

I-3B.1 To assist the program in providing the highest quality of service.

I-3B.2 To do nothing that diminishes the reputation of the program in which we work, unless it is violating laws and regulations designed to protect children or is violating the provisions of this Code.

Principles:

P-3B.1 We shall follow all program policies. When we do not agree with program policies, we shall attempt to effect change through constructive action within the organization.

P-3B.2: We shall speak or act on behalf of an organization only when authorized. We shall take care to acknowledge when we are speaking for the organization and when we are expressing a personal judgment.

P-3B. 4: If we have concerns about a colleague's behavior, and children's well-being is not at risk, we may address the concern with that individual. If children are at risk or the situation does not improve after it has been brought to the colleague's attention, we shall report the colleague's unethical or incompetent behavior to an appropriate authority.

Today's Early Childhood Teachers

Margarita always wanted to be an early childhood teacher, and after high school she went to a community college and earned her Associate in Arts (A.A.) degree. Shortly after her first child was born, she became a licensed family child care provider, and she now cares for infants and toddlers in her own home. It is important to Margarita that she feels she is making a contribution to the family's well-being, as well as enjoying a satisfying career. She hopes to pursue a bachelor's degree in the future.

Paul has a bachelor's degree in special education and spent several years teaching in a school for children with severe developmental delays. He is now a lead teacher for 4-year-olds at the child care center, where he is gaining experience with children whose developmental patterns are typical. Paul wants to remain a teacher but is concerned about the salary levels. He has given himself one more year before he makes a decision to stay or leave the field.

Ginger, a former kindergarten teacher, participated in a parent cooperative nursery school with her three children. She is now the director of a parent co-op where children range from ages 2 to 5. She particularly enjoys leading weekly parent discussion groups.

Elva was the most sought-after parent aide in the city's preschool program. This success stimulated her to get an A.A. degree in early childhood education, then a bachelor's degree in child development. She is now a certified second grade teacher in a bilingual program and is working on her Master's degree.

These teachers had different motivations, yet they all were drawn to the early childhood classroom. They teach in different settings and have different interests. What they share is a commitment to teaching young children and knowing that the work they do is important.

Meeting together helps teachers maintain quality in their programs and reinforces their professional roles and responsibilities.

Comparison with Teaching in Other Educational Settings

The nature of teaching in the early years is unlike that of other age groups. At first glance, the differences in teaching preschool and older children may outweigh any similarities. Common elements, however, link the two:

- Early childhood teachers teach what other teachers teach. The curriculum in the early years is rich in math, science, social studies, history, language, art, and geography, as it is in any other grade.
- Early childhood teachers and their elementary and high school counterparts share many of the frustrations of the teaching profession—long hours, low pay, and a people-intensive workplace.
- They also share the joy of teaching—the opportunity to influence children's lives and the satisfaction of meeting the daily challenges that teaching children provides.

Figure 5-1 highlights the similarities and differences between early childhood teachers and others.

DIVERSITY

Teacher Diversity

According to the U.S. Bureau of Labor Statistics (2010), the following percentages represent the racial and ethnic diversity among early childhood teachers.

Teaching Level	White	Black	Asian	Hispanic/Latino
Child Care Worker	78.3	16.0	3.4	19.1
Preschool and Kindergarten	82.7	13.4	2.7	9.6
Elementary and Middle School	86.7	9.3	2.4	7.3
Special Education Teachers	89.4	6.8	2.0	6.2
Teacher Assistants	81.5	12.7	2.9	15.1
Racial Diversity of Children in the United States (ChildStats, 2011)	54.0	14.0	4.0	23.0

On the surface it appears that most ethnic groups are equitably represented between the teaching and student populations. The one obvious exception is among the Hispanic/Latino teachers and children, particularly in preschools, kindergarten, elementary and middle schools, special education, and teaching assistants. A less obvious exception is among the Asian teaching population. The percentage of Asians teachers is in close alignment with the racial diversity of Asian children, however, a longitudinal study in three California communities from 1994 to 2000 (Whitebrook, et al., 2001) noted that while 50 percent of the classrooms in the study had Chinese-speaking children, only 7 percent had a staff member who spoke Cantonese or Mandarin. Forty-four percent of the classrooms had Spanish-speaking children, yet only half were staffed by Spanish-speaking teachers or caregivers. Parents in these programs reported difficulty in communicating with the staff because of language barriers. This raises the question of how the early childhood field is upholding the Code of Ethical Conduct in their approach to diversity in hiring practices and employment opportunities. The ability of the teaching staff to communicate with the full spectrum of ethnic, cultural, and linguistic backgrounds is a serious issue for today's teachers.

The Early Childhood Teacher's Roles: Professionalism in Action

The variety of roles early childhood teachers perform has been described in many ways:

Storyteller	Traffic director	Conflict mediator
Custodian	File clerk	Mediator
Carpenter	Poet	Plumber
Adult educator	Parent	Musician
Purchasing agent	Resource	Faculty member
Staff supervisor	Nurse	Program planner
Personnel	Business manager	Treasurer
Director	Employee	Employer
Psychologist	Sociologist	Scientist

This diversity is what makes teaching in the early years so appealing. The multiple roles a teacher plays add challenge to the job and underscore the importance of teachers who are well grounded in developmental and learning theory. Knowledge and experience enhances the teacher's ability to think on their feet as they collaborate and interact with children during the intense activity of the classroom. Collaboration reinforces the notion underlying many definitions that teachers are, first and foremost, lifelong learners. The teacher as collaborator is a significant part of the definition of the teacher's role in the schools of Reggio Emilia, Italy (see Chapter 10).

Let's look at the larger role of the early childhood teacher in and out of the classroom.

Interacting with Children

Teacher–child interactions, the spur-of-the-moment crises, the on-the-spot decisions, the caring and nurturing bring both satisfaction and challenges. Helping Rhonda separate from her grandmother, soothing Josh and Benno after they bump heads, and talking with Alexa about her science project are examples of what is at the heart of teaching young children. These encounters help to establish good relationships with the children. It is during these spontaneous, anything-can-happen-and-probably-will times that teachers display their craftsmanship and professionalism.

Early Childhood Teachers: Differences and Similarities

Elements of Teaching and Learning	Early Childhood Settings	Elementary and High School Settings
How teaching and learning occur	Through teacher–child interactions and concrete use of materials	Through lectures and demonstrations that are often teacher dominated
	Guides children toward discovery	Teaches subject matter
Play opportunities	Primary learning medium is play	Usually just at recess
Opportunity for child to make choices	Many choices throughout the day both inside and outside	Few options—all students do same activity most of the day
Classroom environment	Abundant floor space, many activity centers, variety of materials for play	Rows of desks and tables
Daily schedule	Large blocks of time for unlimited exploration of materials and for play	45-minute to 1-hour periods on subject matter
Small group interactions	Majority of teaching	Much less frequent
Large group interactions	Few times a day	Majority of teaching
Outdoor activity	Teachers involved as intensively as they are in the classroom	Others usually supervise play yard—little direct teacher interaction
Parent relationships	Frequent, if not daily, contact	May see them once a year as child grows older
Working with other adults	Often works with aide, assistant teachers, and parents	Usually teaches alone or with part-time aide
Educational materials	Toys, games, natural materials, blocks	Textbooks and worksheets
Evaluating students	Observational and anecdotal assessments, portfolios	Grades, tests, and report cards
	Emphasis on growth of whole child	Standardized academic assessment
Age range of students	May have two- to two-and-a-half-year age span or greater	Usually same age
Art, music, and physical education	Available throughout the day as an ongoing part of curriculum	Restricted to a special class, time, or teacher
Teacher training	Strong child development foundation	Emphasis on subject matter

© Cengage Learning 2011

FIGURE 5-1 The nature of teaching in the early years is unlike that of other age groups.

The art of teaching comes alive on the floor of the classroom. Teachers intuitively use their knowledge base, experience, and proven techniques as they reach back in their minds for all those things they know about children. Throughout the school day they apply that combination of knowledge and know-how. Good classroom management is dependent on how teachers spend their time away from the children and give added depth and strength to the program after children leave.

Managing the Classroom

Being a classroom manager is a little like being a juggler. Both require the ability to think about and react to more than three things at once. With a simple gesture, a significant look, or merely moving nearby, the teacher maintains the ongoing activity.

Anticipating a clash between Nathan and Julie, the teacher, Miriam, intervenes, redirects them, and moves away. At the same time, she has kept a watchful eye on Bobby at the bathroom sink. Passing close to Francie, she touches the child's shoulder in brief acknowledgment, smiling down as Francie struggles with her story writing. Miguel and Lea run up to her, grab her by the skirt and hand, and pull her toward the science display. They need to ask her something about the snake . . . *now!* Jake, the handyman, has come into the classroom wanting to know exactly which of the climbers needs repair. Sarah, the parent volunteer, waves to Miriam: It's time to check on the corn bread baking in the kitchen. Miriam files a mental note of the names of the children who accompany Sarah to the kitchen. As she reaches for a copy of *Ranger Rick* (the book with the great snake pictures in it), she

Teachers model learning, listening, and loving.

observes Angie and her father entering the room. They both look upset. Telling Miguel and Lea she will return, Miriam walks over to greet the latecomers. As she moves past Doug, the student teacher, she comments on how well his language game is going and suggests he continue for another five minutes. Glancing at the clock, she realizes it is almost cleanup time. Assistant teacher Cheryl watches Miriam and a nonverbal signal passes between them. Without a word, they both understand that snacks will be a little late today. Angie's father begins to explain their delay as Miriam bends down to invite the child to come and look at the new snake cage with her.

In this setting, the teacher's role is to supervise a number of people, all of whom add to the richness of a program. But it is Miriam who coordinates and supervises their various functions. Her role as a supervisor and manager includes:

- Caretaker for a safe environment
- Observer of and listener to children
- On-the-spot teacher trainer for students, aides, and volunteers

- On-site supervisor for student teachers
- Liaison and communicator with parents

Setting the Tone

From the moment the teacher steps into the classroom, she sets the **emotional framework**. The use of body language, tone of voice, facial expressions, and verbal and nonverbal communication set the tone for teaching and learning.

Children are sensitive to adult moods and attitudes. When you exude calm and confidence, strength and support, the result is a more relaxed, comfortable atmosphere. When the mood is tense, the tone of the classroom is as well. When you believe that children deserve respect and are intelligent, capable human beings, the learning atmosphere is lively and supportive.

Tantrums, crying, resistance, curiosity, impatience, emotional swings, noise, and self-centeredness are typical behaviors in the early years as children strive to achieve a sense of their separate self. The atmosphere that a teacher creates in the classroom is a key element in helping them through that process.

Planning and Evaluating Curriculum

As teachers move through the school day interacting with children, managing the classroom, and sensing the tone, they consciously or unconsciously evaluate what is happening:

- The relay race outdoors produced more tears than cheers; most of the children were interested in participating when the game started but drifted away. Why?
- The clay was not used today. How can we make this a more inviting activity?
- The toddlers are beginning to participate fully in the "Eensy Weensy Spider" finger play. What might they like to learn next?
- Several children have asked about Sasha's accent. When would be a good time to have him teach the class a few words in Russian?

The teacher notes where and how children played, the quality of their interactions, and possible "next steps" in curriculum. These observations are discussed with other staff members at the end of the day or in weekly planning sessions. This process has its roots in constructivist theory: teachers watching and observing children to give meaning and support to their learning. Early childhood teachers use their observation skills, collect data as they work with children, and build emergent curriculum around their knowledge of actual classroom practice and behavior. Effective ways to develop curriculum planning are further discussed in Chapter 10.

© Cengage Learning

Staying the Course/Shaping Young Minds

Developmentally appropriate practices (DAP) are the basis for high quality early education programs. We know that children are active learners who enjoy hands-on experiences and who learn best in environments that provide opportunities, choices, and challenges for growth. We base our teaching on sound child developmental theory and principles. We recognize that play is fundamental to children's learning. But are our basic tenets compatible with brain research findings?

Several researchers have linked some of the defining elements of DAP with neuroscience in a way that demonstrates the compatibility of what we believe to be best practices and what brain research tells us about how learning takes place. What follows is NAEYC's position statements on DAP and brain research principles (Rushton et al., 2010), with our added applications for classroom use.

1. DAP: Development in one domain influences and is influenced by development in other domains.

    Brain-Based Research: Each region of the brain consists of a highly sophisticated neurological network that interconnects one portion of the brain to another.

    Classroom Applications: Use integrated curriculum to allow for individual differences; make use of the five senses and Gardner's multiple intelligences as much as possible.

2. DAP: Development proceeds at varying rates in each child as well as unevenly within different areas of each child's functioning.

    Brain-Based Research: Each brain is unique; learning new skills and knowledge changes the brain's structure; a spread in differences up to 2 or 3 years is normal in a developing brain.

    Classroom Applications: Give children choices that meet their developmental needs; make time for discussion, movement, and active learning; encourage mixed-age groups or looping.

3. DAP: Optimal periods exist for certain types of development and learning.

    Brain-Based Research: "Windows of opportunity" exist in the brain and the brain's plasticity allows for greater information to be processed and stored.

    Classroom Applications: Repeated experiences in various activity centers help develop problem-solving skills and long-term memory: large blocks of time give children time to absorb both new and familiar information; class and group discussions allow children to interact with each other on a regular basis.

4. DAP: Children are active learners, drawing on direct physical and social experience as well as culturally transmitted knowledge to construct their understanding of the world.

    Brain-Based Research: Learning does not take place as separate and isolated events in the brain.

    Classroom Applications: Learning environments must include opportunities for children to interact with diverse people of all ages and cultures; field trips, guest speakers, and multicultural curriculum help children better understand society and themselves.

Questions

1. What other elements of DAP reflect what you know about brain research?
2. How important do you think brain-based research is? Why?
3. How does this information linking DAP with brain research help you respond to those who promote a more academic structure to young children's learning?

Record Keeping

The type and variety of records vary from program to program. Report writing and record keeping are essential to any good early childhood program. Record keeping is based on a number of factors:

- *The purpose for which the records are used.* In programs that rely on government funding, record keeping is not optional. Children's progress, teacher's performance, and the program itself must be evaluated on a regular basis to ensure continued funding.
- *The philosophy of the school.* In many programs, but especially in laboratory schools and teacher-training centers, teachers write periodical progress reports on the children to guide them in planning and to share with families.
- *As part of a teacher-training process.* Documentation is necessary in some early childhood training programs. Child Development Associates (CDA) candidates submit a written portfolio of their experiences in the classroom as supporting evidence of their competency as teachers of young children.
- *As part of an accreditation process.* NAEYC's accreditation procedures require documentation of the school's operation, ranging from governance and management issues to teacher effectiveness, space usage, parent involvement, school philosophy, and curriculum.

- *As a commitment to quality and developmentally appropriate practices.* A brief note taken on the run, a thoughtful anecdote written after class, or a checklist of the child's playmates for one day give teachers information and insights for a greater understanding of the children's needs and development.
- *As a means of family information and education.* Recorded observations, notes, and similar data may show that Abraham is not participating in any strenuous physical activity and avoids activities that involve balancing and climbing. This information, when shared with parents, could lead to a medical evaluation and diagnosis of possible perceptual problems.
- *As a means of developing curriculum.* Emergent curriculum plans and learning activities sprout from such reports and records. It was not until such data were collected for entry into first grade that the kindergarten teacher realized most of the children in the class were not sufficiently proficient with scissors. A project approach remedied the need and the class learned a necessary skill.

Attending Meetings

Teachers need to communicate with the other people who are involved in the lives of the children as well as attend professional meetings. Figure 5-2 lists the most common types of meetings.

Organizing and Collecting Materials

Some of a teacher's after-hours activities fortify and vitalize the classroom by adding additional materials such as photos for the bulletin board, replenishing curriculum materials, new books from the library, and researching a field trip to the organic farm. In some programs teachers serve on committees and assist with ordering supplies and materials. All of these responsibilities fall to the family child care provider.

Making Contacts

Teachers may call or e-mail families to check on children who are sick or absent, return calls from parents and colleagues, or update a parent about a child's progress. For children with special needs, teachers may need to contact doctors, therapists, and other specialists. The popularity of e-mail has made some communications with families much faster and easier.

Working with Families

Working with families may include working on multicultural events and curriculum or organizing class fairs or school fund-raising events. These duties are a part of the job of teaching young children, but many will be shared with staff. Though time-consuming, these responsibilities add to the creativity and care that teachers express for the children and their families. Chapter 8 discusses the teacher–family relationship in depth.

Common Types of Meetings

Staff Meetings

Held usually once a week for individual teaching teams. Purpose is to plan curriculum, set goals, and discuss children's progress. Faculty meetings for all school personnel may be held less frequently.

Parent–Teacher Conferences

May be offered on a scheduled basis or they may be called by either parents or teachers as needed. Each school defines its own policy as to the number and frequency of parent contacts.

Parent Education Meetings

Many schools offer evening programs for parents. Teacher attendance may or may not be required.

Professional Meetings

Attendance at workshops, seminars, in-service training. Local, state, and national conferences are sponsored by the National Association for the Education of Young Children, Association for Childhood Education International, and Child Care Coordinating Council.

Student–Teacher Conferences

In schools used as training sites, teachers arrange time with individual students assigned to their classes.

Home Visits[1]

May or may not be optional. Some schools schedule them before opening day. Otherwise teachers must arrange them on their own time.

[1] Many parents welcome teacher's visits. Others may fear criticism or judgement about their home environment or family practices.

FIGURE 5-2 Teachers attend many different types of meetings, which help them create better programs, learn more about children, and learn how to become better teachers.

Sharing insights with colleagues helps the early childhood professional become more self-aware.

Personal Attributes of Early Childhood Educators

All good teachers have dedication, compassion, insight, a sense of humor, flexibility, patience, energy, and self-confidence. Other hallmarks of a true professional are physical and mental well-being, a sense of ethical responsibility, and reliability. Well-rounded teachers also know that their interest in the world at large transmits itself to children. The following are some other essential characteristics.

Self-Awareness

How do I make a difference in the lives of the children I teach? Asking that, you have taken the first step toward **self-awareness**. Reflective and critical thinking about your teaching experiences gives you insights that foster your growth and learning. Implicit in the NAEYC's standards (see Figure 5-2) is that early childhood professionals are lifelong learners, pursuing the skills and knowledge they need through coursework, professional development, degree programs, training, and licensing. You have a greater appreciation of learning when you have a sense of it in your own life. You affect children's lives when you know the answers to these questions:

Do I see myself as a learner? Where does my learning take place? How?
Do I learn from other adults?

Do I learn from children?
What happens to me when something is difficult or when I make a mistake?

Opening yourself up to the possibility of learning from students stretches your capacity to grow into relationships with children based on mutual respect and trust. This is especially important when teachers do not share the same cultural background or have no experience with a particular disability. Opening yourself to learning from other teachers creates a foundation for mutual support, collegiality, professional development, and deepening of friendships.

Self-knowledge—examining values and personal qualities—takes courage and a willingness to take risks. Accepting oneself is where to begin in accepting children.

Attitudes and Biases

Values and attitudes weave their way into every relationship and reflect the ethical framework by which we live and teach. This can be both positive and negative. Personal beliefs concerning race, culture, gender, abilities, and economic status may negatively affect our teaching in ways we are not aware. Facing prejudices about children and families based on long-held beliefs may be one of the most difficult things for a teacher to do. Most teachers will not have lived through the significant expe-

In addition to working with children, teachers support parents when they keep in touch. A brief, friendly phone call can make a family feel included in their child's education process.

rience of adapting to a new culture, learning a new language, surviving on food stamps, or living in a wheelchair. They may be uncomfortable with people who have faced these challenges.

Personal histories are filled with biases. We have opinions of what is "good" or "naughty" behavior, about children who are messy, who have odors, whose clothes are too big or too small, who eat strange food, who don't do what girls or boys are supposed to do. Some of these biases can be resolved, but only if a teacher takes the time to examine personal beliefs and biases.

The **anti-bias** approach to teaching young children (Derman-Sparks & Edwards, 2010) is an important teaching method. Widespread racial and ethnic prejudice is still prevalent in this country and causes concern about the harm they do to children's self-identity and self-esteem.

The anti-bias movement promotes the concept that all children are worthy of our respect and challenges teachers to examine beliefs, attitudes, and actions that might deny any child that unconditional respect. (See sections in Chapters 9, 11, and 15 for further discussion.)

The anti-bias approach affords teachers an opportunity to confront their own anxieties and biases through questions that promotes greater self-awareness:

- Am I aware of my identity and its influences on my beliefs and behaviors?
- Do I have ethical beliefs that I follow? Is there a system of ethical behaviors related to working with children and families that I could learn?
- Do I foster respect for the value of those who are different from me? How?
- Do I examine my biases and look at ways I can change my own attitudes? When? How?
- Do I show preference for children who most closely fit my own ethnic, cultural, and religious background? When? How?
- Do I somehow pass along my biases to the children I teach? When? How? With whom?
- Do I truly enjoy differences in human beings? When? With whom?

As you reflect on your answers and gain more insights into your teaching, you are enhancing children's culture and family by learning to understand your own.

Teacher Burnout

Teacher burnout results when teachers are faced with a demanding workload, uncertain or inadequate rewards, and other pressures that prevent work effectiveness. Low morale, stress, and disillusionment occur too often in a profession in which staff quality is the most important single factor in program quality. At its most extreme, teacher burnout can drive a good professional out of the field altogether, a common situation in early childhood settings and one that creates *one of the highest occupational turnover rates in the nation.* Between 25 percent to

Teachers' values and attitudes are reflected in the way they work with children.

40 percent of child care workers leave the field each year (National Association for Child Care Resources & Referral, 2011).

Bloom (2005) cites 10 characteristics that produce a healthy and positive school climate that, in turn, promote high morale among the teaching staff:

- Friendly, supportive, and trusting staff relationships
- Emphasis on personal and professional growth
- Leadership with clear expectations who encourage and support staff
- Clearly defined roles and policies
- Fairness and equity regarding promotions, raises, and other rewards
- Staff involvement in decision-making
- Agreement among staff on philosophy, goals, and objectives
- Emphasis on efficiency and good planning
- A physical environment that promotes responsible teaching and learning
- The ability to adapt to change and solve problems

Directors and staff must take the responsibility to work together to create the kind of climate that enhances success and satisfaction in the workplace. These issues are further explored in Chapter 15.

Becoming a Professional: What You Need to Know

Becoming a professional teacher takes time and the integration of knowledge, training, and experience. The strengths and convictions one has as a person blend with those values one holds for working with children and their families. Professional standards and well-defined teaching attributes form the basis for the beginnings of professionalism.

Professional Standards for Teacher Preparation

NAEYC has developed standards for the field of early childhood education to ensure that teachers receive the best possible professional preparation available. Highly trained teachers define the quality in early education and the programs, not the curriculum, assessments, or environmental setting that have the greatest effect on children's learning and development. These standards for professional preparation identify common expectations of what today's teachers should know and do as they pursue

education, specialized training, and ongoing professional development. The standards parallel the professional values found in the Code of Ethical Conduct, including the diversity of age ranges and programs in the early childhood field and emphasizing a multidiscipline approach to educating teachers. On the inside covers of this text is a handy chart that shows where to find the standards in each chapter. Figure 5-3 outlines the aspects of NAEYC's **professional standards**.

Essential Attributes of a Professional Teacher

There are essential attributes that shape the professional formation of a teacher. Each characteristic is echoed in the Standards for Professional Preparation and the Code of Ethical Conduct.

1. Possess the knowledge and skills
2. Abide by a code of ethics
3. Participate in continuing education; professional development and professional affiliations
4. Have knowledge of career options
5. Engage in reflective teaching
6. Become culturally competent
7. Advocate for children and their families
8. Practice intentional teaching

Possess the Knowledge and Skills

There is a body of knowledge and educational foundation that is assumed of anyone entering the early childhood profession, as noted in Figure 5-3: the NAEYC's Standards. Some basic teaching skills are also necessary. These include methods and techniques appropriate for teaching the very young child, your ability to relate to other adults, the quality of your interactions with children, and skills in program planning.

The NAEYC Standards for Early Childhood Professional Preparation outline other key elements that begin with having a common background with others that comes from studying child development and human behavior, family relations, parent education and development, and curriculum planning.

Teaching experience under the guidance of a master teacher is expected, as is familiarity with observation and recording techniques. Standard 3 provide the framework for professional development as teachers acquire further skills on the job, and Standard 5 encourages lifelong learning that advances teaching practices.

Becoming a professional teacher involves progressing along a continuum of development. The state you

NAEYC's Standards for Initial and Advanced Early Childhood Professional Preparation

What Today's Teachers Should Know and Do

1. Promote Child Development and Learning.
   - Know and understand young children's characteristics and needs
   - Know and understand the multiple influences on development and learning
   - Use developmental knowledge to create healthy, respectful, supportive, and challenging learning environments
2. Build Family and Community Relationships.
   - Know and understand diverse family and community characteristics
   - Support and engage families and community through respectful, reciprocal relationships
   - Involve families and communities in their children's development and learning
3. Observe, Document, and Assess to Support Young Children and Families
   - Understand the goals, benefits, and uses of assessment
   - Know about and use observation, documentation, and other appropriate assessment tools and approaches
   - Understand and practice responsible assessment to promote positive outcomes for each child
   - Know about assessment partnerships with families and professional colleagues
4. Use Developmentally Effective Approaches to Connect with Children and Families
   - Understand positive relationships and supportive interactions as the foundations of working with children
   - Know and understand effective strategies and tools for early education
   - Use a broad repertoire of developmentally appropriate teaching/learning
   - Reflect on your own practice to promote positive outcomes for each child
5. Use Content Knowledge to Build Meaningful Curriculum
   - Understand content knowledge and resources in academic disciplines
   - Know and use the central concepts, inquiry tools, and structures of content areas or academic disciplines
   - Use your own knowledge, appropriate early learning standards, and other resources to design, implement, and evaluate meaningful, challenging curricula for each child
6. Becoming a Professional
   - Identify and involve oneself with the early childhood field
   - Know about and uphold ethical standards and other professional standards
   - Engage in continuous, collaborative learning to inform practice
   - Integrate knowledgeable, reflective, and critical perspectives of early education
   - Engage in informed advocacy for children and the profession

FIGURE 5-3 What today's teachers should know and do. (The Standards and Key Elements are from NAEYC, "NAEYC Standards for Early Childhood Professional Preparation." Position Statement. Washington, DC: NAEYC. Reprinted with permission from the National Association for the Education of Young Children [NAEYC]. Copyright © 2009 by NAEYC. Full text of all NAEYC position statements is available at www.naeyc.org/positionstatements. These correlations are suggested by the authors.)

live in may or may not have regulations for early childhood teachers; some states offer a specialized certification for those in the early childhood field. Professional expectations mandated by the states provide some degree of professionalization of early childhood teachers.

Figure 5-4 is an example of the California statewide certification program. This *career matrix* has a number of levels, each with alternative qualifications for meeting the requirements. Within each level, there are a variety of teaching roles. Each state defines its own certification standards. Information is available through the state's department of education.

Look back to the teachers you met at the beginning of the chapter. Margarita is making plans to move from being a licensed home caregiver to pursuing a bachelor's degree. Match her plans with Figure 5-3 to see what other options she will have.

Experience and education work together to refine the skills and knowledge of the early childhood professional as shown in Figure 5-4. In addition, Figure 5-5 has some useful descriptions of the various roles teachers have in early childhood programs. This chart also shows how the progression from teacher aide to master teacher is matched to increasing responsibilities and education.

A Career Lattice: Child Development Permit Matrix

Level	Education Requirement	Experience Requirement
Assistant	6 units of ECE or CD	None
Associate teacher	12 units ECE/CD, including core courses	50 days of 3+ hours/day within 2 years
Teacher	24 units ECE/CD, including core courses + 16 general education (GE) units	175 days of 3+ hours/day within 4 years
Master teacher	24 units ECE/CD, including 16 GE units + 6 specialization units + 2 units adult supervision	350 days of 3+ hours/day within 4 years
Site supervisor	A.A. (or 60 units) with 24 ECE/CD units, including core + 6 units administration + 2 units adult supervision	350 days of 4+ hours/day including at least 100 days of supervising adults
Program director	B.A. with 24 ECE/CD units, including core + 6 units administration + 2 units adult supervision	Site supervisor status and one program year of site supervisor experience

© Cengage Learning 2011

FIGURE 5-4 A combination of education and experience work together to form a career ladder for early childhood professionals in California who want a child development permit.

General Role Definitions for the Early Childhood Teacher

Title	Description	Minimum Qualifications
Apprentice/ Teacher Aide	Is responsible to teacher for implementing program	**Entry level,** no previous formal training but enrolled in early childhood education classes
Assistant or Associate Teacher	Is part of the teaching team under the direction of teacher; may implement curriculum, supervise children, and communicate with parents.	Child Development Associate (CDA) credential
Teacher	Is coleader who plans and implements curriculum, works with parents, and evaluates children's progress	Associate's degree in early childhood education or related field
Lead Teacher	Creates a model classroom, applies good early childhood education practices, supervises other team members, develops new curriculum, provides leadership to team	Bachelor's degree in early childhood education or related field; supervised teaching experience; additional coursework work in family life, assessment, supervision, etc.

FIGURE 5-5 There are many ways to reach the top of a career ladder. Each role has its own job description that varies with the type of early childhood education setting. The qualifications are based on individual programs and their needs. (Adapted from *Blueprint for Action: Achieving Center-Based Change through Staff Development*, by P. J. Bloom, © 2005 New Horizons.)

Abide by a Code of Ethical Conduct

Every day, situations arise with parents, children, other teachers, and administrators that cause genuine conflict about behavior. Some cases are clearly ethical dilemmas: suspected child abuse by a parent or teacher, talking about children and their families outside of school, or the firing of a staff member without due cause. Others may not seem as obvious. Some examples are:

When parents:

● Ask you to advance their child into the next class against your advice.

- Want you to use discipline practices common to their family and culture but at odds with your own sense of what children need.
- Attempt to gossip with you about another child, staff member, or family.

When another teacher:

- Suggests a private staff meeting outside of school with a select group of teachers.
- Refuses to take a turn cleaning out the animal cages.
- Regularly misses staff meetings.
- Disagrees with the school's educational philosophy and continues to teach in ways that differ from the approved methods in that setting.
- Goes to the school administrator with a complaint about a staff team member.

When the administrator:

- Insists on adding one more child to an already over-enrolled class.
- Makes personnel decisions based on friendship, not performance.
- Backs a parent who complains about a teacher without hearing the teacher's side of the story.

Doing what is right becomes difficult at times; knowing what is right may be elusive. Even identifying what is right—an ethical conflict—may not be obvious. The NAEYC Standard 5 points out that professionals are guided by an ethical code, such as the NAEYC Code of Ethical Conduct (see Appendix A and the beginning of each chapter).

Ethics are the moral guidelines by which we govern our own behavior and that of society. We can strictly define ethics as *the system* that suggests that a personal code of ethics can be supported by a professional code of ethics. A code of ethics is a set of statements that helps us deal with the temptations inherent in our occupations. A code of ethics provides collective wisdom and advice from a broad base in the profession. It states the principles by which each individual can measure and govern professional behavior. It says that a group or association has recognized the moral dimensions of its work. It provides teachers with a known, defined core of professional values—those basic commitments that any early childhood educator should consider inviolate. This protects teachers and administrators from having to make hard ethical decisions on the spur of the moment, possibly on the basis of personal bias. An established professional code supports the teacher's choice by saying, "It isn't that I won't act this way: No early childhood educator should act this way" (Kipnis, 1987).

NAEYC's Code of Ethical Conduct and Statement of Commitment includes four sections: 1) ethical responsibilities to children; 2) ethical responsibilities to families; 3) ethical responsibilities to colleagues; and 4) ethical responsibilities to community and society. The Code of Ethical Conduct and Statement of Commitment may be found in Appendix A at the back of this text. Figure 5-6 shows a basic list of **core values** that has emerged from this work.

Participate in Continuing Education, Professional Development, and Affiliations

Creative and stimulating classrooms are the product of teachers who continue to learn more about how to teach. After the initial stage of teaching, many teachers begin to seek new challenges and new ways to improve the quality of their teaching. Usually this search leads to some form of **continuing education**, such as participation in workshops, courses, or seminars. Standard 5 reinforces the concept of teachers as lifelong learners.

A classic work by Katz (1999) describes four distinct stages of teacher development, ranging from Survival to Maturity. The beginning teacher often feels inadequate and ill-prepared during the first year of teaching (survival) but soon begins to focus on individual children and specific behavior problems (consolidation). By the third or fourth year (renewal) the teacher is ready to explore new ideas and resources and, within another year or two, has come to terms with teaching

---

Core Values of NAEYC's Code of Ethical Conduct

- Appreciating childhood as a unique and valuable stage of the human life cycle.
- Basing our work with children on knowledge of child development.
- Appreciating and supporting the bond between the child and family.
- Recognizing that children are best understood and supported in the context of family, culture, community, and society.
- Respecting the dignity, worth, and uniqueness of each individual (child, family member, and colleague).
- Respecting diversity in children, families, and colleagues.
- Recognizing that children and adults achieve their full potential in the context of relationships that are based on trust and respect.

© Cengage Learning 2014

FIGURE 5-6 These core values form the basis of agreement in the profession about standards of ethical behavior. See Appendix A for a full version.

The Code of Ethical Conduct is shared with all members of the center or school staff.

and searches for insights and perspectives (maturity). At each stage, teachers need differing degrees of on-site support (mentoring), with increased exposure to professional conferences and organizations.

There are many ways to pursue continuing education:

- In-service training programs in the school setting. Special resource personnel who provide specific information about relevant topics and lead the staff in discussions about children's behavior, family relationships, assessment charts, science curricula, and creating multicultural classrooms.
- The teaching staff develops a program of their own, offering their expertise to fellow faculty at an in-service meeting.
- A computer specialist, art resource teacher, or multicultural expert visits the classrooms, instructing children and providing staff with some useful ideas and plans.
- A family therapist speaks at a staff meeting about strategies for supporting families in crisis.
- A library for teachers, stocked with professional books, journals (such as *Young Children*), newspapers (such as *Education Week*), and e-letters such as *Exchange Every Day*, provides the staff with the means to keep up with current trends and practices.
- Parents who are professionals in a variety of fields can be utilized whenever possible to enrich the knowledge and skills of the staff.

Look back at the career matrix (Figure 5-4) and see how many opportunities there are for advancement with the right education and experience. As you achieve each

level, there are challenges to be met. A course in group dynamics, cultural sensitivity, or adult assessment portfolios enhances your chances to move into more satisfying work and enlarge your contributions to those you work with and to the profession as a whole.

Standard 6 of the NAEYC Standards for Initial and Advanced Early Childhood Professional Preparation encourages professional development by joining one of the organizations related to the early childhood field. One of the largest, the National Association for the Education of Young Children (NAEYC), has local and state affiliate groups through which one can become a member. NAEYC offers a range of services to its members, including conferences and publications such as the journal *Young Children*. The Association for Childhood Education International (ACEI) has a similar function, whereas the Society for Research in Child Development (SRCD) focuses on child psychology, research, and development. Abundant resources are available from these groups, and their websites are at the end of this chapter and on the textbook website.

Have Knowledge of Career Options

The need for quality programs for young children has never been greater, and the demand for early childhood specialists will continue, fostered by national attention to the issues of children and families. If you are considering a career in early childhood education (ECE), the options are many and varied. Several of the Standards point to specific early childhood careers. For instance, Standard 1 suggests a teaching and/or consulting job, or Standard 2 may lead toward a calling as a family–child therapist or community organizer. Figure 5-7 lists some of the possibilities that exist in this profession.

TeachSource Video

Watch the TeachSource Video Case entitled "Teaching as a Profession: An Early Childhood Teacher's Responsibilities and Development." After you study the video clip, view the artifacts, and read the teacher interviews and text, reflect on the following questions:

1. One of the primary values in the NAEYC Code of Ethical Conduct is that children are best understood in the context of their family, culture, and society. Where and how does teacher Samantha Brade weave this into the interview?

2. In the case, Samantha defines many roles and responsibilities that challenge her as a professional. Comment on her ability to be self-reflective as she talks about teaching.

Career Options in Early Childhood Education

Direct Services to Children and Families

Teacher in early childhood program
Director of child care facility nursery school,
    Montessori program
Family day-care provider
Nanny or au pair
Foster parent
Social worker/adoption agent
Pediatric nurse/school nurse
Family therapist/parent educator
Pediatrician
Parent educator
Early intervention specialist
Recreation leader
Play group leader
Home visitor

Community Involvement

State/local licensing worker
Legislative advocate
Child care law specialist
ECE environmental consultant
Interior designer for children's spaces
Government planning agent on children's issues
Consultant in bilingual education, multiculturalism
Nutrition specialist for children
Child care referral counselor

Indirect Services to Children and Families

Curriculum specialist
Instructional specialist—computers
Child development researcher
ECE specialist
Program consultant
Consumer advocate
Teacher trainer, two- and four-year colleges
Consultant
Resource and referral programs
State and national departments of education and/or
    human services

Other Options

Communications consultant
Script writer/editor
Freelance writer
Children's book author
Children's photographer
Microcomputer specialist/program consultant

FIGURE 5-7 There are many challenges in a variety of careers awaiting the early childhood professional. (Adapted from "Career Options in Early Childhood Education" by Dianne Widmeyer Eyer. In *Beginnings & Beyond: Foundations in Early Childhood Education*, 3rd Ed., Clifton Park, NY: Thomson Delmar Learning.)

Engage in Reflective Teaching

A reflective teacher stops, looks, and listens. **Reflective teaching** is the process of thinking seriously and thoughtfully about your teaching and how children learn and how these are expressed in what and how you teach. A reflective teacher ponders each experience, probing more deeply for a greater understanding of what was taught and what was learned and how this informs the teaching process. Reflective teaching is the result of insightful examination, self-awareness, and self-assessment. Reflective dialogue with fellow students, colleagues and coworkers, supervisors, and mentors provides the opportunity to challenge yourself and strengthen your professional knowledge and understanding of the meaning of teaching.

Become Culturally Competent

Throughout this text, you will be exposed to cultural awareness and sensitivity in many contexts: in Chapter 1—diversity, immigrant children, class differences; in Chapter 3—cultural sensitivity and family cultural influences; in Chapter 7—culturally appropriate guidance; in Chapter 8—the changing American family; in Chapter 10—culturally appropriate curriculum, inclusive curriculum, multicultural curriculum, and culturally responsive teachers; and in Chapter 15—multicultural education, bilingual education, the challenges for immigrants, class differences, equal play and gender issues, and sexuality.

The culturally competent early childhood professional must be aware of the issues addressed in those chapters. The population trends within the United States have changed dramatically over the past few decades and the ability to adapt to a diversified group of families is the challenge for the teachers of the 21st century. Today's teachers need to build strong family and community relationships (Standards 2, 4, 5) across all types of cultural diversity.

Teaching With INTENTION

Practice Intentional Teaching

Intentional teaching means that everything you do as teacher has specific goals and a purpose; that you have given your actions a great deal of thought; and that if anyone asks you why you have done something, you have a sound explanation (Epstein, 2007). Just as the teacher is deliberate in choosing furniture placement and specific guidance strategies, so too does intentionality play a part in what makes for the best kind of learning experience. We know that children can and should learn by choosing to work and play in an area of interest to them. We also know that there are concepts and content that is best learned through teacher-directed learning experiences. Both experiences are important to the growing child. Through intentional teaching, a teacher sets goals, plans the lesson, selects teaching strategies, and focuses on the most effective way to help children learn. As children react and get involved, the teacher maintains the focus and control on the experience.

Intentional teaching can and should be fun. It allows for creative thinking on the part of the teacher and the class. Jim wants his kindergarten class to focus on creating and extending patterns as part of the math curriculum, to learn that math can be fun, and to involve the class in creating the next steps. He begins by laying out pattern cards and colored blocks to match, which is an activity most of the children have mastered. Next, he adds textured squares to the activity and suggests the children make up their own patterns. Several days later, Jim adds a box of shells. Lena and Tony have been intrigued with each addition to the activity and ask Jim "What else can we add?"

At group time, Jim poses the question to the class: "What else would you like to add to the pattern table?" Jody wants feathers, Jesus wants bigger blocks, Mike wants string, and Paola wants spaghetti. As the children called out further suggestions, Jim added them to the list he was making, and said that he wanted some beans. The children became more animated and made more suggestions of food. "Okay," said Jim. "Those are great suggestions but some of them seem more like lunch than math! Let's vote on four that you like the most." The class voted and the four items were added to the math table. "My pattern is so pretty I want to keep it," said Carly. The next day Jim added construction paper and glue to the table. At group time the children shared their patterns by describing them to the class. Ryan went first: "I've got a brown shell, a red bean, a yellow spaghetti, and green string, and then I have it all over again." As they finished group time, Jim asked them to think about what they would do if one of the choices for their pattern ran out. The next day, he found out.

As Jim explained to one of his colleagues, part of his plan was to assess which children were grasping the concept of patterning and were ready for more challenges and to see what experiences other children might need to further understand patterns. This is intentional teaching at its best.

In each chapter of this text you will find a "Teaching With Intention" box that expands the definition of intentional teaching.

Think About This
1. How does "teaching with intention" alter your teaching strategies?
2. What is the most comfortable style for you right now: child-guided learning or teacher-guided learning? Why?
3. Describe your own definition of "teaching with intention."

Advocate for Children and Their Families

Children need advocates to speak for them and their families on issues ranging from health care to education to poverty to professional quality, staff, and wages. It is up to the early childhood professional to give voice to the issues concerning our young children and to educate the public about those issues. Public policy makers on the local, state, and national level need to hear from those who can speak out for those who cannot. Part of the role of a professional early childhood educator is to join the voices that support educational and teaching reforms as specifically stated in Standard 5. Volunteer with a local organization and make a difference in the lives of teachers and caregivers. Local NAEYC affiliates need volunteers to support *The Week of the Young Child* campaign each year and to monitor public policy at the local and state levels. Some early childhood professionals find it useful to sit on the boards of child care and health organizations.

Team Teaching: Professional Collaboration

Numerous adults are included in the early childhood setting. Some of these people may be:

- Other teachers, aides, and student teachers
- Volunteers
- Program directors and administrators

- School support personnel: clerical and janitorial staffs, food-service workers, bus drivers
- Families
- Consultants and specialists

That list defines the broader meaning of **team teaching**. The majority of classroom interactions, however, are with other teachers, and these relationships are among the most important a teacher can have. The beginning teacher may join a team of teachers or may teach in a small class alone. This depends on:

- The age level of the children
- Licensing or accrediting requirements
- The size of the classroom
- The school's philosophy and practices

Team teaching is defined as two or more adults working together in one classroom with one group of children (Browne & Gordon, 2009). The team approach is common in many nursery schools and child care centers where larger groups of children attend. Kindergarten and first- and second-grade teachers generally teach alone in self-contained classrooms, sometimes with an aide. In extended-day and after-school programs, high school and college students may make up the rest of the team.

Team Composition

Most teams are composed of people with varying skills, experience, and training. A typical group has a lead or head teacher—someone who is trained in child development or early childhood education. Assistants with less experience and training add support. Student teachers, interns, and volunteers may round out the group. A resource teacher—someone who specializes in art, music, or physical development, for instance—may also be available on a part-time basis.

Many state regulations mandate a minimum number of adults in the early childhood setting, and this minimum varies with the ages of the children. In infant programs, for instance, there is a higher ratio of adults per child (NAEYC suggests an optimal a ratio of 1:4), so it is more likely there are several teachers in one classroom. Together the teachers shape, direct, and participate in that program as a team of teachers.

The prescribed ratio of adult to children changes as the children mature and become able to function in more independent ways. (See Chapter 2 for more examples.)

Role Definition and Satisfaction

In order to function successfully, each person on the team must have a satisfying role to play and to be appreciated for the special something he or she brings to the team. All teachers want to know how their special talents and experiences contribute to the success of this program.

A written job description helps teachers understand the scope of their own position, as well as those of other staff members. Clearly defined roles also serve as a guard against legal and ethical problems, especially if children are injured at school. A clear understanding of the roles and responsibilities a teacher has is essential for the teacher's own sense of well-being and for the smooth functioning of the program.

Flexibility

It is important to adapt to the varying needs of children and equally important to respond to the needs of other staff members. Flexibility involves a willingness to offer and accept negotiation and compromise to preserve the effectiveness of the whole staff's effort. A professional teacher has a willingness to change with the changing needs of coworkers, to be open to new ideas proposed by others, and to help children become comfortable with flexibility and change.

Open and Frequent Communication

The ability to communicate thoughts, concerns, and feelings to others honestly and openly is perhaps the most important factor in promoting good team relationships. Good teachers work at becoming better teachers by developing skills in interpersonal relationships with other adults, just as they promote good social relationships among the young children they teach.

Communication problems and conflicts arise in every teaching situation. The Code of Ethical Conduct provides a road map for navigating some of the issues that create conflicts. The Code outlines clear expectations for professional and collegial behavior among staff members and employers. Review them in Appendix A. Communication takes many forms: verbal and nonverbal, written and spoken, and body language.

The three basic reasons for developing successful communication links with others on the teaching staff are:

1. *To share information*—about children and their families ("Sheila's grandmother died yesterday"), about changes in the schedule ("The dentist is unable to visit today; who wants to conduct group time?"), and about child development strategies ("Remember, we are all going to observe Leah's gross motor skills this week").
2. *To contribute new ideas*—teachers encourage one another to keep teaching fresh and alive when they

share a recent article of interest, reports from a conference they attended, or a successful art activity.

3. *To solve problems*—accepting differences in opinions, approaches, personality, and style among people is part of the challenge of working closely with others. Open communication is an ongoing process in which people have honest and frequent discussions of their differences, respecting each other's feelings and integrity and working together for mutually agreeable solutions. If the problem relates to another staff person, Section P-3A.1 of the Code of Ethical Conduct states that when we have concerns about the professional behavior of a coworker, we let that person know of our concerns and attempt to resolve the problem in a collegial manner.

Who Am I?

As noted earlier, self-awareness is a prerequisite to becoming a professional teacher. The kind of self-knowledge that contributes to success as a member of a teaching team is your knowledge of how your strengths and weakness complement or conflict with other team members. How you perceive yourself as a leader and your ability to follow others can affect team relationships. Be aware of what you have done lately that caused you to learn more about yourself, especially as a member of a teaching team.

Mutual Respect and Acceptance

Appreciating and accepting the individuality of other team members are as important to the success of the program as are appreciating and accepting the individuality of each child. The climate of trust created through mutual respect allows each staff member to contribute openly and

Professional attitudes and behaviors enhance team teaching.

innovatively to the program. It helps to know what you have in common with your coworkers, whether or not their teaching philosophies differ from you and from one another, and what values they hold dear. You want to be clear about what you want them to respect and accept about you as well. Section P-3B.1 of the Code of Ethical Conduct makes it clear that when we do not agree with program policies, we first work within the organizational structure to effect change.

Collegiality

A sense of being a team does not happen by accident, but by conscious effort. Every member of the staff must be committed to working together on a daily basis, as well as to the long-term goals of the program. Jorde-Bloom (2005) defines collegiality as the extent to which a team is friendly, supportive, and trusting of one another. Teachers can find support from one another as they share planning problems and achievements and grow in admiration and respect for one another.

Sharing the Spotlight

Tension among staff members can arise from a sense of competition. Teams function best when members learn how to share their strengths in ways that support the team without creating a competitive atmosphere. There must be a feeling of shared success when things work well, just as there is a shared responsibility when problems arise. One of the challenges of working on a team is to deal with feelings that may come from judging another teacher's abilities and/or successes. It helps to know how you feel and react when a parent praises another teacher in front of you or a child prefers another teacher to you. Section P-3A.2 of the Code of Ethical Conduct reminds us to base our views regarding the personal attributes or professional conduct of others on firsthand knowledge and its relevancy to the children and the program.

Evaluations

Evaluations are part of the privilege of claiming membership in the teaching profession. No teacher can become truly successful unless provisions are made for ongoing evaluations that provide a clear picture that confirms strengths and pinpoints areas for growth. The evaluation process is discussed in depth later in this chapter.

Why Team Teaching Works

There are many reasons why teaching in teams is such an integral part of so many early childhood programs. The advantages are numerous:

- *Variety of adult role models.* Teachers who are male, female, disabled, young, middle-aged, older, and varying in ethnic backgrounds bring equally diverse attitudes, approaches to children, interests, skills, and knowledge to share. This teaches children to accept differences in people as they watch adults interact with others on the teaching team.

- *Support for children.* The absence of one teacher is not as disruptive when the children can count on other familiar faces. This enables children to learn to trust the teaching environment because someone they know is always there.

- *Lightened workload.* There is a sharing of all the teaching tasks, from curriculum planning and cleanup to parent conferencing and record keeping.

- *Enriched program.* Talents and resources of the team are used to best advantage so that team members teach to their strengths, adding richness to the program.

Performance Assessment: Key to Improved Teaching Practices

Teachers are the single most important factor in determining program quality, and annual performance assessments promote continual professional improvement and growth. Timely and objective feedback guides teachers toward more effective teaching in their work with children, coworkers, parents, and administrators.

Purposes for an Annual Performance Review

Many programs require an annual assessment of the teaching staff. An evaluation is a professional expectation and reflects the NAEYC's Standards for a well-prepared early childhood professional. Personal performance reviews lend support to self-awareness, lifelong learning, and reflective teaching. There are a number of purposes for a performance review.

To Define and Clarify Job Responsibilities

A clearly defined job description outlines a teacher's duties and responsibilities and forms the basis for the evaluation. Assessing specific job responsibilities is a part of one's professional self-definition, as well as a clarification of actual duties. Studying ourselves helps us know who we are and what we do. Assessing job responsibilities aids in this process and holds us accountable for our work.

To Monitor Teacher Effectiveness

Once clear guidelines are set for teaching expectations, a method is needed to monitor teacher effectiveness. This process may vary from school to school. In some schools, teaching effectiveness is measured, in part, by child achievement, such as how children score on tests. Other centers may solicit the opinions of parents and coworkers. Direct observations while teachers are working with children form a significant part of the assessment.

To Identify Strengths and Challenges

Timely feedback about teaching practices and other job responsibilities is helpful to all teachers, whether beginners or experienced personnel. An assessment that offers teachers information about how to perform their job better

Evaluations are a professional responsibility that help to clarify job performance, professional growth, and challenges.

contributes to job competence and satisfaction. By recognizing strengths, teachers receive positive feedback for high-quality work. By identifying areas of concern, they can begin to set realistic goals for improvement.

To Create a Plan for Professional Development

One function of teacher evaluation is to foster professional development. Teachers do not become "good" and then stay that way for life. Regardless of their stage of development, teachers need to establish annual goals to continually improve. To be effective, goal setting must be embedded in an ongoing system of professional development. Reflect back on Figure 5-3, which shows how education and experience work together to form a career ladder that can be used for goal setting purposes. Figure 5-6 outlines many career options as well.

To Determine Employment

An evaluation can also be used to decide whether teachers should be retained, promoted, or released. Assessment procedures are an administrator's most valuable tools in making that decision. A clear and effective evaluation tool enables the administrator to monitor performance and target specific areas for improvement. The administrator then has a fair and equitable way to determine the promotional status of each employee.

To Meet Accreditation Requirements

Many programs seek accreditation by organizations whose standards they embrace. NAEYC is the leading accrediting body for early childhood programs through its National Academy of Early Childhood Programs. The self-study aspect of the accreditation process includes a teacher's self-assessment, the director's assessment of the teaching staff, and the teacher's assessment of the director. The criteria in the self-study provide the standards by which these evaluations are made, providing concrete ways to measure quality.

Components of an Effective Assessment

An effective evaluation process helps to challenge methods and assumptions and to identify ways to provide support for growth and change. Certain elements are common to all evaluations, such as those found in Chapter 6 for child assessments and in Chapter 2 for program assessments. In the assessment of teachers, the important components are: purpose (as described earlier), evaluators, type of assessment, follow-through, and cultural sensitivity.

Who Are the Evaluators?

Several models have been developed around the issue of who assesses teacher performance.

Self-Evaluation

Self-assessment encourages reflective thinking and self-awareness and can be an important step in the evaluation process. Your insights and perspectives and self-identified strengths and challenges help you to define your goals and objectives for the coming year.

Goals are the learning outcomes you want to achieve, such as improving your ability to help children resolve conflicts. Goals are broad-based challenges that improve your teaching practices.

Objectives are observable and define how you will achieve your goals. Action might include practicing observation skills to become more aware of a potential crisis before it erupts and intervening earlier in children's interactions. Objectives provide the detail for achieving your goals.

Figure 5-8 is an example of a staff evaluation form, which can also be used as a self-assessment tool.

Supervisor Evaluation

Job performance is an administrator's responsibility; therefore, teachers can expect their supervisor, director, or head teacher to be involved in their evaluation. Supervisors often use a single form combining a teacher's self-assessment and the supervisor's evaluation, such as Figure 5-8. This kind of form assures the teacher and supervisor that both are using the same criteria for evaluation and includes appropriate categories for assessment, as noted in Figure 5-8. In some programs, videotapes and portfolios add to the assessment process.

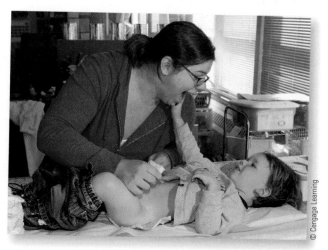

A teacher's self-evaluation provides an opportunity to improve his or her effectiveness with children.

Staff Evaluation

Employee _____

Evaluation Period _____

Key

How often observed:
C – Consistently
F – Frequently
O – Occasionally
N – Never

	C (90–100%)	F (60–89%)	O (30–59%)	N (0–29%)
General Work Habits				
1. Arrives on time				
2. Reliable in attendance; gives ample notice for absences				
3. Responsible in job duties				
4. Alert in health and safety matters				
5. Follows the center's philosophy				
6. Open to new ideas				
7. Flexible with assignments and schedule				
8. Comes to work with a positive attitude				
9. Looks for ways to improve the program				
10. Remains calm in a tense situation				
11. Completes required written communication on time				
Professional Development, Attitude, and Efforts				
1. Takes job seriously and seeks to improve skills				
2. Participates in workshops, classes, groups				
3. Reads and discusses distributed handouts				
4. Is self-reflective with goals for ongoing development				
Attitude and Skills with Children				
1. Friendly, warm, and affectionate				
2. Bends low for child level interactions				
3. Uses a modulated, appropriate voice				
4. Knows and shows respect for individuals				
5. Is aware of development levels/changes				
6. Encourages independence/self-help				
7. Promotes self-esteem in communication				
8. Limits interventions in problem solving				
9. Avoids stereotyping and labeling				
10. Reinforces positive behavior				
11. Minimal use of time out				
12. Regularly records observations of children				
Attitude and Skills with Parents				
1. Available to parents and approachable				
2. Listens and responds well to parents				
3. Is tactful with negative information				
4. Maintains confidentiality				
5. Seeks a partnership with parents				
6. Regularly communicates with parents				
7. Conducts parent conferences on schedule				
Attitude and Skills with Class				
1. Creates an inviting learning environment				
2. Provides developmentally appropriate activities				
3. Develops plans from observation and portfolio entries				
4. Provides materials for all curriculum components				
5. Provides an appropriate role model				
6. Anticipates problems and redirects				
7. Is flexible and responsive to child's interests				
8. Is prepared for day's activities				
9. Handles transitions well				
Attitude and Skills with Co-Workers				
1. Is friendly and respectful with others				
2. Strives to assume a fair share of work				
3. Offers and shares ideas and materials				
4. Communicates directly and avoids gossip				
5. Approaches criticism with learning attitude				
6. Looks for ways to be helpful				

Comments:

FIGURE 5-8 The quality and effectiveness of teaching is affected by the quality and effectiveness of the evaluation process. This form is useful for a self-evaluation and supervisory evaluation and can be downloaded from the Education CourseMate website. (From *The Visionary Director: A Handbook for Dreaming, Organizing, and Improving Your Center,* by Margie Carter and Deb Curtis, pp. 266–277. Copyright © 1998 by Margie Carter and Deb Curtis. Reprinted with permission from Redleaf Press, St. Paul, Minnesota, www.redleafpress.org.)

Types of Assessments

Many evaluations are based on observable, specific information about a teacher's activities and responsibilities. This is known as a **performance-based assessment**. Figure 5-9 is an example of performance-based assessment in regard to a teacher's work with children. When paired with specific goals and expectations, this system is known as **competency-based assessment**.

Competency-based assessments outline exactly what teachers must do to demonstrate their competency, or skill, in their job responsibilities. Criteria are set and areas are targeted that pinpoint what knowledge, skills, and behaviors the teacher must acquire.

The evaluation tools or format determine the validity of the gathered information. Informal techniques may result in unreliable conclusions. A process that is formalized and systematic, related to goal setting and professional development, has a greater chance of success. Although it is important to select an appropriate method and assessment tool, keep in mind that it is the process through which the evaluation is conducted that matters most.

Creating a portfolio is a developmentally appropriate practice that reflects your professional growth and your insights about the nature of teaching young children.

The Classroom Assessment Scoring System (CLASS) (Pianta et al., 2008) is an observation tool that evaluates teachers on two critical aspects of performance. CLASS measures the emotional climate, and as noted earlier in this chapter, setting the tone, or the emotional climate, is the teacher's responsibility. A supportive and positive climate fosters children's learning. CLASS also focuses on a variety of teaching strategies and how they set the stage for optimum learning.

Follow-Through

What follows an evaluation is critical to the overall success of an evaluation process. The important thing to remember is that assessment should be a continuous process because without follow-through, long-lasting improvement in unlikely to occur. Figure 5-10 shows how the circular process works in a **feedback loop**. Data are collected on teacher behavior and given to the teacher in person. Goals are set to improve teaching. A follow-up check is done periodically to see how—and if—goals are being met. Teaching improves as recommendations are put into practice.

Follow-through makes the feedback loop complete as information about improvement is communicated.

Evaluations take hard work, time, and dedication to a higher quality of teaching. It is also a shared responsibility. The supervisor must be explicit about a teacher's performance and be able to identify for the teacher what is effective and what is problematic. Teachers themselves must value the process and understand its implications for their professional growth.

Cultural Sensitivity

Cultural sensitivity affects how a teacher interacts with others, and this needs to be taken into consideration when assessing a teacher's performance. Insight about a

---

Performance-Based Assessment

Teacher Goal	Example
To help each child develop a positive self-concept	I greet each child with a smile and a personal comment.
To help each child develop socially, emotionally, cognitively, and physically	I have goals for each child in each developmental area, fall and spring.
To help provide many opportunities for each child to be successful	My parent conference sheets have examples; for instance, Charlie didn't want to come to group time, so I had him pick the story and help me read it—he comes every day now!
To encourage creativity, questioning, and problem solving	This is my weak point. I tend to talk too much and tell them what to do.
To foster enjoyment for learning in each child	I do great group times and give everyone turns.
To facilitate children's development of a healthy identity and inclusive social skills	I participated in our center's self-study and am taking an anti-bias curriculum class.

© Cengage Learning 2011

FIGURE 5-9 Performance-based assessment ties the goals of the program to the teacher's work. This example asks the teacher to do a self-assessment; a director, parent, or peer could observe and make a second assessment.

DAP   Portfolio-Based Assessment

Portfolio-based assessments are a popular tool for helping teachers consolidate the experiences that help them become better teachers. A **portfolio** is not an assessment tool in and of itself. It is the display or collection system used to demonstrate evidence of professional growth. Folders, boxes, files, and binders are all used to house the collection of data. It is an intentional compilation of materials and resources collected over a period of time that provides evidence of your professional growth.

Documentation is an important part of creating a portfolio because it provides concrete evidence of how you understand and implement developmentally appropriate practices and how you translate theory into action.

Your portfolio is ever changing and reflects your individuality by virtue of what it contains. As an assessment tool, a portfolio is useful in many ways. It helps you clarify your values, keeps you focused on the goals you have set, provides an avenue for self-reflection, and demonstrates

growth. By what is included and what is omitted, a portfolio shows an evaluator tangible evidence of your abilities, provides a framework for setting new goals, and gives a more personal sense of your commitment and professionalism. A portfolio may include but is not limited to the following:

Materials developed by you for use in the classroom

A videotape of your teaching performance

Lesson plans with an evaluation of a specific activity

Samples of conference hand-outs and programs, notes from in-service training, articles, and other materials you use as professional growth

Articles written for newsletters and for families and colleagues

A journal of teaching experiences

Photos of field trips or projects

Self-reflective notes on your teaching

Professional articles

---

teacher's social and cultural background is particularly useful if the evaluator is a member of the majority population and the teacher is not.

There are five specific cultural factors that can affect communication, particularly where supervisors and staff

FIGURE 5-10 A feedback loop is a continuous cycle in which teacher behavior is observed for a performance evaluation. The evaluation is offered through growth goals, which are set in order to affect teacher behavior. Thus, the circle is continuous, with each part helping the next.

members are concerned (Caruso and Fawcett, 2006). They are:

1. *Time sense.* Being on time and doing tasks in a timely fashion are high priorities for many people raised in mainstream American culture. Each culture has its own concept of time, and the teacher who is always late for meetings may be reflecting the cultural context in which he or she was raised.

2. *Space.* How close you get to someone while talking is also a function of cultural context. In some cultures, invading another's personal space (the "comfort zone") is considered rude. If a teacher backs away, she may be considered cold and unfriendly. If the teacher is the one getting too close, he may be seen as forward and aggressive. These perceptions may be innocent reactions based on their cultural sensibilities and should be considered in that light.

3. *Verbal and nonverbal communication.* Eye contact is seen in some cultures to be disrespectful if prolonged; to others it may be a sign of interest and attentiveness. Other facial expressions, such as smiling (or not), gestures, and body language, communicate different things from culture to culture. Silence, too, is used in different cultures in a variety of ways with an assortment of meanings. Speaking loudly may be a cultural norm or it may communicate anger and accusations. Teachers and their supervisors need to learn each other's communication styles and be particularly aware of those that are culture-bound.

4. *Values.* Our values drive our behavior and responses. If a teacher comes from a background that emphasizes dependency in the early years and the school philosophy is one that encourages early independence, a cultural conflict can erupt and affect a teacher's evaluation adversely. Supervisors and teachers must understand each other's value system and what causes each of them to make certain decisions.

5. *Concepts of authority.* The way people deal with authority is also culture-specific. Early childhood professionals who supervise and evaluate staff members from cultures different than their own need to be aware of what cultural expectations surround the issue of authority. In some instances, authority figures are often male, and females are raised not to question authority. A correct answer may be more culturally appropriate than expressing one's true feelings or ideas. The supervisor can avoid misunderstandings if he or she is aware that the teacher is used to an authoritarian style of leadership from supervisors and thus gear the conversation accordingly.

Evaluators have a rare opportunity to create bridges of understanding between and among many cultures. Within their school community, they can create a two-way interchange about culturally relevant issues.

Field Experience: Practice What You Teach

Professional preparation standards either require or recommend at least one practicum or field experience of supervised work with young children in a group setting. For some students, a practicum may be the first hands-on opportunity to work with children.

Learning Through the Practicum Experience

The student practicum experience provides opportunities to test yourself out as a teacher. Through this professional preparation, you learn to:

- Connect knowledge and theory with classroom experience: Children's behavior exemplifies the child development principles learned in textbooks. Theory becomes alive as you observe children play and learn.
- Discover how children function in groups and with other children and adults: The range of children's social skills is apparent as they interact with peers and teachers. You notice how differently children behave as they work alone, in small groups, or participate in a large group time experience.

Through experience, teachers learn how to handle large groups of children. Learning to develop story time and reading skills is an ongoing process.

- Collaboration techniques for working as a team member: Learning to be part of a team takes patience and practice. You learn to work with a variety of adults who have different skills and who model diverse teaching strategies.

- Intensive self-searching through self-assessment and reflective dialogue: You come to understand more about yourself and your abilities as you explore the broader meaning of teaching. You gain new insights as you take time to think about your role, attitude, behavior, and responses to the children you teach.

- Work with an on-site supervisor or mentor teacher: You and your supervising teacher will forge a working relationship based on the goals the two of you set for your practicum experience. Your supervisor observes, guides, and evaluates your experience, as well as encourages and supports your progress.

- Conduct group times and plan curriculum: Your first opportunity to plan curriculum is both exciting and challenging. Your knowledge of child development helps you create activities that are meaningful learning experiences. As you evaluate the activity with your supervising teacher, you gain greater understanding of the children you teach and your own skills as a teacher.

- Gain insights into yourself through ongoing feedback: Throughout your practicum you receive feedback from your supervising teacher that helps you identify the strengths you bring to the teaching experience and the areas in which you need to improve. Evaluations and feedback promote reflective teaching, increase your skills, and tell you what progress you are making in meeting your goals. Feedback increases your confidence and promotes the standards of the early childhood profession.

- Approaches and strategies for developing relationships with children: The teachers you work with model highly polished skills as they relate to children. As you observe them and gain experience you learn to help children solve conflicts, lead them in group discussions, and soothe their hurts. You also learn to ask a lot of questions of the teaching staff to find out why this approach didn't work and that strategy was successful.

- Engage in developmentally appropriate practices: Your practicum experience should lead you to a greater understanding of DAP. You see how teachers plan reasonable goals for each child, based on the individual's developmental levels. You come to see that DAP is more than a definition of what to do; it is a way to meet children where they are.

- Appreciate the role of families in their children's development and learning: Through the family we gain greater knowledge and understanding of the individual child. You learn how teachers build strong relationships with families in order to strengthen the bond between home and school. You also find a broad definition of "family" as it pertains to the diversity of the children in the classroom.

(Based on Browne and Gordon. (2012). *Early childhood field experience: Learning to teach well*. New York: Pearson.)

A field experience can be a productive and valuable asset to your professional growth. Theory evolves into practice, knowledge and skills are polished, and the living laboratory provides rich opportunities to focus on professional preparation.

Summary

LO1 Today's early childhood teachers have much in common with other teachers. The format may differ but the curriculum is similar and includes math, science, language, social studies, geography, and literacy. Early childhood teachers have multiple roles. They supervise and manage the classroom, interact with children and adults, and set the emotional tone. There are meetings to attend, reports to write, parent conferences to hold, and materials to purchase. These after-hours duties add to the depth of classroom experiences the teacher provides for the children. Personal attributes of the early childhood professional should include a high degree of self-awareness, including attitudes and biases that would inhibit good teaching practices.

LO2 Becoming a professional teacher means that there are professional guidelines and standards to follow. NAEYC's Standards for Professional Preparation serve as a challenge for what today and tomorrow's teachers should know and be able to do. The Code of Ethical Conduct fosters professionalism as teachers apply its ideals and principles to everyday situations. A professional code of ethics sets standards of behavior based on core values and commitments all early childhood professionals share. It can support decisions individuals have to make in the best interests of children. Professionalism is enhanced by a teacher's knowledge and skills, professional development, reflective teaching, and the practice of intentional teaching.

LO3 Team teaching is common in many early childhood programs. Creating a successful team effort is based on collaborative skills, which include role definition and satisfaction, flexibility, open and frequent communications, self-awareness, mutual respect and acceptance, and evaluations of the team.

LO4 An annual assessment that is linked to professional growth is a key to maintaining quality programs for children. Some purposes of annual performance reviews are to clarify roles and responsibilities, monitor teacher effectiveness, identify teacher strengths and challenges, plan for professional development, determine employment, and meet accreditation requirements.

The process should include a self-evaluation by the teacher who, with a supervisor, sets appropriate professional goals that relate to the program's philosophy and mission. Continuing growth within the professional field includes understanding the cultural context from which teachers relate to the children, families, other staff members, and supervisors.

LO5 Through a field experience, students gain valuable practice working directly with children under the supervision of a mature teacher. The student practicum helps beginning teachers connect knowledge and theory to the classroom reality of how children learn and behave, find approaches and strategies for relating to young children, and plan developmentally appropriate group times and curriculum. Working with a supervising teacher, students learn collaboration techniques for working on a team and gain insights as they become more aware of who they are in the lives of children.

Key Terms

emotional framework	core values	competency-based assessment
self-awareness	continuing education	feedback loop
anti-bias	reflective teaching	portfolio-based assessments
professional standards	intentional teaching	portfolio
entry level	team teaching	
ethics	performance-based assessment	

Review Questions

1. What are the most important characteristics that today's early childhood professional should possess?
2. How do the professional standards for teaching preparation and the NAEYC Code of Ethical Conduct foster a sense of professionalism?
3. What are the most important collaboration skills that help build positive relationships for team teaching?
4. How does an annual performance assessment guide and inform best teaching practices?
5. What is the value of field experience?

Observe and Apply

1. Survey a classroom where you teach or observe. How many different cultures are represented? How does the teacher respond to the cultural diversity?
2. Read the ethical situations posed in the section, "Abiding by a Code of Ethical Conduct." Think about how you would solve them. Discuss your answers with a member of your class, a teacher, and a parent.
3. Observe a teacher working in a team situation and one who works alone in a classroom. What seem to be the advantages of each? Disadvantages? Which

would you prefer for your first year of teaching? Why? Your third year? Your seventh year?

4. In small groups, discuss the popular images of teachers as reflected in current movies and literature. Is there a consensus of the portrait of teachers today? Where do early childhood professionals fit into the picture? Are issues raised about teachers being addressed anywhere? Where? How? By whom? What would you conclude about your role as a member of the teaching profession?

Helpful Websites

Center for Child Care Workforce   **www.ccw.org**

Council for Professional Recognition (CDA)
   www.cdacouncil.org

National Association for the Education of Young
   Children   **www.naeyc.org**

Association for Childhood Education International
   www.acei.org

Child Care Information Exchange   **www.ccie.com**

ERIC Clearinghouse on Elementary and Early
   Childhood Education   **www.eric.ed.gov**

National Black Child Development Institute
   www.nbcdi.org

The Education CourseMate website for this text offers many helpful resources and interactive study tools. Go to CengageBrain.com to access the TeachSource Videos, flashcards, tutorial quizzes, direct links to all of the websites mentioned in the chapter, downloadable forms, and more.

References

Bloom, P. J. (2005). *Blueprint for action: Achieving center-based change through staff development*. Lake Forest, IL: New Horizons.

Browne, K. W., & Gordon, A. M. (2009). *To teach well: An early childhood practicum guide*. Upper Saddle River, NJ: Prentice.

Caruso, J. J., & Fawcett, M. T. (2006). *Supervision in early childhood education: A developmental perspective*. New York: Teachers College Press.

Derman-Sparks, L., & Edwards, J. O. (2010). *Anti-bias education for young children and ourselves*. Washington, D.C.: National Association for Education of Young Children.

Epstein, A. S. (2007). *The intentional teacher: Choosing the best strategies for young children's learning*. Washington, D.C.: National Association for the Education of Young Children.

Eyer, D. (1989). Career options in early childhood education. In A. Gordon & K. W. Browne (Eds.), *Beginnings and beyond: Foundations in early childhood education*. Clifton Park, NY: Thomson Delmar Learning.

Katz, L. G. (1999). *Talks with teachers of young children*. Norwood, NJ: Ablex.

Kipnis, K. (1987, May). How to discuss professional ethics. *Young Children*, pp. 26–30.

National Association for the Education of Young Children. (2011). *Code of ethical conduct and statement of commitment*. Washington, D.C.: National Association for the Education of Young Children.

National Association for the Education of Young Children. (2010). NAEYC Standards for Early Childhood Professional Preparation Programs. http://www.naeyc.org/files/ncate/file/NAEYC%20Initial%20and%20Advanced%20Standards%203_2011.pdf. National Association for the Education of Young Children. (2005). *Core values*.

National Association of Child Care Resource & Referrals Agency. (2011). *Child care workforce*. http://www.naccrra.org, Retrieved November 2011.

Pianta, R. C., La Paro, K. M., & Hamre, B. K. (2008). *Classroom assessment scoring system (CLASS)*. Baltimore: Paul H. Brookes.

Rushton, S., Juola-Rushton, A., & Larkin, A. (2010). Neuroscience, play and early childhood educations: Connections, implications, and assessment. *Early Childhood Education Journal*, 37, pp. 351–361.

U.S. Bureau of Labor Statistics. (2010). *Labor force characteristics by race & ethnicity, 2007*. Report # 1032 Washington, D.C.: U.S. Government Printing Office.

Whitebrook, M., Sakai, L., Gerber, E., & Howes, C. (2001). *Then and now: Changes in child care staffing, 1994–2000*. Washington, D.C.: Center for the Child Care Workforce.

Observation and Assessment of Children

Learning Objectives

LO1 Define the key elements and purposes of child observation.

LO2 Explain the various contexts of what is observed.

LO3 Identify common types of observation systems.

LO4 Examine the goals and tools of child assessment.

naeyc Standards For Professional Development

The following NAEYC Standards for early childhood professional development are addressed in this chapter:

Standard 1 Promoting Child Development and Learning

Standard 3 Observing, Documenting, and Assessing to Support Young Children and Families

Standard 4 Using Developmentally Effective Approaches to Connect with Children and Families

Standard 5 Using Content Knowledge to Build Meaningful Curriculum

Standard 6 Becoming a Professional

naeyc Code of Ethical Conduct

These are the sections of the NAEYC Code of Ethical Conduct that apply to the topics of this chapter:

Core Values: Helping children and adults achieve their full potential in the context of relationships that are based on trust, respect, and positive regard.

Section I:

P-1.5   We shall use appropriate assessment systems, which include multiple sources of information, to provide information on children's learning and development.

P-1.6   We shall strive to ensure that decisions such as those related to enrollment, retention, or assignment to special education services, will be based on multiple sources of Information and will never be based on a single assessment, such as a test score or a single observation.

Section II:

P-2.7   We shall inform families about the nature and purpose of the program's child assessments and how data about their child will be used.

P-2.8   We shall treat child assessment information confidentially and share this information only when there is a legitimate need for it.

Key Elements and Purposes of Observation

Children are fascinating. They are charming, needful, busy, creative, unpredictable, and emotional. At school, at home, in the grocery store, and in the park, children demonstrate a variety of behaviors. There is the happy child who toddles toward the swing. The angry, defiant child grabs a book or toy and runs away. The studious child works seriously on a puzzle.

These pictures of children working, playing, and living together flash through the mind, caught for an instant as if by a camera. Good observational skills can help teachers capture both typical and exceptional moments in a child's life. Memory leaves just the impression. Documentation with visual samples and the written word are opportunities to check impressions and opinions against the facts. In this chapter, you learn about observing and recording the behavior of young children and how to apply these skills to assess children, to collect their work in a way that reflects each of them, and to evaluate their growth.

What Is Observation?

Teachers learn to make mental notes of the important details in each interaction:

- That's the first time I've seen Karen playing with Bryce. They are laughing together as they build with blocks.
- For five minutes now, Teddy has been standing on the fringes of the sand area where the toddler group is playing. He has ignored the children's smiles and refused the teacher's invitation to join in the play.
- Antonio stops climbing each time he reaches the top of the climbing frame. He looks quickly around and if he catches a teacher's eye, he scrambles down and runs away.

Through their behavior, these three children reveal much about their personalities. The teacher's responsibility is to notice all the clues and put them together in meaningful ways. The teacher sees the obvious clues, as well as the more subtle ones. The way observations are put together with other pertinent information becomes critical.

- Karen has been looking for a special friend. Now that she has learned some ways to approach other children that don't frighten and overwhelm them, children want to play with her.
- Teddy's parents divorced two weeks ago. It appears he is just beginning to feel some of that pain and has become withdrawn at school.
- At home, Antonio is expected to do things right the first time. Because climbing over the top of the frame might be tricky, he does not attempt it at all. At school, he generally attempts only what he knows he can do without making a mistake.

These simple observations, made in the midst of a busy day, give vital information about each child's abilities, needs, and concerns. It is a more developed picture. Children are complex human beings who respond in many ways. Teachers can observe these responses and use their skills to help each child grow and learn. The ability to observe—to "read" the child, understand a group, "see" a situation—is one of the most important and satisfying skills a teacher can have. As Curtis (2008) states:

Learning to see children takes time and practice, both when I am with them and when I take time to reflect on my work. The extra effort is worthwhile as it is much better to share in children's insatiable curiosity, deep feelings, and pure delight than it is to be the toddler police, focusing only on fixing behaviors, teaching to outcomes, or checking boxes on official forms.

A consistent practice of observation helps teachers develop a "child-sense" that gives adults a picture of how both individuals and groups of children are feeling and functioning (Cohen et al., 2008).

Observation is the basis of so much of a teacher's work:

- The environment—how to set it up and when to change it.
- The schedule—how to build the sequence and time periods for activities.
- The atmosphere—how to sense and respond to interactions and relationships.

What can teachers learn by observing children's interactions? The way they make friends, deal with problems, or balance the needs of self with those of others?

You will find examples of observations in every chapter of this book.

Observation also plays an important role in **assessment**, either by replacing (in the case of young children) or by supplementing standardized **evaluation** tools (for elementary-aged children). In fact, authentic assessment can be done only on the basis of good observations. In more reflective and less structured ways, teachers observe how they react and feel, observing themselves and their own values.

Observation is more than ordinary looking. It takes energy and concentration to become an accurate observer. Teachers must train themselves to record what they see on a regular basis. They need to discipline themselves to distinguish between detail and trivia and learn to spot biases that might invalidate observation. Once acquired, objective observation techniques help give a scientific and professional character to the role of early childhood educator.

Play is the work of childhood. It is the way children express themselves and how they show what they are really like. By observing play, teachers can see children as they are and as they see themselves. Behavior reflects inner thought and brain functioning. The stage is set; the action begins as soon as the first child enters the room. Here, teachers can see children in action and watch for important behavior. All that is needed is to be alert to the clues and make note of them:

Teddy, a toddler, walks up to Brooke. He grabs Brooke's toy, a shape sorter, away from her. Then he begins to place shapes into the sorter. He has difficulty placing the shapes into the container. He then throws the shapes, his face turns red, and he kicks the container away.

Karen kneels on the chair placed at the puzzle table, selecting a 10-piece puzzle. She turns the puzzle upside down, allowing the pieces to fall on the table. She selects one piece at a time with her left hand and successfully puts every piece in the frame the first time. She raises both hands in the air and yells to Bryce, "I did it!"

What are children telling us about themselves? Which actions are most important to note? Understanding children is difficult because so many factors influence their behavior. A child's stage of development, culture, health, fatigue, and hunger can all make a difference in how a child behaves. Additionally, environmental factors such as the noise level, congestion, or time of day can add to the complex character of children's actions. Therefore, the teacher must make it a point to observe children at critical moments.

First, *notice the way a child begins each day*. Teddy always clings to his blanket after his dad leaves him at school. Karen bounces in each day ready to play the moment she walks in the door. Antonio says good-bye to his grandmother and then circles the room, hugging each adult before settling into an activity. These children show something about their needs. A good observer continues to watch, taking note of these early morning scenes. One can interpret these behaviors later, seeing how they apply to each child and how behavior changes over time.

Second, *watch how children use their bodies*. The basic routines of eating, napping, toileting, and dressing show how they take care of themselves. Whether or not Karen knows how to put her jacket on by herself may indicate her skills in other areas that require initiative and self-sufficiency. It may also indicate how she is developing an awareness of herself as a separate, independent being.

Third, *focus on how children relate to other people*. Teachers see Teddy choose Brooke as a playmate even when he fights with her, but he seems to avoid the other toddlers. The observant teacher makes note of the adults in each child's life. Who does Teddy seek for comfort? For answering questions? Who takes care of the child outside of school? Who picks the child up from school each day?

Finally, check for *what children like to do, how well they use the environment*, and *what they avoid*. Specific observations about the various areas of skill development—physical-motor, intellectual, affective—can be mirrors of growth. Teachers observe whether a child picks materials that are challenging or exhibits the tendency toward the novel or the familiar. Antonio starts each morning in the art area and then plays with puzzles before taking care of the animals. Karen prefers the blocks and dramatic play areas and lately has been spending more time in the cooking corner. Observing children at play and at work can tell us how they learn and what methods they use to gain information.

Why Observe?

Classrooms are busy places, especially for teachers who plan many activities and share in hundreds of interactions every day. There is so much that demands attention and response; at the same time, by building in systematic observation, teachers can improve their teaching, construct theory, assess children, assist families, and solve problems.

Improve Your Teaching

It is difficult to monitor our behavior while we are in the midst of working with children and time-consuming to reflect on that behavior afterward. Yet, the most effective teachers are those who are thorough in their preparation and systematic in evaluating their own work. It takes a certain level of awareness—of self, of the children, and of the environment—to monitor our own progress. This includes carefully checking what is happening, looking for feedback, and then acting on it. Professionals can do this by asking others to observe them through videotaping, by observing each other at work with the children, and by self-observation.

Bias and Objectivity Observing children helps teachers become more objective about the children in their care. When making observational notes, teachers look first at what the child is doing. This is different from looking at how a child ought to be doing something. The teacher becomes like a camera, recording what is seen without immediately judging it. This **objectivity** can balance the intense, personal side of teaching.

Bias is inherent in all our perceptions. We must acknowledge this truth without falling prey to the notion that because our efforts are flawed, they are worthless. Observing is not a precise or wholly objective act (see Figure 6-1). No two people see something in identical ways. For instance, reread the segments about Teddy and Karen. One teacher sees in Teddy a child demonstrating an age-appropriate response to frustration; another sees someone who is too aggressive; a third focuses on Brooke as a victim, rushing to comfort her and ignoring Teddy altogether.

Observing can never be totally objective or independent of the observer. Whatever you see passes through your filters of your past experiences, assumptions, biases, understanding, and knowledge. Your beliefs and ideas dictate what you see, coloring your perception and interpretation to the observation. Teachers, like all adults, are influenced in their work by their own early childhood experiences. They have notions about how children learn, play, grow, or behave because of the way they were raised and trained. The same behaviors might be labeled "assertive and independent" by one teacher and "bossy and uncooperative" by another (see Diversity Box).

To pull back, take some notes, and make an observation give the teacher a chance to see the larger scene. Team teaching can help. One teacher can step in and manage a situation so that another can get out of the thick of activity and observe from a distance. Teammates can help each other gain perspective by comparing notes on the class, an individual, or a time of the day. Observations can be a means of validating one teacher's point of view or changing it by checking out an opinion or idea through systematic observation.

Guidelines Three guidelines come to mind as one begins to observe:

1. *Practice "intensive waiting."* Cultivate an ability to wait and see what is really happening instead of rushing to conclusions about what it means, where such behavior comes from, or what should be done. These hurried impressions hinder a teacher's work toward understanding. Try to suspend expectations and be open to what is really happening, whether this concerns behavior, feelings, or patterns.

2. *Become "part scientist."* A good observer makes a clear distinction between fact and inference, between real behavior and an impression or conclusion drawn from it. Awareness of the difference between what actually happens and one's opinion and conclusions about those events is critical to good teaching.

3. *Engage in "slowing down."* Ask yourself while you are observing:
   - What is happening for this child in this play?
   - What is his agenda?
   - Does he have the skills and materials he needs to accomplish his intent?

No one can be free from bias, nor is that the point. The impressions and influences made can provide valuable insights into children. Self-awareness, coupled with observation and recording skills, prepares teachers to focus on actual behaviors. By separating what happens from what you *think* about it or how you *feel* about it, you are able to distinguish between fact and inference (see Figure 6-2). This does not mean teachers have to become aloof; your body language can reflect both warmth and a measure of objectivity at the same time.

Construct Theory

Observations are a link between theory and practice. All teachers gain from making this connection. New teachers can see the pages of a textbook as they match what they see with what they read. By putting together psychology and medical research with in-class experiences, professionals gain a deeper understanding of the nature of children.

Early childhood education is the one level of education that systematically bases its teaching on child development. Observation of children has a long history in early childhood teaching:

- Froebel wanted kindergarten teachers to be observers of children so that they could learn how children think and learn.
- G. Stanley Hall of the Child Study Movement asked teachers to observe and interview children to understand their developmental stages.
- John Dewey encouraged educators to see the seeds of democratic social relationships in the classroom play of young children.

Check Your Lenses!

What we see is in the eye of the beholder. What do you behold?

A two-year-old screams "Mine!" and fends off a boy trying to grab the blanket she's holding.

You see: "She's obviously protecting her security blanket; she is standing up for herself."

*Believing in private property.

Or: "Look at that selfish child; she disturbs the group and is unkind."

*Believing in group harmony.

A four-year-old shouts at another, "No; don't knock it down; we just built it ourselves!"

You see: "He's protecting his space; he takes pride in what he creates."

*Believing in self-expression and low frustration tolerance.

Or: "He is rude; he hurts others' feelings and is unfriendly."

*Believing in group affiliation and building community.

Kindergartners are sifting and sorting rice at a sensory table.

You see: "They are learning pre-math concepts through their senses."

*Believing children learn best by doing, by using their hands.

Or: "They are playing with food, and rice is sacred."

*Believing people must take care of food and treat it with respect.

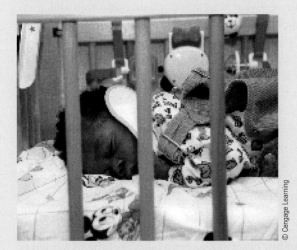

Infants sleeping in cribs in a child care center.

You see: "It is wonderful how the room is set up for quiet napping."

*Believing in children sleeping independently, on their own.

Or: "How sad that the babies are left alone like that."

*Believing in children being held, cared for always.

FIGURE 6-1 Observers watching the same scene, seeing the same behavior, think of it in very different terms. Seeing through a different pair of cultural eyes, each of us is thus affected in our reactions and assessments. (Excerpted from Gonzalez-Mena, J., in *Beginnings and Beyond*, 5th Ed, by A. Gordon & H. W. Browne. © 2000. Reprinted with permission of Delmar Learning, a division of Thomson Learning: www.thomsonrights.com. Fax 800-730-2215.)

DIVERSITY

Do You Have a "Diversity Bias"?

All teachers develop ideas and impressions about children when they spend time with them. Some children seem shy, some helpful, some affectionate, aggressive, cooperative, stubborn, and so on. These opinions influence the way teachers behave and interact with children. The child thought to be aggressive, for instance, is more likely to be blamed for starting the quarrel when one occurs nearby. Children who teachers consider polite are often given special consideration. Teacher bias may cause assumptions that stereotype rather than illuminate the child or group.

The same thing is true in children. When school-aged children are asked how they'd respond to a hypothetical situation, such as one child bumping into another in the cafeteria and spilling a drink on someone, those who assume others are out to get them do not access other conflict-resolution solutions, even if they know them. "They have what researchers call a *hostile attribution bias*," says Galinsky (2010). "These words are a mouthful, but what they mean is that some children immediately interpret ambiguous situations as hostile when there isn't enough information to be certain—they jump to conclusions."

If children and adults are both subject to this bias, it is crucial that teachers practice what they preach; when it comes to perspective, they must themselves step back and make sense of the situation before attributing cause or intention. Look for clues to understand before making a judgment and help children do the same. Circumstances of diversity—age, culture, language, family beliefs and habits—can contribute to biased observations and conclusions. By practicing patience and using appraisal skills that slow down judgment, you can avoid making mistakes of "diversity bias."

- The McMillans used frequent descriptions of children's activities to reflect teachers' use of observation (Reifel, 2011).

If we are to develop programs that work for young children—what they can do, how they think and communicate, and what they feel—we need to be able to apply sound child development knowledge to the classroom. "Each one of you has inside yourself an image of the child that directs you as you begin to relate to a child. This theory within you pushes you to behave in certain ways; it orients you as you talk to the child. . . . We must move beyond just looking at the child to become better observers, able to penetrate into the child to understand each child's resources and potential and present state of mind. We need to compare theirs with our own in order to work well together" (Malaguzzi, 1993).

Use as an Assessment Tool

Recording observations often takes the form of written or visual documentation that serve as informal ways to assess children's skills and capabilities. Assessment is a critical part of a teacher's job, and evaluating children includes observing and assessing their behavior and their development. **Authentic assessment**, done when children are in their natural setting and performing real tasks, fits best with the overall goal of developmentally appropriate practice. Portfolio use and other kinds of work-sampling systems are discussed later in this chapter.

Observation can be used as a tool for teachers to assess the accuracy of their own impressions. Comparing notes with others refines a teacher's objective observation skills. The results lead directly into environmental design, daily scheduling, and curriculum planning as demonstrated in the following situations:

- Does the traffic flow easily or are the toddlers stuck and unable to get out?
- When and where does the trouble start at preschool clean up? Who participates or avoids it?
- What are the second-graders doing to show what sorting and classifying skills they know and what math concepts they have yet to master?

By using observation to assess children and the program, teachers are accountable to their clients: the children, the parents, and the public. Assessment issues and early learning standards are described later in this chapter.

Assist Families

Families benefit from teacher observations. Detailed records collected over time reveal growth in many areas and can be used in family–teacher conferences.

1. The teacher shares fresh, meaningful examples that demonstrate the child's growth and abilities. Families then know more about the child as a *school-person* and are reassured that the teachers value and understand their child.
2. The families share their personal stories and ideas about the child as a *home-person*, and the teachers gain perspective. Problems become clearer, and

Can You Spot the Bias?

Poor Observation

Julio walked over to the coat rack and dropped his sweater on the floor. He is *shy* (1) of teachers, so he didn't ask anyone to help him pick it up. He walked over to Cynthia *because she's his best friend* (2). *He wasn't nice* (3) to the other children when he started being *pushy and bossy* (4). He *wanted their attention* (5), so he *nagged* (6) them into leaving the table and going to the blocks *like four-year-old boys do* (7).

Good Observation

Emilio pulled out a puzzle from the rack with his right hand, then carried it with both hands to the table nearby. Using both hands, he methodically took each piece out of the frame and set it to his left. Sara, who had been seated across from Emilio with some table toys in front of her, reached out and pushed all the puzzle pieces onto the floor. Emilio's face reddened as he stared directly at Sara with his mouth in a taut line. His hands turned into fists, his brow furrowed, and he yelled at Sara in a forceful tone, "Stop it! I hate you!"

Analysis and Comments

1. Inference of a general characteristic.
2. Inference of a child's emotion.
3. Observer's opinion.
4. Inference with no physical evidence stated.
5. Opinion of child's motivation.
6. Observer's inference.
7. Overgeneralization; stereotyping.

Analysis and Comments

Emilio was clearly *angry* as demonstrated in his facial expressions, hand gestures, and body movements. The way a child speaks is as revealing as what a child says when one wants to determine what a child is feeling. Muscular tension is another clue to the child's emotions. But the physical attitude of the child is not enough; one must also consider the context. Just seeing a child sitting in a chair with a red face, one doesn't know if he is embarrassed, angry, feverish, or overstimulated. We need to know the events that led to this appearance. Then we can correctly assess the entire situation. By being open to what is happening without judging it first, we begin to see children more clearly.

© Cengage Learning 2011

FIGURE 6-2 Two observations. The first example contains numerous biases, which are numbered in the left column and explained in the right column. The second example has clear descriptions and is relatively free of biases.

plans can be made to work together. Results can be further tested through continuing observation.

Chapter 8 discusses family–teacher relationships in detail.

Wonder Why and Solve a Problem

In the spirit of being part-scientist, teachers can become researchers in their own classrooms. A scientist, like a child, sees something and wonders why. This curiosity leads to thinking about the various components of a problem and looking at the parts as well as the whole. Next comes the "head-scratching" part—a time of reflection, developing hunches or intuitions about the problem, and generating alternatives. The teacher is then ready to try out an alternative, known in scientific terms as "testing the hypothesis." Finally, the teacher gets results, which feeds back into rethinking the problem or celebrating the solution.

Using observation to research a problem can turn frustration into a more productive approach. For instance, without extensive training, the parent co-op group noticed that the children avoided clean up. They realized that the "parent-helpers" were doing most of the work, and the children kept playing until the teacher called them to the circle. They wondered what would happen if all the adults stopped putting things away and then tried it out. The children were surprised and upset to see the room such a mess, with no place to sit for circle time. This "action research" motivated everyone to find another system for restoring the environment after play.

Contexts for Understanding Observations

The goal of observing children is to understand them better. Teachers, students, and parents collect a great deal of information by watching children. Observational data help adults know children in several significant ways. The **contexts** of observations—the various aspects of settings and situations—helps us understand the child or group better.

Children as Individuals

How do children spend their time at school? What activities are difficult? Who is the child's best friend? Observing is watching a child with the purpose of trying to understand that child from the inside out—to see the world from that child's viewpoint and how it is experienced. By watching individual children, teachers help them learn at their own pace, at their own rate of development, in their own time. When teachers know who each child is, they can choose activities and materials to match interests and skills. This is called **individualized curriculum**: tailoring what is taught to what a child is ready and willing to learn.

This kind of curriculum gives children educational experiences that offer **connected knowledge**: a curriculum that is real and relevant to the individual child and is part of developmentally appropriate practices (see Chapters 1, 2, 9, and 10). It is also part of a program for children with special needs; in these cases, an individualized education plan (IEP/IFSP) is developed jointly by teachers, education specialists, and parents to better serve the child.

Observing helps a teacher spot a child's strengths and areas of difficulty. Once these are known, teachers plan **intervention** measures, helping to make the school experience successful for the child. The **accommodations** made on behalf of individual needs are important for all developmentally appropriate programs and crucial for children with special needs.

Dowley (not dated) suggests that an observation of a child can be made on three levels. First, a teacher tries to report exactly what the child *does*: Note exactly what actions the child takes. Second, express how the child seems to *feel* about what happened: Note facial expressions, body language, and quality of the behavior. Third, include your own *interpretation*: This last and separate step brings in your personal responses and impressions (see Figure 6-3).

Children in General

When recording behavior, teachers see growth patterns emerge. These trends reflect the nature of human development. Both Piaget and Erikson used this technique to learn how children think and develop socially and emotionally. Gesell studied large numbers of children to get a developmental **norm** of physical growth. Parten (1932) and Dawes (1934) watched hundreds of preschoolers and arrived at the definitive description of children's play patterns and quarreling behavior. For today's early childhood educator, observing children can provide the answer to these questions:

- What might you expect when a 2-year-old pours juice?
- How will the second grade class respond to a field trip?
- What kind of social play is typical for the 4-year-old?
- How does an infant move from crawling to walking upright?

Observation and Analysis

Gabriel [2.4 years]: Observations of Psychosocial Development-Temperament

I have seen patterns of quiet and timid behavior all throughout the course of my observation. I suppose that Gabriel belongs to the "slow to warm up" temperament cluster. From what I've observed, Gabriel usually withdraws from the crowd. He prefers to play alone, preferably in quiet spaces. He also likes to play with toys as if they are his own. In one situation, a fellow toddler approaches while Gabriel is playing with an abacus. The fellow toddler tries to participate and play with quiet Gabriel, but as soon as this other kid starts playing with the beads, Gabriel quickly grabs the abacus, knocks it down, picks it up, walks away, and plays it alone for himself.

Gabriel also appears "slow to adapt." When introduced in playtime situations with others, he does not respond promptly to what the others are asking him to do. His usual response would be a stare, or sometimes, no response at all. For example, two children were playing a game of filling up buckets with sand. When they saw Gabriel, one of them gave him a bucket; he held it without movement for a minute, then dropped it and wandered away. In another scenario, one of the caregivers pushed a child in a cart; Gabriel watched closely and seemed to wait for her to play with him. The caregiver, however, suggests Gabriel push the cart and play with the kid. In response, he just looks blankly, and afterwards, complies but reluctantly begins to push the cart and only while the caregiver watches.

FIGURE 6-3 Making an observation involves three levels: reporting exactly what the child does, how the child seems to feel, and your own interpretations. (Notes courtesy of M. Duraliza, 2007.)

Observation gives a feeling for group behavior, as well as a developmental yardstick to compare individuals within the group. Teachers determine age-appropriate expectations from this. It is important, for example, to know that most children cannot tie their own shoes at age 4 but can be expected to pull them on by themselves. A general understanding aids in planning a thoughtful and challenging curriculum. Teachers of young preschoolers, for instance, know that many children are ready for 6- to 10-piece puzzles but that the 20-piece jigsaw will most likely be dumped on the table and quickly abandoned (see DAP Box).

Developmental Relationships

Observing brings about an understanding of the various developmental areas and how they are related. Development is at once specific and integrated. Children's behavior is a mix of several distinct developmental domains (see Chapters 3 and 4) and, at the same time, an integrated whole with parts that influence each other. When we say the *whole child*, we mean a consideration of how development works in unison.

When observing children, one must focus on the major domains of physical-motor, cognitive/language,

DAP Taking Observations into Practice

From observing many children comes an awareness of each child's progression along the developmental scale.

- Experienced teachers of toddlers do not put out watercolor sets, but the second grade teacher does so routinely.
- Teachers learn that it is typical of 4- and 5-year-olds to exclude others from their play because they have seen it happen countless times.
- The 3-year-old who is sure she is "too little" to use the toilet does not concern the knowledgeable teacher, who knows that this is developmentally appropriate behavior.

Decisions about an individual child come from watching and knowing many children. This understanding is a valuable asset when talking to families about their child's skills, challenges, and progress. The results of teachers' observations of children, clinical interviews, collections of children's work samples, and their performances on authentic activities give them concrete examples. These methods of assessment are also appropriate to the developmental status and experiences of young children, and they recognize individual variation in learners and allow children to demonstrate their competence in different ways.

and affective development. Thus, preschool teachers look to ascertain the language abilities of 3- to 5-year-olds and also the social skills that preschool children acquire. They need to know which self-help skills children can learn before age 6 and the expectations and experiences the children have at home. They must observe how fine motor development may interact with intellectual growth, or if gross motor skill affects successful cognitive learning. Overarching for all, teachers observe how self-concept relates to all of the other areas.

Observing helps teachers see how the pieces fit together. For instance, when given a set of blocks in various sizes, colors, and shapes, a 4-year-old has no difficulty finding the red ones or square ones, but may be puzzled when asked to find those that are both red and square. No wonder that same child has difficulty understanding that someone can be their best friend and someone else's at the same time.

Practiced observation shows that a child's skills are multiple and varied and have only limited connection to age. Karen has the physical coordination of a 4½-year-old, the language skills of a 6-year-old, and the social skills of a 2-year-old—all bound up in a body that just turned 3. Sharing the picture of this whole child between parents and teachers can be helpful to both.

Influences on Behavior

Careful observation gives us insight into the influences and dynamics of behavior:

Boaz has a hard time when he enters his child care each morning, yet he is competent and says he likes school. Close observation reveals that his favorite areas are climbing outdoor games and the sandbox. Boaz feels least successful in the construction and creative arts areas, the primary choices indoors, where his school day begins.

Mari, on the other hand, starts the day happily but cries frequently throughout the day. Is there a pattern to her outbursts? Watch what happens to Mari when free play is over and group time begins. She falls apart readily when it is time to move outdoors to play, time to have snacks, time to nap, and so on.

The *environment* influences both these children. The classroom arrangement and daily schedule impact children's behavior, because children are directly affected by the restraints imposed by their activities and their time.

Boaz feels unsure of himself in those activities that are offered as he starts his day. Seeing only these choices as he enters the room causes him discomfort, which he shows by crying and clinging to his dad. By adding something he enjoys, such as a sand table indoors, the teacher changes the physical environment to be more appealing and positive. Boaz's difficulties in saying good-bye disappear as he finds he can be successful and comfortable at the beginning of his day. The physical environment was the primary cause.

The source of Mari's problem is more difficult to detect. The physical environment seems to interest and appeal to her. On closer observation, her crying and her disruptive behavior appear to happen just at the point of change, regardless of the activities before or afterward. The teacher makes a special effort to signal upcoming transitions and to involve her in bringing them about. Telling Mari, "Five more minutes until naptime" or "After you wash your hands, go to the snack table" gives her the clues she needs to anticipate the process of change. Asking her to announce clean up time to the class lets her be in control of that transition. It was the temporal environment, the *time* aspect of the environment, that caused difficulty for her.

Adult behavior affects and influences children. Kindergartner Annika has days of intense activity and involvement with materials; on other days she appears sluggish and uninterested. After a week of observation, teachers find a direct correlation with the presence of Chip, the student teacher. On his participation days, Annika calls out to him to see her artwork and watch her various accomplishments; when Chip is absent, Annika's activity level falls. Once a pattern is noticed, the teacher acts on these observations. Chip offers Annika ideas for activities she could work on to show him when he returns to class. When he is absent, the teacher lets her write him a note or draw him a picture and then reminds Annika of the plan and gets her started.

Children's behavior is a powerful influence. Anyone who has worked with toddlers knows how attractive a toy becomes to a child once another has it. The first grader who suddenly dislikes school may be feeling left out of a friendship group. Teachers need to carefully observe the social dynamics of the class as they seek to understand and figure out how to handle problem situations.

Understanding of Self

Observing children can be a key to understanding ourselves. People who develop observational skills notice human behavior more accurately. They become skilled at seeing small but important facets of human personality. They learn to differentiate between what is fact and what is inference. This increases an awareness of self as a teacher and how one's biases affect perceptions about children. Teachers who become keen observers of children apply these skills to themselves. As Feeney and colleagues (2008) note:

> In a less structured but no less important way, you also observe yourself, your values, your relationships,

Learning to look requires a certain awareness so that the teacher does more than simply watch or become completely involved in an activity.

and your own feelings and reactions. When you apply what you know about observation to yourself, you gain greater self-awareness. It is difficult to be objective about yourself, but as you watch your own behavior and interactions you can learn more about how you feel and respond in various situations and realize the impact of your behavior on others.

The values and benefits of observation are long-lasting. By practicing observations—what it takes to look, to see, to become more sensitive—teachers can record children's behavior fully and vividly, capturing the unique qualities, culture, and personality of each child.

Common Types of Observation Systems

Once teachers and students understand why observing is important, they must then learn how to record what they see. Although children are constantly under the teacher's eyes, so much happens so fast that critical events are lost in the daily routine of classrooms. Systematic observations aid in recording events and help teachers make sense of them.

Although it is true that teachers rarely have the luxury of observing uninterrupted for long periods of time, they can often plan shorter segments. Practice by paying attention to the content of children's play during free periods—theirs and yours.

Next, try your hand at jotting some notes about that play. It is easy to get discouraged, especially if you are unaccustomed to writing. The language of recording gets easier as you practice finding synonyms for common words. For instance, children are active creatures—how many ways do they run? They may gallop, dart, whirl, saunter, skip, or hop. Or think of the various ways children talk to you: they shriek, whisper, whine, shout, demand, whimper, lisp, or roar. Once you have a certain mastery of the language (and be sure to record what you see in the language that comes easiest to you), describing the important nuances of children's behavior becomes easier (see Figure 6-4).

Key Elements of Observations

The key ingredients in all types of observations used in recording children's behavior are 1) defining and describing the behaviors and 2) repeating the observation in terms of several factors such as time, number of children, or activities. All observational systems have certain elements in common:

Focus

- What do you want to know? (motor skills or play choices)
- Whom/what do you want to observe? (child or group)
- What aspects of behavior do you want to know about? (pincer grasp or social problem solving)
- What is your purpose? (use of environment or snags in the daily schedule)

System

- What do you do?
- How do you define the terms?
- How do you record the information you need? How detailed is your record? Do you need units of measure? What kind?
- For how long do you record?

Tools

- What do you need for your observations?
- How do you record what you want to know?
- Where do you watch? When is the best time?
- What restraints are inherent in the setting?

In particular, the tools for observation and documentation are crucial because you miss everything that is happening if you have to scramble to find something to

---

Narrative: The Child Alone

Unoccupied Behavior. SH slowly walks from the classroom to the outside play area, looking up each time one of the children swishes by. SH stops when reaching the table and benches and begins pulling the string on the sweatshirt. Still standing SH looks around the yard for a minute, then wanders slowly over to the seesaw. Leaning against it, SH touches the seesaw gingerly, then trails both hands over it while looking out into the yard. (Interpretive comments: This unoccupied behavior is probably due to two reasons: SH is overweight and has limited language skills compared with the other children. Pulling at the sweatshirt string is something to do to pass the time since the overweight body is awkward and not especially skillful.)

Onlooker Behavior. J is standing next to the slide watching her classmates using this piece of equipment. She looks up and says, "Hi." Her eyes open wider as she watches the children go down the slide. P calls to J to join them but J shakes her head "no." (Interpretive comments: J is interested in the slide but is reluctant to use it. She has a concerned look on her face when the others slide down; it seems too much of a challenge for J.)

Solitary Play. L comes running into the yard holding two paintbrushes and a bucket filled with water. He stops about three feet away from a group of children playing with cars, trucks, and buses in the sandbox and sits down. He drops the brushes into the bucket and laughs when the water splashes his face. He begins swishing the water around with the brushes and then starts wiggling his fingers in it. (Interpretive comments: L is very energetic and seems to thoroughly enjoy his outside playtime with water. He adds creative touches to his pleasurable experience.)

FIGURE 6-4 The narrative form of observation gives a rich sample of children's behavior; even though it risks teacher bias, it still records valuable information.

record what is right in front of you. Keep handy (but not in reach of children) these items:

Pencil and paper on a clipboard or a spiral notebook
Camera, with extra memory card/stick
Video/flip camera, with extra batteries
Computer or laptop, regularly charged

Types of Observations

There are several types of observations you can conduct, depending on the situation or purpose you are trying to achieve. Four major methods of observing and two additional information-gathering techniques are discussed. They are:

1. Narratives
2. Samplings
3. Ratings
4. Modified child study techniques

Narratives

At once the most valuable and most difficult of records, **narratives** are attempts to record nearly everything that happens. In the case of a young child, this means all that the child does, says, gestures, appears to think about, and seems to feel. Narratives maintain a **running record** of the excitement and tension of the interaction while remaining an accurate, objective account of the events and behavior. Narratives are an attempt to actually re-create the scene by recording it in thorough and vivid language. Observers put into words what they see, hear, and know about an event or a person. The result is a full and dynamic report.

Running records and narratives are the oldest and often most informative kind of report. Historically, as Arnold Gesell reported (see Chapter 1), they were used to set basic developmental norms. They are a standard technique in anthropology and the biologic sciences and were used by Pestalozzi (1700s) and Darwin (1800s). Jean Piaget watched and recorded in minute detail his own children's growth, which became a lifelong study of thought processes. Baby biographies, narratives written by parents, were some of the first methods used in child study and reached their peak of popularity in the early 1900s.

Diary descriptions are another form of narrative. Just as the term implies, it is, in diary form, a consecutive record of everything children do and say and how they do it. The process is a natural one. In the classroom, this means describing every action observed within a given time period. It might be a five minute period during free play to watch and record what one child does. The child who is a loner, the child who is a wanderer, and the child who is aggressive are prime candidates for a diary de-

scription. Another way to use this type of running record is to watch an area of the yard or room, then to record who is there and how they are using the materials.

Specimen description, a modified version of a running record as it is often called in research, is a more common form of the narrative. The procedure is to take on-the-spot notes of a specific child each day. This task lends itself easily to most early childhood settings. The teachers carry with them a small notebook and pencil, tucked in a pocket. They jot down whatever seems important or noteworthy during the day. These anecdotal notes are the most familiar form of recording observations (see Figure 6-4). They often focus on one item at a time:

- A part of the environment—how is the science area used?
- A particular time of day—what happens right after nap?
- A specific child—why is a child hitting others?

This system may be even less structured, with all the teachers taking "on-the-hoof" notes as daily incidents occur. These notes then become a rich source of information for report writing and parent conferences.

Logs or **journals** are the final forms of the narrative. Teachers write in detail about each child or a critical incident. Because this is time-consuming and needs to be done without interruption, it helps to write immediately after the program is over. Sometimes teaching teams organize themselves to enable one member of the staff to observe and record in the journal during class time. The important point is that children's behavior is recorded either while it is happening or soon afterward.

The challenging part of the narrative recording technique is to have enough detail so the reader is able to picture whole situations later. Using language as a descriptive tool requires a large vocabulary and skillful recorder. Whatever notes the teachers use, however brief, need to be both clear and accurate.

There are many advantages to this type of observation. Narratives are rich in information, provide detailed behavioral accounts, and are relatively easy to record. With a minimum of equipment and training, teachers can learn to take notes on what children do and say. To write down everything is impossible, so some selection is necessary. These "judgment calls" can warp the narrative. The main disadvantages of narratives are the time they can take, the language and the vocabulary that must be used, and the biases the recorder may have. Even though the narrative remains one of the most widely used and effective methods of observing young children today, many teachers prefer more structured procedures. These more definite, more precise techniques still involve some personal interpretation, but the area of individual judgment is diminished. The observational techniques discussed in the following sections also tend to be less time-consuming than the narrative.

Samplings

Sampling methods examine specific types of behavior and divide the observation into measurable units. Two types of this observational method are time sampling and event sampling.

A **time sampling** is an observation of what happens within a given period of time. Time sampling appears to have originated with research in child development. It has been used to record autonomy, dependency, task persistence, aggression, and social involvement. Developed as an observational strategy in laboratory schools in the 1920s, time sampling was used to collect data on large numbers of children and to get a sense of normative behaviors for particular age groups or sexes. It has been used to study play patterns and to record nervous habits of school children, such as nail biting and hair twisting.

The definitive study using time sampling is Mildred Parten's observation in the 1930s of children's play. The codes developed in this study have become classic play patterns: solitary, parallel, associative, and cooperative play. These codes are used throughout this text (see Chapter 14), as well as in the professional field to describe the interactions of children. In a time sample, behavior is recorded at regular time intervals. To use this method, one needs to sample what occurs fairly frequently. It makes sense to choose those behaviors that might occur, say, at least once every 10 minutes (see Figure 6-5).

Time sampling has its own advantages and disadvantages. The process itself helps teachers define exactly what it is they want to observe. It helps focus on specific behaviors and how often they occur. Time sampling is ideal for collecting information about the group as a whole. Finally, defining behaviors clearly and developing a category and coding system reduce the problem of observer bias.

Yet, by diminishing this bias, one also eliminates some of the richness and quality of information. It is difficult to get the whole picture when one divides it into artificial time units and with only a few categories. The key is to decide what it is teachers want to know and then choose the observational method that best suits those needs. When narratives or time samplings will not suffice, perhaps an event sampling will.

Sampling: Time to Play

P = Parallel
A = Associative
C = Cooperative

Child	Time Unit												Totals		
	9:00			9:15			9:30			9:45					
	P	A	C	P	A	C	P	A	C	P	A	C	P	A	C
Jamal															
Marty															
Dahle															
Keith															
Rosa															
Cameron															
Hannah															

© Cengage Learning 2011

FIGURE 6-5 Time sampling of play with others involves defining the behavior and making a coding sheet to tally observations.
You can download a copy of this form from this text's Education CourseMate website.

An **event sampling** is another sampling method. With this method, the observer defines an event, devises a system for describing and coding it, then waits for it to happen. As soon as it does, the recorder moves into action. Thus, the behavior is recorded as it occurs naturally.

The events that are chosen can be quite interesting and diverse. Consider Helen C. Dawes's classic analysis of preschool children's quarrels. Whenever a quarrel began, the observer recorded it. She recorded how long the quarrel lasted, what was happening when it started, what behaviors happened during the quarrel (including what was done and said), what the outcome was, and what happened afterward. Her format for recording included the duration (*x* number of seconds); a narrative for the situation; verbal or motor activity; and checklists for the quarrel behavior, outcome, and aftereffects (see Figure 6-6).

Other researchers have studied dominance and emotions. Teachers can use event sampling to look at these and other behaviors such as bossiness, avoidance of teacher requests, or withdrawal. Like time sampling, event sampling looks at a particular behavior or occurrence. But the unit is the event rather than a prescribed time interval. Here again, the behavior must be clearly defined and the recording sheet easy to use. Unlike with time sampling, the event to be recorded may occur a number of times during the observation.

For these reasons, event sampling is a favorite of classroom teachers. They can go about the business of teaching children until the event occurs. Then they can record the event quickly and efficiently. Prescribing the context within which the event occurs restores some of the quality often lost in time sampling. The only disadvantage is that the richness of detail of the narrative description is missing.

Rating Methods

Rating methods record either the presence or absence of a behavior or the degree to which a behavior is exhibited. The two most common forms are checklists and rating scales.

Checklists contain a great deal of information that can be recorded rapidly. A carefully planned checklist can tell a lot about one child or the entire class. The data are collected in a short period of time, usually about a week.

Sampling: Events in the Classroom

1. Behavior to be observed: *children's accidents [spills, knockovers, falls].*
2. Information you want to know: *[who, where, when, causes, results].*
3. Recording sheet. *[use M–F morning for 2 weeks]*

© Cengage Learning

Time	Children	Place	Cause	Outcome
8:50	Shelley, Mike	play dough	M steps on S toes	S cries, runs to Tchr
9:33	Tasauna, Yuki	blocks	T runs through, knocks over Y's tower	Y hits T, both cry
9:56	Spencer	yard	S turns trike too sharply, falls off	S cries, wants mom
10:28	Lorena, Shelley	doll corner	L bumps table, spills pitcher that S has just set there	S cries, runs to Tchr
Totals and Analysis: 4 problems	*Shelley-2 Mike, Yuki, Tasauna, Spencer, Lorena-1*	*Inside: Pd, Bk, Dolls Outside: trike*	*Property: 1 Territory: 2 Power: 1?*	*Crying: 4 Seeking Tchr: 2 Seeking Parent: 1*

© Cengage Learning 2011

FIGURE 6-6 Event sampling can be helpful in determining how frequently a specific event takes place. For instance, sampling the number and types of accidents for a given child or time frame helps teachers see what is happening in class.

With data collected for a week, teachers have a broad picture of how these children spend their time and what activities interest them. At other times, yes/no lists are preferable (see Figure 6-7).

Checklists can vary in length and complexity depending on their functions. To develop one, teachers first determine the purpose of the observation. Next, they define what the children will do to demonstrate the behavior being observed. Finally, they design the actual checklist, one that is easy to use and simple to set aside when other duties must take precedence.

Although they are easy to record, checklists lack the richness of the more descriptive narrative. In Figure 6-7, teachers know which activities children have chosen but cannot see how they played in each area, the time spent there, or whether and with whom they interacted. The advantages of checklists are that they can tally broad areas of information and teachers can create one with relative ease. Checklists are often used in child evaluation (see Figure 6-8).

Rating scales are like checklists, planned in advance to record something specific. They extend checklists by adding some quality to what is observed. The advantage is that more information is gathered. A potential problem is added because the observers' opinions are now required and could hamper objectivity.

Rating scales differ from checklists because they can identify the degree to which a behavior is exhibited. Using numbers to rate the occurrence or strength of a characteristic (such as using a scale of 1–5), the rating becomes a kind of **continuum**, (see Figure 6-9). The result is a detailed description of 1) each child's behavior as each teacher sees it; 2) the group's overall attention level; and 3) an interesting cross-teacher comparison.

Rating: An Activity Frequency Count

Observer_____ Date_____ Time_____

Learning Center	Anna	Charlie	Leticia	Hiroko	Max	Josie	Totals
Indoors Science/Pets	1		1		1	1	4
Dramatic Play	1	1	1			1	4
Art	1		1				2
Blocks		1					1
Table Toys			1	1	1		3
Easels & Self Help				1			1
Music			1		1		2
Outdoors Sand/Water		1	1			1	3
Blocks				1	1		2
Wheel Toys		1			1		2
Climbers	1		1			1	3
Woodworking					1		1
Games	1						1
Total	5	4	7	3	6	4	

© Cengage Learning 2011

FIGURE 6-7 With data collected over the course of a week, teachers have a broad picture of how children spend their time at school and what activities interest them.

You can download a copy of this form from this text's Education CourseMate website.

Rating: A Yes/No Checklist

Motor Skills Observation (ages 2–4) Child _____

Date _____ Observer _____ Age _____

	Yes	No
Eating:		
1. Holds glass with one hand		
2. Pours from pitcher		
3. Spills little from spoon		
4. Selects food with pincer grasp		
Dressing:		
1. Unbuttons		
2. Puts shoes on		
3. Uses both hands together (such as holding jacket with one hand while zipping with the other)		
Fine Motor:		
1. Uses pincer grasp with pencil, brushes		
2. Draws straight line		
3. Copies circles		
4. Cuts at least 2" in line		
5. Makes designs and crude letters		
6. Builds tower of 6–9 blocks		
7. Turns pages singly		
Gross Motor:		
1. Descends/ascends steps with alternate feet		
2. Stands on one foot, unsupported		
3. Hops on two feet		
4. Catches ball, arms straight, elbows in front of body		
5. Operates tricycle		

© Cengage Learning 2011

FIGURE 6-8 A yes/no checklist gives specific information about an individual child's skills. You can download a copy of this checklist from this text's Education CourseMate website.

Modified Child Study Techniques

Because observation is the key method of studying young children in their natural settings, it makes good sense to develop many kinds of observational skills. Each can be tailored to fit the individual child, the particular group, the kind of staff, and the specific problem. Teachers who work in complex, creative classrooms have questions arise that need fast answers. Modified child study techniques can define the scope of the problem fairly quickly. Some of the techniques are shadow studies, experimental procedures, and the *methode clinique*.

The **shadow study** is a type of modified technique. It is similar to the diary description and focuses on

Rating: Circle Time Continuum

Rating: <u>Circle Time</u>   Child: _____   Dates: _____

NEVER ATTENDS (wiggles, distracts others, wanders away)

SELDOM ATTENDS (eyes wander, never follows fingerplays or songs, occasionally watches leader)

SOMETIMES ATTENDS (can be seen imitating hand gestures, appears to be watching leader about half the time, watches others imitating leader)

USUALLY ATTENDS (often follows leader, rarely leaves group, rarely needs redirection, occasionally volunteers, usually follows leader's gestures and imitations)

ALWAYS ATTENDS (regularly volunteers, enthusiastically enters into each activity, eagerly imitates leader, almost always tries new songs)

© Cengage Learning 2011

FIGURE 6-9 A rating scale measuring attention at group times requires data in terms of frequency, adding depth to the observation

one child at a time. An in-depth approach, the shadow study gives a detailed picture. Each teacher attempts to observe and record regularly the behavior of one particular child. The notes are then compared. Before starting a shadow study, give some form and organization to the notes (see Figure 6-10).

The data in a shadow study are descriptive. In this, it shares the advantages of narratives. One of its disadvantages is that teachers may let other matters go while focusing on one child, and a shadow study can be quite time-consuming. Still, one interesting side effect often noted is how the behavior of the child being studied improves while the child is being observed. Disruptive behavior seems to diminish or appear less intense. It would appear that in the act of focusing on the child, teacher attention has somehow helped to alter the behavior. Somehow the child feels the impact of all this positive, caring attention and responds to it.

Two additional strategies are used to obtain information about a child. Because they involve some adult intervention, they do not consist strictly of observing and recording naturally occurring behavior. Still, they are very helpful techniques for teachers to understand and use.

Modified Technique: Shadow Study

Child's Name ___*Jeff*___

Time	Setting (where)	Behavior/Response (what and how)
9:00	Arrives—cubby, removes wraps, etc.	"I can put on my own nametag" (enthusiastically). Uses thumb to push sharp end of pin, grins widely. Goes to teacher, "Did you see what I did?"
9:15	Blocks	Precise, elaborate work with small cubes on top of block structure, which he built with James. "Those are the dead ones," pointing to the purple cubes outside the structure. Cries and hits Kate when her elbow accidentally knocks tower off.
9:30	Wandering around room	Semidistant, slow pace. Stops at table where children are preparing snack. Does not make eye contact with teacher when invited to sit; Ali grabs J's shirt and tugs at it. "The teacher is talking to you!" J blinks, then sits and asks to help make snack. Stays 10 minutes.

© Cengage Learning

© Cengage Learning 2011

FIGURE 6-10 A shadow study profiles an individual child in a class and can be very helpful when communicating with families.

Experimental procedures are those in which adult researchers closely control a situation and its variables. Researchers create a situation in which they can:

1. Observe a particular behavior
2. Make a hypothesis, or guess, about that behavior
3. Test the hypothesis by conducting the experiment

For instance, an experimenter might wish to observe fine motor behavior in 7-year-olds to test the hypothesis that these children can significantly improve their fine motor skills in sewing if given specific instructions. Two groups of children are tested. One group is given an embroidery hoop, thread, and needle and asked to make 10 stitches. The other receives a demonstration of how to stitch and is then given the identical task. The embroidery created by both groups is then compared. Some previously agreed-on criteria are used to quantify the fine motor skill demonstrated by the two groups' work.

The major criteria for a scientific experiment may be applied to this procedure as follows:

- The experimenters can control all relevant aspects of the behavior. (In this case, the materials can be controlled, although previous experience with embroidering cannot.)
- Usually, only one variable at a time should be measured. (Only fine motor skill as it relates to embroidery is observed, not other skills such as language or information processing, or even fine motor proficiency in printing or drawing.)
- Children are assigned to the two groups in a random manner. (In other words, the groups are not divided by sex, age, or any other predetermined characteristics.)

Few teachers working directly with children use the stringent criteria needed to undertake a true scientific experiment. However, it is useful to understand this process because much basic research conducted to investigate how children think, perceive, and behave utilizes these techniques. Moreover, the "action research" described earlier attempts to follow the scientific method described here.

The *methode clinique* is the final information-gathering technique that involves the adult directly with the child. This method is used in psychotherapy and in counseling settings, as the therapist asks probing questions. The master of this **clinical method** with children was Piaget, who would observe and question a child about a situation (see Chapter 4). Note how the adults wonder "what or why" and then insert their own actions to find out what they want to know in these examples:

- Three-month-old Jenna is lying in a crib looking at a mobile. Her hands are waving in the air. Her dad wonders whether Jenna will reach out and grasp the mobile if it is moved close to her hands. Or will she bat at the toy? Move her hands away? He tries it to see what happens.
- A group of preschoolers are gathered around a water table. Their teacher notices two cups, one deep and narrow, the other broad and shallow, and asks, "I wonder which one holds more, or if they are the same?" The children say what they think and why. Then, one of the children takes the two cups and pours the liquid from one into the other.

In both examples, the adult does more than simply observe and record what happens. With the infant, her father wonders what Jenna's responses might be and then watches for the answer. For the preschoolers, the teacher intervenes in the children's natural play to explore a question systematically and then listens and observes their answers. The clinical method is not strictly an observational method, but it is an informative technique that, when used carefully, can reveal much about children's abilities and knowledge.

Observation and its various methods are used extensively in early childhood programs and, increasingly, in elementary education to assess children (see Figure 6-11). It is safe to say that whenever a teacher encounters a problem—be it a child's behavior, a period of the day, a set of materials, or a puzzling series of events—the first step toward a solution is systematic observation.

How to Observe and Record Effectively

Learning how to observe and record is a serious activity and requires a great deal of concentration. Some preparations can be made beforehand so that full attention is focused on the observation. Thinking through some of the possible problems helps the teacher get the most out of the experience.

Observing While Teaching

There are *many* effective ways to observe. Some teachers find certain times of the day easier than others. Many prefer to watch during free play, whereas others find it easier to watch individual children during directed teaching times. Most teachers keep a pencil and paper handy to record observations throughout the day; others choose to record what they see after school is over for the day. Contemporary teachers often keep a digital camera nearby, and some have hand-held video cameras. The professional team that is committed to observation finds ways to support its implementation.

Observational Techniques

Method	Observational Interval	Recording Techniques	Advantages	Disadvantages
1. Narratives				
Running Record	Continuous sequences	Use notebook and pencil, clipboard; can itemize activity or other ongoing behavior; can see growth patterns.	Rich in detail; maintains sequence of events; describes behavior as it occurs.	Open to observer bias; time-consuming.
Diary description	Day to day	Same as running record.	Rich in detail; describes behavior after it occurs.	Sometimes need follow-up.
Specimen descriptions	Continuous sequences	Same	Usually documents behavior within a time frame [ex 1 hour].	
Log/Journal	Regular, preferred daily or weekly	Usually has space for each child; often a summary of behavior.	Less structured than other narratives.	
"On-the-hoof" anecdotes	Sporadic	Ongoing during class time; using notepad and paper in hand.	Quick and easy to take; short-capture pertinent events/ details.	Lack detail; need to be filled in at later time; can detract from teaching responsibilities.
2. Samplings				
Time sampling	Short and uniform time intervals	On-the-spot as time passes; prearranged recording sheets.	Easy to record; easy to analyze; relatively bias free.	Limited behaviors; loss of detail; loss of sequence and ecology of event.
Event sampling	For the duration of the event	Same as for time sampling.	Easy to record; easy to analyze; can maintain flow of class activity easily.	Limited behaviors; loss of detail; must wait for behavior to occur.
3. Rating methods				
Checklists	Regular or intermittent	Using prepared recording sheets; can be during or after class.	Easy to develop and use.	Lack of detail; tell little of the cause of behaviors.
Rating scales	Continuous behavior	Same as for checklists.	Easy to develop and use; can use for wide range of behaviors.	Ambiguity of terms; high observer bias.
4. Modified techniques				
Shadow study	Continuous behavior	Narrative-type recording; uses prepared recording sheets.	Rich in detail; focuses in-depth on individual.	Bias problem; can take away too much of a teacher's time and attention.
Experimental procedures	Short and uniform	May be checklists, prearranged recording sheets, audio or video tape.	Simple, clear, pure study, relatively bias-free.	Difficult, hard to isolate in the classroom.
Methode clinique/ clinical method	Any time	Usually notebook or tape recorder.	Relevant data; can be spontaneous, easy to use.	Adult has changed naturally occurring behavior.

FIGURE 6-11 Summary chart of the major observational techniques that the early childhood professional can use to record children's behavior.

BRAIN
Research Says...

Observation: Capture the Brain at Work or Overload

Early childhood education is built on the belief that the whole child, in all developmental domains, provides a greater understanding than only a narrow or single-domain view. Information about the brain has provided new insights into the biological basis of behavior and development. Stress and its impact on children's behavior is of special interest, along with the role that caregivers can take to respond to stress.

The human stress system has two branches, the hypothalamic-pituitary-adrenocortical system (HPA) axis and the autonomic nervous system. The HPA axis stimulates the production of the stress hormone cortisol, which can be influenced by "the Big Three:" [which are] controllability, predictability/familiarity, and social support (Davis & Gunnar, 2000). Knowledgeable teachers can use this information to work with families to provide for these three factors in early experiences.

A second application involves the autonomic nervous system, which gives physical cues to the observant teacher about a child's stress level. Specifically changes can be seen with heightened stress. "Fluctuations in skin color, breathing patterns, sweating, yawning, or the need to go to the bathroom can be cues to the burden a current demand places on a particular child. Similarly, observation of the quality of motor behavior and attention offers insight into how the child experiences the complexity of the task and what support he needs" (Gilkerson, 2001).

So, when a child is wiggly, uncooperative, or inattentive, consider the child's behavior to be important clues to that child's experience. Observing closely can reveal brain activity and help understand and respond well to a child's individual sensory profile.

Questions

1. What might it feel like to be that child in those moments?
2. How can observation assist the teacher in ascertaining a child's capacity to engage?
3. Do you remember being overloaded in school? And what did that feel/look like?

© Cengage Learning

Observation skills are honed when teachers have opportunities to work with a few children at a time.

Creating opportunities for regular observations can be difficult. Centers are rarely staffed so well that one teacher can be free from classroom responsibilities for long periods of time. Some ask for parent volunteers to take over an activity while a teacher conducts an assessment. In one center, the snack was set up ahead of time to free one teacher to observe during group time. The environment can be arranged with activities that require little supervision when a teacher is interested in making some observations.

When children know they are being observed, they may feel self-conscious initially, asking pointed questions of the observer and changing their behavior as if they were on stage. When a teacher begins to write, some of the children pay immediate attention. "What are you writing about?" is a common question children ask. "I'm writing about children playing," is an accurate and brief response. Young children are often pleased; older children may move away. In both cases, teachers make themselves less noticeable by looking away or concentrating elsewhere for a moment. When effective observation strategies are used and familiar adults do regular observations, children soon ignore the observer and resume normal activity.

Teachers can improve their observation and recording skills outside the classroom as well. Taking an "Observational Skills" class is helpful; so is visiting other classes in pairs and comparing notes afterward. Staff meetings take on added dimension when teachers role-play what they think they have seen and others ask for details.

The teacher who makes notes during class time has other considerations. Be ready to set aside your recording when necessary. Wear clothing with at least one good pocket. This ensures the paper and pencil or camera is available when needed and the children's privacy is protected. Take care not to leave notes out on tables, shelves, or in cupboards for others to see. They should be kept confidential until added to the children's records. Some teachers find the "low-tech" materials of pen and notebook or 3 × 5 cards easiest to find, carry, use, and set aside. Others find a camera, tape recorder, or flip video camera helpful, although the expense, storage, and distracting nature of such equipment need to be considered. Regardless of what teachers use, they must organize themselves for success:

- *Gather and prepare the materials ahead of time:* This may mean getting everyone aprons with large pockets, having a spiral notebook, or keeping the camera in a central location.
- *Consider where you observe:* Set up observation places (chairs, stations); in a well-equipped yard and room, you can plan strategically.
- *Plan when you observe:* In a DAP day, teachers can have the freedom to practice observing regularly during playtime.
- *Prepare every adult to be an observer:* Give everyone some regular opportunities to observe and reflect on children's play.

Beginning to Observe

In some schools, observers are a normal part of the school routine. In colleges with laboratory facilities on campus, visitors and student observers are familiar figures. They have only to follow established guidelines for making an observation (see Figure 6-12).

Many times students are responsible for finding their own places to observe children. If so, the student calls ahead and schedules a time to observe that is convenient. Be specific about observation needs, the assignment, the ages of children desired, the amount of time needed, and the purpose of the observation.

If you are planning to observe in your own class, several steps are necessary for a professional observation and a believable recording.

- *Plan the observation.* Have a specific *goal* in mind, and even put that at the top of your recording sheet. (For example, "Observe conflicts in the sand area.")
- *Be unobtrusive.* The success of the observation depends on how inconspicuous the observer can be. Children are more natural if the observer blends into the scenery. By staying back, one can observe the whole scene and record what is seen and heard, undisturbed and uninfluenced (see the photo on page 188).
- *Observe and record.* To be objective, be as specific and detailed as possible. Write only the behavior—the "raw data"—and save the analysis and your interpretation for later. (For instance, make a two-column chart: Title the left side "Observations" and the right one "Interpretation.")

Guidelines for Observing

1. Please sign in with the front office and obtain a visitor's badge. **Your badge must be worn and visible at all times while at the center.**

2. Inform the front office when you have completed your visit.

3. **Be unobtrusive.** Please find a spot that doesn't infringe on the children's space.

4. If you are with a small group or another person, **do not observe together;** consciously separate and space yourselves. Do not talk to other visitors during observation, please.

5. Respond to the children, but **please, do not initiate conversations with them.**

6. **If a child seems upset that you are near him/her, please remove yourself from the area.** If you receive direct requests from a child to leave, please respond that you realize that he said you are in **his** space and will move.

7. **Please do not interfere with the teaching/learning process** during your observation. Either ask when you check out in the front office or leave a note in the teacher's mailbox requesting a time to meet. Please understand that we welcome questions but cannot interrupt the program to answer them immediately.

8. **Walk around the periphery of the outdoor area or classrooms rather than through them.**

9. **When possible, do not stand. Please do not hover over children.** Sit, squat, or bend down at the knees so you are at the children's level.

10. **Taking photographs is not permitted.** In special classes, permission for photographs may be given by the Dean of Child Development and Education.

Thank you for your help and consideration in making your visit to the center a pleasant one for everyone involved.

FIGURE 6-12 Establishing guidelines for observers and visitors helps remind us of the importance of teaching as watching, not just telling. (Courtesy of De Anza College Child Development & Education Department.)

- *Interpret your data.* Reread your notes and make some conclusions. Your observation was *what* happened; the interpretation is the place for your opinions and ideas of *why* it happened. (Be sure to transcribe them into something legible if anyone else might need to read them.)
- *Act on what you observed.* To implement your solutions, plan what you will do next, and then follow through with your ideas.

Wherever an observation is planned, it is critical to maintain **professional confidentiality**. If observing at another site, call ahead for an appointment. Talk about the purpose and format of your observation with both director and teacher. Respect the privacy of the children and their families at all times. Any information gathered as part of an observation is treated with strict confidentiality. Teachers and students are careful not to use children's names in casual conversation. They do not talk about children in front of other children or among themselves. It is the role of the adults to see that children's privacy is maintained. Carrying tales out of school is tempting but unprofessional; change the names of the children and school to protect those involved.

© Cengage Learning

Learning to observe and record effectively takes time and practice. Knowing how to stay unobtrusive yet available allows children to continue their natural behavior without distraction and the teacher to ascertain noteworthy behavior.

Goals and Tools of Child Assessment

How do we evaluate children? What do we look for? How do we document growth and difficulties? How do we communicate our findings to families and agencies?

An increased emphasis on child and program assessment is a result of the trend toward increasing **accountability**. In the United States, both the federal No Child Left Behind legislation and NAEYC accreditation criteria have raised the bar on assessment. How can early childhood educators make sure they are on the right track? These questions focus our attention on children's issues, assessment tools, and the evaluation process.

Why Evaluate?

There are four purposes of early childhood assessment:

To support children's learning
To identify special needs
To evaluate and monitor programs
To provide high-stakes accountability, in which the outcome has major consequences for the child, teacher, or organization

Children are evaluated because teachers and parents want to know what the children are learning. Evaluations set the tone for a child's overall educational experience. Highlighting children's strengths builds a foundation from which to address their limitations or needs. The process of evaluating children attempts to answer several questions: Are children gaining appropriate skills and behaviors? In what activities does learning take place? What part of the program supports specific learning? Is the school philosophy being met? Are educational goals being met?

Dial down to child assessment, and three goals stand out:

1. To better understand their overall development
2. To monitor children's progress through the curriculum
3. To identify children who are at risk for failure or who may need special education services (Gullo, 2006)

In other words, evaluation processes can help teachers discover who children are, what they can (and cannot) do, and how to help them grow and learn.

First, teachers decide *what it is they want to know about each child and why.* With an understanding of children in general, teachers then concentrate on individual children and their unique development. These observations establish a baseline and document children's learning.

Second, *goals for children stem from program objectives and drive curriculum and children's progress.* For instance, if the school philosophy is, "Our program is designed to help children grow toward increasing physical, social, and intellectual competencies," an evaluation measures children's progress in those three areas. One that claims to teach specific language skills wants to assess how speaking and listening are being accomplished. Planning curriculum and monitoring program quality should occur through this process.

Third, *evaluations provide teachers with an opportunity look at children in a more professional way and share their observations with others.* Teachers can use the results to share their opinions and concerns about children with each other, with families, and with important agencies or specialists. For instance, an infant and toddler center schedules parent conferences around a sequence of child evaluations: the first, a few weeks after the child begins; the second, six months after the child's admission into the program; and the third, just before the move up to an older age group (such as moving from the infant to the toddler class).

As with observations, evaluations contain varying degrees of subjectivity and opinion. For an evaluation to be reliable and valid, multiple sources of information should be used. Observing young children in action is the key to authentic assessment; note that most of the child evaluation instruments described in this chapter are based on what children do spontaneously or in their familiar, natural settings. A proper evaluation of a child documents a child's growth over time (e.g., keeping a portfolio of the child's creations, dictations, and anecdotes of behavior and emergent play activities and photos of children engaged in skills. In general, evaluations are made to:

- Establish a baseline about each child
- Document children's learning
- Determine guidance and intervention
- Plan the curriculum
- Communicate with families
- Monitor program accountability and quality

Establish a Baseline

One purpose of evaluating children is to establish a starting point of their skills and behavior. This is the beginning of a collection over a period of time of important information on each child. Through this cumulative record, teachers learn a great deal about the children: whom they play with, how they spend their time, how they handle problems, what fears and stress they show. In other words, they learn a lot about how children live their lives.

A **baseline** is a picture of the status of each child—an overview of individual development. It shows where the child is in relation to the school's objectives because the child is being measured according to program expectations. Baseline data give a realistic picture of a child at that moment in time, but there is a presumption that the picture will change.

A Baseline Tool The beginning of the school term is an obvious time to start collecting information. Records of a child are established in the context of the child's history and family background. Parents frequently submit this information with an application to the school. Teachers can gather the data by visiting the child at home or holding a family conference.

An **entry-level** assessment made during the first few weeks of school can be informative, particularly when added to the child's family history. The evaluation itself should be done informally, with teachers collecting information as children engage naturally with materials and each other. Many agencies ask for an initial assessment within the first 60 days of enrollment (see Figure 6-13).

Application Teachers then use this information to understand children and their development. They can see children's strengths and weaknesses and where future growth is likely to occur. When the information is shared with families, they feel more relaxed about their child and even laugh when they recall those first few days of school. One must remember, however, that the entry assessment is only a first impression. Care must be taken to avoid creating a self-fulfilling prophesy by labeling children so that they become shaped into those beginning patterns. Again, teachers must be mindful of the cautions associated with all assessments as they document children's early behaviors. Still, so much happens in that short period of time; the rich information we gain from documenting this growth is invaluable.

Goals and Plans Teachers use baseline data to set realistic goals for individual children. They tailor the curriculum to the needs and interests they have observed. An entry-level assessment is a vehicle for

Entry-Level Assessment

1. Child's name __Mariko Meade__ Teacher __Kristin Franklin__
   Age __3.0__ Sex __F__
   Primary language __Japanese__ Fluency in English? _____
   Any previous school experiences? __none__
   Siblings/others in household __sister Hiromi, 6 months__
   Family situation (one/two parents, other adults, etc.) __Mother at home, father full-time outside home,__
   __maternal grandmother, baby sister.__

2. Separation from parent:
   Smooth _____ Some anxiety _____ Mild difficulty _____ Unable to separate _____
   Did parent have trouble separating? __mother/no; grandmother/yes; father/no__
   Comments: __grandmother stays and has trouble leaving if M. protests__

3. How does child come to and leave from school?
   Parent __grandma 2x/wk__ Car pool _____ Babysitter _____ Bus _____

4. Physical appearance [general health, expression, clothing, body posture]: *M. is carefully dressed, excellent health, cautious expression, opens up over morning and through week.*

5. Self-care [dressing, toileting, eating, toothbrushing, sleeping]: *M. dresses and toilets without assistance; little appetite, resists toothbrushing; still lays quietly but no sleeping yet.*
   Allergies/other health-related problems: __none reported or observed__

6. Child's Interests: *Indoors—books, easel, art   Outdoors—swings, animals, sandbox*
   Group times (level of participation): *M. comes to circle, sits on my lap, watchful without any participation yet.*

7. Social-emotional development: *M. plays alone, seems happy, but has to be invited to any activity with other children; seems tense unless near me.*
   a. Plays mostly with children of: *No play with other children yet.*
   b. Moves into environment: *Hesitantly, but is getting around a little; tends to follow me.*
   c. Special friends: *none yet.*
   d. Does the child follow teachers? __yes__ Anyone in particular? _____

8. Cognitive development: *follows directions, does not speak yet, points & nods.*

9. Physical development: *prefers R-hand; uses scissors & brushes well; have not yet observed climbing or running.*

10. Goals/points to remember: __Does she have a security object to bring? What does she love to do at home__
    __that we could have here? What Japanese terms should we learn & use? Schedule a home visit this month.__

FIGURE 6-13 Entry-level assessments collect baseline information. Once teachers and children have had some time together, these first impressions can be documented.
⊙ You can download a copy of this form from this text's Education CourseMate website.

watching children's growth throughout the year. For instance, after setting a baseline of Mariko's language ability in English, teachers plan activities to increase her understanding and use of language. Then, they make periodic checks on her increased vocabulary as the school year progresses.

Document Children's Learning

Teachers use evaluations to document children's growth. Data collected provide evidence of children's growth or lack of progress. A careful evaluation of each child furnishes the teaching staff with the necessary foundation from which they can plan the next steps.

© Cengage Learning

© Cengage Learning

Assessments that include photos of children in action offer a snapshot of a child at a particular moment, which can serve as a baseline or as a mid-year evaluation.

Hita has mastered the brushes at the easel. Now we can encourage her to try the smaller brushes in table painting.

Enrico has been asking how to spell simple words. Let's see that he gets some time away from the blocks to work at the writing center.

All the 2-year-olds seem able to separate from their families and say good-bye comfortably now. How can we celebrate this progress with the group?

A Progress Tool A *midyear evaluation* includes criteria for each area of development to build a profile of the whole child. Teachers note the intervention and guidance steps they plan, where appropriate. Many states, national programs such as Head Start, school districts, and individual programs are developing and using assessment tools to establish and monitor progress. Called "essential learning," "developmental guidelines," or "learning goals," they serve to articulate expected standards. One such tool, the California Desired Results Developmental Profile (DRDP), has profile forms for infant/toddler (birth through 36 months), preschool (age 3 to kindergarten), kindergarten through age 7, and 8 to 10 years. The DRDP describes four desired results for children; they are:

- Children are personally and socially competent.
- Children are effective learners.

- Children show physical and motor competence.
- Children are safe and healthy.

For each age group, the tool outlines several indicators and describes growth along a continuum so that the phases children experience as they move toward accomplishing the desired result can be documented. (For examples, see the websites listed at the end of the chapter.)

Application Information about a child is used to assess growth and change. How often this happens varies. Although many changes occur in rapid succession in these early years, it takes time for a child to integrate life experiences and for teachers to see them expressed as a permanent part of behavior. Evaluating too frequently does not reveal sufficient change to make it worthwhile and places an added burden on the teaching staff as well (see Figure 6-14).

Goals and Plans Goals are established for children as a result of an assessment. These goals are changed as growth takes place. A good assessment tool monitors progress in each developmental area so that plans can be made to challenge the child physically, socially, emotionally, creatively, and intellectually.

At the same time, theory reminds us that the child develops as a whole, with each area of growth influencing

A Tool for Monitoring Children's Progress

Check one of the evaluations below for each skill area; for those that need work, document with specific examples.

Developmental Area	Age Appropriate	Highly Skilled	Needs Work
Self-Management			
Personal care	Can feed, dress, toilet self well		
Making choices	prefers indoors to outside		
Following routines	Does fine in routines		
Physical/Motor			
1. Fine Motor	Uses easels—brushes good grasp, pens also		
Art materials	Likes blocks, table toys		
Woodworking tools	Hasn't chosen woodworking, but watches often		
Manipulatives			
2. Gross Motor		Very cautious, seems fearful	
Ball handling		Won't swing, slide, use climber	
Balancing		Wanders outdoors, sometimes does music	
Jump/hop/skip		Runs away when wheel toys are rolled down hill	
Communication and Language			
Vocabulary		Exceptionally strong	
Articulation		Converses with adults daily	
Comprehension		Responds to children but rarely initiates talk	
English as a second language		Outstanding at group time—lots of ideas	
Converses with children		Talks around fears, but fears seem to keep him from trying	
Converses with adults			
Listens			
Expresses self (needs, ideas, feelings)			
Cognitive Development			
Sees cause and effect			
Processes and uses information			
Solves problems with:	Dylan has so much information to share, and lots of interest in		
objects	problem-solving with indoor materials and interactions with teachers.		
peers	We wish he could extend these skills into work with children and		
adults	open up a bit more.		
Premath (sequencing, measuring, numbers)			
Prereading concepts (size, colors, shapes, letters, position)			
Social-Emotional			
Independence/initiative			
Positive self-concept	Does well on own, gets around		
Recognizes/accepts own feelings	Is comfortable and confident		
Deals with frustration	around adults		Seems hesitant/fearful outdoors
Flexibility			Is more solitary or onlooker; is
Leadership			this self-esteem or just fear?
Initiates social contacts			Don't know about leadership yet;
Prosocial behaviors (friendly, sharing, inclusive, cooperative, empathic)			have seen little because of lack
Child–child interactions			of interaction with children
Child–adult interactions			

OVERALL STRENGTHS: GOALS

FIGURE 6-14 A midyear evaluation is a more detailed description of the child. It highlights areas of concern and progress.
⊙ You can download a copy of this form from this text's Education CourseMate website.

and being influenced by what changes take place in other areas. Evaluations that document growth include information so that all teachers see the interrelationships among areas of development. By assessing growth in individual areas, teachers relate that development to the child's collective abilities. An example follows:

Dylan's report shows he lacks dexterity in running and climbing and is quite strong in verbal and listening skills. This influences his development in the following areas:

Emotionally. He appears to lack self-confidence, and his self-esteem deteriorates the longer he feels inept at physical skills. He may even be afraid to master the art of climbing and running for fear he will fail.

Socially. Children tease Dylan because he often cannot keep up with them while playing outside. He often ends up playing alone or watching the other children in more active pursuits.

Intellectually. There is a lack of risk-taking in Dylan's whole approach to play. Because of his slow physical development he seems unlikely to challenge himself in other ways.

Goals: Focus on physical/motor skills. Help him talk about what he likes and dislikes about the outdoors and bring in picture books that depict characters persisting to master difficulties (such as *The Little Engine That Could*), using his language strength as a springboard for growth.

Some programs conclude the year with a summary report. This evaluation serves as an overview of what a child has accomplished, what areas of strength are present, and what future growth might occur. These records are useful to families as a summary of their child's learning experiences. Teachers may use them as references should they ever be consulted by another school about the child. Again, it is critical to assess a child in a sensitive and accepting manner, to keep the time period as brief as possible, and to communicate the results in the same tone. If this is not done, the child's self-esteem may be damaged and the family trust may be lost. The disadvantages of these tools parallel those of standardized tests (see Testing and Screening section).

Determine Guidance and Intervention

A third purpose for evaluation is to help teachers determine guidance procedures. These are based on insights and perceptions brought into focus through the evaluation (see Teaching With Intention). This process serves as a primary tool on which guidance and planning are based. When teachers see a problem behavior or are concerned about a child, they plan for further assessment (see Chapter 7). If a developmental **screening** is done to assess if a child has a learning problem or needs

special services, teachers either refer the family to a proper specialist or agency or administer the screening themselves (see Testing and Screening section).

A Guidance Tool Evaluations help in behavior management. Once a need has been pinpointed, the teaching staff decides how to proceed. Individual problems are highlighted when teachers make a point of concentrating on the child's behavior. Such tools are used at a team meeting to outline steps to be taken in addressing the concern directly. It also helps teachers clarify how to talk to parents in a concerned and supportive manner (see Figure 6-15).

Application Using evaluations for guidance need not be elaborate. For instance, Trevor's parents report that he says he has no friends at kindergarten. At their staff meeting, the teacher and aide share their observation notes,

Child Guidance Form

Problem [present in behavioral terms; limit to three]
Elizabeth has increased toilet accidents in the last 2 weeks.

Family History [ask family, include home, medical, changes]
Dad reports that she is wetting the bed at home, refuses to use toilet at night before bed.

Center History [child's relations to adults, children, materials, activities]
Higher incidence during midmorning snack, often at table or right afterwards.

Intervention [what has been tried with details; what has/not worked; child's strengths]
Teachers started to remind her to use toilet before washing hands for snack; she is resistant to suggestion.

Plans
1. In center: *check her comfort level—does she want privacy? teacher will walk her to bathroom or she can take a friend.*
2. With family: *parents will take her to toilet before bath, offer bedtime stories after she tries, will ask if she wants company/privacy, or take her teddy bear along.*
3. Date for reviewing results: *check-in 2 weeks.*

FIGURE 6-15 One purpose of evaluating children is to plan for behavior management. A good evaluation form includes follow through plans for intervention. (Adapted from McLaughlin & Sugarman, 1982.)

From Observation to Intention and Action

Meet Jody, age 5.

Observations:
- He uses scissors in a "hedge-clippers" fashion.
- He has an awkward grip when using a pencil.
- He finds it difficult to fit puzzle pieces together.
- He does not choose the woodworking table, manipulative table, or cooking project during free choice.

Questions: What would you do? Does he need intervention? How would you address this situation?

Intention and Action: The caregivers in his kindergarten after-school class were concerned about his fine motor skill development. They need to investigate the possible causes of their observations and then make deliberate steps to adjust their teaching, with the intention of helping him increase his skills.

1. A check with his parents revealed two important facts: Jody had trouble handling table utensils and could not button his sweater. They said there was no provision at home for him to pursue any fine motor activities. Jody's parents supplied him with a special art box at home, full of crayons, scissors, pens, watercolors, and stencils at the teachers' suggestion.

2. Knowing of Jody's interest in airplanes, the teachers used that to draw Jody into areas of the curriculum he did not ordinarily pursue. Small airplanes were added to the block corner, and airplane stencils were placed near the art table. A large mural of an airport was hung on the fence, and children were invited to paint on it. One day, children cut airplane pictures out of magazines and used them on a collage. Simple airplane puzzles were placed on the puzzle table. Felt shapes and small plastic airplanes in the water table helped draw Jody toward activities requiring fine motor skills.

As his fine motor skills increased and refined, Jody became a more confident and happier child. By the end of three months, he was a regular participant in all areas of the school and

© Cengage Learning

seemed to be enjoying his newfound interest in art materials. Teaching with intention matters!

Think About This

1. Do you think that intervening after observing was the proper course of action? Why or why not?
2. How do you determine when to talk with a family about what you have observed about their child? What goes into making such a decision?

---

noticing that Ryan and Brooke have shown interest. Teachers have seen both children approach him, but he did not seem to know how to respond. They suggest that Trevor's parents invite the children to play with Trevor at home. At school, the teachers give Trevor verbal cues when children make attempts to play with him, scaffolding the invitations so that he can make small steps toward responding.

Goals and Plans An evaluation tool helps teachers set goals for children (see Figure 6-15). Narrowing the focus to include only those behaviors that concern the staff enables the staff to quickly review the needs of many children.

Plan Curriculum

Teachers plan the curriculum on the basis of children's evaluations. Translating the assessment to actual classroom practice is an important part of the teacher's role. A thorough evaluation helps teachers plan appropriate activities to meet children's needs. More importantly, observation itself drives curriculum development, particularly in the program models of Reggio Emilia, the Project Approach, and Emergent Curriculum (see Chapter 10 and Figures 6-16 and 6-18). **Documentation** of children's work activity shows both classroom curriculum (Figure 6-16) and individual growth (Figure 6-18).

Documentation Board

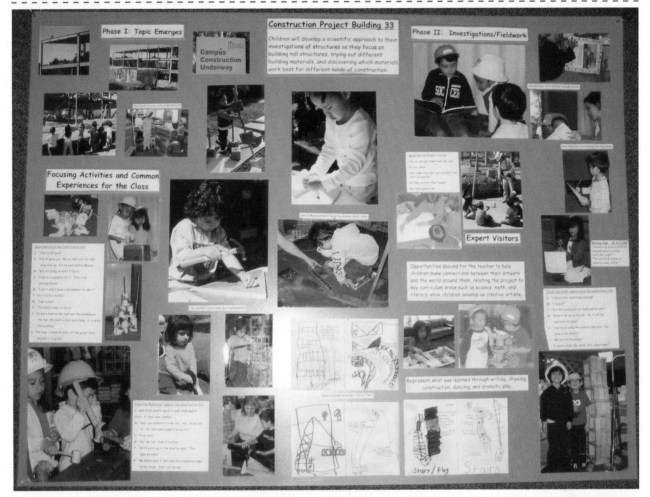

FIGURE 6-16 Thanks to the observational skills of teachers, a group of children were able to develop their interest and knowledge about building construction through curriculum development. Documentation panel by Margaret Lam and Kären Wiggins-Dowler (2006). Reprinted with permission from Mary Meta Lazarus Child Development Center, College of San Mateo.

Planning Tools All three of the previous evaluation tools can be used to plan curriculum. The entry-level assessment and midyear report can be summarized in a group chart. One such chart, made at the end of the first semester of a prekindergarten class, revealed this pattern:

At least one-third of the class was having trouble listening at group time, as evidenced by the group chart that identified "Group Time" and "Language Listening Skills" as areas for growth for nearly half the children. The staff centered their attention on the group time content. It was concluded that a story made the group times too long; the children were restless throughout most of the reading. It was agreed to move story time to just before nap and shorten the group time temporarily.

Evaluation also applies to daily events, such as individual projects and the day as a whole. Chapter 10 discusses curriculum planning in further detail.

Application Evaluation results assist teachers in seeing more clearly the strengths and abilities of each child in the class. Curriculum activities are then planned that enhance growth. Also, areas of difficulty are identified:

Jolene has trouble mastering even the simplest puzzle. *Provide her with common shapes found in attribute blocks (small plastic shapes of varying color, thickness, size), and do some matching exercises with her.*

The younger children in the class are reluctant to try the climbing structures designed by the older ones. *Build an obstacle course with the youngest children, beginning with very simple challenges and involving the children in the actual planning and building as well as rehearsing climbing techniques with them.*

There are practical connections to be made in learning to "read" the children and actual curriculum planning. Reflective work is critical for making curricular connections.

Goals and Plans Each of the previous case studies demonstrate how evaluation tools can be used to plan curriculum. By analyzing both group and individual skills through periodic assessment, teachers maintain a secure environment and challenging program.

Communicate with Families

Plans for evaluating children should include the means by which families are to be informed of the results. Once the teachers have identified a child's needs and capabilities, parents are entitled to hear the conclusions. The teaching staff has an obligation to provide a realistic overview of the child's progress and alert the family to any possible concerns. Using the child guidance form (see Figure 6-15), teachers define problem behavior for a child and work closely with the parents to reach a solution:

Yum-Tong refuses to let his mother leave. The teachers agree that there are two issues: 1) Y.-T.'s screaming and crying as his mother leaves and 2) his inability to focus on an activity while she attempts to go (though she stays as soon as he starts screaming). The family has told them that their other two children had separation problems as preschoolers. The previous school asked the parents to stay until the children stopped protesting, although the parents report that this took nearly six months, so it was a hardship for them in their workplaces.

The teachers choose to intervene by asking Yum-Tong's mother to plan ahead with Y.-T., deciding before school how they spend five minutes together each morning. After playing and helping him to settle in, she then says goodbye and leaves Y.-T. with Pete, his favorite teacher. Pete is prepared to be with him at the departure and stay with him until he calms down. They also plan to have a conference date after two weeks of this intervention plan to follow through and review how it is working for everyone.

A Tool with Parents Teachers and parents need to talk together, especially when problems are revealed by the evaluation. As parents and teachers share knowledge and insights, a more complete picture of the child emerges for both. Each can then assume a role in the resolution of the problem. The role of the teacher is defined in the context of the parents' role, and the family is guided by the teacher's attitudes and actions (see Chapter 8).

Application Aside from identifying normal behavior problems, evaluations may raise questions concerning a child's physical development, hearing and visual acuity, or language/cognitive problems. Recall that one purpose of assessment is to identify children who may need special education services (all ages), who may demonstrate issues of school readiness (prekindergartners), or who are at risk for academic failure (elementary-aged children). Potentially serious problems may emerge from the evaluation, and families are then encouraged to seek further professional assessment or intervention. Evaluation tools can help parents target areas in which their child may need special help.

Goals and Plans Because evaluation is an ongoing process, re-evaluation and goal setting are done regularly. Communicating both progress and new goals is critical for the feedback loop of an evaluation form to be effective, as shown in Chapter 5 on teacher evaluation.

Monitor Program Accountability and Quality

Evaluation results can help a program determine its quality and be accountable to others for its effectiveness. They can lead to changes in the overall program or in the school's philosophy. For example, a child care component might be added to the half-day program after learning that most children are enrolled in another child care situation after nursery school. Or an evaluation might conclude that there is too little emphasis on developing gross motor skills, so the program might decide to remodel the play yard and purchase new equipment.

Child assessments can, therefore, be one measure of program quality. Other measures include evaluating the environment and schedule (see Chapter 9), the teaching staff (Chapter 5), and the curriculum (Chapters 11–14). The accreditation process developed by NAEYC, based on the application of developmentally appropriate practices in programs, is a comprehensive program evaluation tool.

As regards assessment of children, early educators are reminded that, although evaluation is a central part of quality programs, the assessments must be ethical, appropriate, and valid. NAEYC and NAECS/SDE (2003) made specific, evidence-based recommendations concerning early childhood assessment. No matter what is used, the primary goal is to benefit children (see Figure 6-17).

Types of Assessments

With increased pressure for accountability, assessment issues have arisen in both public schooling and early care programs. Regardless of agency or funding source, all early childhood programs must be knowledgeable about assessment and its purposes, tools, and complications. Whether you intend to improve children's learning, identify children with special needs, or defend your program, it is likely you need to engage in some kind of child assessment.

Two Types of Assessments

Generally there are two types of assessments: formal assessments (sometimes referred to as standardized or norm-referenced) and informal assessments (sometimes referred to as authentic).

Indicators of Effective Assessment Practices

- Ethical principles guide assessment practices.
- Assessment instruments are used for their intended purposes.
- Assessments are appropriate for the ages and other characteristics of children being assessed.
- Assessment instruments are in compliance with professional criteria for quality.
- What is assessed is developmentally and educationally significant.
- Assessment evidence is used to understand and improve learning.
- Assessment evidence is gathered from realistic settings and situations that reflect children's actual performance.
- Assessments use multiple sources of evidence gathered over time.
- Screening is always linked to follow-up.
- Use of individually administered, norm-referenced tests is limited.
- Staff and families are knowledgeable about assessment.

FIGURE 6-17 Principles of appropriate assessment in early childhood education. (NAEYC & NAECS/SDE [2003, pp. 2–3])

Formal assessments include standardized, **norm-referenced tests** and various "screening" instruments. The yearly tests taken in elementary and secondary school, using a #2 pencil, are an example of such procedures. "Standardized, norm-referenced assessments follow a standard set of administration rules so that each child theoretically experiences the assessment similarly (for example, each person administering the test gives the same instructions). Norm-referenced assessments permit a child's performance to be compared to those of other children his age" (Maxwell & Clifford, 2004). These are often used to identify special needs or to evaluate programs. **Informal assessments** include observations, note taking, self-assessments, parent interviews and surveys, samples of children's work, and teacher-designed forms (checklists, etc.). Teachers note what children do, say, try, and show.

As with the various observation methods, there are advantages and disadvantages to each type of assessment. Standardized types do allow for comparisons and diminish some of the bias among many observers. Yet, they may not accurately reflect a child's skills due to administration outside the child's usual experience or setting. There are problems associated with testing and screening of young children (see "Testing and Screening"

section). **Naturalistic assessments** do not disrupt children, and a child has multiple opportunities to demonstrate mastery. They do not allow for easy comparison between children or in a group, and bias can affect the results.

It is important to choose assessment tools and techniques that are appropriate for the group or the child under consideration. Informal observations can be made more systematic or comprehensive to gain more information about a specific problem. Formal, commercially developed instruments need to be used more carefully. There are several instruments that are widely used in the United States. The High/Scope Child Observation Record (COR), Work Sampling System (Meisels/Pearson), and Creative Curriculum's Developmental Continuum are three of the most well known (see the websites listed at the end of the chapter). There are a wide variety of assessments to choose from; at the same time, many are not easily adaptable to individual programs or purposes, and many take considerable preparation and training.

"In choosing an appropriate assessment system, it is important to understand what a developmentally appropriate, valid, relative, and ethical assessment looks like. Some background research can provide this information" (Shillady, 2004), and the references at the end of the chapter can help. Before choosing any assessment tool or procedure, know the age group and the purpose as well as the children's cultures, languages, abilities, and disabilities. Assessing special populations is important but challenging, as the procedures need to account for cultural and linguistic differences (see CLAS website at the end of the chapter).

Authentic Assessment: The Portfolio

The dictionary defines "authentic" as "of undisputed origin, genuine . . . made or done in a way that faithfully resembles an original" (*New Oxford American Dictionary*, 2005). For a child assessment to be authentic, it must try to capture who the child is, and what that child knows (or does not) and can (or cannot) do. Teachers must assess to know the child better in order to improve learning.

Many early childhood educators have embraced the idea that children's work samples in a portfolio form are an excellent way to document children's learning and faithfully capture the child's development. In light of the concerns you have read in this chapter about the mis-assessment of young children and the "test mania" that standardized tests in the primary grades have fomented, many professionals have looked for alternative assessment measures.

"**Portfolios** are an excellent visual aid for showing the dispositions, strengths, and interests of a child as

Know the reasons for making an evaluation. Evaluations should avoid unfair comparisons, acknowledge individual differences and uniqueness, and not look at children in a comparative manner.

Child Portfolio

- Identify the purpose of the portfolio (improving communication with families, connecting with other teachers or programs).
- Identify the types of items to be collected (artwork, photos of block or dramatic play, etc.).
- Specify who will collaborate to create the portfolio (teacher, other caregivers, the child, family).
- Set a timetable (for instance, the first set by November 15, second set by April 30).
- Establish any standards or tool you will use (for example, Desired Results or Child Outcomes).
- Have in writing when any portfolio conferences will take place and who will be there (teacher, family, child?).
- Identify procedure for maintaining confidentiality and for release of items.

FIGURE 6-18 Having a set of guidelines for developing and using portfolios keeps the process clear for all involved.

well as what universal skills and knowledge they have acquired under your care" (Wiggins-Dowler, 2011). Although they take considerable planning, they help you collect children's work intentionally. You can evaluate children on their work and play as they are spontaneously, rather than with standardized tests or unnecessary screening.

There are several types of portfolios:

1. Display portfolios—scrapbooks that collect items without teacher comments.
2. Showcase portfolios—the best pieces of the child's work.
3. Working portfolios—include selections of typical work along with teacher documentation to show the child's progress.

Gronlund (2008) recommends a **working portfolio** that combines work samples with teacher commentary. Wiggins-Dowler (2011) describes this type of portfolio:

1. Make a portfolio plan. This includes a brief set of guidelines for collecting items for saving (see Figure 6-18). Mere collection of work is not enough; look for samples that demonstrate goals and the child's progress. Do not try to collect everything.
2. Be organized when storing work samples. Pocket folders or even pizza boxes can keep the material intact; consider creating a folding document with sections for each developmental domain or desired result/goal.
3. Collect children's work with purpose. Look for work in all developmental domains (Chapters 3 and 4), each interest area (Chapter 9), or other categories, such as those you are accountable for teaching. Many suggest you collect a piece of each child's work two or three times a year. Each child's individual portfolio may have completely different work samples from others in the program, but every portfolio still shows growth over time in every developmental area.
4. Add written comments to the work samples. The commentary enhances the documentation by giving the information necessary to assess the process of learning that is going on. Remember to keep your writing legible; a Post-It note can conveniently attach to lesson plan or work sample, but a scribble cannot be recalled later. Be sure to include names of those involved and the time and date. A picture may be worth a thousand words; but for assessment purposes, the words are essential, not just the photo.

Early Learning Standards

Standards, standards everywhere! . . . Child outcome standards that define what young children should be learning. . . . "What are the reasonable expectations that guide early educators in planning curriculum for preschool children and in assessing their progress in achieving these expectations?" (Gronlund, 2008)

The standards movement in K–12 that began in the 1980s has arrived at the early childhood doorstep. More than half the states now have standards that describe results, outcomes, or learning expectations for children younger than kindergarten age, and Head Start has a framework for Child Outcomes. Standards are used to improve the odds that a program increases school readiness as well as serves as a guide for building skills for later achievement. Yet the results are that more children are being denied entrance to a school system, being put in extra-year or pull-out programs, or being placed in kindergarten twice.

Using standards to clarify what children ought to learn and know how to do and to hold programs (and teachers) accountable is here to stay. **Early learning standards** are statements that describe expectations for the learning and development of young children across all developmental domains. This includes health and physical-motor skills and social and emotional well-being; approaches to learning; language and cognitive development; and general knowledge about the world around them.

Tools for Standards

One of the outcomes of the standards movement in education as a whole (see Chapter 15 on Educational Reform) has been to develop and use tools to better describe learning so that it can be assessed and scored more easily. Two tools used in higher education that can be useful in early education are 1) learning domains, as described by Bloom's taxonomy, and 2) rubrics.

Learning Domains: Bloom's Taxonomy Benjamin Bloom, an American psychologist, worked with a committee of colleges in the mid-1950s to identify the broad domains of educational activities (Bloom, 1956). Then, to flesh out these categories, descriptions of knowledge, skills, and attitudes were developed to name the many learning behaviors that could then be observed and assessed. Finally, in a kind of stair-step hierarchy, the behaviors were defined from simplest to most complex thinking.

In other words, what do we see in the learner to show what they know and are able to do or how they feel? The three domains of activities are:

Cognitive: mental skills (*Knowledge*)
Affective: growth in feelings or emotional areas
  (*Attitude*)
Psychomotor: manual or physical skills (*Skills*)

Many of the actions that demonstrate these learning categories are more detailed than most early educators need. The domains are used extensively in higher education to establish learning outcomes for coursework, so that students have a clear idea of what they are to learn in a particular course and what they can expect to be assessed to determine if they have mastered the concepts. **Bloom's taxonomy** is easily understood and is probably the most widely applied one in use today (see Figure 6-19).

Scoring Guides: Rubrics The term "rubric" comes from a heading that was printed in the color red, or rouge, in French. In educational circles, a **rubric** is a scoring guide that is used in assessment. It describes in detail what the learner does to demonstrate various levels of a task or assignment. In this way, the teacher communicates expectations so that the learner can understand, self-assess, and see the criteria for grading the quality of a task. It also provides objective feedback for a goal of more accurate and fair assessment.

As with Bloom's taxonomy, rubrics are used in higher education frequently. For instance, a teacher assessment rubric often describes what "beginning, developing, and proficient grouptime skills" look like. A student teacher might self-assess at the "developing" category with a rubric indicating that this level includes:

- Materials organized ahead of time
- Pace and timing somewhat effective
- Hesitant or harsh handling of off-task behavior
- A mid-level of enjoyment

Using an instrument for child assessment such as California's Desired Results Developmental Profile (http://www.cde.ca.gov/sp/cd/ci/desiredresults.asp) outlines categories that can be used as a rubric when including the examples provided. Program assessment that uses a rating scale, such as the Environmental Rating Scale (http://ers.fpg.unc.edu/), can transform the tool into a rubric by using the indicators to create models of each level of work.

Challenges and Benefits

The challenge is determining standards for children in the early years because the ways children learn and what they are learning is different from those in elementary school. "In early childhood, the development of foundational skills (skills that lay the foundation for later learning) is just as important as mastery of content matter" (Bodrova

Bloom's Taxonomy for Cognitive Assessment

Outcome Category	Definition	Example in ECE
Knowledge recall	To remember previously learned material	Child begins singing once teacher starts the song
Comprehension	To grasp the meaning of the knowledge and be able to explain it	Child can say what "eensy-weensy" means when teacher asks
Application	To use the learned material and information	When asked at lunchtime for serving size of broccoli, child responds "eensy-weensy"
Analysis	To break down the information into parts and understand its organization	Child can put the 4 stanzas of song in the proper order and describe why
Synthesis	To combine this information with new material to form a new structure	Child can use the song-story to describe a weather cycle.
Evaluate	To rate or compare the material with current knowledge	Child can solve a problem such as what insects should do when it rains.

© Cengage Learning 2014

FIGURE 6-19 Bloom's taxonomy describes in active verb form what a person may show or do to demonstrate various levels of learning domains.

et al., 2004). It is essential that effective early learning standards (NAEYC & NAESC/SDE, 2003):

- Emphasize significant developmentally appropriate content and outcomes
- Are developed and reviewed through informed, inclusive processes
- Gain their effectiveness through implementation and assessment practices that support all children's development in ethical, appropriate way
- Require a foundation of support for early childhood programs, professionals, and families

There are benefits to early learning standards, as well as potential problems. On the positive side, early learning standards "reinforce the fact that there is an incredible potential for learning and growth in the infant, toddler, and preschool years and that there is value and importance in providing quality early childhood programs for children's long-term success in school and in life" (Gronlund, 2008). They can articulate both the sequence of typical development and set reasonable expectations for children at different ages. Learning standards are intended to set the bar for student achievement, and in the primary years, they can be crafted to apply brain

and developmental research in their implementation (Schiller & Willis, 2008).

At the same time, standards can result in standardization, the notion that "one size fits all" about a vulnerable and tender population. They can lead to curriculum that is rote and set only to teach the specific sub-skill, often in a direct instruction, whole-group manner that can be stultifying and inappropriate. The challenge is to implement standards that are developmentally appropriate and good for all children and that allow teachers to be creative and enthusiastic as they take good care of children (see Figure 6-20).

Testing and Screening

The practice of testing and screening for readiness, retention, and special needs has increased dramatically in the last decade. With the passage of Public Law 94-142 (Education for All Handicapped Children Act) and the early childhood amendment to the law (Public Law 99-457), U.S. states now have the responsibility to establish specific procedures and policies to identify, evaluate, and provide services to all children with learning problems. Moreover, testing for admittance to kinder-

---

Early Learning Standards

Pros

- They can provide richness to our conversation about children's growth and learning.
- We can match standards to what we are already doing.
- They can be linked to primary standards so that we are indeed contributing to children's school readiness.
- They help us identity next steps and transitions.
- They are a strategy for professionalizing our field.
- They help us communicate across the grades, among ourselves, and with our public.
- They help us to have higher expectations for children.

Cons

- They lead to teaching to the standards only in a cookie-cutter curriculum.
- They bring a pressure of accountability with the risk of a push-down in curriculum and inappropriate expectations for younger children.
- Direct instruction is assumed as the only way that standards are addressed.
- Learning in self-directed, exploratory ways is not trusted.
- They contribute to a "we/they" mentality between preschool and elementary teachers.
- They take time for early educators to learn and work through, to figure out how to integrate into good practices.
- They result in testing and other inappropriate assessment methods being used.
- There is little money to support education and training of early educators in the standards and how best to use them.

FIGURE 6-20 There are both benefits and problems with early learning standards, so teachers should use standards intentionally to inform their planning. (Adapted from Make Early Learning Standards Come Alive: Connecting Your Practice and Curriculum to State Guidelines, by Gaye Gronlund, pp. 4–5. Copyright © 2006 by Gaye Gronlund. Reprinted with permission from Redleaf Press, St. Paul, Minnesota, www.redleafpress.org.)

garten or promotion to first grade has become more common.

Ethical and appropriate principles state that early childhood educators shall not participate in practices that are "emotionally damaging, physically harmful, disrespectful, degrading, dangerous, exploitative, or intimidating to children" (NAEYC & NAECS/SDE, 2003). As mentioned previously, decisions about children must be based on multiple sources of information and not based on a single test score or single observation. One assessment could never tell all that is needed to know about a child or a group.

Testing

Ironically, standardized tests fail to reflect adequately what children learn (National Commission on Testing and Public Policy, 1998) even as more are being developed and used. "Standardized testing captures one part of what children know and understand" (Rushton et al., 2009). What is tested may not be what they have learned or is important to them or their families. Howard Gardner, whose work on multiple intelligences is described in Chapters 4, 10, and 12, affirms:

> Over the past several decades the assumptions underlying the current testing edifice have been challenged by developmental, cognitive, and educational studies. There's a considerable body of scientific findings telling us that if we want to understand people's competence or knowledge about something, we should not examine them in an artificial way in an artificial setting (Gardner, 1988).

Most formal testing engages only two (linguistic and logical mathematical) of the eight intelligences Gardner has identified. Such practices raise some practical and serious philosophical issues:

- Young children do not function well in common test situations, nor do the test results necessarily reflect children's true knowledge or skills.
- These practices (often based on inappropriate uses of readiness or screening tests) disregard the potential, documented long-term negative effects of retention on children's self-esteem and the fact that such practices disproportionately affect low-income and minority children. (National Center for Fair and Open Testing, 2006)
- Although the most needed and appropriate tests (teacher-made) are the hardest to create, the standardized ones are frequently misused and misunderstood by teachers and parents.

- Teachers are pressured into running programs that overemphasize the testing situation and test items.
- Most tests focus on cognitive and language skills; such a narrow focus ignores other areas of development.
- Special training to administer tests is imperative yet often overlooked, and standardized tests require specific protocols.

The practice of **standardized testing** has caused early childhood curricula to become increasingly academic. Early childhood educators and parents are alarmed that:

> Many kindergartens are now structured, "watered-down" first grades, emphasizing workbooks and other paper-and-pencil activities that are inappropriate for 5-year-olds. The trend further trickles down to preschool and child care programs that feel that their mission is to get children "ready" for kindergarten. Too many school systems, expecting children to conform to an inappropriate curriculum and finding large numbers of "unready" children, react to the problem by raising the entrance age for kindergarten and/or labeling the children as failures. (NAEYC, 2003)

The implications of such testing further erode the curriculum when teachers, wanting their classes to do well on the test, alter activities to conform to what is tested. They then begin teaching children to learn "right" answers rather than to engage in active, critical thinking. Rather than making teachers more accountable, "the overuse (and misuse) of standardized testing has led to the adoption of inappropriate teaching practices as well as admission and retention policies that are not in the best interests of individual children or the nation as a whole" (NAEYC & NAECS/SDE, 2003).

Screening

Many kindergartens and some nursery schools use various kinds of screening tests before children can enter the program. The usual purpose of these evaluations is to determine readiness: that is, to verify that the child is able to cope with school and succeed. These tools are best devised with the individual child in mind. Their purpose is to highlight the skills the child has and to identify the areas in which the child may need help in the next class.

Using valid screening tests to identify children who, because of the risk of possible learning problems or a handicapping condition, should proceed to a more intensive level of diagnostic assessment is an appropriate and necessary procedure. Note that screening tests are *not* diagnostic tools; a properly developed screening only indicates if more investigative work is needed. Such instruments are not achievement tests and are not meant to describe child learning outcomes:

> Developmental screening tests identify at an early point which children may have learning problems or disabilities that could keep them from realizing their potential. . . . By triggering in-depth assessment, screening instruments help teachers and other professionals decide who needs additional support for learning, rather than potentially being used to judge whether classrooms are meeting standards set from the outside. (Meisels & Atkins-Burnett, 2005)

Head Start programs use an "Ages & Stages Questionnaire," for instance, so parents/adult family members can inform teachers about children's behaviors that allow for more accurate child monitoring.

Perhaps most important is the reminder to all teachers that tests have no special magic. Assessment is more than testing. A standardized test, a homemade tool, or a screening instrument should be only one of several measures used to determine a child's skills, abilities, or readiness. Any test result should be part of a multitude of information, such as direct observation, parental report, and children's actual work. "There are many ways that children can demonstrate learning, creativity, social skills and emotional intelligence, but these strategies are more time consuming to assess, and open to biased interpretation. Despite these thorny challenges, authentic expressions of knowing that grow naturally out of children's engagement with the curriculum can produce satisfaction for learners, parents, and teachers alike" (Rushton et al., 2009).

Concerns about Assessment

Assessment is challenging! Of all the functions performed by teachers, probably none calls for more energy, time, and skill than evaluation. Anyone involved in evaluation should avoid:

- *Unfair comparisons.* Evaluations should be used to identify and understand the child involved, not to compare one with another in a competitive manner.
- *Bias.* Evaluations can label unfairly or prematurely the very people they are intended to help. Typecasting does not produce a useful assessment. Insufficient data and overemphasis on the results are two areas that need close monitoring. Evaluation tools should be free of language bias or other cultural bias. For instance, an evaluation of children should

not include experiences unfamiliar to the cultural group being assessed.
- *Overemphasis on norms.* Most evaluation tools imply some level of normal behavior or performance, acceptable levels of interaction, or quantities of materials and space. People involved in an evaluation must remember to individualize the process rather than try to fit a child into the mold created by the assessment tool.
- *Interpretation.* There is sometimes a tendency to over interpret or misinterpret results. It must be clear what is being evaluated and how the information will be used. It is particularly important to be sensitive to the feelings of those being evaluated when communicating the results of the assessment. Parents and teachers need to interpret evaluations clearly and carefully if they are to understand the findings and feel comfortable with them.
- *Too narrow of a perspective.* An evaluation tool may focus too much on one area and not enough on others. Moreover, no single occasion or instrument tells teachers all they need to know about a child's abilities, a teacher's performance, or a program's effectiveness. It is essential that information be gathered in many ways and on several occasions. Sampling only children's skills as the single measure would lead to conclusions that were neither reliable nor valid. An imbalanced assessment gives an incomplete picture.
- *Too wide of a range.* An evaluation should be designed for a single level or age group and not cover too wide of a range. It is appropriate to measure a child's ability to print at age 6 but not at age 2. What is expected of the person or task should be taken into account and the evaluation method modified accordingly.
- *Too little or too much time.* The amount of time necessary to complete an evaluation must be weighed. The evaluation that is too lengthy loses its effectiveness in the time it takes. Time for interpretation and reflection must be included in the overall process.

Goals for children encompass all areas of development, and one measurement will not describe every area. Using a single yardstick to measure a child ignores the fact that young children do not always demonstrate what they know in a "testing" or single situation. The tail should not wag the dog; that is, the test should not drive curriculum.

Chapter 15 includes a discussion about the No Child Left Behind legislation.

Using Observation and Assessment Information

Applying our observations to work in the classroom and with families and other professionals is a time-consuming, yet essential, aspect of teaching young children. Information gathered through direct observation and appropriate assessment reveals who children are, where their strengths and interests lie, and what challenges they have that need addressing in the program. Teachers use their observations to plan relevant space, materials, and curriculum for children. In addition, they adjust the environment and schedule based on what they have seen of the group in action. Finally, teachers adjust their interactions with children because of what they see.

Helping special populations and individuals is another way to use information gleaned from observation and assessment. Children with identified special needs require an individualized plan for their educational experience, based on formal assessment and adjusted with accurate direct observation. Many children in early education and care may not have identified special needs but require special handling. For instance, a child with a sensitive temperament may be repelled by ordinary cuddling; one adjusting to a new baby may need more teacher interaction for awhile; the children whose soccer team just won a game might be rambunctious that day. Observant teachers use what they see to good advantage.

There are four principles that guide our assessment practices in order for them to benefit young children, their families, and us as teaching professionals:

1. Standards should identify the important and developmentally appropriate outcomes we want for the children in our care.
2. Processes should be in place to develop and review the standards and our techniques for assessing children with them.
3. Assessment strategies must be ethical and appropriate for young children as they work and play in our settings.
4. Communication about both the standards and the observations and assessments we use must be in place and include teachers, families, and relevant professionals.

Observation and assessment of children can be done appropriately and can tell us so much about children; we owe it to ourselves and the children we teach to use both to benefit all.

SUMMARY

LO1 Observation is key for early childhood teaching. Systematic observation and recording of children's behavior are fundamental tools in understanding children. What children do and say and how they think and feel are revealed as they play and work. By learning to observe children's behavior, teachers improve, become less biased, construct theory, use observation as an assessment tool, assist parents, and solve problems.

LO2 Outlining the major contexts of observations assists in understanding what is recorded. Observational data help adults know children as individuals, children in general, developmental relationships, various influences on behavior, and an understanding of self.

LO3 There are four types of observations systems. All of them have common elements of focus, system, tools, and environment. Narratives, such as a running record or diary/log, are the most common type, followed by samplings (time or event). A third type is rating method, such as checklists and rating scales, followed by modified child study techniques that include shadow studies, experimental procedures, and the clinical method. Certain procedures should be followed to observe and record effectively.

LO4 Child assessment meets several goals and involves many tools. The goals include establishing a baseline, documenting children's learning, determining guidance and intervention, planning curriculum, communicating with families, and monitoring programs. Two types of assessment, formal and informal, differ in their approach and the data collected. With the advent of early learning standards, testing and screening is on the rise, and concerns regarding comparisons, bias, and overemphasis on norms and test results need addressing. There are several guidelines to follow in order to assess children appropriately.

Key Terms

assessment
evaluation
objectivity
bias
authentic assessment
context
individualized curriculum
connected knowledge
intervention
accommodations
norms
narratives
running record

diary descriptions
specimen descriptions
log/journal
time sampling
event sampling
checklists
rating scales
continuum
shadow study
experimental procedure
methode clinique (clinical method)
professional confidentiality
accountability

baseline
screening
documentation
formal assessments
norm-referenced test
informal assessments
naturalistic assessments
portfolio
early learning standards
Bloom's taxonomy
rubric

Review Questions

1. In recording observations, teachers must be careful of bias. Poor observations usually contain inferences, overgeneralizations, and/or opinions that cloud a complete, objective sampling of a child's behavior. Read the following segment and underline the language segments that contain such passages:

   C is sitting on the rug with four friends and he is playing with cars and he starts whining about his car. He is just having a bad attitude about its not moving correctly. C is crying because he just got hit with the car. Let me tell you something about him. He is a big whiner about anything and he always wants it his way. Then he goes over to the book corner and is very quietly reading a book and he is happy by himself.

2. Put this chapter to the test! Match the behavior with the category it describes:

Category	Behavior
Children in general	Matthew cries when his grandma says good-bye.
Influences on behavior	Most 4-year-olds can pull up their pants on their own.
Understanding of self	To really know Celia, I'll have to observe her with scissors, at the climber, figuring out a problem, with her friends, in our small group time, when her mom leaves, and doing a painting.
Developmental relationships	I wonder why Mondays are so hard on Serena? Which weekends does she stay with her dad?
Children as individuals	You know, I just overreact when I see children playing with their food.

3. To see children through observations, teachers use several observational methods. List four and describe the advantages and disadvantages of each. Which would you prefer? Why? Which one(s) might best suit a beginning teacher? A parent? An experienced teacher? The director of the school?

4. Why and how can children's learning and skills be assessed? What are the reasons for assessing children's progress? Describe some of the problems with testing or screening of young children. How can you address these problems if you are required to administer a standardized test to your class?

Observe and Apply

1. Perceptions of a person's character are in the eyes of the beholder. These perceptions affect how teachers behave with children. What color are your glasses tinted? Divide a piece of paper in half, lengthwise. On one side, list some words to describe your feelings about childhood, school, teachers, children, authority, making friends, losing friends, hitting, and playing. On the other side, describe how these feelings may have influenced your teaching and helped create your own biases.

2. Observe a child for 10 minutes. Using language as your paintbrush, make a written picture of that child's physical appearance and movements. Compare the child's size, body build, facial features, and energy level with those of other children in the class. In narrative form, record as many of the body movements as you can, noting seemingly useless movements, failures, and partial successes, as well as final achievements.

3. Try a time sample of children's play in your classroom. Observe 10 children for one minute each during free-play times, and record the type(s) of social behavior they show. Using Parten's categories, your chart would look like this one. Compare your results with the impressions of the other teachers with whom you work. Did you come to any conclusions on how children develop socially?

4. Does your own setting have an evaluation plan for child assessment? Analyze the goals of your plan and how the tools or implementation meet (or do not meet) those goals. Be sure to address the concerns about assessment.

Child/Age	Unoccupied	Solitary	Onlooker	Parallel	Associative	Cooperative
1.						
2.						
3.						
4.						
5.						
6.						
7.						
8.						
9.						
10.						
Totals						

Helpful Websites

California Department of Education Desired Results Developmental Profile—revised (2006).
www.cde.ca.gov

Creative Curriculum assessment system
www.TeachingStrategies.com

Culturally and Linguistically Appropriate Services (CLAS) Early Childhood Research Institute
clas.uiuc.edu

Early Childhood Journal　**www.springer.com/ed**

Early Childhood Research Quarterly
   www.naeyc.org/publications/ecrq

Early Childhood Education Assessment (ECEA)
   Consortium & Council of Chief State School
   Officers   **www.ccsso.org**

Environmental Rating Scale   **ers.fpg.unc.edu/**

High/Scope   **www.highscope.org**

National Association for the Education of Young
   Children   **www.naeyc.org**

National Center for Fair and Open Testing
   www.fairtest.org

National Institute for Early Education Research
   (NIEER)   **nieer.org**

Work Sampling System
   www.worksamplingonline.com

● The Education CourseMate website for this text offers many helpful resources and interactive study tools. Go to CengageBrain.com to access the TeachSource Videos, flashcards, tutorial quizzes, direct links to all of the websites mentioned in the chapter, downloadable forms, and more.

References

Bloom, B. S. (1956). *Taxonomy of educational objectives, handbook I: The cognitive domain*. New York: David McKay Co Inc.

Bodrova, E., Leong, D., & Shore, R. (2004, March). Child outcome standards in pre-K programs: What are standards: What is needed to make them work? In *Preschool Policy Matters*. National Institute on Early Educational Research (NIEER), www.nieer.org. Issue 5.

Cohen, D. H., Stern, V., Balaban, N., & Cropper, N. (2008). *Observing and recording the behavior of young children* (5th Ed). New York: Teachers College Press.

Copple, C., & Bredekamp, S., Eds. (2009). *Developmentally appropriate practice in early childhood programs serving children from birth through age 8*. Washington, D.C.: National Association for the Education of Young Children.

Council of Chief State School Officers (CCSSO) (2005). *The words we use: A glossary of terms for early childhood education standards and assessment*. Washington, D.C.: Early Childhood Education Assessment Consortium.

Curtis, D. (2008, November/December). Seeing children. Beginnings Workshop: Assessment and Documentation, *Exchange*, pp. 37–42.

Davis, E. P., & Gunnar, M. (2000). Stress, coping and caregiving. In L. Gilkerson (Ed.) *Teaching and learning about the brain and early development*. Chicago, IL: Erikson Institute.

Dawes, H. C. (1934). An analysis of two hundred quarrels of preschool children. *Child Development*, 5, pp. 139–157.

Dowley, E. M. (not dated). Cues for observing children's behavior. Unpublished paper.

Feeney, S., Christensen, D., & Moravcik, E. (2008). *Who am I in the lives of children?* (8th Ed). Englewood Cliffs, NJ: Prentice Hall.

Galinsky, E. (2010). *Mind in the making*. Washington, D.C.: NAEYC.

Gardner, H. (1988, September/October). Alternatives to standardized testing. *Harvard Education Letter*.

Gilkerson, L. (2001). Integrating an understanding of brain development into early childhood education. *Infant Mental Health Journal*, 22(1-2), pp. 174–187.

Gonzalez-Mena, J. (2000). Focus Box: Understanding what we observe: A multicultural perspective. In A. Gordon & K. W Browne (Eds.). *Beginnings and beyond: Foundations in early childhood education* (5th Ed). Clifton Park, NY: Thomson Delmar Learning.

Gronlund, G. (2008, July). Creative and thoughtful strategies for implementing learning standards. *Young Children*, pp. 10–13.

Gronlund, G. (2006). *Making early learning standards come alive.* St Paul, MN: Redleaf Press.

Gullo, D. F. (2006). Assessment in kindergarten. In D. F. Gullo (Ed.). *KToday: Teaching and learning in the kindergarten year.* Washington, D.C.: NAEYC, 138–147.

Lam, M., & Wiggins-Dowler, K. (2006). *Documentation panel: Our construction curriculum project.* San Mateo, CA: MML Children's Center, College of San Mateo, 2005–2006.

Malaguzzi, L. (March, 1994). Your image of the child: Where teaching begins. *Exchange,* pp. 52–56.

Maxwell, K. L., & Clifford, R. M. (2004). School readiness assessment in *Spotlight on Young Children and Assessment.* Washington, D.C.: NAEYC, 29–37.

McLaughlin, K., & Sugarman, S. (1982). Personal communications.

Meisels, S. J., & Atkins-Burnett, S. (2005). *Developmental screening in early childhood: A guide* (5th Ed). Washington, D.C.: National Association for the Education of Young Children.

National Association for the Education of Young Children (NAEYC) and the National Association of Early Childhood Specialists in State Departments of Education (NAECS/SDE). (2003). Position statement on early childhood curriculum, assessment, and program evaluation—building an effective, accountable system in programs for children birth through age 8. http://www.naeyc.org/about/positions/pdf/CAPEexpand.pdf

National Center for Fair and Open Testing (NCFOT). (2006). Cambridge, MA: Fair Test. http://www.fairtest.org

New Oxford American Dictionary (2nd Ed). England: Oxford University Press, 2005.

Parten, M. B. (1932). Social participation among preschool children. *Journal of Abnormal and Social Psychology,* 27, pp. 243–269.

Reifel, S. (2011, March). Observation and early childhood teaching: Evolving fundamentals. *Young Children,* 66(2).

Rushton, S., Juola-Rushton, A., & Larkin, E. (2009). Neuroscience, play and early childhood education: Connections, implications and assessment. *Early Childhood Education Journal,* 37, pp. 351–361.

Ryan, K., Cooper, J.S., & Tauer, S. (2013). *Teaching for student learning: Becoming a master teacher* (2nd Ed.). Belmont, CA: Wadsworth/Cengage.

Schiller, P., & Willis, C.A. (2008, July). Of primary interest: Using brain-based teaching strategies to create supportive early childhood environments that address learning standards. *Young Children,* pp. 52–55.

Shillady, A. L. (2004). Choosing an appropriate assessment system. *Spotlight on Young Children and Assessment.* Washington, D.C.: NAEYC, 54–59.

Special thanks to the following Early Childhood Education students for their observation samples: M. Duraliza, J. Gallero, C. Grupe, L. Hutton, C. Liner, C. Robinson, & M. Saldivar.

Guiding Children's Behavior

 Standards For Professional Development

These are the NAEYC Standards for Initial and Advanced Early Childhood Professional Preparation that are addressed in this chapter:

Standard 1 Promoting Child Development and Learning

Standard 2 Building Family and Community Relations

Standard 3 Observing, Documenting, and Assessing to Support Young Children and Families

Standard 4 Using Developmentally Effective Approaches to Connect with Children and Families

Standard 5 Using Content Knowledge to Build Meaningful Curriculum

naeyc Code of Ethical Conduct

These are the sections of the NAEYC Code of Ethical Conduct that apply to the topics in this chapter:

Core Values: We have committed ourselves to helping children and adults achieve their full potential in the context of relationships that are based on trust, respect, and positive regard.

Section I:

I.1-4   To appreciate the vulnerability of children and their dependence on adults.

P-1.1   Above all, we shall not harm children. We shall not participate in practices that are emotionally damaging, physically harmful, disrespectful, degrading, dangerous, exploitative, or intimidating to children.

I-2.6   To acknowledge families' childrearing values and their right to make decisions for their children.

1-3A.2 To share resources wth co-workers, collaborating to ensure that the best possible early childhood care and education program is provided.

Learning Outcomes

LO1 Demonstrate an understanding of the factors that influence children's behavior.

LO2 Compare and contrast guidance, discipline, and punishment and their appropriate use.

LO3 Identify practices that promote a caring classroom through developmentally and culturally appropriate guidance methods.

LO4 Examine effective guidance strategies that promote positive interactions, social learning, and problem-solving skills.

LO5 Become familiar with strategies for helping children who have challenging behaviors.

Understanding Children's Behavior

In the toddler class, 2-year-olds Shawnsey and Kim are playing in the dress-up area. Kim grabs at one of the many necklaces Shawnsey has draped around her neck. Startled, Shawnsey lets out a cry, grabs Kim's arm, and bites her.

Malcolm, a 5-year-old, rushes through the room, heading for the block area. For just a moment, he stands and watches Lorraine balancing blocks on top of one another in a tall column. With a swift wave of his arm, Malcolm topples the structure.

Mac, a 3½-year-old, is busy with a puzzle. When a teacher stops at the table to tell the children it is nearly time to clean up for snacks, Mac replies, "My daddy says that cleaning up is a girl's job and I don't have to do it." He throws the puzzle on the floor and dashes away from the teacher.

These are typical scenes in any early childhood setting. No matter how plentiful the materials, how many or well trained the adults, or how good the program, conflicts are sure to occur. Teaching children to respect themselves and each other is a complex and difficult task. It takes experience, skill, and practice. Look at the examples again. What do they say about Shawnsey, Malcolm, and Mac? How should teachers respond to these children? How did these situations happen?

The Guidance Lens

Guidance is the ongoing process of helping children learn to control their basic impulses, express their feelings, channel their frustrations, and solve their problems. There are no quick fixes or strategies that apply to all circumstances. Positive guidance methods are created to fit a child, an adult (parent, teacher), and a situation. These three elements, when considered together, suggest the most appropriate guidance strategies. Figure 7-1 shows these three factors in relation to one another. Throughout this chapter, the relationship between the child, the adult, and the situation is reflected in guidance theory and practices.

Theories

There are several ways of explaining what people do and why. One idea is that people's behavior is mainly a result of heredity (nature). Another is that experience and environment shape behavior (nurture). A third theory suggests that children go through "stages" at certain times of their lives regardless of their genes or home background.

For guidance to be successful, a teacher must first understand children's behavior.

© Cengage Learning

All sides have valid arguments in the nature/nurture debate, and both heredity and experience affect behavior. Age and stage theory is also familiar. People speak of the "terrible 2s" or say that all 4-year-old girls are silly. There may be some truth to those generalities, but that does not excuse the inappropriate behavior at the various developmental stages. Teachers and parents cannot ignore misbehavior (unless it is a specific guidance strategy) just because children are the "right" age or because of their home situations. That attitude implies adults are powerless to help children form new behavior patterns. Not true! Adults can do something about children's behavior if they understand what is happening to the child.

Factors That Affect Behavior

Knowing what affects children's behavior and feelings helps adults understand and manage the child who is misbehaving. The following factors combine aspects of both nature and nurture theories, as well as the theories of ages and stages of development. The three vignettes at the beginning of the chapter provide examples of all five

The Guidance Lens

In establishing effective guidance practices, adults take into consideration three important elements: the child, the adult, and the situation. For instance, a 2-year-old needing assistance is more likely to respond to the intervention of a familiar teacher than one who is substituting for the day.

Child

- Who am I?
- What are my developmental levels? Skills?
- Who is my family?
- What is my culture?
- How do I fit in the classroom?

Adult
- What is my role and relationship to the child?
- What guidance strategies work best for this child in this case?
- What is my goal for these children and what will be culturally congruent for them?
- What is my role in relationship to the group?

Circumstances
- What is happening?
- At what time?
- Who is involved?
- Where is it taking place?
- What is the social situation at the time?

© Cengage Learning 2014

FIGURE 7-1 A snapshot of three important factors to consider when choosing effective guidance techniques.

factors, which are: 1) developmental; 2) environmental; 3) individual; 4) emotional and social; and 5) cultural.

1. *Developmental Factors.* Adults should be aware of developmental theory to know what type of behavior to expect of children at various ages. Developmental theory helps teachers anticipate what children will do so that they can maintain reasonable expectations. To see behavior as predictable and developmentally appropriate is to understand it more completely and guide it more effectively.

   The facts are that Shawnsey, Kim, Malcolm, and Mac have been in a group setting for more than three hours

and it is nearly snack time. We know that preschoolers cannot be expected to be in control of themselves over extended periods of time. Conflicts and disagreements happen in any group of children. Hungry children are often ineffective problem solvers; Mac might be more manageable after snack. It is also clear to the teacher that the toddlers do not have the language or social development skills to talk problems out with other children, as do Malcolm and Mac.

2. *Environmental Factors.* Through the intentional use of the environment, the teacher indirectly influences behavior in the classroom. The goals for positive

behavior should be reflected in the classroom setting. The physical environment should tell children clearly how to act in that space. Child-size furniture that fits the preschool body encourages sitting and working behavior. Room arrangements avoid spaces that encourage children to walk from place to place. Low, open shelves create an expectation that children take materials out and put them away after use.

Materials and equipment should be adequate and interesting to the age group. When children are occupied with stimulating age-appropriate materials, there are fewer opportunities for misbehavior. Materials can challenge children, overwhelm them, or bore them. If materials and equipment are suitable, children feel more at ease with themselves and more willing to accept adults' limits and controls. Adding materials and equipment can help prevent arguments over a favorite toy, create new and interesting challenges, and extend children's play ideas.

Shawnsey and Kim's teacher will want to add more necklaces to the dress-up area if there are not enough to outfit several children. Perhaps the block area needs to be moved to a more protected section of the room.

Changing the environment when needed can help avert behavior problems. Removing attractive but breakable items reduces tears and conflicts. Some materials may prove to be too stimulating and may need to be removed for a while. Some activities may need to be limited to specific locations to control the level of activity and behavior. Look at Figure 7-2 to evaluate how the environment is related to your guidance philosophy and children's behavior. Chapter 9 contains a detailed discussion of many factors that should be considered when designing spaces for young children. Many of these environmental considerations directly influence children's behavior.

The daily schedule and timing of events indirectly influence classroom behavior. When there are blocks of

---

Classroom Checklist to Enhance Positive Behaviors

Time

____ Does the daily schedule provide enough time for unhurried play?

____ Are those periods that create tension—transitions from one activity to another—given enough time?

____ Is cleanup a leisurely process built in at the end of each activity, with children participating?

Program Planning and Curriculum

____ Is there enough to do so that children have choices and alternatives for play?

____ Is the curriculum challenging enough to prevent boredom and restlessness?

____ Are there activities to help children release tension? Do the activities allow for body movement, exploration, and manipulation of materials?

____ Are children included in developing the rules and setting guidelines? How is their inclusion demonstrated?

Organization and Order

____ If children are expected to put things away after use, are the cabinets low, open, and marked in some way?

____ Are the materials within easy reach of the children, promoting self-selection and independence?

____ Are there enough materials so that sharing does not become a problem?

____ Are the areas in which activities take place clearly defined so that children know what happens there?

____ Does the room arrangement avoid runways and areas with no exits?

____ Do children have their own private space?

____ Are children able to use all visible and accessible materials? Are there materials about which children are told "Don't touch"?

Personnel

____ Are there enough teachers to give adequate attention to the number of children in the class?

____ Are the group size and makeup balanced so that children have a variety of playmates?

____ Are the teachers experienced, and do they seem comfortable in setting limits and guiding children's behavior?

____ Do teachers use their attention to encourage behavior they want, and do they ignore what they want to discourage?

____ Do all adults consistently enforce the same rules?

FIGURE 7-2 By anticipating children's needs and growth patterns, teachers set up classrooms that foster constructive and purposeful behavior.

time to choose activities, children can proceed at their own pace without feeling hurried.

Mac, for instance, had just settled in at the puzzle table when the teacher told him that it was time to clean up. Uncooperative behavior is sometimes related to time pressures.

The physical needs of eating, sleeping, and toileting are met by careful scheduling so that children are able to play without concern for the necessities of life. Schedules that do not allow enough time for clean up and transitions produce a frantic climate.

3. *Individual Factors.* Teachers of young children soon learn the temperamental characteristics of each child in the class.

Hondi works and plays with great intensity; Norman is easily distracted. Tawana fears any change, whereas Enrique thrives on challenges. The consistent patterns of temperament that emerge help define each child's individual style. The teacher wants to support and comfort Kim at the same time she lets Shawnsey know that biting is not tolerated. It is important to maintain a level of trust with Shawnsey so that she can help learn better ways to communicate her needs.

Malcolm is enthusiastic and plunges into activities spontaneously, sometimes without looking ahead or surveying the wreckage he leaves behind. His teacher is aware that he can be personable and cooperative if he is given options and a chance to make decisions. As they talk together about Lorraine's blocks, the teacher offers Malcolm a choice: to talk with Lorraine to see if she would like to have him help rebuild the same structure or start a new one. Both Malcolm and the teacher find satisfaction in working together in ways that acknowledge and respect Malcolm's personal style.

4. *Emotional and Social Factors.* Some behavior problems stem from the child's attempt to express social and emotional needs. These include the need to feel loved and cared for, the need to be included, the desire to be considered important and valued, the desire to have friends, and the need to feel safe from harm. Young children are still working out ways to express these needs and feelings. Typically, because they are only just learning language and communication skills, it is often through nonverbal or indirect actions that children let us know what is bothering them. It is also important to provide children with models of language for resolving these conflicts and to let them know that we recognize they can be angry, jealous, or hurt. The supportive adult helps children find satisfying ways to cope with their social and emotional feelings.

Shawnsey is an only child of older parents and has little opportunity outside of school to interact with others her age. Malcolm comes from a big, boisterous family in which taking care of one's desires and needs is instilled early on. Mac's parents are divorced, and he is now living with his grandmother while his mother looks for work in another town. Their teachers understand their bids for attention and weigh each child's social and emotional history as they guide them toward positive behavior.

Other influences affect behavior. Weather seems to affect children. Wild, windy, rainy days seem to stimulate children into high and excitable behavior. Bright, sunny days also seem to influence a child's mood and temperament. Problems that upset adults can make an impression on a child. A family crisis, a new baby, or a recent divorce has impact. Sharing a bedroom, visits from relatives, illness, television, videos or movies, siblings, nutrition, and health affect children's behavior. The longer teachers work with children, the more adept they become at seeing how

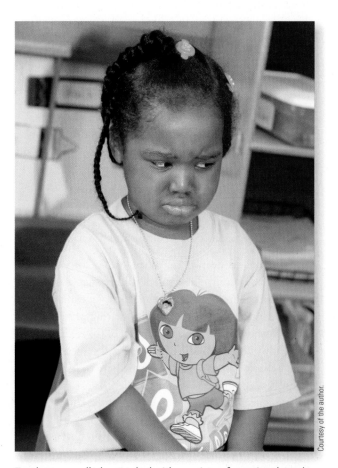

Teachers are called on to deal with a variety of emotional needs.

 **DIVERSITY**

Types of Temperament

According to research, each child, beginning at birth, has temperamental characteristics that we can observe through their activity level, attention span, regularity and rhythm of bodily routines, adaptability, physical sensitivity, intensity of reaction, ease of distraction, and mood. These differences were observed in very young infants and seem to remain consistent as the child grows. Researchers Thomas and Chess (1977) identified these characteristics and defined three types of temperament: the easy child, the difficult child, and the slow-to-warm-up child. Today they are often referred to as:

The *flexible* child (about 40 percent of all children) is adaptable, optimistic, cheerful, and easily trained in eating, sleeping, and toileting; has mild reactions to frustration.

The *fearful* child (about 15 percent) seems shy and adapts to new situations by observing and watching; needs to go at own pace and is slow to express negative mood.

The *feisty* child (about 10 percent) is the opposite of the flexible child with irregular sleeping and eating habits; is fussy in new situations, adapts slowly, and is often disagreeable and prone to temper tantrums.

Children's temperament affects the way people deal with them. If adults identify the nature of a child's temperament, guidance measures can be tailored to meet the individual child. The strategies for dealing with a slow-to-warm-up child and a difficult child are different from techniques used to discipline the easy child. An easy child is easy to respond to; a slow-to-warm-up child may be harder to reach. Difficult children may be blamed for things they did not do. Identifying traits can be useful as long as adults are careful not to label children unfairly or prematurely. As you come to know and understand the diverse reactions of the children you teach, you gain insights into their behavior and find guidance techniques that match their individual temperaments.

these various factors shape the behavior of the individual children in their class. In Chapter 14, the young child's social and emotional growth is further explored.

5. *Cultural Factors.* Today's children are growing up in a country of unparalleled diversity. Many different cultures are converging and creating a nation of peoples, cultures, languages, and attitudes. We are living in a world of continual cross-cultural interactions, so the ability to communicate across cultures is a critical skill to have when guiding children's behavior. (See also discussions in Chapters 2, 5, 8, and 15.) A review of Erikson's and Vygotsky's theories in Chapter 4 and Bronfenbrenner's theory in Chapter 15 underscores the connection between culture and behavior.

Discipline is deeply embedded within the values and beliefs of the family. The family's culture shapes how they raise their children, and each family is unique in the way it interprets its cultural values. Child-rearing practices such as physical punishment to the timing of toilet training are culturally influenced. The messages children receive about their behavior should be consistent between school and home. Yet, conflict may be inevitable because the culturally influenced child-rearing practices of the family may be at odds with a teacher's ideas and expectations.

In some cultures, children are encouraged to challenge adult opinions, whereas this would be considered disrespectful in other cultures. Each child must be valued as part of a family system, no matter the origin or structure, and the teacher's role is to support the child's sense of security and identity within the family. Children bring their unique individuality to the classroom, but they are also bearers of the context in which they are being raised: their family, culture, ethnicity, religion, socioeconomic status, and neighborhood. When we are aware of these influences, we are better able to match who the child is with the most effective guidance approach.

In some families, a sense of community is valued over individualism, a concept that can create difficulty in the early childhood classroom unless it is understood and appreciated. Early childhood educators, for the most part, do not force children to share personal possessions before they seem ready to, and they encourage children to become autonomous at an early age. This is at odds with families in which cooperation and sharing are valued concepts, as is dependency on other family members. We need to become culturally sensitive to some of the long-held assumptions of teaching young children. The sections on "Self-Awareness" and "Attitudes and Biases" in Chapter 5 suggest ways in which teachers can address stereotypes and prejudices that may interfere with their effectiveness in guiding children's behavior.

Schools must be inviting and safe places in which families from all cultures can express their perceptions, concerns, and expectations about their children. Teachers need to be flexible and nonjudgmental as they work with the cultural implications of children's behavior. Figure 7-3 shows how different

Family Patterns and Children's Behavior

Family Culture	Child's Experience and Behavior	Guidance Strategy
Power Structure		
Democratic family—members share in decision making	Child is encouraged to negotiate and compromise.	Offer real choices; use problem-solving techniques.
One family member makes all of the decisions	Child is expected to obey, follow commands, and respect adult authority. Child may be unable to choose activities, look adults in the eye, or call them by name.	Don't insist on eye contact. Child may need help in selecting an activity. Work with the family members who make the decisions.
Values		
Strong, close-knit family	Child learns that the family comes first; the individual sacrifices for the family.	Recognize that family matters may take precedence over school.
Honor, dignity, and pride	Child's behavior reflects family honor; child is disciplined for rudeness or poor manners.	Share achievements with parents; help child learn manners; be sensitive when discussing child's behavior problems.
Expressing feelings is accepted	Child is allowed to cry, scream, throw temper tantrums.	Accept child's crying as you give comfort; stay with child until he is calm.
Issue of Discipline		
Clear, direct discipline	Child learns to respect authority and does what he is told to do; child may not take positive guidance strategies seriously or ignore them.	Use a sense of humor; make firm statements.
Discipline motivated toward inherent goodness	Child has freedom to explore consequences and is warned of possible embarrassment due to behavior.	Child may be passive if disciplined harshly. Use natural consequences; ask rather than demand.
Discipline motivated from inherent self-interest	Child is scolded, threatened, and controlled by promises.	Model desired behavior; use "if/then" statements: "If you finish eating, then you can play." Praise good manners and good behavior.

FIGURE 7-3 Sample of culturally diverse family patterns that affect guidance and discipline. Knowledge of culturally diverse family patterns and guidance strategies to parallel these child-rearing styles can allow you to begin a dialogue with the children you teach. (From *Roots and Wings*, Revised Edition, by Stacey York, pp. 66, 68, 69, 70. Copyright © 2003 by Stacey York. Adapted with permission from Redleaf Press, St. Paul, Minnesota, www.redleafpress.org.)

family cultural patterns relate to a child's behavior and an appropriate guidance strategy. Kim (who was playing with Shawnsey) has a family culture that views the teacher as a respected authority figure and one who must be obeyed. This places Kim in an uncomfortable position if her teacher does not understand why Kim does not make activity choices easily and prefers to have the teacher tell her where to play and work each day. As teachers become familiar with the customs and beliefs of the families in the program, they gain insights into children's behavior and understand the reasons for the way a child responds.

Guidance, Discipline, and Punishment: What Works

The overall process of guidance includes the use of guidance strategies, discipline methods, and appropriate punishment. What is the difference among them?

What Is Guidance?

Guidance is an ongoing system by which adults help children learn to manage their impulses, express feelings, channel frustrations, solve problems, and learn the difference between acceptable and unacceptable behavior (Browne & Gordon, 2009). The children we meet in early childhood programs are just learning how strong their emotions can be and what impact they have on their own behavior and on others. Behavior is the unspoken language through which children act out feelings and thoughts. Until they learn to express themselves vocally, they use a variety of behaviors to communicate. Using words (for instance, a resounding "No!" when someone takes a toy away) is slowly replacing biting, hitting, crying, and tantrums as a way to respond to frustration. Caring and respectful adults create a supportive atmosphere to help young children explore alternative behaviors, develop social skills, and learn to solve problems. This is called a positive approach to guidance. Consider the following examples:

- Tell children what it is you want them to do. Make directions and suggestions in positive statements, not in negative forms.
  "Walk around the edge of the grass, Hilla, so you won't get hit by the swing" instead of "Don't get hit!"
- Reinforce what children do right, what you like, and what you want to see repeated. This helps build the relationship on positive grounds.
  "Good job, Sammy. You worked hard on that puzzle."

- Give indirect suggestions or reminders, emphasizing what you want children to do. Help them refocus on the task without nagging or confrontation.
  "I know you are excited about the field trip, Mickey. Looks like you are almost finished putting on your jacket so we can go" instead of "Hurry and button that jacket so we can go."
- Use positive redirection whenever possible.
  "Let's get a basket for you to toss those balls in. That way you won't bother other children who are playing nearby."
- Use encouragement appropriately, focusing on helping children achieve success and understanding what it is you want them to learn.
  "Harry, I notice you are being careful about where you put your feet as you climb that tree. It looks to me like you are finding good places to stand" communicates a supportive attitude and tells the child what he is doing well. Global praise, such as "Great climbing, Harry. Good for you!" may leave children wondering what exactly it is they have been praised for and omits the learning they can derive from the experience.
- Give reasons for your request. Let children know in simple, straightforward statements the reasons behind your request. Children are more likely to cooperate when they can understand the reason why.
  "Tom, if you move those chairs, then you and Dee will have more room to dance" instead of "Move the chairs, Tom."

Through daily experiences, children construct their moral and social world, and they need adult guidance. The concept of a guide—one who leads, explains, and supports—is an important one. A guide points out directions, answers questions, and helps you get where you want to go. This is what teachers do as they help children learn to balance impulse and outer controls.

A positive guidance approach requires the active participation of both child and adult in order to be successful. Adults help children learn appropriate behavior by serving as models of behavior. Good role models deliberately vary their teaching styles and strategies to accommodate different learning styles and cultural patterns.

Inductive Guidance

There are a number of guidance approaches woven throughout the chapter that have many similar components and fall under the definition of **inductive guidance**. The key elements of inductive guidance are:

1. Guidance is an interactive process that actively involves children, as well as adults.
2. Children are increasingly held responsible for their actions as they begin to understand the impact of their behavior on others.

3. Inductive guidance helps a child learn thinking and reasoning skills, which fosters self-control and the development of a conscience.
4. Children learn to reflect on their feelings and their actions.

These four elements of inductive guidance are supported when teachers provide choices for children, ask open-ended questions ("What would happen if you took her book?" "How do you think he would feel if you said you did not want to play with him?"), and communicate trust and confidence in children's ability to solve problems.

The inductive guidance principles are based on the theories of Erikson and Piaget but owe particular credit to Vygostsky, who placed children's learning in the context of social interactions. The zone of proximal distance (see Chapter 4), for instance, reinforces the reciprocal relationship between adults and children implied in most inductive guidance techniques. Thomas and Chess's (1977) concept of "goodness of fit," in which the adult addresses the child's unique temperament in choosing guidance strategies, is reflected as well in inductive guidance.

© Cengage Learning

Having a hard day.

Family context also continues to be a priority when selecting appropriate guidance methods.

By integrating these principles into a positive guidance approach, teachers enlarge the child's capacity to become increasingly self-directed and self-reliant.

What Is Discipline?

Discipline is a part of the guidance strategies adults use to help children become responsible for their actions, learn self-control, and behave appropriately. **Discipline** stems from the word *disciple*, that is, a pupil, a follower, and a learner. This suggests two important concepts: that of following an example versus following rules and that of positive discipline. Discipline and guidance are similar in that effective discipline has the same foundation of thoughtful, nonpunitive methods that promote children's empathy and moral reasoning (Browne & Gordon, 2009).

What Is Punishment?

Punishment is a consequence for inappropriate behavior and a power assertive technique that relies on children's fears rather than the use of reason and understanding. Punishment is too often a knee-jerk reaction by an adult and may be based on negative strategies such as threats, shaming, and spanking, which are damaging to children's self-esteem. To be effective, punishment should be related to the behavior and help children learn from the situation. For instance, when Georgia grabs a book from Ruthie, the teacher wants to help Georgia learn to negotiate for a turn rather than punish her with a time out. Georgia learns new strategies for controlling her impulses. To maintain a positive approach to guidance, always avoid:

- Methods that shame, frighten, or humiliate children.
- Physical abuse; physical punishment.
- Comparisons among children. Comparisons foster competitiveness and affect self-esteem.
- Carryovers from the incident. Once it is over, leave it behind; do not keep reminding children about it.
- Consequences that are too long, too punitive, or postponed. Children benefit most from immediate, short consequences.
- Making promises you cannot keep.
- Being overly helpful. Let children do as much as they can by themselves, including solving their own conflicts.
- Threatening children with the loss of your affection.

To some, the words discipline and punishment are synonymous. They are not, and Figure 7-4 shows how these terms mean very different things.

Inductive Guidance and the Firefighter Rules

Out in the yard, the firefighter dramatic play was in full swing until Rocco was accidently hit by a two-foot piece of hose. At the teacher's planning meeting after class, Enrico suggested a plan that could help alleviate the rough play that had caused the accident. At group time the next day, before going outside, Enrico ask the class for their ideas on what they might do to prevent such accidents. Emboldened, the children called out solutions, which Enrico wrote on the board: "Get rid of the hoses." "No swinging the hoses." "No climbing on ladders with the hoses." "Make everyone wear a firefighter helmet." "No running with hoses." "Put up a sign to watch for the hoses." "Put up a sign that says firefighters only." "Only kids who have hoses can be firefighters." Enrico then asked the class where would they suggest the hoses be used. "Only on the hill." "All over the yard, so we can run to the fires." "By the little shed where we keep the trikes." "At the side of the yard where children don't play." He then asked what they thought the rules should be about the firefighter play. As children responded with reasonable suggestions, Enrico's role was to encourage open-ended conversation, exploring of ideas, and reaching consensus. At the end of the group time, the class had agreed to three rules: The hoses were to be used to put out fires, not to run with or swing around; firefighter play could take place in most parts of the yard, but not near the swings, slides, or climbers. The following week, the class reviewed the rules and added one more: Firefighters had to take turns with the hoses.

***

Think About This

1. What parts of the vignette were "intentional teaching" moments?
2. Why was Enrico's plan successful and what examples of inductive guidance did he use?
3. What ideas from this vignette will you use?

TeachSource Video

Watch the TeachSource Video Case entitled, "Elementary Classroom Management: Basic Strategies." After you study the video clip, view the artifacts, and read the teacher interviews and text, reflect upon the following questions:

1. Kindergarten teacher Amy spoke of building teamwork. What examples did you observe in this video case that supported teamwork as a way to promote positive behavior?

2. How do you think Amy's attitude toward behavior problems affects her relationship with the children in her class?

Toward Self-Discipline

One of the major goals of a good guidance process is to help children achieve self-discipline. This happens only if adults lead in ways that support children's developing ability to control themselves. By gradually handing over to children the opportunity to govern their actions, adults communicate trust. For young children with their emerging initiative, this is an important step to take. With added responsibility and trust comes an added dimension of self-respect and self-confidence so that children feel capable and worthwhile.

Children do not learn to handle freedom by being told what to do all the time. Only when they have an opportunity to test themselves and make some decisions on their own will they know their capabilities. Young children must learn this in safe places with adults who allow them as much freedom as they can responsibly handle.

An effective guidance approach is interactive. Adults and children both learn to change as they interact with one another toward a common goal. Figure 7-5 summarizes some of the ways children and adults can learn from a guidance and positive discipline philosophy.

The Language of Guidance and Discipline

Guidance has a language all its own. As teachers gain experience in handling problem behaviors, they learn to use that language. The result, in most cases, is **interdependence**: The more practiced teachers become in the language of guidance, the more comfortable they become in developing their own approach to guidance situations. The more comfortable they are in that approach, the more effectively they use language to solve behavior problems.

The language and communication techniques in guidance are both spoken and unspoken. Teachers discover how potent the voice can be—what words work best and when. They become aware of facial expressions and what a touch or a look conveys to children. How they use their

Differences Between Positive Guidance and Punishment

Positive Guidance	Punishment
Emphasizes what the child should do	Emphasizes what the child should *not* do
Is an ongoing process	Is a one-time occurrence
Sets an example to follow	Insists on obedience
Leads to self-control	Undermines independence
Helps children change	Is an adult release
Is positive	Is negative
Accepts child's need to assert self	*Makes* children behave
Fosters child's ability to think	Thinks *for* the child
Bolsters self-esteem	Defeats self-esteem
Shapes behavior	Condemns misbehavior

© Cengage Learning 2011

FIGURE 7-4 Positive guidance encourages children's interaction and involvement; punishment is usually something that is done to a child.

Guidance: An Interactive Approach

We Teach	Adults Learn to	Children Learn to
Values	Express	Internalize
Self-control	Maintain own	Practice
Respect	Give to child	Accord to others
Appropriate behavior	Model	Observe and imitate
Limits	Be clear and consistent	Accept consequences
Feelings	Accept own and child's	Identify and label
Problem solving	Offer meaningful choices	Make decisions
Self-esteem	Protect and enhance	Respect and appreciate self
Rule setting	Share power	Participate in creating behavior controls
Taking another's viewpoint	Be sympathetic and understanding	To be empathetic
Collaboration	Involve child in solutions	Problem-solve cooperatively

FIGURE 7-5 Guidance is an interactive process in which both children and adults may learn. Everyone benefits from disciplinary practices that foster changes in attitudes and behaviors. (From Ann Gordon & Kathryn Williams Browne, *Guiding Young Children in a Diverse Society.* Published by Allyn and Bacon, Boston, MA. Copyright © 1996 by Pearson Education. Reprinted with permission of the publisher.)

body reflects a distinct attitude and approach to discipline. Through experience, new teachers learn how to use these tools in ways that work best for them and the children.

Voice

Some adults feel that when they are speaking to children they must assume a different voice from the one they normally use. Talk to children in the same way you talk to other people. Learn to control the volume and use good speech patterns for children to imitate. Get close enough to speak in a normal tone; get down to the child's level. Often, lowering volume and pitch is effective.

Words

The fewer the words, the better. Simple, clear statements, spoken once, have more impact. The child is able to focus on the real issues involved. A brief description of what happened, a word or two about what behavior is acceptable and what is not, and a suggestion for possible solutions are all that is necessary.

Choose words carefully. They should convey to the child exactly what is expected. "Richy, move the block closer to the truck so that Sarah will not bump into it again" tells Richy in a positive, concrete way what he can do to protect his block building. If he had been told, "Richy, watch where you are building," he would not know what action to take to solve the problem.

Body Language

When working with young children, the teacher must be aware of body height and position. Sit, squat, or kneel—but get down to their level. It is difficult to communicate warmth, caring, and concern from two or three feet above a child's head or by shouting from across the room.

Guidance is founded on a loving, caring relationship between child and adult. To help children gain control over their impulses and monitor their behavior, teachers must establish a sense of trust and well-being with children. The way teachers use their body invites or rejects close relationship and familiarity. A child finds teachers more approachable if they are seated low, with arms available, rather than standing, with arms folded.

Making full use of the senses can soften the impact of words. A firm grip on the hand of a child who is hitting out or a gentle touch on the shoulder tells children the adult is there to protect them from themselves and others. Eye contact is essential. Teachers learn to communicate the seriousness of a situation through eye and facial expressions. They also show reassurance, concern, sadness, and affection this way. Physical presence should convey to the child a message that the teacher is there, available, and interested.

Body height and position are important. Getting down to the child's eye level provides for greater impact and involvement.

Attitude

Attitudes are derived from experience and are part of the unspoken language of guidance. You should examine the way you were disciplined and acknowledge your experiences and feelings about it, particularly assumptions you may have on how children behave depending on their race, gender, or culture.

Promoting a Caring Classroom Community Through Guidance

Teaching practices that promote a caring classroom community are grounded in developmental theory and expressed in both direct and indirect guidance and discipline techniques.

Developmentally Appropriate Guidance

Each developmental stage has shared characteristics, modified by a child's individual rate of growth. It is as typical for 4-year-olds to test limits as it is for toddlers to have a strong sense of ownership about their possessions. Identifying the behaviors that are typical to a specific age

Fostering Developmentally Appropriate Guidance

In a DAP environment, the relationships between child and teacher is warm and nurturing. School becomes a place where adults are consistent and react sensitively when children are upset or under stress. Supportive adults who intervene with positive attitudes and positive guidance strategies exemplify the best of DAP. You foster developmentally appropriate guidance when you:

- Allow plenty of time for children to respond. Give them an opportunity to decide their course of action.
- Review limits and rules periodically. Modify them as children's growth and maturation indicate. Change them as circumstances change; be flexible.
- Encourage children to talk things over. Be open to their point of view even if you cannot accept it. Let them know you are willing to listen to all sides of the conflict.
- Become aware of the climate in the room or yard. Anticipate the need for a change of pace or a different activity before children become bored or troublesome.
- Remember, it takes time and numerous opportunities for changes in behavior to occur. By using consistent positive guidance techniques, you help children practice new behavior repeatedly.

group provides a context in which to understand the child and behavior that can be seen as normal and predictable. Guidance based on a developmental approach tells us that first and second graders have an ability to consider others' points of view, so we help them problem-solve by asking them to think of how their behavior affects others.

A developmentally appropriate approach also means that the teacher considers what is known about the individual child, as well as what is typical for the age group. This ensures that the guidance techniques match the capabilities of the child and that adult expectations remain reasonable.

Culturally Appropriate Guidance

In today's diverse world, teachers may be confronted by parents whose guidance practices are contrary to the school's philosophy. Families may apply pressure on teachers to use some of the techniques that they use at home. The question becomes how do teachers maintain the school's, as well as their own, standards without communicating to the family that their values are wrong

or have children feel that something about their home and family is diminished in the teacher's eyes. Gonzalez-Mena (2008) emphasizes the teacher's responsibility to learn cross-cultural communication when child-rearing practices are in conflict between home and school and suggests the following strategies:

- Accept that both viewpoints are equally valid.
- Work together to figure out a solution to the situation.
- Resist assigning meaning and values to the behavior of others on the basis of your own culture.
- Remember that your behavior does not necessarily convey your own meaning and values.
- Educate yourself about the different cultures represented in your classroom. Learn how and what is communicated through facial gestures, touch, eye contact, physical closeness, and time concepts.
- Observe, ask, and talk about what the differences are; learn from the parents of the children in the classroom what you need to know about their culture.
- Maintain an open attitude that promotes respect and appreciation for each other's views.

Ethical issues involving culture-based differences are discussed in Chapter 5. The anti-bias curriculum, as described in Chapters 5 and 9, suggests some strategies as well. Also see "Child Development and Cultural Diversity" in Chapter 4. The NAEYC Code of Ethical Conduct (Appendix A) is a useful resource for ethical concerns when working with families from many cultures.

Behavior Models

The teacher as a **behavior model** is an important element in guidance. Children pattern their responses after adult behaviors. They are aware of how teachers respond to anger, frustration, and aggression and how they solve problems and conflicts. Adults must be sure to model the desired behavior around the children they teach. To be successful models, teachers should be aware of their emotions and feelings; they do not want to compound a problem by their reaction. Adults who express negative feelings to children must proceed carefully, stating their position clearly, honestly, and objectively in a low, calm voice:

- It bothers me when you call Roberto a dummy.
- You do not need to yell at me. I can hear you from right here. Tell me again in a quieter voice.
- I am serious about this—no biting.
- Sometimes I get angry when children try to hurt each other.
- It makes me sad to see all that food going to waste. Please put just enough on your plate so that you will eat it all.

Remember that children are frightened by strong feelings; do not overwhelm them with your behavior.

Consistency

Being *consistent* is one of the key elements in good guidance practices. If adults want to develop mutual trust, the rules must be clear, fair, and enforced consistently and regularly. It is important that all members of the teaching team reinforce the same rules and not undermine another teacher's problem solving. At the same time, children need to know what happens if rules are not followed. Consequences, too, should be consistent.

Realistic Expectations

Teachers should have *realistic expectations* for children, neither too high nor too low. Sometimes they presume children have abilities and skills they do not yet possess, and this may cause children to respond in inappropriate ways. It can be helpful to rehearse with children how they are expected to act. Practice sessions are especially useful when introducing a new topic or plan.

> One teacher rehearsed the children for their first bus ride to go on a field trip. They practiced singing, looking out the windows, having snacks, and talking with friends. A large outline of a bus was drawn with chalk on the patio floor. The children pretended to board the bus, walk down the narrow aisle, find a seat, and remember to take big steps getting up and down the steps. When the field trip day arrived, children knew several appropriate ways of behaving while on the long bus trip.

> Many times children are asked to do jobs that are too complicated for them. The young child who is just learning to put on a jacket is a good example. Children may not be able to accomplish the entire job at first; it is helpful to them if the task is broken down into smaller steps. Start out small: Let Gordie learn to zip up the jacket. Little by little, teach Gordie how to get his arms in the sleeves. Soon he will be doing the task by himself.

Actively Observe

As *active observers* in their classroom, teachers can learn a great deal about the effects of their guidance efforts. When teachers observe, they can time interventions or move into a situation before it becomes problematic. Observations can also be used to help children see how their actions impact others. Chapter 6 has many good observation forms for teachers to use.

Courtesy of the author.

Effective guidance practice involves children as active participants. How would you help this child solve the problem of being excluded from play?

Preventing Misbehavior

Preventing **misbehavior** is another part of the teacher's role. Effective guidance practices call for teachers to be alert to potential problems and situations before they result in children's inappropriate behavior. Even then, unpredictable situations occur: A child becomes tired in the middle of snack time; one of the teachers is called out of the room; rain forces an activity to move indoors; or a scheduled event gets postponed. At these trying and typical times, a teacher's full range of abilities is called into play. Ways to help children maintain positive behavior patterns in these situations include:

1. *Recognize and label the problem or situation.* Acknowledge the difficulties it presents to the children. Example: "You seem tired, Gus, and I know you had to wait a long time for your snack. When you have finished your juice and cracker, put your head down on the table and rest for a minute."

2. *Ask children for their help.* Get them involved in working out the solutions. Example: "Mr. Gallo had to leave for a while. How can we continue with this math project when I need to help out in the writing area too? Who has an idea? What do you think would work?"

3. *Assign a job or a task to the children who are most likely to react to the crisis.* Example: "Lorraine and Paul, will you carry the special drums inside, please, while I help the others put the wagons away?"

4. *Always be prepared with a story to tell, songs to sing, guessing games to play, or exercises to do.* Help children pass the time in an appropriate way modeled by the teacher. Give a new focus. Example: "The fire truck hasn't arrived at school yet; we'll have to wait another five minutes. While we are waiting to go and see it, show me how firefighters climb ladders and slide down poles."

5. *Say what you would like to have happen.* Admit what you wish you could do to correct the situation. Example: "Oh, little Riko, I wish I could bring your mommy back right now but I can't. She has to go to work, but I will hold you until your crying stops."

These guidance practices apply equally to infants and toddlers, but there are some *special considerations* that teachers should remember. Infants cry—sometimes a great deal. It is their only means of communication. When they cry they should not be ignored or chastised, but comforted. It is helpful to talk to the baby, no matter how young, and begin to identify the steps you will take to ease the distress. "Fernando, you are crying and I don't know what's wrong. Let's take a look at your diaper; maybe a change will make you more comfortable. Perhaps you are teething; I know that can hurt. Maybe you are hungry; is it time for your bottle yet?" Those soothing words as a teacher changes diapers, rubs the baby's back, or cuddles and rocks ease this time of stress.

Toddlers, too, need adults to use words to express problem situations, and the preceding examples readily apply to working with this active and lively age group. One word of caution, however: Removing infants and toddlers from the group or confining them to a playpen or crib is not appropriate. Very young children do not understand that kind of isolation. To be effective, guidance should be helpful, not punitive.

Indirect Guidance

Children's behavior is influenced by the people and places where they live, work, and play. Each setting sends out indirect messages of where to sit, work, eat, rest, and play. Desks lined up in a row or a circle say "Sit here and work." A room with a long, open corridor invites children to run through the space. Rigid time schedules cause anxiety and tension during cleanup times. The presence of too few teachers leaves children unsupervised or ignored. All of these are recipes for inappropriate behavior.

An environment that supports positive behavior does not just happen. It is the teacher's responsibility to anticipate children's response to the environment and create a place that fosters positive behaviors. **Indirect guidance** is the teacher's way of establishing control and setting the stage for what they want to happen in the classroom. Direct guidance strategies are those that involve the teacher interacting with the children. Through indirect methods teachers help ensure that learning is maximized and disruptions are minimal. Chapter 9 has more suggestions on using indirect guidance to set up early childhood environments.

Ten Effective Strategies: The Guidance Ladder

How do you decide which guidance strategy is the most appropriate for the situation? **Direct guidance** methods involve a decision to interact with children by applying one or more of the following strategies. These techniques are along a continuum that starts with the least intrusive, hands-off approach and moves to those that require greater intervention. They are valuable tools to help children become increasingly self-directed and self-reliant and to help teachers choose the most appropriate methods for the situation. Figure 7-6 illustrates how guidance techniques may be used to the best advantage.

Ignoring Behavior

When misbehavior is of a less serious nature—for instance, when a child whines constantly—it may be best to ignore it. This kind of behavior, although mildly annoying, is not harmful. To use the technique successfully, the adult chooses not to respond to the child in any way and may even become occupied elsewhere while the behavior persists. This method is based on the learning theory that negative reinforcement (the adult ignoring the child) eventually causes the child to stop the undesirable behavior. At first, there might be an increase in the misbehavior as the child tests to see whether the adult truly ignores the action. Once the child sees there is nothing to gain, the behavior disappears.

Active Listening and "I" Messages

Parents and teachers can learn the art of **active listening** to respond to a child's feelings as well as words. The adults listen carefully, trying to understand what the child is saying beyond the words being used. Then they reflect back in their own words what it is they think the child has said. The child has an opportunity to correct

The Guidance Ladder

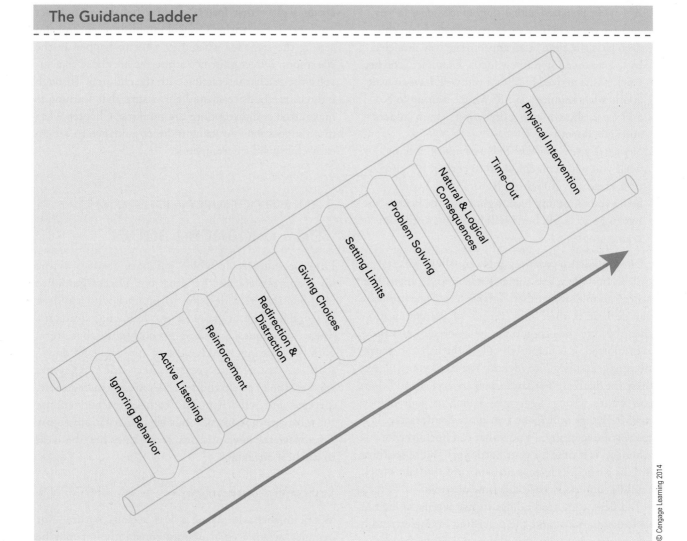

FIGURE 7-6 Climb the ladder to use the guidance strategy that is the least intrusive necessary, moving from the "hands-off" approach to those that require more adult intervention.

any misinterpretations. Further dialogue helps to clarify what the child meant. For example:

Rita:	I hate school!
Teacher:	Sounds as if you are really disappointed you didn't get a turn cooking today.
Rita:	I really wanted to help make pancakes.

"I" messages are an adult's way of reflecting back to children how their actions have affected others.

Parent:	When you scream indoors, it really hurts my ears.
Parent:	I feel sad when you tell me you don't like me.

"I" messages are honest, nonjudgmental statements that place no blame on the child but that state an observation of the behavior and its results.

Reinforcement

In Chapters 1 and 4, you met Pavlov, Watson, Thorndike, Skinner, and Bandura, who formulated behaviorist theory. Behavior modification is based on the premise that behavior is learned through experiences and can be changed by **reinforcement**. Reinforcement is the process in which a behavior is followed by a consequence that is likely to make the behavior repeated. If Jonah gets a smile from the teacher for saying, "Thank you," he is likely to say it again. A pleasant consequence is often called a reward, and unpleasant consequences are often called punishment, but the impact is in the consequences. If Angie is given an unpleasant consequence (such as being sent to her room for hitting her little brother), she may actually enjoy being isolated so that she can read books or

BRAIN
Research Says...

Do Rewards Work?

When you achieve a goal you feel good when someone says, "Well done!" or "Here's a smiley-face sticker." As teachers, we constantly encourage children's behavior through such positive—or negative—reinforcement. But does it work?

The brain makes its own rewards through the "pleasure pathway" and emits good feelings every day (Jensen, 2005). The brain may have different types of reward systems (Fiorillo, Tobler, & Schultz, 2003), one of which predicts pleasurable outcomes, activates the pleasure network (Tremblay & Schultz, 2000) and produces dopamine, the neurotransmitter that pro-

duces pleasure. The brain stores these experiences of prediction and pleasure and learning improves after the first experience. However, student performance drops as they are rewarded time and again because the dopamine is activated as much by the anticipation of pleasure as by the pleasure itself (Berridge & Robinson, 2002). The brain is in a constant state of change and what worked as a reward one or two times, may not work long-term (Koob & LeMoal, 1997). In other words, a piece of candy escalates into a cheeseburger with french fries.

Most brain-related research on rewards has been for simple tasks, and

the findings suggest that rewards can be used successfully for short-terms tasks. The best use of rewards (Jensen, 2005) is for short lengths of time and for a specific reason; the use of tokens or boxes of raisins that are concrete and inexpensive. Consider using more abstract rewards, such as certificates, notes, verbal compliments, and privileges, to reinforce behaviors.

Questions
1. Describe how you feel when someone rewards you.
2. How does this research alter your thinking about giving out rewards and the concept of reinforcement?

---

watch videos in her room. In her case, the punishment is actually a reward.

Positive reinforcement is used to teach new and different behaviors to a child and to help the child maintain the change. Initially, the reinforcement (or reward) must be swift and consistently applied, as often as the behavior occurs. If the desired behavior is for Janie to always hang her coat on the hook, acknowledge the effort each time Janie hangs up her wraps. Once this is a well-established routine, the reinforcement (praise) becomes less intense.

Reinforcers, or rewards, must be individualized to meet the needs of the child and the situation. Social reinforcers, such as smiling, interest and attention, hugging, touching, and talking, are powerful tools with young children. Food, tokens, and money are sometimes used as reinforcers in home and school settings. The goal, however, is that inner satisfaction becomes its own reward regardless of the type of reinforcer one might use initially. If that does not occur, then other positive guidance measures should be explored.

Parents and teachers often take for granted the positive, desirable behavior in children and may forget to acknowledge these behaviors frequently. Behavior modification helps to correct that oversight. Whenever adults focus on a negative aspect of a child's behavior and make an attempt to change it, they also look at the positive qualities the child possesses and reinforce them. This keeps a balanced perspective while working on a problem.

Behavior modification enables adults to invite children to be part of the process, giving them an active part in monitoring their own behavior. Children are capable of keeping a chart of how many times they finished their plate, made the bed, or fed the dog. This chart serves as a natural reinforcer.

Redirection and Distraction

Sometimes the adult wants to change the activity in which the child is engaged to one that is more acceptable. If Pia and Elena are throwing books off the reading loft, the teacher wants to redirect them and may suggest throwing soft foam balls into a makeshift basket. This technique calls for the adult to make an accurate assessment of what the children really want to do. In this case, it appears they enjoy throwing from a height. Now the teacher can consider alternatives that permit the desired activity while changing the expression or form it takes: "It looks as if you two are enjoying dropping things from up there. Let's figure out a way you can do that so that books will not be damaged."

The substitute activity must be a valid one, acceptable to the adults and fulfilling to the children. In most cases, children are not being deliberately malicious or destructive. More than likely, they are expressing curiosity, imagination, and the need to explore. Positive redirection satisfies these needs in a way that enhances children's self-concept and self-control.

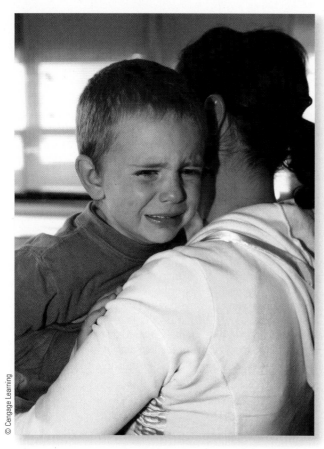

"I know you want to stay and play, but it is time to go home now. Do you want to get your jacket by yourself or do you want your daddy to help?" Choices allow children to gain some control over a stressful situation.

Distraction is similar to redirection and is used when the adult wants to focus the child's attention on an activity that may or may not relate to the previous behavior. Very young children, especially infants and toddlers, can easily be distracted from undesirable actions. Consider the example at the beginning of the chapter in which Kim grabs at one of the necklaces Shawnsey has. A quick-thinking teacher could present Kim with another attractive one. This method calls for well-timed intervention.

Giving Children Choices

Giving choices is a time-honored and popular method for helping children who are being resistant. Choices help children practice self-reliance, self-direction, and self-discipline. "Seth, the cooking area is too crowded. It looks like there is plenty of room at the clay table or the writing table. Which one would you like to go to while you wait for a turn?"

You must give a choice only when you mean for children to make the choice and be prepared to accept the answer. "Some of the children are going in for music now. Would you like to join them?" This is a reasonable choice if there is another adult to supervise the outside.

Suggest two choices when there is the possibility of resistance. This lets a child know you expect him or her to comply with the request but allows some decision making on their part. "It's time to go home now. Would you like to get your artwork before or after you put on your jacket?"

The choice must be valid and acknowledge children's growing ability to deal with responsibility and help them practice making reasonable choices. "It's rest time for everyone now. Do you want to pick out some books before or after you brush your teeth?"

Children should be aware of the consequences of the choices they are making. "If you choose the computer now, you won't have time to finish your rain forest project." Helping children make reasonable choices gives them a foundation for decision making throughout their life.

Setting Limits

Limits are the boundaries we set to help children know what behavior is appropriate. Teachers generally have two reasons for setting limits: 1) to prevent children from injuring themselves or others; and 2) to prevent the destruction of property, materials, or equipment.

Limits are like fences; they are protective structures that help children feel secure. If children know where the fences are, they are free—and safe—to try out many behaviors.

Children may not like fences and may resist attempts to limit their behavior. A natural part of growing up is to stretch those limits and push those fences aside. Limits are self-protective when behavior goes out of bounds. Children are just beginning to exert that inner pressure (self-control) that helps them monitor their own actions. Until then, they need adults to help them learn when and how to apply self-restraint. Limits keep them from going too far.

Children can frighten themselves and others with anger, frustration, and fear. They need adults to stop them from doing physical or emotional harm to themselves or others. Well-considered limits give the child freedom to try out, test, and explore avenues of self-expression in ways that promote growth and protect budding autonomy.

Teachers must learn to set and maintain limits with confidence and authority. To be successful:

- Set a limit appropriate to the situation. Example: "Andrew, get down from the table. You may finish your work either sitting in your chair or standing next to me. You may not stand on the table."
- Match the limit to the child's age, history, and emotional development. Example: "Sheila, you have

interrupted the story too many times today. Find a place at the puzzle table until we are finished. Remember, I told you earlier that you would not be able to hear the end of the story if you yelled again."

- See that all adults apply limits consistently. Example: "I know you want to bat the ball again, but both teachers have said it is Jordan's turn now."
- Reinforce the rules consistently. Example: "Judy, remember everyone walks inside. You can run later when you are outside."
- Follow through and support your words with actions. Example: "I cannot let you tear the books. Since this is the second page this morning, you will need to leave the book nook. I will walk with you while you look for another place to play."
- State limits simply, clearly, and directly. Example: "Roger, use your quiet voice indoors. When you are too loud, other people cannot hear one another."
- Respect and acknowledge the child's feelings. Example: "I know you want your Dad to stay, Megan. He has to go to work now, but I will stay with you while you feel sad."
- Act with authority, purpose, and confidence. Example: "Put the block down, Nick. I cannot let you hurt other people, and I will not let them hurt you."
- Maintain the limit and accept the consequences. Example: "I am sorry, Sarah. You will not be able to play here any longer because you keep calling Geneva 'fatty' and it hurts her feelings."
- Do not give in if the child threatens to fall apart or create a scene. Example: "I am sorry that makes you cry, Sarah, but I cannot let you make fun of one of your classmates. When you finish crying, we can talk about it some more."
- Involve children in creating the limits. Example: "We will be visiting our first grade reading buddies today. What are some of the rules we should follow when we are in their classroom?"

Active Problem Solving

Active problem solving engages children in confronting their differences and working together to solve their problems. The adult guides children toward solutions but does not solve problems for them. Posing open-ended questions, the adult helps keep the child focused so that they can suggest alternate solutions, for example:

"What could you do . . . ?"
"How might she feel when . . . ?"
"What might happen if . . . ?"
"How can you . . . ?"

All of the children's suggestions must be acknowledged seriously, even if they seem unreasonable. Young children may start the discussion by suggesting extreme solutions. In the case of Malcolm, for instance (see the second example at the beginning of this chapter), they might initially suggest: "Do not let Malcolm come to this school anymore." These suggestions are tempered as other children respond; fair and reasonable solutions eventually emerge: "Anyone who knocks over somebody else's blocks has to help them build it back up again."

Rather than assessing blame, teachers help children think through a number of alternatives, including the consequences of their suggestions: "If we close the block area, what will happen when you want to play with your favorite trucks this afternoon?" By assisting them in anticipating the results of what they suggest, teachers can help children understand how their behavior influences and affects others. This is an early lesson in a lifelong quest to become responsible for one's own behavior.

Conflict resolution should become part of the child's daily life. Teachers can help children solve disagreements nonviolently and explore alternative ways to reach their goals. Figure 7-7 outlines a process for active problem solving and conflict resolution (see also Figure 7-6). It is useful for resolving differences through group discussion, as noted earlier, or when one or more children become embroiled in conflict. By following such a process, children learn to respect others' opinions, to express their own feelings in appropriate ways, and to learn tolerance for doing things in a different way.

The process also suggests an important guidance principle: The adult role is to intervene as little as possible, allowing children the opportunity to come up with an acceptable solution.

TeachSource Video

Watch the TeachSource Video Case entitled "Guidance for Young Children: Teaching Techniques for Encouraging Positive Behavior." After you view the clip, view the artifacts, and read the teacher interviews and text, reflect on the following questions:

1. How do the problem solving techniques in the video compare with the Six-Step Approach to Problem Solving in Figure 7-7?

2. What did Linda mean by the term "unconditional attention"? Why might this be an effective technique? Why not?

The Six-Step Approach to Problem Solving

Scenario: Two children run outdoors to get the available wagon. They reach it simultaneously and start pulling on the handle, yelling, "Mine!" One child starts shoving the other child out of the way.

Step One: Approach (Initiate Mediation)

- Approach the conflict, signaling your awareness and availability.
- Get close enough to intervene if necessary; stop aggressive behavior or neutralize the object of conflict by holding it yourself.

Step Two: Make a Statement

- Describe the scene. "It looks like you both want the wagon."
- Reflect what the children have said. "You both say you had it first."
- Offer no judgments, values, or solutions.

Step Three: Ask Questions (Gather Data, Define the Problem)

- Do not try to pinpoint blame.
- Draw out details; define problems: "What is happening here?" "What seems to be the problem?"
- Help children communicate: "How did this happen?" "What do you want to tell her?" "How did that make you feel?"

Step Four: Generate Alternative Solutions

- Help children think of ways to work this out: "Who has an idea of how we could solve this?"
- Let children offer suggestions: "We could take turns." "We could use it together." "We could tell her she can't play here."

- Ask questions: "How do you think that would work?" "What would happen if you told her she can't play?"
- Avoid the common mistake of rushing this stage; give it the time it deserves.

Step Five: Agree on Solution

- When both children accept a solution, rephrase it. "So you both say that you will work on it together."
- If any solution seems unsafe or unacceptable, you must tell the children. ("It is not safe for you both to stand up and ride downhill together. What is another way you can agree?" "We can't close the block corner because other children want to play there."

Step Six: Follow Through

- Monitor the activity to make sure agreement is going according to plan. If the decision involves turn taking, you may need to be the clock-watcher. "Okay, Maggie. Your three minutes are up, and it's Cleo's turn now."
- Make a positive statement to the children who were in conflict and others who may have seen it. "Looks as if you solved your problem. Good for you."
- Use the power of language to reinforce the idea that solutions can be found to problems and that children are capable of solving them.

FIGURE 7-7 Using these guidelines to help children solve problems, teachers listen more than talk, allow children the time to make mistakes and figure out solutions, and point out that diversity of viewpoints is natural, normal, and workable.

When children help create a solution, they come away with a sense of commitment to it. This process also gives children a sense of power and control, a sense of independence, and a feeling of self-worth.

Natural and Logical Consequences

Natural consequences enhance children's ability to take responsibility for themselves. As implied, this approach lets children experience the natural consequences of their actions. Designed by Rudolf Dreikurs, it emphasizes the opportunity children have to learn from the way their environment functions:

"If you do not eat your dinner, you might be hungry later."

"If you do not study your words, you might fail your spelling test."

"If you grab the book away from Ben, Ben may retaliate."

This method allows adults to define the situation for children without making judgments and lets children know what to expect. The consequences are a natural result of the child's own actions.

Logical consequences, on the other hand, are a function of what adults impose. For the adult, this means a commitment to follow through; consequences, once stated, must be enforced. It is important to give children an opportunity to choose their own course of action once they have some understanding of what is likely to happen. Nelson (2006) suggests three criteria for using logical consequences: It must be related to the child's behavior; it must be respectful; and it must be reasonable. For example:

"If you bother Sally again, you will have to leave group time."

"If you take your favorite book to school, it might get lost."

"If you want dessert, you will have to eat your dinner."

Time Out

Removing a child from the play area is particularly appropriate when, owing to anger, hurt, or frustration, the child is out of control. Taking children away from the scene of intensity and emotion to allow them time to cool off and settle down is sometimes the only way to help them. The teacher is firm and consistent as the child is quietly removed from play. It is important that, if used, this technique be used with a positive attitude and approach, not as punishment.

Used appropriately, the time-out period is very much like that used in athletic events: a brief respite and a chance to stop all activity and regroup. There is no time-out chair. The teacher's role is to help the child talk about the incident—the feelings involved and the need for self-control—and to give the child an opportunity to gain self-control before resuming play. Children can monitor themselves and choose when they are ready to return to classroom activity. Noah, who persists in knocking down other children's block structures, might be told, "You may come back to the block area when you think you are ready to play without knocking over other children's work." Noah can then assume some responsibility for how he behaves and when he is ready to return to play.

Too often, time out is punitive. Children are pulled from an activity, pushed into a chair, and told to "Watch how the other children are playing nicely," or "Sit there until you can behave." There is no link made between the behavior and the consequences, so the child does not learn the strategy or skills he needs to change his behavior. One study notes that classrooms that used alternatives to time out were more likely to qualify as caring communities (Howes & Ritchie, 2002).

Time out is an invasive strategy and should be used judiciously. Adults can misuse it and leave the child with a sense of rejection.

Physical Intervention

There are times that a teacher must physically intervene to prevent children from injuring themselves, others, or property. Jude often gets out of control, and his playing becomes too rough. Today, Ramon pushed him away after telling him to stop. Jude retaliated by punching Ramon. The teacher intervened immediately, pulling Jude off Ramon and saying, "Stop! Stop hitting Ramon!" Jude raises his arms toward Ramon again, and the teacher puts her arms around him to hold his arms at his side. "I cannot let you hurt other children. Let's go over here and talk about this." The teacher gives Jude time to calm down before she talks with him.

Almost simultaneously, the teacher has assessed Ramon to see if he is hurt. If so, she calls another teacher over to provide comfort and assistance to him. There may be times when it is appropriate to talk with both boys together or deal with each of them separately. Once the sequence of events has been sorted out, the teacher can begin the conflict resolution process. Ideally, both boys would be able to participate in this discussion as they learn to solve problems without hitting and fighting.

For children who have a history of aggression, a more long-term approach is required that would include regular observations and assessments of the child. Outside professional advice may be necessary if the aggression persists.

The guidance continuum provides a number of choices from which to select the most effective method. Figure 7-8 indicates how some of these guidance strategies can be used.

Behavior That Is Challenging

Every teacher has experienced the child who disrupts the class, throws tantrums, hurts other children, and provides wear and tear on equipment, materials, and the adult's patience. Children with a high degree of energy and stress and a short attention span who are distractible and demanding are some of the children who challenge our skills in guiding their behavior. These children often do not respond to the usual guidance strategies. It takes a skillful teacher to work with children whose behaviors are often challenging, and it takes extra effort, patience, and perseverance.

The reasons for such behavior vary, as indicated earlier in the chapter when five factors that influence behavior were discussed. It is important to take these influences into consideration and understand the impact of children's development, environment, individuality, emotional and social growth, and culture on their ability to behave appropriately. Children who tend to act out frequently need extra support reassurance as they learn to live in a group and become responsible for

A Variety of Strategies

If This Is the Behavior	Try This	For Example
Whining	Ignore	Do and say nothing while whining persists. Pay attention to child when whining stops.
Playing cooperatively	Positive reinforcement	"You two are sure working hard on this garden! What a good team you make."
Refusing to cooperate	Provide a choice	"Reva, do you want to pick up the Legos off the floor or help Charlie empty the water table?"
Restlessness, inattentiveness	Change the activity	"This story seems long today; we'll finish it later. Let's play some music and dance now."
Daydreaming	Indirect suggestion	"As soon as you get your coat, Winona, we'll all be ready to go inside."
Arguing over the use of a toy	Active listening	"You really wanted to be the first one to play with the blue truck today, didn't you, Lief?"
Dawdling, late for snack	Natural consequences	"Sorry, Nate, the snacks have been put away. Maybe tomorrow you'll remember to come inside when the other children leave the yard."
Pushing, crowding, running inside	Change room arrangement	Create larger, more open spaces so children have greater freedom of movement and do not feel crowded together.
Unable to take turns, to wait	Review daily schedule, equipment	Buy duplicates of popular equipment. Allow enough time for free play so children won't feel anxious about getting a turn.
Boisterous play	Positive redirection	"You and Sergio seem to want to wrestle. Let's go set the mats out in the other room. If you wrestle here you disturb the children who are playing quietly."

FIGURE 7-8 The astute teacher selects from the options available and individualizes the responses.

their actions. That support and guidance comes in many forms:

1. *See and hear the uniqueness in each child.* Look at the five factors noted earlier, and assess their influence on the child who is causing disruption or behaving aggressively. What do you know about each of those influences on the child that challenges you? Be sure to note areas of strengths, as well as problems. Jake, for instance, tests every limit, disrupts class meetings and circle time, kicks the furniture, and yells at his classmates. However, Jake is a fast runner, climber, and jumper. He works puzzles that are difficult for most of his classmates and has a keen mind. So far, his teachers have been unable to create a trusting relationship with him.

2. *Build caring relationships with children and their families.* Respect for the individual child and family is where a relationship begins. Jake's teachers start with that premise and build a nurturing and responsive relationship from there. There may be a teacher on the team who is especially sensitive to children with more extreme behavior and offers to work with Jake and his family. She finds attributes in Jake that she likes and uses them to develop his trust and to be a supportive presence to him and his family. Collaboration between home and school fosters Jake's self-confidence and improves his ability to change his behavior.

3. *Make observations.* Collect information about the individual child. When does Jake lose control? What leads up to his outburst? How long does it last?

What cues does he give that he is becoming over-whelmed? Who usually intervenes and for how long? When is Jake's behavior appropriate? How is it acknowledged and by whom? Is Jake's behavior predictable?

4 . *Modify the classroom and schedule.* Make legitimate opportunities for Jake to move about and use large muscles when inside. Are materials and curriculum challenging and age-appropriate? Do children select their own activities and make choices where they work and play for at least part of the day? Is there advanced warning when activities will conclude?

Challenging behaviors often occur during structured activities, such as group times or class meetings. What fits a teacher's agenda does not always fit a child's abilities. Children lose interest and become restless, creating a recipe for frustration and outbursts. Does the schedule call for too many or too lengthy group meetings? How could meetings be modified to be flexible in length and content? What behaviors or activities could be included that help children participate longer? What appropriate alternatives can children suggest if they need to leave the group?

5. *Teacher attention and language.* Take care of any injured party first; then use short, direct sentences, without judgment and without lecturing to the aggressor:
"Jake, that's not acceptable here."
"I cannot hear you when you are screaming."

Look at and speak to the child at eye level. Do not shame, ridicule, or use physical punishment. Give children the support they need to change rather than punish them. Talk with the child about alternatives to their inappropriate behavior:

"Next time, Jake, tell someone you are angry instead of hitting."
"What could you say to Corey instead of hitting him?"

Pay attention to disruptive, nonattentive, aggressive children when they are behaving appropriately:

"You look like you are trying to figure out where that puzzle piece goes. I know you are good at working puzzles, and I am sure you will find it. There! You did it."

Follow through to help the child return to play, giving choices when possible. Find activities that require energy (clay, woodworking) or those that are more calming (water play, reading, painting), depending on what the child seems to need at the time.

Support the child's choice of activity with involvement and relevant comments, interests, and challenges:

"You can decide where you want to play now, Jake. There's room for you at the clay table. I'll help you get started if you like."
Later: "You look like you are having a good time with that clay, Jake. I bet you can squeeze it so hard it oozes out your fingers. Next time when you feel like hitting something, ask me to get the clay out."

With patience, positive interactions, and appropriate guidance practices, teachers find creative and individual ways to help each child grow in social competence and self-assurance.

Summary

LO1 Guidance and discipline have similar meanings and are used interchangeably. Guidance is the ongoing system by which adults help children learn to manage their impulses, express feelings, channel frustration, solve problems, and learn the difference between acceptable and unacceptable behavior. Positive discipline is based on helpful, caring, and supportive relationships between adults and children. Discipline is the action or strategy used to guide the child's behavior. Punishment is a consequence for behavior that an adult thinks is inappropriate and too often includes negative and harmful methods.

LO2 There are five different factors that influence children's behavior: their developmental maturity level, the environment, their individual temperament and style, social and emotional needs, and the family and culture in which they are being raised. Each of these influences shapes how a child behaves and reacts to guidance and discipline.

LO3 Developmental and culturally appropriate guidance is based on three criteria that adults use to make guidance strategy decisions. These three are: 1) age appropriateness (what we know about how children learn and grow); 2) individual appropriateness (what we know about each child's abilities); and 3) culture and family responsiveness (what we know about the child's family and cultural background). Taken together, these criteria form a basis for determining the best guidance process for each child.

LO4 The guidance continuum defines effective guidance strategies that begin with the least intrusive methods by an adult to those that require greater adult intervention and/or involvement. They range from ignoring behavior, using active listening and "I" messages, reinforcement, redirection and distraction, giving children choices,

setting limits, active problem solving, natural and logical consequences, time out, and physical intervention. Some children do not respond to these strategies and present a greater challenge to adults.

LO5 There are times when the usual guidance techniques do not work, especially for children whose behavior is often challenging. Some strategies to consider are making observations to find out when certain behaviors occur, and possibly modifying the classroom and schedule. The most critical factor is to know the individual child and to build a supporting and caring relationship with that child.

Key Terms

guidance	behavior model	reinforcement
inductive guidance	misbehavior	positive reinforcement
discipline	indirect guidance	limits
punishment	direct guidance	
interdependence	active listening	

Review Questions

1. What factors affect children's behavior? How does a child's individual style affect the choice of guidance strategies?
2. How do guidance, discipline, and punishment differ from one another? How are they similar?
3. What are some of the ways teachers can promote a caring classroom community through the use of positive guidance strategies?

4. Which of the strategies on the guidance continuum help children become more responsible for their own actions? Which help teach children to understand and respect differences?
5. What is the most important thing for a teacher to know about children who have challenging behaviors?

Observe and Apply

1. Observe a group of young children during play. See whether you can identify an example of a child who might be described as an easy child, a difficult child, and a slow-to-warm-up child. What guidance techniques do the teachers use with each child? Are they the same? If they are different, describe the differences. How successful are these techniques that are being used? What might you do differently?
2. Observe a teacher who is helping to resolve a conflict between two children. What strategies along the guidance continuum does she use? How do the

children respond? What problem solving techniques were most successful? Why?
3. Finish this sentence: "When I was 4 years old, the worst thing I ever did was . . ." How did the adults around you react? What would you do if you were the adult in charge? Discuss and compare responses with a classmate.
4. Children's literature helps us focus on guidance and behavior problems. Select a book from the following list. Define the problem behavior and the person creating the problem. Do you agree with the author's

way of handling the situation? Suggest alternatives. When and with whom might you use this story? Suggested books:

Stellaluna by Janell Cannon
Jamaica's Find by Juanita Havill
Fancy Nancy by Jane O'Connor
Tree of Cranes by Allen Say

Shy Charles by Rosemary Wells
Bread and Jam for Frances by Russell and Lillian Hoban
Where the Wild Things Are by Maurice Sendak

5 How do you define your approach to guidance and discipline? What factors shaped your attitudes toward children's behavior?

Helpful Websites

Responsive Discipline
www.ksu.edu/wwparent/courses/rd

National Network for Child Care
www.nncc.org/Guidance

Urban Programs Resource Network
www.urbanext.uiuc.edu

Empowering People, Inc
http://www.empoweringpeople.com

Zero to Three   **www.zerotothree.org**

The Education CourseMate website for this text offers many helpful resources and interactive study tools. Go to CengageBrain.com to access the TeachSource Videos, flashcards, tutorial quizzes, direct links to all of the websites mentioned in the chapter, downloadable forms, and more.

References

American Academy of Pediatrics. (1997). *A guide to your child's symptoms.* Elk Grove Village, IL: Author.

Berridge, K. & Robinson, T. (2002). The mind of an addicted brain. Neural sensitization of wanting versus liking. In J. Cacioppo et al. (Eds.), *Foundations in social neuroscience* (pp. 565–572). Cambridge, MA: MIT Press.

Browne, K. W., & Gordon, A. M. (2009). *To teach well: An early childhood practicum guide.* Upper Saddle River, NJ: Pearson.

Fiorillo, C. D., Tobler, P. N., & Schultz, W. (2003, March 21). Discrete coding of reward probability and uncertainty by dopamine neurons. *Science,* 299(5614), pp. 1898–1902.

Gonzalez-Mena, J. (2008). *Multicultural issues in child care.* Menlo Park, CA: Mayfield.

Gordon, A., & Browne, K. W. (1996). *Guiding young children in a diverse society.* Boston: Allyn and Bacon.

Howes, C., & Ritchie, S. (2002). *A matter of trust: Connecting teachers and learners in the early childhood classroom.* New York: Teachers College Press.

Jensen, E. (2005). *Teaching with the brain in mind.* Alexandria, VA: Association for Supervision and Curriculum Development.

Koob, G. & LeMoal, J. (1997). Drug abuse: Hedonic homeostatic dysregulation. *Science,* 278, pp. 52–58.

Nelsen, J. (2006). *Positive discipline.* New York: Ballantine Books.

Thomas, A., & Chess, S. (1977). *Temperament and development.* New York: Brunner and Mazel.

Tremblay, L. & Schultz, W. (2000). Modifications of reward expectation-related neuronal activity during learning in primate orbitofrontal cortex. *Journal of Neurophysiology,* 83, pp. 1877–1885.

8

Families and Teachers: Partners in Education

Learning Objectives

LO1 Identify strategies that promote strong partnerships and effective relationships between families and schools and examine the importance of such collaborations.

LO2 Understand and value the complexity of today's families and demonstrate skills necessary to collaborate with diverse family situations.

LO3 Demonstrate effective strategies that enhance communication between teachers and families through the separation process and family/teacher conferences.

naeyc Standards for Professional Development

The following NAEYC Standards for Initial and Advanced Early Childhood Professional Preparation are addressed in this chapter:

Standard 1 Promoting Child Development and Learning

Standard 2 Building Family and Community Relationships

Standard 4 Using Developmentally Effective Approaches to Connect with Children and Families

Standard 6 Becoming a Professional

Field Experience

naeyc Code of Ethical Conduct

These are the sections of the NAEYC Code of Ethical Conduct that apply to the topics in this chapter:

Core Values: We appreciate and support the bond between the child and the family.

We recognize that children are best understood and supported in the context of their family, culture, community, and society.

Section II:

I-2.2   We shall develop relationships of mutual trust and create partnerships with families we serve.

I-2.4   To listen to families, acknowledge and build upon their strengths and competencies, and learn from families as we support them in their task of nurturing children.

I-2.5   We respect the dignity and preferences of each family and to make an effort to learn about its structure, culture, language, customs, and beliefs to ensure a culturally consistent environment for all children.

I-2.6   We acknowledge families' childrearing values and their right to make decisions for their children.

I-2.7   We will share information about each child's education and development with families and help them understand and appreciate the current knowledge base of the early childhood profession.

P-2.4   We shall ensure that the family is involved in significant decisions affecting their child.

Promoting Strong and Effective Partnerships

Working with families can be one of the teacher's most satisfying responsibilities, or it can be one of the most frustrating. The potential is present for a dynamic partnership between the most important adults in a child's life because they have the common goal of nurturing the young child.

Note: Throughout this chapter, the terms *parents* and *parenthood* are meant to include mothers and fathers, as well as other extended family members and caretakers who have the responsibility for raising a child.

Historical Overview

There is a historical **precedent** for the partnership between families and teachers. Pestalozzi and Froebel, early 18th century educators, detailed many of their procedures for home use (as noted in Chapter 1). The involvement of the mother in the education of the child was considered important even then. When kindergartens were organized in the United States, classes for parents and mothers' clubs were started. The National Congress of Mothers evolved from that movement. Today, it is the National Parents and Teachers Association. This well-known organization is an integral part of most school systems and continues to promote a union between school and home, teachers and parents.

During the 1930s, parent involvement in education was actively discouraged. Teachers were seen as experts who wanted to be left alone to do their job, and in many cases, teachers felt they did little but remedy parental mistakes. That trend ended in the 1940s when the need for parent support and encouragement was recognized and closer relationships between teachers and parents were established. More than 70 years later, this partnership stands as a commonly accepted principle. By the 1960s, Head Start programs required parental involvement and set about developing parent education and parent training programs. A commitment to teaching children included a commitment to the families of those children.

Parent involvement and education were largely ignored in the education reform movement of the 1990s. That omission was addressed as parents became empowered in the creation of **charter** and **magnet schools**, a mid-1990s phenomenon that has created greater parent involvement in public schools.

Collaborating with parents and working within the family context are significant in today's early childhood programs. NAEYC's standards for professional

A true partnership happens when parents and teachers share their strengths with one another for the benefit of the children they care for and love.

preparation underscore parents' right to be involved in their child's learning and the NAEYC Code of Ethical Conduct clearly outlines a range of ethical responsibilities to families. Learning outcomes designated by individual states also mandate partnerships with the family, child, and community. This **family-centered approach** ensures a more equal and consistent partnership between home and school.

Strengthening the Partnership

The early childhood professional and the child's family have knowledge, skills, and a sense of caring to bring to the relationship. Each has a need for the other. Partnerships usually begin with such a need, so families and teachers become coworkers and colleagues in a joint effort to help each child reach full potential.

What Families Contribute to the Partnership

Families have a unique contribution to make in their child's learning. They know the child's physical, medical, social, and intellectual history. They know the child as a member of a family and the role that child plays in the family dynamic, the extended family, and the community.

Families provide the context with which the teacher can view the whole child. They already know what makes their children happy or sad or how they react to changes in routines. Thus, families have a wealth of intimate knowledge about their children that the teacher is only just beginning to discover. Figure 8-1 highlights strategies for effective interactions that strengthen the family–school partnership.

Strategies for Strengthening the Partnership

Treat all families with dignity and respect their differences.

Listen—and learn from families. Ask, don't tell.

Clarify and articulate expectations of one another.

Share the responsibility and power in making decisions about the child's needs and concerns.

Identify and articulate your values and beliefs.

Keep an open mind; move out of your comfort zone in approaches and attitudes.

Keep informed and stay informed with frequent communication with families.

Educate families about their children's needs at each stage of development.

Demonstrate your understanding of the feelings families express. Be empathetic.

Find common ground for agreement when discussing differences.

© Cengage Learning 2014

FIGURE 8-1 All families are interested in the education and well-being of their children. Nurture the relationship through effective interactions that benefit everyone.

How Families Benefit One of the greatest values of a strong family–school partnership is the opportunity for families to meet each other. They find that they share similar problems and frustrations and that they can support one another in finding solutions. Friendships based on mutual interests and concerns about their children can help them forge new relationships.

Through positive home–school relationships, families find ways to become more effective as their children's first and most important teachers. Families benefit from involvement in their children's education in many ways: They:

- Observe teachers model successful techniques when working with children.
- Learn what behaviors are appropriate at certain ages.
- Begin to know how their children make friends and extend their social relationships.
- Become more aware of school and community resources that are available to them and, in the person of the teacher, they now have access to a consultant who knows and understands their child and can help them when they need it.

Family members teach by word, by example, by all they do and say. Through closer home–school relationships, families can be helped to see that their everyday experiences with their children provide teachable moments, those spontaneous opportunities for educating children

A family-centered approach to school relationships supports the growth of the family as well as the child. When families have a meaningful partnership with their children's teachers, it raises their sense of importance and diminishes some of the isolation and anxiety of child rearing. By empowering families to participate in decisions affecting their children's education, teachers can help families see themselves as a vital part of the education process.

Family Cultural Influences Families represent a wide range of cultural backgrounds, so it is important that their contributions be sought out, acknowledged, and used. All of the subtle communication styles that exist within various cultures can be blocks to good family–school relationships, or they can be the basis on which teachers and families connect with each other. This is one of the most pressing issues in teaching effectively today. In Figure 8-2 Bradley and Kibera (2007) explore four different characteristics of family culture to consider when working with families from diverse backgrounds.

Families whose linguistic and cultural backgrounds are different from the teacher need to share their perspectives so that issues relating to basic routines such as eating and sleeping may be understood in their cultural context. The same is true for a family's expectations about their child's experiences in the classroom. Only through forging such a partnership can families of diverse cultural backgrounds become true contributors to their children's education and care. Chapter 10 discusses Culturally Responsive Teaching on pages 312-314.

What Teachers Contribute to the Partnership

Early childhood professionals share similar goals with families but come from a different perspective. Teachers see a child in relation to normal milestones and appropriate

Cultural Dimensions of Families

Cultural Dimension	Questions for Reflection
Values and Beliefs	How is *family* defined? What roles do adults and children play? How does the family make sense of the child's behavioral difficulties? How does culture inform the family's view of appropriate and inappropriate ways of dealing with problem behavior and guidance? What is most important to the family?
Historical and Social Influences	What strengths and stressors does the family identify? What barriers do they experience?
Communication	What is the family's primary language? What support is required to enable communication? How are needs and wants expressed? How are unhappiness, dissatisfaction, or distress experienced or expressed?
Attitudes Toward Seeking Help	How does the family seek help and from whom? How do members view professionals, and how do professionals view them?

FIGURE 8-2 Exploring the cultural dimensions of families is part of an ongoing process to develop greater cultural awareness. (From Closing the Gap: Culture and the Promotion of Inclusion in Child Care, by J. Bradley and P. Kibera, 2007, in D. Koralek, Ed. *Spotlight on young children and families.* Washington, DC; National Association for the Education of Young Children.)

© Cengage Learning

Families appreciate their culture being represented in all areas of school life.

behaviors. They notice how each child plays with other children, what seems to challenge Mickey, and when Ramon is likely to fall apart. Unlike families, teachers see individual children from a perspective that is balanced by the numerous other children they have taught. They observe how the child behaves with a variety of adults, sensing children's ability to trust other adults through interactions with them at school. When families need help, teachers become resources and work with families to find behavioral specialists, psychologists, hearing and speech specialists, or other educational programs, if warranted.

Look at the excerpts from NAEYC's Code of Ethical Conduct at the beginning of this chapter to review ethical responsibilities to families. Note the ideals and principles stated in Section I, P-1.4, Section II, I-2.5 and 2.6. These three passages call for building mutual trust, communicating children's progress in developmentally appropriate terms, and the right of parents to participate in decisions that affect their child. Supporting and encouraging families is part of the teacher's role. Good teachers are sensitive to parent concerns and understand their needs.

Families want to learn the best ways to raise their children and to improve their child-rearing skills. There are numerous opportunities for the early childhood teacher to help families achieve these goals. Figure 8-3 cites a multitude of ways a school, center, or family child care home can become a family-friendly early childhood program.

What Children Gain Children reap the rewards of parent involvement. Decades of research show the positive effects on achievement when children's families are involved in their education. The family is the primary source from which the child develops and grows and is needed to reinforce the learning, attitudes, and motivation if children are to succeed. Family visibility is especially important for low income and minority children; their family's presence can heighten a sense of belonging. Children gain when families are able to monitor

A Checklist for Making Your School "Family Friendly"

_____ Hold an orientation for familes at a convenient time.

_____ Provide a place for families to gather.

_____ Create a parent/family bulletin board.

_____ Give annual family awards for involvement.

_____ Create a family advisory committee.

_____ Allow families to help develop school policies and procedures.

_____ Schedule events on evenings and weekends.

_____ Provide child care for meetings.

_____ Establish a book or toy lending library.

_____ Make informal calls to families, especially to share a child's successes.

_____ Provide transportation for families who need it.

_____ Provide translators for families who need them.

_____ Send appropriate duplicate mailings to noncustodial parents.

_____ Survey families for issues of interest and need.

_____ Develop links to health and social support services.

_____ Provide resource and referral lists.

_____ Publish a school newsletter on a regular basis.

_____ Provide multilingual written communications as needed.

_____ Hire teachers with a strong commitment to supporting families and parents.

_____ Provide in-service training for teachers in working with families and parents.

_____ Hire teachers who are respectful of social, ethnic, and religious backgrounds of families.

_____ Hire staff that is reflective of the cultural background of students and families.

_____ Encourage regularly scheduled conferences between parents/family and teachers.

_____ Offer a variety of family support programs.

_____ Provide many opportunities for family members to volunteer.

_____ Provide frequent opportunities for parents/families to air their concerns.

_____ Encourage parents/families to ask questions, to visit, and to call.

_____ Encourage families to know what goes on in the classroom.

_____ Encourage families to report back on what works well.

_____ Encourage families to attend social events.

_____ Encourage teachers to make home visits.

FIGURE 8-3 A checklist for a family-oriented approach to meeting children's needs.
You can download a copy of this checklist from this text's Education CourseMate website.

their children's progress and reinforce the educational goals at home.

Families come to an early childhood program looking for teachers who know about children and who will help them in raising their children. Children benefit when teachers respond to family concerns with caring and encouragement.

Becoming Full and Equal Partners

Families and schools are natural allies; together they claim the primary responsibility in educating and socializing children. They can and should be equal partners in that effort.

Early childhood educators have long recognized the importance of providing families with child-rearing information and support to strengthen families to meet the challenges of parenting in the years ahead. The early childhood program is often the first time a family has the opportunity to collaborate in their child's education, so it is important that the experience be meaningful and effective.

The increase in the divorce rate, the growing number of single-parent families, families in which both parents work, and increasing numbers of immigrant families all support the need for a more family-centered approach. (See the following section, "Today's Families," and Chapter 15 for examples and discussion.) Long-held school

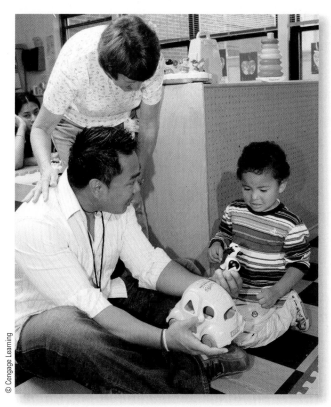

A parent's participation in his or her child's school life can heighten the child's sense of belonging.

perceptions of what constitutes a family may no longer correspond to the reality of today's definition of a family. Family support takes on new meaning when the differences in family styles are acknowledged and supported.

Public Recognition

A growing awareness of the need for a family-centered approach to parent education has been recognized by several government agencies. From its beginning in 1965,

Head Start mandated parent involvement as necessary for the health and welfare of many young children. The Education of the Handicapped Amendments (Public Law 99-457) in 1986 required early intervention services aimed at the family, not just the child. Public Law 99-457 includes parents as members of a team of professionals who develop an individualized plan related to the child and family's needs. Some states have developed comprehensive, family-centered early childhood programs funded through local school districts.

The Complexity of Today's Families

The complexity of today's families reflects the cultural changes in the United States over the past 50 years. The nuclear family, made up of a father, mother, and two children, has become blended, mixed, and extended. Look around your neighborhood to see the variety of family units. Parents today may or may not be married to one another, may have the same sexual orientation, and may include foster parents and adoptive parents. Grandparents, aunts and uncles, and/or siblings may be

Because half of the women with children younger than age 6 work outside the home, fathers often bring children to child care.

TeachSource Video

Watch the TeachSource Video Case entitled, "Communicating with Families: Best Practices in an Early Childhood Setting." After you study the video clip, view the artifacts, and read the teacher interviews and text, reflect on the following questions:

1. A family-centered program acknowledges the critical influence of the family unit on the child's growth and development. What examples does teacher Mona Sanon talk about and model that strengthen the family-centered relationship?

2. What lessons can be learned from the discussion Mona had with a father about his son's block building skills?

Reggio Emilia: An Exemplary Partnership

One of the best examples of a successful school–family partnership are the schools of Reggio Emilia, Italy. Strong and active family involvement is found at every level of school functioning. This is not surprising because the schools were originally founded as parent cooperatives, part of the philosophy that continues to uphold a model of equal and extended partnership. Malaguzzi, the founder and guiding force behind the schools, refers to this balanced responsibility of teachers, parents, and children as a "triad at the center of education" (Edwards, Gandini, & Forman, 1993).

School-based management fosters meaningful participation of all families because all decisions are made by the teachers and parents within each school setting. No area seems the exclusive property of either parents or teachers. Curriculum planning, for instance, depends on the family's involvement, interest, and contribution.

Parents are the core of the individual school boards and on the city-wide school board as an integral part of the decision making process. Frequent meetings inform families of the school's program and bring them up to date on what their children are doing. Smaller groups of parents meet throughout the year with the teachers to talk about their children and the program; individual parent–teacher conferences, which either can request, are held to deal with specific concerns.

There are opportunities to be actively involved in the daily life of the school. Family members, teachers, and town residents build furnishings and maintain materials for the classrooms and the schoolyard and rearrange the space to accommodate program needs. In sessions with teachers and **pedagogistas**, parents learn various educational techniques necessary to the program, such as photography and puppet making, and they use these new skills in the classroom with their children. Using the whole town as a backdrop, families participate in many of the field trips to city landmarks or as small groups visiting a child's home. Recording and transcribing children's activities and projects are often a parent's responsibility (see Chapter 10). Photographs of children and families abound. These elements are the vehicles used to ensure a rich flow of communication.

The schools of Reggio Emilia exemplify the basic tenets of developmentally appropriate practices in the unique relationship with the families they serve. Families have influence and help affect change; in turn, the schools influence and change families. Each becomes a stronger voice for what is in the best interest of the child.

---

the parental figures in a household. Two people can be defined as a family and so can those that include half- and step-siblings, close friends, and gays and lesbians (Browne & Gordon, 2014).

The term "parent" usually means a mother, father, or someone who is a legal guardian. That definition, too, has been stretched to accommodate the complexities of today's lifestyles. Browne & Gordon (2014) define parents as those individuals who are raising biological children, foster children, adopted children, and children of other family members and/or friends.

Understanding Parenthood

The role of a parent is ever-changing. Parents grow and develop along with their children and adapt to the size of their family and the ages and stages of the each child. Every family has its own unique systems and patterns for raising their children. Two of them are worth exploring as you focus on working with parents and families.

Patterns of Child Rearing

Baumrind (1972) defined three types of parental styles: *authoritative, authoritarian,* and *permissive.* These styles differ in the ways parents accept the child and are involved

in the child's life, their control of the child, and how much autonomy they grant (adapted from Berk, 2009).

The most successful approach is the *authoritative* parents who foster the highest levels of self-esteem, self-reliance, independence, and curiosity in children. They are warm, responsive, attentive to children's needs, and set clear limits and high expectations. Authoritative parents are consistent in reinforcing rules and allow their children to make reasonable decisions appropriate to their age and experience.

In contrast, *authoritarian* child-rearing patterns reflect high control and demands combined with relatively low communication and nurturance. They rarely listen to the child's point of view. Authoritarian parents are strict; they expect and demand obedience and may lack warmth and affection. They exert control through belittling, threats, and criticisms and may resort to force. Children become hostile when frustrated, anxious, and withdrawn and may resort to force when they do not get their way.

With *permissive* parents there is a high level of over-indulgence or inattentiveness, warmth, and affection but little control. Clear standards and rules are not set, nor are they reinforced consistently. Permissive parents allow children to make decisions that are not appropriate for their age. Children may be impulsive, disobedient, rebellious, overly demanding, dependent on adults, and have poor task persistence.

The positive effects of the authoritative parent model demonstrates that using reason over power, maintaining appropriate limits yet supporting appropriate autonomy, and encouraging give-and-take create more successful children.

What makes a healthy and successful family? In Figure 8-4 Gonzalez-Mena (2008) lists some characteristics that promote strong families.

Stages of Parent Development

Just as children have various stages of development, parents, too, grow and change throughout the course of raising their children. The parent of one child has different knowledge and feelings than does a parent with three children. Older first-time parents' experiences differ from those of teenage parents. Galinsky (1987) defined six distinct phases that parents go through. During pregnancy, they fantasize about what kind of parent they would like to be and prepare to include a baby into their lives. During the first two years attachment is a key issue as they also reconcile their child-rearing fantasies with their actual experience. From toddler to adolescence, parents establish their authority style and family rules and teach the values, knowledge, and skills they want to pass on. Rules and authority are renegotiated during the teenage years as parents and children create new relationships with one another. Another redefinition of roles occurs when children leave home and parents reflect on their relationships with their children.

As you work with families, it is helpful to look at what stage or stages through which parents might be going. Depending on the size of the family, they may be going through several stages at once. In some cases, boundaries are being readjusted, relationships are in flux, and issues of autonomy are being questioned all within the same time period. Each family has different needs, concerns, and experiences depending on the age of their children and their own stage of parent development. The early childhood professional's role is to support and understand the various forces within the family that affect their journey of parenthood.

Families with Diverse Needs

Parents are parents the world over and have mutual problems and pleasures as they go about bringing up their young. There are some families who face additional challenges in child rearing who may need added teacher support. These are:

- Families of children with developmental delays and disabilities
- Single-parent families
- Adoptive and foster families
- Parents who both work outside the home
- Divorced families
- Gay/lesbian families
- Homeless families
- Teenage parent families
- Grandparents raising grandchildren
- Families who are raising children in a culture different from their own, families who do not speak English, and families whose child is in a setting in which English is not the predominant language

Characteristics of Successful Families

1. There is a healthy attachment and involvement with each other. Family members have a deep sense of commitment to one another and give time and attention to the family.

2. There is mutual nurturing that supports appropriate independence and healthy interdependence on one another. All family members get their needs met.

3. Self-esteem is important for all family members. It is cultivated in all interactions.

4. Effective communication allows family members to express and respond to feelings, resolve conflicts, and problem-solve together. They have the coping skills to deal with daily stress.

5. A secure, safe environment protects all family members, allowing them to connect with the rest of society in healthy ways.

6. The importance of passing on the culture, values, and goals of the family is accomplished through modeling, discussion, teaching, problem solving, and communication.

FIGURE 8-4 Enhancing healthy and successful families creates a supportive atmosphere for children. (Gonzalez-Mena, J. [2008]. *The child in the family and the community.* Upper Saddle River, NJ: Pearson Education.)

- Multiracial families
- First-time older parents

Many of these family characteristics place parents in situations in which they do not have access to an extended family support system. Any one or combination of these situations can create added challenges to the family. For the most part, teachers can help these families by focusing on the many interests and concerns they share with other families. In some cases, additional support for the family is needed, such as:

- Help them locate community resources to address their needs.
- Connect them with other families who have similar circumstances.
- Assist them in exploring school settings for the future.
- See that they are included in all school functions.
- Learn about their special needs.
- Seek their help and advice.
- Help them establish contact with other families who may be willing to assist in translating, transporting, babysitting, and sharing friendship.

Supporting Single Parent Families

- Sixty-five percent of children younger than age 18 live in a household headed by a female.
- Eighty-four percent of single parents are women.
- Sixteen percent of single parents are men. (U.S. Census Bureau, 2012)

Faced with the economic necessity to work, single parents must cope not only with raising children alone, but also with child care arrangements and costs. Particularly hard hit are women who head single-parent households. They are more likely than men to live below the poverty level, to never have married, not to have finished high school, and to be members of a minority population.

Early childhood educators must be sensitive to the unique aspects of raising children alone. This means reexamining school policies and attitudes that ignore the needs of single parents. Overburdened child care professionals, some of whom are single parents themselves, need to be flexible in exploring new avenues of home–school collaboration. We need to ask:

- What kind of involvement in a child's classroom is possible for a working single parent?
- How can I help families feel connected even if they are unable to be at the center?
- What is appropriate support for single parents?

- Am I judgmental about single parents? About single mothers?
- How do I help parents and children deal with the absent parent?
- What are some of the best strategies for helping children cope with the transitions when visiting one parent or the other?

These and other similar questions must become an agenda of staff meetings, in-services for teachers, and parent/family-group meetings.

Valuing Family Culture

One of the most important things teachers can do when working with nontraditional families and families from cultures different from their own is to recognize that they share many of the same values and aspirations as other families and that there are commonalities among them. All parents want their children in environments that value and accept their family.

Depending on the family's situation, communication may be difficult. In many instances, nontraditional families and families from some other cultures may not want to divulge personal information. They may be influenced by previous negative experiences when they have talked about their lifestyle, values, or culture. In these cases, the early childhood educator must work hard to assure these families of confidentiality, stressing the concept that when we know more about a child's family situation, we are in a better position to support and help the child and the family.

Families sense whether an early childhood environment is truly inclusive and supports and celebrates all varieties of families. The inclusive environment is explored further in Chapter 9. In Chapter 10, curriculum is viewed from an inclusive and culturally appropriate point of view. Dealing with attitudes and biases among staff members is discussed in Chapter 5 and Chapter 9. These are all important considerations for working with families with sensitive issues as we help their children achieve their potential. Eisenbud (2002) suggests some ways to create an environment that supports family diversity:

- Ask family members what names the child has for their caregivers, and use these names with the child.
- Create enrollment forms that allow for answers other than "mother" or "father" that indicate the person who is legally responsible for the child and child custody arrangements.
- Find out what the child has been taught about his or her family situation and discuss with the family how you can support their position.

DIVERSITY

Challenges of Immigrant Families

In 2010, 25 percent of U.S. residents younger than 18 were immigrants or children of immigrants. More than 50 percent came from Latin America, 25 percent from Asia, and 13 percent from Europe. The largest individual population of immigrants comes from Mexico, China, India, and the Philippines (DeParle, 2010). The percentage of children who are Hispanic has increased faster than that of any other racial or ethnic group and will reach 25 percent of the school population by 2020 (U.S. Census Bureau, 2008). The future of school population in this century will be defined by the lack of a minority.

These data challenge the early childhood educator to a multicultural sensitivity not yet realized. A willingness to learn various cultural norms and a knowledge of languages are helpful for teachers to communicate with children and parents whose primary language is not English. Teachers should examine their own biases. See the appropriate sections in Chapters 5, 9, and 10 for discussion of teacher bias, anti-bias curricula, and anti-bias environments.

When cultural perspectives of the family and the school differ markedly, teachers can easily misread a child's attitude and abilities because of different styles of languages and behaviors. Teachers may also use classroom practices that are at odds with a child's cultural norms. For example, in some preschool settings, children are encouraged to call their teachers by the teacher's first name. This informal style of addressing authority figures may make some parents uncomfortable. Learning the meaning of behavior from another perspective expands one's view of the world. How adults and children interact with children, the language they use, and the strategies they use to guide children's behavior are areas in which immigrant parents can help teachers learn some of the important cultural differences. We must challenge the profession to aggressively recruit and train early childhood professionals from cultures that represent the family populations whose children attend their schools.

- If one or the other parent is absent, find out if and how that parent(s) is involved with the child's life.
- Be aware of any drug use/addiction related to the child's health and welfare.
- Treat all adults who care for the child, such as grandparents, guardians, caregivers, or adoptive parents, as the child's parents.
- Review the curriculum, books, and physical environment on a regular basis to ensure that all types of families are represented in the classroom.
- Adapt your conversations with children to reflect the diversity of families; for instance, "two mommies, step-brother, foster dad," and so forth.

Look around at the classroom where you are teaching and add other suggestions to strengthen all family units, no matter their makeup.

Enhancing Communication to Support Learning

Families can be an invaluable source of information, support, and affirmation to the teacher and to the school. There are many ways to foster effective communication between home and school that contribute to a caring learning community.

Education and Involvement

Almost any contact between the teacher and the family can be perceived as parent/family education. Teachers interpret children's behavior to their family, suggest alternative ways for dealing with problems, show them toys and games that are appropriate, hold workshops on parenting skills, mention books and articles of interest, and reinforce family interest and attention to their children's education. All of these activities are considered parent/family education. Some are planned; some are spontaneous.

Parent/family education happens frequently, whether in a meeting that focuses on positive discipline or in an informal chat about car seat safety. Many early childhood settings offer family support programs based on the needs of families and their children. Again, the Code of Ethical Conduct in Appendix A can be useful, especially the sections that outline the teacher's professional role to families.

Family involvement may range from high to low participation depending on the family's availability. At the lower end of the scale, some family members may stay and observe before or after school; visit the class and help with an activity; attend school events; collect and make materials for classroom use; help with school events; work in the office or library; write the class newsletter; participate weekly in the classroom; and, for the greatest involvement, take a leadership position.

BRAIN
Research Says...

What Shall We Tell the Parents

What is it that families really need to know about their children's brain development? Thanks to the media and popular press, brain research stories abound, and parents' interest is captured by headlines that call out "Make your baby smarter through Mozart!" and "These toys will increase your child's brain power!" We can help families understand what they most need to know by telling them a few simple facts.

First, families need to know the *significant role of the parent/family/ caregiver* in providing the kind of stimulation and care babies and young children need for their brains to grow and be healthy. Parents are the child's first caregivers and teachers and through their sensitive nurturing, they build secure attachments with their child. Babies are wired to feel, think, respond, and move, and the gestures, reactions, and touching by their families is critical to their brain development and learning. Parents need to respond quickly to their children's cues when they cry for attention or support because this builds children's trust in their caregivers, in themselves, and in the world about them. Touching is important. Children feel more secure and reassured when they are held, cuddled, and snuggled.

Too much stress elevates cortisol levels in the brain to a degree that can destroy or reduce brain cells. Encourage families to reduce and/or remove as much stress from their children's lives as possible. This often means that families need to address their own stressful situations as well.

Second, families need to know the *significance role of the environment*. Nature and nurture do not operate separately but in partnership in the brain's architecture. Genes and the environment work together to influence learning. The brain is in constant motion, growing new connections based on the activities and experiences of the child.

Families can be encouraged to provide an enriched learning environment that offers hands-on activities that include the five senses. Daily activities offer challenges for growth. When a parent asks, "How can we make more room for your new puzzles?" this helps children learn to think, solve problems, and listen to other people's suggestions. Children love repetition (How many times do you read "Goodnight Moon" or sing "Eensy Weensy Spider"?). The brain loves repetition too, because it creates more neural pathways for learning. Language, and lots of it, also help the brain grow new connections, so parents should talk, sing, make up silly songs, recite poetry, talk, chat, and play language games with their young children. Music—all kinds of music—stimulates all aspects of the brain. Art activities prompt the part of the brain that deals with cognition, memory, and emotion. All physical activity stimulates brain growth and helps to fight obesity.

Families are fundamental teachers in every day situations. They need to know that much of what they are already doing is helping their children's brain activity in just the right way. They should feel confident that they are able to provide the stimulation for brain growth. Expensive toys and CDs are not the answer. Parents are.

Questions

1. What do you think of the claims being made about enhancing a child's brain power? Which ones make sense to you after reading through the articles in this text?
2. How would you encourage families to support their child's expanding brain?

Strategies for Keeping in Touch

Personal communications through phone calls, e-mails, notes, home visits, conferences, and day-to-day interactions help to maintain the close contact that strengthens the relationship between home and school. Five of the most common ways teachers can involve and inform families are:

1. *Classroom newsletters* provide information on what the children are doing in class, any special events taking place, personal information about new babies, vacations, or other important events in the lives of the children. Be sure the newsletter is written in the language of the families in the class. See Figure 8-5 for some examples of information that can be provided in newsletter.

2. *Bulletin boards* are posted where families can see them and contain notices about parent/family meetings, guest speakers, community resources, child care, babysitting, clothing and furniture exchanges, and library story hours. Information regarding health programs, automobile and toy safety, and immunization clinics is also publicized. There is often information on cultural events appropriate to the ethnic makeup of the school community.

3. *Classroom website/blogs* are common avenues on which to post pictures and updates, field trip notices, and other information that might be part of a newsletter. A classroom website keeps families aware of daily activities and curriculum. Facebook provides yet another way to communicate in this world of technology and social media.

Families need to know that providing new experiences for their children is the best way to help brain growth.

A well-placed bulletin board with helpful information provides a resource for children and their families.

4 *A parent/family place* may be provided in an area or room at the school set aside for family use and can be an important way to let families know they are wanted and needed. Some schools provide space for a parent/family lounge, complete with a library of resource books on child rearing. If there is no available space, set up a coffee bar in the office or hall. The smallest amount of space—even a countertop with magazines—is a start.

5. *Informal contacts* are the easiest and most useful lines of communication with families. All it takes is a phone call, a note, an e-mail, or a brief talk on a daily basis. For families who have difficulty attending meetings or who do not accompany their child to and from school, teachers can send home a note along with a sample of artwork, or a story the child has dictated, or a photograph of the child with friends.

5. *Home visits* can be useful depending on their purpose. The visit might be set up to focus only on the relationship between the teacher and the child. Or the visit might have a purely social function—a way for teachers to meet the whole family and for them to get acquainted with the teachers. In any event, the teacher can use this as a bridge to build a pleasant, casual beginning with a family.

The Separation Process: Learning to Trust One Another

Each year, as school begins, a child enters a classroom and says good-bye to a loved one. This is a new experience for that child, no matter how long he or she might have been enrolled in school. Even children returning to the same classroom find some changes. There may be new teachers and new children, along with some familiar faces or the room, the teachers, and the children may all be strangers. Some children have had previous group experience to draw on; others have never before have been part of a group. It is usually the younger children who may be starting a program for the first time for whom separation is the hardest.

Each child reacts differently, and it is difficult to predict how a child will respond: Marco clings to his dad's leg; Sherline bounces in and runs off to play, leaving her grandmother standing alone. Taryn is crying and clutching a stuffed dog as her mother carries her into the toddler room. The toddler teacher greets them and spends a few minutes talking to Taryn before her mother leaves. Every child has a natural way of dealing with the anxieties of separating from someone they trust. Their behavior is as varied as they are.

The transition from home to school or child care settings is an important time for children and their families. Leaving familiar adults and learning to trust other adults is a major milestone in a child's life. The **separation process** is often as hard on the parents or family members as it can be on the child. Emotions run high as the time comes to say good-bye. Feelings of guilt, sadness, anger, and unhappiness may emerge as the parent/family member and child deal with the pain of separation.

In Chapter 4, Figure 4-5 is a helpful reminder of how patterns of attachment affect the separation process. For most children, the separation is a struggle between their nature desire to explore the world and their equally natural resistance to leaving what is "safe." It is during these years that children are learning to move about under

The Importance of a Classroom Newsletter

Why	Newsletter Example
To Keep Families Informed	Next Thursday is our first nature walk around the school and the neighborhood. Make sure your child wears boots or waterproof shoes to keep feet dry while we explore. Join us on our walk, if you can.
For Insights into Learning	The nature walk is part of our science curriculum. We want the children to explore the out-of-doors to stimulate their natural curiosity and delight in their discoveries. Firsthand experiences with the texture of tree bark or birds' nests help a child create a base of knowledge on which to build their understanding of the natural world around them.
To Bring Learning Home	You might want to try this at home with the whole family. Walk around your neighborhood and look at what is growing. Take a bag or basket to collect leaves and other natural materials. The children can make a collage out of them when you return home. Comment as the children make discoveries: "I wonder what makes the leaves so green." "What do you think happens to that flower when it snows?" Open-ended questions such as these help children clarify their own thinking and learning.
To Keep Communication Flowing	Several questions about our guidance philosophy came up at the last family meeting. We are putting together an insert for next month's newsletter and we would like your help on one of the topics. How do you deal with bedtime issues (delaying tactics, such as one more story, another glass of water, etc.) in your home? What works for you? Talk with Mrs. Olga or Miss Leona if you want to participate.

© Cengage Learning 2011

FIGURE 8-5 Classroom newsletters enlarge a family's understanding of what their child is experiencing and extends the learning between home and school.

their own power and trust themselves. Coming to school or child care provides each child with the opportunity to grow, starting with the separation from their family. Through careful planning, close communication, and sensitivity to one another, families, teachers, and children master this task.

Written school policies and procedures for separation are helpful so that families know what to expect and can go over the information with a teacher one-to-one or at a general parent meeting before the child enters the program. Separation time is when families and teachers must be especially clear with one another.

Parent/Family–Teacher Conferences

Parent/family–teacher conferences are the backbone of any good family–school relationship. A conference is a mutually supportive link between the adults who are most concerned about a child and should be a regular part of the communication process in all early childhood programs.

Conferences are held for many reasons. The initial conference, when the child first enrolls in school, may focus on the child's development, daily habits, and interests, as well as the family's hopes and expectations. Further into the school year, the teacher shares observations and assessments of the child and works with the family to develop mutual goals that are reinforced at home and at school. Individual conferences may be called at any time by the family or the teacher to express concerns, resolve conflicts, and problem solve together.

Every occasion when families and teachers get together to talk about a child is a step toward building trusting relationships between home and school. A successful conference is the result of good planning and clear communications, such as:

- Be prepared, organized, and have a clear purpose. Use a written format to maintain focus. Ask for other staff input and up-to-date examples. Invite the family to help set the agenda.
- Put the family at ease with a warm welcome and thanks for their time. Help them relax by stating

The separation process is successful if the parents and children know that teachers are there when children need comfort and support.

some of their child's strengths, citing examples. Compliment them on something you have noticed, either with their child or when in the classroom with other children. Be sensitive to any cultural differences that may arise.

- Ask—don't tell. Begin with open-ended questions ("How is that new bedtime schedule working out?" or "Can you tell me more?"). Learn how to listen carefully to what is being said.
- Keep the focus on the child. Keep the conversation based on mutual concerns and how to help each other. Make a plan of action together and discuss ways to follow through and stay in touch.

- Write a brief report after the conference. Make a special note of the important issues that were discussed, solutions that were agreed on, and dates for checking progress. Many of the child assessment forms used in early education programs require teachers to keep these records along with information about child progress.
- Student and beginning teachers should find a good role model in a more experienced teacher who acts as a mentor. Ask that person to sit in on a conference with you and afterward have them reflect on it with you. Learn from your experiences.

Maintaining Privacy and Confidentiality

The more involved families are in the workings of the school, the more important it is to establish guidelines for protecting the privacy of all the families enrolled. Family members who volunteer in the office, the classroom, or on a field trip must understand they cannot carry tales out of school about any of the children, the teachers, the administration, or other parents. The school must be clear about its expectations for ensuring such privacy and communicate policies to families. Family members who work on advisory boards, planning committees, or other activities that allow them access to the school office should be sensitive to the confidentiality issue and respect the privacy of every family enrolled in the school.

TeachSource Video

Watch the TeachSource Video Case entitled "Communicating with Parents: Tips and Strategies for Future Teachers." After you view the clip, view the artifacts, and read the interviews and texts, reflect on the following questions:

1. How do you feel about Margie's philosophy of always being available to parents?
2. What examples did the video show that served to build bridges between the home and school?
3. What are the positive effects of sharing details and insights about children with their families?

Saying Good-Bye

The key to a successful separation process is a trusting and respectful relationship between the teacher and the family. This relationship is intentionally heightened during the time that the child and family are trying to separate from one another. The adjustment is a gradual process and families need encouragement and guidance as their child moves toward independence.

Hint: Listen carefully to the family's concerns and assess the kind of support that they need to help them through this transition. Adrienne's mother worries, "I'm afraid Adrienne won't stop crying when I leave. I don't want her to cry for hours." The teacher responds, "She may cry for a little while, but I will stay with her until she stops. Adrienne and I will find a great place to play in a few minutes. I will phone or e-mail you in a while to tell you how things are going. Don't worry. We will stay in touch."

It can be helpful if the teacher and the child can spend some time getting to know each other before the child enters the program. Sometimes teachers can make home visits.

Hint: The parent introduces the teacher: "Mrs. Hernandez has come to our home to meet you today, Carlos. When you feel comfortable, why don't you get your favorite book and show it to her." The teacher responds: "I would love to look at your book with you or anything else you might want to show me. You and I can have this time all to ourselves."

Other ways to accomplish the initial meeting is a special orientation before school starts where children can come to the school and meet their new teachers. In some settings, the children are scheduled for half-day sessions in small groups that allow teachers to have more individual time with a child and observe his or her interactions with others. The other half of the class comes in the second part-time session. This schedule may continue throughout the first week during which many separations are made.

The best way to accomplish the actual separation is for the teacher and family member to meet ahead of time and talk about what will happen during the first few weeks. This is especially important for infants and toddlers.

Hint: The teacher to child's mother: "I know you need to be at work by 8:30 AM, so I would suggest you bring Trey into the center by 8:00. That way we'll have some time together with him before you have to leave. If he has a favorite blanket or security toy, please bring that too." Trey's mother responds: "But what do I do? Just walk out when it is time?" The teacher reassures Trey's mother that a well-thought out, step-by-step process takes place and that they create the timetable together.

Trey's mother carries him into the infant room at 8:00 on his first day at the center. The teacher immediately makes contact with Trey while he is still in his mother's arms. They walk about the classroom, showing Trey's mother where to put Trey's belongings.

Hint: Trey begins to warm up to the teacher. She sits down on the floor with Trey and his mother and talks with Trey about his "blankie." "Oh, that is a nice warm blankie you have and we'll keep it right next to you. Here's a ball. Can you push it on the floor?" Trey grabs the ball and begins a short interaction with the teacher. After a few minutes, the teachers tells Trey's mother: "I think you could say goodbye in a couple of minutes if Trey keeps playing with me this way. I'll pick him up and you can tell him you'll be back soon. I'll reassure him that I will stay with him until you return. Keep your goodbye short and sweet and then leave immediately. Are you okay with this? Do you think it would be a good time to try it?" Trey's mother nodded her approval.

When the teacher gave Trey's mother a signal, she rose from the floor and let the teacher pick Trey up. "Goodbye, Trey. I love you and I'll see you in a little while." She hugged him, turned, and left the room.

Hint: As Trey began to cry the teacher soothed and held him and told him she would stay with him until his mother returned. His crying persisted until he caught the eye of another baby on the floor. "That is Jackelin, Trey. Let's sit down by her and see if she wants to roll the ball to us." Trey was quiet for a time, cried a little more, and then began to watch the other children. Later, the teacher called Trey's mother to let her know he had eaten his lunch and was napping. They agreed that if she could pick him up a little early that day, it would help him realize she was indeed coming back for him. They also agreed to repeat this process for another few days and then see if they had to make any adjustments.

The teacher's intention is to help the parents assess the situation and come to an agreement on when to actually separate. When a teacher acts with warm conviction, families appreciate the firmness and confidence at a time when their feelings may be ambiguous. At times, separation may take longer and a family member may have to stay for a little while for several days or a week, taking longer and longer breaks away from the child. Children begin to realize their family member does return each day, and they become more and more trusting.

Although this process is a good model to follow, there are times and situations when family members do not have the time to help the child make the adjustment readily. Separations are particularly hard on working parents who have a short period of time to leave the child and get to work on time. During those times, the teaching staff take on extra responsibility while one teacher who has made a connection with the child works through the separation process with the family.

Think About This

1. What are your feelings about parents leaving crying children?
2. How would you describe your approach to helping a child and parent separate?
3. Why do you think a separation process is valuable for families?

Summary

LO 1 A strong and effective partnership between families and teachers begins when each appreciates the unique contribution and role they play in the life of the child. Families provide history and intimate knowledge while teachers bring a perspective based on knowledge and experience with many children.

LO 2 The complexity of today's family present numerous challenges to the teacher/family relationship. Today's definition of parents includes all of the people who care for and nurture young children in their homes. The diversity in families calls on early childhood professionals to adapt their attitudes and programs to meet the needs of single, divorced, adoptive, foster, teenage, and gay and lesbian parents, as well as families of children with disabilities, those whose parents both work outside the home, those who are homeless, and

grandparents raising their grandchildren. Understanding and valuing each family unit and its culture is critical to a positive relationship as is knowing the various stages of parenthood and children rearing practices.

LO 3 Communications between school and family are enhanced when family members become actively involved in their child's education and learning. Keeping in touch through e-mail, telephone calls, newsletters, bulletin boards, home visits, and participating in the class provide opportunities for frequent and open communication. The separation process is one of the most sensitive times for teachers and family members to work together for a smooth transition to the program. Family/teacher conferences offer the occasion to set mutual goals for the child, resolve questions and conflicts, and participate in solving problems together.

Key Terms

precedent
charter school

magnet school
family-centered approach

pedagogista
separation process

Review Questions

1. What are the unique contributions families make to the family/school partnership, and how do they enhance a child's ability to learn? How do teachers promote strong partnerships?
2. What is the definition of today's family, and how does a school/home partnership support the unique needs of families?

3. How does frequent communication between home and school support children's learning? What are some of the most effective strategies for maintaining open communication?

Observe and Apply

1. Discuss the following in small groups, and then share your responses with the rest of your classmates. Finish the sentences:
   "For me, the most difficult part of being a parent today is or would be . . ."
   "When I have children, I plan to (work/stay at home/do both) because . . ."
   "If I were a single parent, I would want my child's teacher to . . ."
2. Are there immigrant families in your school setting? How are these families supported or not supported by school practices and policies? What changes would you make?

3. Reflect on Baumrind's styles of parenting. Which do you think your parents used? Would you use the same style with your children? Why? How do you see these different styles affect the children you teach? How and why does it affect your relationship with the parents?
4. The last step in conducting a successful parent/family conference suggests that you find a good role model. Look around at the teachers you know and select one. Discuss with him or her your own concerns and/or experiences with parent/family conferences.

Helpful Websites

Especially for Parents   **www.ed.gov/parents**

National Coalition for Parent Involvement in
   Education   **www.ncpie.org**

Culturally and Linguistically Appropriate Services
   www.clas.uiuc.edu

Zero to Three   **www.zerotothree.org**

Canadian Childcare Federation   **www.cfc.efc.ca**

Family Communications, Inc.   **www.misterrogers.org**

KidSource Online   **www.kidsource.com**

The Education CourseMate website for this text offers many helpful resources and interactive study tools. Go to CengageBrain.com to access the TeachSource Videos, flashcards,
tutorial quizzes, direct links to all of the websites mentioned in the chapter, downloadable
forms, and more.

References

Baumrind, D. (1972). Socialization and instrumental
competence in young children. In W. W. Hartrup
(Ed.), *The young child: Review of research (Vol. 2)*.
Washington, D.C.: National Association for the
Education of Young Children.

Berk, L. (2009). *Child development*. Boston: Allyn and
Bacon.

Bradley, J., & Kibera, P. (2007). Closing the gap: Culture and the promotion of inclusion in child care.
In D. Koralek (Ed.) *Spotlight on young children and
families*. Washington, D.C.: National Association
for the Education of Young Children.

Browne, K. W., & Gordon, A. M. (2014). *To teach well:
An early childhood practicum guide*. Upper Saddle
River, NJ: Pearson Education.

DeParle, J. (2010, June 26). A world evermore on the
move. *The New York Times*.

Edwards, C., Gandini, L., & Forman, G. (1993). *The hundred languages of children: The Reggio Emilia approach
to early childhood education*. Norwood, NJ: Ablex.

Eisenbud, L. (2002, March). Working with nontraditional families. *Child Care Information
Exchange*, pp. 16–20.

Galinsky, E. (1987). *Between generations*. Reading, MA:
Addison-Wesley.

Gonzalez-Mena, J. (2008). *The child in the family and
the community*. Upper Saddle River, NJ: Pearson
Education.

U.S. Bureau of the Census. (2012). *American Fact-
Finder*. http://www.factfinder2.census.gov.
Retrieved on February 14, 2012.

U.S. Bureau of the Census (2008). *Population estimates
and projections (2008)*.Washington, D.C.: U.S.
Government Printing Office.

Creating
Environments

© Cengage Learning

 **Standards For Professional Development**

The following NAEYC Standards for early childhood professional development are addressed in this chapter:

Standard 1 Promoting Child Development and Learning

Standard 4 Using Developmentally Effective Approaches to Connect with Children and Families

Standard 5 Using Content Knowledge to Build Meaningful Curriculum

 **Code of Ethical Conduct**

These are the sections of the NAEYC Code of Ethical Conduct that apply to the topics in this chapter:

Section I:

P-1.2. We shall care for and educate children in positive emotional and social environments that are cognitively stimulating and that support each child's culture, language, ethnicity, and family structure.

Section II:

I-2.5 To respect the dignity and preferences of each family and to make an effort to learn about its structure, culture, language, customs, and beliefs to ensure a culturally consistent environment for all children and families.

Section III:

Based upon our core values, our primary responsibility to colleagues is to establish and maintain settings and relationships that support productive work and meet professional needs.

Learning Objectives

LO1 Outline the major criteria that are used in creating a developmentally appropriate learning environment.

LO2 Examine the central elements of children's health, safety, and well-being when planning environments.

LO3 Analyze basic arrangements and materials for the physical, temporal, and interpersonal aspects of the environment.

Criteria for Creating Environments

What does it mean to create an environment appropriate for young children? The environment is the stage on which children play out the themes of childhood: their interests, triumphs, problems, and concerns. An environment for children includes all of the conditions that affect their surroundings and the people in it.

Each environment is unique. Rather than a single model, there are many good settings for all children. Each program has goals that reflect the values and priorities of its teachers, families, and communities. When growth goals and the setting mesh, the atmosphere encourages enthusiasm and engagement.

The environment includes not only physical space and materials but also aspects of time and interpersonal relationships such as who plays together and how much time they need to engage deeply in the play.

Definition and Characteristics

The environment speaks volumes to children, and their development is strongly influenced by settings and materials. Our ideas about the environment have been influenced by educators such as Montessori, Vygotsky, and Malaguzzi (see Chapters 1 and 4). As Wurm (2009) notes:

> Each of these educators has left their own influence: from child-sized furnishings, to the creation of social spaces for language development, and the importance of a stage for storytelling. These details, when woven together, have shown us both in theory and practice that schools for young children are spaces that attend to social interaction, problem solving, dramatic play, storytelling, fantasy, conflict and its resolution, and communication as a few of the vehicles for children to build their repertoire and further their understanding of the world.

Definition

The **environment** is the sum total of the physical and human qualities that combine to create a space in which children and adults work and play together. Environment is the content teachers arrange; it is an atmosphere they create; it is a feeling they communicate. Environment is the total picture—from the traffic flow to the daily schedule, from the numbers of chairs at a table to the placement of the guinea pig cage. It is a means to an end. The choices teachers make concerning the **physical** environment (the equipment and materials, the room arrangement, the playground and the facilities available), the **temporal** environment (timing for transitions, routines, activities), and the **interpersonal** environment (number and nature of teachers, ages and numbers of children, types and style of interactions among them) combine to support the program goals.

Teachers arrange the environment to promote what they feel is best in children. Whether the environment is an adapted church basement, an elementary school classroom, or a space made especially for young children, it is a powerful force in their lives. After the family and teacher, it is the child's third teacher. It is the canvas on which children create their work.

Characteristics

All settings for the care and education of young children have similar basic environmental components and goals—meeting the needs of children—despite the fact that programs vary widely in the size of the group, age of children, length of day, program focus, and number of staff. Although physical environments vary on the surface, all high quality, **prepared environments**:

- Convey a welcoming feeling
- Give clear cues about what can be done in each area
- Provide varied spaces that let children concentrate, as well as letting them experience lively group interactions and vigorous physical activity (Hyson, 2008)

Such variation on this common educational theme is one of the reasons why our field is so diverse and interesting. Caution must be exercised, however, to ensure a quality experience for all children. For instance, *size does matter*. Research conducted more than 40 years ago (Prescott, Jones, & Kritschevsky, 1972) found that when a center gets too large, rules and routine guidance are emphasized, outdoor areas often have little variety, and children are often less enthusiastically involved and more often wandering. *Group size* is now recognized as one of the most important indicators of quality child care (Howes, Phillips, & Whitebook, 1992; Copple & Bredekamp, 2009). Too many of us know the problems associated with crowding and cramped conditions, little rooms that become institutions that dehumanize.

The National Association for the Education of Young Children (NAEYC) continues its work with program accreditation of programs and developmentally appropriate practices (DAP). In addition, standards have been set both for group size and for optimal **adult–child ratios** (see Figure 9-1).

Physical Plant

Before creating an environment for children, the early childhood teacher must analyze the physical plant. The building that is inviting and beautiful beckons children to enter; a space with color and light encourages children to play with both. The size and shape of the designated space determine how to plan for safe and appropriate use.

To rescale the space, teachers shift from an adult perspective to a child's scale. Getting on one's knees provides a glimpse of the environment from the child's point

Teacher[a]–Child Ratios within Group Size

Age Group	Group Size									
	6	8	10	12	14	16	18	20	22	24
Infants										
Birth to 15 months[b]	1:3	1:4								
Toddlers/Twos (12–36 months)[b]										
12 to 28 months	1:3	1:4	1:4[c]	1:4						
21 to 36 months		1:4	1:5	1:6						
Preschool[b]										
2.5–3s (30–48 months)				1:6	1:7	1:8	1:9			
4-year-olds						1:8	1:9	1:10		
5-year-olds						1:8	1:9	1:10		
Kindergarten								1:10	1:11	1:12

NOTE: In a mixed-age preschool class of 2.5-year-olds to 5-year-olds, no more than two children between the ages of 30 months and 36 months may be enrolled. The ratios within group size for the predominant age group apply. If infants and toddlers are in a mixed-age group, the ratio for the youngest child applies.

Ratios are to be lowered when one or more children in the group need additional adult assistance to fully participate in the program (a) because of ability, language fluency, developmental age or stage, or other factors or (b) to meet other requirements of NAEYC Accreditation.

A group or classroom refers to the number of children who are assigned for most of the day to a teacher or a team of teaching staff and who occupy an individual classroom or well-defined space that prevents intermingling of children from different groups within a larger room or area.

Group sizes as stated are ceilings, regardless of the number of staff.

Ratios and group sizes are always assessed during on-site visits for NAEYC Accreditation. They are not a required criterion. However, experience suggests that programs that exceed the recommended number of children for each teaching staff member and total group sizes will find it much more difficult to meet each standard and achieve NAEYC Accreditation. The more these numbers are exceeded, the more difficult it will be to meet each standard.

[a]Includes teachers, assistant teachers, and teacher aides

[b]These age ranges purposely overlap. Programs may identify the age group being used for on-site assessment purposes for groups of children whose ages are included in multiple age groups.

[c]Group sizes for this age group would require an additional adult.

FIGURE 9-1 Group size and staff–child ratio are two aspects of the environment that affect the quality of children's experience. (*NAEYC Early Childhood Program Standards and Accreditation Criteria: The Mark of Quality in Early Childhood Education*, Table 2, p. 83. Reprinted with permission from the National Association for the Education of Young Children.)

of view; child space is measured from the floor and playground up. A child's stature determines what is available to and noticed by that child. For crawling infants, space consists primarily of the floor, whereas school-aged children can use and learn from the space up to about five feet, roughly their own height. It is this perspective that teachers must remember as they plan the physical space for children.

Resources

In planning the environment, the teacher must know what kinds of resources are available. Rarely do teachers have unlimited dollars: "This year we can only afford . . ." determines many of the decisions made about the environment. Priority must be given to teachers' salaries and benefits, equipment and materials for the school, and other related services (maintenance, office help, bus service). Despite budget constraints, teachers must beware of operating on too low of a materials budget. Lack of necessary materials can create increasingly passive, angry, and unhappy children out of sheer boredom. Only by knowing the extent of the fiscal boundaries and budget limits can a teacher plan a complete environment.

There are ways to stretch the budget. Good environmental principles do not depend on numerous or expensive equipment, materials, or buildings. A creative child-centered environment can happen in any setting, regardless of financial resources.

- Some equipment can be made, borrowed, or purchased secondhand. In church-based schools, annual rummage sales at the church provide a wealth of dress-up clothes, books, toys, and some appliances.
- Resource books are filled with ideas for recycling materials into usable equipment for young children.
- Parents can provide computer paper, wood scraps, photo paper.
- Community sources, such as the public library storyteller or a senior citizens group, may be available for extended experiences for the children.
- Effective fund raising provides an added source of revenue in many schools and centers.

The human resources must also be identified. Adults do their best with children when their abilities, experience, and availability are matched with what is expected of them. Volunteers, for instance, feel satisfied if their time is organized and spent in ways meaningful to them. A first-year teacher's resources are best expended in the classroom rather than on administrative projects. A master teacher is ready for the challenges of orienting parents or evaluating curriculum materials. When the entire community values its children, as in the case of Reggio Emilia, the school is a showcase, sending a strong message of how important children are in the life of its citizens. Just as we try to match children's developing skills to the tasks at hand, so, too, should we consider individual people as part of an environment's resources.

Program Goals

The goals and objectives of the program are expressed directly in the arrangement of the environment. Three general goals in designing environments are:

1. To have responsive settings that avoid behavior problems;
2. To establish predictable environments that encourage independence;
3. To create stimulating spaces for active learning.

The physical space and materials should tell the children exactly what is going to happen and how they are to go about their work. In every program, consideration of what children are to accomplish puts goals and environments together. For example, if cognitive and fine motor skill development are the program goals, a space with games using pre-reading and writing materials should be prominent. Puzzles and table toys should have a central place in the classroom. Enough time should be dedicated to these activities every day, and teachers should be available to reinforce and encourage children as they play.

The goals of an early childhood program vary widely. Some programs are housed in large centers, others in homes; children may attend all day or part of it; the purpose may be educational, recreational, or even custodial. In every case, good environments for children must reflect clear and reasonable program goals. Once we know what we wish to do and why we want to do it, we can create space, timing, and an atmosphere in which to meet those goals.

Goals into Action

Creative teachers plan a program directed toward goals for each dimension (physical, temporal, and interpersonal) of the environment (see later in this chapter).

1. The room and yard are arranged to give maximum exposure to the materials and equipment they want children to use.
2. They take care to arrange the daily schedule in ways that provide the time blocks needed to teach content when and how they want to teach it.
3. They see that a warm relationship exists among the teachers and in their interactions with children.

When children walk into a center, the environment should communicate how they are to live and work in that setting. Children should receive clear messages about what they can and cannot do there as well as cues that tell them:

- Where they are free to move to and where they cannot go.
- How they will be treated.
- Who will be there with them.
- What materials and equipment they can use.
- How long they have to play.
- That they are safe there.
- What is expected of them.

The teacher is the key element in creating the environment. It is not the facility alone that counts, as much as it is the teacher's understanding of all the environmental factors and how they are related to one another (see Figure 9-2). A room is just a room and a yard is just a yard until a teacher makes them environments for learning. The teachers are the most responsive part of the

Messages from the Environment

Children Need to...	So the Environment Should...
Be treated as individuals, with unique strengths and developmental goals.	Have low teacher–child ratio for one-to-one interactions. Provide private as well as public spaces for group and solitary play. Place teachers and materials for ready access. Be staffed by teachers who set goals for each child based on observation and assessment. Have materials that match the developmental level of the group. Provide a balance of quiet and active times.
See themselves and their family culture represented positively and be exposed to cultural diversity in meaningful ways.	Include pictures, books, dolls, dramatic play materials, activities, and people that reflect many cultures and life experiences. Have teachers who understand and value home cultures and diverse family practices. Provide opportunities for various cultural habits, activities, and celebrations to occur.
Make choices and independent learning.	Be arranged with clearly marked available choices. Offer a variety of activity centers for exploration. Allow large blocks of time for child-initiated choices. Provide an adequate number of trained teachers to support self-discovery.
Learn to be part of a group.	Be set up for group play—several chairs around tables, easels next to each other, more than one telephone and wagon. Regularly schedule small and large group times and encourage participation. Include trained staff who can create engaging group activities. Allow children to use each other as resources. Provide activities that emphasize cooperation and social interaction.
Become responsible for the setting.	Schedule cleanup times as part of the daily routine. Include teachers and children working together to restore order. Allow time for children to be instructed in the proper use of materials and care.
Be aware of the behavioral limits.	Ensure that teachers and the daily schedule reflect important rules of behavior. Have teachers who deal with behavior problems in a fair and consistent way. Allow plenty of time during transitions that reduces stress during changes. Be arranged to avoid runways and dead ends.
Be with adults who will supervise and facilitate play and encourage learning throughout the day.	Be set up before children arrive so teachers are free to greet them. Encourage teacher–child interactions through the use of small groups. Create a daily schedule that allows time for in-depth interactions.

FIGURE 9-2 The goals of the program are mirrored in the environment.

environment; they converse, hug, appreciate, give information, and see the individuality of each child. They are the ones who create the space, time, and atmosphere that engages children's curiosity and involvement. Indicators of program quality, such as group size, adult–child ratio, the stability, education, and experience of the caregiver all contribute to an environment that meets its goals for children (see Chapters 2 and 5).

Developmentally Appropriate Learning Environments

Because children live in the world of the senses, actions, and feelings, they are greatly influenced by their immediate surroundings. Therefore, we must pay attention to what is in their environment and what happens during their stay there. The following are 15 elements of developmentally appropriate learning environments:

1. *Create brain-compatible environments.* Positive neurological changes occur when a child is engaged in a learning experience. "By immersing a child in a highly motivating and challenging room, we may be able to engage the brain, especially the pre-frontal cortex [where] higher-order thinking skills take place such as comparing and contrasting or making connections between size and shape" (Rushton et al., 2010). A child at the sand table adds water to build a castle [stimulating the motor cortex], sizes it up [occipital lobe], then gauges how high to build it before it collapses [prefrontal lobe]. Children with language or learning disabilities are often over stimulated by excessive noise or harsh lighting. Acoustics, light, colors, and other stimuli may affect the brain.

2. *Build culturally responsive environments.* The environment reflects the cultures of the children in the program and introduces them to those outside of their experience. A self-help focus reinforces a Euro-American cultural value of independence; an antibias goal brings in values of group harmony and interdependence. Even if the teachers do not look like the children, or the space does not look like home, it is critical that the environment complement children's home culture. (See Figure 9-3 and the next sections of this chapter.)

3. *Consider children's developmental levels.* Recognize that there are many things young children are not able to do on their own, but allow them the chance to do all they can. Be developmentally aware—know what children in the class are capable of, at what point they are now in their development, and what

the next step should be. Three-year-old Sophie can only zip her jacket now, so having dressing frames helps her put the zipper in the housing. Kindergartener Andrew needs time for both independent work and cooperative peer play

4. *Give families ways to identify their children's space.* Label cubbies, storage bins, or baskets with names, a photo, or a familiar picture so that children can see where to put jackets, artwork, and other personal belongings.

5. *Provide access to enough toys and materials.* Make sure that supplies are stored in such a way that adults do not have to hand them to children each time they are used. "A developmentally appropriate learning environment is designed for individual children to be messy, noisy and quiet, alone and social, and active and still," says Greenman (2000). "It is designed to accommodate much *stuff*—loose parts—the raw materials of discovery for active hands and minds." Equipment placed at a child's height on open, low shelving permits children to proceed at their own pace and to select materials without depending on adults to serve them.

6. *Give opportunities for making choices.* Both indoors and out, children should be given an abundance of materials and a range of activities from which to choose so that they may decide how to spend their time. Choosing to feed the hamster instead of painting at the easel helps 2- to 7-year-olds practice self-regulation. Choosing who to play with and which teacher to join gives children experience in establishing close relationships.

7. *See that children are responsible for caring for the environment.* Have a clean up time in the daily schedule and allow children time to help restore the room and yard. Label shelves and cupboards with pictures or symbols of what is stored there so that children can readily find and return things. Outline the specific shapes of the blocks that are stored on each shelf and make a "parking lot" for wheel toys. An accessible drying rack with large clothespins tells children that they are expected to care for their own artwork.

8. *Involve children in planning and setting up the environment.* Let the children help decide what they want to learn. When Sarita's cat had kittens, the center encouraged a visit to school, then sent a newsletter asking for other pets, arranged a field trip to a pet store, and organized a pet hospital for dramatic play.

9. *Provide children with enough time.* One of the ways children learn is to repeat an activity over and over

Culturally Responsive Environment Checklist

Overall Environment

1. In general, is the classroom hospitable?

2. What is on the walls?
   *If there is work done by children, does it all look alike? For example, are there teacher-made shapes that the children colored, or is the art *genuinely* done by the children?
   *Are all of the pictures for children and the art hung *at children's eye level*?
   *Are the pictures of people hanging on walls or bulletin boards representative of a multicultural community?
   *Even if pictures *do* represent a diverse population, are they stereotypic in any way? For example, is there an alphabet chart that uses "Indian" to symbolize the letter "I"?

3. Is there evidence of families in the environment?

Social Studies

1. Does the curriculum as a whole help the children increase their understanding and acceptance of attitudes, values, and lifestyles that are unfamiliar to them?

2. Are materials and games racially or sex-role stereotypic—for example, black people shooting dice or boys playing war games? Are women depicted only as caregivers while men do lots of exciting jobs?

Music and Games

1. Do the music experiences in the curriculum reinforce the children's affirmation of cultural diversity?

2. Are fingerplays, games, and songs from various cultural groups used in the classroom?

3. Are there many varieties of musical instruments, including ones made by children?

Dramatic Play

1. Is there a wide variety of clothes, including garments from various cultural groups?

2. Are the pictures and the props representative of a diversity of cultures?

3. Are the dolls representative of a broad variety of racial groups?
   *Are they just white dolls with changed skin color?

Blocks

1. Are the accessories representative of various cultural groups and family configurations?

2. Are the people block accessories stereotypic in terms of sex roles?

Language Arts

1. Does the classroom have a wide variety of age-appropriate and culturally diverse books and language-arts materials?

2. Are there stories about a variety of people from each of the following groups in the book corner?
   _____ Native-American cultures
   _____ Asian-American cultures
   _____ Black cultures
   _____ White ethnic cultures
   _____ Spanish-speaking cultures
   _____ Biracial or multiracial people
   _____ Family configurations, including biracial and multiracial families and gay and lesbian families

3. Are there any books that speak of people of diverse cultures in stereotypical or derogatory terms (e.g., describing Latinos as "lazy" or Japanese as always taking photographs)?

Cooking

1. Do the cooking experiences in the classroom encourage the children to experiment with foods other than those with which they are familiar?

2. Are the cooking experiences designed to give young children a general notion of the connections between cultural heritage and the process of preparing, cooking, and eating food?

FIGURE 9-3 An environment checklist provides questions for teachers to evaluate and monitor progress toward an anti-bias environment for children. (Adapted from Frances E. Kendall, *Diversity in the Classroom: New Approaches to the Education of Young Children.* New York: Teachers College Press. Copyright © 1995 by Teachers College Press, Columbia University. Reprinted with permission.)

You can download a copy of this checklist from this text's Education CourseMate website.

again. They explore, manipulate, experiment, and come to master a puzzle, to shape a lump of clay, or how to brush their teeth. Large blocks of time in the daily schedule—especially for routines—let children learn at an unhurried pace (see Temporal Environment section).

10. *Make expectations clear and consistent.* Use both the environment and your words to let children know what you want them to do. Putting on a clean up song that lasts several minutes communicates both verbally and nonverbally, without pressure. Give clues that indicate how to proceed. For example, Isaac usually has someone dress him at home, yet when he comes to the toddler class, he sees the poster of a child dressing himself, then plays a dressing game in circle time. So when the teacher prompts him, "If you pull up your underpants first, it will be easier to get your pants up," and then gives feedback on what is working, "Good. You've got the back up. Now reach around the front," he hears the teacher's confidence in his ability to finish the task.

    Be sure staff expectations are consistent. The teaching team should set common goals for each child and reinforce them consistently. Children become confused if one teacher expects children to get their cots ready for nap, then another does it for them.

11. *Let children teach one another.* Encourage children to share the skills they have mastered with their peers. Actively seek out each child's way of doing things; support a diversity of approaches. Those who can tie shoes enjoy helping their friends with stubborn laces or slippery knots. Whether reading or telling stories to one another, or showing a friend a fast way to put on a jacket, children benefit from helping each other.

12. *Allow children to solve their own problems whenever possible.* Piaget reminds us that we rob a child of the joy of self-discovery when we do things for them. See how far a child can go in discovering how to manipulate a pin so that it closes, or to work out with another child who uses the red paint first. A good teacher tries not to intervene too early and can let a child struggle sufficiently with a problem before stepping in to help.

13. *Accept children's efforts.* To support children in their quest for independence, the adult must be satisfied with children's efforts. Be ready to accept that Shelley put her boots on the wrong feet, if they are right to her.

14. *Make it safe to make a mistake.* Children learn from their own actions and their own experiences. Let them know it is perfectly acceptable, indeed inevitable, that they at times make mistakes. Help them deal with the consequences of their mistakes. When Chelo spills her juice, she is encouraged to find a sponge and clean up the table, then reinforced by commending her for scrubbing ability and swift action.

15. *Give credit where it is due.* Provide feedback so that children know when they have been successful. Compliment Chaz on how carefully he sorted through the nails to find the one he wanted. Let children take pride in their own accomplishments.

A final note: *Include beauty in your planning.* The environment in which children grow and learn should also be visually appealing and relaxing. There are so many assaults on our visual senses in schools: concrete, barred windows, heavy doors, clutter, to name a few. People become numbed to balance, shape, form, line, and color. While resources are limited, beauty does not need to be ignored. The environment is one of the few things that teachers can control and use to everyone's advantage.

Three Core Aspects of DAP Environments

When creating engaging, appropriate environments for young children, teachers keep in mind the concepts of anti-bias, self-help, and inclusion.

The Anti-Bias Environment

One of our ethical responsibilities is to create and maintain settings for children that respect their dignity and their contributions. Children learn to value one another's uniqueness, the differences as well as the similarities when culturally relevant experiences are embedded in the environment and curriculum.

The **anti-bias** curriculum, developed at Pacific Oaks College, encourages children and adults to:

- Explore the differences and similarities that make up our individual and group identities.
- Develop skills for identifying and countering the hurtful impact of bias on themselves and their peers. (Derman-Sparks & Edwards, 2010)

The physical and interpersonal environment can be used to help children see that culture consists of the various ways people do similar activities. This approach is different from the "tourist curriculum," which provides only superficial information that is often detached from the child's own life. It is also different from an approach that is based only on the interests of the class and gender, racial, and cultural groups represented therein. The anti-bias environment incorporates the positive aspects of a multicultural curriculum and uses some of the activities that highlight other cultures, but it provides a more inclusive, ongoing approach. This approach avoids patronizing or emphasizing trivial, isolated, exotic differences. There is an inherent feeling of fairness to self and others in the anti-bias approach, as children explore the many ways people do the basic human tasks of everyday life. Think of the diverse cultures expressed in how babies and things are carried from place to place in different parts of the world. How many ways do people eat? Cook? Shop for food?

The anti-bias approach to creating environment has its roots in the theories of Maslow, Piaget, and Erikson (see Chapter 4). Research data reveal that children begin to notice and construct classifications and evaluative categories very early; indeed, 2-year-olds begin to notice gender and racial differences and may even notice physical disabilities (Froschl, Rubin, & Sprung, 1984). Early childhood programs must develop a child's basic sense of trust and mastery so that children can learn to understand themselves and become tolerant and compassionate toward others (see Figure 9-3).

With the prevalence of stereotyping in society, and the impact of bias on children's development, early childhood educators have a responsibility to find ways to prevent, even counter, the damage done by such stereotyping. Teachers do this by arranging an anti-bias physical environment, as well as creating an atmosphere of problem solving and learning in the day-to-day conflicts and interactions that arise naturally. Think about how teachers provide the materials and encourage an atmosphere of trust and time for conflict resolution in these examples:

- A kindergarten teacher shows the children a magazine picture entitled "Brides of America." All of the women pictured are Caucasian. She asks, "What do you think of this picture?" Sophia responds, "That's a silly picture. My mom was a bride, and she's Mexican" (Derman-Sparks & Edwards, 2010).
- A toddler teacher sets up the water play table for washing babies. Choosing dolls that represent several racial and ethnic groups, she invites the children to soap and rinse them. One 2-year-old begins to wash the teacher's arm, then scrubs it hard. "Do you wonder if my color will wash off?" the teacher asks. The child nods, and several others look up. "Does it? Go ahead and try . . . See, a person's color is her own and stays with her. Try yours, too. That's one way people look different: we all have skin, and yet we

each have our own color" (Gutierrez, personal communication, 1987).

The anti-bias approach takes a broad view of a classroom, as a kind of "mini-society" in which children and adults work together. Injustices from the outside world are sometimes addressed. For instance a teacher helps children ticket parents' cars who improperly park in the class-made handicapped parking space (Derman-Sparks, 1989). An anti-bias classroom fosters:

- *Positive self-concept.* Curiosity and creativity stem from being able to affect the environment and what is in it. When Jamal says his baby's hair is fuzzy like his, his smile tells how good he feels about the similarity.
- *Awareness.* All people have interests and feelings, both about themselves and about others. Yoko notices that her classmate Julie runs and throws her arms around her dad, but she prefers a less demonstrative greeting.
- *Respect for diversity.* This stems from the ability to classify similarities and differences and then to appreciate both. For example, when the children create self-portraits for their class books, some choose different colors of paper for drawing faces, but all of them use the same markers to draw in their features.
- *Skills in communication and problem solving.* Learning how to express thoughts and feelings includes being able to hear others and finding peaceful ways to resolve conflicts. Jim and LaNell are quick to tell Eben he cannot play, but they find out that telling him he is "too little" does not work. He does not accept that simply being 3 years old is enough reason to leave him out, so they must either try to include him or make a claim for privacy.

Self-Help Environment

A **self-help** environment has as one of its fundamental goals the development of children's own skills—fostering their mastery of basic abilities that allow them to become responsible for their personal care, learning, emotional controls, problem solving, and choices and decisions. A self-help environment gives children the feeling that they are capable, competent, and successful. It allows children to do for themselves, to meet the challenge of growing up. A self-help environment reflects the belief that autonomy and independence are the birthright of every child.

I Can Do It Myself "I can do it myself" is heard frequently in preschoolers. Nothing renders people more helpless than not being able to maintain their own needs or to take care of themselves in basic ways. Children are

© Cengage Learning

The anti-bias environment encourages girls and boys to play together, respecting differences and including others in new ways.

still in the process of learning about what they can and cannot do. They need many different kinds of experiences to help them learn the extent of their capabilities. Most of all, they need adults who understand their tremendous drive to become self-reliant, adults who not only encourage their abilities and provide the time for them to practice skills, but adults who understand that it is the nature of the child to develop this way.

Self-concept is based on what we know about ourselves, which includes the ability to take care of our own needs. To care for oneself, to feel capable of learning, to solve problems, are all related to feelings of **self-esteem**. Self-esteem is the value we place on ourselves; how much we like or dislike who we are. Helping children achieve a positive self-concept and self-esteem is the most important part of teaching. The development of a strong sense of self-esteem is a lifelong process; its origins are in the early years.

A program designed to promote self-help skills uses every aspect of the environment, from the room arrangement to the attitudes of the teachers. Each activity is designed to foster self-reliance, thereby building self-esteem. A supermarket is a real-world example of an environment created for maximum self-reliance. Shelves are accessible and the products are clearly marked and attractively displayed.

That kind of thoughtful preparation can create spaces that say to children, "Try me. Master me. You are capable." Teachers want to communicate to children that they value self-help skills as much as they appreciate an art project or science experiment. If Claudia feels that

learning to tie her shoes is worth doing just because of the pleasure it gives her to manipulate the strings, weave them through the holes, and bring them together in a knot, then that becomes her reward. She becomes capable of reinforcing herself.

The Inclusive Environment

In 1975, the Education for All Handicapped Children Act (Public Law 94-142) called for an end to segregation for disabled students from kindergarten through high school. This policy filtered down to preschools and child care centers with an amendment (Public Law 99-457, 1986) that mandated all preschoolers with special needs be placed in the **least restrictive environment** (LRE). The practice of placing children with disabilities in the same classroom as children without disabilities is called **mainstreaming**. A more comprehensive method is known as **full inclusion**, in which both typically developing children and children with diverse abilities are taught together by a teaching staff with expertise in both normal child development and special education (see Chapter 3). The "Americans with Disabilities Act" (1990) prohibits child care centers from denying admission to a child simply because the child has a disability. Together, these federal laws form part of the rationale for early childhood centers to become more inclusive environments.

Children with diverse abilities need the same things in their environment as their more typically developing peers. They need an environment that is safe, secure, and predictable and one that provides a balance of the familiar and novel so that there are materials and activities that

DIVERSITY

A Place at the Table

The pluralistic view assumes that 1) people are different from each other and 2) differences are valuable; they add to the richness of everyone's experiences. The anti-bias aspect of the environment is the message that all children are included. The environment and the activities are derived from three sources: the children and their activities, the teachers' awareness of the developmental needs and learning styles of the group, and societal events.

All of the children are asked to bring something that shows their culture, so we have foods, clothing items, and toys throughout the environment on a daily basis. We ask about regular routines and special days in their cultures, such as Kwanzaa, Ramadan, and Hanukkah. Children share to educate us on why these days are special and what they do to celebrate them. We try to be sensitive; for example, during Ramadan you are not allowed to eat while the sun is up. If a family wants their children to participate in a cultural ritual, you have to make accommodations. And you watch the other children's reactions; if they seem to view it as "not normal," you take this opportunity to teach everyone so that it becomes familiar.

The various cultural learning moments include families.

- One of our African American families came in to educate us on black history month;

- Two Hispanic families explained Dia de los Muertos, and we all made a place in our environment for photos and items of special family members;
- Our new family from Shanghai helped us learn to make *zongzhi* and celebrate the Dragon Boat Festival by making boats to race.

Teachers make general selections of what children are to learn and arrange the environment for learning to begin. If unity is the completed puzzle, then diversity are the many pieces—with a place at the table for everyone. (Special thanks to Professor Elizabeth Jones and Student Leah Navarre Johnson.)

---

provide for their development. At the same time, a child with disabilities may be at a different level or need special help, so accommodations must be made. These may require either adding something to the environment that is not already there or using something in the environment in a different way. As noted at the chapter opening, we make adaptations in teaching strategies, learning environment, and curriculum so that each child can play and learn in an inclusive environment that meets the needs of children with and without disabilities.

Environmental adaptations are changes that make the environment fit the child better, so they vary with the children. Children with motor disabilities need different adaptations than those with hearing or language disabilities or with visual impairments. Physical changes may be necessary, modifications in the schedule may be recommended, or individualizing activities may be best. Parents are the best source of information about the child; other readings or specialists can be further guides (see Figure 9-4).

Three key concepts are helpful to remember—access, usability, and maximizing learning:

1. Can the child get where s/he needs to be in the classroom to learn something?
2. Once the child is in that location, can s/he use the materials and equipment and participate in the activity as independently as possible to learn something?

3. Are the learning activities arranged and scheduled to meet the individual learning needs of the children, including the child with disabilities?

Come Together for a Child "Come together for a child" is an adage for including children with special needs. Consider Andrew, who at 5 years of age had a motor/muscle disability with some speech difficulties. His cognitive skills were very strong and his social skills very weak. Andrew's mother talked to everyone during "Kinder Circle" about Andrew's needs and fears. If he fell down, he had a hard time righting himself. He needed help sitting and standing. He was afraid of getting bumped because he could not catch himself before falling very hard and then could not get up. The children all agreed to be careful about **roughhousing** around him. *The setting for success was being created.*

Because Andrew did not have much control of his fine motor skills, the teachers provided him with painting and play dough. They set up a crafts table; soon he was gluing pictures on paper, with or without order, and was very proud of his accomplishments. He even started using scissors on simple patterns. *The physical environment was responding to his needs.*

He was a wonderful puzzle builder, and the other children asked for his help often when they were stuck. It was wonderful to watch how they included him in

Checklist for an Inclusive Environment

Physical Environment:

Questions to think about:
- How can we enhance or adapt the physical environment for children who have difficulty moving (or who move too much)
- How do different children use their bodies or the space around them for learning?
- How can we capitalize on the physical environment for children who learn by moving?

Accessing the environment safely:
_____ Doorway widths in compliance with local building codes
_____ Ramps in addition to or instead of stairs
_____ Low, wide stairs where possible (including playground equipment)
_____ Hand rails on both sides of stairs
_____ Easy handles on doors, drawers, etc.
_____ Kids' chairs with armrests, "cubes" or footrest and/or seat strap
- When adapting seating, mobility, and/or motor activities for a specific child with physical disabilities, consult a physical therapist.

Learning through the environment:
_____ Toys and equipment physically accessible
_____ Magnets glued to backs of puzzle pieces and attribute blocks and use on a steel cookie tray
_____ Large knobs or levers attached to toys with lids, movable parts
_____ Tabs attached to book pages for easier turning
_____ Tray for boundaries for art activities

- An occupational therapist can provide specific suggestions for adapting materials and activities.

Visual Environment

Questions to think about:
- How do different children use their vision for learning?
- How can we enhance the visual environment for a child with low or no vision?
- How can we capitalize on the visual environment for children who learn by seeing?

Accessing the environment safely:
_____ Contrasting colors are used on edges and when surfaces change (e.g., tile to carpet, beginning of stairs, etc.)
_____ Windows shaded to avoid high glare
_____ Darker nonglossy floors and tabletops.
_____ Visual clutter is avoided on walls, shelves, etc.
_____ "Spot lighting" (e.g., swing arm lamp) available on some table tasks
- Orientation and mobility specialists help children with visual impairments learn to navigate the environment.

Learning through the environment:
_____ Large-print materials, textured materials, and auditory materials available (e.g., big books, sandpaper letters, books on tape)
_____ Daily schedule represented in words and pictures (e.g., a Velcro schedule with photos/pictures for children to post the schedule, then remove items as activities are completed)
_____ Children with low vision are seated close to the center of activity and away from high glare

FIGURE 9-4 When designing an inclusive environment, providing environmental support means altering the physical, temporal, and interpersonal environment to promote participation and learning. (Based on Brault et al., 2009, and Haugen, 1997.)
🌐 You can download a copy of this checklist from this text's Education CourseMate website.

Auditory Environment

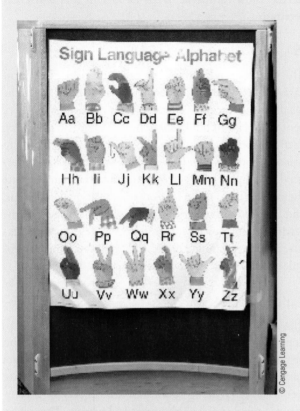

Questions to think about:

- How do different children use their hearing for learning?
- How can we enhance the auditory environment for a child who is deaf, hearing impaired, or has poor auditory discrimination skills?
- How can we capitalize on the auditory environment for auditory learners?

Accessing the environment safely:

_____ Eliminate or dampen background noise (using carpeting, closing windows and doors, etc.)

_____ "Auditory competition" is avoided (e.g., instead of raising one's voice to get attention, use a "silent signal," such as holding up a peace sign and encouraging children who notice to do the same until the room is focused)

_____ Nonauditory signals, such as turning lights on and off, are used to alert children

Learning through the environment:

_____ Auditory messages are paired with visual ones (e.g., simple sign language, flannel boards, picture schedules)

_____ Children with hearing impairments are seated so they can see others' faces and actions

Social Environment

Questions to think about:

- How do different children use social cues for learning?
- How can we adapt the social environment for children with impulsive behavior, attention deficits, or other behavior problems?
- How can we capitalize on the social environment for children who learn by relating to others?

Accessing the environment safely:

_____ Predictable schedule with children informed of changes

_____ Schedule provide a range of activity levels (e.g., adequate opportunities for physical activity, activities simplified into small steps)

Learning through the environment:

_____ Environment has a positive impact on self-esteem (capitalizing on child's interests and favorites, inviting adaptive equipment, invites peer support)

_____ Learning materials and toys include representations of all kinds of people, including children and adults with disabilities

_____ Schedule includes opportunities for a variety of groupings (pairs, small groups, whole class) as well as quiet time or time alone

_____ Schedule provides both structured and open activity times

- School psychologists and behavior specialists can help analyze misbehavior and modify the environment or schedule.

FIGURE 9-4

many things. They accepted his differences right from the beginning and treated him just like all the rest—except they were careful when running and playing around him. His fear was apparent, and they respected it. *Thus, the interpersonal environment was emerging.*

There was a regular physical education time each day in the big room where the group jumped rope, played "Simon Says," played "Red Light, Green Light," and ran obstacle courses. At first, Andrew sat on the sidelines and watched. He cheered and looked interested, so one teacher started asking him if he'd be her partner because she was a little afraid. At first he refused and told her to use someone else. The teacher kept asking but would drop it as soon as he gave his answer; then one day he said, "OK." The two of them ran and jumped over the snake (rope), and all the kids laughed. They hugged and that was the beginning. *When given the time that is needed (the temporal environment), the child triumphs.* (Special thanks to Cindy Rogers)

Central Elements In Environment Planning

Planning environments is a complex task for early childhood teachers. There are many people who use the environment, and the children's health, safety, and well-being are the primary focus.

Who Is in the Environment?

Many people live and work in the early childhood environment. Cooks, bus drivers, office personnel, and yard and building maintenance people are but a few. Each person has special demands on the environment to do the job they are hired to do. Three key groups of people are the children, their teachers, and the families.

Children

Children's needs are met through the environment. The physical, social, emotional, and intellectual requirements of children suggest the type of building, the size of the furniture, the choice of equipment, the size and age range of the group, the number of teachers who lead and supervise, and the budget allocations. Guided by child development principles, teachers match the setting to the children who learn and play there. The individuality of a particular group of children, of a school, and of its philosophy is expressed by

the arrangement of the environmental factors. Who are the children who use this space? What are their needs? How can those needs be met in this particular setting?

Teachers

The working environment is a predictor of the quality of care children receive. What has been done to meet the needs of the teachers? Do they have an office? A teachers' room? A place to hold conferences? Where do they keep their personal belongings or the materials they bring to use at school? Do they have a place to park? All teachers need room to create curriculum materials, to evaluate their programs, to review other educational materials, and to meet with their peers. The general context of the setting, opportunities for professional development, status, and wages are factors of how well teachers are provided for in an educational setting.

Families

The needs of children's parents and other adults vary, depending on whom the program serves. Adults who bring their children to child care or school need adequate and safe parking facilities. In settings in which adults are free to stay, a reading room, resource library, or a comfortable place to talk with others is desirable. Those who participate in the class are welcomed by a teacher, shown a place to put their belongings, and given a name tag and appropriate directions.

Children develop a sense of self when they have their own space, labeled with a photo or other visual clue so that they can easily identify it as their own.

There are many reasons families may need to contact the school or center. Are there ways to reach teachers and children in emergencies? How welcoming is the environment as they enter the building? The office? The classroom? What does the environment say about family involvement and interest?

The environment can be accessible and welcoming in several ways.

- Post contact information for school authorities and teachers where they can be reached after hours or in an emergency.
- Have a bulletin board for community notices, pertinent announcements, and for family use, along with mail pockets.
- Provide a place for families to talk with each other or wait outside the classroom.

The center that offers parents both an authoritative teacher and other useful resources helps them feel that their children are important. (See Chapter 8 for more suggestions.)

Regardless of how many children are in the setting and for how long, the first priority is to provide for their health and safety. Health, safety, and nutrition are closely related because the quality of one affects the quality of the others (Marotz, 2009). Programs for children must establish policies that provide for the protection, service, and education of child health and safety at all times. Government regulations and professional recommendations vary, but all establish some kind of standards to ensure good health and safety practices.

Keeping Children Healthy

Sanitation

When groups of people live in close quarters, proper sanitary conditions are imperative to prevent the spread of disease. For an early childhood center, the physical plant must have adequate washing and toileting facilities for both children and adults. The number and size of toilets and wash basins are usually prescribed by local health or other regulatory agencies. Children do not realize their role in spreading germs, especially as their moist and warm hands touch and handle everything. Set regular times, use gentle reminders, and role model hand washing to help children learn the habit of washing their hands at important times.

Sanitation depends on frequent, systematic cleaning. The classrooms require daily cleaning, and equipment

TeachSource Video

Watch the TeachSource Video Case entitled "Creating a Safe Physical Environment for Toddlers." After you study the video clip, view the artifacts, and read the teacher interviews and text, reflect on the following questions:

1. List five safety practices you noticed in the video. What potential problems might arise in implementing these practices into a program?

2. Choking hazards are a particular risk when working with children younger than 3 years of age. Identify three circumstances when there might be choking hazards and how to address them.

3. Director Doreen Dubique talks about being "a second set of eyes" in an environment. Create a 10-point safety checklist and observe a center or home.

that is used regularly should be sanitized on a periodic basis. Nontoxic paint must be used in all circumstances, including on outdoor equipment, cribs, and for art activities with children. Classroom dress-up clothing, pillows, nap blankets, and cuddle toys all need regular laundering, either at school or at home.

The nature of preventive health care in educational settings has expanded in the last decade. Knowledge of how disease is spread and concern over communicable diseases (see following discussion) have increased awareness of the kinds of practices teachers must en-

Spaces should be arranged according to the needs—and dimensions—of the children, so they can see and relate to things of interest at *their* level.

gage in on a daily basis. These include hand washing (the number-one way to prevent unnecessary spread of germs) and an approach known as **universal infection control precautions**. All teachers should receive training in using universal health precautions with all children.

Because we cannot be guaranteed of the infectious state of an individual, it is very important to always follow universal safety procedures with all children. The steps that keep a barrier between persons and blood can apply to more than blood-borne infections. All programs should be equipped with sets of latex gloves and plastic bags to properly handle and dispose of anything with blood or fecal material. Because intact skin is a natural barrier against disease, it may not always be necessary or possible to use gloves, but it is essential that hands be washed immediately after any toileting activity. All areas for eating, diapering, and toileting must be cleaned and sanitized, using a water-diluted bleach solution after cleaning away visible soiling.

Temperature, Ventilation, and Lighting

Heating and ventilation should be comfortable for the activity level of the children and should change when weather conditions do. Adequate, nonglare lighting is a necessity. Uniform, fluorescent lighting may not be the best environment for children; therefore, a mixture of lighting, such as is in homes, is preferable. Rooms should have some means of controlling light (e.g., shades, blinds). Cross-ventilation is necessary in all rooms where children eat, sleep, or play. Proper heating and insulation are important.

Communicable Disease

This is an important issue when dealing with young children in group care. Some people question the advisability of early group care on the grounds that it exposes children to too much illness. Others claim that such exposure at an early age helps children build up resistance and that they are actually stronger and healthier by the time they enter primary grades. In the largest U.S. study to date on children's health, the Environmental Protection Agency and Centers for Disease Control and Prevention concluded that, although infants and toddlers face a higher risk of colds and viruses, day care was not seen as increasing children's illnesses at older ages and not a risk overall (CDC, 2010).

Families should be notified when normal childhood diseases (such as chicken pox) or common problems (such as head lice) occur in the classroom. Infections of special concern to adults include chicken pox, hepatitis, cytomegalovirus (CMV), and human immunodeficiency virus (HIV). Regular education about disease is helpful; a handout on a specific infection that describes symptoms, dates of exposure, and incubation informs families who can then help prevent the spread of infectious disease.

In group care, children can contract a fair number of colds and viruses, especially when they are eating and sleeping close to each other (see Figure 9-5). The school and its staff have responsibility to ensure that good health standards are instituted and maintained to keep illness to a minimum.

Health Assessment and School Policies

Every early childhood center should establish clear health policies and make them known to families. A daily inspection of each child helps adults spot nasal discharge, inflamed eyes, and throat and skin conditions of a questionable nature. This daily check screens out more serious cases of children too ill to remain at school and may be done by a teacher, nurse, or administrator. Educating families about the warning signs of illness encourages sick children to be cared for at home.

It is very important for the school to inform families about what happens when children are refused admittance or become ill during the school day. Every school should provide a place for sick children where they can be isolated from others, kept under supervision, and be made comfortable until they are picked up. For their part, parents must arrange to have sick children cared for elsewhere if they are unable to take them home. School policies on these issues must be explicit and upheld consistently and compassionately for the sake of all the children.

Teachers must be sensitive to families' feelings and situations when sending a sick child home. This situation often produces guilt feelings in parents and work-related stress. Working families may need school assistance in locating alternatives for care of a sick child.

Most schools require, under state or local laws, a doctor's examination and permission to participate in an early childhood education program before a child can enter the program. This includes a record of immunizations and the child's general health. Parents, too, should submit a history of the child, highlighting eating, sleeping, and elimination habits. It is critical to note any dietary restrictions or allergies and then post them in the classrooms for a reminder.

Tips for Common Children's Health Problems

Condition	Tips
1. Allergies and asthma	Post a list of all children with chronic conditions; check ingredient lists on foods; watch what triggers reactions.
2. Scrapes and cuts	Reassure and sympathize with child; supervise child's washing with soaped pad and caring comments; use packs of ice or frozen peas in towel for swelling.
3. Bumps on the head	Notify parents of any loss of conciousness and watch for signs for two to three days.
4. Sand in eyes	Remind child "Do not rub!," have child wash hands and cover eyes with tissue; normal eye tearing will bring sand to inside corner of eye; remove with clean tissue.
5. Splinters	Clean area with alcohol and remove with tweezers or cover with adhesive strip and let parent remove.
6. Conjunctivitis	"Pinkeye" is highly contagious; watch for excess eye rubbing and red eyes; have child wash hands; isolate with washable toys until parent takes child home and gets treatment.
7. Head lice	Distressing but not dangerous; wash shared clothing, stuffed animals, bedding; vacuum rugs and furniture; remove hats, combs, and brushes from dramatic-play area; send notices home and inspect children's hair for two to three weeks.
8. Chicken pox	Isolate child until parents pick up; alert all parents about contagious period; watch for signs on all children for three weeks after exposure.
9. Strep throat	Send home notices; wash all equipment that might carry germs.
10. Lingering coughs	At onset, send child home until evaluated; frequent drinks will soothe; coughs may last up to two weeks; if longer, may suggest infection or allergy.

FIGURE 9-5 Common health problems require effective solutions. (Adapted from Needlman, R., & Needlman, G. [1995].)

Nutrition

What children eat is also important for proper health. Places where food is prepared and stored must be kept especially clean. The child who has regular, nutritious meals and snacks is likely healthier and less susceptible to disease. Many children do not have the benefits of healthy meals and snacks. Some do not receive adequate food at home; others are used to sugar-laden treats and fast foods. Education about child nutrition is needed for families and teachers in all programs, regardless of social or economic status. Some centers establish food regulations in an attempt to ensure that nutritionally sound meals are served to children. Most schools attempt to provide a relaxed atmosphere at meal and snack time. Children are asked to sit and eat, sharing conversation as well as food. Because lifelong eating patterns are established early in life, teachers of young children have a responsibility to understand the critical role nutrition plays in the child's total development.

Clothing

The health and safety of children are affected by the clothing they wear. A simple way to be sure children stay healthy is to encourage them to dress properly for play and for varying weather conditions. Children need clothing in which they can be active—clothing that is not binding and is easy to remove and easy to clean. To promote a self-help environment, parents and teachers should provide clothes the children can manage themselves (elastic waistbands, Velcro™ ties, large zippers). Pants are a good choice for both boys and girls; long dresses can become a hazard when climbing, running, or going up and down stairs. The safest shoes for active play should have composition or rubber soles. Whenever possible, it helps to keep extra clothes at school.

Children need clothing in which they can be active, playful, and messy!

Health of the Staff

A responsible early childhood center is one that supports and maintains a healthy staff. Teachers should be in good physical and mental health to be at their best with children. It is wise to check the health regulations and benefits of the individual center when employed there. Many states require annual chest X-rays and tuberculosis clearance as a condition of employment. Sick leave policies should be clearly stated in print. Early childhood education is an intense job involving close interpersonal contact. Most teachers work long hours, often with low wages and few health benefits, and with clients in various stages of health. Such working conditions produce fatigue and stress, which can lead to illness or other stress-related problems.

Guarding Children's Safety

Beyond the continual supervision of indoor and outdoor space, everything is planned with the children's safety in mind. Creating a hazard-free environment that still allows for risk and challenge for children takes careful observation and attention to detail. A quick walk around the room and yard reveals potential problems. Sharp corners, loose rug edges, and gated stairwells are sample indoor items; fences and broken equipment in the playground, use of scissors/hammers, and appliances everywhere are just some of the examples (see Figure 9-6).

Most importantly, there must be safety rules that are explained to children and upheld by adults. Outdoors is especially important because children are physically active. Approximately 200,000 children are sent to an emergency room every year as a result of a playground accident (Consumer Product Safety Commission, 2009). With an estimated 27 to 30 million children between 5 and 14 years of age participating in organized sports each year, safety issues are paramount for school-aged children. The adults serve as the link between children and sports and are the chief means of prevention of injuries and accidents (see Chapter 11).

Field trips are an extension of the program, and "safety first" is the motto. Preparing children for the trip includes rehearsal of safety procedures.

First Aid

Every school should establish procedures for dealing with children who are injured on the property. First aid and CPR training should be required of all teachers and made available as part of their in-service training. Teachers should know how to handle a child who is not breathing as well as treat bumps and bruises, minor cuts and abrasions, bleeding, splinters, bites and stings, seizures, sprains, broken bones, and minor burns. Each classroom should be equipped with two first aid kits. One is for use in the classroom and yard; the other should be suitable for taking on field trips. Each kit should be readily available to adults but out of children's reach, and supplies should be replenished regularly.

Emergency numbers to be posted near the telephone in each room include those of the ambulance squad, fire department, police, health department, nearest hospital, and a consulting physician (if any). All families enrolled at the school should be aware of center policy regarding injuries at school and should provide emergency information for each child: the name of their physician, how to locate the family, and who else might be responsible for the injured child if the parents cannot be reached. The program, in turn, must make sure they notify families of any injuries the child has incurred during the school day.

Natural Disaster

Most adults are familiar with the most common disaster preparation: the fire drill. Most local fire regulations require that fire extinguishers are in working order and placed in all classrooms and the kitchen area. Exits, alarms, and escapes should be well-marked and functioning properly. Children and teachers should participate in emergency drills regularly. Other natural disasters vary by geographical location; helping children prepare for earthquakes, tornadoes, hurricanes, floods, and snowstorms includes participating in drills for those disasters. Proper preparedness includes eliminating potential hazards (e.g., bolting down bookcases); establishing a coordinated response plan (a "Code Blue!" emergency plan should involve children, parents, all staff, and local emergency agencies); and, in some areas of the country, conducting

Safety List for Indoor Environments

_____ Person monitoring children (at entrances, indoors, outdoors)

_____ First aid and emergency

    _____ Materials readily available to adults, out of children's reach, and regularly stocked and updated

    _____ Adults trained in first aid and CPR regularly and familiar with emergency routines

_____ Safety plugs on all outlets

_____ Cords

    _____ Electrical cords out of children's reach; avoid using extension cords

    _____ Curtain and window cords, window pulls and poles out of children's reach

_____ Floormat and carpet tacked down to avoid slippage

_____ Doors

    _____ Made to open and close slowly

    _____ All clear access, marked exits, and not blocked

_____ Cubbies and storage cabinets

    _____ Bolted to walls (or back-to-back together)

    _____ Any dangerous materials in locked area

_____ Toys

    _____ In good repair; no splinters or sharp, broken edges

    _____ Check for size with younger children (purchase safety-sizing gadget or estimate to keep at the size of a child's fist)

    _____ Check for peeling paint

_____ Plants and animals

    _____ Nonpoisonous plants _only_

    _____ Check animal cages regularly

    _____ Supervise animal handling carefully

    _____ Store animal food away from children's reach

_____ Adult materials

    _____ Keep adult purses, bags, and so on, away from children

    _____ Avoid having hot beverages around children

    _____ No smoking in children's areas

_____ Kitchen and storage

    _____ Children allowed in _only_ with adult supervision

    _____ Poisonous or hazardous materials stored in a locked area

© Cengage Learning 2011

FIGURE 9-6 Children's safety is of primary importance to teachers and caregivers. Careful evaluation and regular safety checks eliminate dangerous materials and conditions in children's spaces.

🔄 You can download a copy of this checklist from this text's Education CourseMate website.

regular earthquake and tornado drills. These experiences can reinforce in parents the need for establishing similar procedures at home.

Automobile Safety

Automobile safety is a related concern when considering potential hazards for preschool children. The use of approved car seats and restraints for children riding in automobiles has received national attention in recent years. Some states have passed legislation requiring the use of specific devices to ensure safer travel for young children. Whether or not they walk to school, children should also be aware of basic rules for crossing streets. The street and parking lot can be a source of danger unless the program articulates policies to parents regarding the safety needs of children. There are potential risks when cars and children occupy the same space. Children should not be left unattended in parking lots.

Maintaining Children's Well-Being

The overall environment for children takes into consideration many factors. To provide for children's health and safety, teachers look at the physical environment carefully, then review the schedule, and finally assess the overall atmosphere of well-being. Young children are growing up in a world threatened by violence abroad and at home, drug abuse, unresolved conflicts among adults, and constant bombardment of television and other media.

Because young children do not easily separate the home and school parts of their lives, early childhood educators learn about children's lives and family details readily. They are often at a loss as to what to do, either with information that a child shares or with the child's behavior in the program. Yet, a situation does not need to be a crisis to affect a child's well-being. As a rule of thumb, when you feel the child's physical or emotional development is in jeopardy, you have a responsibility to take further action.

Difficulties in the Program

Children's well-being can be threatened by a difficult situation at school, such as being bitten, left out, or ridiculed. Although the situation may be remedied quickly and seem resolved, it may linger in a child's mind and get triggered later or when looking ahead to another day in the program.

Problems at Home

Children are at risk for myriad crises from home—problems with family members, separation or divorce, violence, or substance abuse. Community problems, such as closure of a local grocery store or a neighborhood crime incident, can affect children. Bronfenbrenner's ecological theory (see Chapter 4) is applicable to conditions of well-being. Although much of our response is with adults—families, community resources, professional supports—we are also responsible for trying to provide a psychologically safe and positive environment. By design (physical and temporal) and by responsiveness (interpersonal), teachers provide an environment that soothes and cares for young children.

Basic Arrangements and Materials for Creating the Environment

The environment is more than just the space provided or even the things put into it. When planning a place for children's growth and development, teachers consider three aspects of the environment: the physical elements, the temporal (time) dimensions, and the interpersonal atmosphere.

The Physical Environment

Every educational setting is organized fundamentally around physical space. The building itself may be new and designed specifically for young children. In Reggio Emilia, for example, it is the environment that creates an atmosphere of discovery. As founder Louis Malaguzzi explains (Edwards et al., 1993):

> There is an entrance hall, which informs and documents, and which anticipates the form and organization of the school. This leads into the dining hall, with the kitchen well in view. The entrance hall leads into the central space, or piazza, the place of encounters, friendships, games, and other activities

that complete those of the classrooms. The classrooms and utility rooms are placed at a distance from but connected with the center area. Each classroom is divided into two contiguous rooms . . . to allow children either to be with teachers or stay alone. . . . In addition to the classrooms, we have established the atelier, the school studio and laboratory, as a place for manipulating or experimenting.

More than likely, however, the space is a converted house or store, a parish hall, or an elementary classroom. Sometimes a program shares space with another group so that furniture has to be moved. Family child care programs are housed in a private home, so adaptations are made in the space both for the children and for the family that lives there. There may be a large yard or none at all. Some playgrounds are on the roof of the building, or a park across the street may serve as the only available playground (see Chapter 11).

Constraints also come in the form of weather conditions. Outside play—and therefore large-muscle equipment—may be unavailable during the winter, so room for active, vigorous play is needed inside during that time. Hot summer months can make some types of play difficult if there is little or no shade outdoors. Weather conditions must be considered when planning programs for children.

Early childhood programs have specific needs that must be met by the buildings they occupy. Although the choice of building is generally determined by what is available, at a minimum the setting should provide facilities for:

playing/working	food preparation
eating	washing/toileting
sleeping/resting	clothing and wraps
storage	office/work space

Ideally, the setting should have enough space to house these various activities separately. In practice, however, rooms are multipurpose, and more than one event takes place in the same space. A playroom doubles as an eating area because both require the use of tables and chairs. When a room serves many functions (playing, eating, sleeping), convenient and adequate storage space is a necessity.

General Requirements

Ground floor classrooms are preferable for young children to ensure that they can enter and leave with relative ease and safety. For noise reduction, the walls and ceilings should be soundproofed. Carpeting, draperies, and other fireproof fabrics in the room help absorb sound. Floors must be durable, sanitary, and easily cleaned. They should be free from drafts. Rugs should be vacuumed each day. Room size should be sufficient to allow for freedom of movement and the opportunity to play without interference.

Many local and state agencies have regulations regarding the use of space for children in group care settings. Licensing agencies often recommend or mandate minimum room and yard size standards. The fire marshal, health department, and similar agencies must be consulted and their regulations observed.

The National Academy of Early Childhood Programs (NAEYC, 2005) has developed guidelines for indoor and outdoor facilities that promote optimal growth. Besides floor and play space (minimum 35 [and recommended 50] square feet indoors and 75 square feet outdoors), the guidelines suggest how to arrange activity areas to accommodate children and what kinds of activities and materials are safe, clean, and attractive. This document, along with *Inspiring Spaces for Young Children* (Deviney et al., 2010), *The Creative Curriculum* (Heroman et al., 2010), and the *Environmental Rating Scales* (Harms et al., 2005-2009) are used extensively to develop this material. There are several key dimensions to any environment that are helpful to consider. If we are to offer children both balance and variety, these criteria need to be included in developing space both indoors and out (see Figure 9-7).

Indoors

Interest Areas/Learning Centers Interest areas or learning centers are **activity centers**, with a classic definition that holds today.

Key Environmental Dimensions

1. Softness/Hardness

   Soft: rugs, pillows, play-dough, finger paints, grass, sand, swings

   Hard: tile floor, wooden furniture, asphalt, cement

2. Open/Closed

   Open (no one right way to use it): sand and water, dress-up, collage materials, painting

   Closed (manipulated only one way to come out right): puzzles, many board games, most Montessori equipment

   In between: many manipulatives such as Legos®, Tinkertoys®, blocks, balls

3. Simple/Complex

   "Play equipment can differ in its holding power; i.e., the capacity to sustain attention . . . A simple unit has one manipulable aspect; a complex unit has two different kinds of materials combined; and a super unit has three different kinds of materials that go together."

      Simple: swings, climbers, sand pile with no toys

      Complex: dramatic play with only a kitchen

      Super: climbers with slides and ropes, playhouse with kitchen, dress-up clothes, dolls, and/or play-dough; sand area with equipment and/or water

   As you add more features to a unit, you increase its complexity and the children's interest in it. To simple play-dough, add cookie cutters; then add toothpicks or a garlic press and it becomes a super unit.

4. Intrusion/Seclusion

   Intrusion: places where children can enter or go through easily; blocks, housekeeping, even the entire environment are often highly intrusive areas

   Seclusion: places where children can be alone or with only one child or adult; cubbies, a fort, or under a table become secret places

5. High Mobility/Low Mobility

   High: whole-body places and activities, outdoors, climbers, trike lanes, gym mats

   Low: sitting-still places and activities; puzzles and games, story and group times, nap time

   In-between: dramatic play, block corner, woodworking

FIGURE 9-7 Key dimensions when considering an early childhood environment. (Adapted from *Exchange Magazine*, E. Prescott, 1994.)

"An activity area has five defining attributes. Physical *location,* with visible *boundaries* indicating where it begins and ends, within which are placed *work and sitting surfaces,* and the *storage and display of materials* used to execute the activities for which the area is intended. An area, like a room, has a *mood* or personality distinguishing it from contiguous spaces" (Olds, 1989).

Deciding what interest centers you want, reflective of program philosophy and children's interests, and what kind of space you need is good preparation to making a basic floor plan and sketching in the interest centers.

Start with an assessment of the way space is set up now. "First draw a simple floor plan of the room you are currently working in, one you are familiar with, or one you imagine using in a new job. As you sketch out the arrangements of the room, do not include a lot of detail. . . . Put yourself in the shoes of the children who spend their days in your space" (Carter & Curtis, 2003).

You consider their ages and needs of the group, and make a list of "I can" and "I like to" statements as if *you* are those children. Now check your floor plan; if you had trouble finding any of the components in your room, make some changes.

Most programs include basic areas for play and engagement in a variety of dimensions. **Learning centers** are areas of the environment focused on different activities for different developmental experiences. For infants and toddlers, areas for movement and for sensory experiences dominate; preschoolers want more creative and manipulative choices; school-age children might include areas for academic stimulation or practice.

Teachers must create learning centers that are interesting; accurately reflect the goals for children; and take into consideration space, traffic flow, the number of people, and availability of equipment and materials. Teachers use environmental cues to communicate to children what may happen there, and make good use of the learning centers as places for observation and assessment (see Figure 9-8). Creating learning centers is a standard early childhood practice that has tremendous potential in school-age and primary settings.

Environmental Components that Frame the ECE Curriculum

Infants, Toddlers & Twos

Routines

Hello/goodbye, diapering/toileting, eating

Sleeping/napping, getting dressed

Experiences

Playing with toys, imitating/pretending

Enjoying stories, connecting with music

Creating with art, tasting food, exploring

Sand and water, going outdoors

Partnering with Families

Plenty of display space

Preschoolers

Physical learning environment

Time for play, routines, transitions, groups of several sizes

Interpersonal considerations with peers and teachers

School-Agers

Being with Friends

Quiet area for just talking, tables for being in groups, large area for whole group

Completing Homework

Place with lighting, computer access, teacher availability, away from noise

Special places for either older [10+] or younger [K only]

Preschoolers

Infants, Toddlers & Twos

Interest and Activity Centers
Art
Blocks
Cooking/sensory
Discovery/science
Dramatic play
Library/literacy
Media/computers
Music and movement
Outdoors/garden and pets
Toys and games/math

School-Agers

Research & Theory

© Cengage Learning 2014

FIGURE 9-8 Environmental features in the environment are set in a framework that helps build appropriate experiences for children in the early years.

Bathrooms Bathrooms should be adjacent to the play and sleeping areas and easily reached from outdoors. Child-sized toilets and wash basins are preferable, but if unavailable, a step or platform may be built. In most settings for children younger than age 5, the bathrooms are without doors, for ease of supervision. Toileting facilities for children should be light, airy, attractive, and large enough to serve several children at a time. An exhaust fan is desirable. Paper towel holders should be at child height and wastebaskets placed nearby.

If diapering is part of the program, areas for this purpose should be clearly defined and close to hand washing facilities. Hand washing regulations for the staff should be posted, and an area should be provided for recording children's toileting and elimination patterns. Closed cans and germicidal spray must be used, and diapering materials should be plentiful and handy.

Room to Rest Room to rest means providing nap and sleeping facilities with adequate storage space for cots and bedding. Movable screens, low enough for teacher

supervision, allow for privacy and help reduce the noise level. Cots or cribs should be labeled with children's names and washed regularly. They should be placed consistently and in such a way that children feel familiar, cozy, and private—not in the center of the room or in rows. Teachers can develop a "nap map" that places children so that they can get the rest or sleep they need while still feeling part of the group.

Food Service This aspect includes routines and choices around food. "Good nutrition affects the health and well-being of individuals of all ages," states Marotz (2009). "Small children need nutrients for growth and energy . . . regardless of the guideline selected, the common factor necessary for good nutrition is the inclusion of a wide variety of foods." As early childhood classrooms have become more diverse and multicultural, educators must take into consideration families' cultural practices and preferences.

Feeding young children and teaching toddlers and older children about good food choices can be a challenge throughout the early childhood span. In an infant

All photos © Cengage Learning

Early childhood programs provide for children to play and work alone and together, with friends and teachers, indoors and out.

program, storing formula and milk is a necessity. As toddlers assert their independence, they begin to make their preferences known. Care must be taken to offer a variety of foods at regular times, but avoid a battle of wills over what the child eats. Preschoolers are influenced by a teacher who sets a good example of eating with balance and variety. School-aged children can understand nutritional concepts better but are more influenced by what their peers are eating.

Whether involved in a light snack or full meal program, the center must adhere to the most rigid standards of health protection and safety provisions. Every precaution must be taken to ensure maximum hygienic food service. Daily cleaning of equipment, counters, floors, and appliances is a necessity. Proper disinfecting of high chairs and tables requires an appropriate bleach-to-water ratio, and bottles of this solution should be stored away from children's reach yet handy for teachers. Consult NAEYC or local referral agencies for guidelines on serving nutritional foods and incentives or subsidies.

Each age has its unique food-service needs. Infants need to be held or seated near an adult with enough high chairs or low tables to prevent an unreasonable wait for eating. Toddlers should not be fed popcorn, nuts, or raw carrots because of the hazard of choking. All children must be served food on disposable dishes or on dishes cleaned in a dishwasher with a sanitation cycle. Lunches brought from home by school-age and full-day children must be checked for spoilage. Information about eating patterns, proportions, and nutritional needs should be regularly shared with families.

Adult Space Adult space is rare in early childhood centers. "Oh, for a real 'teacher's desk,'" the early childhood caregiver moans. "I'm lucky if I can find a place to stash my bag in the morning!" A common issue for early childhood education programs is to donate nearly all the available space to child use and materials storage. Yet, the personal and professional needs of adults deserve environmental support. Early education programs sometimes have an adult space in the director's area. An adult bathroom is also common. Elementary classrooms include a desk and a bookshelf for the teachers and a workroom or lounge for staff in the school office. However, in programs for children younger than age 5, even a desk can seem a hazard, taking up precious space for children.

Still, early childhood professionals deserve environmental support for their work. A safe place for their belongings, space for first aid/emergency materials and information for families, and an area for a special adult project goes a long way in respecting the teachers' lives in the classroom. We show our priorities by the space and time we give them.

Outside

Some of our deepest childhood joys—those of running in the grass, wading in a stream, exploring vacant lots, of privacy and secrecy—can only be experienced outside, and nowhere else. Free and fresh air and open space to move about at will are often children's favorite spots in a program. Indeed, many a preschooler has been able to say good-bye easier when the great outdoors beckons.

Traditional playgrounds—typically on a flat, barren area with steel structures such as swings, climbers, a slide, perhaps a merry-go-round or seesaws, fixed in concrete and arranged—are poor places for children's play from both safety and developmental perspectives. Children as young as toddlers and through the primary years much prefer the adventure of a creative playground, spaces that have a variety of fixed and movable equipment. Raw materials, such as sand, water, tires, spools, sawhorses, bowls, or pans, in combination with larger superstructures or open-air "houses" with some flexible parts, stimulate a wide variety of both social and cognitive play (including constructive, dramatic, and games play).

A wide porch or covered patio is ideal for rainy days or days when the sun is too severe. Many activities can be extended to the outside area with this type of protection. The physical plant should include adequate playground space adjacent to the building. A variety of playground surfaces makes for more interesting play and provides suitable covering for outdoor activities. Tanbark can be used in the swing area, cement for wheel toys, and grass for under climbers. Sand is used for play in a large area and also in a sensory table.

No matter what the surface, the yard should be constructed with a good drainage system. Trees, bushes, and other plantings allow for both sunshine and shade. Fences are *mandatory*. They must be durable, an appropriate height, with no opportunity for a child to gain a foothold. Because there are no mandatory standards for the manufacture of play equipment, adults who work with children must assume responsibility for playground design. Given the importance that young children attach to the outdoors, teachers are well advised to concentrate their efforts by visiting high quality playgrounds and consulting with child development specialists when selecting equipment (see Chapter 11).

Materials and Equipment

Selection of materials and equipment is based on a number of criteria. Program budgets are limited, so to make every dollar count, teachers select materials that:

- Are age and developmentally appropriate.
- Are related to program philosophy and curriculum.

- Reflect quality design and workmanship.
- Are durable.
- Offer flexibility and versatility in their uses.
- Have safety features (e.g., nontoxic paints, rounded corners).
- Are aesthetically attractive and appealing to children (and adults).
- Are easy to maintain and repair.
- Reflect the cultural makeup of the group and the diversity of the culture overall.
- Are nonsexist, nonstereotypical, and anti-bias.

Materials should be appropriate for a wide range of skills because children within the same age group develop at individual rates. Simplicity of detail and versatile in use are practical watchwords (Community Products, 2011). Selecting equipment and toys to support development is important because young children typically try to play with everything in their environment. Many of the materials can be **open-ended**; that is, they can be used in their most basic form or they can be developed in a variety of ways. Using the key dimension of simple/complex (see Figure 9-7) elements, unit blocks, clay, and Legos® are examples of materials that children can use in a simple fashion and, as skills develop, these materials can be manipulated in a more complex manner.

Toys and materials need to reflect the diversity of the class, the families, and the community:

- From a DAP perspective, materials need to appeal to individual interests and also respond to children's cultural and linguistic strengths. Homemade materials and a variety of cultural artifacts help the environment feel familiar.
- From a self-help viewpoint, dressing frames and plenty of workable doll clothes help children learn those self-care tasks.
- Children's books that demonstrate social values and attitudes that expand gender roles and family lifestyles show a value for an anti-bias environment.
- An inclusive viewpoint might include materials to highlight tactile, auditory, and olfactory experiences for children with visual impairments.
- Educational philosophy, including broad curriculum models of Montessori or High/Scope (see Chapter 10), might determine materials. Consider how the Waldorf philosophy contributes to the kindergarten environment (Waldorf, 1995):

The feeling of warmth and security is largely created by using only natural materials—woods, cotton, wool—in the construction of the decor and toys. The curtains transmit a warm glow in the room.

Ideally, the walls and floor of the room are of natural wood. In this warm environment are placed toys which the children can use to imitate and transform the activities that belong to everyday adult life. In one corner stands a wooden scale and baskets for children to pretend they are grocery shopping; a pile of timber stands ready to be constructed into a playhouse, a boat, or a train; a rocking horse invites a child to become a rider; homemade dolls lie in wooden cradles surrounded by wooden frames and cloths the children can use to create a pretend family and play house. Pinecones and flowers are artistically dispersed. Lovely watercolors adorn the walls. The effect of this beautiful arrangement of decorations and toys is the feeling of stepping out of the business and clutter of modern life into a sanctuary where one can breathe easily, relax, and play according to the impulses of one's heart.

Basic materials form a foundation from which individual and program interests blossom (see Figure 9-9).

Try to avoid toys that have limited play value. The organization "Teachers Resisting Unhealthy Children's Entertainment" (TRUCE, 2011) suggests that we steer away from toys that:

- Make electronic technology the focus of play.
- Lure girls into focusing on appearance.
- Model violent and sexualized language or behavior.
- Are linked to commercial products and advertisements.

Children are active learners, and their materials should provide them with ways to explore, manipulate, and become involved. Young children learn through all their senses, so the materials should be appealing to many of the senses. All children need opportunities for quiet, private time and space as well, with materials that parallel the balance of key environmental dimensions.

Organizing Space

There are many different ways to arrange and organize space in an early childhood setting; the final result expresses the diversity of the program. Most early childhood centers are arranged by **interest areas** (learning centers or activity areas). The amount of space devoted to any one activity says a great deal about its value to the staff. For example, teachers at a child care center noticed the high interest in sociodramatic play with several new babies in children's families. They built up the housekeeping area, making sure there were at least six baby dolls, four telephones, and three doll buggies and countless bottles, tippy cups, and pretend baby food. As interests

Basic Materials for ECE Environments

Basic Materials for Indoor Environments

Floors and Seating: Various surfaces (carpet, linoleum or tile, wood floor) kept clean and draft-free, comfortable seating (chairs at tables, rocking chair or sofa, carpet squares)

Areas: Art, blocks, dramatic play, toys and games, library, discovery/science, music and movement, cooking, media

Equipment:
Art: Easels, paints, watercolors; playdough, clay; pens, pencils, brushes; scissors, hole punch; glue, paste; collage materials; assorted paper

Blocks: Unit, hollow blocks; props (people & animal figures); accessories (signage, doll furniture)

Dramatic play: Mirrors; furniture; clothing; dolls, cooking utensils, pretend food items; purses and backpacks; expanded materials beyond house as needed

Toys and games: Puzzles, constructions toys, math toys, Montessori materials, cooperative games

Library/book nook: Picture books; flannel board and items; photos; writing center materials; listening post items

Discovery/science: Nature materials; pets; sensory materials; water/sand table; magnifying glasses and scales, etc.; textured materials or other 'theme/ interest' related displays

Music and movement: CD/tape player and items; instruments, dancing scarves (may also be used in circletime)

Cooking: Food preparation materials (may also be used in discovery or art areas)

Media: Computers, tape/cd deck; TV

Infant-toddler: Limit materials and reduce number of interest areas; offer fewer choices in each area; substitute soft blocks and push/pull toys; have knobbed puzzles and stacking toys

School-age: Increase game area, vary units, add self-help in art and chapter books in library

Basic Materials for Outdoor Playgrounds/ Yards

Grounds: Various surfaces (grass, asphalt, gravel/sand, tanbark), as much natural habitat as possible

Areas: Climbing place, sand/water space, wheel toy/ riding place, games & dramatic play spot, building space, pet/garden area

Equipment: Climbing apparatus with ramps, slide, pole, ladder; swings (various types); house/quiet area; ramps and supports to build; tires, "loose parts"

- Sand and water toys
- Various wheel toys
- Large building blocks
- Dramatic-play props
- Balls and game materials
- Workbench and woodworking/clay materials

Infant-toddler: Have plenty of simple riding toys, eliminate woodworking, have apparatus correct size and simplicity and/or foam wedges

School-age: Increase game area, may eliminate number or kinds of wheel toys; substitute a stage, mural, boat, creek; increase "loose parts" for child-created forts

© Cengage Learning 2011

FIGURE 9-9 All programs should stock both indoor and outdoor environments with developmentally appropriate basic materials.

change, so do the room and yard—someone brings in a hamster and the discovery area blossoms or a family camping trip brings out the tents.

Room and Materials Arrangement Room arrangement and choice of materials play an important role in children's educational experience. A developmentally appropriate room invites children in and welcomes them at their level, as seen in these four examples:

1. *Toddler Class.* Simplicity is a watchword in a toddler room. Room arrangement changes with the age range.
   - A large-motor zone is essential for children aged 12 to 24 months.

- The dramatic-play area for pretend play is advisable for children aged 24 to 30 months.
- The messy zone for liquid materials is recommended for children aged 18-30 months.
- Every toddler room needs a quiet zone, a haven to relax and step back.

2. *Family Child Care Home.* Having a program in a home presents special challenges, both in the space and the mixed age ranges of children. Beyond the general spaces for indoor and outside play, retreats (such as an empty cabinet without its door or behind the couch) allow moderate privacy while still ensuring supervision.

DAP Inventing Toys for Tots

Toys can be used to support development in very young children, although their potential is often overlooked with a focus on safety or an inadequate understanding of infant and toddler development. "Teachers can build on children's play by providing engaging toys," advises Guyton, a special education teacher and infant/toddler specialist (2011). What needs to be kept in mind is the critical factor of engagement. "A little creativity combined with basic materials can stimulate play and facilitate a young child's development across all domains."

Using readily available materials of fabric, boxes, and safe kitchen items, teachers can create toys to stimulate DAP cognitive growth:

- *Use fabric scraps.* A scarf can be a toddler's costume in dramatic play or a cover for a surprise game with older infants.
- *Collect cardboard and paper.* Make boxes from shoeboxes or cereal boxes, even paper bags stuffed with newspaper, especially for toddlers younger than age 2.
- *Hunt for common household items.* Puzzles can be made combining a muffin tin with a variety of measuring cups, plastic jar tops, and clothespins that the 1- to 2-year-old fills and dumps out again.

"Developmentally appropriate" does not need to spell "expensive" or "impossible" when making cognitive connections with infants and toddlers.

3. *Preschool and Kindergarten.* Harms and others (2005) recommend these environmental areas for preschool and kindergarten:
   - Space and furnishings
   - Personal care routines
   - Language-reasoning
   - Activities (motor, cognitive, creative)
   - Interaction (social, emotional)
   - Program structure (schedules)
   - Parents and staff (personal and professional needs)
4. *School-Age Programs.* After-school programs for children from kindergarten through third and sometimes fifth or sixth grade have special requirements, as those environments have an extensive range of physical size, interests, and developmental needs. The National School-Age Core Competencies (NAA, 2011) recommends tables for projects and experiments, homework tables in a quiet corner, a place for snacks and club meetings, art, blocks, house corner, and large group activity area.

Placement of the interest centers is important. Balance the number of noisy and quiet activities, both indoors and out. Some activities are noisier than others, so place the noisier centers together and cluster the quieter ones together. Quieter activities, such as puzzles, language games, and storytelling, take place in areas away from blocks, water play, or dramatic play, because the last three tend to spark animated, active, and sometimes noisy behavior. Some programs create a kind of layered room—entry, quiet, messy, noisy.

Adult needs also should be met through proper organization. How can the teachers supervise all areas while ensuring cozy spots for children's privacy? Are the teachers deployed evenly throughout all the space? Is storage integrated so that equipment is located near the place where it is used? Is the space arranged for cooperation and communication among the adults as well as the children? In other words, is this a work and play place that is accepting, inviting, and challenging to all? (See Figures 9-10 through 9-12.)

Playground Designs Playgrounds must be arranged so that there are enough play spaces for the number of children in the group. Clearly defined boundaries and obvious pathways make it easy for children to live and work in the space. There should be enough space for larger groups to gather together as well as small groups (see Figure 9-13).

Calculating play prospects is part of analyzing the number of play opportunities in program settings. In their classic study, Prescott and others assigned areas and activities a value so that the overall richness of the environment can be calculated (Prescott, Jones, & Kritschevsky, 1972). A simple area (swings, climbers) counts as one play space, a complex area (housekeeping/dramatic play) counts as four play spaces, and a super area (sand and water play combined) counts as eight play spaces. The value assigned an area generally coincides with the number of children who might be accommodated in that space. When the total for the space is figured, it is matched against the actual number of children in the group to see if there is a place for everyone to play.

In summary, the physical environment should be organized around these criteria:

- *Availability.* Open, low shelving with visual cues for placement of toys and equipment aids in clean up and room set up.
- *Consistency in organization.* Neat, systematic, in logical order.
- *Compatibility.* Noisy activities are grouped away from quiet ones; art needs natural light when possible; water play near a bathroom or kitchen; messy projects done on washable floors.

Preschool Classroom

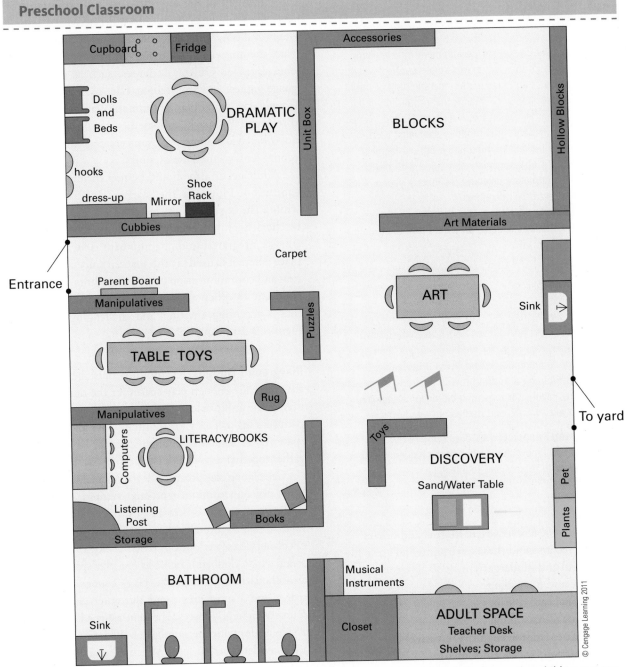

FIGURE 9-10 A preschool child care center needs clearly defined boundaries and obvious pathways so that children can use the space independently.

- *Definition.* Clearly defined boundaries indicating available space and what is to take place; obvious pathways outlined in class and yard; ways to get in and out of an area without disrupting activity in progress; no dead ends or runways.
- *Spacing.* Interest areas with enough space to hold the children who play there; one third to one half of the surface should remain uncovered; materials stored near space where they are used; storage and activity spaces have visual cues.

- *Communicability.* Tells children what to do instead of relying on adult to monitor activities; communicates to children what behavior is expected; arrangement suggests numbers of children, levels of activity.

The Temporal Environment

The second dimension of the environment to consider is the time and timing of a program. What happens, when

Toddler Room

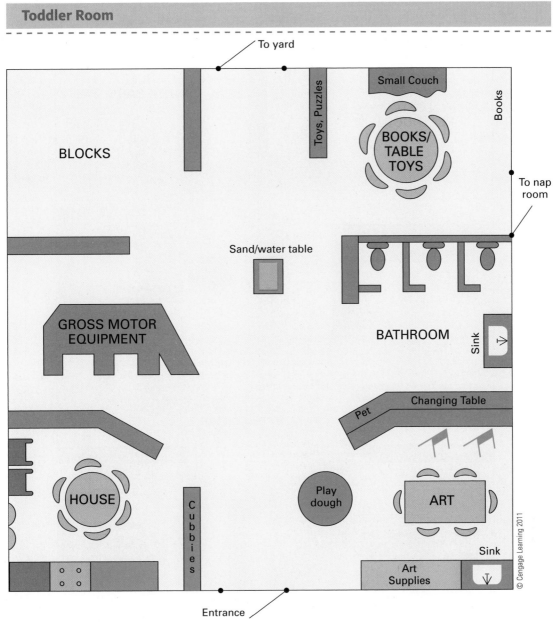

FIGURE 9-11 A toddler environment has safety and accessibility in mind so that children can be maximally involved with a minimum of distraction from others.

it occurs, and how long it takes all affect both individual children and group functioning.

Daily Schedule: Time to Learn

The **daily schedule** defines the structure of each program. It creates the format for how children experience the events of the day—in what order and for what length of time.

No two schedules are alike because each reflects the program it represents. The amount of time devoted to specific activities communicates clearly what value the school places on them. The amount of time given to certain aspects of the curriculum, the variety of events, and the level of flexibility tell children and adults what is important in this particular setting (see Figure 9-14).

Criteria for Scheduling Criteria is used to see how the schedule functions on a daily basis. Teachers first decide what is important for children to learn, how that learning should take place, and how much time to allow in the daily program. If small group work and individual attention are program goals, enough time is set aside to ensure their success. More time is needed to allow children several curriculum choices than if they had only one or

School-Age Center

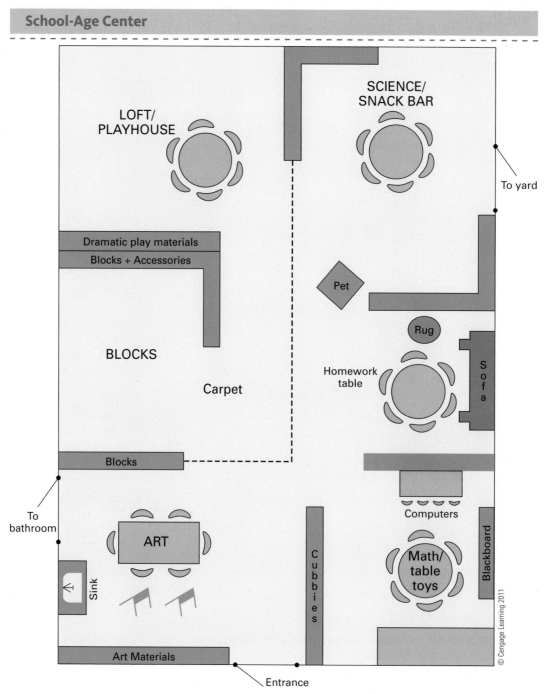

FIGURE 9-12 A school-age center has learning centers to allow children to engage in peer connections and homework constructively.

two activities from which to select. Three-year-olds need more time for toileting activities than do 5-year-olds, who are considerably more self-sufficient.

The physical plant itself may dictate a portion of the daily schedule. If toilet facilities are not located adjacent to the classroom, then more time must be scheduled to travel to and from the bathrooms. If the building or space is shared with other groups, some portion of the program may be modified. For example, a program housed in church

buildings scheduled field trips during the annual church rummage sale to free up the space for the church's use.

Expectations and Flexibility Setting expectations and having flexibility are part of the golden rule for child care, which is to treat children as we want them to treat us. The children in child care today are the adults of tomorrow who will be taking care of us in our old age. Remembering that, it helps to think of how often

PreK-to-Grade 3 Yard

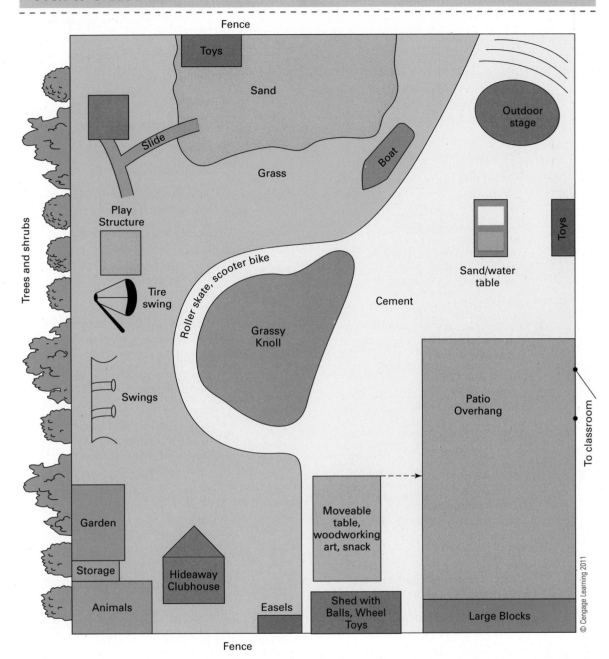

FIGURE 9-13 A playground/yard, suitable for ages 4 and older, gives children a sense of security and adventure, contact with nature, opportunities for social play, and freedom for active physical play. (Adapted from Themes, 1999.)

children are asked to do and finish their tasks on others' schedules, to ask permission to do what they wish, or to participate in activities of someone else's choice. A children's program must be *for* children, on their timetable as much as possible.

1. Suitable choices are built in as much of the time as possible, avoiding the expectation that everyone should do the same thing at the same time.

2. People need time to settle in, whether this is for a child to say good-bye in the morning or a group to get ready for lunch. Different people cope with change and new experiences in different ways.

3. Meaningless activities that simply keep children busy have no intrinsic value and should be avoided.

4. We need a healthy balance between an individual's need for autonomy, freedom, and independence on

Daily Schedules

Half-Day Toddler Program

9:00–9:30	Greet children Inside activities • playdough and art/easel • home living • blocks and manipulatives • books
9:30	Door to outdoors opens
9:45–10:20	Outdoor play • large motor • social play
10:20	Music/movement outdoors
10:30	Snack/"Here We Are Together" song • washing hands • eating/pouring/cleanup
10:45–11:45	Outside
11:15	"Time to Put Our Toys Away" song • all encouraged to participate in cleanup
11:20	Closure (indoors) • parent–child together • story or flannel board

Full-Day Program for Preschoolers

7:00	Arrival, breakfast
7:30	Inside free play • arts/easels • table toys/games/blocks • dramatic-play center; house, grocery store, etc.
9:00	Cleanup
9:15	Group time: songs/fingerplays and small group choices
9:30	Choice time/small groups • discovery/math lab/science activity • cooking for morning or afternoon snack • language art/prereading choice
10:00	Snack (at outside tables/cloths on warm days) or snack center during free play
10:15	Outside free play • climbing, swinging; sand and water, wheel toys, group games
12:00	Handwash and lunch

12:45	Get ready: toileting, handwashing, toothbrushing, prepare beds
1:15	Bedtime story
1:30	Rest time
2:30	Outdoors for those awake
3:30	Cleanup outdoors and singing time
4:00	Snacktime
4:15	Learning centers; some outdoor/indoor choices, field trips, story teller
5:30	Cleanup and read books until going home

Half-Day Kindergarten Plan

8:15–8:30	Arrival Getting ready to start • checking in library books, lunch money, etc.
8:30	Newstelling • "anything you want to tell for news" • newsletter written weekly
9:00	Work assignment • write a story about your news *or* • make a page in your book (topic assigned) *or* • work in math lab
9:30–10:15	Choice of indoors (paints, blocks, computer, table toys) *or* second-grade tutors read books to children • when finished, play in loft *or* read books until recess
10:15	Snack
10:30	Recess
10:45	Language: chapter in novel read *or* other language activity
11:15	Dance *or* game *or* visitor
11:45	Ending: getting ready to leave • check out library books • gather art and other projects
12:00–1:30	For part of group each day Lunch, then: • field trips • writing lesson • math or science lab

FIGURE 9-14 Daily schedules reflect the children's needs and ages; the time and timing of the day reflect the program's values and priorities.

the one hand, and the need for group connection and harmony with rules that help us get along together on the other.

5. Staff balances the need for a routine, for the comfort and reassurance of the familiar, with the need for variety and novelty for change. Flexibility makes for a more humane environment.

The daily schedule is important for everyone in the setting. Two important aspects of a schedule are routines and transitions.

Routines

The regular or habitual performance of an established procedure is a **routine**. Routines provide an important framework to a program. Each day, some events are repeated, providing continuity and a sense of order to the schedule. Routines are the pegs on which to hang the daily calendar. When should children eat? Sleep? Play? Be alone? Be together? These questions are answered by the placement of routines. The rest of the curriculum—art activities, field trips, woodworking—works around them.

Program Routines Program routines in an early childhood environment setting include:

- Self-care (eating, rest/sleeping, dressing, toileting)
- Transitions between activities
- **Group times**
- Beginning and ending the day or session
- Making choices
- Task completion
- Room clean up and yard restoration

Routines are an integral part of creating a good environment for children. All three environmental factors are influenced by routines:

1. *Physical.* Child-sized bathroom and eating facilities; storage of cots, blankets, and sleeping accessories; equipment for food storage and preparation.
2. *Temporal.* Amount of time in daily schedule for eating, resting, toileting, clean up.
3. *Interpersonal.* Attitudes toward body functions; willingness to plan for self-care tasks; interactions during activities and transitions; expectations of staff, parents, and children.

Most routines are very personal and individual rituals in children's daily lives. Children bring to school a history firmly established around routines, one that is deeply embedded in their family and culture. Routines are reassuring to children, and they take pride in mastering them; they are also a highly emotional issue for some.

Self-Care Tasks Self-care tasks include eating, sleeping, dressing, and toileting and can be difficult issues between adult and child, virtually from the moment of birth. Everyone can recall vivid memories associated with at least one routine. They seem to become battlegrounds on which children and adults often struggle. Many times this is where children choose to take their first stand on the road to independence.

The early childhood teacher must be able to deal with the issue of self-care routines in sensitive and understanding ways. Children adjust to routines when they are regularly scheduled in the daily program and when there are clear expectations.

Ordinary, everyday routines have learning potential because they teach the young child important skills and habits (see Figure 9-15). In the four curriculum chapters of this book (Chapters 11–14), there is specific planning for routines, transitions, and group times. It is these times that provide a sense of security for children. Beyond the planning for indoor and outdoor activities, careful teachers realize that helping children with the routines of daily living provides a solid underpinning so that other learning can take place.

Sequence with a "Loose Grip" Keeping a "loose grip" on sequencing is important because once the time sequence is clear to all, then everyone can go about the business of learning and teaching. Children are more secure in a place that has a consistent schedule; they can begin to anticipate the regularity of what comes next and count on it. In that way, they are then free to move, explore, and learn without hesitation. Children can freely involve themselves without fear of interruption. Adults, too, enjoy the predictability of a daily schedule. By knowing the sequence of events, they are then free to flex the timing when unforeseen circumstances arise.

It is the unforeseen that often does happen. Amidst the noise of children at work, the play is likely to be interrupted by a number of things that can affect the "best laid plans" of all teachers.

- Chad unexpectedly decides that he does not want Dad to go—just as the teacher was helping Shana onto the toilet for the first time.
- An argument breaks out in the block corner—at the moment a teacher was leaving with a group of children for the kitchen with several cookie sheets full of carefully constructed gingerbread people.
- A visitor comes in the door with a special group time activity—just as two children collide and bump heads.

Routines: Learning Opportunities in Self-Care

● Eating Teaches:

Health: Introduction to new and different foods, good nutritional habits

Social Skills: How to manage in a group eating situation, how to focus on eating and conversing; what is acceptable mealtime behavior and manners

Fine-Motor Skills: Pouring; handling spoons, forks; serving self, drinking, eating without spilling

Independence Skills: Finding and setting one's place, serving self, making choices, cleaning up at snack and lunch

Respect for Individual Differences: Likes and dislikes; choices of food; pace of eating

● Toothbrushing Teaches:

Health: How to keep teeth and tongue clean

Independence Skills: Self-awareness, perceptual-motor to use toothbrush in mouth.

● Resting/Sleeping Teaches:

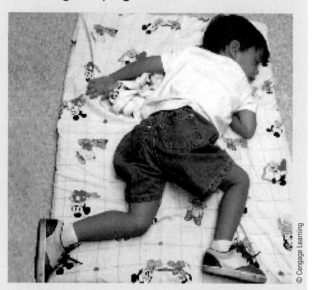

Health: Personal care skills; relaxation habits; internal balance; change of pace; alternating activity to allow body to rest

● Dressing Teaches:

Independence Skills: Self-awareness, how to get one's own area ready—blanket, cuddly, book

Respect for Individual Differences: Comparisons between clothes for girls and boys, younger and older, larger and smaller children, and children in and out of diapers or training pants

Self-esteem: Caring for one's own body; choosing one's own clothes

FIGURE 9-15 Every routine can be used as a vehicle for learning within the environment.

Fine-Motor Skills: How to manage snaps, buttons, zippers; handling all garments; maneuvering in and out of a snowsuit or jacket; matching hands and feet with mittens and boots or shoes

- Toileting/Handwashing Teaches:

   Self-awareness: Body functions, learning the names and physical sensations that go with body functions

   Self-identity: Comparisons between girls and boys (sit versus stand)

   Self-esteem: Caring for one's own body without guilt, fear, shame

   Human sexuality: In a natural setting, promotes healthy attitudes toward the body and its functions, and that adults can be accepting, open, and reassuring about the body and its care

© Cengage Learning

FIGURE 9-15 *(continued)*

Teachers may then need to change the sequence to flex with the changing landscape. Further changes are at the heart of the next aspect of the temporal environment.

Transitions

Humans are known as a species for their adaptability. And yet we are resistant to change. For young children, too, change is difficult. Teachers and caregivers can make the necessary changes easier for children if they focus their attention on those times. Rather than trying to rush through quickly to get to the next event, provide enough transition time. Helping children anticipate, figure out, work through, and successfully manage the changes in their day guides them to maturity (see Figure 9-16).

Preparing children for upcoming transitions is useful, such as using a song or strumming of an instrument and the words, "Get ready to clean up soon." This helps children's perceptions of time, immediacy, and closure to collide with the schedule. Recall the unexpected chaos in the previous section on routines. If Chad does not want his Dad to go, perhaps getting Shana on the toilet has to wait; or Dad can read him another story until Shana's "All done now!" has taken place. The gingerbread sheets can be held up momentarily so that the quarrel can be resolved, or some of the "fighters" could be invited to be door-openers and help to march the group to the kitchen. Perhaps another teacher could help the visitor begin with the rest of the class on the rug while you get ice for the bumped heads.

These examples all illustrate the common clash of adult timetables and children's intentions. Programs need to be designed to allow for both consistency and **flexibility.** Consistency brings security and closure, allowing for teacher authority and expertise to assert themselves; flexibility invites sensitivity to individuals and respectful agreements to be reached. As teachers work with schedules, they continually balance the needs of individuals with those of the group.

Developmentally Appropriate Schedules

Just as the arrangement of space should reflect the group of children within, so does the daily schedule allow for appropriate growth at the developmental level of the group. There are common factors to consider for all children in the early years, as well as some developmental distinctions at the various ages.

There are common elements for all schedules:

- Include time for routines (to eat, rest, wash, toilet) as well as time for transitions (what happens when there is a change from one activity to another) and group times (circle time to begin the day, song time for announcements, or story time as closure).

Transition Times Made Easier

Questions for Planning

- Who is involved in the transition time (child, parents, teachers, other children, visitors, etc.)?
- What kind of activity has preceded the transition time and what will follow?
- What will the children be asked to do during transition?
- What will the teachers be doing during transition?
- How will the children be told or find out what to do *during* the transition?
- What do you know about child development and this particular child(ren) that can help with these questions?

Teaching Strategies

Arrival

- Greet each child with a smile, and welcome child and parent with what activities are available.
- Make name cards and/or an attendance sheet that child and parent can participate in as a starting point.
- Plan with parents, and alert the child, a simple and clear way for them to say goodbye and for the parents to leave (see Chapter 8 for details).

Cleanup Materials

- Give the children a five-minute "warning" to alert them to upcoming changes.
- Have a consistent and calm signal to start putting away toys.
- Use music as background and/or sing during cleanup.
- Consider having necklaces or cards of specific areas for children, or make teams.
- Construct the environment so that it is clear where things go and children can do the majority of it themselves.
- Occasionally thank the children publicly for cleaning up, noting individual efforts and specific chores done well.

Preparing Children to Attend

- Make a chart that shows the choices available.
- Sing a song or familiar fingerplay to get everyone's attention and participation.
- Ask the children to put on "elephant ears" (rabbit, etc.) or lock their lips and put the key in their pockets.

Ready to Rest/Nap Time

- Prepare the environment ahead of time to be restful—darkened room, soft blanket/cuddlies nearby, quiet music, teachers whispering and available to walk children to their places and stay with them.
- Read a story to the group in one place before they are to lie quietly, or split larger groups into small subgroups with a teacher reading to each.

Moving to Another Place/Building

- Gather the group and tell them exactly what will be happening.
- Ask for ideas of how to behave ("What will we need to remember? How can we stay safe and have fun together?") and reinforce with a few concrete rules.
- Have the children be a train, with adults as the engine and caboose, or a dragon with head and tail.
- Have the children choose a partner to stay with and hold hands.
- Ask preschoolers and early primary children to remember the "B" words ("beside or behind") in staying near adults.

Waiting for Others to Finish

- Prepare a part of the room for children to move to, such as a book corner or listening post, having an adult in that space with more than two children.
- Make an apron or hanging with several pockets filled with activity cards or small manipulatives for children to use alone.
- Plan a special table with folders or large envelopes with activities.
- Have a "waiting box" with special small items for these times only.

© Cengage Learning 2011

FIGURE 9-16 Transitions are a regular part of children's routines and should be learning times that are as well-planned as other parts of the day.

- Alternate quiet and active play and work to help children pace themselves.
- Provide opportunities for both inside and outside play.
- Allow children to participate in structured activities as well as those of their own choosing.
- Make it possible for children to work individually, in small groups, or in larger ones.
- Gear the time to the age and developmental levels of the group.
- Provide for flexibility so that children's interests can be maintained and emergencies met.
- Have a beginning and an end (meet and greet to start, close and review to finish, anticipate tomorrow).
- Involve the adults in planning and review (include a regular meeting time for more substantial discussion of children, long-range planning, and evaluation).
- Include time for clean up and room restoration.
- Incorporate the teachers' roles and assignments so that they know their area of responsibility.
- Be posted in an obvious place in the classroom for all to see.

Age-related differences should be taken into consideration as well. They call for schedules to reflect the development and needs of the group (see Figure 9-14). In general, these guidelines help to create a DAP schedule:

- *More choices* are available to children as they grow. *Example:* Two-year-olds could be over stimulated by the selection of materials that is appropriate for school-aged children.
- *Transitions* can be handled differently in the various age groups.
  Example: Older children can move through some transitions as a group, such as changing from one activity area to another or going out with a specialist in pairs or even in a single file. This is difficult for younger children, who would push or wander away. For them, the door to the yard opens quietly, allowing children to go out slowly.
  Example: A child care class of 3- and 4-year-olds is dismissed from song time to snack by the color of people's shirts or the first letter of their names, rather than as one whole group.
- *The structure* of the day changes with age.
  Example: The balance of free play and teacher-directed activities shifts from relatively few directed activities for younger children to more for preschool. A kindergarten schedule provides more structure both in individual work projects and teacher-focused time. A first grade schedule has more whole-group teacher instruction times.
- *The content of group activities* changes with age.

Example: A toddler circle time is simple, with a short finger play, flannel board or puppets story, and a good-bye song. Preschool group times include several songs, a dramatization of a favorite finger play, and a short story. By kindergarten, groups can last 15 to 20 minutes, with announcements and a weather board, children's "news telling," longer dramas, and even chapter stories.

The Interpersonal Environment

A child responds to everything in school: the color of the room, the way the furniture is arranged, how much time there is to play, and how people treat one another. To the child, everything is a stimulus. The feeling in a room is as real as the blocks or the books. Thus, the interpersonal or social aspects of an early childhood setting are powerful components of the environment.

Setting the Tone

Children are the most important people in the setting; they should feel safe and comfortable. A warm, interpersonal environment invites children to participate and to learn. When children feel secure with one another and with the setting, they are able to engage more fully in the total program.

Just how important is the interpersonal environment? Theories of Erikson, Bandura, and Vygotsky (see Chapter 4) emphasize the role of relationships in learning. Although most experts agree that the relationship between teacher and child is important, extensive research has only recently begun to document exactly how teacher–child interactions occur and how variations in such interactions might be related to behaviors or other outcomes in children. With a pattern of positive relationships between children's sensitive, involved interactions with teachers and other children, enhanced development is likely to be seen in cognitive, socio-emotional, and language domains. Brain research confirms that socialization plays a critical role in development. "The circuitry of the brain is developed through stimulations presented with adequate intensity, repetition, and duration to create and amplify the neural connection which are stored in short-term and, eventually, in long-term memory" (Marshall, 2011).

People are at the heart of early childhood education.

Defining Interpersonal Elements

The human component, the connections among the people in a center or home, makes all the difference to young children because they are the barometers of interpersonal tension or openness and freedom.

Noise and Busy-ness

Centers are very busy environments for children. So many things, so much learning, so much to do! Often the children's enthusiastic curiosity mixes with the teachers' focus on transmitting skills and information, creating an intensity that threatens to crush the spirit of play and compress the time.

- Reserve an area of your environment for those who want to sit quietly. This should include children and adults, both alone and with each other.
- Make meals a time for peace and quiet. This doesn't mean silence, but rather a rejuvenating break from the hustle of playtime.
- Wake up children from naps a little sooner than is needed. This gives

them time to transition and allows wakeful children to learn to respect others' styles.

- Don't decorate every window with paintings. These are places to let in light and to contemplate the outdoors.
- Change room displays often. The room can get cluttered when projects are left up while more are added.

Avoid over-scheduling or making too many small time segments. Children may have short attention spans for adult-centered activities and "teacher talk." Yet they need and use longer periods of time to discover their interests and stay focused.

The intentional teacher shows respect for children when putting the temporal environment to work for them.

Think About This

1. Write a sample schedule for a preschool morning program. Mark the times for noise/busy-ness and those for quiet/respite. Count the minutes allotted for each. Is it balanced? Why or why not?
2. Many family child care homes have full-day schedules with children from newborns to 5-year-olds. How would you plan a day with eight children in this age range?
3. If you had an after-school program of 25 kindergarteners through third graders, what would be a balanced schedule for the afternoon? How many teachers would you need?

There are four elements of the interpersonal environment (Conventry, 2011):

Child–child relationship. Children learn from each other, observe and model other's behavior, and react to other children's expressions, especially emotional reactions.

Teacher–child relationship. Because it is understood that the single most important factor in determining the quality of a program is the teacher (see Chapter 5), it follows that teachers are the key ingredient in determining the interpersonal "flavor" of a class. The first component of the NAEYC's Academy criteria for high quality early childhood programs is the interactions among the staff and children (see Chapter 2).

Teacher–teacher relationship. The way staff feel about each other and how they express their feelings have an impact on children. How teachers solve conflicts with one another, how polite or kind they are, and how much positive communication flows makes a difference in the atmosphere.

Teacher–family relationship. Families matter in the life of a program, especially in the early years. Does the teacher know the family, share resources, and support their parenting?

Crafting the Teacher's Role

Young children develop best through close, affectionate relationships. Although this is true for all young children, it is particularly important for children younger than age 3 and those without facility in the dominant language spoken in the class. The interpersonal aspect of environment is the central element affecting the quality of toddler play. In addition, those who cannot talk about what is going on inside them show their feelings and conflicts through behavior. Teacher sensitivity and calm acceptance is critical. In this regard, every issue is a relationship issue.

The Reggio Emilia approach emphasizes relationships, as seen here (Caldwell, 2011):

I love Loris Malaguzzi's image of thinking with children as being a little like a game of tossing a ball back and forth. A child or a group of children have an idea or are drawn to something. If we are listening, we notice. Then perhaps we want to play a game, so we "toss" them a twist, a provocation, a wide-open question about their idea. They respond with something marvelous that we did not anticipate, and the game continues. We don't know where the next idea will come from, but the game is fun and challenging for both child and adult, and we get better at playing it in many situations and scenarios.

In a human and humane environment, people are respected, and the focus of the staff is on children's strengths and capabilities; limitations are seen as needs rather than liabilities. Children model their behavior on what they see others doing, so teachers engage children in interactions that include smiling, touching, listening, asking questions, and speaking on eye level. The language and tone of voice used are respectful and friendly, with children treated equitably across lines of culture, language, ability, and gender. Staff use positive guidance rather than punitive discipline techniques (see Chapter 7) and develop warm relationships with families (see Chapter 8).

Including Family Contributions

Teachers have to see children within the family context. To do so, they must establish stability and consistency through mutual learning, open dialogue, and exchange of information. Note the struggle, and ultimate shift, for these teachers:

- No matter how many times you tell Kai's grandfather that school starts at 9 AM, he continues to bring him between 9:30 and 10 . . . until you find out that in China, old people are often late and people respect their habits and sense of time. Now your realize you need to flex your schedule to allow for this late arrival and support this family custom.
- Elena's father speaks with such an accent you can hardly understand him. You would like to just avoid talking with him, but then you would connect only when there is a problem. You discover that, in his Central American culture, "good parents" are those that ask for teacher's opinions. You understand it is for you to overcome your discomfort and converse more, asking him respectfully to repeat what he is saying a bit more slowly so that you can understand.
- Every day Maryam brings her lunch, and it is so difficult to manage. These Iranian foods are not the same as the other children's, and the kindergartners tease each other about what they bring in their lunch boxes. You wonder if you should simply tell her auntie to send her with a sandwich. Only you realize that every child wants familiar foods, and letting Maryam eat what her parents send should be coupled with teaching tolerance to the other children. Now you move to use lunch as a time for everyone to get curious and interested in new foods.

The interpersonal connection between families and teachers cannot be overstated. Good relationships create a positive mood and can bolster what happens to the child within the classroom and can provide a smooth

The teacher's posture and facial expressions show respect for children and their learning pace and style.

© Cengage Learning

Space and Time for Brain Work

Advances in neuroscience have been touted in both the popular press and in educational conferences. Educators are urged to base their teaching practices on such research. But which research and what practices?

There are ways of improving learning based on brain research evidence. Good early childhood education has been implementing "teaching methods that respect the way the brain functions" (Jalongo, 2008):

- *An attentional mindset.* It is essential to pay attention. The more the mind wanders, the less it focuses on learning. Notes Jalongo (2008): "ECE has a long history of inventing materials to maximize the learner's attentional mind set. Whether it is unit blocks, outdoor play equipment, a dress up corner, toy animals or live classroom pets, early childhood is all about captivating children's attention and capitalizing on their curiosity."
- *Low to moderate stress.* Children need some choice over what they engage with. DAP and early childhood traditions emphasize the whole child and do not focus on academic achievement only. "The physical learning environment is non-threatening, yet stimulating" (Rushton et al., 2009).
- *Engagement in coherent, meaningful tasks.* Hands-on, experiential learning gives children real toys and events to explore. Children are not bored, so they don't have to be convinced to engage in the tasks. Even the literature mirrors their lives.
- *Repetition for repeated practice.* Large blocks of time are made available to use materials over and over. Basic materials are available daily. "The brain will create new connections when there's new learning, but these connections must be reinforced and strengthened or they deteriorate" (Jensen, 2006).
- *Learner-controlled feedback.* Montessori materials are self-correcting, as is some of the best computer software, so that children can guide both the pace and quantity of the "lessons" they are learning.

The study of the brain can now "assist educators in understanding how children learn best and what connects the learning environment with neurobiological changes in the child brain" (Rushton et al., 2009). We just need to give children the space and time so that they have a brain-friendly environment.

Questions

1. What parts of a physical environment might be considered "brain-friendly"? Why?
2. Which time blocks in a typical preschool program might be "brain-busters"? Why?
3. Look at the four components of the interpersonal environment, and list teacher behaviors that could be positive for brain compatibility and those that would be considered negative factors. Justify your list.

---

transition between school and home. Learning is enhanced when parents and teachers come to communicate in supportive, nonthreatening ways.

Noting Interpersonal Learning Moments

The attitudes and behaviors of teachers affect children's behaviors. Questions teachers can ask themselves as they evaluate the quality of the environment are:

- Is there a feeling of mutual respect between children and adults?
- Do teachers pick up on nonverbal and verbal expressions of both girls and boys? Of children with varying abilities? Of children of color?
- How do children treat one another?
- Do teachers model cooperative behavior with other adults and children? Do they show by example how to work through a disagreement or problem?
- Does the physical set up allow the teacher to focus on the children?
- Do housekeeping details keep teachers disconnected from children?

- Do teachers encourage children to use one another as resources?
- Do teachers take time to show children how to accomplish a task by themselves?
- Are girls complimented only on appearance and boys just for achievement? Are all children helped to appreciate similarities and differences?
- Do teachers use reasoning and follow-through?
- How and when do teachers interact with children?
- What are the teacher's posture and facial expression when involved in a problem situation?
- If I were a child, would I like to come here?

The answers to these questions provide a sense of the atmosphere of positive social interaction. The most important thing to remember is that the way people feel about each other and how they express their feelings have an impact on children. Teachers must focus as much attention on the interpersonal part of the environment as they do on buying equipment or arranging the room.

Summary

LO 1 The major characteristics of an environment are its physical plant, available resources, and program goals. Developmentally appropriate learning environments must adhere to several key principles that are expressed in the core aspects of anti-bias, self-help, and inclusion.

LO 2 The central elements in planning for the environment are children's health, safety, and well-being. Keeping children healthy has several components: Guarding children's safety involves first aid, natural disaster, and automobile safety and maintaining children's well-being means responding to both program and family challenges.

LO 3 Basic arrangements and materials for the environment revolve around three components. The physical environment addresses indoor and outdoor space, arrangement, and materials. The temporal environment refers to all aspects of time and schedule. The interpersonal aspects of the environment pinpoint the relationships and the tone created.

Key Terms

environment	self-concept	activity centers
physical environment	self-esteem	learning centers
temporal environment	least restrictive environment	open-ended
interpersonal environment	mainstreaming	interest areas
prepared environment	full inclusion	daily schedules
group size	environmental adaptation	routines
adult-child ratios	roughhousing	group times
anti-bias	universal infection control	transition
self-help	precautions	flexibility

Review Questions

1. What are the major principles in creating developmentally appropriate learning environments?
2. Who and what is involved in planning safe and healthy environments?
3. Write a definition of environment in early education including the three aspects to consider when planning programs for young children.

Observe and Apply

1. Hunch down on your knees and look at a classroom from the child's perspective. Describe what you see in terms of the principles of successful environments.
2. Discuss three school health and safety policies that help keep illness and injury to a minimum. Interview a director or head teacher about their policies, how they explain the guidelines to parents, and how they handle problems that have arisen.
3. Examine a daily schedule from an early childhood center. What do you think are the program goals of the school? How can you tell? Compare this with a daily schedule of a family day care home. How are they alike? How are they different?

Helpful Websites

American Alliance for Health, Physical Education, Recreation & Dance **www.aahperd.org**

Canada Institute of Child Health **www.cich.ca**

Centers for Disease Control and Prevention **www.cdc.gov**

Children's Health **www.kidshealth.org**

Consumer Product Safety Commission
www.cpsc.gov

National After School Association **www.naaweb.org**

National Association of Child Development
www.nacd.org

National Institute on Out-of-School Time
www.niost.org

National Program for Playground Safety
http://playgroundsafety.org

National Safety Council **www.nsc.org**

Teachers Resisting Unhealthy Children's Entertainment
www.truceteachers.org

Zero to Three **www.zerotothree.org**

🖲 The Education CourseMate website for this text offers many helpful resources and interactive study tools. Go to CengageBrain.com to access the TeachSource Videos, flashcards, tutorial quizzes, direct links to all of the websites mentioned in the chapter, downloadable forms, and more.

References

Brault, L. (2009). *Inclusion works! Creating child care programs that promote belonging for children with special needs.* Sacramento, CA: Child Development Division of California Department of Education.

Caldwell, L. (2011). Thinking about the environment: I nspirations from the Reggion approach. In A. Gordon & K. W. Browne, *Beginnings and beyond* (8th Ed). Clifton Park, NY: Thomson Delmar Learning.

Carter, M., & Curtis, D. (2003). *Designs for living and learning: Transforming early childhood environments.* St. Paul, MN: Redleaf Press.

Centers for Disease Control and Prevention. (2011). *The ABCs of raising safe and healthy kids.* Atlanta, GA: Author.

Community Products, LLC. (2008). *Children come first: Selecting equipment for early childhood education.* Rifton, NY.

Consumer Product Safety Commission. (2009). *Public playground safety checklist, CPSC Document #327.* Washington, D.C.: Author.

Conventry, A. (2011). Creating a calming environment in a preschool setting. http://www.brighthub.com/education/early-childhood/articles/65480.aspx. Accessed June 1, 2011.

Copple, C., & Bredekamp, S. (Eds.). (2009). *Developmentally appropriate practice in early childhood programs serving children from birth through age 8* (3rd Ed.). Washington, D.C.: National Association for the Education of Young Children.

de Melendez, R. W., & Ostertag, V. (2012). *Teaching young children in multicultural classrooms* (4th Ed.). Clifton Park, NY: Thomson Delmar Learning.

Derman-Sparks, L., and Olson Edwards, J. (2010). *Anti-bias education for young children and ourselves.* Washington, D.C.: NAEYC.

Deviney, J., Duncan, S., Harris, S., & Rody, M. A. (2010). *Inspiring spaces for young children.* Lewisville, NC: Gryphon House.

Froschl, M., Rubin, E., & Sprung, B. (1984). *Including all of us: An early childhood curriculum about disabilities.* New York: Educational Equity Concepts.

Greenman, J. (2000). What is the setting? Places for childhood. In A. Gordon & K. W. Browne, *Beginnings and beyond* (5th Ed). Clifton Park, NY: Thomson Delmar Learning.

Gutierrez, M. E. (1982). *Chicano parents' perceptions of their children's racial/cultural awareness.* Unpublished master's thesis, Pacific Oaks College, Pasadena, CA.

Guyton, G. (2011, September). Using toys to support infant-toddler learning and development. *Young Children, 66*(5), 50–56.

Harms, T., Clifford, R. M., & Cryer, D. (2005–2009). *The early childhood (revised), family day care, infant/toddler, and school age environmental rating scales.* New York: Teachers College Press.

Heroman, C., Dodge, D. T., Berke, K-L., & Bickart, T. (2010). *The Creative Curriculum® for preschool* (5th Ed). Washington, D.C.: Teaching Strategies.

Heroman, C., & Copple, C. (2006) Teaching in the kindergarten year. In D. F. Gullo (Ed.), *Teaching and learning in the kindergarten year.* Washington, D.C.: NAEYC, 59–72.

Howes, C., Phillips, D., & Whitebook, M. (1992). Thresholds of quality: Implications for the social development of children in center-based care. *Child Development, 63*(4), 449–460.

Hyson, M. (2008) *Enthusiastic and engaged learners: Approaches to learning in the early childhood classroom.* NY: Teachers College Press.

Jalongo, M. R. (2008). Editorial: Enriching the Brain— The link between contemporary neuroscience and early childhood traditions. *Early Childhood Education Journal, 35,* pp. 487–488.

Jones, E. (1984). *Personal notes about pluralistic and developmental viewpoints.* Unpublished.

Kendall, F. (1996). *Diversity in the classroom* (2nd Ed). New York: Teachers College Press.

Marotz, L. (2009). *Health, safety, and nutrition for the young child* (7th Ed). Clifton Park, NY: Thomson Delmar Learning.

Marshall, J. (2011, May). Infant neurosensory development: Considerations for Infant child care. *Early Childhood Education Journal, 39,* pp. 175–181.

National After-School Association (NAA). (2011). National School-Age Care Alliance Core Knowledge and Competencies for After-School and Youth Development Professionals. http://www.naaweb .org.

National Association for the Education of Young Children. (2005). *Position statement: Code of ethical conduct* (Appendix A is the entire text of the Code). Washington, D.C.: Author.

National Institute for Early Education Research. (December/January, 2006). Blueprint for new

research: Classroom design and achievement. Volume 4, No. 1: 3.

Navarre Johnson, L. (2011). The interpersonal environment. Unpublished paper.

Needlman, R., & Needlman, G. (1995, November/ December). Ten most common health problems in school. *Scholastic Early Childhood Today.*

Olds, A. (1989). Psychological and physiological harmony in the child care center design. *Children's Environments Quarterly,* (6)4, p. 13.

Prescott, E., Jones, E., & Kritschevsky, S. (1972). *Group care as a child-rearing environment.* Washington, D.C.: National Association for the Education of Young Children.

Ritchie, S., & Willer, B. (2008). *Accreditation performance criteria (revised).* Washington, D.C.: National Association for the Education of Young Children.

Rogers, C. (1994, Spring). *Mainstreaming: Special needs—Special experiences.* Unpublished paper.

Rushton, S., Joula-Rushton, A., & Larkin, E. (2010). Neuroscience, play, and early childhood education: Connections, implications and assessment. *Early Childhood Education Journal, 37,* pp. 351–361.

Teachers Resisting Unhealthy Children's Entertainment (TRUCE). (2011-2012). *Toys and toy trends to avoid.* West Somerville, MA: Author.

Waldorf School (author unknown). (1995, January). *What is a Waldorf kindergarten?* Los Altos, CA: Author.

Wurm, J. (2009). *Working in the Reggio way.* Redmond, WA: Redleaf Press.

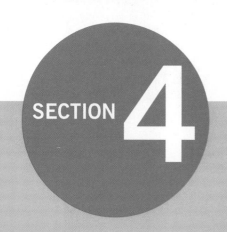

What Is Being Taught?

© Cengage Learning

VPG/ Toddlers/Cengage Learning

10

Curriculum: Creating a Context for Learning and Play

Learning Objectives

LO1 Demonstrate knowledge and understanding of the framework for creating curriculum that is developmentally and culturally appropriate, and identify essential elements that engage children of all ages and abilities to learn on many levels.

LO2 Articulate the relationship between play-based curriculum and the development of skills, knowledge, and learning.

LO3 Describe techniques that foster development and learning, including written curriculum plans, and how they are supported through learning standards, goal setting, and teacher-directed activities.

LO4 Investigate curriculum models that support play-based learning and describe their specific strengths and characteristics.

naeyc Standards For Professional Development

The following NAEYC Standards For Initial and Advanced Early Childhood Professional Preparation are addressed in this chapter:

Standard 1 Promoting Child Development and Learning

Standard 2 Building Family and Community Relationships

Standard 3 Observing, Documenting, and Assessing to Support Young Children and Families

Standard 4 Using Developmentally Effective Approaches to Connect Children With Families

Standard 5 Using Content Knowledge to Build Meaningful Curriculum

Standard 6 Becoming a Professional

Field Experience

naeyc Code of Ethical Conduct

These are the sections of the NAEYC Code of Ethical Conduct that apply to the topics of this chapter:

I-1.2 To base program practices upon current knowledge and research in the field of early childhood education, child development, and related disciplines, as well as on particular knowledge of each child.

1-1.3 To recognize and respect the unique qualities, abilities, and potential of each child.

1-1.10 To ensure that each child's culture, language, ethnicity, and family structure are recognized and valued in the program.

1-1.8 To support the right of each child to play and learn in an inclusive environment that meets the needs of children with and without disabilities.

I.4.1 To provide the community with high quality early childhood care and education programs and services.

Curriculum: The Framework for Teaching and Learning

Ira, a 2-year-old, is more interested in the process of pouring milk (especially what happens after the cup is filled) than in eating and conversing at snack time.

Kindergartners Bert and Leo become absorbed in watching a snail make its way across the sidewalk, ignoring for the moment the lesson on running relays. Each of these children are involved in the curriculum of an early childhood program.

What Is Curriculum?

In an early childhood setting, the curriculum consists of the art activity and language game; it is also the spontaneous investigation of pouring liquids at snack time, the song that accompanies digging in the sand, and the teacher's explanation of why the hamster died. Young children absorb everything going on about them. They do not discriminate between what is prepared and structured for them to learn and whatever else happens to them at school. It is *all* learning.

The **curriculum** is the framework around which planned and unplanned activities and lessons are created. The process of creating curriculum includes how, when, where, and why an activity or subject is being taught. Creating a good curriculum for young children is not simply a matter of writing lessons plans. It is understanding the process of how children interact with people and materials to learn. It is the sum of a teacher's knowledge about children's needs, materials, and equipment and what happens when they meet.

Curriculum must also be relevant to the child. Head Start classes on Native American reservations develop curricula that represent the history and traditions of the tribes the students represent. Relevant curriculum for a preschool in Seattle may include field trips to the Pike Street Market to see the recent salmon catch, whereas a transportation unit for inner city Boston children may include subway rides.

Developmentally Appropriate Curriculum

Appropriate early childhood curriculum is based on the theory, research, and experience of knowing how young children develop and learn. As noted in Chapter 2, developmentally appropriate programs, curricula, or practices

Children respond to curriculum materials that are inviting and accessible.

Courtesy of the author

are defined by NAEYC (Copple & Bredekamp, 2009) as having the following core considerations:

- What is known about child development and learning of a particular age group so that the curriculum has appropriate experiences and learning activities to help children achieve and to challenge them.
- What is known about each individual child, the individual rate of growth, and the unique learning style so that the curriculum will reflect their needs, interests, and preferences.
- What is known about the social and cultural context of each child so that the curriculum provides meaningful and relevant learning experiences that are respectful of the backgrounds of the children and families in the group. The foundation for **developmentally appropriate practices (DAP)** and curriculum content is historically rooted in John Dewey's vision that schools prepare students to think and reason in order to participate in a democratic society (see Chapter 1). Figure 10-1 lists recommendations jointly endorsed by the National Association for the Education of Young Children and the National Association of Early Childhood Specialists in State Departments of Education to

Recommendations for Developmentally Appropriate Curriculum

NAEYC and the National Association of Early Childhood Specialists in State Departments of Education recommend implementing curriculum that is thoughtfully planned, challenging, engaging, developmentally appropriate, culturally and linguistically responsive, comprehensive, and likely to promote positive outcomes for all young children. The indicators of effectiveness for developing curriculum are:

- *Children are active and engaged.* Children of all ages and abilities can become interested and engaged, develop positive attitudes toward learning, and be supported in their feelings of security, emotional competence, and links to family and community.
- *Goals are clear and shared by all.* Curriculum goals are clearly defined, shared, and understood by program administrators, teachers, and families. The curriculum, activities, and teaching strategies are designed to help achieve the goals in a unified, coherent way.
- *Curriculum is evidence-based.* The curriculum is based on evidence that is developmentally, culturally, and linguistically relevant for each group of children and is organized around principles of child development and learning.
- *Valued content is learned through investigation, play, and focused, intentional teaching.* Children learn by exploring, thinking about, and inquiring about all sorts of things that are connected to later learning. Teaching strategies are tailored to children's ages, developmental capabilities, language and culture, and abilities or disabilities.
- *Curriculum builds on prior learning and experience.* The content and implementation builds on children's prior individual, age-related, and cultural learning, is inclusive of all children, and is supportive of the knowledge learned at home and in the community. The curriculum supports children whose home language is not English by building a base for later learning.
- *Curriculum is comprehensive.* All developmental domains are included in the curriculum, such as physical well-being and motor development, social and emotional development, language development, and cognition and general knowledge. Subject matter areas are included, such as science, mathematics, language, literacy, social studies, and the arts.
- *Professional standards validate the curriculum's subject-matter content.* Curriculum meets the standards of relevant professional organizations (for instance, The American Alliance for Health, Physical Education, Recreation and Dance, The National Council of Teachers of English, The National Science Teachers Association) and are reviewed so they fit together coherently.
- *Curriculum is likely to benefit children.* Research indicates that the curriculum, if implemented as intended, will likely have beneficial effects. These benefits include a wide range of outcomes.

FIGURE 10-1 NAEYC & NAECS/SDE (National Association of Early Childhood Specialists in State Departments of Education). 2003. *Early childhood curriculum, assessment, and program evaluation: Building an effective accountable system in programs for children birth through age 8.* Washington, D.C.: National Association for the Education of Young Children.

ensure developmentally appropriate curriculum. It can be used as a checklist as you move through the next three chapters, which focus on curriculum.

Culturally Appropriate Curriculum

If meaningful learning is derived from a social and cultural context (as Vygotsky asserts), then a multicultural atmosphere must be created in which awareness and concern for true diversity (including ethnicity, gender, and abilities) permeate the program. Multicultural education is about providing equal opportunities for all groups of students.

Culturally appropriate curriculum is also developmentally appropriate curriculum. The challenge is to

develop a curriculum that reflects the plurality of contemporary American society in general and the individual classroom, in particular, and present it in sensitive, relevant ways.

Figure 10-2 highlights the differences between creating curriculum from a Eurocentric or dominant culture point of view and from a transformative curriculum approach.

Effective Curriculum: Five Basic Elements

Effective curriculum consists of any number of factors. Five important features of curriculum are that it is 1) inclusive, 2) integrated, 3) emergent, 4) based on multiple

DIVERSITY

Transformative Curriculum

Creating a truly multicultural classroom calls into question the familiar ways of doing things and provides new insights and ways of thinking about culture. Banks (2006) describes this approach as **transformative curriculum**.

Transformative curriculum helps teachers develop critical thinking skills so that they question some of the opinions and images of people and cultures that are represented in the Eurocentric curriculum that dominates American schools. For instance, this approach encourages teachers to look at Christopher Columbus from the perspective of a Native American Indian before creating a curriculum about Thanksgiving, the pilgrim, or Native Americans. Transformation curriculum is a way to help develop more positive attitudes toward all racial, ethnic, and cultural groups.

The common practice in many early childhood programs of cooking ethnic foods or celebrating ethnic or cultural holidays as isolated experiences often trivializes or stereotypes groups of people. Folk tales, songs, food, and dress are symbols and expressions of a culture, not the culture itself. For children to gain any meaningful knowledge, the content must contribute to a fuller understanding of human diversity, not just a special occasion topic. Including diverse food, music, and clothing are important artifacts in the curriculum only when they expand a concept of diversity and serve as a link to discuss other aspects of a culture. Songs and dances of one culture could lead to a discussion of what games children play in different parts of the world.

Characteristics of a Multicultural Classroom

Common Practices of Dominant Culture	For a Multicultural Approach
Focuses on isolated aspects of the histories and cultures of ethnic groups	Describes the history and cultures of ethnic groups **holistically**
Trivializes the histories and cultures of ethnic groups	Describes the cultures of ethnic groups as dynamic wholes
Presents events, issues, and concepts primarily from Anglocentric and mainstream perspectives	Presents events, issues, concepts from the perspectives of diverse racial and ethnic groups
Is Eurocentric—shows the development of the United States primarily as an extension of Europe into the Americas	Is multidimensional and geocultural—shows how many peoples and cultures came to the United States from many parts of the world, including Asia and Africa, and the important roles they played in the development of U.S. society
Content about ethnic groups is an appendage to regular curriculum	Content about ethnic groups is an integral part of regular curriculum
Ethnic minority cultures are described as deprived or dysfunctional	Ethnic minority cultures are described as different from mainstream Anglo culture but as rich and functional
Focuses on ethnic heroes, holidays, and factual information	Focuses on concepts, generalizations, and theories
Emphasizes the mastery of knowledge and cognitive outcomes	Emphasizes knowledge formation and decision making
Encourages acceptance of existing ethnic, class, and racial stratification	Focuses on social criticism and social change

FIGURE 10-2 A comparison of two different approaches to multicultural curriculum, one from a Eurocentric point of view, the other from a culturally sensitive perspective. (Reprinted with permission of James A. Banks from James A. Banks, 2006, *Cultural diversity and education: foundations, curriculum, and teaching*, 5th Edition, Boston: Pearson Allyn and Bacon, page 238.)

intelligences, and 5) bears in mind differences in learning styles. With these in mind, the curriculum becomes more flexible and suited to all children in the class.

Inclusive Curriculum

Inclusive curriculum challenges teachers to provide opportunities for all children, regardless of gender, abilities, disabilities, language, culture, ethnicity, and religion. The activities and materials are chosen to enhance the potential of each child and are reflective of the diversity and abilities within the classroom. All activities are adjustable to a wide range of skills and abilities; are flexible enough to accommodate the needs of each child; and are ones in which children can participate at their developmental level, yet be challenged enough to help them learn. Chapters 3, 9, 10, and 11 have further information on inclusive classrooms.

Integrated Curriculum

The *whole child* approach that you learned about in Chapter 3 makes the point that interaction and relationship of the developmental domains are interconnected and work together to help children find meaning in and mastery of their world.

Developmentally appropriate materials fit the abilities of all children.

© Cengage Learning

Think of integrated curriculum in the same way because it weaves across many subject areas throughout the school day so that skills and concepts are developed in the context of other learning. Subjects such as math, science, reading, writing, and social studies are planned components of the daily curriculum and not taught as separate topics. An integrated curriculum makes it possible for teachers to include skill development activities in context, not in isolation. For instance, tracing square shapes in the Writing Center and cutting out squares with scissors can expand the concept of a square. A book about shapes shows squares in many configurations to make a picture; and in the Block Center, fences and building are constructed in square shapes. In this way, each activity center supports the concept of squares in different ways. The guidelines for developmentally appropriate curriculum found in Figure 10-1 contain many of the characteristics of an integrated curriculum.

It is easy to see how an integrated curriculum works. Experiencing a concept in a variety of contexts is a natural rather than a contrived way for children to learn. Unit blocks, a staple in most early childhood programs, are a good example of how much learning potential is available in one activity, as noted in the DAP Box.

An integrated curriculum supports developmentally appropriate learning by fostering children's wide range of abilities, skills, and knowledge and allowing them to proceed at their own level of development in meaningful activity.

Emergent Curriculum

Emergent curriculum is just what it says: curriculum that comes from or slowly evolves out of the child's experiences and interests. The emphasis is on children's interests, their involvement in their learning, and their ability to make constructive choices. Teachers set up materials and equipment in the room and the yard, sometimes planning a few activities each day that capture children's attention. For the most part, teachers then watch and evaluate what children do and support and extend what use children make of their experiences.

The curriculum begins with the children rather than with the teacher, who observes what children do, how they play, and what captures their interest and imagination. The point is to deepen and extend children's learning as they discover meaning and understanding in their play. The following example shows how emergent curriculum can be developed by following the children's lead.

Taking Cues from Children   A lively group time discussion one day in the 4-year-old classes involved a new bridge that was being built near the school. The teachers had noticed

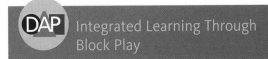

Integrated Learning Through Block Play

DAP includes engaging all of the developmental domains of the whole child. Social, emotional, cognitive, physical, language, and creative areas are drawn into action during block play. The significance of what children learn while building with blocks cannot be underestimated.

While playing with blocks, children learn about many concepts.

- *Science:* weight, gravity, balance, stability, height, inclines, ramps, interaction of forces
- *Mathematics:* classification, order, number, fractions, depth, width, height, length, fractions, size relationships, volume, area, measurement, shape, size, space, mapping
- *Social Studies:* symbolic representation, mapping, grids, patterns, people and their work
- *Art:* patterns, symmetry, balance, design, texture, creativity, drawing
- *Language:* making comparisons, recognition of shapes and sizes, labeling, giving directions, communicating ideas and needs, writing and drawing plans, using books as resources
- *Physical Development:* eye-hand coordination, clean up, hand manipulation, fine motor, visual perception
- *Social Development:* cooperation, sharing, clean up, conflict resolution, negotiation, respect for the work of others
- *Cognitive:* planning, naming, differentiation of sizes, shapes, inductive thinking, discovery

It is easy to see why one teacher has called block play "the perfect curriculum: It has everything children need to learn!"

What math and science concepts did the 4-year-olds use while creating this block building?

Courtesy of the author

that the block area had sat unused during the week, so they added books on bridges, paper, crayons, and scissors to the shelves near the blocks and put up pictures of different kinds of bridges. These additions drew children to the block area where they built bridges, made paper bridges, and counted the number of different kinds of bridges that were in the books nearby. Further conversations between the children and the teachers led to a woodworking project to create wooden bridges. Songs and poems about bridges became a routine part of circle time. Outdoors, the sand pit became a waterway with bridges and was soon followed by projects with boats and other water transportation. The curriculum content in this example is apparent, but an end product is not the focus. It is an example of integrated curriculum as well as emergent curriculum because the process children go through in creating knowledge through the

extension of bridge play fosters new insights and learning. The focus is on the child, not on the activity.

This practice of taking cues from children—noting what they play with, what they avoid, what they change—is one of the components of emergent curriculum and stems from the belief that in order to be a meaningful learning experience, the curriculum should come out of the daily life in the classroom. Based on the principles of Erikson, Piaget, and Vygotsky, emergent curriculum assumes that children are active, curious learners, capable of taking the initiative and constructing their knowledge through experience. Children are encouraged to use whatever style of learning is most natural to them, making use of the variety of materials in their own way. A materials-rich environment in which play is valued forms the foundation for the curriculum. For example,

- Anton, a first grader, noticed how dark the sky was as he and his classmates waited for the school bus to take him home. His teacher responded that the days were shorter in winter, so there was less daylight. The children began to ask questions about how this happened. The next morning many of the Activity Centers had materials for exploring light/dark;

charts for tracking the changes of light to dark; and a new outdoor thermometer. Over the next few months, children were immersed in the seasonal changes that occurred outside their windows.

- Four new babies were born to families with children in the 3-year-old class. The dramatic play area teemed with dolls, blankets, bottles, and baby beds. As the children talked about their new siblings, the teachers posed questions about the care and feeding of a newborn and how different it is from what the 3-year-olds ate. Children were asked to bring in pictures of themselves as babies and created a collage that was hung on the wall near the dramatic play area. During music, the children moved like babies and, outside, the wagons became baby carriages. As long as their interest held, the curriculum was deepened and extended.

In each instance, the curriculum followed the children's curiosity and became more complex in order to maintain their interests and learning potential. The teacher's role was to be a co-creator with the children to ensure that learning goals and objectives were met.

Planning emergent curriculum requires good observation and listening skills and the ability to interpret children's play. Webbing, which is discussed later in the chapter, is a good way to clarify with children what they know and what ideas they have for further exploration. Webbing also helps integrate the activity to include all learning domains.

Fostering Collaboration and Mutual Learning The emergent curriculum calls for collaboration on the part of the teachers with children and on the part of children with other children and with adults who offer suggestions and ideas. When children work collaboratively, they help each other succeed as well as to negotiate and solve problems together.

The accent is on mutual learning for both children and adults. For example, when the first grade class took a subway to the museum, this prompted a great many questions about subways and how they work. Because of the children's interest and the teacher's awareness of their developmental and educational needs, a project emerged and was developed over the next few weeks. Teachers learned more about what the students wanted to know about subways, so they could facilitate the children's learning and define the goals and objectives. The children helped plan the project. They asked questions; investigated; researched; explored; and, with the teacher's support and encouragement, formed small groups and completed assigned tasks. Books became an important

resource, as did people. The teacher, knowing what the children needed and were ready to learn, guided the discussion to ensure that educational goals would be met.

For emergent curriculum to be successful, teachers listen and observe carefully as children generate new ideas and then respond to what they hear and see that children have learned. Many observations methods were described in Chapter 6 and are appropriate ways to find ways and materials to advance and deepen what children learn. While emergent curriculum calls for collaboration and negotiation between children and teachers, it is the teacher who knows what is necessary for children's education and development and sets the goals for learning.

Finding Curriculum Ideas   Children are only one of many sources of curriculum possibilities. A number of other sources feed into emergent curriculum, as noted by Jones (1994) in her classic work on emergent curriculum:

- Teachers' and parents' interests and skills
- Developmental tasks of the age group
- The physical and natural environment as well as people and things
- Curriculum resource books
- Family and cultural influences
- Serendipity or the unexpected
- Daily issues of living together, problem solving, conflict resolution, routines
- Values expressed by the school philosophy, the families, and the community

Emergent curriculum seems to capture the spontaneous nature of children's play and blend it with the necessary planning and organization. In the discussion of curricular models that follows in this chapter, you see that emergent curriculum has many applications.

TeachSource Video

Watch the TeachSource Video entitled "School Age: Emergent Curriculum." After you view the clip, reflect on the following questions:

1. What would you do to further the "cloud" discussion?

2. Describe the teachers' conversation regarding the weather. How would you have added to that conversation with regard to extending the children's interest?

3. How would you rate the teachers' planning process? Why?

Multiple Intelligences

In Chapter 4, you read about Gardner's theory of multiple intelligences (MI). According to this theory, children are capable of distinct categories of intelligence. That is, they have many different ways of knowing or of being "smart." Refresh your memory by reviewing Chapter 4. The potential for developing the various intelligences is based on the child's experience, culture, and motivation. The following is a summary of this theory (adapted from Armstrong, 2000 and The New City School, 1994). The MI categories with examples are:

1. *Linguistic Intelligence.* Sensitivity to the sounds, structure, meanings, and functions of words and language.

    Example: Children who enjoy word games, understand jokes, puns, and riddles, and enjoy the sounds and rhythms of language. They have a good vocabulary, spell easily, memorize readily, and are good storytellers.

    Examples: Adults such as Maya Angelou, Amy Tan, Martin Luther King, Jr.

2. *Logical-Mathematical.* Sensitivity to and capacity to discern logical or numerical patterns; ability to handle long chains of reasoning.

    Example: Children who notice and use numbers, patterns, and shapes and explore the relationships in them; they have a systematic approach to problem solving and organize their thoughts well. They think conceptually and are able to move easily from the concrete to the abstract. They like puzzles and computer games.

Logical-mathematical intelligence.

Examples: Adults such as Stephen Hawking, Madame Marie Curie, Bill Gates

3. *Spatial.* Capacity to perceive the visual-spatial world accurately and to perform transformations on one's initial perceptions.

    Example: Children who like to draw, build, design, and create things. They enjoy patterns and geometry in math as well as maps and charts. They think in three-dimensional terms and enjoy color as well as design. They love videos and photos.

Linguistic intelligence.

Spatial intelligence.

Examples: Adults such as I.M. Pei, Maria Martinez, Frank Lloyd Wright

4. **Bodily-Kinesthetic.** Ability to control one's body movements and to handle objects skillfully.

Example: Children who are agile, coordinated, have good body control and who take in information through bodily sensations. They are hands-on learners with good motor skills. They like to touch things, run, and use body language.

Examples: Adults such as Jackie Joyner-Kersee, Marcel Marceau, Kristi Yamaguchi

5. **Musical.** Ability to produce and appreciate rhythm, pitch, and timbre; appreciation of the forms of musical expressiveness.

Example: Children who like to sing, dance, hum, play instruments, and move their bodies when music is playing. They remember melodies, are able to keep and imitate a beat, make up their own songs, and notice background and environmental sounds. They enjoy listening and differentiating patterns in sounds and are sensitive to melody and tone.

Examples: Adults such as Stevie Wonder, Carrie Underwood, and Yo-Yo Ma

6. **Interpersonal.** Capacity to discern and respond to the moods, temperaments, motivations, and desires of other people.

Example: Children who have a lot of friends, who like to talk, who prefer group problem solving, and can mediate conflicts; who like to hear someone else's point of view; who volunteer to help when others need it.

Examples: Adults such as Marion Wright Edelman, Mother Teresa

Musical intelligence.

Bodily-kinesthetic intelligence.

Interpersonal intelligence.

7. ***Intrapersonal***. Access to one's own feelings and the ability to discriminate among one's emotions; knowledge of one's own strengths and weaknesses.

   Example: Children who pursue personal interests and set goals; who identify and label feelings; are insightful, sensitive, reflective, intuitive; who may daydream and are comfortable being alone. They know their own strengths and weaknesses.

   Examples: Adults such as Sigmund Freud, the Buddha, Maria Montessori

8. ***Naturalist***. Expertise in distinguishing among members of a species; recognizing the existence of other neighboring species; and charting out the relations, formally or informally, among several species.

   Example: Children who enjoy all the features of the outdoor world. They recognize and classify plants, animals, rocks, clouds, and other natural formations; they garden and like to have animals at home and school to care for. They enjoy zoos, aquariums, and places where the natural world is on display and can be studied.

   Examples: Adults such as John Muir, Jane Goodall, George Washington Carver

9. ***Existential***. Individuals who think about the deeper aspects of life: questions such as the infinite or unexplained phenomenon and people who are drawn

Naturalist intelligence.

to issues of life and death, morality, and other matters of the spirit.

   Examples: Children who ask questions about God, death, and war, and who raise questions about the ethics or "rightness" of a situation or discussion.

   Examples: Adults such as Billy Graham, Bishop Desmond Tutu and other Nobel Peace Prize winners, Joan of Arc.

In a classroom it is easy to notice the different strengths children have in the MI categories. Some children excel at puzzles and manipulative games while others are busy dictating stories, building a boatyard with blocks, or holding the guinea pig. There are children who cannot be still for very long and need to be actively and physically involved in play and work for much of the day. We all have the capacities for the categories of MI, but we are not equally proficient in all of them.

Through a wide variety of meaningful learning experiences, children's strengths (and primary intelligences) can be assessed, and curriculum can be developed that fosters new knowledge and thinking. Jmel is strong in spatial intelligence, and that can serve as a context for other learning in different intelligence categories. Her intrapersonal and linguistic intelligences can be encouraged through activities that include her telling or writing stories about something she drew and what it means to her. Bodily-kinesthetic and music abilities can emerge through dancing and moving the body through space in different ways. This allows Jmel to experience and reinforce her own strengths and increase her strengths in other areas as well.

The relationship of curriculum based on MI to integrated curriculum is fairly clear from the example of Jmel and from Figure 10-4. If children have different ways of knowing, they should experience a concept, lesson, or subject matter in a variety of ways. As teachers

Intrapersonal intelligence.

Sounds of the City

Multiple Intelligences Context: Students from diverse communities need to develop an awareness and appreciation for the unique nature of the urban environment.

Learner Outcomes: Student will recognize the sounds of the city.

Procedure

1. Elicit from students the sounds that are unique to an urban area and list these sounds on chart paper. Show pictures of different urban settings to enhance the activity. Some sounds that might be included in this list are airplanes, traffic, emergency sirens, and street vendors.

2. Have students record city sounds on their empty playground if the school is located in an urban area. For homework, they could record city sounds from their neighborhoods or from the television.

3. Instruct the students to create a rhythm chant based on the sound word list created earlier, and use the taped examples to enhance the mood of the chants. Percussion instruments may be used to accompany portions of the chants. Students perform their musical numbers for the class.

Materials

Pictures of city scenes, tape recorders, cassette tapes, percussion instruments, chart paper, markers

Assessment/Reflection

Are the students able to identify urban sounds? How are the sounds the students collected from the various locations the same and different? What generalizations are the students able to make from this information?

Multiple Intelligences Extensions

Interpersonal: Help the students develop an awareness of how these city sounds affect their relationships with others.

Intrapersonal: How do city sounds affect moods?

Bodily-Kinesthetic: Use movement to complement the compositions.

Linguistic: Read *Apt. 3* by Ezra Jack Keats. List all the sounds that are heard within the story and who made those sounds. Use the sound hints to determine who lives on each floor.

Logical-Mathematical: Collect data on the number of times specific sounds can be heard within a community. Interview people and graph their reactions to these sounds. Propose a hypothesis as to how the frequency of sounds might affect the lives of the people they interviewed.

Spatial: Create cityscape murals that capture the city and its sounds.

A practical guide created by the faculty of The New City School © 1994

FIGURE 10-3 Planning curriculum around Multiple Intelligences. (From *Celebrating multiple intelligences: Teaching for success* [paper] by the faculty of the New City School. Copyright © 1994 New City School. Reprinted by permission.)

and caregivers expand their own thinking about children's abilities, they can vary what and how they teach and teach to many intelligences and developmental areas instead of just one. An integrated MI curriculum makes it possible to involve many intelligences in a wide range of activities and enable more children to succeed by drawing on their own capacities to learn. The lesson plan in Figure 10-3 is a good example of planning curriculum with an MI emphasis.

Gardner (Woolfolk, 2001) has written about the good uses of MI theory when it is applied to teaching. "Schools should cultivate those skills and capabilities that are valued in the community and the broader society," he says, and, "At the heart of the MI perspective—in theory and in practice—[is] taking human difference seriously." In both comments, Gardner affirms criteria for DAP.

Multiple Intelligences are also discussed in Chapter 4 and Chapter 12.

Learning Styles

Some people like going to lectures to learn about a new culture or country. Others prefer to watch a travelogue. Still others get the most out of traveling to that country and living among its people, eating the food, absorbing the atmosphere. Each of these is a legitimate method of learning and processing information, and each indicates the preferred style of that particular person. In Chapter 3, the discussion was about **learning styles** related to differences in children's behavior. In this chapter, we focus on how basic learning styles affect curriculum planning. These are the preferred mode of each child but not the only method by which the child can integrate knowledge.

Sensory Style

1. *The Visual Learner.* These are children who prefer pictures to words; photos, charts, and graphs provide the necessary clues; they like to represent their

learning by reading, writing, and drawing; the finished product is important.

2. *The Auditory Learner.* These are children who listen to others to learn and speak and discuss what they are learning. They are good at following directions in the appropriate sequence from one task to another.

3. *The Tactile-Kinesthetic Learner.* These children are active, full-body learners; they need hands-on activity and learn by doing, not listening or sitting still.

These modalities are the favored ways children learn through the use of their five senses. It seems clear that an integrated, emergent curriculum would be easily adaptable to all three learning modes. In fact, most early childhood experiences are heavily weighted toward the development of the five senses that provide many opportunities for children to learn through their preferred style.

Field Dependent/Independent Learning Style The two facets of this model, with examples (McNeely, 1997; Ramirez & Casteñada, 1974), are:

Field Dependent Learning Style (FD). These children are able to grasp broad distinctions among concepts, and they see relationships through a social context, working with others to achieve a common goal. They learn best through material that is related to their own experiences. FD learners are more person-oriented in their play and engage in social interactions sometimes for the sake of the interaction itself. They often use social conflict to make a social contact. They learn concepts through watching others, and their learning is reinforced by rewards such as verbal praise, helping the teacher, and showing the task to others. They depend on authority, seek guidance and demonstration from teachers, and need to have the performance objectives of the curriculum carefully explained.

Field Independent Learning Style (FI). These children look at things analytically, creating their own structure, and learn things for their own sake. They prefer self-defined goals and reinforcements and are motivated through competition and their own values and are more assertive than FD learners. FI learners prefer to work independently, and rarely seek physical contact with teachers; they are more idea-oriented than people-oriented. They like to try out new tasks without help. These children like the details of concepts because they find meaning in the various parts. They focus on the materials and their uses; social interactions are not as important to them.

A Teacher Provides Opportunities for:

Field Dependent Children to:	Field Independent Children to:
• Engage in global thinking	• Engage in analytical thinking
• Follow a given structure	• Generate own structure
• Be externally directed	• Be internally directed
• Attend to social information	• Be inattentive to social information
• Resolve conflict	• Think things through philosophically
• Be social	• Be distant in social relations
• Work with others	• Work alone
• Have friends	• Have acquaintances
• Work with a provided hypothesis	• Generate own hypothesis
• Work with facts	• Work with concepts
• Use others' decisions	• Use own decisions
• Be sensitive to others	• Be insensitive to others
• Use stress for learning	• Ignore external stress for learning

FIGURE 10-4 A teacher must make use of learning styles for field dependence/independence. (Adapted from McNeely, S.L. [1997], *Observing students and teachers through objective strategies.* Boston: Allyn & Bacon, Boston.)

Figure 10-4 suggests some curriculum approaches that work well for these two learning styles.

Play-Based Curriculum: Developing Skills, Knowledge, and Learning

In Chapter 4, you learned about the value and process of children's play. You may want to review that section to refresh your understanding of why play-based curriculum enhances children's potential for learning and is, in fact, the foundation for learning.

The vast knowledge of human development and behavior comes from researchers who spent countless hours observing and recording children playing. As noted by many, from Froebel to Vygotsky to Gardner, children need meaningful materials and activities in order to learn. They need to be physically as well as mentally and emotionally involved in what and how they learn, and they need to play. Through the use of activity centers, a variety of play opportunities that develop skills, knowledge, and learning are available throughout the school day (see Figure 10-5).

The Teacher's Role in Learning Through Play

Classroom teachers learn about children by listening to and observing spontaneous play activity and planning curriculum that encourages play. They discover each child's individual personality, learning style, and preferred mode of play.

Interest and Understanding

Genuine interest is one way teachers show their approval of the play process. Creating a safe environment in which children feel physically and emotionally secure is another. To establish play as an important part of the curriculum, teachers must:

Understand, appreciate, and value play experiences for young children;

Focus on the process of learning rather than on the process of teaching; and

Reflect on their observations in order to know what activities, concepts, or learning should be encouraged or extended.

Erikson (1972), one of the most notable contributors to the field of human development, advises that play has a very personal meaning for each individual. Perhaps the best thing that we as adults can do to discover this meaning is to go out and play; to reflect on our own childhood play; to once again look at play through the eyes of the child.

Involvement in Play

One of the most difficult tasks teachers face is knowing when to join children at play and when to remain outside the activity. They must ask themselves whether their presence supports what is happening or whether it inhibits the play. Sometimes teachers are tempted to correct children's misconceptions during play:

Abby and Salina, deeply involved in their grocery store drama, are making change incorrectly. A teacher must judge whether to explain the difference between nickels and quarters at that time or to create an opportunity at a later date. Teachers must be aware of what happens if they interrupt the flow of play and how they influence the direction it takes. If Abby and Salina begin to talk about their coins, showing an interest in learning how to compute their change, the teacher can move into the discussion without seeming to interfere.

Many adults enjoy playing with the children in their class; others feel more comfortable as active observers. But every teaching situation demands the teacher's involvement at some level. The hesitant child may need help entering a play situation; children may become too embroiled in an argument to settle it alone; play may become inappropriate, exploitative, or dominated by a particular child.

Vygotsky gives us other reasons to be involved with children as they play, particularly in relation to the interpersonal nature of teaching (see Chapter 4). The belief that learning is interpersonal and collaborative is exemplified by the teachers of Reggio Emilia (see Chapters 2 and 5), who guide and support children's learning by engaging in play and knowing what strategy best helps an individual child reach the next level of skill (zone of proximal development). The Reggio Emilia approach to curriculum (discussed at the end of this chapter under "Curriculum Models") finds an appropriate and appealing blend of Vygotsky's concern for individual exploration and assisted discovery.

The teacher's role in facilitating play is about balance: how to allow children the space and time to create their own play while still taking advantage of the teachable moments in which further learning is enhanced. Use the following guidelines to maintain a good balance:

- Guide the play, but do not direct or dominate the situation or overwhelm children by participation.
- Capitalize on the children's thoughts and ideas; do not enforce a point of view on them.
- Model play when necessary; show children how a specific character might act, how to ask for a turn, how to hold a hammer.

Play-Based Curriculum: Enhancing Children's Learning

Cognitive/Language

Distinguishes between reality and fantasy
Encourages creative thought and curiosity
Allows for problem solving
Encourages thinking, planning
Develops memory, perceptual skills, and concept formation
Learns to try on other roles
Acquires knowledge and integrates learning
Learns communication skills
Develops listening and oral language skills

Creative

Fosters use of imagination and make-believe
Encourages flexible thinking and problem solving
Provides opportunity to act upon original ideas
Supports taking risks
Learns to use senses to explore
Re-creates images in buildings and art media
Sharpens observational skills
Provides variety of experiences
Learns to express self in art, music, and dance
Develops abilities to create images and use symbols
Acquires other perspectives

Social

Tries on other personalities, roles
Learns cooperation and taking turns
Learns to lead, follow
Builds a repertoire of social language
Learns to verbalize needs
Reflects own culture, heritage, values
Learns society's rules and group responsibility
Shows respect for others' property, rights
Teaches an awareness of others
Learns how to join a group
Builds awareness of self as member of a group
Gives sense of identification
Promotes self-image, self-esteem
Experiences joy, fun

Physical

Releases energy
Builds fine- and gross-motor skills
Gains control over body

Provides challenges
Requires active use of body
Allows for repetition and practice
Refines eye–hand coordination
Develops self-awareness
Encourages health and fitness

© Cengage Learning

Emotional

Develops self-confidence and self-esteem
Learns to take a different viewpoint
Resolves inner fears, conflicts
Builds trust in self and others
Reveals child's personality
Encourages autonomy
Learns to take risks
Acts out anger, hostility, frustration, joy
Gains self-control
Becomes competent in several areas
Takes initiative

© Cengage Learning 2011

FIGURE 10-5 Play is the cornerstone of learning.

- Ask questions; clarify with the children what is happening.
- Help children start, end, and begin again.
- Give verbal cues to enable children to follow through on an idea.
- Focus children's attention on one another; encourage them to interact with each other.
- Interpret children's behavior aloud when necessary.
- Help children verbalize their feelings as they work through conflicts.
- Expand the play potential by making statements and asking questions that lead to discovery and exploration.

Setting the Stage for Play

Teachers set the stage for learning through play by developing curriculum that includes many forms of play, some of which is spontaneous, some of which is guided and/or directed by the teacher. The environment (physical, temporal, and interpersonal) is a key element in reinforcing a play-based curriculum.

Structuring the Environment

To structure the environment for play, teachers include uninterrupted time blocks in the daily schedule (at least 45 minutes to an hour) for free play time. This allows children to explore many avenues of the curriculum free from time constraints. It is frustrating to young children to have their play cut off just as they are getting deeply involved.

Established routines in the schedule add to the framework of a day planned for play. The raw materials of play—toys, games, and equipment—are changed periodically so that new ones may be introduced for further challenge:

- In choosing materials, teachers select dress-up clothes and accessories that appeal to all children's needs, interests, and emotions.

- Props are required for a variety of roles: men, women, babies, doctors, nurses, grocers, mail carriers, teachers, and firefighters.
- Hats for many occupations help a child establish the role of an airline pilot, tractor driver, construction worker, police officer, or baseball player.
- Large purses are used for carrying mail and babies' diapers; they also double as a briefcase or luggage.
- Simple jackets or capes transform a child for many roles.

Props that represent aspects of the child's daily life are important; children need many opportunities to act out their life stories.

For younger children, teachers make sure there are duplicates of popular materials. Group play is more likely to occur with three telephones, four carriages, eight hats, and five wagons. Social interaction is enhanced when three space shuttle drivers can be at the controls.

Materials that are open-ended further enlarge play. These are materials that expand the children's learning opportunities because they can be used in more than one way. Blocks, a staple of the early childhood curriculum, are a case in point. Children explore and manipulate blocks in many ways. The youngest children carry and stack blocks and also enjoy wheeling them around in wagons or trucks. They also enjoy the repetitious action of making small columns of blocks. Older preschoolers build multistoried structures as part of their **dramatic play**—offices, firehouses, and garages.

Classroom Activity Centers

The **activity centers** in most early childhood programs consist of:

Indoors	*Outdoors*
Creative arts	Climbing equipment
Blocks	Swings
Table toys	Sand/mud/water
Manipulatives	Wheel toys
Science/discovery	Woodworking
Dramatic play	Hollow blocks
Language arts/books	Music
Math	Nature/science
Music	Organized games

All of these centers offer activities and materials for children to choose from during free play time—the greatest portion of their school day. (See typical daily schedules in Chapter 2.) Paints are in the easel trays, puzzles on the tables, dress-up clothes and props in the housekeeping/dramatic play center, blocks and accessories in the block corner, and books and tapes in the language area. Teachers plan the resources and materials and place them so that children readily see the alternatives available to them. Some of these activities might be teacher-directed, such as cooking snacks in the housekeeping area. For the most part, however, these activities are self-initiating and child-directed. At all times, the emphasis is on providing a child-centered curriculum.

Whatever the activity center, it needs attention and planning. Wherever children are present, learning and playing are taking place. Because each play space makes a contribution to children's experiences, teachers should develop appropriate curriculum for that learning area.

Go back and review what Chapter 9 describes as the important principles in creating environments that reflect curriculum goals, and see Chapter 2 for daily schedules.

Just as focusing on the activity or learning centers can develop curriculum, so, too, can an early childhood program be planned around the skill levels of the children in the class. The next three chapters provide a more in-depth identification of the types of skills that children need to learn.

The first decision teachers must make concerns what particular skill they wish to help children develop. The skill can be in the area of physical, cognitive, language, creative, social, or emotional development.

The nature of the individual class and the program philosophy helps teachers establish priorities for these skills. Teachers then select the activities and materials that enhance the development of any one or more of those particular skills. Figure 10-6 shows how the cognitive skill of classification can be implemented in the classroom, making it the focus of the entire curriculum.

The next three chapters provide a more in-depth identification of the types of skills that children need to learn.

Planning Curriculum: Engaging Teaching and Learning

The aim of the curriculum is to help children acquire the skills and behaviors that promote their optimal growth physically, socially, emotionally, and intellectually. Teachers consider a number of factors in developing a curriculum to provide maximum learning opportunities. Among these are the *educational philosophy and goals* of the program. A family child care provider plans activities for a few children in an intimate setting while the kindergarten teacher arranges small working groups so that the large group does not seem overwhelming. The activities

should support the goals of the program and result in the accomplishment of those goals.

Ways to Foster Skills, Knowledge, and Learning

1. The single most important determinant the teacher must consider is *the children themselves*. Their ages, developmental levels, individuality, and learning styles are barometers of what is a successful and stimulating curriculum.

2. The *number* of children in the class affects the teacher's planning as does the number of teachers, aides, and volunteers who help out in the classroom.

3. A **prerequisite** for planning is the *availability of people and material resources* and ways to use them. The strengths of the teaching staff, adequate supplies and equipment, and enough adults to supervise the activities are taken into consideration.

4. The *ethnic and cultural backgrounds* of the children must be taken into consideration. To be effective, curriculum experiences should draw on children's background and cultural experience.

5. Curriculum planning stems from *a knowledge of young children*. Teachers look at how, when, and what concepts children should learn and how they teach those concepts; what the child already knows, and how they can build on that. In many ways, teachers start at the end: They look at children's developmental levels as they focus on what they want the child to accomplish or to learn as a result of this experience and then plan the curriculum to lead toward those results.

6. Planning for a *broad range of developmental skills and interests* is important. Because the abilities of children even of the same age vary, activities must be open-ended and flexible enough to be used by a number of children with varieties of skills. Remember, too, that some children may not be interested in formal or organized art projects or science experiences. These children may learn more easily through self-selected play.

7. The developmental word pictures of children from birth through age 8 found in Chapter 3 can be useful in determining *what kinds of activities appeal* to young children. Activities should be conducted in a variety of modes so that all children can connect with what they need to learn.

8. The *amount of time* available in the daily schedule and *the amount of space* in the room or yard affect a teacher's planning. Finger painting requires time for children to get involved, proximity to water for clean up, and an area in which to store wet paintings.

Developing Classification Skills through Integrated Curriculum

ART: size, shape, texture, color of materials; properties and functions of art materials (e.g., paste or glue).

MUSIC/GAMES: description of music for tempo, volume; description of rules of the game, similarities to and differences from other known games.

BOOKS AND LITERATURE: attributes of size, shape, and color of books; comparison of plot, characters, subject matter.

COOKING: comparison of food by flavor, texture, color, consistency; comparison of food before and after cooking/refrigeration.

GROUP TIME: description of children by hair, eye color, size; comparison of types of shoes, clothing, and closures (e.g., tie, buckle, Velcro, zipper).

GROSS MOTOR: description of speed, method of moving; comparison of distance, height, speed; comparison of wheel and other transportation vehicles.

CLASSIFICATION

BLOCKS: size, shape, weight of blocks; comparisons of curves in blocks (e.g., quarter circle vs. ellipse).

BATHROOMS: descriptions of toilets, sinks, soaps; comparison of size and function with those at home.

MANIPULATIVES: descriptions of size, shape, color, variety of table toys; comparison of uses of materials (puzzles, things for building, things for lacing, things to stack).

DISCOVERY/SCIENCE: description of attributes of animal (e.g., guinea pig has eyes, ears, feet, hair); comparison with other animals; descriptions of sensory materials and how they feel, smell, taste, look.

DRAMATIC PLAY: descriptions of dress-up clothing by size, color, role; comparison of kitchen equipment by what is used for cooking, for eating, for cleaning; comparison of what needs to be in freezer, refrigerator, cabinet.

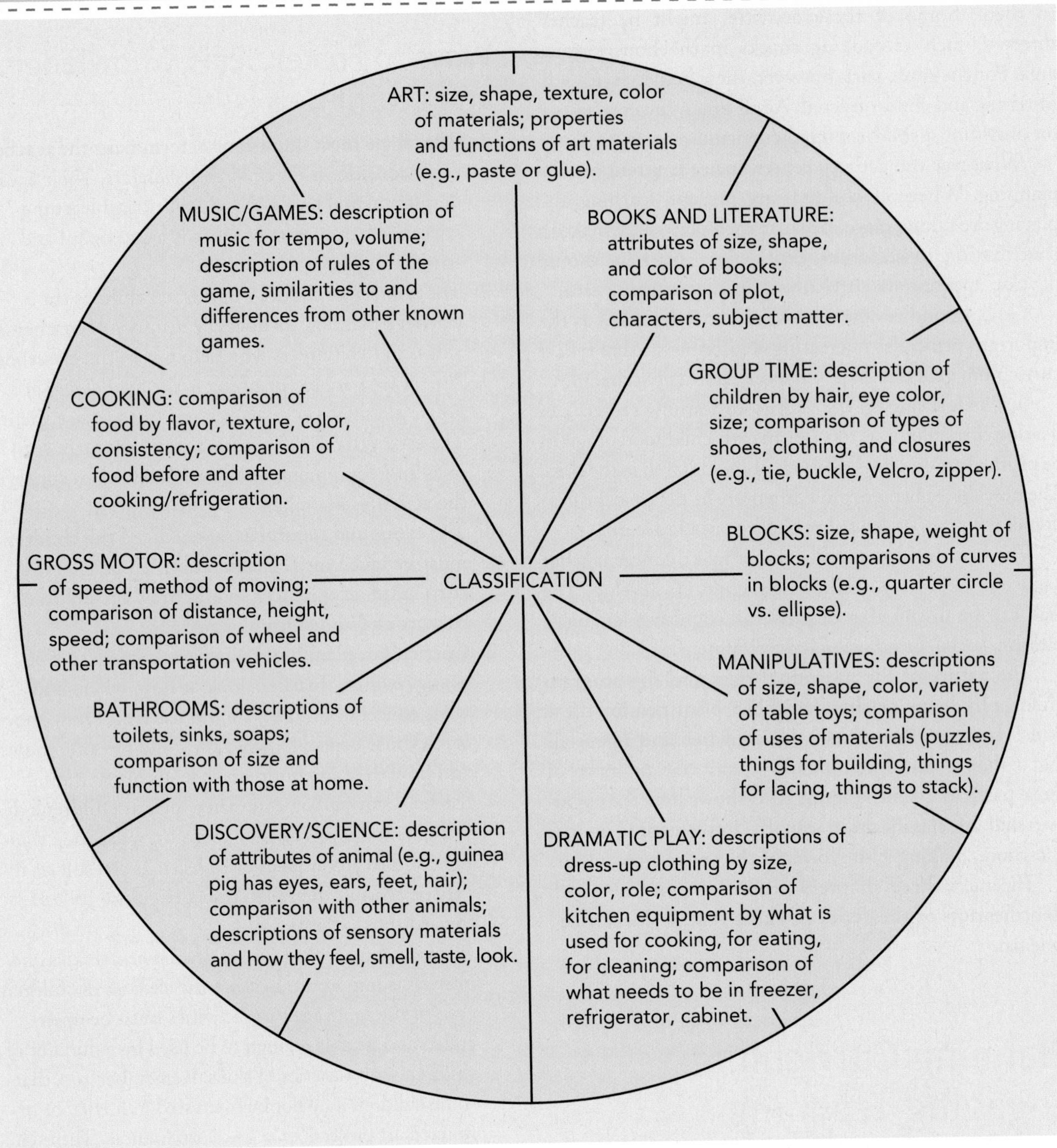

© Cengage Learning 2011

FIGURE 10-6 Curriculum can be developed with a focus on a particular skill. Classification skills can be enhanced throughout the curriculum and in activity centers. Note: This is a graphic way to demonstrate an integrated curriculum, not an example of how to write curriculum plans.

Culturally Responsive Teaching

Positive attitudes toward self and others emerge when children know they are valued for their individuality and appreciated as members of a family and a culture. The school environment can reflect this in a number of ways. Figure 10-7 lists ways in which an early childhood program can use culturally diverse materials on a daily basis to foster the relationship between home culture and school.

Banks (2006) identifies five important characteristics of the effective teacher in a multicultural society. They are teachers who:

1. Seek pedagogical knowledge of the characteristics of students from diverse ethnic, racial, cultural, and social class groups; of prejudice and prejudice reduction theory and research; and of teaching strategies and techniques.

Play Materials to Enhance Cultural Diversity and Inclusivity

Curriculum Area	Materials and Equipment
Music	Rainstick (Chile), marimba (Zulu), balaphon (West Africa), ankle bells (Native American), maracas (Latin America), Den-den (Japan), Shakeree (Nigeria), drums (many cultures), ocarina (Peru), songs of many cultures
Literature	Books on family life of many cultures, stories of children from far and near, legends and folktales from many countries, stories with common childhood themes from many lands, favorite books in several languages, wordless books, sign language, Braille books
Blocks and accessories	Variety of accessories depicting many ethnic people, aging people, community workers of both sexes in nonstereotyped roles and with various disabilities; Russian nesting dolls, Pueblo storytellers, animals from around the world
Art	Paints, crayons, markers, and construction paper in variety of skin-tone colors; child-size mirrors
Dramatic play	Anatomically correct dolls representing many ethnic groups; doll accessories, including glasses, wheelchairs, crutches, walkers, leg braces, and hearing aids; doll clothes, including cultural costumes and dress-up clothing from many cultures; cooking utensils, such as a wok, tortilla press, cutlery, chopsticks
Games	Language lotto, dreidel game, lotto of faces of people from around the world, black-history playing cards, world globe
Outdoors	Elevated sand and water tables and ramps for wheelchair access, lowered basketball hoops, sensory-rich materials
Classrooms	Carp banners (Japan), paper cuttings from Mexico and China, photographs and magazine pictures of daily life from many cultures, artwork by artists from a variety of ethnic backgrounds, pictures of children from many ethnic backgrounds and cultures

© Cengage Learning 2011

FIGURE 10-7 A child's family and culture can be brought into the classroom through a variety of curriculum materials; so, too, can children with disabilities be included.

2. Have reflected on and clarified an understanding of their own cultural heritage and experience and have knowledge of how it relates to and interacts with the experiences of other ethnic and cultural groups.
3. Have reflected on their own attitude toward different racial, ethnic, cultural, and social class groups.
4. Have the skills to make effective instructional decisions and reduce prejudice and intergroup conflict.
5. Devise a range of teaching strategies and activities that facilitate the achievement of students from diverse racial, ethnic, cultural, and social class groups.

Children with special needs also need their life mirrored in the school setting with dolls, books, and play accessories that signify acceptance and belonging.

Throughout this text, especially in Chapters 2, 5, and the upcoming chapters, cultural sensitivity on the part of teachers and curriculum goal is emphasized. Woolfolk (2001) suggests the following guidelines for culturally relevant teaching. They provide an accurate summary of many of the points found elsewhere in this book:

- Experiment with different group arrangements to encourage social harmony and cooperation.
- Provide a range of ways for children to learn material to accommodate a wide range of learning styles.
- Use direct teaching methods for important information that everyone should know, such as telling children how to take care of materials, acceptable ways to disagree, and how to get the teacher's attention.
- Learn the meaning of different behaviors of your students; find out how they feel when they are praised or corrected; talk with family members to discover the meaning of gestures, expressions, or other responses that are unfamiliar to you.
- Emphasize meaning in teaching; that is, make sure students understand the concept by using examples from everyday experiences.

- Get to know the customs, traditions, and values of your students; analyze different traditions for common themes; attend community fairs and festivals.
- Help students detect racist and sexist messages, analyze the curriculum for biases, and help children discuss ways that their communication with each other may be biased. Discuss expressions of prejudice.

A sound curriculum is the **linchpin** of a quality program for children. Curriculum planning and development is a creative act, one that is rewarding for teachers. Figure 10-8 highlights some of a teacher's thoughts in the planning process. In the next four chapters, curriculum implementations are explored from another perspective, that of the major areas of development in the child's growth. In Chapter 11, the focus is on how curriculum affects the growing body. Chapter 12 emphasizes the curricular role in developing the mind, and Chapters 13 and 14 explores the curricular issues surrounding social and emotional growth.

Integrating Learning Standards

Curriculum planning may be affected by a set of standards mandated by states. Most states have developed some sort of explicit learning expectations for children to meet at various age and grade levels, often termed "outcomes" or "desired results." At the federal level, there is the Head Start Child Outcomes Framework and the content standards that other national organizations have created for math, science, and literacy. **Standards** describe the kinds of learning that should take place and often, but not always, includes most areas of developmental domains.

There are several benefits of standardization (Gronlund, 2006). When linked to primary grade standards, early childhood standards may enhance school readiness. Standards help to define the foundational skills for learning and help teachers identify the next steps in their learning. To the public, they could reinforce the potential for learning in very young children and the importance of quality early childhood programs. Standards also provide a vehicle for demonstrating the breadth of learning that takes place in the early years and, if used with thought and planning, they can work hand in hand with developmentally appropriate practices.

Many early childhood professionals have concerns over the potential misuse of these standards. They may foster "teaching to the test" rather than a more developmental approach to teaching and cause pressure on the child through inappropriate expectations. They may promote testing and other assessment methods inappropriate for

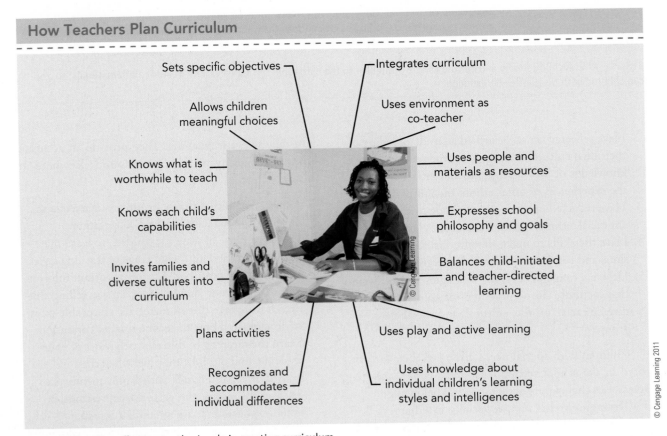

How Teachers Plan Curriculum

Sets specific objectives

Integrates curriculum

Allows children meaningful choices

Uses environment as co-teacher

Knows what is worthwhile to teach

Uses people and materials as resources

Knows each child's capabilities

Expresses school philosophy and goals

Invites families and diverse cultures into curriculum

Balances child-initiated and teacher-directed learning

Plans activities

Uses play and active learning

Recognizes and accommodates individual differences

Uses knowledge about individual children's learning styles and intelligences

© Cengage Learning

FIGURE 10-8 The effective teacher's role in creating curriculum.

young children as noted earlier in Chapter 6. Too often, standards do not address all of the developmental domains but focus only on literacy and/or math and science. Children's sociocultural experiences are a significant part of their learning and standards need to recognize this when determining what children should know and be able to do (Bowman, 2006). We do not want to deprive children from recess and play because of the national emphasis on high stakes testing and the belief that play is less important than academics (Frost, Wortham, & Reifel, 2008).

A joint position paper by NAEYC and the National Association of Early Childhood Specialists in State Departments of Education (NAECS/SDE) (2002) cites four essential features that early learning standards should include: 1) significant, developmentally appropriate content and outcomes; 2) informed, inclusive processes to develop and review the standards; 3) implementation and assessment strategies that are ethical and appropriate for young children; and 4) strong support for early childhood programs, professionals, and families. By following these guidelines, standards could contribute to more positive outcomes for all children.

Today's teachers need to learn more about their own state's requirements and reflect with other early childhood professionals on the tension between meeting the standards and remaining true to developmentally appropriate practices. Figure 10-9 is an example of how a developmentally appropriate curriculum includes learning standards.

Setting Goals

The process of developing curriculum begins with setting goals and then choosing the most pressing ones for attention. The following five steps are guidelines to setting and achieving curriculum goals:

1. *Set goals.* Decide what it is you want children to learn. What do you want them to know about themselves? About others? About the world? State goals clearly, preferably in behavioral terms so that results can be measured.

2. *Establish priorities.* Make a list of three to five goals or objectives you consider most important. State the reasons for your choices; your own values and educational priorities will emerge more clearly.

3. *Know the resources.* A rich, successful, and creative curriculum relies on a vast number of resources. To create a health clinic in the dramatic play area, for instance, you might need the following resources:
   Materials. Props, such as stethoscopes, X-ray machines, tongue depressors, adhesive strips, medical gowns, and masks.
   People. Parents and/or community people in the health care professions to visit the class.
   Community. Field trips to a nearby clinic, hospital, dentist's office.

4. *Plan ahead.* Set aside a regular time to meet for curriculum planning. This may be on a weekly, monthly, or seasonal basis. Discuss the curriculum

Early Learning Standards

Standard	Activity	Demonstrates Mastery
Personal and social competence: Identifies self by categories of gender, age, or social group.	1. Graph children's ages. 2. Make an "All about Me" book. 3. Create self-portraits with dictation.	1. Says correct age and shows correct number of fingers. 2-3. Says, "I'm a girl," "I'm 4 years old," or "I'm Vietnamese."
Effective learner: Completes increasingly complex puzzles.	Play with knob-puzzles, puzzles with and without frames, and floor puzzles.	Uses puzzles with interlocking pieces without the help of frames.
Physical and motor competence: Manipulates two or more objects at the same time.	String beads; play with Legos or Duplos; practice buttoning, zipping, lacing cards, and cutting paper.	Two hands manipulate object at the same time to complete task successfully.

FIGURE 10-9 Early learning standards are beneficial when they can be linked to developmentally appropriate curriculum and have clear goals and outcomes. (Source: Adapted from Kim Yuen, San Mateo County Office of Education, San Mateo, CA. From Browne, K. W., & Gordon A. M., 2009. *To teach well: An early childhood practicum guide.* Upper Saddle River, NJ: Pearson Learning.)

activities as well as the daily routines in order to integrate the two.

5. *Evaluate.* Reflect on the outcome of your planning. Consider what worked and what did not, why it was successful or not. Look at the part of the experience that did not work as well as you would have liked. How can it be improved?

What can you change about it? An evaluation should be immediate, precise, and supportive. Teachers need feedback about their planning and implementing skills. The needs of children are best served when the curriculum is refined and improved. Figure 10-10 is a useful example of how to evaluate an activity.

Evaluating Classroom Activity

Activity _____

How many children participated?_____ Did any avoid the activity? _____

How involved did children become? Very _____ Briefly _____ Watched only _____

What were children's reactions? Describe what they said and did. _____
_____
_____
_____
_____

What did you do to attract children? To maintain their interest? _____
_____
_____

How would you rate the success of this activity? Poor _____ Adequate _____ Good _____ Great _____

Why? _____

What skills/abilities were needed? Did the children exhibit the skills? _____
_____
_____

What parts of the activity were most successful? Why? _____
_____

Describe any difficulty you encountered. Give reasons and tell how you would handle it if it happened again.
_____
_____
_____

If you did this activity again, what would you change? _____
_____

In light of your evaluation, what would you plan for a follow-up activity? _____
_____
_____

How did this activity compare with your goals and expectations? _____
_____
_____

FIGURE 10-10 Evaluating daily activities lets teachers use assessment as a curriculum planning tool. Although not every activity needs this scrutiny on a daily basis, careful planning and evaluation create effective classrooms. (Originally adapted from Vassar College Nursery school. From *Beginning Essentials in Early Childhood Education.* Figure 10-18, p. 393. Copyright © 2007 Wadsworth, a part of Cengage Learning, Inc. Reprinted by permission. www.cengage.com/permissions.)

Ⓢ You can download a copy of this form from this text's Education CourseMate website.

Teacher-Directed Learning

This text promotes teaching through active learning where children have a part in creating the curriculum. This does not exclude, however, the need for teacher-planned experiences in order to further the educational goals of the program. When materials and information are complex or the concept is unfamiliar to the children, teachers provide specific directions and knowledge to illustrate what they are teaching.

Teaching certain skills, such as cutting with scissors and writing lower and upper case letters, requires teacher guidance. The continuum that is shown in Figure 10-11 suggests a broad range of teaching behaviors, including teacher demonstration and directive teaching.

Different activities require different teaching strategies to meet the needs of all children. Helm and Katz (2001) observe that teachers using the project approach often use teacher-directed instruction for teaching certain skills and concepts while keeping a high degree of child choice and initiative in the project.

Group Times

There are certain times within the daily routine when teachers call children together. The size of the group is determined in part by how many teachers there are and how they want to present various learning experiences. The reverse is also true. Various types of learning experiences best lend themselves to small or large group discussions. In using the project approach, for instance, small group work seems to provide the best format for developing ideas and listening to one another's opinions. A presentation by a visiting parent or expert on the project theme would be more appropriate for the large group. Smaller groups could then form to discuss in greater detail the ideas presented.

Large group times are used for a variety of reasons. Teachers may use them as opportunities to bring the entire class together to:

- Provide transitions in the daily schedule.
- Bring in a special guest or presentation.
- Introduce new ideas and materials.
- Sing, dance, and do fingerplays.

A Continuum of Teacher Behavior

Nondirective			Mediating			Directive	
Acknowledge	Model	Facilitate	Support	Scaffold	Co-construct	Demonstrate	Direct
Give attention and positive encouragement to keep a child engaged in an activity	Display for children a skill or desirable way of behaving in the classroom, through actions only or with cues, prompts, or other forms of coaching	Offer short-term assistance to help a child achieve the next level of functioning (as an adult does in holding the back of a bicycle while a child pedals)	Provide a fixed form of assistance, such as a bicycle's training wheels, to help a child achieve the next level of functioning	Set up challenges or assist children to work "on the edge" of their current competence	Learn or work collaboratively with children on a problem or task, such as building a model or block structure	Actively display a behavior or engage in an activity while children observe the outcome	Provide specific directions for children's behavior within narrowly defined dimensions of error

FIGURE 10-11 There are many ways for teachers to respond to and support children's growth and learning. (From Bredekamp S. & Rosegrant, T., Eds. [1995]. *Reaching potentials: Appropriate curriculum and assessment for young children*, Vol. 2. Figure 2, p. 21. Reprinted with permission from the National Association for the Education of Young Children.)

A Balancing Act: Child-Directed and Teacher-Directed Experiences

Intentional teaching involves deciding if a child-directed or adult-directed experience is best under particular circumstances. One researcher (Epstein, 2007) explored the similarities between both approaches to teaching and learning. It turns out that neither way is controlled exclusively by the teacher or by the child; both are actively involved in the activity and process. When the experience is teacher-directed, children are encouraged to make suggestions, ask questions, and otherwise actively participate. The teacher deliberately keeps the focus on the purpose of the lesson while responding to the children's involvement. For a child-directed experience, teachers are similarly intentional in their involvement. As children investigate and explore, the teacher is primed to observe and get involved when it seems appropriate. Neither teaching strategy is a passive approach, but in both, the teacher times suggestions and interactions with the children and the activity. The teacher's role is to help advance the experience and guide their learning to greater depths.

As we think about the learning experience, we ask ourselves:

Which method best suits the goals for learning?

Which method is best for this particular group?

Which method extends children's knowledge and deepens their understanding of this particular lesson or information?

Which method am I most comfortable with for this experience?

There is no right or wrong answer to these questions. Both methods are developmentally appropriate and children learn through both ways. Whether child- or adult-directed, teaching with intention fosters children's initiative and learning.

Think About This:

1. Describe a teaching situation where you would use teacher-directed methods. How would you get the class involved and keep interest high?
2. Describe a situation where you would interact with a child-directed activity. How would you establish your involvement and keep children focused without dominating the activity?

- Read stories.
- Plan activities with children.
- Review the day's events.
- Initiate group problem solving.

Small groups, on the other hand, are opportunities for teachers and children to have a closer and more personal experience. This setting provides the teachers with ample opportunities to:

- Help children practice a specific skill, such as cutting with scissors.
- Encourage children in their social interactions with one another.
- Enjoy conversations with children.
- Teach a new game to a few children at a time.
- Closely observe each child's growth and development.
- Hold discussions regarding their project work, and move the project along.
- Explore topics in depth.
- Eat a meal or have a snack with children and encourage the social process.
- Provide close supervision for some experiences, such as cooking.

What is common to all group times is the occasion for teachers to encourage listening and speaking skills; provide an arena in which children share thoughts and ideas with one another; and introduce any number of cognitive and social activities.

Written Curriculum Plans

A written plan is an organized agenda, an outline to follow, a framework for the curriculum. It may include a list of activities, goals for children's learning experiences, the

Group times are more meaningful when children's home language is used for story time. One teacher reads the book in English, the other reads it in Spanish.

process or method of instruction, the teacher's responsibilities, the time of day, and other special notations. A plan may be developed for a day, a week, a month, or a specific unit or theme. Figure 10-12 illustrates a weekly curriculum. The four chapters that follow also contain many examples of written plans.

Advantages of Written Plans

Setting lesson plans to paper helps teachers focus on the nature of the children they teach—their interests, their needs, their capabilities, and their potential. A written plan encourages thorough, in-depth planning of curriculum in a logical progression, provides a direction, and helps teachers clarify thoughts and articulate a rationale for what they do. Team teaching is more stimulating when teachers plan together, sharing their ideas and resources; everyone knows what is happening; in case of absences, a substitute teacher can carry out the plans. Changes can easily be made to allow for flexibility, adaptation, and on-the-spot decisions.

When plans are written down, it is easy to see what resources are needed and to have the time to prepare materials. Written plans serve as a communication tool for the teaching staff, for parents, and for the governing agency and provide a concrete format from which evaluation and assessment can be made.

A clearly written lesson plan serves as a curriculum map that guides the daily experiences and agendas. It should reflect the program's goals and priorities as well as the teachers' objectives for each student, such as what skills the activity fosters. The activities themselves should provide for first-hand learning experiences that promote discovery through active exploration of materials. A written lesson plan is a good way to demonstrate how well the curriculum is integrated, inclusive, and culturally sensitive.

The plan should present a balance to the day in which activity and play alternate with opportunities for quiet times, including the time spent outdoors. Large and small group times that are teacher-directed are included, as well as blocks of time in which children select their own activities. The plan should also note when and where teachers are able to work individually with children. Many written lesson plans also include any changes that need to be made to the environment or schedule.

Figure 10-12 demonstrates many of the key elements for a weekly lesson plans. Figure 10-13 shows a written plan for a curriculum that individualizes a child's specific needs and experiences, and Figure 10-14 is a lesson plan for an individual activity.

Planning by Objectives

One approach to curriculum development requires more formal, organized planning. Comprehensive lesson plans are developed, sometimes for the whole year, and usually include objectives, the stated concepts that children learn through this experience. These are commonly called behavioral objectives. The lesson plans include specific, stated, observable behaviors that children are able to demonstrate to show that the teaching objective has been met. In other words, a behavioral objective states clearly what children actually do (e.g., be able to hold scissors properly; grasp a pencil between thumb and first two fingers). If the behavioral objective is to improve fine motor skills, the lesson plan includes activities and events that foster children's use of their fine motor skills. Several objectives may apply to a given activity. It is then important to order the objectives so that the purposes of the lesson remain in focus. To plan successfully, the teacher needs to know developmental and behavioral theory (Chapter 4), to have good observational strategies (Chapter 6), and to possess tools to assess whether the objective has been accomplished (Chapter 6).

One example of using behavioral objectives is Figure 10-9, which shows the use of behavioral objectives when meeting learning standards. A more developed plan found in early childhood classrooms would include activities for the full range of curriculum areas, such as art, motor activities, and dramatic play, for each of the objectives. Important factors in developing curriculum objectives are how much knowledge and understanding children have, what children are interested in, and what standards are mandated by the individual state for the specific age group.

Webbing

Webbing is the process through which teachers develop a diagram based on a particular topic or theme, highlighting key ideas and concepts (Katz and Chard, 2000). Ideas generated from **brainstorming** sessions flesh out the topic with many subheadings and lists of curriculum possibilities. Webbing is a planning tool that provides depth to a topic and creates a map of possible activities and projects. A web may be organized around a theme (water), into curriculum areas (language arts, music), or around program goals (problem solving, cooperation). By their very nature, webs foster an integrated curriculum approach and help teachers extend children's learning and experiences.

Creating a web can be fun because it allows teachers to use their imaginations and calls into play their knowledge, resources, and experience. Katz and Chard (2000)

SAMPLE PRESCHOOL-KINDERGARTEN LESSON PLAN

TEACHER(S): **DATES:** **THEME:** Magnificent Me!

CONCEPTS: I am unique, special, and part of a family

SKILLS: Prewriting, writing, measuring, graphing, problem-solving, and-awareness of similarities/differences

CENTERS & ACTIVITIES	MONDAY	TUESDAY	WEDNESDAY	THURSDAY	FRIDAY
MORNING GROUP ACTIVITY	Sing "Good Morning." Introduce "My Body."	Take individual instant photos. Introduce "My ends."	Read On the Day You Were Born. Introduce "My Family."	Make breadsticks formed in initials. Introduce "My Home."	Healthy snack chart: finish & discuss.
AFTERNOON GROUP ACTIVITY	Identify body parts and what they do.	Animal friends: share stuffed animals and/or pets.	Chart birthdays of the children and family members.	Read **How My Parents Learned to Eat.**	Bring and share something about yourself.
LANGUAGE & LITERACY	Begin "All About Me" books.	Write about photo and put into "Me" book with photo.	Add family photo to book. Write or draw about photo.	Write class story about field trip experience.	Finish "All About Me" books and share. Finish class story.
ART	Make life-sized self-portraits.	Make thumbprint and footprint pictures.	Make puppet papercup family pop-ups.	Make kitchen gadget puppets.	Mix playdough to match skin color.
MUSIC & MOVEMENT	"Name Song" Body parts move to music.	Sing "I'm A Special Person and So Are You" and "Friends Go Marching."	Beanbag toss and Kitchen marching band	Sing "So Many Ways to Say Good Morning" and dance.	Dance in hats with streamers to music.
DRAMATIC PLAY HOME LIVING	Home living center with a full mirror and baby pictures of children.	Add phones, paper, and pencils for message-taking.	Bathe baby dolls in warm sudsy water. Add stuffed animals to area.	Add a Wok and other cookware to center.	Add hats to dress-up clothes.
MATH MANIPULATIVE	Measure and record height of each child.	Graph the children's heights.	Use puzzles of family celebrations.	Gather items from home and play "What's missing?"	Estimate number of pennies in a jar, then count them.
SCIENCE & DISCOVERY	Listen to heart with stethoscope. Examine picture or model of skeleton.	Magnifying glasses to see thumbprints. Exploring shadows.	Food colors, eye droppers, and ice trays	Weigh on scales for "Me" book. "What's That Sound?"	Magnets and what sinks, what floats?

OUTDOOR/LARGE MUSCLE
Nature walk: obstacle course on playground Hop, run, skip, jump

BLOCKS
Add: people figures, animal figures, boxes, houses, cars

SOCIAL STUDIES
Invite family members to visit. Field Trip to grocery store. We are all alike. We are all different.

TRANSITIONS
Puppet helper of the day Variations on "Name Song"

SENSORY CENTERS
Water table with warm, soapy water Multicultural skin colored playdough. Healthy snacks "Tasting Tray"

BOOKS OF THE WEEK
My Five Senses, Big Friend, Little Friend, Mommy's Office, William's Doll

SPECIAL ACTIVITIES & NOTES Field trip to grocery store. Children decide which healthy snacks to buy. Explain decisions.

Week-long project: Make chart or diagram re: food groups. Prepare and eat snacks. Write class story.

FIGURE 10-12 Weekly lesson plan. (Source: Jackman, H.L., 2012. *Early education curriculum: A child's connection to the world*, 5th Ed. Belmont, CA: Wadsworth/Cengage Learning Inc., p. 66.)

Individualized Child Planning Form

Teacher: *Marlene*
Child's Name: *Rosie*

Group: *Fours*
Date: *Week of Jan. 7-11*

Developmental Information: *Rosie's physical/motor and cognitive skills seem to be age appropriate. Her language skills are well-developed with adults but Rosie does not speak to other children except in two or three-word sentences. Her social development seems limited with her peers but not her teachers.*

Current Observation: *Rosie prefers to play and work alone. She participates in groups but with limited response to her peers. She observes adults as they interact with other children and enjoys one-to-one conversations with teachers, telling them stories about her cat, Patches. Rosie was most animated last month during a project where she could work on her own along side others.*

Curriculum Plan:

- *Arrange a week-long small group experiences that include Rosie and 2 or 3 other children. Using animal photo cards, play a matching game to help Rosie begin to interact with others. Ask each child to talk about the animal on their card, making sure that Rosie gets one with a picture of a cat. Prompt her with questions and comments that help expand her discussion, especially about her own cat.*
- *Follow up with discussions about cat's names, their coloring, and their habits. As children become more involved in the topic, include larger members of the cat family. Make sure that Rosie has opportunities to contribute to the discussion.*
- *As Rosie becomes more comfortable with the group, ask her to work with Marley on an art project about wild cats. Support her interactions as she and Marley begin to work together.*
- *Teachers need to model for Rosie how to participate in an activity and to learn what to say and how to react to other children's suggestions.*
- *Suggest to Rosie's family that Marley be invited over to play. They are both quiet and enjoy less boisterous and crowded activities.*

FIGURE 10-13 The most effective curriculum grows out of the child's needs and experiences and the teacher's observations.

---

suggest the following process to develop a web about the fall season:

1. *Brainstorming.* Using small slips of paper, teachers write down theme or topic ideas that the children suggest—each idea on a separate piece of paper. For the topic "Things that happen in fall and winter," for instance, the slips would contain ideas such as "cut jack-o-lanterns" or "rake leaves."

2. *Grouping.* The slips of paper are organized into groups of similar ideas, and, on a colored piece of paper, a heading is given to each group. "Canning and preserving" and "seasonal recipes" fall under the heading of "Cooking." Subgroups can be created, if necessary.

3. *Sharing.* Teachers can share their ideas with one another, rearranging the headings and subheadings as they share skills, resources, and information with one another.

4. *Drawing.* The ideas can be transferred to a piece of paper, placing the topic or theme in the center and drawing lines radiating out to the headings (group time, manipulatives, dramatic play). *This creates a visual record* of the relationships between and among the ideas and becomes a flexible resource that changes and grows.

Jones and Nimmo (1994), in their early work with webbing, emphasize the organic nature of a web. First created as a response to children's ideas, it creates a picture in which ideas emerge and connect in any number of ways. It is, of course, a tentative plan, for what happens next depends on the children's responses. The web creates a flexible plan that can be altered and adapted as teachers observe children and evaluate their interests.

Figure 10-15 is an example of children and teachers working together on a curriculum web that grew out of the children's involvement with play animals. The project that evolved is featured in Figure 10-17 on page 326.

Themes

A traditional method of developing curriculum is to focus on a broad, general topic or theme, also known as a unit. Though used interchangeably, themes are generally a smaller part of a unit, allowing for a more specific focus. For example, a unit on the body may have "What I can do with my hands" as one theme. This mode of planning is used in many early childhood and elementary settings. Focusing on themes, however, can and

---

Lesson Plan for an Individual Activity

- -

Teacher Name: _____
Date: _____

Name of Activity and Brief Description: _____
Classroom/Outdoor Location _____
Class or Group _____
Goal of Activity _____
Materials Needed _____
Changes Need in Environment _____
Teaching Methods and Process _____
Developmental Domains Included _____
Ways to Extend Learning _____

Evaluation:
Children's Involvement _____
Goals Realized _____
Problems that Emerged _____
Follow-up Suggestions _____
Clean Up _____

FIGURE 10-14 Good planning takes time and thought. A single activity can lead to other activities.

© Cengage Learning 2014

---

should be much more than an in-depth study of a topic and should be integrated into the whole curriculum.

A thematic approach can utilize many of the attributes of an integrated curriculum:

- Children can help choose and plan themes, thereby constructing their own learning.
- Activities can be chosen to reflect the curriculum goals.
- The emphasis is on active learning.
- The most appropriate themes are those that have a meaningful connection to children's lives.
- Many subject areas can be integrated in the different activities.
- The program lends itself to flexibility, teacher permitting.
- It provides for an in-depth study of a topic.
- It can support the use of multiple learning styles through different media.
- It adds coherence and depth to the curriculum.
- It has the potential for good multicultural curriculum emphasis.

Figure 10-16 is an example of a theme on the five senses for toddlers.

Gestwicki (2007) cites some disadvantages of using a traditional theme approach to curriculum. It can be restricted and narrow and too adult-directed, not allowing for children's curiosity and initiative. There is a danger of creating an artificial unit that has no relevancy to the children's experiences or interests. Teachers may find it hard to deviate from the curriculum plan and not be flexible enough to extend the topic further. When too rigidly applied, themes can isolate the experience into a particular subject or concept and miss the opportunities to broaden the learning potential. At its worst, a theme can be recycled every year without regard for the different group of children and their needs and interests.

Holiday Themes

An inappropriate use of themes is to limit them to specific times of the year, such as Thanksgiving or Valentine's Day, or to celebrate holidays. Themes are not just for special occasions because they tend to isolate and narrowly define the topic.

Some holiday themes may not be appropriate to every family represented by the group. One teacher decided that making Easter baskets on Good Friday (a religious day for many Christians) was offensive to those who practiced Christianity and was uncomfortable for the non-Christians in the class. The practice was dropped throughout the school in the name of cultural and religious sensitivity.

Some schools have adopted policies that do not permit celebrating holidays as part of the school curriculum. Holidays do provoke a particularly sensitive time for celebrating. There are many who believe that celebrating holidays from around the world brings a sense of multiculturalism to the curriculum. York (2003) suggests that when done with thought and care, holidays can be an important addition to the curriculum. To ensure the most positive outcomes, according to York, all holidays are celebrated with equal importance; only those that have importance to the children and families in the class are observed; parents are enlisted to help; the celebration takes place within the context of the daily life of people and families; and sensitivity to the children and families who do not celebrate a particular holiday is observed.

Others might say this is a tourist approach to cultural diversity or that it is a quick visit to another culture without follow-up and depth of exploration. Too often in early childhood programs, holiday curriculum units are the only expression of cultural diversity. According to Derman-Sparks & Edwards (2010), there are no meaningful developmental reasons for the strong emphasis on celebrating holidays in most early childhood programs today. She further argues that this overuse of holiday

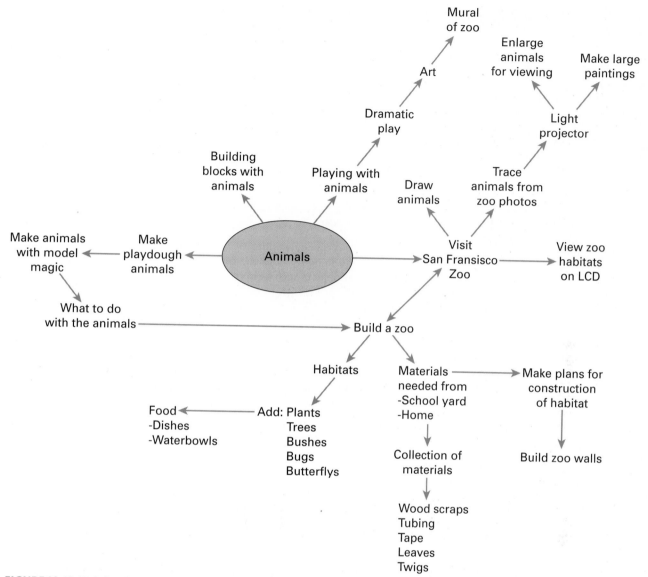

FIGURE 10-15 Web for elementary school children. (Tracy Pierce, Geo-Kids, Menlo Park, CA. Used by Permission.)

themes actually interferes with a developmentally appropriate curriculum because too many foods or songs are used, bypassing the opportunity for children to learn about common areas of life. It seems that holiday themes paint a flat picture of a cultural or religious event without taking into account how people in those cultures live, work, sleep, or play in ways that are familiar or similar to other cultures.

Life-Oriented Themes

Themes that are of great interest to young children are those that directly concern them. The body as a theme suggests many avenues for development: Body parts may be emphasized; exploration using the senses may be stressed; measuring and weighing children may be used to demonstrate growth of the body. Another subject to which children readily respond is that of home and family. Animals, especially pets, are appealing to young children and can lead into further curriculum areas of wild animals, prehistoric animals, and so on.

The more in touch with children the teachers are, the more their classroom themes should reflect the children's interests and abilities. Children who live in Silicon Valley in California, in Houston, Texas, or in Central Florida may have a local interest in computers and space shuttles. The urban child of New York, Detroit, or Washington, D.C., relates more readily to themes about subways, taxis, and tall buildings. Children's interests often focus on, but are not

Curriculum through Play for the One-and-a-Half-Year-Old

Sensory Stimulation

Objective: To help toddlers begin to explore and understand the five senses.

	Activity	Small-Group Focus	Optional Activities
Monday	Soap painting	Guessing game: textures. Distinguish soft from hard using familiar objects.	Play hide-and-seek with two or three
Tuesday	Water table play	Guessing game: smells. Identify familiar scents in jars.	Blow bubbles.
Wednesday	Fingerpainting	Guessing game: weights. Distinguish heavy/not heavy using familiar objects such as book or doll.	Take walk to collect collage materials of different textures.
Thursday	Making collages of textures collected day before	Guessing game: shapes. Using puzzles of shapes and shape-sorting boxes.	Have a parade of sounds from many musical instruments.
Friday	Play dough	Food fest of finger foods: Try different textures, sizes, shapes, and flavors	Make foot or hand prints on large mural paper.

© Cengage Learning 2011

FIGURE 10-16 Example of teacher-directed activities to help toddlers explore their sensory skills.

necessarily limited to, what they have experienced. By choosing themes that coincide with children's daily lives, teachers promote connected and relevant learning. Take another look at Figures 10-4 and 10-8 from this perspective.

Some themes in an early childhood setting can address children's own issues. All young children share similar fears and curiosity about the world they do not know but imagine so vividly. The cues children give, particularly about their concerns, suggest to the observant teacher some important themes of childhood. During Halloween, for example, it can be helpful and reassuring to children if the theme of masks is developed. Select some masks that have a function, such as hospital masks, ski masks, safety glasses, sunglasses, snorkel masks, or wrestling and football helmets. Children can try them on and become comfortable with the way their appearance changes. They can laugh with friends as they look in the mirror to see how a mask changes the appearance but does not change the person.

Themes can be inclusive, integrated, and appropriate. It takes a teacher with a child-centered approach to respond to children's innate excitement and curiosity about learning.

The Project Approach

Much of what you have just learned about emergent and thematic curriculum as an integrated approach applies equally to projects. As you read ahead, keep in mind what you have learned about the advantages of an integrated curriculum (page 300), how to take cues from children as explained in the discussion on emergent curriculum (page 300), the concept of children and teachers collaborating (page 302), and the sources for curriculum ideas found on page 302. A **project approach** embodies these characteristics as well. On the continuum of teacher-directed versus child-directed learning, a project requires the greatest amount of child involvement.

Projects are the epitome of an integrated curriculum, embracing all of the key characteristics of integrated learning and allowing for the incorporation of a wide range of subject areas. In her now classic work, Katz (1994) defines the "project approach" as:

. . . an in-depth investigation of a topic worth learning more about . . . usually undertaken by a small group of children within a class . . . the whole class . . . or even an individual child. The key feature . . . is that it is a research effort deliberately focused on finding answers to questions about a topic posed either by the children . . . or the teacher.

A recent revival of this curriculum approach used in progressive schools (see Dewey, Chapter 1) is worth noting here. Based on the belief that "children's minds should be engaged in ways that deepen their understanding of their own experiences and environment" (Katz & Chard, 2000), the project approach consists of exploring a theme or topic (such as babies, dinosaurs, riding the school bus) over a period of days or weeks.

Preplanning by the children and teachers is the first step: They observe, question, estimate, experiment, and research items and events related to the topic. Together, they make dramatic play and display materials they need. Children work in small groups throughout the process and have the opportunity to make numerous choices about their level of participation. The teacher often records the activity on tapes and with photographs. Project work has different levels of complexity, so it meets the needs of children of different ages and abilities.

In the small town of Reggio Emilia in northern Italy, a similar approach to curriculum has received worldwide attention. The project approach is used in even greater depth as it permeates the entire curriculum and school environment. It will be discussed later in this chapter.

Projects emerge from children's own interests, teacher observations of children's needs and interests, and parents' suggestions. The topics reflect the local culture of the children. In fact, Chard (1998) suggests that because life experiences and interests of the teacher and of the children are so strongly reflected in the project itself, it is a singular occurrence relevant only to that group. Another group may adopt the same topic, but it is not a duplicate process due to the individual nature of the children and teacher planning the project.

This approach to teaching and learning easily lends itself to an inclusive classroom and curriculum, responding to diverse points of view as well as diverse cultures. Projects created by the children of Reggio Emilia, for instance, differ from those of American children due to many cultural influences—in particular, the children's ability to argue their point and defend their ideas to others as the project emerges. In the Italian culture, this is a natural part of discourse and is usual in the beginning of conversation between people; in American mainstream culture, it is usual when two people "agree to disagree" for the conversation to end.

The planning process is crucial to the success of the project approach as is the underlying philosophy that children can be co-constructors of their own education. This approach has much in common with the approaches

of both Dewey and Neill's *Summerhill* (see Chapter 1). The teacher helps children explore what they already know about the topic, what they might need to know, and how they can represent that knowledge through various media, reinforcing Vygotsky's theory that interaction and direct teaching are important aspects of intellectual development. Teachers pose questions for children that lead them to suggest a hypothesis: What might happen if you do that? What do you think you could do to make that work? Children are encouraged to evaluate their own work and learn to defend and explain their creations to others. Figure 10-4 on field dependent/independent styles exemplifies this process.

The following is a summary of the process involved in a project approach as outlined by Chard (1998), Katz and Chard (2000), and Helm and Katz (2001). There are four phases to a project approach:

1. *Representation.* Children express and communicate their ideas. Through the use of drawing, writing, construction, dramatic play, maps, and diagrams, children share their experience and knowledge. Representation documents what children are learning.
2. *Fieldwork.* Investigations take place outside the classroom, through events, objects, places, and people so that children build on their own knowledge through direct experiences.
3. *Investigation.* Using a variety of resources, children explore and research the topic. This includes fieldwork as well as closely analyzing, sketching, and discussing what they find.
4. *Display.* Exhibits of children's work on the project serve as a source of information and provide an opportunity to share their work and ideas with others. As the project progresses, the children are kept up to date on their progress by displays of their work.

Using Technology in the Classroom

Many children come to early childhood settings having some knowledge and competency with today's technology tools. The digital age is part of their home setting as they see parents with cellphones, computers, cameras, DVD players, and a host of interactive tablets, games, and music devices. Many of these tools have found their way into the early childhood classrooms and challenge the early childhood professional to assess their usefulness and potential for learning. As with any other aspect of curriculum, teachers need to use their knowledge of child development principles and awareness of how children learn as guidelines for integrating technology and media into the curriculum. The National Association for the Education of Young Children and the Fred Rogers Center for Early Learning and Children's Media's

Playing with animals in classroom

Making animals from Model Magic

Making animals from Model Magic

Using their animals with blocks

Visiting the zoo

Drawing plans for building the zoo

Drawing plans for building the zoo

Building the zoo

Making the zoo habitat

The zoo

FIGURE 10-17 This project evolved from the web shown in Figure 10-15 and took several months to accomplish. We thank the children at Geo-Kids in Menlo Park, CA, and photographers Tracy Pierce and Michele McMath.

position statement (2012), *Technology and Interactive Media as Tools in Early Childhood Programs Serving Children from Birth through Age 8*, sets out guidelines that help inform a teacher's decision of how and when to use technology and **interactive media** with children, noting that these activities should never replace "creative play, real-life exploration, physical activity, outdoor experiences, conversation, and social interactions."

1. Choose and evaluate interactive media tools intentionally, keeping in mind their developmental appropriateness and their potential for an interactive experience.
2. Use interactive media as a way to intentionally extend and support hands-on activities to enhance children's engagement with their real world and expand their ability to gain to new information.
3. Avoid the passive use of television, videos, DVD's and other **non-interactive media** in early childhood programs for children under age 2. Among two-to-five-year olds, discourage use of media in which children do not take an active part.
4. In programs for children under age 2, only use technology and interactive media that supports responsive and positive interactions between children and caregivers.
5. Follow **screen time** recommendations from public health organizations that limit how much time children should spend in front of media screens.
6. Help ensure equitable access to technology and interactive media for children and their families.

Chapter, 13, and 15 also include more in-depth discussions of this topic.

Play-Based Curriculum Models

Five distinct models demonstrate curriculum that embrace the five guidelines for developmentally appropriate practice: creating a caring community, teaching to enhance development and learning, planning curriculum to achieve important goals, assessing children's development and learning, and establishing reciprocal relationships with families. Each model is unique with its own strengths and characteristics, and each is play and development integrated.

High/Scope: Cognitively Oriented Model

The High/Scope curriculum stresses active learning through a variety of learning centers with plenty of materials and developmentally appropriate activities. The schedule includes extended periods of free play time and guidelines for teacher's intervention in play activities (Frost et al., 2008). Active problem solving is encouraged as children plan, with teacher's assistance, what they will do each day, carry out their plan, and review what they have done. Appropriately, this is known as the "plan-do-review" process. Teachers use small groups to encourage, question, support, and extend children's learning while emphasizing communication skills.

There is a balance between child-initiated experiences and teacher-planned instructional activities. Teachers use observational techniques to focus on children and to understand children's play. Teachers are responsible for planning curriculum organized around key experiences that reinforce and extend the learning activities the children select for themselves. These key experiences form the basis of the curriculum and include creative representation, language and literacy, initiative and social relations, movement, music, classification, seriation, number, space, and time (Hohmann & Weikart, 2002).

Children with special needs are integrated readily into High/Scope programs and with a curriculum developed especially for K–3 grades and early adolescents. High/Scope extends its active learning philosophy into further school years.

High/Scope's approach to children's learning is deeply rooted in Piagetian theory and supports Vygotsky's theory of social interaction and cognition: Children learn when interacting with the people and materials in their environment. The schools of Reggio Emilia share core elements of the High/Scope philosophy. Both philosophies stress the importance of children's constructing their knowledge from activities that interest them; team teaching is an important concept, to allow the children access to adult support; and the process of planning, acting, recording, and reassessing is one that both approaches use to foster critical thinking skills.

To document children's growth using a portfolio system (see Chapter 6), the High/Scope program uses the following categories (Schweinhart, 1993; Brewer, 1995):

- *Initiative:* Expressing choices, engaging in complex play.
- *Creative representation:* Making, building, pretending.
- *Social relations:* Relating to children and adults, making friends.
- *Music and movement:* Exhibiting body coordination, following a musical beat.
- *Language and literacy:* Showing interest in reading, beginning reading, beginning writing.
- *Logic and mathematics:* Sorting, counting objects, describing time sequences.

BRAIN
Research Says...

The Brainy Teacher

What does it mean to be a "brainy teacher"? How can we use current brain research to enhance children's learning and increase our own understanding of good teaching? One researcher (Jensen, 2005) developed a model that begins to answer some of these questions. The three-step model gives us an outline of what to do before, during, and after teaching that gives greater support to children's brain functions.

First Step: Preparation Before Class

The brain must be in the right "state" to activate the networks for learning. You learn more when you are in a clear and positive state of mind than when you are depressed or tired. To get yourself and children in the right "state" of mind, try the following:

Prepare yourself mentally, academically, and emotionally. Think about what students need and create a lesson plan that is appealing and involving.

Prepare the environment: Create a comfortable space, where children can move about, with bright lights and cool temperature.

Second Step: The Lesson

Teachers use a five-step approach to engage the brain to absorb knowledge. The steps and examples are outlined here:

Engage the whole child—mind and body. Get children ready for learning by capturing their attention and getting them excited about the lesson. This increases the heart rate and raises the dopamine and cortical levels of the brain and improves children's emotional state for learning. Engagement activates more of the pleasure structures in the brain than do tasks that require memorization (Poldrack et al., 2001).

Example: "Okay, everyone. Take a deep breath and hold it. Hold it. Hold it. Now let it out! Hold it again. Let it out! Hold it again."

"Good. Do it again, but think about this one thing when you begin to let your breath out: Alaska! Okay, breathe! Now look to your right and share with your friend what the word Alaska meant to you both. Good. Now stand up and show me with just your body what word you thought of. Aha, Carlos is walking like a big polar bear. Willy is walking like a penguin. Elsie is shoveling snow. Jacquie is fishing. Sit down now and let's make a list of all the words that come to mind about Alaska."

Frame the learning. Capitalize on children's curiosity and excitement:

Example: "Now that our list is made, we're going to focus on just one of these words today. Who has a guess?" "Those are all good guesses and Antony picked the right one, so he can come circle the word 'polar bear.' Do you remember the book about polar bears that Megan brought to school last week? You liked it so much I had to read it twice, so I thought we might learn more about polar bears today."

Knowledge acquisition. This is where the intentional teaching part of the lesson begins with teacher-directed learning. As children and teacher engage in dialogue, a more child-directed activity may emerge. Asking the brain to engage in nonstop attention hinders learning. For teacher-directed instructional learning of new content, Jensen (2005) suggests five to eight minutes for kindergarteners through second grade, and eight to twelve minutes for third through fifth grades.

Example: "You have a lot of questions about polar bears, so why don't we go on a bear hunt? Look around the classroom and find pictures and books, or draw something that bears like to eat or where they live. You have 10 minutes and then we'll talk some more about how polar bears hibernate."

Elaborate to extend the learning. Brain connections made at the synapse

from the lesson solidify within the first hour of learning. Check to see if children have grasped the basic concepts and if they are correct in their understanding of the content. It is better to check for accuracy right away before the synapse sets with misinformation. The brain is also limited in how much a child can hold in short-term memory. Use quizzes, true/false statements, and other quick methods to ensure that the children have the correct information.

Strengthen the memory and correct the learning. The brain recalls more in the first hour after learning than in the next few days, so help the children recall the who/what/when/how of the lesson. An interactive method, such as acting out the story of the polar bear, helps the child retain the lesson.

Third Step: Settle and Review

The brain needs time for processing and rest after learning.

1. Plan the lesson just before snacks or lunchtime, recess, outdoor play, or nap time.
2. Give the children time to let the lesson settle.
3. The brain synapses have made connections, but you need to create time to review the lesson over the next few days in order to ensure that the synapses adapt to the new information the brain has received.

Questions

1. How does Jensen's model help teachers "teach with the brain in mind"? Why do you think the process works? Which stages is the most challenging for you?
2. How does Jensen's model relate to developmentally appropriate practices? Emergent curriculum? Integrated curriculum?

Teachers evaluate these abilities as they observe children's use of key experiences and plan the curriculum accordingly.

Bank Street: Developmental-Interaction Model

Bank Street was founded by Lucy Sprague Mitchell (see Chapter 1), and its roots reflect the thinking of Freud, Dewey, Erikson, Vygotsky, and Piaget, among others. It is a developmental approach as child development principles influence the curriculum planning, and it is an interactive model because of the connections made between children, adults, and the greater environment. The cognitive and social-emotional relationship stresses the link between education and psychology.

The Bank Street model originated the play-based approach used in many early childhood settings today through the use of interest centers, water and sand play, blocks, puzzles, painting, and small and large group play. Teachers use play to enhance children's cognitive and language skills through frequent conversations and interactions (Frost et al., 2008).

Children are seen as active learners who learn by interacting with and transforming the world about them. Play is the primary vehicle for encouraging involvement between and among children, adults, and materials. The teacher's primary role is to observe and respond to activities initiated by the children. Classrooms are organized into learning centers, in which children can work individually or in groups.

The Bank Street model exemplifies an integrated curriculum. Children learn about the world in which they live through concrete, first-hand experiences. Community and neighborhood connections are stressed. Units and themes are used to focus the curriculum, and children have access to materials and are free to choose where to play. A teacher's knowledge and understanding of child development principles is crucial to this approach. Educational goals are set in terms of developmental processes and include the development of competence, a sense of autonomy and individuality, social relatedness and connectedness, creativity, and an integration of different ways of experiencing the world.

The Schools of Reggio Emilia

Respect for children's investigative powers and for their ability to think, plan, criticize, collaborate, and learn from all they do is the hallmark of the Reggio Emilia approach and is an excellent example of an integrated and emerging approach to learning. This collection of schools in Italy, with separate programs for infants to 3-year-olds and 3- to 6-year-olds, has commanded worldwide attention for its philosophy and practices. "Nowhere else in the world," states Gardner (in the classic work of Edwards, Gandini, & Forman, 1993), "is there such a seamless and symbiotic relationship between a school's progressive philosophy and its practices." The curriculum takes the project approach to its highest levels.

Influenced by Dewey's progressive education movement, the philosophies and practices of Reggio Emilia owe a great deal as well to Piaget's constructivist theory, Vygotsky's belief in social discourse as a method of learning, and Gardner's theory of multiple intelligences (see Chapters 1, 4, and 13). Children are actively engaged in long-term projects that they initiate, design, and carry out with the support of the teacher. Art is the primary medium for learning.

Some of the key components of the Reggio Emilia approach are: a materials-rich environment that is aesthetically appealing; a community-based attitude involving the entire city; a family support system; and a commitment to process.

These elements are manifested in the program through astonishingly beautiful school settings, replete with the work of children and evidence of their projects elegantly displayed throughout; by support realized through a large portion of the city's budget; through small groups of children who stay together for a three-year period with the same teacher; and through intentionally bringing the children's culture into school life.

Play, in the Reggio Emilia classroom, is focused on children's ability to represent their experiences through the arts. As such, play is more collaborative with several children working on one project while another group is working elsewhere. "Working" in this context is playing; art is the form that play often takes in this model. The

Courtesy of St. Louis–Reggio Collaborative. Copyright © 2001

The Reggio approach: order and beauty.

Reggio Emilia: a materials-rich environment.

teacher's role is more involved than in other models because the philosophy of Reggio Emilia is to work with children and assist them with their activities.

Cadwell (1997) identifies eight fundamentals of the Reggio Emilia approach. Each has implications for creating a curriculum that is fully integrated and one that emerges from children's interests and ideas. These eight essential points are:

1. *The child as protagonist.* All children are strong and capable and have the potential and preparation to construct their learning. They are protagonists (i.e., central characters) with teachers and parents in the educational process.
2. *The child as collaborator.* There is an emphasis on working in small groups. This stems from the belief that we are social beings and form ourselves through interactions with people and things.
3. *The child as communicator.* Symbolic representation, through dance, art, painting, sculpting, building, dramatic play, music, and words help children discover and communicate what they know and what they question. Teachers support the use of these "many languages" to help children make their thinking visible.
4. *The environment as third teacher.* Every corner of the environment has an identity and purpose and encourages encounters, communication, and relationships. There is order and beauty in the design of the equipment, the space, and the materials.
5. *The teacher as partner, nurturer, and guide.* Teachers listen and observe children closely in order to facilitate and guide their process of open-ended discovery. They ask questions to find out about children's ideas and theories and then provide the opportunities for their learning.
6. *The teacher as researcher.* Teachers work in pairs and collaborate with other members of the staff, engaging in continuous discussion and interpretation of their work and the work of the children. This provides ongoing staff development and deeper exploration of theoretical foundations. Teachers see themselves as researchers who prepare and document their work. They consider children researchers as well.
7. *The documentation as communication.* Thoughtful care is given to ways in which the thinking of children is presented. Teachers make transcripts of children's dialogue, take series of photographs of their projects, and arrange them in panels that hang throughout the school or in books. This documentation is a way to communicate to the rest of the school what the children's work is about, to help parents become aware of their children's work, to assist teachers in evaluating children's work, and to show children that their work is valued.
8. *The parents as partner.* Parent participation is considered essential, and parents discuss their ideas and skills with the teachers. This underscores the collegiality and collaboration between home and school and ensures a curriculum that represents the diversity of the children and their families.

The teacher's role is unique: Two coequal teachers work with a class of 25 children. There is no head teacher or director of the school. The teachers are supported by a **pedigogista**, a person trained in early childhood education who meets with the teachers weekly. Also on the staff of every school is an **atelierista**, a person trained in the arts who teaches techniques and skills the children learn for their projects.

The process of the activity is highly respected as the way to plan and work together. Teachers and children—collaborators—listen to one another, and many points of view are encouraged. Debate and discussion are key elements in the process of deciding what project to do and how to go about it. The attitude that a child is a natural researcher as well as an able learner and communicator has molded the organization and structure of the schools.

The schools of Reggio Emilia are worth knowing about just for the strong and powerful view they hold of the child and the concept of teacher and student learning from one another. There are a growing number of American models as well.

Cadwell (1997), who has assisted two schools in St. Louis, Missouri, to adopt the Reggio Emilia approach

TeachSource Video ▶❚❚

Watch the TeachSource Video entitled "The Reggio Emilia Approach and Purpose-Built Schools." After you view the clip, reflect on the following questions:

1. How does the Reggio Emilia philosophy promote the community's responsibility to work together for quality child care and education?

2. What do you think is the most important aspect of the Reggio Emilia approach to care and educating young children?

described on these pages, offers a hopeful challenge: "We can learn from the Reggio educators to look at children differently, to expect more of them and of ourselves, and to offer them many more possibilities for full development."

Waldorf Schools

The Waldorf curriculum, shaped by Rudolf Steiner in 1919 (see Chapter 1), emphasizes the development of the whole child through "the head, heart, and hands." Based on the belief that young children learn primarily through observation, imitation, and experience, the curriculum provides a rich environment for children to explore and role models who provide appealing activities. Waldorf schools are play-based: A hallmark of the curriculum is learning through play, and large periods of time are devoted to creative play. Steiner agreed with Froebel and others that education should begin where the learner is: Whatever the child brings to the educational experience is to be worked with, not against. Academics are de-emphasized in the early years of schooling. Looping is common in the elementary school years as the teacher stays with the class for up to eight years. Other defining features (WECAN, 2005) of a Waldorf curriculum include:

- *Strong rhythmic elements based on the cycles of life and nature*: A daily rhythm of play, work, circletime, and outdoor play, ending with a nature or folk tale creates a consistent pattern for each session. The weekly rhythm evolves from activities, with one day for baking, another for crafts, and another for painting, and so on. Seasonal activities, such as planting bulbs, harvesting produce, or gathering leaves, stress nature's impact on our lives.

- *Environments that nourish the senses*: The walls of the classrooms are usually painted with soft watercolors, curtains may be made from plant-dyed fabrics, and tables and chairs are made of solid wood. The materials used are natural and real; the surroundings are simple and calming.

- *Extensive use of natural materials*: Wood, cotton, and wool are used throughout the classroom. Most of the toys are handcrafted from these natural materials, encouraging children to use their imagination. A piece of wood becomes a ticket to ride the train, which is made from chairs and pieces of wood. It may also become a telephone, a piece of food, or animal in a barn made of similar materials. The Waldorf philosophy suggests that other, more "finished" toys limit the power of fantasy, imagination, and creativity that is natural in a young child.

- *Play as an imitation of life*: The curriculum fosters skills that imitate the work of adults. Children participate in activities focused on the home—cooking and baking, cleaning, washing and sewing, and gardening and building. Engaging in meaningful life activities are seen as preparation for later academic challenges.

- *Enhancement of a sense of reverence and wonder*: Children's natural sense of awe and wonder is fostered and deepened, primarily through activities, stories and festivals that celebrate the cycles of the seasons. In the fall, the classroom may be decorated with corn stalks and sheaves of grain; the seasonal table is draped with beautiful fabrics in fall colors and hold gourds, pumpkins, acorns, and leaves. When parents join them for a harvest festival, songs of thankfulness and praise are sung before the feast begins. Each season this is repeated in order to expand the child's sense of reverence for life.

A Waldorf curriculum has much to offer, especially to those who put a premium on the use of imagination and an appreciation for the natural world. Learning is noncompetitive with no grades or set textbooks. There are many elements in the Waldorf method that are common to the Montessori method and to the Reggio Emilia schools.

Montessori Schools

In Chapter 1, Maria Montessori was discussed in relation to the history of early childhood education. What follows here is an explanation of the Montessori Method as a curriculum model for young children.

Montessori's approach to learning has had a continuing influence in education since those early years. Of her work, three features stand out: 1) adapting school work to the individual rather than molding the child to fit the curriculum; 2) insisting on freedom for children in selection of materials and choice of activities; and 3) training of the senses and on practical life issues.

Montessori programs may not be play-based in the way the four previous models are, but they are certainly child-centered and child-based in philosophy and practice. Montessori held that the choices children make during free activity time is work that others might rightly identify as play. Montessori programs have art activities as well as music, movement, and some group games. Fantasy play, a staple in other early childhood settings, is not part of the Montessori curriculum. Instead, the Practical Life area, where children learn personal care and care of the environment, is the closest Montessori comes to dramatic play. In the Practical Life area, children imitate adult activities, such as pouring and food preparation, but with real glasses, pitchers, and utensils readily available to them.

The Program

A common misunderstanding is that all schools with the Montessori name are the same. They are not. There are many variations and types of Montessori schools throughout the United States, reflecting an infinite variety of interpretations of the Montessori Method. Within the Montessori movement itself, there are at least two factions claiming to be the voice of the true Montessori approach to education.

Although the most common form of Montessori program is one in which 3- to 5-year-olds are grouped together, there are a growing number of schools for 6- to 9-year-olds and even 9- to 12-year-olds. Teacher education programs now prepare Montessori teachers to work with infants and toddlers as well as high school students.

The most striking feature of the Montessori classroom is its materials. Many are made of wood and designed to stress the philosophy of learning through the senses. Color, texture, and quality of craftsmanship of the materials appeal to the hand as well as the eye; they demand to be touched. "Smooth" and "oval" take on new meaning as a child runs a finger around Montessori-designed puzzle shapes.

Montessori materials have other unique characteristics besides their **tactile** appeal. They are self-correcting; that is, they fit together or work in only one way so that children know immediately whether they are successful. The Montessori curriculum presents the materials in a sequence, from simplest to most difficult. Many of the learning tasks have a series of steps and must be learned in a prescribed order. Whether sponging a table clean or using the number rods, the child is taught the precise order in which to use the materials. Montessori developed curriculum materials and tasks that are related to

real life. Practical Life activities range from cleaning tasks (hands, tables) to dressing tasks (lacing, buttoning, or tying garment closures).

In a Montessori classroom, children work by themselves at their own pace. They are free to choose the materials with which they want to "work"—the word used to describe their activity. Children must accomplish one task before starting another one, including the replacing of the materials on the shelf for someone else to use.

The prepared environment in a Montessori program has child-sized furniture and equipment—one of Froebel's ideas that Montessori used. Materials are set out on low shelves, in an orderly fashion, to encourage children's independent use. Only one set of any materials—their shape, form, and the way they are presented for children to use—are the vehicles for learning.

The teacher in the Montessori setting has a prescribed role, one of observing the children. Teachers become familiar with skills and developmental levels, and then match the children to the appropriate material or task. There is little teacher intervention beyond giving clear directions for how to use the materials. Group instruction is not common; learning is an individual experience.

Program Changes

Many changes have taken place in Montessori practices over the years, and today's best Montessori programs are those that are true to philosophical traditions of the Montessori method but constantly make small changes and adjustments. Many Montessori schools are adding curriculum areas of art, dramatic play, gross motor development, and computers. There is also greater teacher flexibility to promote social interaction.

For years, Montessori was separated from the mainstream of American education. Today that has changed, with more than 100 public school districts offering Montessori programs in their elementary schools and with the increased interaction between Montessorians and other early childhood professionals.

Maria Montessori has found her way into nearly every early education program in existence today. Whether labeled so or not, much of the material and equipment, as well as many of the teaching techniques, in use today originated with this dynamic woman nearly 100 years ago. She is firmly established in early childhood history and its future. The Montessori method should be weighed in light of contemporary knowledge and should be tailored to meet the needs of vigorous, eager, often needy children of the 21st century.

Summary

LO 1 Developmentally appropriate curriculum is age-appropriate, individually appropriate, and framed in the context of a child's culture. Culturally appropriate curriculum reflects the children, their families, and their community and enhances children's ability to view events and situations from a different perspective. Integrated curriculum provides opportunities for children of diverse skills and abilities to learn through the same experience. Inclusive curriculum ensures that all children are able to participate fully in all aspects of the program. Integrated curriculum fosters learning concepts through many curriculum subjects and activities. Emergent curriculum takes its cues from the children's interests, and the teacher helps them to explore their ideas in more depth. Multiples Intelligences and learning styles help teachers create a curriculum that covers a broad range of interests and abilities.

LO 2 Play-based curriculum is the foundation for learning in early childhood settings. Skills, knowledge, and learning take place in a setting where teachers support play by their interest, involvement, and setting the stage for children's experiences. Play is recognized as the curriculum of the child through activity centers and hands-on activities where discovery and experiment are the basis for learning.

LO 3 Planning curriculum includes setting goals, establishing priorities, knowing what resources are available, and evaluating the process. As teachers develop their curriculum plans, they may focus on the classroom activity or learning centers and the skills of the children. All three lend themselves to a basis for curriculum planning, and all are important vehicles for creative and effective curriculum for young children. State mandated learning standards influence curriculum development in the early childhood and elementary years. Although standards have the potential to improve teaching and learning, they carry the risk that inappropriate teaching and testing take the place of developmentally appropriate practices.

LO 4 Various curriculum models, such as High/Scope, Bank Street, the schools of Reggio Emilia, Waldorf schools, and Montessori schools are unique yet they have some common characteristics. They all model developmentally appropriate practices, and the development of skills and knowledge through play-based learning.

Key Terms

curriculum
developmentally appropriate
   practice (DAP)
culturally appropriate curriculum
transformative curriculum
holistically
inclusive curriculum
emergent curriculum

learning styles
dramatic play
activity centers
prerequisite
linchpin
standards
webbing
brainstorming

project approach
interactive media
non-interactive media
screen time
pedigogista
atelierista
tactile

Review Questions

1. Define developmentally and culturally appropriate curriculum for early childhood programs. What three core considerations determine whether a curriculum is DAP?
2. What are the most compelling arguments that play-based curriculum is the foundation for learning?
3. What elements do you include when you plan curriculum to meet the needs of all students? What is the importance of written plans, and how do they support teaching and learning?
4. Describe five play-based curriculum models that are developmentally appropriate, including the elements that foster development through play. How do these five models differ? How are they similar?

Observe and Apply

1. Observe an infant/toddler program, a preschool program, and an early elementary grade program. How do these programs exemplify developmentally and culturally appropriate curriculum? What is missing? What would you suggest they do to improve their program(s) to meet the DAP criteria?
2. Observe teachers as children play. What is the difference in the play when 1) a teacher interacts with children in their play and 2) a teacher intervenes? What happens to the play immediately after teacher contact is made? How long does the play last? What is your conclusion?
3. Develop a written plan for a week for 1) a 3-year-old class; 2) a family child care home; and 3) an after-school program for 6, 7, and 8 year olds. Use a nonholiday theme.
4. Use Gardner's Multiple Intelligences to determine your own ways of knowing. How has this style affected your abilities as a student? How do you think it affects your abilities as a teacher? What did you learn from this activity?
5. Observe a teacher-directed activity in an early childhood setting. What was the focus and what strategies did the teacher use to communicate the concept? Do you think this activity was a success or failure? Why?

Helpful Websites

High/Scope   www.highscope.org
NAEYC   www.naeyc.org

The Creative Curriculum®
   www.TeachingStrategies.com
Reggio Emilia   **www.reggiochildren.org**

🖲 The Education CourseMate website for this text offers many helpful resources and interactive study tools. Go to CengageBrain.com to access the TeachSource Videos, flashcards, tutorial quizzes, direct links to all of the websites mentioned in the chapter, downloadable forms, and more.

References

Armstrong, T. (2000). *Multiple intelligences in the classroom.* Alexandria, VA: Association for Supervision and Curriculum Development.

Banks, J. (2006). *Cultural diversity and education: Foundations, curriculum and teaching.* Boston: Allyn & Bacon.

Cadwell, L. (1997). *Bringing Reggio Emilia home.* New York: Teachers College Press.

Copple, C., & Bredekamp, S. (Eds.) (2009). *Developmentally appropriate practice in early childhood programs serving children from birth through age 8.* Washington, D.C.: National Association for the Education of Young Children.

Derman-Sparks, L., & Edwards, J. O., (2010). *Anti-bias education for young children and ourselves.* Washington, DC: National Association for the Education of Young Children.

Edwards, C., Gandini, L., & Forman, G. (1993). *The hundred languages of children: The Reggio Emilia approach to early childhood education.* Norwood, NJ: Ablex.

Epstein, A.S. (2007). *The intentional teacher: Choosing the best strategies for young children's learning.* Washington, D.C.: National Association for the Education of Young Children.

Erikson, E. H. (1972). Play and actuality. In M. W. Piers (Ed.) *Play and development* (pp. 127–168). New York: Norton.

Frost, J. L., Wortham, S. C., & Refifel, S. (2008). *Play and child development.* Upper Saddle River, NJ: Pearson Education, Inc.

Gestwicki, C. (2007). *Developmentally appropriate practice: Curriculum and development in early education.* Clifton Park, NY: Thomson Delmar Learning.

Gronlund, G. (2006). *Making early learning standards come alive: Connecting your practice and curriculum to state guidelines.* St. Paul, MN: Redleaf Press.

Helm, J. H., & Katz, L. (2001). *Young investigators: The project approach in the early years.* New York: Teachers College Press.

Jensen, E. (2005). *Teaching with the brain in mind.* Alexandria, VA: Association for Supervision and Curriculum Development.

Jones, E. (1994). An emergent curriculum expert offers this afterthought. *Young Children, 54,* p. 16.

Jones, E., & Nimmo, J. (1994). *Emergent curriculum.* Washington, D.C.: National Association for the Education of Young Children.

Katz, L. G. (1994). *The project approach.* Champaign, IL: ERIC Clearinghouse on Elementary and Early Childhood Education.

Katz, L., & Chard, S. (2000). *Engaging children's minds: The project approach.* Norwood, NJ: Ablex.

McNeely, S. L. (1997). *Observing students and teachers through objective strategies.* Boston: Allyn & Bacon.

National Association for the Education of Young Children (NAEYC) & National Association of Early Childhood Specialists in State Departments of Education (NAECS/SDE). (2002). Position Paper: Early Learning Standards: Creating the Conditions for Success. http://www.naeyc.org. Retrieved March 2009.

National Association for the Education of Young Children (NAEYC) & the Fred Rogers Center for Early Learning and Children's Media (2012). Position Paper: Technology and Interactive media as Tools in Early Childhood Programs Serving Children from Birth through Age 8. http://www.naeyc.org. Retrieved May 31, 2012.

New City School. (1994). *Celebrating multiple intelligences: Teaching for success.* St. Louis, MO: The New City School.

Poldrack, R. A., Clark, J., Pare-Blagoev, E. J., Shohamy, D., Creso Moyano, J., Myers, C., & Gluck, M. A. (2001, November 29). Interactive memory systems in the human brain. *Nature, 414,* pp. 546–550.

Ramirez, M., & Casteñada, A. (1974). *Cultural democracy, bicognitive development, and education.* New York: Academic Press.

WECAN (Waldorf Early Childhood Association of North America). (2005). *The Waldorf kindergarten: The world of the young child.* Retrieved from www.waldorfearlychildhood.org, March, 2012.

Woolfolk, A. (2001). *Educational psychology.* Boston: Allyn & Bacon.

York, S. (2003). *Roots and wings: Affirming culture in early childhood programs.* St. Paul, MN: Redleaf Press.

VPG/Lawrence/Cengage Learning

11

Planning for the Body: Physical/Motor Development in Action

 naeyc Standards For Professional Development

The following NAEYC Standards for Initial and Advanced Early Childhood Professional Preparation are addressed in this chapter:

Standard 1 Promoting Child Development and Learning

Standard 2 Building Family and Community Relationships

Standard 4 Using Developmentally Effective Approaches to Connect With Children and Families

Standard 5 Using Content Knowledge to Build Meaningful Curriculum

naeyc Code of Ethical Conduct

These are the sections of the NAEYC Code of Ethical Conduct that apply to the topics in this chapter:

Core Values: We have committed ourselves to basing our work with children on knowledge of child development.

Section I:

1-1.5 To create and maintain safe and healthy settings that foster children social, emotional, cognitive, and physical development and that respect their dignity and their contributions.

1-1.8 To support the right of each child to play and learn in an inclusive environment that meets the needs of children with and without disabilities.

Learning Objectives

LO1 Know how to maximize the importance of learning through physical activity and movement that enhances the mind–body connection, and articulate how that affects children's health and self-concepts.

LO2 Examine patterns of physical growth and development that include knowledge of gender issues, ethnic variations, and special needs concerns.

LO3 Identify and implement effective approaches that foster motor skills through appropriate curriculum strategies throughout the school day.

LO4 Analyze the teacher's role in promoting physical play through gender equity, an enriched playground, and a safe and challenging environment.

Maximizing Learning Through Movement

One of the first things you notice about young children is their energy and movement. Teachers often characterize children through their movements. "Trina never walks . . . she runs!" Pregnant mothers are aware of fetal motions and often assign personality traits to their children by these movements: "This baby is so active I think it must be in training for the Olympics." Infants show the extent of their full-bodied, random movements when they cry, roll over, and reach for a crib mobile. Physical growth and motor development are partly determined by a child's genetic makeup. Equally important are environmental factors, such as nourishment, health, safety, stimulation, opportunity, practice, encouragement, and instruction. The crucial interplay of heredity and environment guides the child's progress through life.

Integrated Learning

Motor abilities affect other areas of development. As noted earlier, research reinforces the notion that physical and motor development is integrated with a child's cognitive development. Factors that affect children's physical growth, such as poverty and malnutrition, can affect their ability to learn. Complex movements such as dancing or throwing a ball engage areas of the brain used for problem solving, planning, and sequencing new things to do. This mind–body integration can be seen in other areas of development as well:

Tim is reluctant to climb outside. He is frightened when he—or anyone else—is up in a tree or on a climber. Because he cannot risk using his body in space, he stops

Children are the picture of movement, spending the greatest portion of their day in physical activity.

himself from playing with anyone who invites him to try these activities. Tim's lack of gross motor development is affecting his social skills and his self-confidence.

Samantha loves to draw and cut. She chooses the art area every day. Not only are her fine motor skills well developed for her age; she takes great pride in her creations. Her motor skills enhance her self-confidence in school. In turn, she receives praise and attention from others as she communicates with both adults and children through her work.

What Movement Exploration Teaches

The greatest portion of the young child's day is spent in physical activity. Quality early childhood programs recognize this, providing for a full range of physical and motor experiences, planned and spontaneous. Indoors, children use puzzles, scissors, and dressing frames as they practice fine motor skills. They dance with scarves and streamers to music. Perceptual motor development, as with body awareness, occurs when children learn songs and games ("Head and Shoulders, Knees and Toes" or "Mother May I Take Two Giant Steps?") or while finger painting. Outdoors, gross motor skills are refined by the use of climbers, swings, hopscotch, and ring-toss. Movement exploration enhances children's ability to:

- Solve problems.
- Exercise divergent thinking.
- Respond at their individual age and developmental level.
- Learn to cooperate with others.
- Become more aware of others' viewpoints and ideas.
- Share, take turns.
- Be self-expressive.
- Be creative.
- Gain confidence.
- Develop strong muscles.
- Refine motor skills.

Children need time as well as equipment and activities to practice these skills. The value teachers place on physical and motor development is directly related to the time allotted in the daily schedule for children to pursue them.

The Importance of Physical Activity and Movement

Physical activity should be part of every child's daily life, in school and at home. "Movement is as necessary to their learning as air and light," says Jim Greenman (2000), noted authority on children's environments.

BRAIN
Research **Says...**

Linking the Mind and the Body

If you are an athlete, you are probably aware how energized you become when participating in a sport. Physical activity raises blood pressure, brings more oxygen to the brain, and increases the number of connections between neurons. At the same time, there is increased cognition and better memory (Kempermann, 2002).

Physical activity and exercise are strongly correlated with increased brain mass, mood regulation, and reading ability (Jensen, 2005). The reason for this is that the cerebellum is the part of the brain that processes movement as well as cognition. The connection between the two is powerful and demonstrates how domains of growth are deeply interconnected. Look back in Chapter 3 in the section "The Whole Child" to see how each area of growth affects and is affected by each other.

Early movement experiences are critical for optimal brain development.

The primary motor circuits that connect to the cerebellum—which controls posture and coordination—are formed during the first two years of a child's life. Early motor stimulation fosters attention, listening, reading, and writing skills (Palmer, 2003). If children do not develop basic movement skills during the early years, these skills often remain unlearned.

In older children, research has shown a connection between physical fitness and the brain. Children between the ages of 9 and 10 years old tend to have a bigger hippocampus and better memory than their peers who are less fit (University of Illinois at Urbana-Champaign, 2010). The hippocampus is in the central brain area and part of the foundation for learning and memory. A study by the American Heart Association (2010) connected physical fitness in seventh graders with higher academic performance than students who were not as fit.

Children move—constantly. It is in their nature. As educators, we need to understand that when they move, they learn. Learning is taking place when we all go on "A Bear Hunt" or play "Five Little Pumpkins." Movement activity stimulates brain growth as children physically experience up and down, or five minus one. The bottom line is: Learn to move so that you can move to learn.

Questions

1. How have you experienced the mind–body connection when you exercise or participate in sports?
2. What would you say to administrators who want to cut physical education from the curriculum?
3. As an early childhood educator, how can you support greater movement exploration for young children?

Childhood Obesity

American children are exposed to a value system in which physical/motor fitness is not always a high priority. Children are often encouraged toward sedentary activities at an early age, such as watching television and videos and playing computer games.

The frequency of children who are overweight and childhood obesity has increased alarmingly. According to the National Center for Health Statistics (2011), the prevalence of childhood obesity among children ages 2 to 5 has increased from 5 percent in 1980 to 10.5 percent in 2008. In children from age 6 to 11 years, there is an even greater increase since 1980, when the percentage rose from 6.5 percent to 19.6 percent in 2008. Health risks for these children include heart disease, high blood pressure, diabetes, depression, and low self-esteem.

Although there are many factors influencing obesity, such as socioeconomic status, family eating habits, heredity, and television viewing, a key factor seems to be whether or not one of the parents is obese (Berk, 2009). The American Academy of Child and Adolescent Psychiatry (2011) notes that if one parent is obese, there is a 59 percent chance the child will be obese in adulthood; if

both parents are obese, there is an 80 percent chance. The dramatic increase in childhood obesity only serves to underscore the need for regular physical exercise in programs for young children. Children do not learn by play alone. Many outdoor areas in schools contain few challenges, perhaps only a blacktop for bouncing balls and a small metal climber. Structuring physical activity into the curriculum helps children maximize their movement

Physical activity is an antidote to obesity.

DAP for Preschool and Elementary School Movement Programs

Movement is the planned and spontaneous curriculum goals that promote appropriate physical activity. The following guidelines and examples support developmentally appropriate practices for children from ages 3 to 12.

DAP for children from ages 3 to 5

Movement programs are designed for a child's individual developmental level.

Example: Equipment of different sizes and weights with multiple levels of complexity and difficulty accommodates children's varying skill levels and body sizes. Activities are adapted for children who are overweight and those who have special needs.

Children learn by moving and doing, interacting with people and objects, and teachers understand that movement can occur in any learning environment.

Example: Math concepts are given meaning when children are asked to take four steps forward and three steps backwards or count the number of stairs to the reading loft.

Learning experiences in movement are integrated with other areas of development.

Example: Learning to print your name is both a cognitive and fine motor activity.

Planned movement experiences enhance play experiences.

Example: When a teacher helps a young child learn to toss a ball to another child, the visual and verbal information fosters repetition during later play.

Teachers serve as guides, facilitators, and models for young children.

Example: Teachers support physical activity and movement when they model joy and interest in children's activity, when they allow children to make choices and when they encourage exploration and creativity.

DAP for Elementary School Children

The ultimate goal is to help children develop the skills, knowledge, and desire to enjoy a lifetime of physical activity.

Example: Teachers demonstrate enthusiasm for active, healthy lifestyles and encourage all children to experience the joy and satisfaction that can come from regular physical activity.

Children should engage in physical activity that is appropriate for their developmental levels.

Example: All children, regardless of developmental level and ability, are challenged at an appropriate level. Both boys and girls are encouraged in all activities, which are adapted for children who are overweight or those with special needs.

Recess and physical education are important but different aspects of the school program.

Example: Recess provides an unstructured opportunity in the school day for children to play and socialize. Physical education is a planned instructional program with specific goals and objectives.

Physical activity and physical education are not the same.

Example: Physical education is an instruction program taught by teachers with professional credentials and is designed to teach fundamental motor skills that form the foundation for physical activity. Physical activity includes a variety of movements that children use throughout the day. Elementary school children should have 60 minutes or more of daily physical activity.

Physical education and youth sports programs are different.

Example: Youth sports programs provide opportunities for children to choose one or more sports and refine their skills in competition with others. DAP physical education programs are designed for all children to have opportunities to learn motor skills appropriate to their developmental levels.

From *Appropriate Practices in Movement Programs for Young Children, Ages 3–5*, 2000, pages 4-11, and *Appropriate Instructional Practice Guidelines for Elementary School Physical Education*, 2009, pages 4-21. The Council on Physical Education for Children, Reston, VA: A position statement of the National Association for Sport and Physical Education/NASPE.

---

experiences and provides skill development that unstructured play cannot.

The National Association for Sport and Physical Education (NASPE) and the Council on Physical Education for Children (COPEC) established developmentally appropriate guidelines for preschool-age children. See the DAP Box for a discussion of these guidelines.

A Child's Self-Concept

The image of physical self is an important part of self-concept. How people feel about themselves is rooted in the way they feel about their bodies and what they can or cannot do with them. Attitudes about the body and its abilities directly affect the types of activities children try. Studies show that skill in games appears to be tied to peer group acceptance (Gallahue, 2003). Psychologists and teachers often notice a link between learning problems and clumsiness. Skilled early childhood educators carefully observe children, document their observations, and make referrals if a child needs an individual assessment.

Physical ability, then, contributes to a child's self-concept. With practice comes a sense of competence.

Children can learn to relax as they gain experience in physical activities, and thus reduce the stress of anticipating failure. Competence breeds self-confidence and a willingness to try greater challenges. As children try new activities, they learn more about themselves. And physical activity increases awareness of what fun it is to move—to run through a field or pump a swing just for the sheer joy of it!

Teachers support positive self-concept through physical and motor development in several ways. They let children discover their physical limits, rather than warning or stopping them from trying out an activity:

- *"I'm stuck!"* A child shouts across the yard. Rather than rushing to lift the child down, the teacher walks over to the child and replies, "Where can you put your foot next?" "How can you find a way to get across that branch?"
- *"I'm afraid!"* The teacher stands close to the child who is climbing and responds to the fear. "I will stand close to the climbing ropes so that you will feel safe."
- *"Look what I can do!"* Teachers reinforce children who try something new. "Greg, it's good to see you cutting out that pumpkin all by yourself."
- *"I tried."* Teachers congratulate efforts for the achievement they really are. "Your hands reached the top this time, Shannon. I bet you are feeling proud of yourself."
- *"I can't do it."* Children who stand on the side lines observing others may need some encouragement from the teacher to take the first step in mastering the climbing frame or slide. "Here is a good place for you to put your foot, Arturo. I will hold on to your hand until you ask me to let go."

It is not so much what teachers say to children that influences their feelings about themselves as it is the way in which children are treated. Children value themselves to the degree they are valued by others. The ways in which teachers show how they feel about children actually builds their self-confidence and sense of self-worth. Children create a picture of themselves from the words, attitudes, body language, and judgment of those around them.

Patterns of Physical and Motor Development

Children do not need encouragement to participate in physical activity. They need the opportunity, time, and support of their teachers to learn the fundamental fine and gross motor skills necessary for a healthy, active life.

Physical Growth

The average preschooler grows 2½ inches and gains five to seven pounds each year (Santrock, 2010), so understanding how physical development affects learning is important to teachers and parents. For example:

- New behavior is made possible through physical change: A toddler can be toilet trained once the anal sphincter muscles develop.
- Growth determines the child's experiences: Observe the new vistas that open up when children learn to climb.
- Growth changes the way people respond to the child: The mobility of crawlers and toddlers leads to more restrictions from parents, and teachers choose materials that are more challenging and complex.
- Self-concepts are profoundly related to physical development: An obese first grader avoids the running and chasing games during recess.

Growth Patterns

Development follows a directional and sequential pattern, even with children who are physically or mentally disabled. Variations in growth patterns are influenced by environment and genetic makeup. Large muscles develop before smaller ones—one reason why most preschoolers are more proficient at running than at cutting with scissors. Growth also starts at the center of the body and moves outward. Watch a toddler walk using whole-leg action and compare that with a 5-year-old whose knees and ankles are involved in a more developed response. Children also tend to develop in a head-to-toe pattern. Infants move their eyes, head, and hands long before they learn to creep or crawl. It is important to remember, however, that growth does not occur in a smooth and unbroken pattern.

By the age of 5, a child's brain is almost adult size. As the brain matures between the ages of 2 and 6, children gain greater impulse control, speed, and coordination of arms and legs. Eye–hand coordination is complete around the age of 4 years (Berger, 2006).

When looking at these growth patterns and brain development, parents and teachers must keep in mind the wide individual differences in the rates at which children grow and in the timing of each change. As a general rule, the pattern within individuals is consistent; that is, a child who is early, average, or late in one aspect of physical development is so in all aspects of growth. Figure 11-1 shows the range of dramatic changes in growth for children up to age 8.

See also Chapter 3 for an overview of developmental norms.

Growth Patterns of the Young Child

Age	Weight	Height	Proportion	Teeth
Newborn	7 lb.	20 in.	Head = 1/4 of length	None
Infancy (up to 18 months)	Gains 15 lb. (now 20–25 lb.)	Adds 8 in. (now 28–29 in.)	About the same	6
Toddler (18 mo. to 2½ years)	Gains 5 lb. (now 28–30 lb.)	Adds another inch or two (now 29–33 in.)	Legs = 34% of body	20
Preschool (2½– 5 years)	About 5 lb./yr. (now 30–40 lb.)	Add 14–15 in. from birth; at age 2 = half of adult height (now 35–40 in.)	Head growth slows; legs at age 5 = 44% of body	20
Early-middle childhood (5–8 years)	Doubles before adolescence (age 6 = 45–50 lb.)	Adds 9–10 in. (age 6 = 44–48 in.)	Continues to move slowly toward adult proportions	Begins to lose baby teeth; replaced by permanent teeth (age 6 = 20–24 teeth)

© Cengage Learning 2011

FIGURE 11-1 An overview of growth shows how rapid physical growth is in childhood.

Gender Differences

From infancy, boys and girls have similar body size and proportion, however, boys have a larger proportion of muscle tissue than girls, are more physically active and participate in more rough-and-tumble play than girls. Girls have more fat tissue than boys and are smaller and lighter until puberty (Santrock, 2010). Girls mature earlier than boys, and their growth is more regular and predictable. In motor skills, preschool girls have an edge in fine motor skills, such as writing and drawing, and gross motor skills, such as hopping and skipping. By age 5, boys can jump slightly farther, run slightly faster, and throw a ball about 5 feet farther than girls. These gender differences remain small until adolescence (Berk, 2009).

During middle childhood, motor development becomes smoother, more controlled, and coordinated. In gross motor skills, boys usually outperform girls through speed, strength, and agility. Fine motor skills increase as hands become steadier and more precise in both boys and girls (Santrock, 2010).

Ethnic Variations

There is some indication that physical development differs among ethnic groups. We need to be aware of the possibilities in the way children grow, but be careful not to stereotype them. African American infants and toddlers seem to walk earlier and as a group are taller than Euro-Americans. Asian children also seem to develop physically earlier than Euro-American babies but are smaller and shorter overall (Bee & Boyd, 2009). Some researchers suggest that because African American children have longer limbs, they have better leverage, which accounts for their superior performance in running and jumping (Berk, 2010). In the United States, children of African descent tend to be the tallest, followed by Europeans, Asians, and Latinos (Berger, 2006). Health and nutrition are factors that influence growth, and their effect is evident in the smaller size and weight of children in underdeveloped and/or poor nations.

Children with Special Needs

Every classroom is likely to have children who have special needs that must be met. It has already been established (see Chapters 3 and 9) that inclusion of children with special needs in early childhood programs is not only appropriate but is mandated by law. Physical education is the only subject area cited in the definition of an "appropriate education" in Public Law 94-42 that provides an opportunity for children to grow and develop through movement and physical activities.

Children with physical, cognitive, emotional, or learning disabilities are faced with a variety of challenges, many of which may be met by adapting the environment and planning for activities that help children function within their range of abilities. "The Inclusive Environment" and Figure 9-4 in Chapter 9 offer a number of ways for teachers and caregivers to individualize the

© Cengage Learning

To learn a motor skill, children must combine memory with experience, taking advantage of opportunities to try something new, and practice what has already been learned.

FIGURE 11-2 Many physical activities are appropriate for all children and encourage those with special needs to take an active part in the daily program. (From Gallahue, D.L., 2003. *Developmental physical education for today's children.* Madison, WI: Brown and Benchmark.)

setting for a variety of needs. In Chapter 3, many types of disabilities are discussed.

There are a number of teaching strategies that can enhance the participation of children with special needs in regular classroom activities in Figure 11-2. These brief examples make it clear that including children with special needs takes some careful thought about what kinds of movement experiences and physical development activities are within their abilities. Many of the suggestions are appropriate for all children, reminding us that the needs and interests of all children are essentially the same.

Motor Skills and Development

Motor development is a lifelong process of continuous change based on the interaction of 1) maturation (i.e., the genetically controlled rate of growth); 2) prior experiences; and 3) new motor activities. Like physical growth, motor development is a sequence of stages that is universal but still allows for individual differences. Each stage is different from, yet grows out of, the preceding level. Figure 11-3 charts motor development through the early years.

Any discussion of motor development should include reference to bodily-kinesthetic intelligence, part of Gardner's multiple intelligence theory (see Chapters 4, 10, and 12). Bodily-kinesthetic intelligence occurs when children use their bodies to help them process information and communicate their understanding of school. For instance, children who learn best through bodily-kinesthetic intelligence need active manipulation of materials. Drama, creative movement, dance, manipulatives, games, and exercises, both indoors and outdoors, benefit the bodily-kinesthetic learner.

Gross Motor Development

Gross motor activity involves movements of the entire body or large parts of the body. Using various large muscle groups, children try to creep, crawl, roll, bounce, throw, or hop. Activities that include balance, agility, coordination, flexibility, strength, speed, and endurance foster gross motor development.

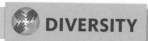
DIVERSITY

Kareena's Story: Adapting the Curriculum for Children With Special Needs

Adapting the environment and curriculum activities that help children function within their range of abilities is an important responsibility of the teacher. To plan physical activity for children with special needs, a teacher needs to:

- Evaluate the child's physical and motor development, focusing on the child's capabilities and needs. *Kareena is a 4-year-old girl who is blind, with age-appropriate motor skills except when she is in a new environment. She has a hesitant and unsteady gait as she learns furniture placement and activity area layout. Kareena is at ease with the teachers and is willing to approach other children, some of whom seem uncomfortable with her. She is generally cheerful and has a strong sense of herself and her abilities.*

- Set appropriate goals. *Involve Kareena in more group activities that promote social relationships. Pair her with a child who is sighted but whose physical development needs are similar. Playing with peers supports learning and a growing sense of competence.*

 In this way both children can build confidence and friendships. Utilize outside play for balancing activities, obstacle courses, and music and movement with scarves. Involve other children to help Kareena move from one activity to another and support her by modeling conversations that aid her in becoming oriented to materials and equipment: "There are a lot of fish in the water table, Kareena. Let's see if you can find the shark. Renee and Leo, can you tell Kareena what other fish and toys are in the water and who else is playing here?"

- Consider what modifications need to be made to materials and equipment that individually support children's wide range of capabilities. Use multisensory toys and objects when possible. *The balance beam may need to be wider or possibly placed on the ground for Kareena's first attempts. Add textured materials (cotton balls, velvet, rubber, and plastic objects) to the obstacle course and other equipment that will help direct Kareena as she moves. A wind chime hanging near the beginning of the obstacle course and balls with bells or other noisemakers inside will also guide her. Simplify activities by starting with what Kareena can do. For instance, kick a ball that is stationary before kicking a moving ball.*

- Make space modifications as necessary. *Check to see if walkways are clear and if equipment is readily accessible. Be consistent in storing classroom materials and equipment. Move equipment* closer to where children can easily reach it. Equip riding toys with bells or beepers. Create physical boundaries, if necessary, and purchase equipment that is specifically designed for an individual child's disability.

- Evaluate children, materials, and activities on a regular basis. *When Kareena masters the balance beam on the ground, how high might you move it for her next attempt? Is the obstacle course too challenging and, if so, how does it need to be modified? Does Kareena seem to enjoy these outside activities, and is she growing in her social relationships?*

Children of varying abilities enjoy difficult tasks and challenges that give them an opportunity to experiment, learn, and make progress.

There are a number of teaching strategies that can enhance the participation of children with special needs in regular classroom activities in Figure 11-2. These brief examples make it clear that including children with special needs takes some careful thought about what kinds of movement experiences and physical development activities are within their abilities. Many of the suggestions are appropriate for all children, reminding us that the needs and interests of all children are essentially the same.

Fine-Motor Development

Fine motor activity uses the small muscles of the body and its extremities (the hands and feet). Such movement requires dexterity, precision, and manipulative skill. Grasping, reaching, holding, banging, pushing, spinning, and turning are all activities that refine these skills.

Perceptual-Motor Development

Perceptual-motor development is a process in which the child develops the skill and ability to take in and interpret information from the environment and respond to it with movement. Children obtain data and impressions primarily through their senses. How often have you seen babies mimic a parent's or caregiver's mouth movements—taking in visually the various expressions, then physically responding in kind?

In a sense, every moment is perceptual-motor activity because the body and mind must work together to complete all motor tasks. The perceptual task is to process information; the motor response activates what is received in a physical way, although perceptual and motor abilities do not necessarily develop at the same time or the same rate (Gallahue, 2003). The complex nature of perceptual-motor development can be seen when

Steps in Motor Development

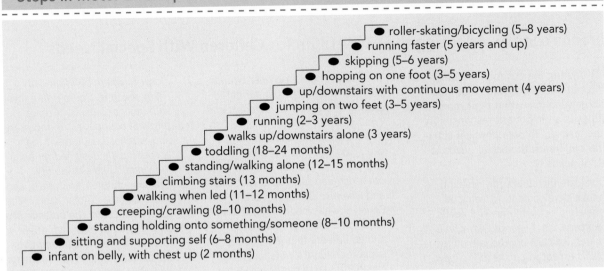

- roller-skating/bicycling (5–8 years)
- running faster (5 years and up)
- skipping (5–6 years)
- hopping on one foot (3–5 years)
- up/downstairs with continuous movement (4 years)
- jumping on two feet (3–5 years)
- running (2–3 years)
- walks up/downstairs alone (3 years)
- toddling (18–24 months)
- standing/walking alone (12–15 months)
- climbing stairs (13 months)
- walking when led (11–12 months)
- creeping/crawling (8–10 months)
- standing holding onto something/someone (8–10 months)
- sitting and supporting self (6–8 months)
- infant on belly, with chest up (2 months)

FIGURE 11-3 Motor development follows a developmental sequence. (Adapted from Allen, K.E., & Marotz, L., 2010. *Developmental profiles: Prebirth through 12.* Belmont, CA: Wadsworth Cengage Learning.)

© Cengage Learning

Fine motor activity requires using the small muscles of the body with dexterity and precision.

examining the three basic categories of spatial, temporal, and sensory awareness, which also include perceptual-motor concepts of body and directional, visual, and auditory awareness.

Spatial Awareness For children, **spatial** awareness means a sense of body awareness and the body's relationship to space, as well as a knowledge of what the body parts can do.

- For the toddler, concepts of spatial relationships are developed through motor activity: dropping objects from a high chair or forcing a large stuffed animal into a small box. Their definition of space is related to the action and movement involved in specific activities.
- A sense of relationship to less immediate things and places (knowing a specific route to school and home, making simple maps) develops in the preschool years. To illustrate, let us look at 3-year-old Tamara. She demonstrates her awareness of spatial relationships as she moves herself up to a table (without bumping into it), reaches to her left to pick up a ball of clay, and turns around behind her to choose a rolling pin.
- Not until ages 6 to 8 do children develop the more abstract spatial ability of distinguishing left from right on their own bodies and on others' bodies. Specifically, directional awareness refers to left and right, up and down, front and behind, over and under.

Temporal Awareness Temporal awareness is the child's inner clock, a time structure that lets the child coordinate body parts. Dancing to a rhythmic beat, speeding up, and slowing down develop this kind of skill. It is also a force that helps children predict time. For instance, 7-year-olds Luis and Aref ask if it is time to clean up as they finish their game of soccer. The after-school center has sports time for about an hour before getting ready for snack; the children have an inner sense of time that parallels their knowledge of the daily schedule.

Sensory Awareness Sensory awareness refers to use of the senses. It is another way the body gives the mind information. Vision is the dominant sense for young children. Visual awareness is the ability to mimic demonstrated movements and to discriminate faces, emotions, sizes, shapes, and colors. It is the ability in 3-month-old babies to recognize their mothers. Auditory awareness includes the ability to understand and carry out verbal directions and to discriminate among a variety of sounds ("Is this loud? fast? soft?" "Is that Josie or Dominick who called you?"). Auditory skills help children process information about language. From infancy, children seem to be able to combine visual and auditory awareness. Further sensory awareness develops through touch. Babies seem to put everything in their mouth to learn. When 4-year-old Stephanie picks up each object at the display table, she is using her sense of touch to discover size, shape, and volume.

Fostering Motor Skills in Young Children

Physical abilities and cognitive growth are intricately connected. Children acquire motor skills by making comparisons between their past experience and new actions. Such comparisons use memory and experience. Physical movement activities require full involvement of the mind and body.

Memory plays an important part in learning motor movements because children need to recall what they just did to make corrections or refinements. The ball that does not reach the basket is tossed farther on the next shot. To get the puzzle piece to fit, a child remembers other ways to manipulate the pieces. A long-term memory of movement is one that may go unrehearsed for long periods of time. The experience of swimming, for example, may be recalled only in the summer.

The experiences children have and the ability to recall those experiences are part of the process of gaining motor skill. Rehearsal is as important to the young child because every day children repeat and practice specific movements over and over as they play and work.

Types of Movement

Physical/motor skills involve three basic types of movement: locomotor, nonlocomotor, and manipulative abilities.

1. *Locomotor* abilities involve a change of location of the body (up, down, and sideways) (Gallahue, 2003) and include the skills of walking, running, leaping, jumping, climbing, hopping, skipping, galloping, sliding, and riding a tricycle.
2. *Nonlocomotor* abilities (sometimes referred to as balancing or stabilizing) are any movements that require some degree of balancing (Gallahue, 2003). These skills are turning, twisting, pushing, bending, stretching, pulling, swinging, rolling, dodging, and balancing.
3. *Manipulative* abilities include the operation and control of limited and precise movements of the small muscles, especially those in the hands and feet. Manipulative skills include throwing, catching, reaching, bouncing, striking, kicking (gross motor manipulation) and holding, grasping, cutting, and sewing (fine motor manipulation).

These three basic movements are necessarily combined when children are active in physical play:

With doll buggy:	Holding onto buggy—Manipulative
	Pushing buggy—Nonlocomotor
	Walking with buggy—Locomotor
Playing ball:	Bending down for the ball—Nonlocomotor
	Throwing the ball—Manipulative
	Running to base—Locomotor
Jumping rope:	Holding and turning the rope—Manipulative
	Jumping—Locomotor
	Balancing self after jump—Nonlocomotor
Breaking a piñata:	Holding the bat—Manipulative
	Swinging the bat—Nonlocomotor
	Running to get the prize—Locomotor

How to Foster Basic Motor Skills

Type of Motor Skill	Infants 0 to 1½ Years	Toddlers 1½ to 3 Years	Preschoolers 3 to 5 Years	Early School 6 to 8 Years
Locomotor: Walking Running Jumping Hopping Skipping Leaping Climbing Galloping Sliding	Safe areas to explore body movements Balls to roll Hanging jumpseats Walkers on wheels Simple obstacle course	Walker wagons Pull/push toys Dancing Wide balance board Toddler gym—stairs and slide "Ring around the Rosey"	Hippity-hop balls Sled Beginning skis Trampoline Roller skates Jump rope Balance beam Climber Dancing	Jump rope Roller skates Ice skates Climbing rope Tumbling mats Hopscotch
Nonlocomotor: Pushing Pulling Bending Balancing Stretching Rolling turning Twisting	Large, safe areas for exploration Parent/caregiver play: holding, pushing arms, legs, sturdy push toys Soft obstacle course of pillows	Pounding board Simple, low rocking horse Ride-on toys Toddler-type swing Large Legos® Sturdy doll buggy Wagon Fabric tunnels Blocks Cars, trucks to push	Shopping cart/doll carriage Wheelbarrow Pedal toys, trike Rakes, shovels Slide Swing Punching bag	Scooter Two-wheel bike Sled, toboggan Exercise mat Acrobatics Diving mask for swimming Doorway gym bar
Manipulative: Grasping Throwing Catching Kicking Receiving/moving objects Bouncing	Mobile attached to crib—kicking feet moves it Rattles, teething rings Crib activity board Soft foam blocks Snap beads Floating bath toys	Variety of balls Stacking, nesting toys Activity box—on floor Shape sorters Large, fat crayons Large pegs and board Water/sand table	Crayons, markers Clay, dough Bowling games Puzzles Woodworking tools Balls Lacing board Water/sand table	Baseball glove/bat Ring toss game Full-size balls Oversize bat Frisbee "Miss Mary Mack"

FIGURE 11-4 Toys and games help develop specific motor skills in young children.

Figure 11-4 shows age appropriate toys and games that foster the development of the three types of basic motor skills.

Practicing Basic Skills

A child's typical day, at home or at school, provides numerous opportunities to practice motor skills. Through play, the child can practice fine motor skills such as:

- Holding a paintbrush, scissors, or rattle.
- Tiptoeing to music.
- Grasping a bottle, a hand, a toy.
- Threading a bead or a wide needle.

The child can also practice gross motor skills such as:

- Pumping on a swing.
- Climbing a tree.
- Digging a garden.
- Balancing on a board, on one foot.

Through self-help activities the child can practice fine motor skills such as:

- Buttoning a coat or doll's clothes.
- Brushing teeth, hair.
- Turning a faucet handle or doorknob.
- Feeding self with utensils.

Gross motor practice includes:

- Moving a nap cot or table.
- Kicking covers off.
- Walking, holding onto furniture.
- Climbing up stairs or on a climber.

Children learning motor skills need experience in basic skills; they must learn simple skills before combining

Practice is challenging and fun.

them into complex activities. Children must have time to try, refine, and try again.

Feedback

Children modify and improve their motor skills as they receive information about their movements, both **intrinsic** (the paintbrush makes marks when it is pushed across the paper) and **extrinsic** ("I notice that your legs are very far apart as you try to somersault; how about holding them together as you roll next time?").

A Range of Developmental Levels

Any group of young children has various levels of motor growth and physical development. An individual child may have different abilities and skills in gross, fine, and

TeachSource Video

Watch the TeachSource Video entitled "Two–Five Years: Fine Motor Development for Early Childhood." After you study the video clip, reflect on the following questions:

1. What activities did you see that lay the foundation for writing?
2. Compare and contrast the video clip's fine motor activities with those described in the text.

perceptual-motor areas; activities should be offered on several developmental levels. Play materials and equipment, such as balls, climbers, and ladders, should accommodate a variety of skill levels, particularly if children with physical disabilities are in the class. Climbing boards put on several levels and puzzles ranging from 6 to 60 pieces are two examples of how teachers can meet the need for success and challenge.

Curriculum Strategies for Physical Development

Teachers plan activities that promote physical/motor skills in the areas of gross motor, fine motor, and perceptual-motor development. They look at the environment, both indoors and out, to see that all three areas of physical growth are encouraged.

Throughout the Day

When thinking of physical/motor development in the classroom, teachers tend to focus on the fine motor (or small-muscle) tasks for the classroom and on gross motor (or large-muscle) tasks for the outdoor play space. The indoor area lends itself more readily to activities with less movement, and the outdoor area encourages whole-body play. Yet children can have a wider variety of activities if teachers remember that both gross motor and fine motor projects can happen everywhere in the environment.

Indoor Areas Indoors, the art area is stocked with pens, crayons, scissors, and hole punches that develop the fine motor skills.

1. Add large brushes or rollers to the easel or plan finger painting, and the art area now includes gross motor development.
2. When children use templates to trace both inside and outside spaces, they practice perceptual-motor skill.
3. In the science area, getting "just a pinch" of fish food is a fine motor activity; cleaning out the turtle house requires larger muscles to move rocks and sand.
4. Perceptual-motor development occurs as children use pitchers to fill the fish tank or turtle tub and learn about water levels.
5. At the manipulative table, when a child puts a peg into a pegboard, fine motor skills are used.
6. Removing puzzles from a shelf and carrying them to a table brings in gross motor skills. Add nuts and bolts, and the child's perceptual-motor skills are called into play.
7. The block area has endless possibilities, from lifting and carrying (gross motor), to balancing and stacking

(fine motor), to building a space so that an animal or car fits through (perceptual-motor).

8. The language and library areas are places for turning pages or looking at words and pictures (fine motor). They also involve taking books off shelves and replacing them and trying out the movements and activities read about in books. For instance, Tana Hoban's *Is It Hard? Is It Easy?* encourages children to act out the scenes pictured in the story, all gross motor tasks. With a listening post nearby, children listen for the "beep" and coordinate what they hear (perceptual) with turning the page (motor).

Outdoor Areas   Outdoors, children develop motor skills of all kinds.

1. In the sand, children dig, a gross motor activity. As they judge how big a hole is or how much water will fill it, they are practicing and improving their perceptual-motor skills. Turning on a faucet, planting seeds, and making mud pies are for fine motor development.
2. Wheel toys offer children opportunities in all motor areas.
3. Pushing someone in a wagon develops arm and leg strength—gross motor development.
4. Guiding tricycles and carts on a path and around obstacles requires perceptual-motor skill.
5. Trying to "repair" or "paint" a wheel toy with tools or with large brushes, tying wagons together, or weaving streamers through the spokes of a bicycle all use fine motor skills.

By looking at the classroom and yard with one eye to physical and motor development, teachers can plan activities that support growth in all skill areas.

Adults support children's self-confidence when they foster physical and motor activity.

Transitions and Group Times   Every part of the daily schedule can be planned to use all physical/motor skills. For instance:

1. Getting in and out of coats and snowsuits is a large muscle activity. Children learn perceptual-motor skills as they try to get their arms in the correct sleeves.
2. Buttoning, zipping, and tying are fine motor activities.
3. As children get ready for group time, often a difficult transition, they might practice drawing faces in the air or making their bodies into the shapes of letters, both perceptual-motor tasks.
4. Group times also include activities for motor development, such as stretching, dancing, jumping, as well as working puzzles, pounding clay, and writing stories.
5. When there are balloons, scarves, or a parachute at music time, children practice gross motor skills.
6. Finger plays at group time are a fine motor task. Activities for developing the senses of hearing and sight are two areas of sensory growth that can be utilized as content for group times.

Focusing on Skills Development

The physical/motor skills include those that use large and small muscles and that coordinate perception and motor response. Teachers planning activities for children can focus on any one of the following skills as a basis for curriculum planning.

Eye–Hand Coordination.   Developing stitchery skill uses the perceptual-motor skill of *eye–hand coordination*. A series of activities can be planned to help children learn these skills.

1. It begins in infancy, when the baby first begins to manipulate and examine an object, learns to grasp with thumb and forefinger (pincer grasp), and shows a hand preference.
2. Stringing large wooden beads is a first step and leads to using pieces of straw and punched paper, with somewhat smaller holes. Macaroni can be strung on shoelaces or on stiff string and then onto yarn, which is softer and more challenging.
3. Sewing cards made by punching holes in polystyrene trays can be introduced as the next activity. Large plastic needles can be used with the lacing cards or with the trays; large embroidery needles with big eyes can be used for stitching yarn onto burlap.
4. Children may be ready to use embroidery hoops with which they can make a design on burlap first

and then stitch over the outlines. Buttons can be sewn on burlap or other fabric. Popcorn or packing material can be strung using a needle.

5. A final project might be to make a group wall hanging, with squares of children's stitchery sewn together. Simple backpacks and coin purses might be made with the children sewing most of it themselves.

Balance Look again at Kareena's story on page 343 or the process teachers use to help Kareena and others with a wide variety of capabilities learn how to use a balance beam.

Figure 11-4 on page 346 lists age-appropriate equipment that fosters the development of motor skills.

Use of Themes

When teachers plan activities, they often have a theme or unit as their focus. Themes can be used to encourage physical and motor involvement. A unit on outer space involves ample opportunity to involve all the motor skills.

- Gross motor skills are used in jumping around on the moon, taking a space walk, getting in and out of the rocket ship, and building a spaceship with large blocks.

- Fine motor skills are needed to manipulate knobs on the instrument panel, to draw maps of the stars, or to write out a countdown on a chalkboard.
- Perceptual-motor skills are needed to work out how to get ready for a trip to Mars, what happens on the trip, and when and how to get back to Earth.
- Use the sample forms in Chapter 10 to develop an outer space unit as well as other appropriate themes to encourage motor skills.

Once teachers realize which physical/motor skills the children possess and what the group is ready to learn, they can plan activities around a classroom unit.

Parents can be a good source of ideas for ensuring that themes and activities reflect the various cultures within the classroom. Figure 11-5 lists many activities that are culturally related.

Curriculum planning for motor and movement skills requires teachers to know principles of physical growth and motor development. They then can use this knowledge to plan activities that encourage children to master their own movements and to learn other skills through movement. In the early childhood setting, curriculum can be planned by concentrating on activity areas, focusing on a specific motor skill, or using a classroom theme.

Appreciating Cultural Diversity through Motor Development

For Indoor and Outdoor Play

Activity	Motor Skill Practice	Culture
Lion or dragon dance	Gross-motor	Chinese (New Year)
Making and flying carp kites	Fine- and gross-motor	Japanese
Dodgeball	Gross-motor	Euro-American
Chinese jump rope	Gross-motor	Chinese
Breaking the piñata	Gross-motor	Latino
Spinning like a dreidel	Gross-motor	Jewish (Hannukah)
Origami art	Fine-motor	Japanese

Activity	Motor Skill Practice	Culture
Weaving	Fine-motor	Native American
Country/Western dance step	Gross-motor	Euro-American
Make mariachi instruments	Fine-motor	Latino
Dancing to mariachi band music	Gross-motor	Latino
Hokey pokey	Gross-motor	Euro-American
Make and twirl a grager	Fine-motor	Jewish (Purim)
Cooking; stir-fry rice	Fine-motor	Chinese
Making fry bread	Fine-motor	Native American
Kick the can	Gross-motor	Euro-American
Making and beating drums	Fine-motor	Native American

© Cengage Learning 2011

FIGURE 11-5 A variety of activities that reflect many cultures can be integrated into the curriculum for motor and physical development. Note: These activities are, at best, an approximation of traditional cultural expressions and not authentic presentations, yet they can enlarge the child's worldview through physical play.

The Teacher's Role

As teachers plan programs for physical/motor development, they reflect on several important issues that go beyond written curriculum plans.

Sex-Role Stereotyping

Is motor behavior different for boys and girls? If so, why? Research indicates that there are differences between girls and boys in these areas. For example, behavioral differences in motor development are apparent in early life: 1-year-old girls already spend more time in fine motor tasks, whereas baby boys are more engaged in gross motor activity. Around the age of 2, children begin to identify people by their gender and are aware of which behaviors are considered more appropriate for their sex (Hill & Flom, 2007). Preschoolers often characterize many toys, articles of clothing, occupations, and behaviors with one sex or the other (Campbell et al., 2001). During preschool and early elementary years, boys seem to prefer rough-and-tumble, aggressive outdoor play (Else-Quest et al., 2006). By age 2, children seem to prefer playmates of their own gender, a tendency that increases in middle childhood (Hay et al., 2004).

Why does this happen? Probably some sex differences are the result of genetics. At the same time, **sex-role stereotyping** expectations profoundly affect the motor and physical development of young children. A gender stereotyping mindset can either encourage or discourage children from developing to their fullest potential, and teachers need to be aware of these attitudes in others and themselves. They might ask themselves:

- What messages do I give children about physical activity? Do I value it for myself? For children? Do I value physical expression for girls as well as boys?
- Do I emphasize sports as a way to have fun? A way to be healthy? Do I praise only the "winner"?
- Can I provide male and female role models for physical activities using parents, grandparents, older siblings, staff, visitors, and guests?
- Do I encourage children to wear clothing that allows them the freedom to run, climb, or tumble? What do I do when girls arrive in long dresses and party shoes? (Be sensitive to family and cultural influences about appropriate clothing.) What should I wear?
- Are all physical/motor activities made equally available and attractive to boys and girls? What should I do if some children dominate these activities, while others never choose them?

- How do I actively engage all children in every form of physical activity? Do I let them know I think it is important?

Pica (2004) notes that children between the ages of 6 and 8 usually play with others of the same sex. She further suggests that this growing gender awareness can be addressed by assigning play partners of the opposite sex for certain games or suggesting that all children take on the roles of people in various occupations (firefighters, police officers, hairdressers, dancers) regardless of gender. By working and playing together, children learn to appreciate not only their own ideas and ways of doing things, but also those of others. See Chapter 15 for further discussion on gender-related issues.

A Safe and Challenging Environment

First and foremost, teachers ensure the safety of the children. To maintain a safe physical environment, they see to it that materials and equipment are in usable condition and that overall traffic patterns are free of hazards. For example, to make a gymnastic activity safe, teachers would provide mats and make sure that only one child is tumbling at a time.

Psychological safety requires an even finer sensitivity on the part of the teaching staff. Fear is a learned response, and teachers must be careful not to discourage children from using their full range of abilities, creating overly anxious and fearful children. The new teacher is often concerned about children's safety, particularly when they are climbing. It helps to remember that children generally climb to heights that are comfortable for them; in other words, they often set their own limits.

Picking children up and placing them on equipment, often at their own request, is questionable. If teachers comply with children's wishes to be lifted and set somewhere high, they are placing those children in situations outside of their natural limits. The children may see this as saying, "You are incapable of climbing up there yourself," or "It is too dangerous for you to try that alone." Also, this does not allow children to gain experience in basic skills first, but puts them in a situation that calls for skills more complex than they have at the time. This denies the child the opportunity to practice those skills and increase their capabilities. When they must seek solutions to getting up, out, in, or down, they learn to handle realistically their current level of physical and motor development. Teachers lend encouragement and confidence to children by saying, "I cannot put you up there, but I will help you try." Making playgrounds safe is a good way

Getting Physical Indoors

"How can we provide more opportunities for children to be physically active for part of every school day? Could it be done in a way that includes all developmental domains?" Teacher Tanya posed these questions at a staff meeting. The team liked the idea of focusing on the various developmental domains to ensure that the whole child was being addressed. They discussed how to individualize the activities, change the room arrangement, and how this would affect their daily planning. The staff unanimously agreed to move forward, and Tanya offered to modify the existing curriculum to see how greater movement activity could be integrated into the daily schedule. Here are her suggestions that the staff adopted after more discussion on ways to implement aspects of the plan.

Motor Development Across the Developmental Spectrum

Language Arts: At group time, have the children make the letter "A" with their body, then other letters, such as C, P, I, S, T, and with a partner, the letters H, M, W, B, and so on.

Math: Have children line up according to their height, tallest to shortest; Compute the number of fingers and toes in the classroom.

Art: Draw outlines of the children's bodies in various positions of walking, running, or crawling and have children cut them out and decorate them. Make a mural across the wall with the body shapes.

Cognitive: Have children lie on the floor and kick their legs high/low and sideways and like scissors, bicycle riding, skiing, and swimming.

Social: Working in pairs, have children play "Mirror" where they face each other and imitate wide arm and leg movements and facial expressions.

Emotional: Have children dance as if they were angry, proud, happy, sad, quiet.

Physical Motor Skills:

Large Motor: Have children build a slide that is appropriate to their age level, play musical chairs, create a "Where the Wild Things Are" dance.

Fine Motor: Create a class quilt and have children cut, draw, color, and sew or paste felt squares to make a community blanket.

Think About This
1. How do each of these activities foster brain development?
2. How would these activities foster children's feelings of success?

to promote physical growth and sets the stage for learning through motor development as shown in Figure 11-6.

Playground Enrichment

The playground is the natural arena for optimal physical development and the ideal environment to promote physical fitness. On the playground, all motor skills are called into play. Outdoor activities should challenge children to use a wide range of motor skills and provide for a wide range of differences among their abilities:

Carmine grabs a scarf and begins to dance, *twirling* and *whirling*, *hopping* and *bending* in time to the music. Following the teacher's lead, Carmine *balances* on his toes and *waves* his scarf high over his head.

Tina *walks* to the climber, *grasps* the highest rung she can reach, *pulls* herself up by *lifting* one leg and then the other until she *stretches* vertically full-length along the climber bars. Satisfied, she *pushes* off with her feet and *jumps* backward to the ground. She *bends* her knees as she lands, *balances* herself to an upright position, and *runs* off.

Ramon *toddles* over to *pick up* the large red ball. Momentarily overwhelmed by its size, he *falls* backward to *sit on* the grass. As a teacher approaches him, he *rolls* the

ball toward her. She *throws* it back to him and Ramon imitates her movements. Soon they are involved in *kicking* and *tossing* the ball to each other.

Using both small and large muscles, children gain control over their bodies as they run and play. The playground provides open space where full-bodied action takes place, providing many opportunities to develop balance and coordination.

Physical skills, however, are not the only benefit of outdoor play. Social and cognitive skills are enhanced as well. On the playground, children must negotiate turns with the wagons, ask for a push on the swing, and wait in line going up the slide. Some of the most intricate and involved dramatic play takes place outdoors. Problems get solved when two tricycles collide. Science experiences are all around—finding a bird's nest or planting a garden. "There are indeed advantages of the outdoors that cannot readily be provided indoors" (Frost et al., 2008).

On the playground, no one says "Be quiet!" or "Quit wriggling!" It is a place of motion and space, filled with the special sensations found only outdoors.

When creating and maintaining a challenging environment, teachers consider both variety and level of challenge. A choice of surfaces encourages a variety of movements, and while cement may be appropriate for

Making Playgrounds Safe

Safety in the yard means:
- Enough room for the number and age of children who will use it.
- Adequate empty space.
- Availability of both hard and soft surfaces.
- Soft surfaces under any equipment from which a child might fall.
- Shady areas alternating with sunny spots.
- No standing water—good drainage.
- No poisonous or thorny plants, or litter or debris.
- Areas of play clearly defined and differentiated from one another.
- Sand area protected at night from animals.
- Fences high enough and in good repair.
- Gates secure with latches out of children's reach.

Equipment is:
- Well maintained—no exposed nails, screws, sharp edges, chipped paint.
- Chosen with children's ages in mind in regard to height and complexity.
- Stable and securely anchored.
- Repaired immediately or removed if damaged.
- Varied to allow for wide range of skills.

- Not crowded.
- Smooth where children's hands are likely to be placed.
- Checked frequently.
- Placed appropriately: sides facing north, swings away from other structures and busy areas.
- Scaled to age level: steps and other openings are 4 inches or less apart or 8 to 10 inches apart.
- Modified for age levels: swings have soft seats.

Teachers:
- Reinforce safe practices.
- Wear appropriate outdoor clothing.
- Check frequently where children are playing.
- Involve children in safety checks of yard, equipment, and grounds.
- Provide continual, adequate supervision.
- Avoid congregating to talk.
- Get involved with children.
- Provide enough activities and challenges.
- Watch for sun exposure, especially with toddlers.
- Assist children when they want to rearrange movable equipment.

© Cengage Learning 2011

FIGURE 11-6 Before children are allowed to use a playground, teachers should use a checklist such as this to ensure that safety standards are met. A safe playground stimulates physical development, social interaction, and full exploration of the materials and environment.

transportation toys, tanbark and rubber mats are better for climbing, hanging, and dropping.

Varying the equipment also stimulates motor activity. Equipment that is mobile allows for greater range of uses and allows children to manipulate their environment. By creating their own physical challenges with wooden crates, children make platforms; caves; and houses to crawl in, over, and through. Another way to provide variety is to focus on the less developed skills, such as catching and throwing, rolling, latching, snapping, or zipping.

When children are encouraged to discover their physical potential, they learn to solve problems of movement defined by the limits of their abilities rather than by performance. This kind of learning encourages self-confidence as children find success.

Encouraging Physical Play

The vital role of physical activity is best fulfilled when teachers:

- Create time in the daily schedule for periods of physical activity, preferably, but not limited to, outdoors.
- Actively participate while supervising and encouraging all children to become involved in strenuous activity.

© Cengage Learning

The outdoor area has great potential for developing gross motor skills (climbing, bending, sliding), fine motor skills (grasping, reaching, holding), and perceptual-motor skills (eye–hand coordination, directionality, tempo).

- Set goals for children's motor development and physical fitness.
- Use a variety of activities on a daily basis, including science, art, and music, to stimulate physical development.
- Select age-appropriate equipment and materials, providing a variety of props to enhance their use.
- Give children opportunities to repeat, practice, and refine the skills they learn.

When children develop their physical and motor skills under this kind of encouragement, their confidence and sense of competence grow. This sense of personal worth is at the core of their being.

Observing children while they play outdoors allows teachers an opportunity to assess potential problems in motor development. The checklist in Figure 11-7 indicates some areas to observe.

Teachers plan activities that promote physical/motor skills in the areas of gross motor, fine motor, and perceptual-motor development. They look at the environment, both indoors and out, to see that all three areas of physical growth are encouraged.

Check Whether Child:

- ☐ 1. Has trouble holding or maintaining balance
- ☐ 2. Appears to have difficulty balancing and moves awkwardly
- ☐ 3. Cannot carry self well in motion
- ☐ 4. Appears generally awkward in activities requiring coordination
- ☐ 5. Has difficulty making changes in movement
- ☐ 6. Has difficulty performing combinations of simple movements
- ☐ 7. Has difficulty in gauging space with respect to own body; bumps and collides with objects and other children
- ☐ 8. Tends to fall often
- ☐ 9. Has poor eye–hand coordination
- ☐ 10. Has difficulty handling the simple tools of physical activity (beanbags, balls, other objects that require visual–motor coordination)

© Cengage Learning 2011

FIGURE 11-7 A checklist of possible problems in physical/motor development serves as a guideline when devising a developmentally specific profile for spotting problems.

Summary

LO 1 Physical growth and motor skills progress at a rapid rate during the child's first few years of life. Children are in motion virtually from conception, and physical activity maximizes their learning potential. The mind–body connection is linked as the brain synapses are reinforced by the repetition of motor skills, such as walking, running, and crawling. Physical and motor development is integrated with a child's cognitive abilities and learning. Complex movements engage the brain in problem solving, sequencing, planning, cooperation, and creativity. The importance of daily physical activity cannot be underestimated and has implication for the rise in childhood obesity, which can result in lower self-concept.

LO 2 Knowing growth patterns and the sequence of development determine how and what teachers provide as physical and motor experiences. Gender differences and the skills of children with special needs influence planning as well. Motor development, like physical development, is a sequence of stages based on maturation, prior experiences, and new motor activities.

Muscular development can be categorized as gross motor, fine motor, and perceptual-motor. Gross motor movements use the entire body or large parts of it, such as the legs for running or the arms and torso for throwing. Fine motor movements, such as manipulating objects, are those that use smaller muscles and that require precision and dexterity. Perceptual-motor movements are those that combine what is perceived with a body movement. Spatial, temporal, and sensory awareness all play an important part in the development of perceptual-motor skills.

LO 3 The three basic types of motor skills are locomotor, which involves a change in location of the body; nonlocomotor, which involve some type of balance; and manipulative. To learn a motor skill, children combine memory and experience and are challenged by new activities that extend their learning. A child who has mastered a 25-piece puzzle needs opportunities to work 60- and 75-piece puzzles. To master the more complex activities, children need time and opportunity throughout the school day to practice and rehearse what they have already learned. Curriculum that provides a wide range of play materials that appeal to a variety of skill levels foster motor development.

LO 4 As teachers plan programs that foster physical motor growth, there are several important issues to consider. Too often, physical activity is hampered by sex-role stereotyping that can discourage children from participating in the full range of physical opportunities. Maintaining a sage physical environment is critical, as is providing a wide variety of movement experiences in a rich and challenging playground. Creating time in the schedule, actively encouraging physical play, setting goals for children to meet, and using the full curriculum to enhance movement development are ways in which teachers encourage physical play.

Key Terms

gross motor	spatial	intrinsic
fine motor	temporal	extrinsic
perceptual-motor development	sensory	sex-role stereotyping

Review Questions

1. How do children learn through physical activity and motor development, and what effect does that have on their health and self-concept?
2. Why is it important to understand physical development and the patterns of growth in young children?
3. How can the teacher of young children foster motor skills in all developmental domains throughout the classroom areas? How can the teacher support acquisition of specific motor skills in young children with special needs?
4. What is the teacher's role in promoting physical activity that is gender inclusive, and what considerations are needed for a safe and challenging environment and playground?

Observe and Apply

1. Map the classroom in which you are currently working. List at least one activity in each area that develops physical motor skills. Add one more activity of your own that widens such development.
2. In what ways does a school program you know reinforce sex-role stereotyping in motor activities? What could be done to change this?
3. Observe an infant/toddler program, a group of 4 or 5 year olds at play, and a first grade recess. How does the environment—inside and out—support or inhibit strenuous physical activity?
4. Do you know a young child who is obese? What factors do you think are responsible for this condition? Do you know if his or her family is aware and/or concerned? If you were the child's teacher, what might you say to the parents?

Helpful Websites

American Academy of Pediatrics   **www.aap.org**
National Program for Playground Safety
  www.playgroundsafety.org

National Association for Sports & Physical Education
  www.aahperd.org/naspe

Ⓔ The Education CourseMate website for this text offers many helpful resources and interactive study tools. Go to CengageBrain.com to access the TeachSource Videos, flashcards, tutorial quizzes, direct links to all of the websites mentioned in the chapter, downloadable forms, and more.

References

Allen, K. E., & Marotz, L. (2010). *Developmental profiles: Prebirth through 12.* Belmont, CA: http://www.sciencedaily.com/releases/2010/03/100302185522.htm. Retrieved February 2, 2012.

Bee, H., & Boyd, D. (2009). *The developing child.* Menlo Park, CA: Addison-Wesley.

Berger, K. S. (2006). *The developing person.* New York: Worth Publishers.

Berk, L. E. (2009). *Infants and children.* Boston: Allyn & Bacon.

Campbell, A., Shirley, L., & Caygill, I. (2001). Sex-typed preferences in three domains: Do two-year-olds need cognitive variables? *British Journal of Psychology,* 93(2), pp. 203–217.

Else-Quest, N. H., Hyde, J. S., Goldsmith, H. H., & Van Hulle, C. A. (2006). Gender differences in temperament: A meta analysis. *Psychological Bulletin,* 132(1), pp. 33–72.

Flanagan, J. R., Vetter, P., Johansson, R. S., & Wolpert, D.M. (2003). Prediction preceded control in motor learning. *Current Biology,* 13, pp. 146–150.

Frost, J. L., Wortham, S. C., & Reifel, S. (2008). *Play and child development.* Upper Saddle River, NJ: Pearson Education, Inc.

Gallahue, D. L. (2003). *Developmental physical education for today's children.* Madison, WI: Brown and Benchmark.

Greenman, J. (2000). Guest editorial: Places for childhoods. In A.M. Gordon & K.W. Browne, *Beginnings and beyond: Foundations in early childhood education.* Fifth Edition. Clifton Park, NY: Delmar Learning.

Hay, D. F., Payne, A. & Chadwick, A. (2004). Peer Relations in childhood. *Journal of Child Psychology and Psychiatry,* 45 (1), 84–108.

Hill, S. E., & Flom, R. (2007). 18- and 20-month-olds' discrimination of gender-consistent and inconsistent activities. *Infant Behavior & Development,* 30(1), pp. 168–173.

Jensen, E. (2005). *Teaching with the brain in mind.* Alexandria, VA: Association for Supervision and Curriculum Development.

Kempermann, G. (2002, February 1). Why new neurons? Possible functions for adult hippocampalneurogenesis. *Journal of Neuroscience,* 22(3), pp. 635–638.

National Center for Health Statistics. (2011). *Obesity and overweight prevalence of obesity among children and adolescents. US Trends, 1963-1965 through 2007-2008.* Hyattsville, MD: U.S. Department of Health and Human Services, Centers for Disease Control and Prevention.

New City School, Inc. (1994). *Celebrating multiple intelligences: Teaching for success.* St. Louis, MO.

Palmer, L. (2003, July 25). *Smart Start program: Evidence from two schools: Vestibular stimulation improves academic performance.* Lecture at Learning Brain EXPO, Chicago, Illinois. As reported in Jensen (2005).

Pica, R. (2004). *Experiences in movement: Birth to age 8.* Clifton Park, NY: Thomson Delmar Learning.

Santrock, J. W. (2010). *Children.* Boston: McGraw-Hill.

University of Illinois at Urbana-Champaign. (2010, September 15). Children's brain development is linked to physical fitness, research finds. *ScienceDaily.* http://www.sciencedaily.com/releases/2010/09/1517/1536.htm. Retrieved February 2, 1012.

12

Planning for the Mind: Cognitive Development in Action

© Cengage Learning

Learning Objectives

LO1 Define cognition and the major developmental perspectives.

LO2 Examine the central elements of children's cognitive skills when planning curriculum.

LO3 Identify effective approaches that foster cognitive skills through appropriate curriculum strategies.

LO4 Discuss the use of technology and media as a special topic of cognitive curriculum.

naeyc Standards For Professional Development

The following Standards for Initial and Advanced Early Childhood Professional Preparation are addressed in this chapter:

Standard 1 Promoting Child Development and Learning

Standard 4 Using Developmentally Effective Approaches to Connect With Children and Families

Standard 5 Using Content Knowledge to Build Meaningful Curriculum

naeyc Code of Ethical Conduct

These are the sections of the NAEYC Code of Ethical Conduct that apply to the topics of this chapter:

Core Values: We have committed ourselves to basing our work with children on knowledge of child development.

Section I: Ethical Responsibilities to Children—Ideals and Principles

I-1.5 To create and maintain safe and healthy settings that foster children's social, emotional, intellectual, and physical development and that respect their dignity and contributions.

P-1.7 We shall strive to build individual relationships with each child; make individualized adaptations in teaching strategies, learning environments, and curricula; and consult with the family so each child benefits from the program.

The Development of Cognition: Multiple Perspectives

Cognitive development encompasses what humans do, say, think, and feel. In other words, everything uses the brain. Understanding how children learn through cognitive experiences includes many perspectives. The theories of Piaget and Vygotsky help make sense of cognition and how to plan for its development in early childhood programs.

Learning Through Cognitive Experiences

Ah, to be a child again! The world is a place of wonder and promise. There are worlds and people to discover, explore, and understand. Childhood is a time:

- *Of self* . . . a baby plays with his hands and feet for hours and rolls over just for the sake of doing it.
- *Of things everywhere* . . . a toddler invades the kitchen cabinets to see what treasures can be found.
- *Of people* . . . a preschooler learns the teachers' names and then makes a first "friend."
- *Of faraway places* . . . a second-grader packs for the first "sleepover."

The amount of learning that takes place in early childhood is staggering. How do children manage to absorb the sheer quantity of information and experience they accumulate in their first few years of life?

Every child accompanies this mighty feat by thinking. **Cognition** is the mental process or faculty that children use to acquire knowledge. To think is to be able to acquire and apply knowledge. By using conscious thought and memory, children think about themselves, the world, and others. Educating the thinking child is a critical function of parents and teachers. Curriculum in the early years must address the thinking, or cognitive, skills.

Cognition is related not only to the developing mind but also to all areas of the child's growth. Young thinkers are at work no matter what they are doing. For example, physical/motor development is also a cognitive process. Learning to rollerblade involves skinned knees and learning to balance (motor tasks), along with analyzing, predicting, generalizing, evaluating, and practicing the art of locomotion on wheels (cognitive skills). When trying to enter into group play (a social task), children think of strategies for how to get started (cognitive skill).

The relationship between cognition and language, two major aspects of the intellectual domain, is particularly important. Typically, we find out what children think by listening to them talk or asking them to tell us what they know. But that isn't always the case:

- Cognition *can* occur without the language to express it. For example, an infant's laughter during a game of peek-a-boo indicates the child's knowledge that the hidden face will reappear.
- The use of language can occur without cognition (i.e., without knowing the meaning). A child's counting from 1 to 20 (". . . 11, 13, 17, 20!") is a case in point.

At the same time, language and thought are intertwined. The growing child communicates through meaningful language. Children get their needs met better when they can name them. Their thoughts are expressed more clearly to adults when they are put in words, and feelings can be mediated through language. Cognition and language generally become more interdependent as development progresses. Children expand their knowledge base through language. They listen, question, and tell. The child with good language skills can thus apply them to widen the horizons of knowledge.

For the purposes of clarity, cognition and language are separated into two chapters. Teachers must remember that they work together. Cognitive development is nurtured through a rich environment of meaningful print (see Chapter 13). Language content is also stimulated by curiosity and inquiry as is discussed in this chapter. This chapter applies cognitive development principles to curriculum planning by elaborating on the development of cognition in the early years, on the skills acquired by children from birth to age 8, the role of the teacher in curriculum plans, and on the special topic of technology and media.

As children investigate the world of people and places, they ask themselves and others what they want to know.

An Eclectic Point of View

In trying to enhance cognitive development, early childhood educators draw on developmental and learning theories and their direct experiences with children. By combining theoretical and practical viewpoints, teachers take a blended, or eclectic, perspective on the development of the thinking process. They work with children to encourage their ability to formulate ideas and to think rationally and logically to develop:

Concepts: Labeling or naming an idea, moving from the specific to the abstract.

Relationships: What is the association between two or more things? How are they similar or different? What are their functions, characteristics?

Generalizations: Drawing conclusions from concepts, grouping things and finding common elements.

Example: "What is a grape?"

"What colors of grapes are there?" "Do all of them have seeds?" "What sizes do you see? Do they taste alike?"

"Are grapes a fruit or meat?" "How do grapes grow?"

The primary perspectives that inform teachers in planning curriculum for cognitive development in early childhood are cognitive-developmental, sociocultural, Multiple Intelligences theories, and current brain research.

A Piagetian Perspective

Developmental psychology, particularly through the works of Jean Piaget, has provided a deeper understanding of cognitive development. Piaget's view of cognition (see Chapter 4) is twofold.

- First, learning is a process of discovery, of finding out what one needs to know to solve a particular problem.
- Second, knowledge results from active thought, from making mental connections among objects, from constructing a meaningful reality for understanding.

Knowledge is an interpretation of reality that the learner actively and internally constructs by interacting with it. Piaget divided knowledge into three types: physical, logical mathematical, and social.

1. *Physical knowledge* is what children learn through external sensory experiences. Watching leaves blow in the wind, grabbing a ball, and sniffing a fresh slice of bread are all instances of children learning about different physical objects and how they feel, taste, smell, move, and so on. The basic cognitive process involved in the development of physical knowledge is **discrimination**. For example, by touching magnets to paper clips, puzzles, and paper dolls, children learn firsthand about magnetism. They learn to discriminate between those objects that "stick" to the magnet and those that do not.

2. *Logical mathematical knowledge* derives from coordinating physical actions into some kind of order, or logic. This is not to be confused with formal mathematics; rather, it is the kind of mathematical thinking children use in making connections about what they see, such as an infant's lifting the blanket to find a hidden toy. The logic of the young child is seen in the coordination of actions to make an **inference**. Think back to the magnets example. If a child deliberately takes a magnet to the metal drawer pulls and metal climbing bars, we can see the logical knowledge used: the child has made the inference that it is the metal things that "stick" on the magnet.

3. *Social knowledge* comes from our culture—the rules of the game, the right vocabulary, the moral codes. It includes learning vocabulary and being taught or told things, as well as knowledge about the social aspects of life. Value-laden and often arbitrary, it can rarely be constructed logically but is learned through life. With the aforementioned magnets, social knowledge would need to be used to decide who gets to play with the magnets, or when it is somebody else's turn.

In developing cognitive curriculum, teachers plan experiences that enhance those types of knowledge. They can teach using different forms of knowledge.

- **Rote knowledge** is information given with no particular meaning to the learner—that which could be learned meaningfully but is not. A teacher talking about magnets or telling children what attracts or repels gives children rote knowledge.
- **Meaningful knowledge** is what children learn gradually and within the context of what they already know and want to find out—like the example of letting the children handle the magnets themselves if they choose and answering their questions as they arise.

Both telling (rote) and asking or allowing (meaningful) can be useful; the question for the children is the balance between the two in everyday educational encounters.

In applying this theory to curriculum, the program likely looks like this:

- *Choice.* Making decisions from a variety of materials or activities lets children focus on formulating their own real questions and learning how to find genuine answers.

- *Play.* Children develop their own thinking because play allows for self-selection and creates situations in which children must exchange views and solve problems.
- *Materials and Activities.* Concepts are developed through interactions and experimentation with real objects, materials, and people, so an environment must provide materials that are both appropriate and interesting as well as many activities that stimulate interaction with peers.
- *Time.* Each day allows long blocks of uninterrupted time for child-initiated activities.
- *Teacher.* The teacher's role is to facilitate and to impart information and social knowledge, along with providing an emotionally safe and intellectually stimulating environment.
- *Curriculum Content.* The content arises from the issues of the students' real lives, their interests, family, and events so that learning is in the context of meaning for each child.

Vygotsky, Thinking, and Culture

Focusing on how our values and beliefs affect what we transmit to the next generation, Vygotsky's sociocultural theory (see Chapter 4) shows that much of children's development and knowledge is culturally specific. The role of social interaction in thinking has spawned a new understanding of group differences and how social experience and language shapes our capabilities (Rogoff, 2003). The most salient sources of knowledge are family members, the media, and school. In order to learn higher mental functions (symbolic thought, memory, attention, and reasoning) children need the mediation of someone who knows the tools of that particular society. "With a growing population of people of color, speaking a variety of different languages, belonging to many religious groups and ethnic and national communities, the question is not can all children learn, but how to teach them" (Bowman, 2007).

Vygotsky adds an important element to our understanding of thinking. If knowledge is connected to what a culture values, then learning must be done in a collaborative style. Teachers and parents must have some agreement about what is important to teach children. The best way of teaching is a kind of assisted learning that allows for scaffolding, a natural learning technique known as *apprenticeship.* An older child or adult serves as a guide who is responsive to what the child is ready to learn.

There are three implications of this theory for curriculum:

1. Mixed-age groupings: A wider age range allows younger children to learn from older ones, and the more advanced children have opportunities to help others. For instance, the most effective strategy for preventing early reading failure is one-to-one tutoring.
2. Play: Playful experiences are valuable ways for children to work with the symbols and other higher forms of thinking. With other people alongside, the child practices what is to be expected and valued in society.
3. The teacher: Adults can be both observer and participant. For instance, if a child builds with blocks, the teacher might sketch the building and then encourage a joint effort to make a map or use measurement tools.

DAP A Teaching Style for Intellectual Development

There are three common styles of teaching young children (Riley et al., 2009). The first is known as a "discovery approach," used traditionally by preparing materials and activities and letting children direct their own play. A second approach is "direct instruction," in which teachers tell children what to do and how to learn, often with practice and drills. In between is the "guided learning approach," which blends some instruction with hands-on experience for the children. The assistance provided scaffolds the child's learning and increases the zone of proximal development by helping organize the child's cognitive processes, with hints provided only as needed.

For example, teacher Daudi carefully chooses which puzzle he offers kindergartener Christa. Too easy, and she dashes through it without thought, too difficult, and she gets overwhelmed and discouraged. Guided discovery offers a challenge, but not too little or too great. "This matching of task difficulty with the cognitive abilities of the child is the essence of great teaching" (Riley et al., 2009). When we don't give away the answer, but guide children to discover it, children then construct their own understanding and learn strategies for solving problems. The guided discovery approach is the height of developmentally appropriate practice because it takes into consideration the age, the individuality, and the cultural context of the child to create the educational opportunity for them to grow.

Gardner's Multiple Intelligences

Research into cognition (see Chapter 4) documents that children possess different kinds of minds, and therefore understand, learn, remember, and perform in different ways. Most experts agree that **intelligence** is complex and that traditional tests do not measure the entire host of skills or abilities involved.

Gardner's theory endorses what teachers have noticed in the classroom. Many intelligences can be nurtured as the curriculum is adjusted and teaching is varied so that it meets the needs of a broader range of children. Multiple Intelligences (MI) theory acknowledges that people learn and use knowledge in different ways. Its classic applied work *Project Spectrum* (Gardner et al., 1998) developed an innovative approach to curriculum and assessment in the preschool and early primary years. If each child exhibits a distinctive profile of different abilities (or spectrum of intelligences), then an environment rich in stimulating materials and activities can provide educational opportunities that enhance multiple intelligences. Because MI is neither a curriculum nor a model of pedagogy, there are many ways that the intelligences can be brought into the classroom. The overall framework involves four steps:

1. Introduction: Introduce children to a range of learning areas
2. Identification: Identify each child's strengths
3. Nurturance: Nurture those strengths
4. Bridging: Bridge their strengths to other subject areas

This does not mean that teachers must develop every activity to all intelligences! A relatively easy start is to create the various learning centers that correspond to the different intelligences. For learning math facts, for example, a drawing center taps into spatial intelligence, while a circle activity with snapping fingers while counting stimulates body-kinesthetic intelligence, and a listening post could use musical intelligence while clapping to the rhythm or beat of counting (see Figure 12-1).

Brain Research

"The human brain is the most fascinatingly organized three pounds of matter on this planet" (Schiller, 2008). The only unfinished organ at birth, it continues to grow throughout the life cycle. The principal task of the brain in early childhood is the connection of brain cells, as a child's brain is two-and-a-half times as active as an adult's. During the first three years of life, an infant's brain creates an estimated one trillion synapses. "Babies are designed to learn—and this evolutionary story would say children are for learning, that's what they're for—we might expect that they would have really powerful learning mechanisms. And in fact, the baby's brain seems to be the most powerful learning computer on the planet" (Gopnik, 2011).

Providing quality experiences and relationships creates lasting effects on how the brain gets wired. Indications are strong that children's brains need to be stimulated for the network of connections to grow and be protected from

The Multiple Intelligences Approach: Sample Early Learning Activities

Learning Center	Sample Activity	Intelligence Area
Blocks/manipulatives	Making wire designs	Spatial
Discovery/science	Tools for biologists	Naturalistic
Music	Sound cylinders match-up	Musical
Movement	Statue game	Body-kinesthetic
Math	Weights and measures	Logical
Social studies	Making silhouettes	Interpersonal
Language	"Reporting the news"	Linguistic
Visual arts	Making an art portfolio	Intrapersonal
Self studies	"Why are we in the world?"	Existential

FIGURE 12-1 Adapted from Project Spectrum Activities, a research project aimed at improving performance of at-risk first graders (Chen, Isberg, & Krechevsky, 1998).

deletion. Connections that have been reinforced by repeated experience tend to remain; those that are not used are discarded. We need to develop curriculum that brings children to interesting places and brings interesting things to children (see Figure 12-2).

In general, teachers of children can keep these ideas in mind:

- *Birth to age 4.* Provide for healthy sensory stimulation. This means all the senses need to be included in a child's exploration of the world. Very young children should live in an enriched environment—visual, auditory, language, and so on, because the executive circuits that are responsible for language, number, and emotional and social functioning come "on line" in the first years of life (Galinsky, 2010).
- *Age 4 to 8.* The brain is eagerly searching for stimulation; it is most flexible, or plastic, early in life to accommodate a wide range of environments and

interactions, but its capacity for change decreases with age (NSC, 2008). Programs from preschool through fifth grade must be richly stimulating with activities that reward the brain's appetite for meaning. Give children plenty of opportunities to use stories, explore ideas, and master tasks rather than use worksheets or other repetitive tasks that kill enthusiasm for learning.
- *All ages.* Develop curriculum that provides for children's well-being. "Neuroscience research . . . has made important contributions to our understanding of cognitive development by demonstrating that the brain is far more plastic at all ages than previously thought—and thus that the speed and extent by which experience and behavior can shape the brain is greater than almost anyone imagined" (Diamond & Amso, 2008). Emotions affect memory and brain function. When a person feels content, the brain releases endorphins that enhance memory skills, and

Brain Research: Influences on Cognitive Curriculum

Brain Research Findings

The brain is strongly run by patterns rather than facts. Children learn best with curriculum developed around themes, integrated learning, and whole experiences. The key to our intelligence is the recognition of patterns and relationships.

Stress and threat affect the brain in many ways. Emotions run the brain, and bad emotions reduce the capacity for memory and understanding, as well as reducing higher-order thinking skills. Good emotions create excitement and love of learning.

The brain runs better when food intake is steady. Insulin levels stay more even, cortisol levels are lower, and glucose tolerance is better. Diet activates memory; children need diets rich in proteins (meats, nuts, cheese), omega-3 fatty acids, and selenium and boron (leafy green vegetables), as well as enough restful sleep so the brain can reorganize itself.

All learning is mind–body. A child's physical state, posture, and breathing affect learning. Our brain is designed for cycles and rhythms. Practice makes permanent, and memory is kept more accurate when information is revisited.

Curriculum Implications

Conclusion: Develop meaningful themes for activity planning. Uninteresting or abstract pieces of information (e.g., drilling young children on alphabet letters) will not provide understanding. Plan some kinds of "immersion experiences" that encourage children to go deeply into their play and work.

Conclusion: Make a positive, personal connection with each child, and avoid threats by loss of approval, hurried schedules, or implying children are helpless or bad. A secure environment counteracts the problems that may occur when the stress regulation mechanisms are triggered too often. Good emotions enhance memory.

Conclusion: Snacks are good! Regular snack times may lead to better cognitive functioning, *fewer* discipline problems, and an enhanced sense of well-being.

Conclusion: Keep track of and teach to children's bodily functions and body states and how long they are expected to sit or nap. Plan a daily schedule with both variety and balance, and work in regular routines and productive rituals.

FIGURE 12-2 Teachers must translate new findings into appropriate curriculum.

Building the Brain, from Masa to Tortillas

Step into a typical, high-quality early childhood program any morning and you are likely to see children moving around a classroom or yard. It may look like chaos as they cruise the activity centers, then select one—or someone—as a focus. From easels to unit blocks, from house corner to the pet table, children choose and change the "soft wiring" of their brains as they gather experiences.

Let's zoom into one activity: making tortillas. A child sees the table, the bag of masa flour, and the pitcher of water. Another notices the teacher and the two friends. A third smells the corn as the water is poured into the masa. All three eagerly put their hands into the mixture, knead the dough, and then roll it into a ball. They wait their turn to put it onto the tortilla press,

pushing the bar down hard, then delicately lifting their tortilla so that it can be helped onto the griddle. They repeat a chant (first in Spanish, then English) while it cooks, then lovingly take their fresh tortilla to a place at the table to eat. ¡Sabroso!

"Forming language, identifying cultural and social norms, and learning to distinguish right and wrong requires intense neurological growth to take place, thus strengthening the connections between neurons"(Rushton et al., 2009). Each region of the brain has a highly sophisticated network of cells and dendrites that interconnect the various parts of the brain to each other; a curriculum that engages all the senses immerses children fully in the learning process. Brain-based research suggests that the brain works to associate new

information with what is already known; hands-on activities stimulate the various regions and help with recall and problem solving.

"Two great responsibilities of the early childhood educator, then, are the development of the learning environment and modeling an engagement . . . that will lead to the release of certain neurotransmitters in the brain that support learning" (Rushton et al., 2009). All this can happen from masa to tortilla on a typical school day.

Questions
1. What aspects of a cognitive curriculum might be considered "brain-friendly"? Why?
2. What kinds of teaching would be incompatible to brain development?

---

undue stress short circuits these skills. Exercise and positive social contacts, such as hugging, music, and the supportive comments of friends create opportunities for collaboration and cooperation.

In summary, research from cognitive developmental psychology and brain research supports curriculum development that is engaging and that encourages exploration. The biological evidence strongly suggests that there are sequences in children's thinking, that there are at least multiple expressions of intelligence, and that the context of learning affects what children know.

Cognitive Skills

The actual skills children acquire as they learn to think are considerable. A basic skill is defined by two fundamental qualities:

- A skill is basic if it is **transcurricular**: that is, if the child can use it in a variety of situations and activities throughout the school day. For example, children who can express their curiosity and opinions clearly—who can let adults know when they are having difficulties or want to know more—have acquired a skill that is useful anywhere.

- A skill is also basic if it has **dynamic** consequences: that is, if it leads to other worthwhile responses. For instance, children who are articulate tend to elicit more verbal responses from adults. Consequently, they are exposed to more verbal stimulation, which in turn strengthens their verbal abilities, and so on. Thus, having this skill leads to major dynamic consequences in a favorable direction, whereas not having the skill leads to dynamic consequences in an unfavorable direction.

Most skills fall into the nine categories that follow. The list, though long, is comprehensive; what children learn in the thinking realm of their development falls into one of these categories. The teacher plans activities for all cognitive skills to ensure challenging children's thinking.

Skills of Inquiry

Young children are curious, watching the world carefully. Through exploration and examination, they increase their attention span. Inquisitive children begin to organize what they see, analyzing and identifying confusions or obstacles for themselves. All the senses function at birth, and both *sensation* and *perception* are used to make sense of the world.

Cognition is one step beyond perception. It occurs when a person actually thinks about what he or she has perceived. Thus, there is a sequence, from sensation to perception to cognition. A baby's sense organs must function if this chain of comprehension is to begin. No wonder the parts of the cortex dedicated to the senses develop rapidly: This is what allows all other developments to occur (Berger, 2009).

Thus, the skills of inquiry include the development of *attention span* and *memory*. Children need to take an active role in questioning and information gathering; they cannot just sit passively while the adults do all the work. The child asks questions, listens, gets ideas, and makes suggestions. They interpret what others communicate, seeking assistance from other people and materials.

Piaget called these skills of **inquiry**; several of Gardner's intelligences would also be included, as would Vygotsky's notion of cultural ways of learning. Organizing and finding patterns, reasoning, and problem solving are also inquiry skills. As children examine alternatives, they choose a course of action, revising their plans as needed. The National Education Standards of Kindergarten–Grade 4 have been translated into early childhood and concentrate on an inquiry-based approach (see Common Core, Chapter 15).

Young children thrill in making educated guesses, then checking their hypotheses by experimenting and taking risks. This means we develop this skill by helping children build on what they already know to construct new knowledge. As Drew and others (2008) describe it:

> Constructive play involves building and making things no one has seen before. As young children fiddle with, sort, and arrange materials, ideas and imagination begin to flow. Questions arise naturally. They wonder: What will happen if I put this here? How tall will it go? Where did the bubble come from? In this way, constructive play serves to focus the minds of children through their fingertips and leads them to invent and discover new possibilities, to fulfill their sense of purpose.

These basic skills of inquiry are the foundation for thinking; as such, they are far more important to develop than are rote letter or numeral recognition.

Knowledge of the Physical World

How do children learn about the physical world? First, they use objects, spending plenty of time exploring, manipulating, choosing, and using toys and natural materials.

- Babies search for something to suck; they begin to grasp objects and let them go.

Being able to explore actual materials and objects encourages children to assimilate and use new knowledge.

- Toddlers pick up and throw things or drop objects from a highchair to see what happens.
- Preschoolers roll out play dough to make snakes, then coil it up flat to make a plate.
- Six-year-olds with balloons and water explore how to fill, roll, throw, and burst the balloons.

This knowledge is part of Gardner's logical mathematical intelligence, for knowledge of the physical world is essential to making order of it.

A stimulating cognitive environment is filled with interesting sights, sounds, and people that enrich a child's schemes of thought and action. As they learn the properties of objects, children gain a better understanding of the concept of cause and effect. Experience with the physical world gives children a base for comparing and contrasting, key skills for mathematical classification and scientific thinking.

Knowledge of the Social World

Relationships are primary to development. Early experience significantly influences social and emotional brain function, and "toxic stress damages developing brain architecture, which can lead to life-long problems in learning, behavior, and physical and mental health" (NSC, 2008). Learning about others is hard work because the social world is not concrete and is often illogical. The child needs an awareness of self before developing an awareness of others and how to interact socially. To Gardner, this kind of knowledge requires both intrapersonal (access to one's own feelings and a range of emotions) and interpersonal (the ability to notice others, making distinctions among individuals, particularly their moods and motivations) intelligence. Attachment relationships are important in the unfolding of the emotional and social development of the child. "Mirror neuron networks throughout the brain confirm the importance of the teacher's moment by moment actions as the child's neurological synapses 'mirror' not only the teachers actions and reactions, [but also] affect the mood of the individual observing" (Rushton et al., 2009).

Infants begin by distinguishing friends from strangers. Toddlers learn to use "mine" and then to use others' names as well. The next step is to expand their knowledge of roles to include those of family, school, and the community. Four and 5 year olds are provided with daily opportunities to cooperate, to help, and to negotiate with others about their needs and wishes. According to Vygotsky, preschoolers learn appropriate actions by playing with older children. Also, make-believe is a major means through which children extend their cognitive skills.

In the best of circumstances, children are encouraged to notice both similarities and differences in people and then are led to develop tolerance for both. School-aged children seek small group teamwork and moments of private time with a close friend. In learning rules for social living, children learn appropriate conduct for various situations—indoors or out, happy or sad, at the grocery store or at the dinner table.

Classification

Knowledge of the physical world teaches children to have different responses to different objects. **Classification** is the ability to group like objects in sets by a specific characteristic. During their first year, infants use their senses to sort and classify their many experiences. As toddlers, they initially classify by sorting groups of completely different objects, using a logic that only the child understands. During the preschool years, they begin to sort objects using consistent criteria. Once they develop language proficiency, they can name and classify objects. Gradually, and with help from adults who stimulate describing and manipulating, they learn that objects have more than one attribute and can be classified in more than one class.

To clarify this process, consider how 2-year-old Tisa learns to classify:

> What can Tisa do to her stuffed bear and the family dog? What can she do with one and not the other? Which are her toys? Which are Rover's? Which ones have fur? What is different about them?

Tisa learns the attributes of the objects by exploring, learning the class names of "toy" and "pet." Tisa makes collections, sorting by similarity those that are Rover's toys and those that are her own. She uses class relationships to understand that both animals have fur, but she

can tug on only one animal's ears without encountering a problem.

Seriation

Seriation is the ability to put an object or group of objects in a logical series based on a property of those objects. Many of the sensorial and practical life materials designed by Montessori were developed to make clear to children exactly what seriation is and how it can be learned. These toys distinguish grades of intensity by size, color, weight, and number. Children build pyramid towers, fit nesting blocks together, and use the counting rods. By noting differences, often through trial and error, children learn seriation systematically. For instance, the pyramid tower is ordered from largest piece to smallest as it is built. Boxes are nested, one inside the other, by their graduated size or volume. The counting rods can be put into a staircase array, the units building on each other from one to 10. Children can arrange several things in order and fit one ordered set of objects to another. Gardner's category of musical intelligence requires seriation, as well as the skill of inquiry ("How do I make noise? Rhythm? Musical song?") and a knowledge of the social world ("How can we make music together? A real band?").

Numbers

Understanding the concept of numbers means learning about quantity: understanding amount, degree, and position. Mathematical knowledge is an emergent understanding of concepts. Once infants develop an understanding of object permanence (that an object exists

Cognition in action! The concepts of the world come to life through Montessori materials.

whether or not it can be seen), they are ready to learn about quantity. Toddlers compare objects, for example, by stacking rings on a stick, sorting by groups (large versus small, hard versus soft), and noticing what is "more."

Preschool children can learn songs, chants, and finger plays that include numbers ("One Potato, Two Potato" or "Five Speckled Frogs"). Once children comprehend numbers, they are ready to use mathematical terms and forms of expression. For instance, after singing about the frog that jumped into the pool in the song "Five Speckled Frogs," Chantel can begin to understand that four is "one less than" five. Embedding math concepts into daily classroom activities gives children a foundation for more complex math and logic skills that are needed throughout their schooling.

A knowledge of numbers is neither complete nor meaningful unless children have direct experience with materials and objects. Number sense includes understanding number and quantity as well as number relationships and operations. Counting is a fundamental skill in children's early understanding of numbers and is important in learning the counting procedure—that objects are counted in a specific sequence and each object is counted only once (CDD, 2010). Learning about quantity means:

- Comparing amounts (as when children work with table toys, blocks, sensory materials, and the like);
- Arranging two sets of objects in one-to-one correspondence ("Each person needs one and only one napkin for snack, Tyler");
- Counting objects and beginning computation ("Parvin, you have three shovels. Here is one more; now how many do you have?").

As with language and pre-reading skills, children who grow up in poverty tend to enter school already lagging behind their middle class peers in key math knowledge. "Research has shown that if children don't have good instruction and effective teachers in early grades, they are more likely to struggle later when they face more complicated concepts" (Banchero, 2011). Teachers use instruction, games, and hands-on activities that focus on five major areas of mathematics: number sense, algebra and functions, measurement, geometry, and mathematical reasoning (CDD, 2010). The importance of math learning in the primary grades and children's potential to learn math have implications for teaching primary grade math. The early years are especially important for math development, as knowledge in math is predictive of both math achievement and later reading success as well (Sarama & Clements, 2009).

TeachSource Video

Watch the TeachSource Video Case entitled "Exploring Math Concepts through Creative Activities." After you study the video clip, view the artifacts, and read the teacher interviews and text, reflect on the following questions:

1. How does preschool teacher Jessi Surette encourage children to develop nine cognitive skills?

2. If identifying shapes and describing spatial relationships are fundamental for understanding geometry, what activities would help these happen?

3. Attaching a visual image to the word label scaffolds children's understanding of math concepts. How could you do this for young preschoolers? For first graders?

Symbols

A symbol stands for something else; it is not what it appears to be! Young children have to think hard and long to symbolize. It is a task of some skill to imitate or use one object to represent something else. They begin by using their bodies. Infants and toddlers love to play peek-a-boo, reacting to "Boo!" with full-bodied excitement. Pretend play is the hallmark of using symbols. Preschoolers revel in playing favorite characters. Primary school children make up plays and puppet shows.

Make-believe helps in the process of symbolizing, as does making sounds to represent objects ("Choo-choo" is a train, for example). The beginning of pretend play is a hallmark of a new stage of thinking for toddlers. Using and making two- and three-dimensional models are other ways children symbolize, when they transfer what they see to the easel or to the clay table. Children are also symbolizing when they dress up in costumes and uniforms. The Reggio Emilia approach (see Chapters 9 and 10) encourages children to use a variety of media to express their thinking and deepen their understanding.

Teachers add to the symbolizing process when they use descriptive words. Description games encourage children to do the same. For example, "It is round and red and you eat it. What is it?" (An apple!) After all these skills have been mastered, children are ready for written symbols when they can use the written word to label, take dictation, or write notes. Using Gardner's and Vygotsky's theories, educational environments for school-age children might take the form of discovery centers, a kind of museum, in which apprentice groups with children of different ages would help children with numerical and computer skills (see Special Topic).

Spatial Relationships

Spatial relationships develop early.

- Infants visually track what they see, trying to reach and grasp. As they experience one object's position in relation to another, they begin to have a mental picture of spatial relationships.
- Toddlers find this out as they learn to steer themselves around tables and seat themselves on the potty. The concept of "close" (the chair) and "far away" (the teacher waiting for me) give clues to length and distance.
- Preschoolers learn to fit things together and take them apart. One of the best ways to learn spatial relationships is with a basic set of unit blocks (Reifel et al., 2010).
- School-age children observe and describe things from different spatial viewpoints. They play hide-and-seek, noticing that what one sees from the side of the hill is not what can be seen from the top.

Adults help children learn such skills by letting them locate things at home, in the classroom, in the department store. Cognitive theories of Piaget and Gardner suggest that body and kinesthetic knowledge are used in this type of activity. In Reggio Emilia, for instance, mirrors are placed around corners, found at the school entrance, and embedded in the floors, giving children a sense of self in space in a number of ways. Teachers encourage children to represent such spatial relationships in their drawings, with pictures, and in photographs.

Time

Understanding time is a complicated affair because time is composed of at least three dimensions: time as the present, time as a continuum, and time as a sequence of events. Children must learn each of these to fully understand the concept of time. In some settings, children learn to stop and start an activity on a signal (when the teacher strikes a chord on the piano for clean-up time). They try to move their bodies at different speeds, indoors and out. Older children begin to observe that clocks and calendars are used to mark the passage of time. Specifically, children come to know the sequencing of events in time: which comes first, next, last. Having an order of events through a consistent daily schedule helps children learn this aspect of time. They also benefit from anticipating future events and making the appropriate preparations. Planning a course of action and completing that plan give meaning to the idea of time.

When considering intellectual development, teachers should keep in mind that, to children, education is exploration. Let children use their imagination to use materials in new and different ways.

What children learn intellectually in the early years is massive in quantity and quality. Yet young children are ready—eager, in fact—to engage themselves with the world around them to acquire these cognitive skills (see Figure 12-3). "Back to basics" is a phrase commonly heard in conjunction with academic and cognitive curriculum. Its intention is to focus attention on what is fundamental to be learned and often refers to intellectual skills. Fondly known as the 3Rs—reading, 'riting, and 'rithmetic—these skills are often taught by whole-group telling and by drill-and-skill repetition.

From what we know of development and the brain, a better way to think about a cognitive curriculum is to give it the classic "child-centeredness test" (Bos, 1983):

- Does this activity help the child's sense of identity?
- Is the activity open-ended—that is, can the child change the material?
- Does this activity allow the child to create?
- Does this activity provide a framework for the child to cooperate with others while retaining a sense of self?
- Is the activity fun? Does it inspire laughter and a love of learning?

By remaining aware of how much is to be learned, educators keep a realistic—and humble—appreciation for the "work" of children.

Cognitive Skills into the Curriculum

Cognitive Skill	Sample Activity	Age
Inquiry: senses, perception, attention, memory	Playing with water: what can you find out?	Toddler, Preschool
Knowledge of the physical world	Take an outdoor sound walk	Toddler, Preschool
Knowledge of the social world	Make a Wheel of Feelings; read Aliki's *Feelings* book	Preschool, School-Age
Classification	Collections: put together, identify describe, and classify a nature collection	Preschool, School-Age
Seriation	Yeast grows: see which expands most, with flour, sugar, salt, juice	School-Age
Numbers	Play "fives" game with playing cards numbered 1–4	School-Age
Symbols	Making shapes: bodies and shape cards	Preschool, School-Age
Spatial relationships	Geoboards	Preschool, School-Age
Time	Play "Stop & Go" with music	Preschool, School-Age

© Cengage Learning 2011

FIGURE 12-3 Every cognitive skill has a place in planning curriculum.

Effective Approaches for Curriculum

Planning a cognitive curriculum requires educators to keep several key points in mind, such as knowing how children learn and how the various contexts "play out" in individual children and the group. Taking into account the setting, schedule, and skill levels of children allow a better match between the themes or activities presented and what teachers want children to learn.

Considerations

When considering children's intellectual development, teachers should keep the following in mind:

● *Education is exploration.* The process of education is more than its products. Teachers enhance learning by allowing children to interact with the environment. The teacher is a source of information and support rather than one who gives answers or commands. A project approach (see Chapter 10), based on the belief that children's minds should be engaged in ways that deepen their understanding of their experiences and environment, may be used. Consisting of exploring a theme or topic (such as shadows, houses, building a table) over a period of weeks, this approach reflects Dewey's progressive education and the British Open Schools (see Chapter 1) and is implemented regularly in the Reggio Emilia schools. The goal is to have children ask their own questions and create their own challenges.

● *Children do not think like adults.* Children think and perceive in their own ways, as Piaget believed (see Chapter 4). They think in sensory and concrete terms and come to conclusions based on what they see and touch.

● *Children's thinking is legitimate and should be valued.* Their thought processes and perceptions are as valid as those of adults. Teachers support those processes by asking questions to stimulate further thought and by providing materials for exploration.

● *The language of the teacher should support cognitive development.* Throughout their interactions with

DIVERSITY

Activity Simplification for Inclusion

"Inclusive child care takes place in many different ways, depending on the setting and the needs of children in the program" (Ong, 2009). Although each child is an individual, and thus the modifications and adaptations are designed with that single child in mind, there are several proven strategies to address the diverse learning of an individual. One such strategy is activity simplification.

"Simplify a complicated task by breaking it into smaller parts or reducing the number of steps" (Ong, 2009). This can include:

- Giving a child one piece at a time, rather than all the pieces at once. (With a puzzle, allow the child to dump out the pieces, then set up the frame and hand single pieces systematically.)
- Preparing a material for easier use. (Wrap duct tape around an easel brush to make the handle larger and easier to grasp.)

- Exchange a difficult material with a simpler one that serves the same function. (Have "helper scissors" at the ready and cardboard books alongside paperback ones.)

A child's individual background and presenting conditions must be paired with services for both child and family. At the same time, a program's cognitive curriculum must address the diversity of all learners in the group.

---

children, teachers help children use words, terms, and concepts correctly:

> Mariko (at water table): I need that suckup.
> Teacher: The baster really does suck up water, doesn't it?

- Their *questions* are open-ended to help children *think* and often leave the child with something to ponder:

> Teacher: I wonder why the turtle's head went back in its shell when you put your finger close?
> Teacher: If you want to play with José, how can you let him know?
> Teacher: What do we need from the woodworking shelf to make a spaceship?

The teacher must match the child's cognitive capacity with the instruction. Child-centered, self-initiated learning (see Chapter 10) is a great motivator, so observing children's intensity with materials and asking questions to extend their thinking is recommended. Use conversation, document children's thinking, use drawing, and incorporate problem solving.

The teacher must consider, include, and plan for children with learning disabilities and other varied learning "styles." Each type of learning disability (see Chapter 3) has its own description and treatment. Teachers must develop a wide range of techniques to address such disabilities. After the identification and assessment phases, teachers and families need to work with specialists and devise options (an individualized education plan, or

IEP) that include the child and establish reasonable learning goals.

Figure 12-4 shows further how teachers' use of language helps children think and develop cognitive skills as part of their early childhood experience.

Curriculum Planning for Cognitive Development

In the Early Childhood Setting

Teachers plan cognitive curriculum for their children much as they do for each of the developmental domains. Consider the setting, both indoors and out, and the daily schedule. Each activity center and time slot can be used to encourage intellectual development with a variety of curriculum materials and methods (see High/Scope in Chapter 10). Another way to plan curriculum is to focus on a specific cognitive skill and prepare activities or to use a theme throughout the environment or schedule. Keep in mind:

- Children ages birth to 2 have a limited attention span and can be over stimulated unless the environment is kept simple.
- Three- to 5-year-olds can absorb more information and finer detail as they have more developed motor and perceptual skills.
- Older preschoolers and kindergartners learn best trying to solve real problems that are right in front of them, such as making a river in the sandbox or building and connecting castles in the block area.

Teacher's Role in Developing Cognitive Skills

Skill	Teachers Can
Inquiry	• Ask questions so children make statements about their conversations.
	Example: "What do you notice about the guinea pig?"
	• Try to be more specific if such questions seem overwhelming or if they elicit little response.
	Example: "What sounds do you hear? What can you find out by touching her?"
	• Ask how children arrived at their answers.
	Example: "How did you know that the marble wouldn't roll up the ramp?"
Social knowledge	• Try not to respond to unstated needs.
	Example: "Do you want something? Can I help you?"
	• Help children define what they want or need, so that they learn how to ask for it.
	Example: Marie: "I wonder who is going to tie my shoes?"
	Teacher: "So do I. When you want someone to tie your shoe, you can say, 'Would you tie my shoe?'"
	Marie: "Would you tie my shoe?"
	Teacher: "I'd be glad to."
Classification	• Ask questions that will help children focus on objects and see differences and details.
	Example: While cooking, ask
	"Which things on the table do we put in the bowl?"
	"What are made of plastic?"
	"Which go in the oven?"
	"What on the table is used for measuring? How do you know?"
	"Now look carefully—what do you see on the measuring cup?"
	"What do those little red lines mean?"
Spatial relationships	• Ask for the precise location of an object the child asks for or is interested in:
	Example: "Where did you say you saw the bird's nest?"
	"You can find another stapler in the cabinet underneath the fish tank."
Concept of time	• Use accurate time sequences with children.
	Example: Teacher: "Just a minute."
	Milo: "Is this a real minute or a 'wait a minute'?"
	Teacher: "You're right. I'm with Phoebe now. I'll help you next."

© Cengage Learning 2011

FIGURE 12-4 Teachers' use of language affects how children develop cognitive skills. The more children are allowed and encouraged to think for themselves, the more their cognitive skills develop.

• Compared with preschoolers and kindergarteners, school-age children are more logical and flexible in their thinking, have more knowledge of the world, have improved memory, and can better sustain their attention.

Figure 12-5 shows how one activity (which can be done with nearly all ages) contributes to the development of children's thought processes.

Teachers can create high activity, low stress, brain-compatible learning environments (see Chapter 9). An optimal environment has several learning centers for the children to choose from so that the brain is stimulated to be attentive, to absorb new information, and to store this information in long-term memory. Teachers should aim to create a balance between meaningful experiences and optimal stimulation of the brain in their classrooms. "Such an environment offers children experiences with

Cooking as a Cognitive Activity

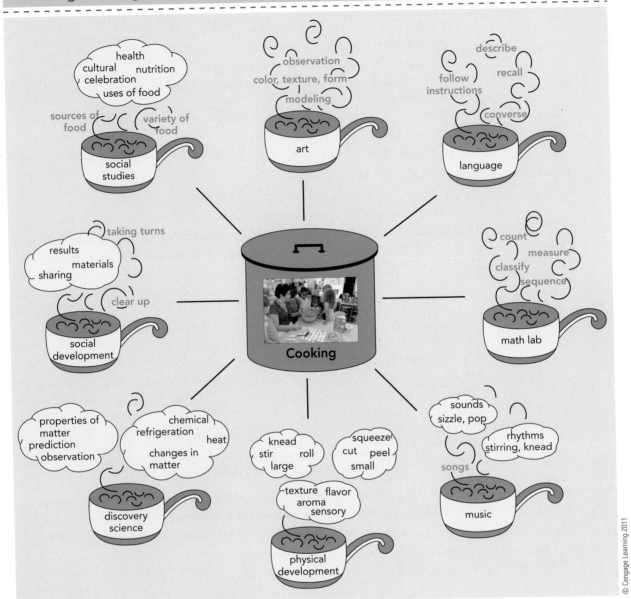

FIGURE 12-5 Each activity, such as cooking, can enhance cognitive development throughout the curriculum. A trip to the market can be an experience in classification and calculation.

real-life, hands-on, theme-based activities oriented to solving problems, such as children counting out play money when shopping at the store in the dramatic play center" (Rushton, 2001).

Indoor Areas Indoor areas provide the basic ingredients of a stimulating cognitive environment, with simplifications for younger children and elaborations for older ones:

- *Art.* Include a "help yourself" shelf for child-chosen projects. A variety of paper, drawing implements, and tools encourage children to re-create their own

reality, using representational art forms that show how children see the physical and social worlds.
- *Blocks.* Have paper models of each block shape on storage shelves to help children with classification by shape and size. Be sure you put a priority on having enough unit blocks (a 600-piece set for a preschool class of 16) and provide enough space (40–80 square feet per group) with a firm carpet that supports balancing towers and controls noise. Accessories, such as animals and homemade trees and lakes, help children symbolize. As they experiment with blocks, they learn about physical laws

and reality and have experiences in cooperative learning and living, all of which are cognitive tasks. Counting blocks, which builds on one-to-one correspondence rather than rote memorization, contributes to genuine understanding. Building structures with young children inspires them as young mathematicians and scientists (Reifel et al., 2010).

- *Discovery/science.* Rotate a display of "touch me" materials. This gives children firsthand experience with plants, seeds, animals, magnets, seashells, foods, and so on. Have a "Fix It" or "Take Apart Shop" with non-working appliances and radios, equipped with plenty of screwdrivers, pliers, and containers for small parts. School-age children can find out which plants grow in saltwater or freshwater by setting up plants in each environment and watching daily ("Today something has changed!" wrote a 7 year old. "The duckweed is not really green anymore. A second root is hanging"). If you can, have a computer or other technology such as touchpads (see special topic later in the chapter) available with developmentally appropriate software.
- *Dramatic play.* Stock this area with materials for role-playing, puppet making, and acting out adult activities. Have anatomically correct boy and girl dolls of a variety of races and some with disabilities. Include clothing for all types of work, equipment for carrying things, and babies that reflect the homes of all the children in the group but also extend the play to include new ways of dressing, eating, and playing. When several prekindergarten children got haircuts, the class developed a "Hairy Heads" theme, transforming this area into a hair salon with brushes, barrettes, and wigs. The dolls got plenty of shampoos that month!
- *Language/library.* Choose books that focus on both the physical and social worlds. Children's interests in numbers, symbols, and time can also be extended by selecting literature that reflects their level of understanding. Look for the message in children's books and choose good stories that reflect diversity, such as *Helping Out* (Ancona) and *George the Babysitter* (Hughes). Be sure to listen to the group's interests, and make a point to place books that respond to those interests in the library.
- *Manipulatives (table toys).* The manipulatives area is an ideal place for materials that encourage cognitive development; highlight this area with both favorites (Legos® or Crystal Climbers®) and new items (Construx® or sewing cards). Counting cubes aid in classification and seriation, whereas puzzles or nesting blocks focus on spatial relationships. Information processing theory emphasizes the importance of experiences that develop children's working memory and familiarity. Manipulative materials and games give children hands-on experiences with counting, sorting, and organizing that are both meaningful and socially natural. Homemade lotto games or puzzles with the children's photos encourage self-esteem and group identity as well as cognitive and motor development.

Outdoor Areas Outdoor areas provide opportunities for children to plan and organize their own thoughts. Offer your yard as a place for discovery, with both structured and wilder places. Remember that cognitive toys include sticks and dirt.

Toddlers can classify what they find as they look for balls, sand buckets, and toy trucks hidden around the yard. Preschoolers in the sand pit predict how water affects the sand, using their growing knowledge of the physical world. Children learn to classify water table and wheel toys and learn seriation when they select sand buckets by size. Counting shovels to see that there are enough to go around; building with large, hollow blocks; and watching the seasonal changes are all cognitive skills children gain as they play outside.

Physical and logical mathematical activities are easily incorporated into the curriculum outdoors. Piaget's *methode clinique* (see Chapter 4) inspires experimenting and reasoning: "I wonder why?" or "What would happen if . . . ?" are common teacher inquiries. The water table outdoors could have a large block of ice; a variety of materials such as wood, cotton balls, straws, and cardboard; or containers of colored water and eyedroppers. Balancing activities might mean hollow blocks, milk cartons, or beanbags (or all three). A hillside or long plank can become a site for predicting and trying out rolling, using different sizes of balls or even bodies.

Daily Schedule

Teachers plan environments, activities, and grouping of children to give the class experience in cognitive challenges. Teachers use signs, their words, and helpful tips that illuminate for children what is happening, what is expected of them, and how they can express themselves in all segments of the day.

Groups, transitions, and routines are more structured times and all play a part in developing children's knowledge of the social world. As children learn to conduct themselves in school, they learn:

- To enter a room and start to play (transition).
- To take care of their own belongings and those of their school (routines).
- To concentrate on an activity with others around (group times).

- To interact with others while at the same time paying attention to a leader or task (group times).
- To end an activity, an interaction, a school day (transition).

Moreover, many routine activities offer wonderful opportunities for cognitive learning. For example, consider the snack table. Incorporating math concepts into snack time engenders enthusiasm and skill development. Whether as a part of free choice time or a time period on its own, snack time becomes "think time" as children:

- Fill out and use menu cards ("What are we eating today?").
- Learn the concept of sets ("*Everyone* needs five of *everything*").
- Work with the concept of uniform units ("Are the ham and cheese pieces the same?").
- Understand the concepts of equal, less, and more ("How will it be fair for everyone?").
- Learn how to count "wet stuff" and to count by the spoonful or handful.
- See geometry and fractions at work (circles for raisins, triangles for sandwiches, break the graham cracker in the right number of pieces).

Focus on Skills

How can teachers help children develop specific cognitive skills? After observing the children carefully, teachers identify a particular skill and then list those processes, concepts, and vocabulary involved. For instance, the skill of inquiry can be encouraged in every part of the curriculum by asking questions (see Figure 12-6). Teachers model curiosity by observing and asking questions about what they see and what children may be thinking. This stimulates children to look, wonder, and interact:

Teacher: I wonder which piece of wood you will choose to glue on your board next.

Teacher: What part do you want to play in our grocery store?

Teacher: How can we find out how long your road of blocks is?

The processes of mathematical literacy involve using representation, performing manipulations, making sense in math reasoning, and problem solving.

- Help children as they use markers to "stand for" people or animals or dolls in place of real babies— this representational thinking is a hallmark of the

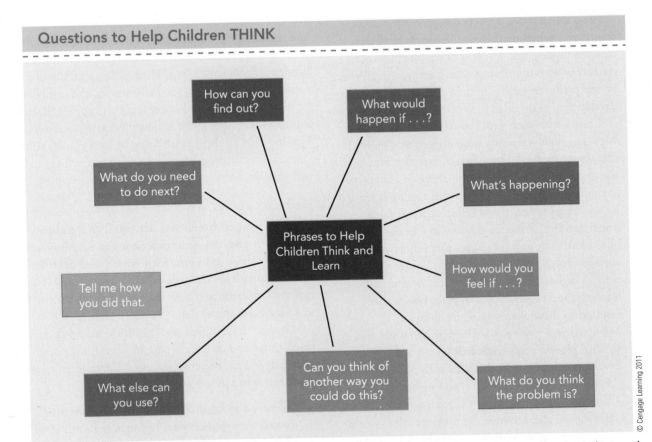

Questions to Help Children THINK

How can you find out?

What would happen if . . .?

What do you need to do next?

What's happening?

Phrases to Help Children Think and Learn

How would you feel if . . .?

Tell me how you did that.

What else can you use?

Can you think of another way you could do this?

What do you think the problem is?

© Cengage Learning 2011

FIGURE 12-6 Teachers encourage children's thinking when they ask questions. Posted in the classroom or given to students and parents, this chart serves as a reminder that to TEACH is to ASK more often than to TELL.

preschool period, and fantasy play can help in mathematical thinking if the teacher makes children aware.

- Use manipulatives to help children add and subtract; it makes such operations understandable.
- Guessing games can be a fun way to elicit reasoning; ask "How did you know that?" once the child has made a guess. Remember that children have limited knowledge and need to be encouraged to keep guessing, while you stimulate them to offer, justify, and question their ideas.
- Develop math games based on children's literature to invite new math experiences, such as using Ormerod's *Joe Can Count* or McMillan's *Eating Fractions* with a small group and have circle time follow through.

Problem solving is mentioned often in early childhood education circles, in social and artistic contexts as well as for cognitive development. For this to be successful, two issues must be addressed: problem posing and making investigations.

- Problem posing is difficult for many children, and children need guidance so that the problem is clear before the group or individual launches into looking for a solution.
- Investigations are authentic problem solving situations in which children work as mathematicians or engineers.

For example, a group of 7 to 8 year olds were asked how to make a bridge. The teacher worked with their answers and eventually drew a trestle on the board. Then each child was given a box of Legos and flat sticks to start their part. The teacher observed, participated to scaffold their individual work, and then helped them put their parts together to make a bridge at the end of the session.

Outdoors, inquisitive children explore their environment. Children ask questions: "Can we turn on the water? What if we bury all the toy bears in the gravel? Could we use the ladder to see over the fence? Let's all hide from the teacher!" The way teachers handle inquiries from children about what they want to do sends a message that supports—or discourages—this cognitive skill. When there is no harm in asking (though the answer may be "No"), children are encouraged to develop further the skill of inquiry (see Figure 12-7).

Use of Themes

A specific theme can be chosen for cognitive development. Themes that emerge from the children's interests engage their thinking more than those imposed by the teachers. Units based on things in the physical world (season changes, pets, the garden), on unexpected or current events (a new load of sand, a community fair, road work nearby), or on the special interests of the children (sharing the African masks, swimsuits, or dinosaurs) are all appealing. Current events must be chosen carefully because young children may have only passing knowledge or interest in most of them. Meaningful events might be a space shuttle mission or a solar eclipse. More likely, the event is a local one, such as the discovery of ants on the playground or someone's new baby (see Teaching With Intention Box).

The critical point is to have a meaningful theme for children; rehashing the same old themes year after year may be easy for adults but can crowd out other interests of each unique group. The project approach (see Chapter 10) describes the use of themes in curriculum, making it accessible so that the children can interact and "own" it. Infants and toddlers have less need for a theme; curriculum ideas for them concentrate on cognitive stimulation at their particular level of development.

Special Topic: Technology & Media

"Advances in technology and **interactive media** rapidly are transforming how we communicate and use information in our homes, offices, and early childhood settings" (NAEYC & FRC, 2012). Thus begins a Position Statement co-written by two well-known groups—the National Association for the Education of Young Children and the Fred Rogers Center for Learning & Children's Media (see chapter 15). A wide variety of organizations are attempting to address the issue of young children and **screen time**, which affects both children and the environments of school and home. Digital decisions must be made by educators (Simon & Nemeth, 2012); choosing whether or not to include technology and media in the program and, if so, the right technology tools is an important part of creating cognitive curriculum.

Computers in the Classroom

A computer can be as nonthreatening as a watercolor brush. In the hands of a child, it can be a tool for experiencing the world. Early childhood classrooms are arranged so that children learn about the world directly by piling blocks, molding sand and clay, and bouncing a ball. Through these experiences, children gradually form concepts about how the world works and how they can affect it. As children touch the keys of a computer, they are

Problem Solving: An Intellectual Pursuit

The Concepts:
    Selecting a course of action
    Making educated guesses
    Making and revising a plan
    Risking and evaluating the results

The Vocabulary:
    Guess
    Plan
    Problem
    Solution/solve
    What? why? how?

The Process:

Activity area	Process question
Art	How many ways can you use the brush (pen, squirt bottle) to make a mark on the paper? Why is it dripping? How can you stop it when you're ready?
Bathrooms/cubbies	You found Paul's sweater. . . . How can you find where it goes? Where did the water come from? How can you clean it up?
Blocks	What makes the tower of blocks fall over? How can a block be used to connect two others?
Cooking	How do we mix these ingredients together? What will happen when it is put in the oven?
Discovery/science	Why did the magnet pick up the nail and not the pen? What is the difference between the rabbit and the guinea pig? How are they alike?
Dramatic play	Who will be the dad? What happens when these other children want to play? How can you get to wear the costume you want?
Language/library	What happens next in the story? Why do you think so? Why did the child feel unhappy at first? Then what happened?
Large group	Why can't you see/hear the leader? What can you do about feeling too crowded? What can you do when your friend keeps whispering to you during storytime?
Gross-motor	How do you jump rope? What do you use to pump yourself on a swing? How will you find a ball?
Manipulatives	How do you figure out what puzzle piece fits? Do you see a pattern on the peg board? What is it?
Sensory	How do you get the water from the large pitcher to the small cup? How will you get the wet sand through the funnel?

FIGURE 12-7 Problem solving is a cognitive skill that involves problem posing and making investigations.

challenged to explore and discover in ways never before possible.

There are two reasons why every classroom or child care center should have a computer—children love them, and they can provide a positive learning experience for every child, even the most difficult or contrary. NAEYC's Position Statement on Technology and Young Children for Ages 3–8 (2012) notes that "computers will have the most positive impact when they provide concrete experiences; children have free access; children and teachers

An Inquiry-Based Project

Incorporating science into the curriculum is intimidating to many early educators who feel they have an inadequate grasp of physical, life, or earth sciences. Yet "science is a wonderful gateway for children to discover more about the world and their place in it. Extending our classrooms to include the outdoors opens up new possibilities and opportunities for children to learn" (Jacobs & Crowley, 2010) and can meet the national science content standards (2008) at the same time.

Using the steps of the project approach (see Chapter 10), note how the topic of "rocks and sand" takes an intentional teaching plan and engages children in scientific thinking (adapted from Ogu & Schmidt, 2009).

Think About This:

1. Brainstorm five topics you think would be interesting to a group of kindergartners. Why did you choose those? How would you determine if they were "good" topics?

2. Many family child care homes have children from ages 0 to 5. How would you plan an inquiry-based project for children in this age range?

3. If you could provide digital cameras for children to use as a tool of inquiry, what topics might you have them investigate? What would you have them do with the photos? What culminating experience would reflect on the journey?

Rocks and Sand: An Inquiry-Based Project in Cognitive Curriculum

An inquiry-based project uses the discovery method to engage the children in scientific thinking and is related directly to their own thinking (adapted from Ogu & Schmidt, 2009).

A Topic Emerges

Kindergarten cubbies and pockets have collections of rocks and pebbles in them.

We Investigate It

- Make a rock vocabulary list [boulders, crystals, fossils].
- Take a rock walk.
- Display our findings with a table and poster.
- Make a rock gift store that has job opportunities.
- Set up a trading game and its rules.
- Take photos for documentation boards and newsletters.
- Have a rock show and invite families.

Reflecting on the Journey

- Ask questions that invite constructive input and validate prior knowledge. ["What do you know about rocks?"]
- Ask open-ended questions. [What do you notice? What might happen if . . .?]
- Encourage children to wait a few seconds before giving an answer to allow time for thinking. ["Close your eyes and think before you say your idea."]
- Repeat or paraphrase what the children say without praising or criticizing. ["Joe thinks sand comes from rocks, and Andrea says it is dirt from the ocean. What do you think?"]

© Cengage Learning

learn together; peer tutoring is encouraged; and children control the learning experience."

Discovery-oriented experiences with computers enhance children's learning, especially in stimulating their cognitive thought processes. Unlike a teacher or playmate, computers and screen games can wait patiently for a child in a nonjudgmental way, do not tease or exclude, and often can adjust to children's diverse abilities and styles. Children design and control places and things of their own choosing, such as a house, the seashore, or a face. Then, they create events that challenge them to think through the consequences of their actions. Moreover, computer programs can be process highlighters for children; the program can speed up or detail hidden processes and cause-and-effect relationships that are more difficult to observe, such as a plant growing, a face changing expression on command, or a dance put together with a special sequence of steps.

Technology use is especially meaningful in primary classrooms. School-age programs can create a website, make newsletters, and build interesting curriculum webs.

To integrate computers and take advantage of what they can offer children, educators should select developmental software, select appropriate websites, integrate using the computer as a resource into the program, and select the actual computers and support items.

At the same time, many professionals are skeptical of computers and other screen media. They worry that children become passive for long periods of time, unwilling and unable to disengage and become involved in physical and social play. Young children learn best through firsthand experiences with objects and people; "regardless of content, what children see or interact with on the screen is a symbolic representation of first-hand real world experience, so it can never provide as full an experience as interactions with the real world" (Carlsson-Paige, 2012).

In addition, many worry that play is being undermined by media saturation. "Media, especially when it is tied to toys and products, is making children's play less original and creative. In the last 25 years, children's play has become more imitative. Teachers describe how kids' play copies media themes and characters and seems like a script of something they've seen on a screen" (Carlsson-Paige, 2012). One way to think intentionally and cautiously might be to consider the stages of thinking from 0–8 years.

(See Chapter 4 and Figures 12-3 & 12-4). Both the American Academy of Pediatrics (AAP, 2011), and the White House Task Force on Childhood Obesity (White House, 2010) recommend that children younger than age 3 be as screen-free as possible.

Children 3–5 years are all-or-none thinkers, and imitation may become rote. As they mature, they move into more logical, symbolic, and concrete operational thinking, so that they are ready to use media to think in more abstract ways.

Developmentally Appropriate Software

Along with blocks and paints, the computer can become an expressive medium that encourages skills in a variety of ways. Once children have had many experiences with *concrete* items such as paint, crayons, and markers, they are then ready to try their creative hand at computer graphics.

To use computers appropriately in the classroom, teachers must first be *comfortable* with the computer themselves.

1. Put the computer area in a quiet spot of the classroom (such as in or near the library/listening spot) and against a wall to minimize damage to the equipment or cords.
2. To introduce the computer, show small groups of children the basic care and handling of the computer.
3. The computer can be one of many choices offered during free play, or it can be a more limited choice with a waiting list.
4. Interaction between children can be encouraged by including space for two or more at the computer; assigning turns to a pair or small group of children, particularly if the computer seems to be dominated by a few; and watching to ensure that no one becomes "stuck" at the computer or any other area.

Once the computer is a regular part of the environment, teachers can use it to develop curriculum. Arleen Prairie has written extensively about the use of technology in the classroom, and offers these key points (Prairie, 2010):

With technology a group of children can generate ideas and develop plans: While developing the new topic about the study of earthworms, the group listed what they knew about earthworms as the teacher entered them on computer using a computer program. To add to the list, one child announced, "They have eyes." Several children agreed. Others did not. The group posed several questions they could explore to determine whether worms have eyes. This started a lengthy investigation over several days, looking at them through the magnifying glass, looking at diagrams, taking close-up photos and enlarging them using PhotoShop, and asking the worms if they see their reflection in the mirror they held up to it.

It is in the area of **software** that teachers of young children have many choices. These choices must be carefully made. Not every program intended for children is developmentally appropriate, and teachers must pay thoughtful attention to the program and to what they know about their own group of children. Computer software should:

1. Be age appropriate.
2. Allow children to control it (children setting the pace and being active participants).
3. Include clear instructions.
4. Have expanding complexity.
5. Support independent exploration.
6. Be "process oriented" (having the software program be so engaging that the product of using it is secondary).
7. Include real world representation.
8. Have high quality technical features (colorful, uncluttered, and realistic).
9. Provide trial-and-error opportunities.
10. Have visible transformations (the ability to affect the software, for example, by transposing objects).

Selecting software can become easier by using a website to help with software recommendations.

The Internet

Many centers use a computer simply with software; others, particularly those with primary-age children, may be interested in using the Internet. The Internet has been less researched than software, and its potential is untapped. There are a variety of learning opportunities using the Internet; however, the sheer volume of Internet sites is overwhelming, and there has been no screening.

There are four types of children's websites:

1. *Information.* Information sites are great reference resources; for instance, the National Zoo from the Smithsonian (http://nationalzoo.si.edu) would be a wonderful introduction or follow up to a field trip.
2. *Communication.* These sites connect children to experts to answer questions on projects, such as "Ask an Astronaut" (http://coolcosmos.ipac.caltech.edu) for an outer space theme.
3. *Interaction.* These work like software programs, only more slowly. The program "Name-Jumping" asks children to jump around a floor-sized keyboard.
4. *Publication.* These sites can post children's work, such as Kid Pub® (http://www.kidpub.com).

Again, Prairie (2010) gives an example of appropriate use of the Internet:

With technology, teachers, along with the children, can find more information and view pictures on practically any topic through accessing the Internet: When a small group of children found a strange-looking tiny insect on the classroom wall, the teacher heard the children's attempt to label it. "It's a-a-a ant," "A frog 'cause it has back legs." "I know. It's an ugly spider." Mr. Ed had no idea what it was. They put the strange creature in a collection jar for the afternoon. With children excitedly looking on, Mr. Ed downloaded photos and a large diagram of an ant, a frog, a spider, and an insect. They compared the pictures and the creature. They discussed the body parts and counted legs. "You found out it was an insect. Let's search the Internet some more."

Integrating Technology into Learning

Specific methods have been devised for teaching young children to work successfully with computers. For instance, a child must be able to maneuver a joystick or mouse, find the keys on the keyboard, or even insert a DVD into the computer correctly. Because very young children cannot read, they need help getting started. Teachers must be able to help children learn by setting up their classrooms with a computer positioned in a safe yet accessible place, structuring activities and the daily schedule to give children plenty of time to manipulate the machinery and programs, and choosing specific hardware and software that work with the class.

© Cengage Learning

Using the computers in a classroom can individualize a program and offer social experience.

One of the most exciting aspects of technology in the classroom is the ability to support other learning. Kindergartners can listen to a story by a teacher, read the same one on an iPad, then play vocabulary games on the computer (Hand, 2012). Teachers who use the computer effectively as an educational tool integrate their program goals to use the computer with individual children. To maximize the benefit computers can give children, teachers should attend to three components: access, availability, and home collaboration. In the classroom, be sure the computer is open regularly, enough so that the issue of crowding or frantic behavior around access is eliminated. Pay close attention to who is using the computer: By the time children are age 10, boys spend more time at computers than do girls. Although this difference is not significant at preschool age, teachers need to ensure that girls get access and that selected software is not catering to males only. With careful scrutiny, teachers can use online resources to assist them in using technology tools (see Helpful Websites).

Recognize that many of your families may not have a computer at home, yet computer use can be helpful to all children. One study found that a group of underperforming children whose families were provided with a computer and free Internet access had higher scores on standardized reading tests after six months and higher grade point averages nearly one and a half years after the start of the study than those who used one less (Jackson in Packard, 2007). Regardless of your family population, be sure to communicate to parents about computer use and learning, and be ready to offer ideas, when appropriate, about quality software, supervision, and using the Internet. A final example from Prairie (2010):

> With technology, teachers can communicate the ideas and learning of children with parents: When the children returned from their short trip to visit "their class tree" in December, Renee was particularly concerned about what she called "our dead tree." When Ms. Jones, her teacher, sent a photo of the tree from this short trip via e-mail to parents, she also suggested that parents and children together look at trees around their house. She added a note to Renee's mother about her daughter's comment. Later that evening, Renee's mother viewed the e-mail and the photo with her daughter. Together they looked out the window at trees and bushes nearby. Renee noted the difference between the green of the "growing trees" (evergreens) and "dead trees." Outside they found dead leaves and small branches from "dead" and "alive" trees. Back inside, Renee looked at, smelled, and bent the deciduous branch. Later Renee thought aloud, "Maybe it's sleeping in the cold."

Technology in the early childhood classroom can relate to children's learning in powerful ways. Ferry-Perata (2012) lists 10 strategies to extend the learning process; we added examples that make technology use an engaging cognitive activity:

- Help children see themselves as thinkers.... *What are you thinking about, Juan, when you click on that button?*
- Respond to their curiosity ... *What do you notice, Elisa, on that screenshot?*
- Use mirror talk ... *I see you scrolling through the page, Sarita, and then you stopped on that part.*
- Have conversations ... *So Sam drew the tree on the touch tablet, and Cassandra added a nest. Ask Francisco what he wants to put in the tree.*
- Inspire imaginative play ... *Everyone wants a Cinderella dress. Could we find out how to make them on the Internet?*
- Solve problems together ... *I have a basket of apples; how can we find out more about the apples? Let's brainstorm—how many, their size, and favorites— great ideas, now how can we show it on the IWB [Interactive whiteboard]?*
- Use rich vocabulary .... *What media would work best for writing your story? A tape recorder or a touch tablet? Would a powerpoint presentation help? What about importing pictures?*
- Laugh with children ... *Ha! Tarek was the big bad wolf in that recording of the* <u>Three Pigs.</u> *Wasn't he scary? And funny?*
- Ask questions ... *We will make a class book about our field trip to the park, sending it to everybody at home and printing it for us. How did we get ready? What did we need to take? How did we get there? Who fell down?*
- Link the new to the familiar ... *If you second graders are going to make a presentation about dinosaurs to your kindergarten buddies, what format will you use that will interest them and teach them what you already know?*

Summary

LO 1 Cognition is the ability to learn, remember, and think abstractly. The understanding of cognitive development includes multiple perspectives, including theories of Piaget, Vygotsky, and Gardner and current brain research.

LO 2 Cognitive skills include the nine categories of inquiry, knowledge of the physical world, understanding of the social world, classification, seriation, numbers, symbols, spatial relationships, and time.

LO 3 Effective approaches to curriculum involve several teacher considerations and planning curriculum for cognitive development. The teacher's role is to understand how cognition develops in children and to put that knowledge to work in the classroom. While creating curriculum, teachers keep certain attitudes and ideas in mind while planning by area, schedule, skill, or theme.

LO 4 A special topic in cognitive curriculum is computers in the classroom. Issues around developmentally appropriate software, use of the Internet, and integrating technology into learning are key considerations.

Key Terms

cognition
physical knowledge
discrimination
logical mathematical
    knowledge
inference

social knowledge
rote knowledge
meaningful knowledge
intelligence
transcurricular
dynamic

inquiry
classification
seriation
screen time
software
interactive media

Review Questions

1. Write a working definition of cognition, listing at least three theories that offer a perspective on cognition.
2. Match the cognitive skill with the appropriate activity.

    inquiry   being aware of others
    physical world   learning to locate things
    social knowledge   pretending to be a puppet
    classification   asking questions
    seriation   sequencing events
    numbers   using nesting blocks
    symbols   expressing amounts
    spatial relationships   sorting objects
    time   manipulating materials

3. What is an activity in each environmental area that stimulates cognitive development?
4. Name three considerations when planning for computer use in a classroom.

Observe and Apply

1. Look at the program in which you now teach, or recall your own first classrooms. Find at least one example of rote knowledge, social knowledge, and meaningful knowledge.

2. Take one cognitive skill and trace how it could be developed in each curriculum area of an early education setting.

3. Make a list of the classroom areas. Beside each, name one activity that would foster cognitive development.
4. Consider the use of a computer in the following programs, and then answer the questions below:
   - Toddler child care program
   - Preschool half-day program
   - Kindergarten
   - After-school primary program

   Is a computer appropriate in each of them? Why and how? What guidelines, if any, would be needed in each setting? What would be the adult's role in each?

Helpful Websites

American Academy of Pediatrics **www.pediatrics.org**

Center for Media Literacy **www.medialit.org**

Children and Computers **www.childrenandcomputers.com**

Common Sense Media **www.CommonSenseMedia.org**

I Am Your Child **www.iamyourchild.org**

National Association for the Education of Young Children **www.naeyc.org**

Beyond the Journal (NAEYC) **www.naeyc.org/yc/**

National Child Care Information Center of the U.S. Dept. of Health and Human Services **www.nccic.org**

National Scientific Council on the Developing Child **www.developingchild.harvard.edu/**

SuperKids® Educational Software Review **www.superkids.com**

Zero to Three **www.zerotothree.org**

The Education CourseMate website for this text offers many helpful resources and interactive study tools. Go to CengageBrain.com to access the TeachSource Videos, flashcards, tutorial quizzes, direct links to all of the websites mentioned in the chapter, downloadable forms, and more.

References

AAP (American Academy of Pediatrics), 2011b. "Policy Statement—Media Use by Children Younger Than 2 Years." *Pediatrics* 128 (5): 1–7.

Banchero, S. (2011, November 29). New calculation: Math in preschool. *The Wall Street Journal.*

Berger, K. S. (2009). *The developing person through adolescence* (8th Ed). New York: Worth Publishers.

Bos, B. (1983). *Before the basics.* Roseville, CA: Turn the Page Press.

Bowman, B. (2007, May/June). The effects of culture on thinking. *Exchange.*

Carlsson-Paige, N. (Winter 2012), Media & Technology in ECE. *Connections: The Journal of the California Association for the Education of Young Children.*

Child Development Division (CDD). (2010). *Preschool curriculum framework, Volume 1.* http://www.cd.ca.gov/re/pn. Sacramento, CA: Department of Education.

Diamond, A., & Amso, D. (2008, February). Contributions of neuroscience to our understanding of cognitive development. *Current Directions in Psychological Science*, pp. 136–141.

Drew, W., Christie, J., Johnson, J. E., Meckley, A. M., & Nell, M. L. (2008, July). Constructive play: A value-added strategy for meeting early learning standards. *Young Children,* 66(4).

Ferry-Peralta, E. (2012, Winter). How to Extend the Learning Process with Young Children and Technology. *Connections: The Journal of the California Association for the Education of Young Children.*

Galinsky, E. (2010). *Mind in the making.* New York: HarperCollins.

Gardner, H., Feldman, D. H., Krechevsky, M., & Chen, J.-Q. (1998). *Project Spectrum: Early learning activities (Project Zero Frameworks for Early Childhood Education, Volume 2).* New York: Teachers College Press.

Gopnik, A. (2011, September). What do babies think? TedTalk. http://www.ted.com/talks/lang/en/alison_gopnik_what_do_babies_think.html.

Hand, A. (2012, Winter). Technology in K-2 Classrooms. *Connections: The Journal of the California Association for the Education of Young Children.*

Jacobs, G., & Crowley, K. (2010). *Reaching standards and beyond in kindergarten.* Thousand Oaks, CA: Corwin/Washington, D.C.: NAEYC.

National Association for the Education of Young Children (NAEYC) & the Fred Rogers Center (FRC) for Early Learning and Children's Media (2012). Position Paper: Technology and Interactive Media as Tools in Early Childhood Programs Serving Children from Birth through Age 8. http://www.naeyc.org. Retrieved May 31, 2012.

National Scientific Council on the Developing Child. (2008). *In brief: The science of early childhood development.* Cambridge, MA: Author.

Ogu, U., & Schmidt, S.R. (2009). Investigating rocks and sand: Addressing multiple learning styles through an inquiry-based approach. *Young Children,* 64(2), pp. 12–18.

Ong, F. (Ed). (2009). Inclusion works! Creating child care programs that promote belonging for children with special needs. http://www.ca.cde.gov/re/pn. Sacramento, CA: Department of Education.

Packard, E. (2007). It's fun but does it make you smarter? In E. Junn & C. Boyatzis (Eds.). *Annual Editions: Child Growth and Development,* 09/10, 16e. New York: McGraw Hill.

Prairie, A. (2010). Technology in the early childhood classroom relate to children's learning? In A. M. Gordon & K. W. Browne. (2010). *Beginnings & Beyond* (8th Ed.).Belmont, CA: Wadsworth Cengage.

Reifel, S., Miller, K., & Chormann, C. (2010). Foundations: The value of unit block play. Community Playthings, www.communityplaythings.com.

Riley, D., Carns, M., Ramminger, A., Klinkner, J., & Sisco, C. (2009). *Intellectual development: Connecting science and practice in early childhood settings.* St Paul, MN: Redleaf Press.

Rogoff, B. (2003). *The cultural nature of human development.* New York: Oxford University Press.

Rushton, S., Juola-Rushton, A., & Larkin, E. (2009, November). Neuroscience, play and early childhood education: Connections, implications, and assessment. *Early Childhood Education Journal,* 37, pp. 351–361.

Sarama, J., & Clements, D. H. (2009, March). Teaching math in the primary grades: The learning trajectories approach. In *Beyond the Journal, Young Children on the Web.*

Schiller, P., & Willis, C. (2008, July). Using brain-based teaching strategies to create supportive early childhood environments that address learning standards. *Young Children,* 63, 4.

Schiller, P. (2001, July). Brain research and its implications for early childhood programs. *Child Care Information Exchange,* 140.

Simon, Fran Sokol, and Nemeth, Karen (2012). *Digital Decisions: Choosing the Right Technology Tools for Early Childhood.* Silver Spring, MD: Gryphon House.

White House Task Force on Childhood Obesity. 2010. *Solving the Problem of Childhood Obesity within a Generation.* Washington, DC: Office of the President of the United States. www.letsmove.gov

13

Planning for the Mind: Language and Literacy Development in Action

Learning Outcomes

LO1 Define language and literacy and the major developmental perspectives.

LO2 Examine the central elements of children's language acquisition and literacy skills when planning curriculum.

LO3 Identify effective approaches that foster language and literacy skills through appropriate curriculum strategies.

LO4 Discuss dual language learners as a special topic of language and literacy curriculum.

naeyc Standards For Professional Development

The following NAEYC Standards for Early Childhood Professional Development are addressed in this chapter:

Standard 1 Promoting Child Development and Learning

Standard 4 Using Developmentally Effective Approaches to Connect with Children and Families

Standard 5 Using Content Knowledge to Build Meaningful Curriculum

naeyc Code of Ethical Conduct

These are the sections of the NAEYC Code of Ethical Conduct that apply to the topics of this chapter:

Core Values: We have committed ourselves to basing our work with children on knowledge of child development.

Section I:

I-1.11 To provide all children with experiences in a language that they know, as well as support children in maintaining the use of their home language and in learning English.

Section II:

I-2.7 To share information about each child's education and development with families and to help them understand and appreciate the current knowledge base of the early childhood profession.

The Development of Language and Literacy

Alexis:	Laleña, will you help me full this pitcher up?
Laleña:	No, because my ponytail is keeping me in bothers.
Veronique:	Hey, come here! I accidentally dropped a piece of bread, and the birds yummed it right up!
Abhi:	I know that's what the tooth fairy did to my tooth.
Marty:	I'm going to keep all my baby teeth in a jar and the next time a baby comes along I'll give him my baby teeth.

Learning Through Language Experiences

Language is the aspect of human behavior that involves the use of sounds in meaningful patterns. This includes the corresponding symbols that are used to form, express, and communicate thoughts and feelings. Any system of signs used for communication is language. For the developing child, language is the ability to express oneself. Language is both **receptive** (listening, understanding, and responding) and **expressive** (articulation, vocabulary, grammar, and graphic language). In other words, as illustrated earlier, language is meaningful, enjoyable communication.

Language and thought are closely related (see Chapter 12). Thoughts are produced when people internalize what they experience, and language is a major way to express or describe it. Language shapes the way thoughts are produced and stored.

"Language is a logical and analytical tool in thinking" (Vygotsky, 1962). Farmers who work the land develop tools to till the soil and language to describe their work. The child who comes to the bazaar with her mother learns the language of bargaining better than one who is in a shopping cart in a grocery store. Tribes who are snowbound develop tools to deal with the ice and language to describe the many kinds of water conditions. Language and thought are tools to make sense of and interact with the world.

© Cengage Learning

Research tells us that language experiences during preschool and kindergarten are reflected in later literacy success.

A baby may not start life with language, yet he or she always communicates. Crying, laughing, smiling, and wiggling are body language to express and transmit information. Some communication is nonsymbolic (gestures or pointing), and some is symbolic (words). A child progresses naturally from nonsymbolic communication (pointing at the window to mean go *outside*) to symbolic communication, when the child says "out go" or "me go out," thus demonstrating a shift in their level of cognitive development. Spoken language, as it develops from year to year, becomes the most common form of symbolic language. Once children master a language, they use it to communicate, play, and develop areas of intelligence (see Chapter 4).

Language is also related to other areas of development. Children learn to offer an idea, using language as a prop to get social play started. They begin to label, describe, question, and demand when they tell each other how they feel and what they want, using language to develop emotionally. Anyone who has heard a child talk himself down from a tree knows how language can be a great help in using physical skills.

The Development of Language

Language seems to be an innate characteristic of humankind. Wherever people live together, language of some form develops. Languages worldwide vary remarkably in their sounds, words, and grammatical structure. Nonetheless, young children around the world acquire language.

What Research Tells Us

Research into language development and expression reveals several interesting characteristics.

- *The language of children is different from adult language.* Child language is not garbled adult language, but rather it is unique to the child's age and linguistic level. Children's language deals with the present and is egocentric, taking into account only the child's own knowledge. There appears to be a lack of awareness on the child's part of language form. Preschool children do show awareness of language structure (for instance, "feets" to mark the plural form) but do not seem to know the parts of speech. In other words, children use language to communicate but seem to have no understanding of language as an entity itself.
- *Language is not learned simply by imitating adult speech.* All infants babble ma-ma and da-da sounds at about 6 to 9 months (Goldman in Berger, 2009). Gardner lists language ability as one

form of cognition (linguistic intelligence), and most language development theorists agree that there seems to be an innate human tendency toward language (Chomsky, 1993). Children are not just trying to imitate others and making mistakes but are trying to come to terms with language themselves. A child tries out theories about language in attempts to understand its patterns. In language, as in so many areas of cognition, children are involved as active participants in their learning. The use of speech is not merely imitative but productive and creative.

- *Experiences help build language.* The more experiences a child has, the more she has to talk about; thus, vocabulary is built firsthand. The size of a child's vocabulary is strongly correlated with how much a child is talked to; wide variations are apparent in language fluency. Research endorses the behaviorist theory that adults do teach children language and young children learn it (Berger, 2009).
- *Language experiences during the first five years are reflected in later literary success.* By talking to children and reading to them, adults can prepare children to read because an awareness of letters and sounds at age 4 predicts reading at age 6 (Berger, 2009). There are vast differences in how much children are spoken with, which correlates to vocabulary size. By age 6, linguistic differences are already huge; some know 5,000 words and others know 20,000 (Moats, 2001). Quality programs can reduce the degree of delay for high risk children in communicative skills, and personal interactions in a stimulating environment increase children's communication effectiveness. Building on existing schema assists with the meaning of words, and the more words a child knows, the easier it is to add additional vocabulary (Neuman & Dwyer, 2009). Three dimensions of children's experiences that relate to later literary success are exposure to varied vocabulary; opportunities to be part of conversations that use **extended discourse**; and environments (both home and school) that are cognitively and linguistically stimulating.
- *Language development is a process of experience and maturation.* Teachers must be aware of children's diverse language skills and challenges, particularly in the areas of **bilingualism**, speech or language disorders, and dialects, all of which are addressed in this chapter. Just as in the development of cognitive skills, there are stages of language growth that follow a specific sequence.

There are also variations in timing that are important to remember.

Stages of Language Development

Children follow a six-step sequence in language development (see Figure 13-1). Except in cases of deafness or trauma, this sequence seems *invariable* regardless of what language is being learned.

1. *Infant's Response to Language.* Babies begin by attending to speech and changes in sound, rhythm, and intonation. These are the **precursors** of speech, and young infants are especially sensitive to some sound differences. Infants need to hear speech, and plenty of it, to develop the foundations of sound.

2. *Vocalization.* By 3 to 4 months of age, infants begin cooing and babbling. Babbling increases with age and seems to peak around 9 to 12 months. This is a matter of physical maturation, not just experience; children who are deaf or hearing impaired do it at the same time as those whose hearing is normal. Furthermore, similar vocalization patterns are seen among different languages.

3. *Word Development.* The child must first separate the noises heard into speech and non-speech. The speech noises must be further separated into words and the sounds that form them. The growing infant starts to shift from practice to playing with sounds. The end result is planned, controlled speech.

   Children begin playing with sounds around 10 to 15 months of age. From this point, the development of speech is determined as much by control of motor movements as by the ability to match sounds with objects.

   Most children can understand and respond to a number of words before they can produce any. Their first words include names of objects and events in their world (people, food, toys, animals). Then the child begins to overextend words, perhaps using "doggy" to refer to all animals. Finally, single words can be used as sentences: "Bye-bye" can refer to someone leaving, a meal the child thinks is finished, the child's going away, a door closing.

4. *Sentences.* Children's sentences usually begin with two words, describing an action ("Me go"), a possession ("My ball"), or a location ("Baby outside"). These sentences get expanded by adding adjectives ("My big ball"), changing the verb tense ("Me jumped down"), or using negatives ("No go outside"). Children learn grammar not by being taught the rules but as they listen to others' speech and put together the regularities they hear.

   Child language, although not identical to that of adults, does draw on language heard to build a language base. Children incorporate

Language Skills: Ages and Stages

Stage	Age (approx.)	Sample
1. Response	0–6 months	Smiles, gazes when hearing voices
2. Vocalization	6–10 months	Babbles all types of sounds, creating babble-sentences Uses vocal signals other than crying to get help
3. Word development	10–18 months	Mama, Dada, Doggie Bye-bye, No-no
4. Sentences	18 months–3 years	Me want chok-quit (I want chocolate) She goed in the gark (She went in the dark)
5. Elaboration	3 to 5 or 6 years	You're my best Mommy, you can hold my turtle at bet-bis (breakfast) (Cough) That was just a sneeze in my mouth
6. Graphic representation	5 plus to 8 years	

© Cengage Learning 2011

FIGURE 13-1 Children's language skills develop with both age and experience.

and imitate what they hear to refine their own language structures.

5. *Elaboration.* Vocabulary begins to increase at an amazing rate. Sentences get longer, and communication begins to work into social interaction. In the hospital corner of a nursery school, this conversation takes place:

Chip: I'm a nurse.

Brooke: I'm going to try to get some patients for you.

Megan: Do I need an operation?

Chip: Yeah, if you don't want to be sick anymore.

6. *Graphic Representation.* By late preschool and kindergarten, reading and writing emerge as children become aware of language as an entity itself and of the written word as a way of documenting what is spoken. Awareness of print and emerging literacy are the outgrowth of this last stage of development.

Alphabet knowledge and **phonemic awareness** are predictors of early reading success. Children who learn to read well and most easily in first grade are those with prior knowledge of the alphabet and the understanding of the sounds that letters represent. Within the guidelines of developmentally appropriate practice, the teaching focus must be on creating meaningful experiences.

As children create a linguistic representation of their cognitive understanding, they see the potential of language reading and writing as a tool for communicating. Known as *literate thinking*, this is the hallmark of the last early childhood developmental stage in language development. (See Early Literacy section later in this chapter.)

Dual Language Learning

Children who begin formal schooling ready to learn are more likely to succeed in meeting the academic and social challenges they encounter. A major challenge facing the education system in the United States and other countries is the increased number of students in public schools who speak English as their second language. In the United States, "the majority of these children are born in the United States and thus from a very young age are acquiring both the language of their family as well as the language of the larger community. These very young children are **dual language learners** [DLLs]" (Ballentyne et al., 2008).

These learners may not have had access to those early learning experiences that prepare children for learning in school. They may not have had quality preschool experiences, may live in poverty, have parents with low levels of education, and have not had access to

health care services. Research on instruction indicates that young DLLs:

- Benefit from instructional techniques that work to include them in classroom social interactions and recognize the value of their home language.
- Require sufficient time (4 to 6 years) to become proficient in their second language.
- Benefit from explicit vocabulary instruction.
- Can transfer literacy skills from their first language and retain the benefits of first language literacy through eighth grade measures of reading proficiency (Ballentyne et al., 2008).

Schools, communities, and families can work together to get children ready to succeed in education. Children who are age 3 to 5 are still in the process of acquiring their first language, even as they are also acquiring their second. Because the first five years are crucial for brain development, it is an ideal time to learn a second language. At the same time, DLLs are diverse in their linguistic backgrounds. As Ballentyne (2008) notes:

They may differ in terms of the amount of English that their parents speak (from very little English at all to fluent English). Their parents may also differ in terms of the extent that they speak one or more languages in the home. In some families, parents may speak one language at home and another at work. In other families, parents may speak two languages interchangeably. Family members may come from different language backgrounds, so a child may speak English to a parent but Spanish to a grandparent living in the home. Dual language learners arrive at school with language backgrounds and skills which are substantially different from monolingual English speakers. The strategies for dealing with bilingualism and dialect differences overlap with those of developmentally appropriate practices for helping all children acquire language skills.

Bilingualism In early childhood terms, bilingualism is the ability of a person to communicate in a language other than their native language with a degree of fluency. Baker (2007) explains:

There is not just one dimension of language. We can examine people's proficiency in two languages in their *listening (understanding), speaking, reading and writing* skills. Calling someone *bilingual* is therefore an *umbrella* term. Underneath the umbrella rest many different skill levels in two languages. Being bilingual is not just about proficiency

Providing books that are in tune with all children's cultures and language backgrounds expands everyone's world.

in two languages. There is a *difference* between *ability* and use of language. . . . In practice, a person may be bilingual, although ability in one language is lacking (but improving steadily).

A bilingual child must learn to comprehend and produce aspects of each language and to develop two systems of communication. This is a lengthy and complicated process of getting used to a new culture and a new language before feeling comfortable enough to use it in a classroom.

Second language learning occurs in two general ways. **Simultaneous acquisition** happens if a child is exposed to two languages from birth. These bilingual children tend to lag behind in vocabulary development in the early years, often mixing sounds or words. By 4 or 5 years of age, however, most children have separated the languages successfully.

The second pattern is known as **successive acquisition**. This occurs as a child with one language now enters the world of a second language, as when children with one home language enter a school that uses another language. A common pattern among immigrants and many children in the United States, this learning seems to favor younger children in their accent and grammar, but there is no evidence that younger children are any more successful with vocabulary and syntax.

More bilingual/bicultural children are in early childhood classrooms in the United States than ever before. Indeed, 185,000 English learners enter California kindergartens annually (Olsen, 2011). It helps to understand how children learn a second language and how to apply this research in practical ways (see Figure 13-2).

First and second language acquisitions are similar in many ways. Language acquisition is a natural process. Linguists generally agree that children reach proficiency in their first language by age 5, barring other identified difficulties. Moreover, brain development is at its peak in the early years, so learning a second language is at a premium. Not all children are successful in acquiring a second language, however, because a great deal depends on external and internal factors (CDD, 2007)

- External factors may include access to speakers of a second language, the frequency with which children come into contact with and interact with those speakers, the degree to which the second-language context is emotionally supportive and the messages and pressures present in school and society regarding the mastery of the second language.
- Internal factors may include the children's cognitive abilities and limitations, perceived need to learn a second language, talent in learning language, and individual temperaments and social skills.

For instance, Tjarko is of Swiss-German ancestry, so is it any wonder he pronounces an English "v" like an "f," as in "Can I *haff* one of those?" Sachiko, who has moved from Japan within the year, complains, "My *neck* hurts when I drink," and disagrees that it is a sore throat since "neck" is the word she knows.

- A particularly important point for all early educators to understand is the effect of a new language on a child in the program and at home.
- *Children of linguistically and culturally diverse backgrounds may face isolation at school.* In an English-speaking school, for instance, the child who does not yet understand or speak English may find it difficult to interact appropriately with children and teachers. Lack of a mutual language can result in the child being treated as nearly invisible or like a baby by other children, or as less intelligent or capable by teachers.
- *Children acquiring language in an English-dominant program often begin to isolate themselves from their families.* They may refuse to use their home language anymore, as it is difficult to use both, and English may have greater status in the children's eyes. Families sometimes promote this, as they wish their children to learn English. However, if they themselves do not speak English, they become unable to communicate at length with their children. The lack of a mutual language then grows

Myths & Truths Related to Second Language Acquisition

Myths or Misconception	What We Actually Know
Home language interferes with children's ability to learn English.	There is no evidence for this. In fact, a strong foundation in the home language **positively** impacts the learning of a second language.
Mixing languages is a sign of the child being confused.	'Code switching' is a normal part of bilingual language development and a common communication strategy for bilingual children & adults.
Bilingual children start to speak later than their monolingual peers.	Bilinguals share the same wide range of normal development as their monolingual peers.
If a child learning a second language demonstrates signs of language impairment, dropping the home language will fix the situation.	Research shows that bilingual children with language impairment are typically impaired in both of their languages. (we expect this to be true for L2 children also)
Children can learn a second language very quickly.	Children seem to have an easier time learning languages relative to adults, but we should not underestimate the effort it takes for them to learn a new language. (up to 2 years to reach a conversational level, and up to 5–7 years to achieve an academic level)
Parents who do not speak a language perfectly will pass on their errors and/or accent to their children.	This might be true if the child had no other language models, which is highly unlikely! Moreover, when exposed to various accents, children learn to be more accepting and respectful of diversity from a young age!

FIGURE 13-2 Myths and truths related to bilingualism. (Developed by the Early Childhood Language Development Institute, a project of San Mateo County Office of Education, Redwood City, California. June 2005. Reprinted by permission.)

at home, creating problems of family cohesiveness and harmony.

Teachers need guidance in educating second language learners (see Special Topic: Supporting Dual Language Learners).

Dialect Differences Dialect differences are variations in the way words are pronounced or grammar is used, even among English-speaking children. These differences reflect a **dialect**, or variation of speech patterns within a language. When we travel to New York, for example, our ear is attuned to the unique pronunciation of "goyl" (girl), and when we move north we hear "habah" (harbor). Southern speakers are easy to identify with elongated vowel sounds such as "Haiiiii, yaaw'll!" In addition to regional dialects, there are also social dialects that are shared by people of the same cultural group or social class.

Italian, Russian, and numerous other languages have regional and social dialects. Linguists, the scholars who study languages, argue that there is no such thing as a good or a bad language. Each language and dialect is a legitimate system of speech rules that governs communication in that language.

Some dialects, however, are not viewed favorably within the larger society and often carry a social or economic stigma. The unique linguistic characteristics of African American children is known as **Ebonics**, or black English. Negative views of black English or any nonstandard dialect are of concern to parents who want better opportunities for their children. The early childhood educator would be prudent to develop the goal of "language power for all children, so that each child is a comfortable and capable speaker in any situation demanding 'standard' English or the language of his own 'speech community.'"

The Development of Literacy

Successful readers see a relationship between spoken language and the written word. They are aware that sounds are how language is put together. Teachers plan activities that make connections between what is said and what is written. With the emphasis on early reading, legislation such as No Child Left Behind, and Common Core standards (see Chapter 15), teachers feel pressured to bring direct instruction into their early education programs.

Early Literacy

It is important to emphasize that early literacy is not equivalent to early direct instruction. Yet, much must go on in the early years for a child to be ready to read in primary school.

> Reading is the most natural activity in the world. . . . We read the weather, the state of the tides, people's feelings and intentions, stock market trends, animal tracks, maps, signals, signs, symbols, hands, tea leaves, the law, music, mathematics, minds, body language, between the lines, and above all we read faces. "Reading," when employed to refer to interpretation of a piece of writing, is just a special use of the term. We have been reading—interpreting experience—constantly since birth and we continue to do so. (Smith, 2011)

There is an important role for teachers of young children in the early stages of reading and writing. Teachers can influence positive attitudes toward reading and writing. They encourage children to talk and converse with others about what they see and do; this gives them increasing experience in using and attaching experiences to words. Taking the time to write down what children say and then reading it back gives a sense of importance to children's language and their ability to express themselves. Organizing the environment to support literary development and learning to teach toward reading in developmentally appropriate ways are all part of building an early literacy curriculum. In these ways, teachers can help children get involved with print in natural and unpressured ways (see Figure 13-3). For adults who work with young children, digital literacy is essential (NAEYC, 2012).

A Reading Curriculum A reading curriculum involves engaging children with print in ways that make sense to them. By creating an environment that provides rich opportunities to use the printed word, teachers help motivate children toward reading. High quality preschool is a powerful force in building language and cognitive skills. Research shows that children who attend quality prekindergarten score higher on school readiness measures at kindergarten entry (Karoly et al., 2008). Early literacy experiences are the first step in closing the achievement gap.

Essential Early Literacy Teaching Strategies

Rich teacher talk	Engage in conversation, use rare words, extend their comments.
Storybook reading	Read aloud once or twice a day.
Phonemic awareness activities	Play games or sing songs that involve rhyme, alliteration, match sounds.
Alphabet activities	Use magnetic letters, alphabet blocks and puzzles, alphabet charts and books.
Support for emergent reading	Provide a well-designed book center, repeat reading children's favorites, have functional and play-related print.
Support for emergent writing	Encourage scribble writing, invented spelling, provide a well-stocked writing center and play-related writing materials.
Shared book experience	Read Big Books, draw attention to basic concepts of print such as left-to-right and top-to-bottom, cover and title page.
Integrated, content-focused activities	Investigate topics of children's interest, helping children gather data and record it, engage in dramatic play, use emergent writing to record what they learn.

FIGURE 13-3 The pressure of early reading instruction can be relieved by encouraging early forms of reading and writing that also give play a prominent role (Roskos, Christie, & Richgels, 2003).

Adults encourage children's writing by taking their attempts seriously.

But what are developmentally appropriate early literacy experiences? Adults and even children often have a stereotypical concept of reading. They think the ability to read is only the literal translation of signs and symbols on a printed page (called **decoding**). Learning to read is also attaching experiences and knowledge to words and understanding the use of the written word in daily life. It is a complex process that includes both language and literary competencies. Building on these skills takes time and has tremendous individual variation; thus, it is known as **emergent literacy.** The processes involved in helping children with emerging literacy include beginning literacy awareness and involvement before kindergarten, using reading and writing concurrently and in an interrelated manner and interacting with the written word in everyday activities and using it to interact with the world. Literacy development is part of the total communication process that includes listening, speaking, reading, and writing.

The International Reading Association, in its Joint Position Statement with NAEYC (IRA, 2006) describes five stages of early literacy development:

1. Awareness and exploration
2. Experimenting with reading and writing
3. Early reading and writing
4. Transitional reading and writing
5. Conventional reading and writing

Teachers can help children through these stages (see Figure 13-4).

- First, help children learn that print is a form of language. Read them books filled with magic, messages, and mystery (pre-reading).
- Second, be sure children hear stories, poems, chants, and songs many times. Programs such as *Raising a Reader* and other take-home, book bag pre-literacy programs help children and families access books in an enjoyable, consistent way
- Third, help children rehearse by chanting, singing, re-saying, and "reading along" as we read to them (pre-reading).
- Fourth, observe as children learn to recognize words they read and know the text and begin to use some phonics to discover which words say what (beginning reading).
- Fifth, children start to read more and more on their own or with a friend. Now the task is to make them better readers (reading).

Reading can be seen as a two-stage process:

Stage 1. *Grow up to words and print* (birth to 4 years old). Falling in love with words and using everyday narrative are followed by first attempts: pretending to read, learning about print, and nourishing the mind with high quality books. Toward the end of this period, children know that alphabet letters are a special category of visual graphics and may recognize some. They pay attention to separate and repeating sounds in language, show an interest in books and reading, and display reading (signs in the local environment) and writing attempts (name on a birthday card; taking orders in a pretend restaurant).

Stage 2. *Become a real reader* (kindergarten through third grade). To become real readers, children need well-integrated instruction that focuses on three core elements: 1) identifying words using sound–spelling correspondence and sight word recognition; 2) using previous knowledge, vocabulary, and comprehension strategies to read for meaning; and 3) reading with fluency.

- During kindergarten, children should gain a solid familiarity with the structure and uses of print, be familiar with sound-by-sound and word-by-word analysis of language, and have an interest in the types of language and knowledge that books can bring them.
- First grade makes a transition from emergent to "real" reading. Children continue phonemic awareness, letter knowledge, and print awareness to help with

A Language Experience Chart

When is your birthday?
- Where is your name?
- How many children have birthdays in April? February? December?
- How many children have birthdays on the 10th? the 2nd? At the end of the month?

JAN.	FEB.	MAR.	APRIL	MAY	JUNE	JULY	AUG.	SEPT.	OCT.	NOV.	DEC.
13 Ann	1 José	3 Leon	2 Mrs. K.	16 Brian	11 Katie	5 Mr. W.	2 Carrie	8 Jim	21 Chris	7 Nick	13 Keesha
19 Bill	3 Mary	7 Kirk	10 Peter	27 Adele		9 Panya		29 Danny	30 Jay		25 Carol
26 Judy	6 Sue	15 Roberto	11 Jon			12 Kevin					30 Mrs. M.
24 Tom	11 Andy		18 Jill								
	19 Sean		23 Libby								
			30 Mia								

© Cengage Learning 2011

FIGURE 13-4 A language experience chart involves children through the subject matter and the way in which information is displayed.

writing attempts and fluent reading. Spelling becomes a focus during the year, starting with **invented spelling** and growing into a sensitivity to conventional spelling. Literacy activities are done voluntarily, such as choosing stories to read or writing a note to a friend.

- Second and third grades help children build automatic word recognition, spelling skills, and reading fluency. Comprehension improves, along with recall of facts and participation in creative responses to texts, and children move toward producing a variety of written work. "Learning to read" is now shifting toward "reading to learn."

Early childhood tradition develops curriculum through the emerging interests, needs, and developmental levels of the children (see Chapter 10). This corresponds to the **whole language** approach to reading instruction. In this method, a teacher might read a story to the children and then ask them to make up their own endings. The class

Teachers and children can share intimate moments when they enjoy using language together.

would be *listening* (to the story), *speaking* (telling their ideas), *writing* (trying their hand at spelling and handwriting), and *reading* (their creations to a friend or the class at the end of the lesson).

© Cengage Learning

Contrast that method to a direct teaching approach more often used with **basal readers**. Teaching the decoding skills, which a traditional phonics approach emphasizes, creates lessons around making associations between letters and sounds (phonics). But even before teaching formal reading, teachers can help children develop phonological and phonemic awareness—a sensitivity to the sound structure of the language. Children who can detect and manipulate sounds in speech are beginners in the decoding process. The ability to discern syllables is an important part of learning to understand how sounds translate into individual and combinations of letters (Strickland & Schickedanz, 2009). Regardless of approach, early literacy can be implemented appropriately in early childhood education programs (see Figure 13-5).

Current knowledge concludes that, to learn, primary children benefit from both specific phonics instruction and a rich background in literature (such as being read stories). This approach blends early phonics instruction in the teaching of reading while at the same time stressing the importance of balance (see Figure 13-6). In addition, it must be repeated that children younger than 5 years of age are not yet ready for an onslaught of conventional, direct instruction methods. There is a lack of agreement in the field over what exactly counts as *emergent literacy skills*, and more research is needed along with more refined understanding of the skills involved. Learning graphic language is a creative process that involves both an *art* (literature, rhyming songs, and invented spelling) and a *science* (the nuts and bolts of decoding). It is the teacher's job to be the master craftsperson in helping children put the two together.

Writing Curriculum A writing curriculum involves learning about words in print much the same as learning about reading and other aspects of language; that is, by seeing it used and having plenty of opportunities to use it themselves. Writing can be as natural for children as walking and talking. "What is written language? For a child, print is just another facet of the world, not yet comprehended, perhaps, but not different from all the complex sights, sounds, smells, tastes, and textures in the environment—not especially mysterious or intimidating" (Smith, 2011). Children's **emergent writing** begins when they first take a pencil in hand and start to scribble. Later, they can write a story by drawing pictures or by dictating the words and having someone else write them down.

A *print-rich environment* that includes labels, lists, signs, and charts can make print a meaningful part of the classroom environment. Often, children are involved in making the signs to indicate where things go and what things are. Using the languages of the group expands this "literate room," as do helper charts, daily schedules, and even attendance charts. Road signs can be made for the block corner, recipe cards for cooking. "Do not touch" may be written for an unfinished project, as can "Inside voices here" for the library corner. Labeled picture cards can be used for rhyming games, alphabet puzzles, magnetic letters, and scrabble games, as well as opportunities for children to give dictation, write grocery lists, and compose letters to friends and family.

Writing materials can be available throughout the room and yard. Paper and pencils come in handy in the dramatic play area. Menus, shopping lists, prescriptions, and money are but a few uses children find for writing equipment. The block corner may need traffic signs; the

---

Early Literacy Comes to the Classroom

1. Have a cozy library corner, giving children lots of time to explore and read all kinds of books.
2. Make a writing corner with different kinds of supplies, using this area to develop grouptime activities (children's stories), meaningful themes (post office), and connected learning (writing and sending letters).
3. Take field trips, pointing out print as they find it (street signs, store shelves, bumper stickers) and writing about it afterward.
4. Use large charts for poems, fingerplays, and songs as well as for listing choices available and for group dictation.
5. Plan activities that incorporate print: read recipes for cooking projects, make menus for lunch and snack, follow directions in using a new manipulative toy, write sales tickets for dramatic play units, bring books into science displays.
6. Use written notes regularly, sending a regular newspaper home that the children have written or dictated, writing notes to other team teachers that children deliver, encouraging children to send notes to each other.

FIGURE 13-5 Whole language in the primary classroom means integrating graphic language activities in a natural, meaningful way.

Activities for Phonemic Awareness

Phonemic Awareness Includes	Teachers
1. Oral vocabulary	1. Encourage talking, learning new words and phrases, singing, finger plays, and remembering and reflecting verbally.
2. Auditory discrimination (the ability to detect sound differences)	2. Create sound discrimination boxes in the science area, a "listen-to-the sound" walk, guessing games with musical instruments, and activities that teach letter sounds by using the children's names.
3. Phonological awareness	3. Help children play with individual sounds, both larger and smaller as well as different types of manipulations. The song "Old MacDonald" has 5 sounds (E-I-E-I-O), and playing with "apples/bapples/dapples" focuses attention on sounds.
4. Syllable awareness	4. Encourage children to listen and segment words into syllables, such as playing word games (me-mama-granpapa each have a different number of sounds: You want a drink of wa...*ter*, let's fix a sand...*wich*).
5. Onset-rime awareness	5. A more complex skill, onsets are the consonant sounds that precede a vowel in a syllable (d is the onset in dog, fr in frog) and rimes are a vowel plus any sound that follows it (og is the rime for dog and frog), so games that play with each "end" of a word help children hear the sounds.
6. Phoneme awareness	6. The smallest unit of speech are **phonemes,** which vary widely among languages; English has about 44, Spanish closer to 24 (Yopp & Yopp, 2009). Besides extending children's natural play with sounds, read aloud books, poetry, and songs that play with sounds, and play games such as "I Spy" that focus on a sound (I spy something that begins with /sh/...shoes!)

© Cengage Learning 2011

FIGURE 13-6 Children gain early literacy skills through activities for phonemic awareness.

computer, a waiting list. Outdoors, pictures can label the location of the vegetables in the garden; markers indicate where children have hidden "treasures" or where the dead bird is buried.

The early childhood classroom heightens an interest in writing with a writing center (see Figure 13-7). It can be part of a language area or a self-help art center. Wherever it is located, this center includes a variety of things to write with and to write on and "writing helpers."

- Children write with pencils (fat and thin, with and without erasers), colored pencils, narrow and wide marking pens, and crayons. They enjoy having many kinds of paper products, including old calendars and colored paper.
- Children write on simple books, a few blank pages stapled together. Carbon paper and lined paper add variety.
- "Writing helpers" include a picture dictionary, a set of alphabet letters, a print set, an alphabet chart, a

chalkboard, a magnetic letter board, or an interactive whiteboard. All of these serve to help children practice writing skills.

Emergent writing describes children's first attempts at writing, which includes drawing or scribbling. Writing moves from pictures to words, and drawing helps children plan and organize their thoughts (and, thus, their text). Teachers encourage children to tell them about their stories and can ask for a child's help in "reading" these writings. As children begin to work with words themselves, adults can help them sound out words or spell words for them. Spelling development is similar to learning to speak: Adults support the efforts, do not correct the mistakes, and allow children to invent their own spelling of words. Picture dictionaries and lists of popular words help children use resources for writing. Figure 13-8 is a sample of invented spelling in a kindergarten.

The *language experience* approach involves taking dictation; writing down and reading back to children

Reading *Is* Rocket Science!

An emerging field of research is developing that has particular promise for early childhood education. Blending psychology, neuroscience, and education, neuroeducational studies are attempting to understand neuroscience discoveries and apply them to educational practice. Frey and Fisher (2010) reviewed decades of research and have found five topics that inform preschool and primary teachers about reading acquisition.

Reading is learned, not innate. "Oral language and written language are fundamentally different. This can best be demonstrated by two recurrent findings: first, that even though most young children without disabilities learn to speak or listen, not all become fluent readers and writers. . . . Unlike speech, which develops uniformly across languages and cultures and is directly associated with specific brain and motor structures, reading occurs only through the intentional appropriation of existing structures within the brain." In other words, the reading brain is a relatively new evolutionary habit, and early experiences with print are needed to prepare young children for later reading instruction.

Language learning changes the brain. "Experience changes neural connections. Neuroplasticity, the brain's ability to physically change, is an important consideration given that our

[teaching] actions can permanently alter the learner's brain." Children who are taught well do learn to read and early learning must include background knowledge. Further, with specific instruction, children with reading difficulties had brain changes that persisted for more than one year on brain scans (Meyler et al., 2008).

Repetition can lead to automaticity, making more of the brain available for comprehension. "More cognitive space is needed when learning a new skill, and needed space is reduced over time as the skill becomes automatic. . . . As specific tasks become automatic, working memory is available for meaning making." If teachers can help children create schema or chunk information that make remembering easier and decoding less difficult, children can then shift their attention to comprehension, and thus fluency and enjoyment.

Vision plays an important part in human learning. Medina (2008) asserts that "vision trumps all other senses and is probably the single best tool we have for learning anything." Pictures are easier to remember, more likely to be stored, and more likely to be retrieved than print. Perhaps picture books are superior to basal readers because they pair illustrations with text so well; maybe comics aren't such a bad idea after all.

We are hardwired to imitate. Cognitive behavioral theorist Al Bandura (see Chapter 4) conducted research that showed the powerful effect of modeling. "The brain makes use of specialized cells called mirror neuron systems. These unique cells are active when we do something or when we watch someone do something." Children learn from watching the teacher move his hand across the page of a big book and listening to him sound out a word. It is one of the best strategies for beginning readers to use: watch, listen, and then do.

Reading *is* as complex as rocket science, and we help launch children when early childhood educators know that every brain must be *taught* to read. Neuroscience gives us clues for how to do that well.

Questions

1. What kind of language activity might be considered "brain friendly"? Why?

2. What do you remember about learning to read? What worked for you, and why?

3. List three curriculum activities or strategies that you consider negative for reading acquisition. Justify your list.

---

their own spoken language. It is important to use the child's exact words so that they can make the connection between their speech and the letters on the page. This is true for group stories, for children's self-made books, or for descriptions of their paintings. A useful technique in taking dictation is to say the words while writing them, allowing the child to watch the letters and words being formed. When the content is read back, the child has a sense of completion (see Figure 13-9). This is similar to the **organic reading** system in which the students themselves build a key vocabulary of words they wish to learn to read and write. In her classic book *Teacher*, Sylvia Ashton-Warner, a

kindergarten teacher who believed strongly in children's innate creativity and curiosity, developed this method for her classes of native Maori children in New Zealand, for whom the British basal readers held little meaning. Ashton-Warner's personal, culturally relevant teaching works well because it flows naturally from the child's life and interests.

Story maps help children see the parts and sequencing of the writing process. Depicted as a body, the head serves as the beginning (with facial features called "topic," "characters," and "setting"), the body as the middle, and the legs as the end ("Finally . . ."). A primary child can write in the various parts of the story and

A literate classroom includes plenty of opportunities for experiences with writing.

read it from the map or continue to elaborate with full sentences in a more traditional manner. In these ways, teachers help raise awareness of the use and enjoyment of the printed word.

Many teachers use a combination of key words, journals, and phonics along with holistic strategies such as DEAR (Drop Everything and Read), huddle groups (you choose who to work with), book bragging time (either in large or small groups), and SST (sustained silent reading with a timer, usually done in first through third grades) as they teach reading in developmentally appropriate ways.

Noticing and manipulating the sounds of a spoken language are related to later success in reading and spelling. "In English—and many other languages—the written language is predominantly a record of the sounds of the spoken language. With a few exceptions, the English language is written out by sound" (Yopp & Yopp, 2009). Therefore, children must be able to grasp the sounds of speech if they are to understand how to use a written system that records those sounds.

Children's Literature

Children's books bring us back to ourselves, young and new in the world. Our bones may lengthen and our skin stretch, but we are the same soul in the making. . . . Children's books are such powerful transformers because they speak, in the words of the Quakers, to one's condition, often unrecognized at the time, and remain as maps for the future. . . . In children's books, we preserve the wild rose, the song of the robin, the budding leaf. In secret gardens we know the same stab of joy, at whatever age of reading, in the thorny paradise around us. (Lundin, 1991)

Literature has as important a place in the curriculum today as it did in this classic description written more than two decades ago. Through the use of good books, teachers can help children broaden their interests and concepts. Books that are primarily used for transmitting information expand the child's knowledge base. Thoughtful books that draw on children's everyday experiences widen their understanding of themselves and others.

For instance, five different books describe and illustrate the behavior of cats in five different ways. Exposure to *Millions of Cats* (Gag), *Angus and the Cats* (Flack), and *The Cat in the Hat* (Dr. Seuss), as well as to the cats portrayed in *Peter Rabbit* (Potter) or *Frog Went A-Courtin'* (Langstaff), enlarges the child's concepts of cats. Different cultures are also represented in any number of children's books, teaching a greater awareness of all of humankind (see Figure 13-10).

Teachers have an opportunity to encourage divergent thinking through the use of children's literature. Children gain more than facts from books; they learn all manner of things, providing they can interpret the story rather than just hear the individual words. Quizzing children about whether the dinosaur was a meat- or plant-eater brings about responses that are predictable and pat, but comprehension does not have to be joyless. "Would a brontosaurus fit in your living room?" gets children to think about *Danny and the Dinosaur* (Hoff) or Kent's *There's No Such Thing as a Dragon* or Most's *If the Dinosaurs Came Back* in new ways that get them involved in the story.

Selection of books is important (see Figure 13-11). The wise teacher chooses books that invite participation. Everyone can "roar a terrible roar, gnash their terrible teeth, and show their terrible claws" during a rendition of *Where the Wild Things Are* (Sendak). Meaning for children lies more in action than in words. When Andrea was struggling to find the words to describe a large

© Cengage Learning

Suggested Writing Center Materials

- Alphabet board
- Alphabet stamps
- Binders—yarn, string, "twist ties," to bind homemade books
- Book-binding machine (used by adults to bind special books)
- Cardboard—cereal/cracker boxes provide cardboard for covers
- Clipboards
- Collage materials—magazines, wall paper, and wrapping papers
- Colored pencils
- Crayons
- Envelopes (local card store will sometimes donate leftovers)
- Fabric
- Laminate (factories will sometimes donate end rolls)
- Magnetic letters
- Markers
- Mini books (½- and ¼-size sheets of paper, about 4–5, stapled. Another recommendation: ½ sheets of lined paper, about 30 pages for longer works.
- Name cards (children's names)
- Notebooks, notepads, stationary, odd-shaped/colored papers (printshops will sometimes donate these)
- Office-style rubber stamps and ink pads
- Old cards, invitations, and business cards
- Old date books and calendars
- Paper crimping tool (roll a piece of paper through and it comes out corrugated—found at a rubber stamping or craft store)
- Paper punches (with large button that can be easily pushed by children)
- Recycled paper (different sizes)
- Rulers
- Scissors
- Stamps: wildlife and other nonpostage stamps. (Homemade stamps can be made by painting the backs of pictures with "lick'em, stick'em"—one part strawberry gelatin and one part water. Apply to shiny magazine pictures, dry and then they can be licked and used as stamps.)
- Stapler (kindergarten)
- Stencil shapes
- Stickers
- Word wall (words and their corresponding pictures—whenever the children need to know how to write a new word, it goes up there.)

FIGURE 13-7 A writing center needs plenty of materials to stimulate graphic language development (Chesler, 2011).

amount, Mitra began to recite: "Hundreds of cats, thousands of cats, millions and billions and trillions of cats!" (Gag's *Millions of Cats*). As Trelease (2006) states, "If our first problem is not reading enough to children, our second problem is stopping too soon." Whether age 1 or 10, children need and thrive on being read aloud to

regularly. Teachers could ask for no better activity to promote good listening habits than a wealth of good children's books.

A Rich Literary Environment A rich literary environment can be a challenge to create. The newspaper

Invented Spelling

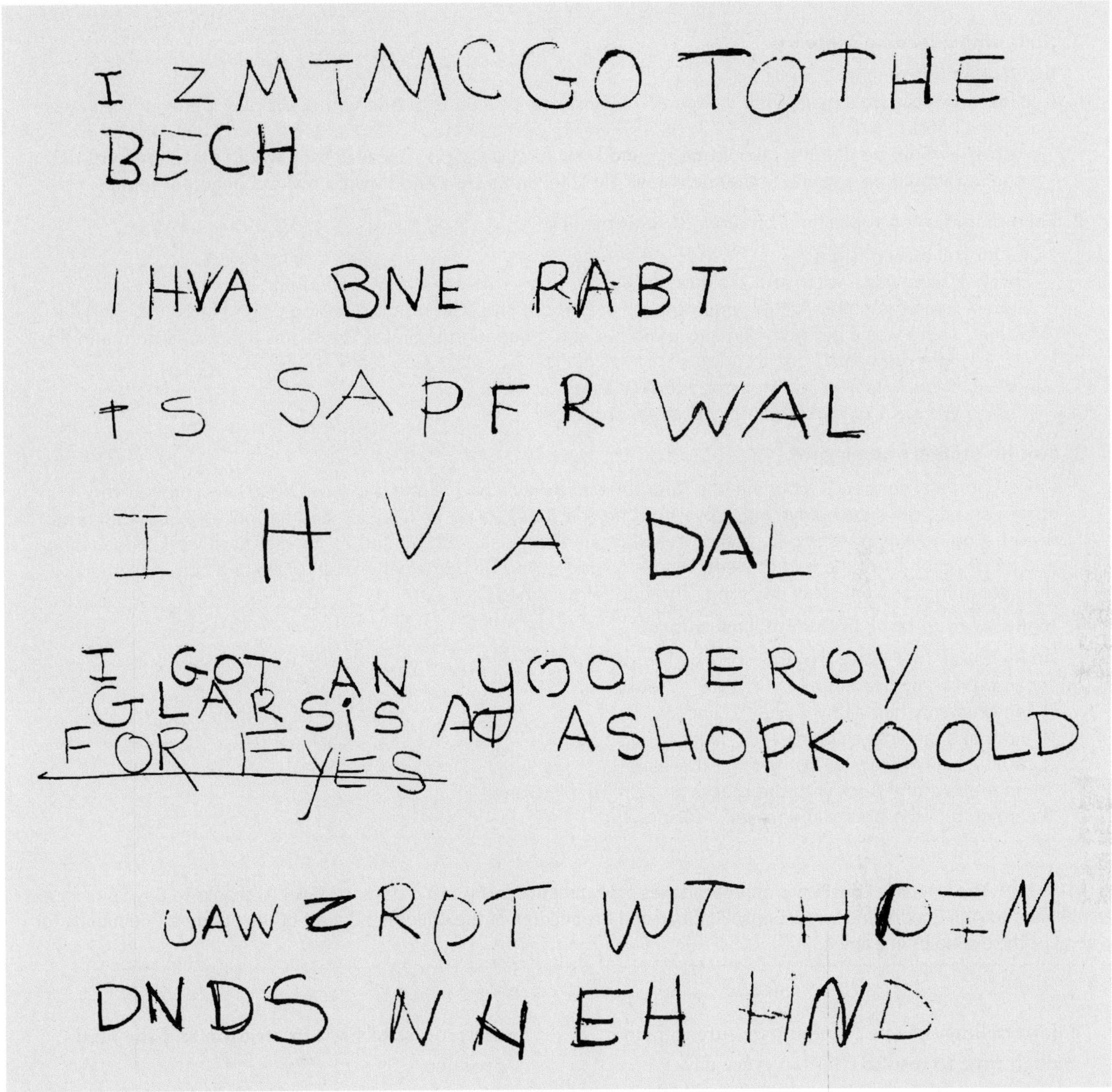

I ZMTMC GO TOTHE
BECH

I HVA BNE RABT

tS SAPFR WAL

I H V A DAL

I GOT AN YOO PEROV
G LARSiS AT ASHOPKOOLD
FOR EYES

UAW Z RDT WT HOTM
DNDS NH EH HND

FIGURE 13-8 Early writing usually involves children's attempts at words of their own invention. Invented spelling can be treated with respect for the efforts and as a foundation for successful writing experiences. (Courtesy of Kim Saxe. Reprinted with permission.)

comics of yesterday are far outdistanced by the television and video games of today. How can teachers give children experiences in literature in the face of such competition?

The field of children's literature is rich in its variety, including both great classic stories and those of present day situations and concerns. Fiction and informational books, children's magazines, and poetry add balance to the literary curriculum. Every classroom should contain representative works from each of these areas and should:

● *Provide plenty of time for using books and other materials.* Children need time to browse, to flip through a book at their own pace, and to let their thoughts wander as they reflect on the story line. They also

The Language Experience Approach

1. Start with a leading sentence.

If I were an instrument . . .
Michelle: I would be a piano with strings and lots of sparklies on top. And you could play me even if you were blind.
Janette: I would be a drum. I would be hit and I wouldn't be happy because they would make me hurt.
Dennis: I would be a violin. Someone would play me with a bow and I would make a beautiful sound.

2. Take dictation on topics and pictures of their making.

"On Our Halloween Nights"
Ehsan: There was a witch and skeleton and ghost in my room on Halloween night.
Lionel: Costume night. A cow jumping over the moon. The little rabbit sleeping.
Martine: There was a big pumpkin and a big bat and a bear and a pirate. There was a jack-o-lantern and the light glowed.
Andrew: There was a smiley monster and Aka-Zam!
Luke: We went to my church for hot dogs and cider.

3. Ask for stories of their own.

Once upon a time there's a boy named Timothy and he punched all the bad guys dead. And he was very strong and he can punch anything down. And he can do anything he likes to. And he makes all the things at winter. And he was so strong he could break out anything else. And he had to do very hard work all day long and all day night. And he had to sleep but he couldn't. And he had a very small house and cup. And then he did everything he want to all day long. The End. Tim (signed)

4. Make a group book (including illustrations).

All By Myself (our version of the book by Mercer Mayer)
"I can put on my overalls all by myself." (Stephanie)
"I can brush my hair all by myself." (Lindsey)
"I can make pictures all by myself." (Jessica)
"I can buckle my jeans all by myself." (Megan)
"I can make a drill truck with the blocks all by myself." (Lionel)
"I can jump in the pool all by myself." (Andrew)

FIGURE 13-9 The language experience approach takes many creative forms in a classroom. (Special thanks to Gay Spitz for example 1 and to Ann Zondor and Lynne Conly Hoffman and the children of the Children's Center of the Stanford Community for several of the examples in 2 and 4.)

enjoy retelling the tale to others. Be sure to plan enough time to read to children every day.

- *Make a space that is quiet and comfortable.* In addition to soft pillows or seats, locate the reading area where there is privacy. Crashing blocks and messy finger painting intrudes on the book reader. A place to sprawl or cuddle up with a friend is preferable.
- *Have plenty of books and supporting materials.* The language arts center might contain a listening post, with headsets for a CD player. Perhaps there is even a puppet stage or flannel board nearby so that stories can be created in new ways.
- *Display children's literary creations.* Establishing a place in the room where they can be seen and read honors the efforts of children's stories and bookmaking. Children then see how adults value

the process of literary creation and the final product.

- *Model how to care for a book and keep classroom books in good repair.* Children can come to realize that a book is like a good friend and should be given the same kind of care and consideration.
- *Foster children's reading at home.* This is one of the important contributions a teacher can make to the reading process. Attitudes about reading are communicated to children from the important people in their lives Family literacy programs are developing for all families to gain skills in English; check your local community for availability. Families whose home language is not English face enormous challenges when encouraging reading; research supports development of the home language as a foundation for learning other languages

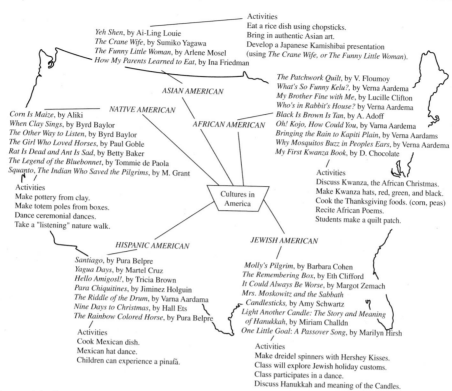

FIGURE 13-10 Using multicultural literature helps each child get connected with books and expands all children's outlooks. (Courtesy of de Melendez & Ostertag, 2012.)

(see Special Topic), so programs should attempt to offer *book bags* to families with books in their home language as well as plenty of picture books that allow parents to "read" the pictures with their children. Posting the local library hours, establishing a lending library, and providing parents with lists of favorites reinforces the child's interest in literature.

- *Use books around the room.* Do not confine them to just the book corner or the bookshelf. Demonstrate their adaptability to all curriculum areas by displaying a variety of books in the activity centers. Ask children to help you retell or emphasize parts of a story (see the Storytelling section), and ask them questions informally afterward: "How many bowls of porridge were on the kitchen table? Which one did Goldilocks like best? How did you know?" (see Figure 13-12).

Literary Extensions Literary extension experiences are excellent ways to use good literature. A creative teacher uses books and literature to develop other curriculum materials. Translating words from a book into an activity helps a child remember them. Books and stories can be adapted to storytelling, the flannel board,

dramatizations, puppets, book games, and audiovisual resources.

Storytelling is as old as humanity. The first time a human being returned to the cave with an adventure to tell, the story was born. Storytelling is the means by which cultural heritage is passed down from one generation to another. Children's involvement with a story that is being told is almost instantaneous. The storyteller is the medium through which a story comes to life, adding a unique flavor through voice, choice of words, body language, and pacing. The oral tradition is strong in many cultures, and the telling of the tale is memorable. Instead of focusing on a book page, the teacher involves the children directly, with expressions and gestures that draw in the children. Repetition and questions get the children so involved they feel that they have created the story. Young readers want to find the book, and young writers want to draw and retell the story or create their own.

Teachers can use any familiar story, be it *The Three Little Pigs* or *Swimmy*. Props can be added to draw attention to the story. Flannel board adaptations of stories are helpful; they give the storyteller a sense of security and a method for remembering the story. Children can be involved in the action by placing the characters on the felt board at the appropriate time. Puppets or an assortment of

Selecting and Reading Children's Books

Before reading:
 Look at the cover.
 Talk about pictures and text.
 Activate prior knowledge.
 Ask for personal connections.
 Set a purpose.

THE LITTLE ENGINE

During reading:
 Make predictions.
 Pause and reflect.
 Create mental images.
 Summarize.
 Read it again, pointing to words
 and pausing.

After reading:
 Make connections.
 Create reenactments.
 Perform retellings.

1. ____ Could I read this book enthusiastically?

2. ____ Are the contents of the book appropriate for the children?
    ____ Is it age appropriate?
    ____ Is it suitable for the individual child(ren)?
    ____ What are the cultures and languages of the group?

3. ____ Is this book biased?
    ____ Are illustrations stereotyped or showing tokenism?
    ____ What is the story line: What is the standard for success; how are problems presented and resolved; what is the role of women, people of color, or the heroes?

4. ____ Is the book written with an understanding of my group's age characteristics?

5. ____ Is the author's style enjoyable?
    ____ Can the children understand the sequence?
    ____ Is there repetition of words or actions?
    ____ Does it end in a satisfying way?
    ____ Are there humorous parts?

6. ____ Does it have educational value?

FIGURE 13-11 Selecting books for children involves careful study. (Derived from Machado, 2009 and Derman-Sparks & Olsen Edwards, 2010.)

hats can be used as props. Good storytellers enjoy telling the story and communicate their enthusiasm to children.

- *Dramatizations* have universal appeal as children act out characters from a favorite story. Two and three year olds are introduced to this activity as they act out the motions to finger plays and songs. The "Eensy Weensy Spider" and its accompanying motions are the precursor for dramatization. Story re-enactment helps children learn to work together so that their social development is enhanced, as is the cognitive ability to engage in collective representation.

As an extension of Steiner's theories, Waldorf kindergartens include fairy and morality tales. These tales,

told on successive days for up to two weeks, culminate in a play (by the children) with the teacher narrating. Whether the child is an observer, walk-on, mime, or actor, the learning is real in each step of the continuum. Older children may choose to write (or dictate) parts or scripts; it is appropriate for 6 to 8 year olds to have their playmates act out original stories. Once the "right" story has been chosen, the teacher helps the children to retell the story together, set the stage, and let the play begin.

- *Puppet shows* can involve a large number of children as participants and audience. Children of all ages enjoy watching and putting on a puppet show. Because puppets are people to young children, they become confidants and special friends.

Literature Across the Curriculum

Living Together: Reflecting Diversity

Knots on a Counting Rope (Martin, Jr., & Archambault)
The Big Orange Splot (Pinkwater)
Mei Li (Handforth)
Gilberto and the Wind (Ets)

Creating Art

Black Is Brown Is Tan (Adoff)
Start with a Dot (Roberts)
Little Blue and Little Yellow (Lionni)

Building Blocks

Changes Changes (Hutchins)
The Big Builders (Dreany)
Who Built the Bridge? (Bate)

Dramatic Play: On Our Heads!

Martin's Hats (Blos)
Caps for Sale (Slobodkina)
Hats Hats Hats (Morris)

Families

When You Were a Baby (Jonas)
All Kinds of Families (Simon)
Whose Mouse Are You? (Kraus)

Discovery/Science: Grow, Growing, Growest!

Growing Vegetable Soup (Ehlert)
The Carrot Seed (Krauss)
From Seed to Pear (Migutsch)

ABC, Just Like Me!

K Is for Kiss Goodnight: A Bedtime Alphabet (Sardegna)
A to Zen (Wells)
Grandmother's Alphabet (Shaw)

Math Lab: 1,2,3, Count with Me!

How Much Is a Million? (Schwartz)
Roll Over! A Counting Song (Peek)
Ten, Nine, Eight (Bang)

Making Music

Hush Little Baby (Aliki)
Ben's Trumpet (Isadora)
One Wide River to Cross (Emberley)

Having Friends

Friends (Heine)
George and Martha (Marshall)
Frog and Toad Are Friends (Lobel)

Books for Zero to Threes

Goodnight Moon (Brown)
Brown Bear, Brown Bear (Martin, Jr.)
Duerme Bien, Pequeno Oso (Buchholz)

Books for Early Primary

Charlotte's Web (White)
How Many Days to America? (Bunting)
Ramona (Cleary)

FIGURE 13-12 When literature is a natural part of the environment, children learn to appreciate and use it.

Children confide in and protect a puppet, engaging in a dialogue with one or more puppets that is often revealing of the child's inner struggles and concerns. Teachers can support their efforts by helping them to take turns, suggesting questions and dialogue to them, and involving the audience. The project of puppet making can be quite elaborate and very engaging for older children.

- *Book games* are a good way to extend the literary experience. Buy two copies of an inexpensive book with readable pictures, such as *The Carrot Seed* (Krauss). Tear out the pages, and cover each page with clear plastic. Children must then read the pictures to put the book into proper sequence. A book of rhymes, such as *Did You Ever See?* (Einsel), lends itself to rhyming games. Children can act out the rhymes from the story line or match rhyming phrases from cards the teacher has made.

- *Media materials* enlarge the child's experience with books. The auditory and visual experiences reinforce one another. Putting in a "listening post" so that a few children can listen to a story with headphones adds interest to stories. Touch tablets can encourage collaboration around making stories together or planning out a show for older children. Music brings literature alive; besides tapping into

Acting out characters from a favorite story is culturally relevant and has universal appeal.

the musical aspect of intelligence, it appeals to all children to move and express themselves and, thus, enjoy literature and books even more. The pictures can show children new aspects of the words; sometimes the music or the voices bring the book to life. Often both happen. Hundreds of children's stories—classics and modern day—have been translated to these media. Be judicious with videos, so that the dominance of the visual images does not erase the images from the children's imaginations.

Language and Literacy Skills

Teachers translate language development theory into practice as they work with children. Language and literacy skills in the early childhood setting include articulation,

receptive language, expressive language, graphic language, and enjoyment. Children's conversations, their ways of talking, some children's lack of expressive language, and their ways of asking questions all offer glimpses into their skills.

Articulation

Articulation is how children actually say the sounds and words. Children's ability to produce sound is a critical link in their connecting the sounds to form speech. Mispronunciation is common and normal, especially in children younger than 5 years of age. The preschool teacher can expect to hear "Thally" for Sally, "wope" for rope, and "buh-sketty" for spaghetti. Children who repeat sounds, syllables, or words in preschool are not stutterers; 85 percent of 2- to 6-year-olds hesitate and repeat when talking. As children talk, teachers listen for their ability to hear and reproduce sounds in daily conversation. Can they hear and produce sounds that differ widely, such as "sit" and "blocks?" Can they produce sounds that differ in small ways, such as in "man" and "mat?"

How adults respond to disfluencies can help a child through this normal stage of language development. Chesler (2011) suggests:

- Pay attention to the child when she talks to you. Do not rush her.
- Do not demand speech when a child is upset or feels stressed.
- Do not put children on exhibition by asking them to recite or talk when they do not want to.
- Avoid interrupting a child when she is talking; avoid completing a sentence for her.
- Statements like "slow down" or "think before you talk" draw attention to his speech and usually cue the child that there is something wrong with the way he talks.
- Do make an example of your speech by talking slowly, smoothly, and distinctly.

Receptive Language

Receptive language is what children acquire when they learn to listen and understand. It is what they hear. With this skill, children are able to understand directions, to answer a question, and to follow a sequence of events. They can understand relationships and begin to predict the outcome of their behavior and that of others. They develop some mental pictures as they listen.

Children begin early and can become experts in reacting to words, voice, emphasis, and inflection. How

DIVERSITY

Speaking with a Stutter

All of us has experienced trouble finding words or expressing ourselves clearly from time to time. Young children experience normal breakdowns when they cannot retrieve a word, they are rushed, or they feel intensely.

Stuttering is different. In that case, the person knows exactly what s/he wants to say but cannot coordinate the speech muscles to communicate.

Panico and colleagues (2011) offer a description of stuttering and strategies for the classroom of children 3 to 8 years of age. Although the cause of stuttering is unknown, the disorder is characterized by "repeating parts of words ("p-p-pizza"), repeating a whole word ("my-my-my name is Molly"), prolonging or stretching a sound ("pleeeeease"), or being temporarily unable to produce sound (pl——ease").

Children who stutter may start to avoid speaking, show nonspeech behaviors such as eye blinking, or start withdrawing from social interaction or group participation. Further, these children encounter reactions from other children, including avoidance, teasing, and even rejection. While as many as 75 to 80 percent of children who stutter eventually outgrow the disorder, the communication breakdowns can have negative effects on the child.

As with other aspects of diversity, teachers play an important role. It is their authority that either accepts these behaviors that exclude or intervenes and models tolerance and acceptance. Panico and his colleagues recommend these four strategies:

Modify the rate of your speech. Model slower speech, rather than asking the child to slow down. The child likely imitates your slower pace, which may help the motor aspects of the stuttering.

Create a relaxed speaking environment. Anxiety-producing conditions often increase (but do not cause) stuttering, and finishing a child's sentence for him can create more stress than it relieves. Teachers should model a safe affective tone so that the child knows not to feel ashamed.

Listen attentively. Answer children about what they say, rather than how they said it. You don't need to focus on how the speech was produced to respond positively.

Modify the linguistic complexity of your speech. "Stuttering tends to occur when children use longer words, infrequently used words, and longer or more grammatically complex sentences." When a child is stuttering, begin to simplify your own speech, allowing the child to modify as well.

These strategies provide a safe place for the child who stutters and teach tolerance of difference and of individual challenges in the program.

---

many times does the child understand by the way the words are spoken?

"You finally *finished* your lunch." (Hooray for you!)
"You *finally* finished your lunch?" (You slow poke.)

Children learn to listen for enjoyment, for the way the wind sounds in the trees, the rhythm of storytelling, or the sound of the car as it brings Mom or Dad home.

Expressive Language

Expressive language in the early years means the process and steps involved in expressing ideas, feelings, and intentions in language. This includes words, grammar, and elaboration.

Words

Expressive language is the spoken word. Children's first words are of what is most important to them (ma-ma, da-da). Adults help children extend their knowledge and vocabulary by using the names of objects and words of action (walk, run, jump) and feelings (happy, sad, mad). By describing objects in greater and greater detail, teachers give children new words that increase their skills. Children are then ready to learn that some words have more than one meaning (the word "orange," for example, is both a color and a fruit) and that different words can have the same meaning (such as "ship" and "boat" as similar objects, or "muñeca" and "doll" as the same word in different languages).

Grammar

Basic grammatical structure is learned as children generalize what they hear. They listen to adult speech patterns and use these patterns to organize their language. It helps to hear simple sentences at a young age, with the words in the correct order. Next, children can grasp past tense as well as present, plural nouns along with the singular. Finally, the use of more complex structures is understood (prepositions, comparatives, various conjugations of verbs).

Elaboration of Language

Elaboration of language takes many, many forms. It is the act of expanding the language. Through description, narration, explanation, and communication, adults elaborate their speech to encourage children to do the same. For instance, communication for children includes talking to themselves and others.

Verbalize a process aloud.	"I'm trying to get the plant out of its pot, but when I turn it upside down it doesn't fall out."
Give and follow directions.	"It's time to make a choice for clean up. You find something and I'll watch you."
Ask and answer questions.	"How do you feel when she says she won't play? What can you say? Do?"
Stick to the subject.	"I know you want to go play kickball, but first let's solve the problem of the wagon."
Use speech to get involved.	"What a great house you built. How do you get inside?"

Graphic Language

"Talk written down" is the essence of graphic language. The child now learns that there is a way to record, copy, and send to another person one's thoughts. Because words and letters are simply "lines and dots and scribbles" to young children, the teacher and parent must demonstrate how meaningful graphic language can be. Moreover, the translation of talk into print is a cognitive task (see Chapter 12), so children's intellectual development as well as their language abilities are at play when learning about the printed word.

Enjoyment

To encourage language is to promote enjoyment in using it. As teachers converse with children, parents, and other adults, they model for children how useful and fun language can be. Knowing the power and pleasures of language gives children the motivation for the harder work of learning to read and write.

Children learn to enjoy language by participating in group discussion and being encouraged to ask questions. Reading and listening to stories and poems every day are essential parts of any program. The program should also include children's literature and stories children dictate or write themselves.

Word play and rhyming are fun as well as educational. Group language games are useful, such as asking the question, "Did you ever see a bat with a hat? A bun

A listening post can provide additional interest in books and stories.

having fun? A bee with . . . ?" and letting the children add the rest. Begin a song, for instance, "Do You Know the Muffin Man?" and add the children's names. Whatever contributes to the enjoyment of language supports its growth, from varying voice and tone to fit the situation (in storytelling, dramatic play, and ordinary activity periods) to spontaneous rhyming songs.

Effective Approaches for Curriculum

Planning a language curriculum requires educators to keep several key points in mind, such as providing a kind of envelope of language for all children, not just the more talkative ones, and inviting the use of home language and dialects to bridge learning the dominant language. Taking into account both the indoor and outdoor space, schedule, and skill levels of children allow a better match between the themes or activities presented and what teachers want children to learn.

Considerations

When considering how to work with young children in language development, teachers should keep several things in mind:

1. *Children need an "envelope of language."* Be a play-by-play announcer, providing language labels for everything the child does and touches. For example, babies need communication from caring adults: "Acknowledge the baby by name, wait for

the baby's response, include your observation of the baby's response in your next message, and say what you see or think you see" (Kovach & Ros-Voseles, 2011). When you expose children to quality literature every day, you ensure that children find both social and linguistic communication are pleasant things to do.

2. *Children must use language to learn it.* Adults often spend much of their time with children talking—to, at, for, or about them. "Be careful not to dominate when talking with children. Lean toward more child than adult talk" (Epstein, 2009). Children's conversations with each other are important in learning the basics of how to take turns and keep to one topic and of saying what they mean, getting their ideas and themselves heard and accepted. Talk time with peers and adults, in both structured (group times) and nonstructured (free play) situations, allow children to practice and refine language skills. Listening and speaking are two of the four language arts (the other two being reading and writing) (see Figure 13-13).

3. *The most verbal children tend to monopolize language interactions.* Research shows that teachers interact verbally with the children who are most skilled verbally. Seek out and support language development in those with fewer skills, generally by drawing them out individually through (a) reading the unspoken (body) language that communicates their ideas, needs, and feelings and (b) helping them express verbally those ideas, needs, and feelings.

Children can use story time as "talk time" as well as for engaged listening.

4. *Adults should know the individual child.* Consistency in adult–child relationships may be as important for language as for effective development during the early years. If so, teachers must have a meaningful relationship with each child. This includes knowing the parents and how they communicate with their child.

5. *Home languages are to be invited into the program.* Language is a powerful way families transmit their love, culture, and identity to their children. When centers do not use the home language, they reinforce existing societal messages that a child's language is

---

Helping Children with Receptive Language

1. *Give clear directions.* "Please go and sit on the rug next to the chairs," instead of "Go sit over there."
2. *Let children ask questions.* Give them acceptable answers. For example, repeat a phrase from the child's last sentence that asks the child to try again: "You want what?" or "You ate what?" Or cast the question back to a child by changing the phrase "Where did you put it?" into "You put it where?"
3. *Give instructions in a sequence.* "Put your lunch on your desk, then wash your hands. Then you are ready to go to lunch." It often helps to ask the children what they think they are to do: "How do you get ready for lunch? What comes first? Next?"
4. *Try to understand what the child means, regardless of the actual language.* Look for the purpose and intent beyond what the child may have said. This is particularly important with toddlers, non-English speakers, and newcomers.
5. *Ask children to state their thoughts out loud.* "Tell me what you think is going to happen to the eggs in the incubator. Why do you think some might hatch and some might not?"
6. *Use literature, poetry, and your own descriptions.* Give children an idea of how words can be used to paint verbal and mental pictures. Ask questions about children's own images and dreams. To older children read aloud from books without pictures.

FIGURE 13-13 Teachers do more than insist "Listen to me" to encourage receptive language.

Contribute to Communication Competence

Research shows that effective communication is a significant skill that contributes to school readiness, academic success, and social success. Early childhood programs are increasingly diverse. "Differences in children's family backgrounds (for example, culture and language) and individual characteristics (such as learning ability and educational experience) pose both challenges and opportunities for early childhood teachers to be creative and flexible practitioners" (Chen & Shire, 2011). More than 150 languages are spoken among American public school children (Batalova & McHugh, 2010), and 13 percent of total student enrollment was served under Individuals with Disabilities Education Act (IDEA) during the 2007–2008 school year (NCES, 2010).

Effective communication is a goal for both children who are dual language learners and children with special needs, and intentional teaching is key (based on Chen & Shire, 2011):

Dual Language Goals	Teaching Strategy
Build respect and positive connections.	Ask about family background (country of birth, languages spoken), culture (food, customs, values), and children's experiences (extended family, prior schooling).
Understand receptive skills likely precede expressive language.	Use pictures of objects, activity areas, and feelings faces to match with words.
Determine the level of individual communication skills in English.	Use individual skill set to provide scaffolding to English.
Be aware that children may communicate well in their home language.	Engage use of home languages to count, name objects, sort by size, and so forth.

Special Needs Goals	
Scaffold children's learning.	Bring a "master player" to assist or be a model.
Build on individual strengths.	Highlight child's knowledge and skills.
Collaborate with other involved adults.	Share observations and strategies regularly.
Create an environment that supports differences in learners.	Answer children's questions about learning differences, read books about children with challenges (e.g., *Cleversticks*)

Think About This

1. You have a child in your kindergarten who has been diagnosed with an articulation speech disorder. Which of these strategies would work with her? Why?
2. Your class has four children who are learning English; two speak Spanish at home, one has home languages of Mandarin and English, and one child speaks Farsi. How will they communicate at first in your program? How can you help each one? What might work well with all of them?
3. What is your home language? What do you remember of your first schooling experiences and language? Was it easy to speak up? How did you interact with your teacher and with other children when using language? What can you remember about learning to read? Was it easy or difficult? Can you recall reading aloud to others? How do these memories inform your educational practices?

lower in status than the dominant language. "Much recent research has found that the home language and cultural practices of your DLL children are fragile and susceptible to dominance by the English language and mainstream culture" (Espinosa, 2010). Having explicit language goals around welcoming and using home languages in the program are important (see Special Topic).

6. *Dialect differences expand your speech community.* Dialects are as much a part of children's culture and identity as is their home language. Providers may mistakenly see children speaking their dialect as less capable, or even delayed. We need to not make the assumption that different means "less than."

7. *Some children may have speech and language disorders.* Early detection of and intervention for speech and language disorders is possible without the teacher being a speech therapist. With a basic knowledge of typical speech development and signposts of speech and language problems, the perceptive teacher can alert

families and recommend specialist assessment and input. Once a child with a disability comes into a program with specific learning objectives, the staff plans how to address those needs in the curriculum and with the children (see Figure 13-14).

8. *The language of the teacher influences the classroom.* What teachers say—and how they say it—is important. Moreover, what they do not say communicates the most to children in their struggle to gain mastery of the language. Teachers provide a rich environment and a high quality of interaction with the child that encourages all language skills. Preschool teachers' use of sophisticated vocabulary and analytic talk about books combined with early support for literacy in the home can predict fourth-grade reading comprehension and work recognition (Dickenson, 2011). Teachers engage in conversations with both individual children and small groups. Whenever possible there are sustained conversations (with multiple conversational turns, complex ideas, rich vocabulary) and *decontextualized language* (talk about events beyond the here and how) concerning what is past or future or imaginary ("What do you think we will see at the firehouse?").

Curriculum Planning for Language and Literacy Development

Teachers who plan curriculum for language skills, just as for cognitive development, focus on the setting, schedule, skills, and themes. They organize the environment and activities to help children acquire linguistic skills of their own (NAEYC, 2005).

In the Early Childhood Setting

Indoors Indoor space is arranged so that children practice speaking and listening and, in programs for older children, reading and writing. Areas can be arranged to enhance language development as follows:

Art
- Have signs and pictures that show where things are kept.
- Ask children to describe the materials they use.

Readiness Checklist for Children with Language Disorders

Ask yourself these questions, then complete the checklist.

	Ready	Not
Is information presented in multiple formats? Use pictures, picture schedules, symbols, and words to communicate with children.	❏	❏
Do teachers supplement spoken words with eye contact and gestures?	❏	❏
Do teachers modify their language to reflect the developmental levels of the children they are speaking to? For example, use shorter sentences when talking with 3-year-olds and longer ones with 5-year-olds.	❏	❏
Do teachers frequently check to make sure children understand what was said? Look for signs such as eye contact and gestures; consider asking children to repeat back what they heard.	❏	❏
Do teachers encourage children to "use their words" and then model appropriate language?	❏	❏
Does the classroom library include a variety and range of books suitable for different ages and developmental levels?	❏	❏
Do teachers read books with children one-on-one in addition to reading aloud to a group?	❏	❏
Do teachers encourage children who use language to ask for materials and join in activities?	❏	❏
Do adults have frequent conversations with children on topics of interest to the children?	❏	❏

FIGURE 13-14 A checklist for getting your program ready for children with communication and language disorders. (Watson, A., & R. McCathren. 2009. Including children with special needs: Are you and your early childhood program ready? *Young Children* 64[2]: 22-28. Reprinted with permission of the National Association for the Education of Young Children.)

🔲 This checklist can be downloaded from the Education CourseMate website.

Blocks

- Ask children to give each other directions for where blocks go and what they are used for.
- Label block shelves with shapes and words.
- Sketch children's structures and then write their verbal descriptions.

Cooking

- Label utensils.
- Describe actions (pour, measure, stir).
- Use recipe cards with both pictures and words.

Discovery/Science

- Label all materials.
- Ask questions about what is displayed.
- Encourage children's displays, with their dictated words nearby.
- Graph growth and changes of plants, animals, children, and experiments.

Dramatic Play

- Provide a variety of equipment for a diversity of gender play, including male and female clothes.
- Set up spaces in addition to a "house/kitchen," such as a "reader's theater" in which children choose a story to act out and eventually write their own scripts.
- Offer cooking and eating utensils, objects, and tools that reflect cultural and linguistic diversity, such as a tortilla press and molcajete in the kitchen and different kinds of combs and brushes for the dolls, beginning with the cultures of the children in your program and then adding other groups.
- Have plenty of child-sized mirrors.

Language/Library

- Label the bookshelf, cassette player, and computer in children's languages.
- Help children make their own books that involve description (My family is . . .), narration (It is winter when . . .), and recall (Yesterday I . . .).
- Have children "write" notes, lists, or letters to one another, the teachers, and their families.
- Develop a writing center with a typewriter, office supplies, and so on.

Manipulatives

- Recognize this area as a place for self-communication, as children talk and sing to themselves while they work.
- Explain similarities and differences of materials and structures.

Outdoors Outdoor space emphasizes gross motor movements, so motor skills can be described and pointed out by teachers and children, as both use words of action and of feeling. For example, what actions does it take to

Small groups are language-intensive activities that call for teachers to provide material and experiences in everyone's home language.

© Cengage Learning

DAP — Set up a Literacy Yard

Taking language and literacy outdoors is a good idea because many children feel freer and interact more actively with each other outdoors. These three curriculum ideas take language and literacy wherever the children may be:

Toddler Tent: Set up a small see-through tent outside, with a soft blanket and a basket of cardboard books.

Preschool Playgrounds: Regularly set up one of these stations outdoors, with cards that describe the actions the children need to take (Beaty, 2009): walking rink, running ring, jumping pad, crawling chamber, leapfrog lodge, throwing booth, dancing ring.

School-Age Spot: Set up a writing nook with plastic milk crates, clipboards, and even a small swimming pool with pillows. Consider adding binoculars or making some from cardboard tubes to focus attention. Read the entries the children create at circle time.

Outdoors is an ideal place to bring in developmentally appropriate props and activities for language curriculum goals.

get a wagon up the hill? How does a child's face feel when swinging up high? How do people sit? Move? Carry things?

Daily Schedule

Language and literacy skills are used throughout the day and are especially useful in transitions and routines, which are more manageable if the children understand what is happening and exactly what they are to do. Teacher language helps talk children through the process so that they can internalize what they are asked to do. Arrival is an easy time to reinforce name recognition. Mark cubbies with names and photos, and comment on the names children find there. Children's belongings should also be labeled. These steps take a little time to make but can increase children's awareness of print.

Snack/lunch tables at one preschool began to exchange notes ("Dear Teacher Adrienne's Table: What are you doing? What are you eating?"). They passed notes to each other's groups, including the sign language two children used ("How do you sign banana? What's the sign for graham crackers?").

A chart that shows in pictures and written language the steps children are to take from lunch to nap is invaluable, and children refer to it daily. Preschool teachers often use this time to have regular and predictable one-on-one conversations with a teacher. The teacher prompts children by asking what they want to talk about and then concludes conversations with a pat and a transition sentence such as "I'll see you when you wake up."

When things feel unfinished or interrupted, a teacher can write a note to "Please save" for the child who does not have time to finish a project, or they can write children's dictated notes to family members on their way out after dropping off a child.

Group times, with finger plays, songs, and stories, are language-intensive activities. Children's articulation skills are strengthened, as is receptive language through listening to others.

- When children discuss daily news and important events, brainstorm ideas about a subject, or report on what they did earlier in the day, they gain experience in listening and speaking.

A language-rich environment includes a welcoming spot for books and reading.

© Cengage Learning

- Children can also dramatize familiar stories and finger plays.
- Using visual aids or name cards gives children experience in graphic language. These might include having felt letters for the song "B-I-N-G-O"; numbers for the finger play "One, Two, Buckle My Shoe"; or name cards for the activity "I'm Thinking of Someone . . ." Children enjoy the cadence and rhythm of language spoken or chanted.

Focus on Skills

Recall that there are four major language arts skills: speaking, listening, reading, and writing. In addition, there are the pragmatics of language, which are the appropriate and effective use of language in social communication.

Teachers can plan curriculum based on any one of the skills:

- To increase speech, vocabulary, and awareness of other languages, get a familiar book such as *The Very Hungry Caterpillar* (Carle) from the Children's Braille Book Club and also make name cards in Braille for every child.
- To encourage receptive listening skills, have children bring a favorite item from home or choose something from the class or yard and hide it in a "guessing bag." Children take turns looking into the bag and describing their item until others guess it. They can then pull it out and talk about it with the group.
- For developing reading skill, use "Readers' Theater" to improve reading comprehension and fluency, enhance motivation, and build social skills (Zambo, 2011). By having authentic opportunities for repeated readings, children are motivated to read and then perform.
- For developing written language, consider activities that extend the age range experiences of the children. For example, a kindergarten class makes a group story about "The Mystery of Space." Then, they separate into small groups with second grade helpers to write their own books in story form, complete with illustrations.
- To emphasize the pragmatics of language, teachers allow children to express themselves by practicing words and grammatical structure and by elaborating on their own expressions. Outdoors, 4-year-old Hadar describes her actions: "Teacher, look at me! I'm taller than you!" The teacher responds, "You called me over, smart girl! You climbed up the ladder to the top of the tunnel. Now, when you stand up, your head is above mine."

Themes

Projects or themes for curriculum planning can be used to develop language and literacy skills by careful selection of topic (see Figure 13-15). Although themes are not typically used with infants or toddlers, many units that elicit an extensive use of language for 3 to 8 year olds are:

1. *Harvest.* Activity: Ask children (2 years and older) to bring food from home for a "feast corner." Make a display of food from a harvest feast in the past or change the housekeeping corner into a "feast for all" area.

   Group time: Begin a group story using the sentence "I am thankful for . . ."

   Special project: Plan a feast, with the children creating the menu and preparing both the food and the table for their families at the school.

2. *Friends.* Activity: Choose a favorite book (3 years and older) to introduce the topic; the *Story Stretchers* book series (Raines & Canady, 1989–2011) has several suggestions, such as *Heine's Friends.*

   Group time: Talk with the children about the kinds of things friends like to do together. Make a list; then read the book. Later, select children to act out the animal parts. Do not worry about reading lines; keep it imaginative!

   Special project: Put a flannel board in the library corner with characters and props from the book. Encourage the children to tell the story from the perspective of the various animals and then the farmer.

3. *The Earth Is Our Home.* Activity: Have the group (5 years and older) make a large circle in a shade of blue, sketching the continents. Provide brown, green, and blue paint in pie tins and let children make a hand print on the ocean or land. Next, have the children bring from home the names of the countries of their family's ancestry. Help them locate those areas and attach their names to those parts of the world.

   Group time: Sing "The Earth Is Our Home" (Greg and Steve) and "One Light, One Sun" (Raffi). Read *Just a Dream* (Van Allsburg) and *Where the Forest Meets the Sea* (J. Baker).

   Special project: Help make a class recycling area or compost heap. Take a field trip to recycle the materials, or visit a garden that uses compost. Young children can learn about endangered species through Burningham's *Hey! Get Off Our Train;* older children can do research on

Theme: Babies

Art: Limit art materials to just what toddlers and infants can use.

Cooking: Make baby food.

Discovery/science: Display baby materials, then bring in baby animals.

Dramatic play area: "The baby corner" with dolls, cribs, diapers.

Manipulatives: Bring in several infant and toddler toys.

Gross-motor/games: Make a "crawling route," an obstacle course that requires crawling *only.*

Field trip/guest: A parent brings a baby to school to dress, bathe, feed.

Large group time: Sing lullabies ("Rock-a-Bye-Baby")

Small/large group: Children discuss "What can babies do?"

Joshua: Babies sleep in cribs. They wear diapers. Babies can't talk.

Becky: They sometimes suck their thumbs. Babies cry when they are hungry.

Dennis: Babies go pee in their diapers.

Stevie: Babies sit in highchairs. Babies eat baby food that looks like squashed bananas.

Corey: Babies sleep in a bassinette. Then they crawl and bite your finger.

FIGURE 13-15 Teachers plan a unit to promote the skills they are focusing on in the class. A "babies" theme brings out the expert in all children and encourages language.

an animal and make its natural habitat in a shoebox.

Although preschool and school-age children are challenged by specific themes, curriculum for infants and toddlers does not usually need this kind of focus. Curriculum for younger children should emerge naturally from their developmental level and interests. A gentle, supportive environment with adults who listen and respond to sounds can be expanded on themes of favorite stories or activities.

Special Topic: Supporting Dual Language Learners

Language and literacy curriculum development is incomplete unless it addresses the special topic of second language learning (see previous section on Dual Language Learning and Bilingualism). Briefly, the research base shows:

- Attending to the social, emotional, and cognitive skills of dual language learners in early childhood enhances their schooling experiences (Ballantyne et al., 2008).
- Dual language learners may learn to read best if taught both in their native language and English

from early in the process of formal schooling (Shanahan & Beck, 2007).

- In addition to clear, intentional interactions that are focused on important instructional goals, DLL children also require adaptations while they are in the process of acquiring English (Espinosa, 2010).

Language Goals

Each program must first decide on its language goals. Is there a full dual language approach, in which half the spoken language is in English and half in children's home language? This 50:50 approach works with bilingual/biliterate staff and a single home language of the children. Or is the program conducted primarily in English with home language support? This 90:10 or 80:20 approach is more likely to be used when fewer of the staff are fluent or if there are multiple home languages spoken in the group. Who teaches in which language and in what spaces and during which parts of the day are other decisions that need to be made.

Environment and Program Strategies

Support for second language acquisition includes environmental organization, language techniques, and classroom activities (see Figure 13-16). The following

Checklist for Language-Friendly Classroom Practices

1. Help children make sense of language.
   _____ What is their "language dictionary"?
   _____ What can their family experts tell you?

2. Provide comprehensible input.
   _____ What information talk can you provide in the moment?
   _____ What multisensory experiences can you plan?

3. Be prepared for the "silent period."
   _____ How do they communicate when they aren't speaking?
   _____ What sign of progress and learning do you see?
   _____ In what ways is the child able to communicate?

4. Be sensitive to the affective filter.
   _____ How can you tell when the child is in emotional discomfort?
   _____ When do you invite participation?

5. Create a connection.
   _____ What is your morning greeting?
   _____ What is the predictable schedule?
   _____ When does the child need your support?

6. Build a community of acceptance.
   _____ Does the environment reflect the child's life?
   _____ How is the child's home language validated?
   _____ Have you helped the child find buddies?
   _____ How have you worked with the family?

7. Examine teacher behaviors.
   _____ When/how are teachers helpful and encouraging?
   _____ When/how have teachers ignored or been unhelpful?

© Cengage Learning 2011

FIGURE 13-16 A checklist for teachers to examine their daily practices with children who are acquiring a second language (with help from Soodie Ansari, 2011).
⊙ This checklist can be downloaded from the Education CourseMate website.

recommendations serve as guidelines for teachers of children who are acquiring a second language:

1. *Understand how children learn a second language.* There is a developmental sequence of second language acquisition. First, children may continue to speak their home language with both those who speak it and those that do not. Next, children begin to understand that others do not understand their home language and give up using it, substituting nonverbal behavior that may appear less mature. Allowing them to watch and listen and also interpreting and inviting children into play helps. Third, children begin to break out of the nonverbal period with a combination of telegraphic and formulaic language. One-word phrases such as "no, yes, mine, hey" all telegraph meaning, as do catchwords such as "ok, lookit, I dunno" that are used as formulas for communicating. Finally, productive use of the new language appears.
   The perceptive teacher sees that it is a positive step in a cumulative process.

2. *Make a plan for the use of the two languages.* Try to have bilingual staff or at least one teacher who specializes in each language. The children are then exposed to models in both the home language and English. Many programs in communities in which the children and educators have the same first language background use the children's home language while learning English in a naturalistic setting. They may start a year with the language of the children and gradually use more English until the languages are equal.

3. *Accept individual differences.* Take note of both the style and the time frame of language learning. Children bring a range of individual differences to learning a second language. Motivation to learn, exposure to the dominant language, the age of the child in relationship to the group, and temperament can all affect language acquisition. Do not insist that a child speak, but do invite and try to include the child in classroom activities. Assume developmental equivalence; that is, that the children, although different, are normal. For example, Maria Elena just does not come and sit at group time. Allow her to watch from a distance and believe that she is learning, rather than be worried or irritated that she is not with the group yet.

4. *Support children's attempts to communicate.* Encouraging children's communication bids rather than correcting them helps children try to learn. Recognize developmentally equivalent patterns. For instance, Kidah may not say the word "car" but can show it to you when you ask. Receptive language precedes expressive language.

5. *Maintain an additive philosophy.* Recognize that children are acquiring more and new language skills, not simply replacing their primary linguistic skills. Asking Giau and his family about their words,

foods, and customs allows teachers to use a style and content that are familiar to the Vietnamese, thus smoothing the transition and adding onto an already rich base of knowledge.

6. *Provide a stimulating, active, and diverse environment.* "A first step in planning a welcoming environment for young DLLs, as well as all children, is to think about the messages and impressions that the classroom communicates. Ask yourself if what hangs on the walls, what is displayed, and the materials offer a welcoming feeling for culturally and linguistically different children" (de Melendez, 2011). Give many opportunities for language in meaningful social interactions and responsive experiences with all children. Have a set routine so that children can anticipate and anchor onto a predictable sequence. Provide a safe haven so that children can spend some time away from communicatively demanding activities and can do things that don't always require language to succeed. Make use of story time, increasing the amount of time when you tell or read aloud stories; the predictable plot and repetitive language help children follow along and understand. Choose chants, finger plays, and songs for the same reasons.

7. *Use informal observations to guide the planning of activities.* Provide spontaneous interactions for speakers of other languages. Teachers need to expand the types of observations used for assessment to see a child's physical, cognitive, or emotional abilities in language-free situations. Additionally, a home visit observation may help to learn how a child is doing in home language development. Also, only by actively watching does a teacher find special moments in a classroom to help a child be accepted and join in. Seeing a group of girls building a zoo, a teacher gives a basket of wild animals to Midori. Walking with her to the block corner, she offers to stock the zoo and then helps all the girls make animal signs in Japanese and English. Thus, Midori enters the play in a positive and strong way.

Family Contacts

Find out about the family. Establish ties between home and school. School learning is most likely to occur when family values reinforce school expectations. Parents and teachers do not have to do the same things, but they must have a mutual understanding and respect for each other and goals for children. For example, Honwyma's parents and his teacher talk together about what of the Hopi language and culture can be brought into the classroom. When there are differences between the Hopi patterns and those of the school, teachers try to accommodate.

Provide an accepting climate. The classroom climate must value culturally and linguistically diverse young children. Teachers must come to grips with their cultural ethnocentricity and learn about the languages, dialects, and cultures beyond their own. It is critical to value all ways of achieving developmental milestones, not just those of the teacher's culture or educational experience.

Use multiple strategies to involve families. Since access to information in the home language helps progress in both languages, digital technologies can help teachers find appropriate materials and games in languages so that children can get active practice. "Technology tools can be effective for dual language learners by providing access to a family's home language and culture while supporting English language learning." (NAEYC, 2012). Finding words in a home language, recording a child's speech for later translation or a parent's expressions to use with a new child can support both access and comfort.

Challenges and Conclusions

The challenge to young children and their teachers is enormous. With informed, open-minded teaching, children can learn a second language without undue stress and alienation. We can conclude that:

- Children can and do learn two languages at an early age, though the process and time vary with the individual child.

TeachSource Video

Watch the TeachSource Video Case entitled "English Language Learners: Partnering with Parents." After you study the video clip, view the artifacts, and read the teacher interviews and text, reflect on the following questions:

1. What do you notice about the interaction style of Teacher Marie Mona Sanon? What effective strategies does she use with the parents?

2. What language-related information is important for teachers and directors to know about a child and family?

3. How can families who are not English-literate help their children to acquire English skills? To keep their home language?

- Instruction in a familiar language can serve as a bridge to success in English and support retention of the home language.
- Two languages can be learned at the same time in a parallel manner. The depth of knowledge of one language may be different from that of the other, or the two may develop equally.

- The acquisition of languages may mean a "mixing" of the two, as heard in children's speech when they use words or a sentence structure of both languages.
- Learning two languages does not hurt the acquisition of either language in the long run.

Summary

LO 1 Planning for language and literacy development is a huge part of a teacher's curriculum work. Language and thought are intertwined and multiple developmental theories are used to describe the sequence of language and literacy acquisition. Research on brain development and early literacy both indicate the importance of the early years.

LO 2 There are several key elements of children's language acquisition and literacy skills. Language skills in early childhood include articulation, receptive and expressive language, graphic representative, and enjoyment, and all are included when planning curriculum. Early literacy involves children in reading and writing experiences. Children and books belong together, so the early years should lay a foundation in literature on which children can build throughout their lives.

LO 3 Effective approaches that foster language and literacy skills require an understanding of several considerations. Knowing language development and the role of home language is critical. Keeping individual children in mind and watching for dominance by the most verbal children helps. The teacher also needs an understanding of bilingualism and dialect differences and a working knowledge of speech and language disorders. The language of the teacher—both spoken and nonverbal—influences children's use of language in a program through appropriate curriculum strategies.

LO 4 Supporting dual language learners is a special topic of language and literacy. Language goals vary and influence curriculum development. Environment and program strategies implement goals, and family contacts are critical. Challenges can be met and positive outcomes can be achieved for children's acquisition of English and retention of home language.

Key Terms

receptive language	simultaneous acquisition	whole language
expressive language	successive acquisition	basal reader
extended discourse	dialect	emergent writing
bilingualism	Ebonics	phonemes
precursors	decoding	organic reading
phonemic awareness	emergent literacy	articulation
dual language learners	invented spelling	elaboration

Review Questions

1. What are the stages of language development?
2. List the five language skills and one way early education can help their development.
3. Describe three curriculum activities for language or early literacy development. Simplify them for infants/toddlers/2 year olds and elaborate for the primary-aged youngsters.
4. Describe dual language learning and how teachers help children who are dual language learners.

Observe and Apply

1. Observe the children in your care. Identify the stages of language development of three children. Give concrete examples that validate your assessment.

2. Teaching reading readiness involves trying to develop receptive (listening) and expressive (elaboration) skills. What could a teacher of toddlers plan for each? A kindergarten teacher?

3. Describe three ways children's books and literature can be extended in the curriculum.

4. Choose a child in your care whose primary language is not English. How is that child processing language? What are you doing to foster the child's emerging English skills? How is that child's first language being supported in your program? What can you do to involve the family?

Helpful Websites

American Library Association   www.ala.org

Braille Institute   www.brailleinstitute.org

Children's Book Council   www.cbcbooks.org

Council for Asian American Children and Families
www.cacf.org

Early Childhood Research Institute on Culturally and Linguistically Appropriate Services
http://clas.uiuc.edu/links.html

National Association for Bilingual Education
www.nabe.org

National Association for Multicultural Education
www.nameorg.org

National Association for the Education of Young Children   www.naeyc.org

National Black Child Development Institute
www.nbcdi.org

National Center for Family Literacy   www.famlit.org

National Task Force on Early Childhood for Hispanics
www.ecehispanic.org

Raising a Reader Early Literacy Program
www.raisingareader.org

Reading Is Fundamental   www.rif.org

The Education CourseMate website for this text offers many helpful resources and interactive study tools. Go to CengageBrain.com to access the TeachSource Videos, flashcards, tutorial quizzes, direct links to all of the websites mentioned in the chapter, downloadable forms, and more.

References

Ansari, S. (2011). *Early Childhood Language Development Institute*. Redwood City, CA: San Mateo County Office of Education.

Ashton-Warner, S. (1986). *Teacher*. New York: Simon & Schuster/Touchstone Books.

Baker, C. (2007). A *parents' and teachers' guide to bilingualism* (3rd Ed). Clevedon, England: Multilingual Matters Ltd.

Ballentyne, K. G., Sanderman, A. R., & McLaughlin, N. (2008). Dual language learners in the early years: Getting ready to succeed at school. Washington,

D.C.: National Clearinghouse of English Language Acquisition. Retrieved from www.ncela.gwu.edu.

Beaty, J. J. (2009). *Preschool appropriate practices* (3rd Ed.). Clifton Park, NY: Delmar Cengage.

Berger, K. S. (2009). *The developing child through childhood and adolescence* (8th Ed). New York: Worth Publishers.

Chen, J. J., & Shire, S. H. (March 2011). Strategic teaching: Fostering communication skills in diverse young learners. *Young Children*, 66(2), pp. 20–27.

Chesler, P. (2011). Bilingualism: Literacy development and activities for the young child. Unpublished.

Child Development Division. (2007). *Preschool English learners: Principles and practices to promote language, literacy, and learning.* Sacramento, CA: Department of Education.

Chomsky, N. (1993). *Language and thought.* Wakefield, RI: Moyer Bell.

Derman-Sparks, L., & Olsen Edwards, J. (2010). *Anti-bias education for young children and ourselves.* Washington, D.C.: NAEYC.

Dickenson, D. K. (2011, August). Teachers' language priorities and academic outcomes of preschool children. *Science,* 333(6045), pp. 964–967.

Epstein, A. (2009, January/February). Think before you (inter)act: What it means to be an intentional teacher. *Exchange.*

Espinosa, L. M. (2010). *Getting it right for young children from diverse backgrounds.* Upper Saddle River, NJ: Pearson.

Frey, N., & Fisher, D. (2010, April). Reading and the brain: What early childhood educators need to know. *Early Childhood Education Journal,* 38, pp. 103–110.

International Reading Association. (2006). Position statement: Literacy development in the preschool years. Retrieved from www.reading.org.

Jacobs, G., & Crowley, K. (2010). *Reaching standards and beyond in kindergarten.* Thousand Oaks, CA: Corwin and Washington, D.C.: NAEYC.

Karoly, L., Ghosh-Dastidar, B., Zellman, G., Perlman, M., & Fernyhough, L. (2008). *Prepared to learn: The nature and quality of early care and education for preschool-age children in California.* Santa Monica, CA: RAND Corporation.

Kovach, B., & Ros-Voseles, D. D. (2011, March). Communicating with babies. *Young Children,* 66(3), pp. 48–50.

Lundin, A. (1991, Summer). Secret gardens: The literature of childhood. *Childhood Education,* 67(4).

Machado, J. M. (2009). *Early childhood experiences in language arts,* (9th Ed.). Belmont, CA: Wadsworth Cengage.

Meyler, A., Keller, T. A., Cherkassky, V. L., Gabrieli, J. D., & Just, M. A. (2008). Modifying the brain activation of poor readers during sentence comprehension with extended remedial instruction: A longitudinal study in neuroplasticity. *Neuropsychologia,* 46(10), pp. 2580–2592.

Moats, L. C. (2001). Overcoming the language gap: Invest generously in teacher professional development. *American Educator,* 25(5), pp. 8–9.

NAEYC. (2005). *Position statement on responding to linguistic and cultural diversity: Recommendations for effective early childhood education.* Washington, D.C.: Author.

NCELA. (2008). Dual language learners in the early years: Getting ready to succeed at school. Washington, D.C.: Author. Retrieved from www.ncela.gwu.edu.

Neuman, S. B., & Dwyer, J. (2009). Missing in action: Vocabulary instruction in pre-k. *The Reading Teacher,* 62(5), pp. 384–392.

Olsen, L. (2011, December). California's long-term English learners: Directions for policy, programs, and practice. Retrieved from www.ncela.gwu.edu.

Panico, J., Daniels, D. E., & Claflin, M. S. (2011, May). Working in the classroom with young children who stutter. *Young Children,* 66(3), pp. 91–95.

Raines, S. C., & Canady, R. J. (1989–2011). *Story stretchers.* Mt. Rainier, WA: Gryphon House.

Roskos, K. A., Christie, J. F., & Richgels, D. J. (2003). The essentials of early literacy instruction. In D. Koralek (Ed.), *Spotlight on young children and language.* Washington, D.C.: NAEYC.

Saxton, R. R. (1998, July). Different dialects. Personal communication.

Smith, F. (2011). *Understanding reading—the psycholinguistics of reading and writing* (6th Ed). New York, NY: Routledge.

Strickland, D.S., & Schickedanz, J. A. (2009). *Learning about print in preschool: Working with letter, words and beginning links with phonemic awareness* (2nd Ed.). International Reading Association. Newark, DE: Retrieved from www.reading.com.

Trelease, J. (2006). *The read-aloud handbook* (6th Ed.). New York: Penguin Books.

Vygotsky, L. S. (1962). *Thought and language.* New York: MIT Press and John Wiley and Sons.

Watson, A., & McCathren, R. (2009, March). Including children with special needs: Are you and your early childhood program ready? *Young Children,* 64(2).

Yopp, H. K., & Yopp, R. H. (2009, January). Phonological awareness is child's play. *Young Children,* 64(1).

Zambo, D. (2011, March). Young girls discovering their voice with literacy and Readers Theater. *Young Children,* 66(2), pp. 28–35.

Special Topic: Supporting Dual Language Learners

Ballentyne, K. G., Sanderman, A. R., & McLaughlin, N. (2008). Dual language learners in the early years: Getting ready to succeed at school. Washington, D.C.: National Clearinghouse of English Language Acquisition. Retrieved from www.ncela.gwu.edu.

de Melendez, W. R., & Ostertag, V. (2012). *Teaching young children in multicultural classrooms* (4th Ed.). Belmont, CA: Wadsworth Cengage.

Espinosa, L. M. (2010). *Getting it right for young children from diverse backgrounds.* Upper Saddle River, NJ: Pearson.

Shanahan, T., & Beck, I. (2007). Effective literacy teaching for English-language learners. In D. August & T. Shanahan (Eds.). *Developing literacy in second-language learners: Report of the national literacy panel on language minority children and youth.* Mahwah, NJ: Erlbaum.

© Cengage Learning

14

Planning for the Heart and Soul: Psychosocial Development in Action

Learning Objectives

LO1 Define psychosocial domain and the major developmental elements.

LO2 Examine the central elements of children's emotional growth and effective approaches when planning curriculum.

LO3 Examine the central elements of children's social growth and effective approaches when planning curriculum.

LO4 Examine the central elements of children's creative growth and effective approaches when planning curriculum.

LO5 Examine the central elements of children's spiritual growth and effective approaches when planning curriculum.

LO6 Discuss emotional intelligence as a special topic of psychosocial curriculum.

naeyc Standards for Professional Development

The following NAEYC Standards for Early Childhood Professional Development are addressed in this chapter:

Standard 1 Promoting Child Development and Learning

Standard 4 Using Developmentally Effective Approaches to Connect with Children and Families

Standard 5 Using Content Knowledge to Build Meaningful Curriculum

naeyc Code of Ethical Conduct

These are the sections of the NAEYC Code of Ethical Conduct that apply to the topics of this chapter:

Core Values: We have made a commitment to recognize that children and adults achieve their highest potential in the context of relationships that are based on trust and respect.

Section I:
P-1.2   We should care for and educate children in positive emotional and social environments that are cognitively stimulating and support each child's culture, language, ethnicity, and family structure.

Section II:
I-2.3   To welcome all family members and encourage them to participate in the program, including involvement in shared decision making.

The Development of the Psychosocial Domain

The heart and soul of any good program for young children is a commitment to help children as they struggle with 1) the reality of emotions, 2) the awareness of the need for social skills, 3) the creative urge, and 4) acknowledgment of the spirit. Together, these four areas comprise the psychosocial, or affective, side of development. The **psychosocial domain** is the third area of human development. It includes the development of emotions, temperament, and social skills. Areas of self-concept and self-esteem are also in this realm. "Family, friends, the community, the culture, and the larger society are particularly central to the psychosocial domain. For example, cultural differences in appropriate sex roles or in family structures are part of this domain" (Berger, 2009). The domain is sometimes labeled **affective** as it deals with feelings, or *socioemotional*, as the social and emotional areas are key components.

Affective growth takes place in the context of personal identity. Identity begins with family—every aspect of child-rearing, such as how a child is held, bathed, fed, dressed, and sleeps, lays a foundation for children of who they are. Families hand down beliefs, attitudes, and behaviors and then hand over their children to us for a time, so identity development becomes a shared responsibility.

It is primarily through psychosocial experiences that children learn who they are; only then can they see themselves successfully in relation to others. Social and emotional competence predict, in part, school readiness and later success. Therefore, early environments and curriculum help build this competence.

Defining Psychosocial Experiences

The first thing one notices on entering an early childhood program is the children at play. A quick survey of the area shows who is playing together, whether there is crying or fighting, and how happy or sad the children look. This overview gives an immediate sense of the affective climate in that early childhood setting.

- *Emotional.* Toddler Abier giggles as she runs her hands across the water table, then cries after she splashes soapsuds in her eyes and needs to be comforted.
- *Social.* Preschooler Danny wants his favorite red wagon, so Pat, the student teacher, helps him negotiate a turn with Christa.

- *Creative.* Kindergartners Fabio, Erika, and Benjy work steadily to build a tall, intricate block structure. When it is finished, the three children stand back and marvel at their creation.
- *Spiritual.* The children see a nest being built in the backyard of Teresa's family child care home. "How do the birds know how to make the nest?" wonder the children. They make daily checks and then hear the peeping sound of the newly hatched baby birds. "It's magic!" whispers Neefara, and the children sit quietly and reverently every time they see the mother return.

Together, these factors—emotional mood, social dynamics, creative, and spiritual tone—define the overall atmosphere in which children play and work.

The components of psychosocial development are woven together in the developing child. Children who are sensitive to their feelings and moods are able to begin understanding other people and, thus, become more socially effective and successful. Children with experience in many creative endeavors have the self-confidence that comes from having an outlet for self-expression. Children who are spiritually curious are likely to ask questions such as "How did the little seed do that?" when gardening, or they want to write a letter to their dead pet to make sure all is at peace.

The division into the three domains (physical-motor, cognitive-language, and psychosocial) makes development easier to study, but growth is holistic, not piecemeal. Note the connections here:

- *Creative/Physical.* Physical skills can define and limit children's creative abilities. Two-year-old Andrea, whose physical skills do not yet include balancing objects, plays with blocks by piling them on top of one another, filling her wagon with blocks, and dumping them or lugging them from place to place.
- *Social/Cognitive.* It is hard for 5-year-old Karena to share her best friend Luther with other children. Her intellectual abilities do not yet allow her to consider more than one idea at a time, so she cannot understand that Luther can be her friend and Dana's at the same time.
- *Emotional/Language.* Tyler is upset with his teacher's refusal to let him go outdoors during story time. "I hate you!" he screams, "and you aren't the boss of me!" Children learn to label and express their emotions through words.
- *Spiritual/Creative.* The children make their daily trek to the henhouse as soon as outside time begins. They first gasp as they discover a raccoon has pried open the wire and killed their pet. After all the queries about what happened, Ellie speaks up,

"I want to make a picture for Henny-Penny to take with her." The group paints a multicolored mural, for which each one dictates ideas. "I am sad you died," says Ellie. "But don't worry, you will rise again!" A child's spiritual notions are allowed to express themselves in creative ways.

It is difficult to measure the child's growth in these areas; it is easier to see physical growth, cognitive skills, and language development. After all, a child has grown to 40 inches tall or not, can rote count to 20 or misses some numbers, and speaks in full sentences or in short phrases. Affective expressions are more subtle and subjective. Talbot may feel rejected and sad if no one greets him as he enters the playhouse. He may mistake the children's busy-ness as an act of exclusion and withdraw or lash out. In reality, the children did not even notice he was there; his social skill expression and self-identity were based on a misunderstanding—one that can change dynamically with a teacher's input or change of scene.

A Sense of Self

Traditionally, early childhood educators have concerned themselves with children's well-being, knowing that in the early years the foundations must be laid for children to understand themselves and others. Social growth, creative expression, and experience with a wide range

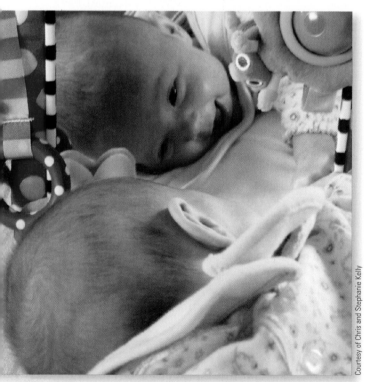

Building self-image is complex, multidimensional, and ever changing.

Growing a Sense of Self		
Age	**Growth Focus**	**Help Children with . . .**
Infants	Relationship	Attachment
Toddlers	Awareness	Self-regulation
Twos	Curiosity	Interactions with others
Preschool	Self-concept	Testing and evaluating self
	Authority	Testing their limits in play, making friends
Kindergarten	Self-in-the-world	Feeling effective
Primary	Competence	Managing failure/mistakes, finding their strengths

© Cengage Learning 2011

FIGURE 14-1 Children's emotional and social growth is an ongoing challenge as they enter new settings in their expanding world.

of emotions also help children develop a strong self-concept with positive self-esteem.

What Research Tells Us

Building self-image is complex, multidimensional, and ever changing. It affects everything we do and is affected by everything we do. Crucial to children's self-image is how children interpret the response of the environment to their actions. And much of a self-image is based on the way society views the child. Teachers play an important role as they provide an essential ingredient of self-image: the quality of human interactions.

Children need to have several key experiences in the early years to develop and consolidate a sense of self (see Figure 14-1). Psychosocial theory (see Erikson, Chapter 4) posits that the early years are critical in the development of conscience; formative experiences must shape a child in terms of moral worth, wrestling with good/nice and bad/mean. The autonomy of the toddler gives way to the initiative of the preschooler and competence of the school-aged child. These developments coincide with a longer attention span and a sense of pride in accomplishments of the tasks that require concentration. "Self esteem is the foundation for practice and then mastery" (Berger, 2009).

Sociocultural theory (see Vygotsky, Chapter 4) asserts that children must learn the ways of their culture to be grounded enough to find their place in the world. Attachment theory asserts that secure attachment is an asset; research confirms that children with high self-esteem are more likely to be securely attached and have parents who are attentive to their needs (Booth-LaForce et al., 2006). Emotional intelligence, "a 21st century skill for children and adults" (Koralek, 2011), requires neurological work to regulate the self (see Special Topic).

Research shows that low self-image is correlated with poor mental health, poor academic achievement, and delinquency. Many experiences can contribute to low self-image.

Transformative education recognizes that all of us are socialized to take our place in society. Our sense of self is influenced by prevailing social values, and our social skills are shaped by social practices. The social realities of sexism, racism, classism, ethnocentrism, and heterosexism shape children's self-identity and the formation of prejudice and discriminatory behavior (York, 2003).

The chronic stress of neglect or abuse, poverty or family disruption all contribute to a child's negative experiences that may lead to poor self-image.

In contrast, a positive self-concept is correlated with good mental health, academic achievement, and prosocial behavior (Salmivalli et al., 2005). As children's spontaneous play becomes more goal-oriented, children encounter success in making projects and making friends.

A psychosocial curriculum prepares children to be active and involved. It promotes social action and problem solving so that children develop into involved citizens with a positive self-identity.

- With infants and toddlers, the emphasis is on relationships.
- In preschool, programs emphasize emotional expression and social self-regulation.
- For school-age programs, it is often known as character education and usually involves conflict resolution and teamwork.

Affirming Identity

As children experience messages from others and through their perceptions, they construct an understanding of race, ethnicity, gender, and ability. This shapes their self-image and, by extension, their relationships to others.

Self-Esteem Self esteem refers to an individual's sense of personal worth and an acceptance of whom one is that helps one make judgments as they confront the world. To the extent that children feel worthy and capable, they are ready to succeed. If children disapprove of themselves, they may feel like failures and expect to do poorly.

Self-esteem develops as a reflection of experiences. The way people respond to you gives you some indication of your importance or value. Newborn infants have no concept of self and no past experience to judge their worth. A young child who has positive experiences with others is more likely to have a higher sense of self-esteem than one who has felt unloved or unnoticed.

The "Four I's" The **"Four I's"** refer to four components of self-esteem:

1. I hold a sense of my identity.
2. I have a sense of my uniqueness.
3. I feel a sense of self (power).
4. I carry a sense of belonging (connectedness).

Early in life, self-esteem is tied to family, friends, and other important people, such as teachers. Curriculum can be developed to foster each of these characteristics (see Figure 14-2).

- *I.* When children enter the classroom, the message they receive is "I am important and this is my place." The physical environment, the daily schedule, and the curriculum are designed to give all children permission to express themselves. This gives children a sense of identity and uniqueness.
- *Initiative.* Children are encouraged to initiate their learning, to make contact with others, to take action, and to make choices. Power is important to young children; they want to know how to take (and when to let go) of control, and how to use power to get what they want and need.
- *Independence.* Self-management tasks of dressing, eating, and toileting are given an important place in the curriculum. Children are assisted in taking care of their belongings and in developing independent judgment about events and activities. Every culture and group has its own intricate rules about when and how to be independent, and an early childhood group can give them experience.
- *Interaction.* Social interaction has a high priority in the program. The room and yard are busy places, with children moving about and talking among themselves and with adults. Conflicts are accepted as a natural consequence of social life. In the spirit of John Dewey (Chapter 1), democratic group living encourages children to interact. In respect for cultures that value collaboration and group harmony, such interaction fosters a consciousness of interdependence. The need for relationships with other people is crucial, and interaction gives children a sense of connectedness.

Children with a positive identity are ready to meet life's challenges. They have the self-confidence to deal with the reality of emotions, the changing nature of social interaction, the joys of creativity, and serenity of spirituality.

Curriculum for Psychosocial Development

Emotional Skill Development

Self Esteem

1. *Identity:* "Look at what I can do, the noise I can make, the weight I can pick up and move!"

2. *Connectedness:* "I can make the same snakes as you; we can all make cakes."

3. *Uniqueness:* "I'm pouring mine; you're dripping yours; and she is squeezing her stuff out her fingers!"

4. *Power:* "I can make this water go anywhere I want; look out for the tidal waves!"

Deal with Feelings

1. *Identification* (to notice and label): "Does it feel very smooth, slippery, slidy? Is it soft and soothing?"

2. *Mastery* (to accept): "She took your baker's dough and that made you angry. You can tell her you don't like it when she grabs what you are using."

3. *Expressing* (to express appropriately):

   Child: "Tami has all the big pitchers."

   Teacher: "How can you let her know you want one?".

   Child: "And she splashed me two times!"

   Teacher: "If you feel too crowded, you need to tell her so."

4. *Feelings* (to deal with others): "Whee! Yuk! Mmm! Ha!"

Curriculum: Activity (Use of Sense)

- Use rocks of various sizes with balances, so that children can touch and hear when they move things around.

- A malleable material such as play dough can be used first alone, then with tools.

- Make "oobleck," a mixture of cornstarch and water, in separate tubs for each child. Children can manipulate it in their own ways.

- Water play offers the child choices: pour into any of several containers, fill or empty the jug, use a funnel or a baster to squirt the water, make waves or splash hands.

- When fingerpainting, the teacher can describe what it appears the child is feeling. Children can identify their feelings as the teacher describes them while they use the materials.

- Whether the sensory material is clay, soapy water, or fine sand, the issues of ownership and use of materials arise. Then, teachers reflect children's feelings and help them take responsibility for their own feelings.

- As children begin to use the sensory materials, they need to communicate to others. Usually the issues are about wanting more material and personal space.

- When children share in a sensory activity, such as a feeling walking through tubs of small pebbles, sand, and soapsuds, they have the delightful experience of enjoying their own feelings with another.

FIGURE 14-2 A psychosocial curriculum offers sensorimotor opportunities to deal with materials in a nonstructured way. Because children relax with open-ended activities, they often share their feelings as they use sensory materials in a comfortable atmosphere.

Curriculum for Emotional Growth

As discussed in the previous three chapters, the curriculum for the emotional domain needs to be built around key developmental concepts.

The Development of Emotions

Emotions are the feelings a person has—joy and sorrow, love and hate, confidence and fear, loneliness and belonging, anger and contentment, frustration and satisfaction. They are responses to events, people, and circumstances. Feelings are an outgrowth of what a person perceives is happening. Emotionally healthy people learn to give expression to their feelings in appropriate ways. They do not allow their feelings to overshadow the rest of their behavior. The optimal time to learn these skills is in the early years.

Research in brain development (Rushton et al., 2010; Thompson, 2001) has identified key areas of the brain involved in emotional expression and development. An area in the limbic section of our brains is the control center of our emotions. Two almond-shaped organs behind our eyes, called the amygdala, are in constant communication with the rest of the brain (for thinking and perceiving).

The emotional brain scans everything happening to us from moment to moment to see if something that happened in the past that made us sad or angry is similar to what is happening now. If so, the amygdala calls an alarm to declare an emergency and to mobilize in a split second to act. And it can do so, in brain time, more rapidly than the thinking brain takes to figure out what is going on, which is why people can get into a rage and do something very inappropriate that they wished they had not. (See the special feature on the brain later in this chapter.)

Children experience this constantly, and educators must help children develop dimensions of **emotional intelligence** (Goleman, 1995): self-awareness, handling emotions generally, motivation, empathy, and social skills (see Special Topic later in this chapter). These grow over time, with maturation and experience both at work.

- In infancy, there are only two identifiable emotions: contentment and distress. Infants respond in agitated emotion whether wet, hungry, hurt, or bored. Gradually, the expression of the emotion becomes more refined and varies with the situation. Curiosity and anger begin to appear.
- A toddler's cry of frustration is different from the cry of discomfort or hunger. Emotions such as frustration and doubt are apparent.
- As children become preschoolers, their emotional expressions change as they gain control over some of their feelings and learn new ways to express them. New emotions appear toward the end of the third year: pride, shame, embarrassment, and even guilt.
- By primary school, children can show all these emotions but are learning to keep their expression in check. Self-regulation and an awareness of how others perceive and react to them are taking place.

These strong external forces include parents, family members, teachers, and friends. They help the young child learn socially acceptable behavior and can mediate aggressive or withdrawing behavior. Much of what children learn is by example and modeling (see Chapter 4). Therefore, children learn more from adult models than from simply being told how to behave and feel. The emotional foundation of the first five years is carried forth into school-age, as a friend, the peer group, and validation from adults help build resilience and coping skills for dealing with stress.

Emotional Skills

The emotional skills children learn in their early years are substantial. Research shows that some emotions—interest, disgust, distress, to name a few—are observable in the newborn, and it is posited that all the **basic emotions** are present within the first few weeks of life. These include happiness, interest, surprise, fear, anger, sadness, and disgust. The more **complex emotions** of shame, guilt, envy, and pride emerge later, once children have had the social experiences of observing these emotions in others or have been in situations that might evoke such feelings. These expressions have been observed in a wide range of cultural and ethnic groups.

In early childhood, children learn to respond to new situations and to react and connect with a teacher, both very emotional experiences. Good teachers stimulate an emotional response to themselves and the curriculum that is a balance between interest and overwhelming fear. Creating the "right" emotional conditions is a primary way to gain access to a child's capacity for learning. Young children are not yet limited by standards of conduct that prevent them from sincere and truthful self-expression. Teachers observe children and learn how they feel about facing their feelings, the feelings of others, and the range of skills categorized as emotional growth.

Ability to Deal with Feelings

Dealing with feelings involves four steps. Each step builds on the other so that they follow a developmental sequence; the learning that takes place at one level affects the development of what follows (see Figure 14-2).

To Notice and Label Feelings This ability is the first step. The sobbing 1 or 2 year old may have many reasons for feeling distress. As families recognize the cries of hunger, hurt, and fear, they may name these feelings. The child learns to notice what the feeling is and recognize it. Teachers know how to "read" children's faces and body language to give them the words for and ways to express those feelings (see Figure 14-3). Toddlers and 2 year olds can be taught simple words for sad, mad, and glad. Preschoolers are quite verbal and curious about language and ready to learn words that describe a wider range of feelings. They can learn "lonely," "scared," "silly," "sad," and "happy." Labeling what one feels inside is a critical skill to learn. It is a healthy first grader who can say, "I have tried to cut this string three times and the scissors aren't working. I am frustrated. I need some help!"

To Accept Feelings Accepting feelings is step two. Teachers recognize that children are capable of strong feelings. Children can feel overwhelmed by the very strength and intensity of a feeling, be it one of anger or of love. Acceptance involves learning how to handle the depth of the feeling and not let it overpower them. The

Learning to "Read" Feelings

Feeling	Behavioral Definition
1. Fear	Pale face, alert eyes, tense mouth, rigid body.
2. Surprise	Wide eyes, eyebrows uplifted, involuntary cry or scream, quick intake of breath.
3. Anger	Red face, eyes staring, face taut, fists and jaw clenched, voice harsh or yelling, large gestures.
4. Joy	Smiling face, shining eyes, free and easy body movements, laughing.
5. Pride	Head held high, smiling face, jaunty walk or strut, tendency to announce or point out.
6. Embarrassment	Red face, glazed and downcast eyes, tight mouth, tense body, small and jerky movements, soft voice.
7. Sadness	Unsmiling face, downturned mouth, glazed and teary eyes, crying or rubbing eyes, limp body, slow or small movements, soft and trembly voice.
8. Anxiety	Puckered brow, pale face, tight mouth, whiny voice, jerky movements, lack of or difficulty in concentration.
9. Curiosity	Raised brow, shining eyes, perhaps tense body in absorption of the object of curiosity; often hand movements to touch and pick up object; sometimes mouth agape.

© Cengage Learning 2011

FIGURE 14-3 As we observe children's behavior, we understand how their feelings are expressed. Expressions of fear, anger, sadness, disgust, and happiness are universal, and learning to read faces and body stance is essential to guiding emotional development.

changing nature of feelings is also part of acceptance; it can be a source of comfort and relief for young children to discover that the strong emotion they are experiencing will pass. Adults who work with young children help them work through those feelings safely.

For instance, 3-year-old Carlos feels sad as his mother prepares to leave. His teacher walks them to the door, then bends down and puts an arm around him as his mother waves good-bye. Acknowledging that he is sad, the teacher stays with Carlos, reminding him that his mother returns and that the teacher will take care of him while he is at school. Because the child is allowed to feel the sadness that is natural in leave-taking, the tense feelings are over in a few minutes. The teacher smiles and encourages Carlos to find something fun to do. Once he has recovered his composure, the teacher can point out that he's "okay now," and Carlos can feel proud for having lived through and grown from saying good-bye. Acknowledgment of the feeling and his ability to accept it help give Carlos the confidence to move on.

To Express Feelings in an Appropriate Way The third step is to express feelings appropriately. Expressing feelings appropriately is a two-part process. First, children must feel free to express their feelings; second, they must learn ways of expression that are suitable to their age and to the situation. Many beginning teachers are uncomfortable because children express themselves so strongly (and often aggressively). Yet the child who is passive and unable to express feelings freely should be of equal concern and should be encouraged in self-expression.

When teachers create a safe emotional climate, they can effectively help children learn to understand and express themselves. "I can see you are upset about Joaquin taking the zoo animal," you might say, "But I cannot let you hit him—and I will not let him hit you, either."

As children grow, they acquire the modes of expression that are developmentally appropriate for their age.

- Babies and toddlers without language cry and call for an immediate response;
- Two year olds express their displeasure by pushes and shoves, which need quick intervention;
- Preschoolers begin to use their verbal power and argue; a teacher can get close to observe first and then intervene if necessary.
- By age 6 or 7, children learn to tell others—clearly and with reasons—what they are feeling. Now the teacher must monitor and mediate as needed.

The ability to express feelings is intact, but the methods of expression change as children grow. Expression of feelings also has a cultural dimension (see Diversity Box).

To Deal with the Feelings of Others This is the culminating step in the development of emotional skills. Feelings are the spark of life in people: the flash of anger, the

All photos © Cengage Learning

Young children feel their emotions strongly. Learning to read faces and body stance is essential to guiding emotional development and for children to be successful socially.

"ah-hah" of discovery, the thrill of accomplishment, the hug of excitement. Because recognizing and expressing emotions are closely interwoven, children who can distinguish among different emotions and have some experience in taking the perspective of others by observing their feelings develop empathy. With increasing social awareness and decreasing egocentrism in the school-age, concrete operational period (see Chapter 4), two other emotions emerge: **empathy**, a true understanding of the feelings of another; and **antipathy**, intense dislike of other people. Toddlers may cry or gather near the teacher when a playmate is hurt or sad; preschoolers smile at another's laughter; and kindergartners imagine themselves vividly in another's predicament during a story.

Like the complex emotions discussed earlier, empathy requires cognitive abilities, such as seeing oneself as both separate from other people and also as connected. Older children, who are better able to put themselves in another's place (see Piaget, Chapter 4) and who understand a wider range of emotions, can respond to others in distress. Empathy is affected by early experience and needs nurturing to grow (see Social section).

Ability to Handle Change

It is remarkable that, as one of the most adaptable species on the planet, we humans resist change so much. Even as our brains are programmed to find pattern and sameness, it is change that is inevitable. The very act of being born is

Children learn to appreciate and understand feelings when teachers who can show them how to deal with feelings and changes accept their feelings.

a change, marking the beginning of a life in which stress is part of the act of developmental achievement. Witness the toddler's numerous falls when learning to walk, the separation of parent and child at the nursery school doorway, the concentration and frustrations of the 6 year old on roller skates. A measure of **positive stress** encourages a child to strive and achieve, to find out and discover.

Stress can arise from several factors—both internal (severe colic) or external (moving to a new home). Some stresses are acute in a child's life, such as a hospitalization, whereas others are chronic, such as living in an alcoholic household. Inadequate housing, poverty, and war are ecological stressors. Family changes—the birth of a sibling, death or loss of a close family member, marriage problems, and divorce—are personal stressors. Inept parenting practices that neglect or abuse children are especially troublesome because they hurt children and provide them with poor role models for learning how to cope with stress (see Chapter 15).

Teachers can help children accept change in several ways:

- *Anticipate changes.* Identify the process children can engage. "Junko, your mother will be leaving soon.

We will go looking for that favorite puzzle after you say good-bye to her."
- *Notify children of changes in the daily routine.* "We will not be having snacks inside today; let's use the patio table instead."
- *Model acceptance of unanticipated changes.* When children are informed that change is anticipated, accepted, and not necessarily disrupting, they become more relaxed about handling the unpredictable. "Whoops, we didn't think it would be raining. Now everyone needs to either find a raincoat and boots or choose something inside."
- *Be a resource for helping children cope.* "It's okay to cry when you are sad or scared, Akbar. It is hard to figure out what to do when they say they do not want to play."

Ability to Exercise Judgment

The ability to exercise judgment is an important skill because it helps children to make decisions and figure out what to do in new situations. On entering a program, a child faces many decisions: Where shall I play? Who shall I play with? Who will I turn to for help when I need it? Judgment is selecting what to do, when to do it, with whom to do it, and when to stop.

Making Choices Making choices is an essential part of decision making. Children are bombarded with choices in America—too many choices, some people say. Some children must decide about issues that, in other times, only adults handled. But children have difficulty discriminating between big choices and little choices. Every choice is a big one for most children. Learning to make good choices takes thought, guidance, and lots of practice.

There is no easy way to teach children how to make decisions because each situation must be dealt with on an individual basis. The judgment a child exercises in choosing a friend to play with today may have other factors to consider tomorrow. Instead, teachers help children base their decisions on the best judgment they are capable of in each instance. One way to encourage decision making is to provide opportunities for choice (see "Focus on Skills").

Internalizing Messages Internalizing messages is second part of exercising judgment. These are the internal messages children are calling on when deciding on a course of action. Some cultures are open in their display of emotions, whereas others are reserved. This must be respected and taken into consideration (see Diversity Box).

DIVERSITY

Feelings: What if the messages are different?

The "appropriate" expression of feelings has many definitions. Over time, children see many different ways people express their likes and preferences, their dislikes and opinions. Early childhood education programs can inadvertently use practices that counter parents' efforts. At the same time, many families do not have articulated explanations of their child rearing. Both may have strong ideas about display of emotions. Encouragement to act out every emotion is not appropriate, for instance, for many African American children. "Living under oppressive conditions mandates learning to handle oppression in ways . . . [such as] to learn where to express feelings and who it is safe to let know your feelings," says Cooper (1992). "Their reluctance to engage should be respected, not viewed as a challenge."

Strong expression of feelings is seen as a sign of disrespect to adult, particularly those of authority, such as teachers. Praising a child for self-expression and avoiding negative remarks may seem fine to a teacher, but Chinese parents may see it as their duty to tell children their errors in direct language (Chua, 2011).

Will the child's emotional well-being be put at risk If the messages are different? Children are resilient, and by the end of the early childhood years, they have already learned that different circumstances call for different behaviors. But in these early years, if the differences between home and school expectations are too great, children are confused, and it leads to difficulties and misunderstandings. Think of yourself as a learner rather than an expert and inquire about family practices around expression of emotions. Share what you have seen as children achieve competence in self-expression. The most important element in bridging children's worlds is for the adults who care for them to be comfortable and accepting of differences.

Enjoying one's self includes being aware of one's power and learning to use it well, making important things happen without harming self or others.

Self-regulation Self-regulation is the third aspect of judgment. Research suggests that children can develop the capacity to plan and guide themselves (Rothbart & Rueda, 2005). In contrast to self-control, in which we teach children to respond to an external rule, children's self-regulation is a combination of the cognitive and emotional realms.

During the early childhood years, there is a great increase in self-regulation. Children are increasingly able to control their behavior in familiar situations, focus their attention, and comply with external requests. Such self-directed thinking and problem solving is an essential life skill. "Focus and self control . . . may be as important as IQ" (Galisnky, 2010).

The teacher can encourage this process by:

- Giving children cues to *be alert and orient* themselves. Start circle time with a song that everyone can move toward and clap with.
- Creating activities that require *cognitive flexibility* so that children practice shifting their attention. Help children pretend roles and then switch back to being themselves.
- Establishing some routines that require children to hold information in their minds develops *working memory*. Story time is good for this, asking them to

think about a detail or character and call it back as the story concludes.

- Working regularly to help develop *inhibitory control*. This is what most people think of when they hear "self-regulation," as this control enables children to resist the inclination to do one thing and instead do the "right" thing. Controlling attention and emotions while also controlling behavior is especially difficult in conflict, so teachers need to be involved in children's disagreements. This skill can help with failure (stop the urge to give up) and with hurting (stop the impulse to hit back).

Enjoying One's Self and One's Power

Teachers want children to feel powerful—to know that they can master their lives and feel confident in their own abilities. This feeling of power is particularly important in the early years, when so much of what a child can see is out of reach, both literally and figuratively.

Responsibility and limits, however, go hand in hand with power. The child who is strong enough to hit someone has to learn not to use that strength unnecessarily. The child who shouts with glee also finds out that noise is unacceptable indoors. By holding children responsible for their actions, teachers can help children gain the self-regulation skills that allow them to enjoy their power and accept its limitations.

Superheroes **Superhero** is a kind of fantasy power play most teachers encounter. Common to children as young as 2 years old, superhero play is exciting and rowdy, usually active and loud, playacting of heroic roles that give children powers they lack in everyday life. Superhero play attracts children who are (Hoffman 2004):

- Investigating power and autonomy
- Balancing the desire for power with the need for friendship
- Testing physical limits
- Exploring feelings
- Answering big questions about the world, such as:
  - What is right and what is wrong, good, and bad?
  - What is fair and what is unfair?
  - What is life and what is death?
  - What is a boy and what is a girl?
  - What is real and what is fantasy?

Imaginary Companions **Imaginary companions** often join superheroes, although they just as often accompany children on their own. This second type of fantasy play sometimes concerns adults. Piaget believed that they reflected immature thinking of the preoperational stage and should disappear around the time a child began

elementary school (see Chapter 4). Imaginary friends offer companionship and entertainment, and can help children through difficult times (see Figure 14-4).

> [T]he creation of an imaginary companion is healthy and relatively common. . . . [C]hildren with imaginary companions appear to be less shy, more able to focus their attention, and to have advanced social understanding when compared with other children. . . . The bottom line is that although imaginary companions and other fantasies have sometimes been interpreted as signs of emotional disturbance, a break with reality, or even the emergence of multiple personalities, they are really just a variation on the theme of all pretend play.

Children need guidance to learn how to express themselves appropriately and exercise their growing powers responsibly. Fantasy play is an important component of children's cognitive and emotional development. Teachers can help children learn to appreciate and enjoy themselves. Each time a child is acknowledged, a teacher fosters that sense of uniqueness: "Carrie, you have a great sense of humor!" "Eric, your power bracelets are helping to collect all the trash here." "Freddie, I love the way you and your 'dog-friend Dan' sing so clearly." Saying it aloud reinforces in children the feeling that they are enjoyable to themselves and to others.

Resilience

Resilience is the ability to bounce back or recover from adversity. Resiliency is a kind of protective mechanism, something that allows a child to "get back

---

Superhero Play: Exercising Power Responsibly

- Help children recognize humane characteristics of superheroes.
- Discuss real heroes and heroines.
- Talk about the pretend world of acting.
- Limit the place and time for superhero play.
- Explore related concepts.
- Help children de-escalate rough-and-tumble play.
- Make it clear that aggression is unacceptable.
- Give children control over their lives.
- Praise children's attempts at mastery.

FIGURE 14-4 Superhero play is a special type of dramatic play that calls for special handling.

on the horse" after being thrown. Research indicates that resilient children are more successful in dealing with stressors than those who are not (Mayer & Ulich, 2009). Terrible circumstances can overwhelm everyone; at the same time, some children who experience serious difficulties become happy, healthy adults. Nurturing children's capacity to develop resiliency is not simple, but teachers can help by knowing the protective mechanisms that promote resiliency. These include:

- *The child's personality and behavior:* Help a child find his strengths and sense of humor.
- *The family attributes:* Find someone or something that reflects the child's capacity to succeed and meet high expectations (Dweck, 2006).
- *The social environment:* Notice and comment on effort rather than ability to develop a "growth mindset" (Pawlina & Stanford, 2011).

Resilient children have hope and good self-esteem. Both of these are under the influence of the teacher and curriculum.

Effective Approaches for Curriculum for Emotional Growth

Considerations

There are several key components in helping children develop healthy emotional growth:

1. *Acquiring good patterns* is an adult's first step. Reflect on these questions:
   - Are you a person who labels others?
   - What happens to you when a child is difficult?
   - How do you feel like reacting when a child does not meet your expectations? Identifying strengths and positive labels for every child helps teachers deal better with the emotions and behavior of the children in their care.
2. *Developing and using a "feeling" vocabulary* makes words of an emotional nature part of the program vocabulary. Identify some of the feelings children express; then describe how the children look and act when experiencing those emotions (see Figure 14-3 and Special Topic on emotional intelligence at the end of this chapter).
3. *Making the classroom a comfortable place* for children is the third step to a healthy emotional climate. Teachers can also become more attuned

Observing children's feelings, such as the joy and pride in this child's face, helps teachers understand the children they teach.

to the emotional climate in the classroom by knowing when and how feelings are expressed:
- What causes children in the class to become excited? Frightened? Calm? Loud? How does this knowledge guide curriculum planning? How can it help a teacher handle an unplanned event or change in the schedule?
- How do I anticipate children's emotional behavior? How do I follow through?
- What can teachers do to handle children's emotional outbursts and crises?
- What happens to the rest of the class when one teacher is occupied in an emotional incident with one or more children?
- What do I do when a child shows emotion? How do I feel when a child displays emotion?
- What types of emotions are most common with the young child?

When teachers perceive that children are ready to talk about their feelings, small group discussions or individual conversations can be helpful.

"It really *hurts* to bend your knees now that you have scraped them."

"I saw some children look so *sad* when their friend was playing with someone else." Good books that touch on sensitive issues (being excluded, being blamed, caring for others) offer possibilities for teachers and children to talk about feelings. Games and joking can help children to feel relaxed and to explore feelings in an accepting way. Classroom problems (not sharing materials, pushing on the climbers) offer topics for discussion (see Figure 14-5).

The ability to express emotions verbally gives children the power to deal with them without resorting to inappropriate behavior. **Social referencing** involves "relying on another person's emotional reaction to form one's own appraisal of an uncertain situation" (Berk, 2011).

"Look! Paul is crying. Let's go over and see if we can comfort him."

"I can see that they are shouting about the red ball, but I can see them talking it out."

Making use of others' emotional cues can help infants to deal with stranger anxiety, toddlers to calm themselves after saying good-bye, preschoolers to avoid overreacting to a fall, and school-aged children to begin to recognize that people can feel more than one emotion at a time. The teacher who runs to the rescue after a minor spill can engender "learned helplessness" and cause children to be overly dependent on others. Conversely, the teacher who fails to respond to children when they express emotions may give children the message that others' distress is to be ignored.

Curriculum Planning for Emotional Development

Setting   Teachers set up their classrooms and yards to promote emotional growth. Indoors, children's inner thoughts and feelings are best expressed through:

- *The Arts.* Clay or dough lets children vent feelings, because it can be pounded, pinched, poked, slapped, and manipulated. Finger painting and painting on broad surfaces with large brushes encourage a freedom of movement that permits children to express themselves fully.
- *Blocks/Manipulatives.* Vary the materials regularly to help children adjust to change and to allow them to exercise judgment about playing with different materials. A variety of props—motor vehicles, animals, people, furniture—gives children the opportunity to reenact what they see of the world.
- *Discovery/Science.* Often, science need not be geared toward only cognitive and language development.

The Teacher's Role in Children's Anger Management

1. Create a safe emotional climate . . . by having clear, firm, and flexible boundaries.
2. Model responsible anger management . . . by acknowledging when you are upset.
3. Help children develop self-regulatory skills . . . by giving children age- and skill-appropriate responsibilities and encouraging problem-solving with support.
4. Encourage children to label feelings of anger . . . start with "mad" and expand to include "upset, annoyed, irritated, furious, steamed," etc.
5. Encourage children to talk about anger-arousing interactions . . . by talking about situations when they aren't happening. "I felt mad when . . . " can start a lively conversation; cards with realistic scenarios can do the same, as can puppets.
6. Use appropriate books and stories about anger to help children understand and manage anger . . . see Figure 14-6.
7. Communicate with parents. . . . Introduce the books or puppets, let them borrow them overnight. Tell them what you do in your program, and ask what they do.

© Cengage Learning

FIGURE 14-5 When children come to grips with their strong feelings, their emotional growth is encouraged (categories from Marion, 2011).

Caring for pets brings out feelings of nurturing and protectiveness. Make "feeling clocks"; the blank clock faces are a base on which children draw or paste pictures of people showing various emotional states.

- *Dramatic Play.* Home-life materials give children the props they need to express how they see their world of family, parents, and siblings. Through play, the child who is afraid of being left with a sitter may become the parent leaving the child-doll at home and then returning; the child who is afraid of the doctor can sometimes be seen gleefully giving shots to all the stuffed animals. Mirrors, telephones, and dress-up clothes encourage children to try out their emotional interests on themselves as well as each other.
- *Language/Library.* Stories and books in which characters and situations reflect a wide range of emotions are readily available (see Figure 14-6). Children enjoy looking at photographs of people and guessing what the person in the photo is feeling; record and post responses nearby.
- *Music/Movement.* Music of all kinds encourages self-expression and permits an endless variety of movement and feelings to be shown openly and freely (see TeachSource Video). Children can be introduced to classical, ethnic, jazz, or rock music

while dancing with scarves or streamers or marching with rhythm sticks, as well as singing and dancing to children's recordings. Because musical knowledge is the earliest of human intellectual competencies (see Chapter 12), music can be part of the curriculum for children as young as toddlers. Pounding on drums and dancing both relieve tension in a socially acceptable manner. More structured activities, such as showing children how to use musical instruments, must be balanced by plenty of freedom for individual musical expression.

Outdoors, the environment itself encourages self-expression. Whether in the sand or on a swing, children seem to open up emotionally as they relax in the physical freedom the out-of-doors fosters. Outdoor games are usually highly emotionally charged. "A Bear Hunt" (also known by many other names) uses the teacher as lead, narrating movements such as going through a gate, swishing in the grass, climbing trees, swimming across creeks, and so on. Running, chasing, and the dramatic play of superheroes provide emotional release for children.

The outdoor area is an ideal place for large, noisy, and messy activities. Tracing body outlines create life-size portraits of each child that reinforce self-concept and

Books for Emotional Skill Development

Anger: *When Sophie Gets Angry—Really, Really Angry* (Bang); *The Grouchy Ladybug* (Carle); *My Name Is Not Dummy* (Crary)

Fear: *There's a Nightmare in My Closet* (Mayer); *Storm in the Night* (Stolz)

Self-Esteem: *The Growing Story* (Krauss); *Ruby* (Glen); *Things I Like* (Browne); *Amazing Grace* (Hoffman)

Loss: *The Maggie B* (Keats); *Amos and Boris* (Steig)

Change: *Changes, Changes* (Hutchins); *Sam Is My Half-Brother* (Boyd)

Friendship: *Two Is a Team* (Bemelman); *That's What Friends Are For* (Kidd); *Big Al* (Clements)

Security: *One Step, Two* (Zolotow); *The Bundle Book* (Zolotow); *Rise and Shine, Mariko-chan* (Tomioka)

Choice: *Best Enemies* (Leverich); *Did You Carry the Flag Today, Charly?* (Claudill)

Death: *Death and Dying* (Stein); *The Dead Bird* (Brown); *Nana Upstairs, Nana Downstairs* (dePaoli)

Divorce: *Two Places to Sleep* (Schuchman)

Doctor/Dentist: *Curious George Goes to the Hospital* (Rey); *Your Turn, Doctor* (Robinson & Perez); *My Doctor* (Harlow)

Moving: *Mitchell Is Moving* (Sharmat); *Jamie* (Zolotow); *The Leaving Morning* (Johnson)

New Baby/Adoption: *Baby Sister for Frances* (Hoban); *I Want to Tell You about My Baby* (Banish); *Peter's Chair* (Keats); *The Chosen Baby* (Wasson)

Nightmares: *Where the Wild Things Are* (Sendak); *In the Night Kitchen* (Sendak); *There's a Nightmare in My Closet* (Mayer)

Spending the night: *Ira Sleeps Over* (Waber)

© Cengage Learning 2014

FIGURE 14-6 Whether 2 years old or in second grade, children learn about their feelings when teachers use books that have a variety of feelings and ways to deal with them.

encourage personal pride. Woodworking is an outdoor activity that allows children to vent anger and tension. Nails will not be hurt no matter how hard they are pounded; there is satisfaction in sawing a piece of wood into two pieces. Even a simple project such as water painting becomes an avenue for self-expression as children use paintbrushes and buckets of water on trees, cement, and buildings, giving them all a fresh coat of "paint."

Daily Schedule Much of the schedule involves routines, transitions, and group times that involve shifts from one kind of activity to another. There is a sense of uncertainty and they are emotionally charged, so children's behavior is most likely to be unfocused. Here, you find the wandering and chasing, even oppositional or withdrawn behavior.

Teachers help children best by giving children ideas of what to do ("Each of you can sponge a table now," or "You can sit on my lap while your dad leaves today"). Specific suggestions for group behavior, including those generated by the class itself, inspire success (see Figure 14-7). In addition, flexibility is the cornerstone of success.

> By remaining flexible, especially to the children's needs, I have built a deep, personal relationship with each of the children I care for. I find ways to adapt to their schedules as much as possible instead of [always] forcing them into a [rigid] routine of the center. (McCormick, 1993)

Skills Emotional development is a lifelong process that requires experience with one's feelings. To help children learn to express and control their emotions, teachers consider each child's emotional skills. The goals teachers set for children determine which emotional skills will be the focus: Maggie has difficulty with changes in the routine; Caroline never cries, no matter how she hurts; and Clyde screams when he is frustrated.

Problem solving is a skill with an emotional focus. This skill can be done directly or indirectly. Both use a step-by-step process similar to interpersonal conflict resolution (see Chapter 7):

Direct Problem Solving: How to Improve a Boring Playground

1. Help children define the situation by turning it into a question. ("What can we do to fix up our playground?")
2. Make a list of options or alternatives. ("Plant flowers, get more bikes, add more sand toys.")
3. Ask the children to think of what might happen for each option. ("Flowers would look pretty, but we would have to water them.")

4. Make a choice. ("Which one should we chose?")
5. Implement the plan. ("OK, today we will plant the flowers from the field trip to the nursery.")
6. Check later to see how the choice turned out. ("Look how nice the yard is!" or "Darn, we forgot to water, and they died.")

Indirect Problem Solving: When Ning Hated School

1. Introduce the main character. "Once upon a time there was a girl named Ning . . ."
2. Tell about the problem. "One day Ning ran away from school because . . ."
3. Talk to a wise person. "Ning's auntie knew just about everything, so . . ."
4. Try out a new approach. "So Ning decided she would try . . ."
5. Evaluate the results: "She liked school better now . . ."
6. Summarize the lesson. "Now Ning felt better. She told her friend . . ."

"Persona dolls" (Derman-Sparks & Olsen Edwards, 2010) encourage language involvement. Each doll has his/her story that can reflect the composition of the class and can offer experiences that extend the children's learning. All dolls are introduced with their own lives, and a teacher introduces each one and tells its story. Children ask questions, which expands the story. The teacher can tell a story that arises from the everyday interactions in class, "hot topics" that parents are talking about or occur in the news, things the teacher decides are important to think and talk about, or stories based on history.

Themes Themes can be useful when developing curriculum for emotional growth. One school-age program developed the themes of "Hurt and Healing," another did "Pitfalls with Pets." For the first, the group brainstormed and came up with throwing water baggies at targets, kicking stacks of boxes, stomping on egg cartons, pounding anger out into clay, and throwing colored water at a painting. For the second, skits were developed to dramatize scared reactions; stories were dictated, pictures drawn, games made up (see Figure 14-8).

Curriculum for Social Growth

Social development is the process through which children learn what behavior is acceptable and expected. A set of standards is imposed on the child at

Dealing with Change in the Daily Schedule

Routines:

Respect children's feelings of anticipation.

- Have a chart of daily activities.
- Discuss upcoming field trips or visitors ahead of time when possible.

When possible, let the children take responsibility for known sequences.

- Set their own snack table.
- Get flowers for the table.
- Help clean a place for the next children.

Transitions:

When unexpected changes occur, discuss them with individuals and the group.

- "Andy isn't here today. He has a sore throat, so he is staying home. Esther will be the teacher in his group today."

Provide time for self-help *without unnecessary hurry.*

- Put on their own name tag.
- Wash and dry their own hands.
- Dress themselves—jacket for outdoors, shoes after nap, and so on.
- Take care of their rest items—blanket and stuffed toy in a labeled pillowcase, books back in a basket or bookshelf, and soon.

Group Times:

Use children's faces as a focus.

- Practice facial expressions with mirrors.
- Call out feelings, having them show you on their faces.
- Sing "If You're Happy and You Know It,..." with a variety of feelings. Ask children what situations have them feel each.
- Show photographs of children's faces; ask the group to tell you how that person is feeling, why, and so on.

Try idea completions.

- "I feel glad when..." (also mad, bad, sad, safe, excited, scared, silly) ● "I like school when..." (also don't like, also my friend, mom, it) ● "I wish...", ● "The best thing I can do..."

Use situations to elicit feelings.

- "Here's a picture of a family. What are they doing? How does each person feel?"
- "I'm going to cover part of the picture of the face to see if you can guess what expression it's going to be."
- "These cards show situations the teachers have seen happen. As I read them think: 'How do I feel? What can I say? What can I do?'"

© Cengage Learning 2014

FIGURE 14-7 Anticipating changes that are likely to occur helps children learn to accept them.

birth that reflects the values of the family and the society in which the child lives. Social growth refers to what happens with the child and others. Theorists from Freud and Piaget to Bandura and Gardner (see Chapters 4 and 12) acknowledge the relationship between social competence and learning. Indeed, enhancing social intelligence builds a set of skills that may be among the most essential for life success of many kinds.

The Development of Social Competence

Social competence is acquired through countless experiences with others. Some children become competent in the early years; even more need the years of childhood and adolescence to achieve it. Still, the early years are a foundation for social growth for all (see Figures 14-9 & 14-10).

Theme: Who Am I?

1. *Art:* Body outlines
   Facial expressions pictures—variations (a) provide handheld mirrors, (b) give a blank face and let them draw in the features, (c) self-portraits: make them throughout the year, using "people colors," (d) cut out faces in magazine for collage
   Face painting
   Fingerprinting (hand and foot)

2. *Blocks:* People, furniture, structures people live in
   Pictures of same

3. *Cooking:* Share ethnic dishes (tortillas, pasta, things you like to cook at home)

4. *Discovery/Science:* Height/weight charts
   Drawing around hands and feet and comparing sizes
   Doing body outlines of a large group of children, each with a different color, and comparing sizes
   Mapping—charting where people live, charts of phone numbers, put out a globe
   Weather—make connections to types of homes

5. *Dramatic Play:* Lots of mirrors
   A variety of dress-up play for taking on a variety of roles and seeing how they feel

6. *Language/Library:* Have children write books about themselves—variations: (a) use *Is This You?* (Krauss) as model (b) loose-leaf binder of their own books they can add to themselves, (c) "Where I Live" as title, (d) families
   Books on children and families with diverse backgrounds (*Corduroy* [Freedman] lives in an apt.)
   Where animals live
   Feelings about where children live

7. *Manipulatives:* Puzzles with body parts, with people and clothing
   Self-help skills with dressing frames
   Encourage children to build a structure that things could live in (e.g., using Lincoln Logs).

8. *Sand and Water Play:* Bubble-blowing
   Using your bodies to build—digging with hands and feet, encouraging sensory exploration
   Use body parts to help you (e.g., using your foot on the shovel).

9. *Swinging/Climbing:* Both of these activities use body parts; teachers help the children become aware of how they do physical activity.

10. *Games:* Rolling the barrel, rolling yourself   Hide and Seek, Tag
    Mother May I?   Dramatic play games with family members
    Guessing games: Make "Who am I?" snapshots of the backs of children's heads or their hands. Use a shoe from each child, having them all tuck their feet under them.

11. *Large Block-Building:* Making house-like structures
    Using vehicles that need your body's force to move

12. *Woodworking:* Using body parts
    Make a map board of school, neighborhood, a city

13. *Routines:* Self-help: Awareness of what you can do by yourself by definition of "Who Am I?" tasks; teachers use verbal and musical reinforcement

14. *Transitions:* Use physical characteristics of children for transitions—"Everyone who has brown eyes/freckles/blue jeans can go outside."

15. *Group times:* "Head and shoulders"
    Description games—describe someone and guess who it is as a game "I'm thinking of someone" or with song "Mary Has a Red Dress"
    "Little Tommy (Tina) Tiddlemouse," voice recognition
    "Good morning little Teddy Bear," with bear going around circle and saying names

16. *Snack time/bedtime:* Mark places with names and pictures, such as beds or placemats
    Try to coordinate the name tag, bed, or placemat with symbol on cubby

FIGURE 14-8 Curriculum activities can strengthen a child's sense of self.

Social Development

Social development begins at birth. Within the first few months of life, the infant smiles, coos, and plays in response to a human voice, face, or physical contact (see "Attachment," Chapter 4). Young children are influenced from birth by a deliberate attempt on the part of adults to guide them in ways that society expects. Parents attempt to transmit behavior patterns that are characteristic of their culture, religion, gender, educational, and ethnic backgrounds. Teachers assist by incorporating some family rituals and traditions into the program.

Children imitate what they see; they adapt social expectations to their personality. "Cooperation, generosity, loyalty, and honesty are not inborn. They must be passed on to the child by older people, [whether] they are parents, other adults, or older youngsters" (Kostelnik et al., 2008). There are many cultural variations in social expectations. How people relate to each other, what feelings are to be expressed, how to deal with personal space, how and who to touch, and how to respond to personal events varies considerably.

The socializing process—called **socialization**—includes learning appropriate behavior in a number of different settings. Children learn very early to discriminate between the expectations in different environments.

- At school, free exploration of play materials may be encouraged, but in a church pew it is not.
- Grocery stores may be places to sit up high and watch, to walk and choose, to tear around with a little cart, to grab and cry about things.
- Libraries and Grandma's home may look very different, but both are for being quiet and looking at books.

Children's understanding of others is critical for their social growth. Very young children show awareness of what other people feel—even infants pay special attention to emotional expressions of adults. Toddlers can ascertain if someone is happy, sad, or angry, and can try to comfort someone in distress. Three year olds know that if someone gets what he wants, he is happy, and if not, he is sad. Older preschoolers begin to understand that what they (or others) believe may turn out to be false. By kindergarten, many children understand that others sometimes think and feel differently than they do.

In general, the socialization process in an early childhood setting revolves around a child's *relationships with people*. During this time of their lives, children work out a separate set of relationships with their teachers, those adults other than their parents. They interact differently with adults than children, and learning to interact successfully with other children is important.

Through socialization, *gender roles* are learned. The customary roles that boys and girls play are transmitted, along with acceptable variations. Children come to understand how teachers, mommies, daddies, grandparents, males, and females are expected to act. Early childhood professionals need to be aware of the difference between a child's gender identity development and a child's sex role development. Various cultures may have differing notions about sex role development.

Children also learn *social attitudes* at an early age. They learn to enjoy being with people and participating in social activities. At the same time, young children can also develop attitudes of bias, and it is in these early years that prejudicial behavior often begins. How the teachers respond to negative comments, unfair acts, exclusivity based on race, gender, or ability is crucial in combating these negative attitudes. Favorable attitudes toward people and a strong desire to be part of the social world interacting with others are established in the early years.

Another important facet of socialization involves the development of a *sense of community*. A program's emotional climate and teacher's behavior contribute not only to children's sense of personal safety and belonging but also to the value of relationships that are sustained by communication. Teachers who strive for community awareness and bonding are adhering to an anti-bias philosophy (see Chapter 9) that promotes empathic interaction with people from diverse backgrounds and standing up for self and others in the face of bias.

All areas of children's development play a part in learning social skills:

- Having the confidence to try joining a group calls on emotional skills.
- Remembering children's names or how a game works is a cognitive task.
- "Using your words" to express an idea or feeling requires language.
- Having the ability to play, chase, or walk in high heels for a dress-up game requires certain physical dexterity.

There are many variations that arise in social situations. For instance, children can sustain complex play without much language, and games can be adapted to include children with a variety of physical skills.

Understanding the principle of interrelated development, however, helps teachers appreciate the process of social learning and recognize opportunities to guide their social development.

In the early years, children mature socially in discernible developmental stages (see Figure 14-9). From birth to age 3, children's interest in others begins with a mutual gazing and social smile in the early months (birth through 8 months), continues with an exploration of others as well as some anxious behavior around strangers in the crawler and walker stages (8 to 18 months), and develops into an enjoyment of peers and adults along with an awareness of others' rights and feelings as a toddler and 2 year old (18 months to 3 years).

In the preschool years, children learn to control their aggressive impulses, think about others beside themselves, and resist doing what they should not. This learning translates into four basic expectations. They:

1. Show interest in others.
2. Learn right from wrong.
3. Learn to get along with others.
4. Learn a role for themselves that takes into consideration their unique self-gender, race, ethnicity, and abilities.

Children of the primary years (5 to 8 years) show an increased interest in peers and social competence, and group rules become important. The development of a social conscience and of fairness rounds out the primary grade developmental milestones.

Social Competence

Social competence involves the skills and personal knowledge children develop to deal with the challenges and opportunities they face in life with others. This includes relationships with all other people, including family, teachers, caregivers, peers, and the community at large. Through their social interactions, children learn a sense of personal identity, adopt family and cultural values, acquire interpersonal skills, and learn how to "live in the world" (see Figure 14-10).

Social Development Timeline

Infant–Toddler	Preschooler	Primary Child
Response to Other's Distress		
Reacts emotionally by experiencing what the other seems to feel.	Begins to make adjustments that reflect the realization that the other person is different and separate from self.	Takes other's personality into account and shows concern for other's general condition.
Peer Interaction		
• First encounters mutual inspection • First social contacts • (18 months) Growth in sensitivity to peer play • (2 years) Able to direct social acts to two children at once (beginning of social interaction)	• Adjustment in behavior to fit age and behavior of other • (More than 3 years) Friendship as momentary • (3–5 years) Beginning of friendship as constant	• Friend as someone who will do what you want • Beginning of friend as one who embodies admirable, constant characteristics
Social Roles		
• (10–20 days) Imitation of adults • (3 months) Gurgles in response to others • (6 months) Social games based on imitation • (18 months) Differentiation between reality and pretend play • (2 years) Makes doll do something as if it were alive	• (3 years) Makes a doll carry out several roles or activities • (4–5 years) Acts out a social role in dramatic play and integrates that role with others (mom and baby)	• (6 years) Integrates one role with two complementary roles: doctor, nurse, and sick person • (8 years) Growing understanding that roles can influence behavior (doctor whose daughter is a patient)

FIGURE 14-9 A timetable of social development for the ages of infancy through the primary years. (Special thanks to Gay Spitz. Reprinted by permission.)

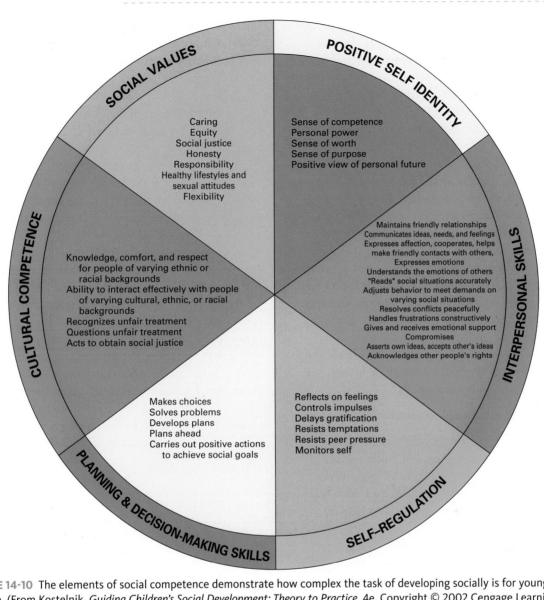

FIGURE 14-10 The elements of social competence demonstrate how complex the task of developing socially is for young children. (From Kostelnik. *Guiding Children's Social Development: Theory to Practice*, 4e. Copyright © 2002 Cengage Learning, Inc. Reprinted by permission. www.cengage.com/permissions.)

There are several components to social competence:

- *Emotional regulation.* The ability to regulate emotions (see earlier in this chapter).
- *Social knowledge and understanding.* Knowledge of enough language and norms to interact successfully; understanding the reactions of others and their feelings (empathy).
- *Social skills.* Social approach patterns, attention to others, exchange of information, handling aggression.
- *Social dispositions.* Habits or characteristic ways of responding to experiences.

Why is social competence important? Such children are happier than their less competent peers. Children's social relations have been linked to academic achievement.

Lack of social competence is linked to rejection by peers, poor self-esteem, and poor academic performance (Kostelnik et al., 2008). It is now widely accepted that young children who do not frequently interact with peers are at risk for a host of later socioemotional difficulties.

Children become socially competent in several predictable ways.

- First, *the brain is wired to look for patterns.* When an infant smiles and is met with a reciprocal smile, a pattern of responsiveness and attachment begins. The preschooler who grabs for toys and usually gets to keep them when he is at home is surprised (and unhappy) when the pattern is broken at the child care center and the toy is returned to the one who was using it. As a result of their experiences, children form ideas about how the social world works. They are active learners who observe and experiment and learn firsthand what happens when they try something. In-the-moment, on-the-spot lessons greatly help children learn socially.

- Next, *children have multiple ways of learning*. Because teachers often do not know each child's ways of learning, it is best to try a variety of approaches when teaching social skills. Talking helps some (linguistic), others learn better by seeing patterns (logical mathematical), and many learn by modeling. Rehearsing how to do or say the words helps the kinesthetic learner.

- Finally, *children learn much of their social repertoires through play*. Dramatizations, role-playing, and dramatic play provide opportunities to act out many roles and help children deal with some of the demands placed on them. In play, the child experiments with options: finding out what it feels like to be the boss, to be the baby, to behave in ways that might otherwise be unacceptable.

See how all three ways are used in this sequence:

Sarda wants to play in the block corner, but stands hesitantly as four boys shout and vroom the cars around. "Do you want to play here?" inquires the observant teacher. When she nods, the teacher helps her move in and the two begin building [acquire approach through modeling]. Soon, the boys notice and come to see a garage being built, so they drive their cars over [a pattern of play they recognize]. The teacher slowly steps aside, and the game continues [learn through play].

Common Social Challenges

Children of each age in early childhood experience a range of social difficulties (see Chapter 7). For instance, toddlers develop many forms of testing behavior, including saying "No" to adult rules and other restraints. Grabbing, biting, and hitting are common forms of aggression and self-expression. Some of this occurs in preschoolers, as well as other forms of self-determination. There are problems children encounter when responding to emotions, both theirs and those of others. Peer status and friendship loom large in primary school, when loneliness and exclusion, teasing and bullying all occur (Gordon & Browne, 1996; Browne & Gordon, 2009).

Teasing and bullying can become disruptive in older groups. Teachers need to be clear about what bullying is, and how to respond to it early. "Bullying is repeated, systematic efforts to inflict harm on someone who is unable or unlikely to defend himself or herself" (Berger, 2009). Children who are exposed repeatedly and over time to negative actions (words, physical contact, making faces, gesturing, or intentional exclusions from a group) on the part of one or more others can develop low self-esteem and may become withdrawn or be rejected by their peers. Not every rejected child becomes a bully victim, and not every child who excludes or teases another becomes a bully. But the antisocial behavior results in difficulties for both sides: "Over time, the social costs to both bullies and victims include impaired social understanding and problems with human relationships in adulthood" (Berger, 2009).

Although bullying is more serious and noticeable late in childhood and adolescence, its roots are in early childhood. Teachers must take notice and do a better job of dealing with the behaviors. Preschool and school-age programs can also implement conflict resolution programs that teach children how to express themselves and listen to others in socially intense situations. Systematic work with children to teach them these social competence skills helps them deal with what might be called the "garden variety" conflicts—issues of property, territory, and power such as teasing, put-downs, hitting, not sharing, and who is the boss (see Figure 14-11).

Talk It Out: Conflict Resolution

1. Stop. Cool off.

2. Talk and listen.

3. Think of ways to solve the problem.

4. Choose the idea you both like. ☺☺

FIGURE 14-11 A "Talk It Out" poster helps teachers mediate conflicts and teach children resolution skills. (From Barbara Pooro, *Talk It Out: Conflict Resolution in the Elementary Classroom*, Fig. 4.11. Copyright © 1996 by ASCD. Reprinted with permission. Learn more about ASCD at www.ascd.org.)

Peer Relationships

For the young child, social development means the steady movement away from the *egocentric* position of self (and parents) as central points toward a more **socio-centric** viewpoint that involves others—both adults and, especially, children. During the early years, the child learns to socialize outside the family; social contacts outside the home reinforce the enjoyment of social activities and prepare the child for future group activity.

Peer interactions, that is, associations with friends of the same age group, become important to the child once infancy and early toddlerhood are past. Through peer interactions, children can identify with models who are like themselves and can learn from each other's behavior. Friends provide models for imitation, for comparison, and for confirmation of themselves, and they are a source of support.

Playing with other children begins with solitary and parallel play at around age 2, in which two or more children are in the same area with each other but do not initiate social interaction. By the ages of 3 and 4, more interaction takes place. There are conversations and conflicts as well as cooperation in playing together. There are stages in children's friendships. In the early years, friendship starts at an **undifferentiated** level, in which children are egocentric and a friend is more of the moment. This gives way to a **unilateral** level; a good friend does what the child wants the friend to do. Toward the end of early childhood, friendship becomes more **reciprocal**, involving some give-and-take in a kind of two-way cooperation. Listen to these children trying out their friendship:

Chris: I'll be the teacher, you be the kid.
Suzanne: NO! I want to be the teacher, too.
Chris: No! No! You can't be the teacher, too, 'cause then there'd be no kids.
Suzanne: OK. Next time, I get to be the teacher.
Chris: Maybe! OK, everybody go wash your hands for snack time. Suzanne, you can pass out your very nutritious snack to everybody.
Suzanne: Superfasmic, I'm the boss of snack.

A peer group is important for a number of reasons. Social development is enhanced because a child learns to conform to established social standards outside of his home setting. The expectations of the larger society are reinforced. To become autonomous, the child must also learn to achieve independence from the family, especially parents. Young children must also come to understand themselves as part of society. Self-concept is enlarged by a group of peers as they see how others respond to them and treat them.

Rejection is a common form of social behavior in young children. In the early years, children need to deal with the feelings that arise when they are told, "You can't play with us."

Making and keeping friends are essential to children's positive social development, so important that children without friends by the primary years are considered at risk for overall school success. Developing friendships is more than teaching general interpersonal skills and is especially important for children with special needs. Facilitating friendship development in inclusive classrooms requires teacher awareness and interaction as well as careful environmental and schedule planning.

Social Skills

Social skills are strategies children learn that enable them to behave appropriately in many environments. They help children learn to initiate or manage social interaction in a variety of settings and with a number of people. **Social cognition** is the application of thinking to personal and social behavior; it is giving meaning to social experience. For example, Nadia wants to play with Paul, a very popular 4 year old. She remembers Paul's interest in the rope swing and challenges him to swing higher than she did. He responds enthusiastically and the friendship begins.

Peer relationships are a source of pleasure and support. Children start with a preoccupation with themselves, move to a curiosity about others, and eventually to an awareness of the thoughts and feelings of their friends.

Social cognition requires children to interpret events and make decisions, to consider the impact of their behavior on others, and to consider the cause as well as the consequence of an action. Cognitive skills are necessary when we ask children to seek alternative solutions to social problems: "How else could you ask him for a turn, Pete?" These are all social cognition skills, and they serve as the basis for the acquisition of other skills.

Social Intelligence

Building on Gardner's multiple intelligences theory (see Chapters 4 and 12), Daniel Goleman outlined five dimensions of emotional intelligence (see previous section and the Special Topic at the end of this chapter). The fifth element of emotional intelligence is social skills. Teachers who can help children handle their emotions (self-regulation) and learn to "read" other people's feelings by their body language or tone of voice (empathy) can then lead children to gain social skills. As mentioned earlier in this chapter, children who bully can be taught better social skills, and the early childhood setting is just the place to do so. Paley's classic works (1992) describe in detail the social climate of classrooms:

> "Are you my friend?" the little ones ask in nursery school, not knowing. The responses are also questions. If yes, then what? And if I push you away, how does that feel?
>
> By kindergarten, however, a structure begins to be revealed . . . certain children will have the right to limit the social experiences of their classmates. . . . Long after hitting and name-calling have been outlawed by the teachers, a more damaging phenomenon is allowed to take root, spreading like a weed from grade to grade.

With more social intelligence than most, Paley as kindergarten teacher decided to post a sign outside her door one year. "You can't say you can't play" turns the class upside down and requires both adults and children to learn new ways to interact.

Social skills can be viewed in different ways. The *Four Hows* is one set of categories for such a complex array of skills:

1. *How to approach.* Getting and being included.
2. *How to interact.* Sharing, cooperating.
3. *How to deal with difference.* Including others, helping, bullying, and teasing.
4. *How to manage conflict.* Handling aggression, problem solving.

Another is to realize that there is a skill set learned in every kind of interaction.

Skills Learned with Adults

In their relationship with adults, children learn:

- They can stay at school without parents.
- They can enjoy adults other than parents and respond to new adults.
- Adults help in times of trouble or need.
- Adults help them learn social protocol.
- Adults keep children from being hurt and from hurting others.
- Adults help children learn about cultural differences and similarities, disabilities, gender identity, and language diversity.
- Adults resist bias and stereotyping and teach children to actively do the same.
- Adults do not always take a side or solve the problem.
- Adults work with them to solve problems.
- Adults believe that every child has a right to a satisfying social experience in early childhood settings.

Skills Learned with Peers

In their relationship with other children, children learn:

- There are different approaches to others; some work, some do not.
- Interactive skills and how to sustain the relationship.
- How to solve conflicts in ways other than retreat or force.
- How to share materials, equipment, other children, friends, teachers, and ideas.
- How to achieve mutually satisfying play.
- Self-defense and how to assert their rights in socially acceptable ways.

"Mirror Neurons" at Work

"A teacher's moment-by-moment actions and interactions with children are the most powerful determinant of learning outcomes and development. Curriculum is very important, but what the teacher does is paramount" (Copple & Bredekamp, 2009). Developmentally appropriate practices are now supported by neuroscience. If you stick out your tongue at a baby, he does the same. The same portions of the human brain activate when a person performs an action as when that person is watching someone perform the action. Monkey see, monkey do. And children do, too.

It appears that certain brain regions contain "mirror neurons." These are neurological networks set up "so that a child's neurological synapses 'mirror' not only the teacher's actions and reactions . . . [but also] these same mirror neurons affect the mood of the individual observing the instructor (Rushton et al., 2009). This implies

that it is not just what the teacher presents that is important, but how and who does the presenting. "The irreducible core of the environment during early development is people" (Thompson, 2001). The greatest dangers to the developing brain in the early years are chronic stressors, including unavailable, depressed, or otherwise coercive or inconsistent adults.

The implications of the discovery of mirror neurons is staggering: Might the mirror neurons affect the mood of the child watching the teacher? "At a subliminal level, children observe the teacher's expressions and dispositions and internalize how the teacher is feeling. Neuroscientists believe that our ability to empathize with another human being is due, in part, to the activation of the mirror neuron networks being activated by what we observe" (Rushton et al., 2010).

Children's behavior and their mirror neurons reflect their external world.

Research suggests that "a positive, enthusiastic teacher sends signals to the child's mirror neurons, which, in turn, can impact how they receive the learning objectives being delivered. How we present not only ourselves, but the phenomenal journey of learning, is critical to the child's emotional development (Rushton, 2011).

Questions

1. What imitative behaviors might you see in young children that indicate mirror neurons are firing?
2. If the research recommends that curriculum be personally meaningful, what kinds of activities would likely be positively meaningful to toddlers? Prekindergartners?
3. Knowing that you influence children's developing mirror neuron networks, how should you behave with them?

- How to take turns and how to communicate desires.
- How to negotiate.
- How to be helpful to peers with tasks, information, and by modeling behavior.
- How to anticipate and avoid problems.
- Realistic expectations of how other children behave and respond toward them.
- Ways to deal with socially awkward situations and with socially difficult situations and children.
- How to make, be, share, and lose a friend.

Skills Learned in a Group

In groups, children learn:

- How to take part as a member and not as an individual.
- That there are activities that promote group association.
- To identify as a member of various groups.
- To follow a daily schedule and pattern.
- To adapt to school routines.
- School rules and expectations.

- Interaction and participatory skills: how to enter and exit from play.
- To respect the rights, feelings, and property of others.
- To become socially active, especially in the face of unfair or biased behavior and situations.
- How to work together as a group, during clean-up time, in preparation for an event, and so on.
- How to deal with delay of gratification: how to wait.

Skills Learned as an Individual

As individuals, children learn:

- To take responsibility for self-help, self-care.
- To initiate their activities and to make choices.
- To work alone, close to other children.
- To notice unfairness and injustice and learn how to handle them.
- To negotiate.
- To cope with rejection, hurt feelings, disappointment.
- To communicate in verbal and nonverbal ways, and when to use communication skills.
- To test limits other people set.

© Cengage Learning

Friendship: "The more we get together, the happier we'll be!"

- Their own personal style of peer interaction: degree, intensity, frequency, quality.
- To express strong feelings in socially acceptable ways.
- To manage social freedom.

Specific skills within these four areas include the social and moral aspects of nurturance, kindness, and sharing. As children get older, these skills include telling the truth, taking turns, keeping promises, respecting others' rights, having tolerance, and following rules.

Another social skill that has taken hold is that of **social action.** In an anti-bias program (see Chapter 9), children can learn how to take social action to make unfair things fair. For instance, preschoolers discover that their adhesive strips are labeled "flesh-colored" but match the skin of only a few children; they take photos and send them to the company (Derman-Sparks & Olsen Edwards, 2010). Promoting activism may not always bring successful results, but the activity and the model are powerful learning experiences.

Curriculum Approaches for Social Growth

A major role for the early childhood teacher is to see that children have enjoyable social contacts and to help motivate children toward a desire to be with others. The early childhood setting affords children numerous learning opportunities for social development. In the role of social organizer, the teacher creates a physical and interpersonal environment that promotes the development of children's social skills.

Considerations

Early childhood teachers consider the physical environment, daily schedule and relational interactions when planning a social curriculum.

Planning and Arranging a Social Environment

Planning the social environment involves placement of furniture in ways that allow children to play alone or with someone, as well as materials and toys available shelves for choosing. The placement of two telephones, three wagons, and eight firefighter hats fosters child–child interactions. Children often act together in a spontaneous way; then get organized toward a planned end when they decide to build a single tower together. The teacher must also allow enough time in the daily schedule for children to get thoroughly involved in playing with one another (see Figure 14-12).

Help Children Develop Trust
Trusting in themselves, their peers, and their teachers, is a part of learning about social relationships. Teachers enhance children's social knowledge as they gradually improve their sense of trust (Figure 14-13). General recommendations are:

1. *Help children recognize their needs.* Notice children who need to clarify their wishes; ask uninvolved children with whom they would like to play; help arguing children say how they feel and what they want.
2. *Increase children's awareness of their social goals and the goals of others.* Teachers can aid children by helping them recognize their choices; they can also mediate so that others can express themselves.
3. *Help children develop effective social skills.* Provide a model for listening, for choosing another place to play, or for going along with another's ideas; help children find ways to stand their ground and also accommodate and learn to use conflict resolution, cooperation, coping, and helping skills.

Arranging a Social Environment

Do	Don't
• Respect individual timetables and feelings.	• Make implied comparisons.
• Establish authority and credibility.	• Issue empty threats.
• Express expectations simply and directly.	• Hover.
• Redefine children's characters in positive terms.	• Make teacher–child interaction be all about misbehavior.
• Encourage impulsive control.	• Motivate children by indirect disapproval.
• Appeal to children's good sense.	• Lose your sense of humor.
• Invoke ground rules.	• Allow a rigid curriculum to narrow possibilities for social interaction.
• Mix it up: Arrange things to get one child next to another.	
• Move it: people, toys, you.	

Question everything you do: Could I open this up for more than one child?

FIGURE 14-12 Planning a social environment is more than furniture arrangement.

Cooperation: "I'll help you, then you'll help me."

4. *Teach children to recognize others' emotions and intentions.* Children become flooded with their own strong feelings and are not likely to notice someone else's emotions in the heat of the moment; teachers can help children see another's face or hear a tone of voice, thus beginning to "read" another person.

5. *Reflect with children on how their behavior affects others by pointing out what is predictable in their interactions.* Young children do not always "connect the dots" between their behavior and others' reactions. When a teacher makes a statement without disapproval, the child can then understand the effects of her or his behavior on others: "Wow! When you use that loud voice, I see the kids looking scared, and then they tell you not to play here."

6. *Highlight children's success by helping them learn to monitor their behavior.* It can help children to see their successful social encounters as well as the strategies that did not work. "When you asked them if you could play, they said, 'No!' But then you went and got shovels for everyone and that worked!"

7. *Avoid telling children who their "friends" are.* Early childhood teachers encourage children to learn about friendship; however, "legislating friendship" often backfires. Telling children "We're all friends here" or "Friends share their things with everyone" denies the distinction between positive, friendly experiences and friendship. "Classmate" and "friend" are not the same word.

8. *Develop a set of strategies to help the socially awkward and troubled in your class.* Although each child is unique, there are certain situations that arise time and again in an early childhood classroom. Children

Curriculum for Social Skill Development

Time	Skill	Activities
Week 1	Developing a positive self-image	Do thumbprint art. Make foot and handprints. Compare children's baby pictures with current photos. Play with mirrors: Make faces, emotional expressions. Dress felt dolls in clothing. Sing name songs: "Mary Wore Her Red Dress." Make a list: "What I like to do best is . . . " Post in classroom. Do a self-portrait in any art medium. Make a silhouette picture of each child.
Week 2	Becoming a member of a group	Take attendance together: Who is missing? Play picture lotto with photographs of children. Play "Farmer in the Dell." Share a favorite toy from home with older children. Tape record children's voices, guess who they are. Have a "friendly feast": Each child brings a favorite food from home to share.
Week 3	Forming a friendship within the group	Provide one puzzle (toy, game, book) for every two children. Take a "buddy walk": Return and tell a story together of what you saw. Play "telephone talk": Pretend to invite your friend over to play. Play "copy cat": imitate your friend's laugh, walk, cry, words. Practice throwing and catching balls with one another. Form letter together with two children's bodies: A, T, C, K, etc. Play tug-of-war with your friend. Build a house out of blocks together. Make "mirror images" movements with your friend.
Week 4	Working together as a group	Play with a parachute; keep the ball bouncing. Make snacks for the rest of the class. Plan and plant a garden. Make a mural together to decorate the hallways. Play "Follow the Leader." Sing a round: "Row, Row, Row Your Boat."
Week 5	Learning a group identity	Make a map of the town and have children place their house on it. Take a field trip together. Print a newspaper with articles by and about each child. Select and perform a favorite story for the rest of the class. Take a group snapshot. Make a "family tree" of photos of children in group. Learn a group folk dance. Make a mural of handprints joined in a circle.

FIGURE 14-13 Build social skills through small-group experiences, beginning with an understanding of self and moving toward an appreciation of group membership.

who are socially inept often do not use nonverbal language effectively and are "out-of-sync" because they miss the signs.

9. *Do not stay uninvolved or ignore teasing and bullying.* A lack of response can signal all children that it is okay to engage in these behaviors and acceptable to fall victim to it. Talk about it; read books such as *Rosie's Story* (Gogoll) or *Oliver Button Is a Sissy*

(de Paola); make an experience chart ("I feel (un)welcome when . . ."); and help the class with fair rules. In noncompetitive games, children learn to help each other rather than trying to win or gain power over others. Finally, foster friendships between girls and boys and actively counter gender bias.

10. *Work to provide a caring community in your class.* Brain research (see Brain Box) confirms this point,

and an anti-bias approach (see Chapter 9) supports the development of social action as an extension of "making right" the classroom and beyond.

11. *Invite parents and families into the process of children's socialization.* Both teachers and families share in the responsibility of helping children develop social skills; neither one can do it alone (see Chapter 8).

Facilitate Children's Interactions and Interpret Their Behavior To help young children understand each other and to pave the way for continued cooperation, the teacher reports and reflects on what is happening along with specific curriculum planning. In the classroom setting, during an active, free-play period, the teacher might:

Reflect the Action:	*Say:*
Call attention to the effect one child's behavior is having on another.	"Randy, when you scream like that, other children become frightened and are afraid to play with you."
Show approval and reinforce positive social behavior.	"I like the way you carefully stepped over their block building, Dannetta."
Support a child in asserting her rights.	"Chrystal is hanging on to the doll because she isn't finished playing yet, Wilbur."
Support a child's desire to be independent.	"I know you want to help, Keyetta, but Sammy is trying to put his coat on by himself."
Acknowledge and help children establish contact with others.	"Omar would like to play, too. That's why he brought you another bucket of water. Is there a place where he can help?"
Reflect back to a child the depth of his feelings and what form those feelings might take.	"I know George made you very angry when he took your sponge, but I can't let you throw water at him. What can you tell him? What words can you use to say you didn't like what he did?"

Adult responses to children's play are particularly critical in supporting positive social development. When children make judgments in error, coming to false conclusions about children on the basis of race, gender, native language, or ability, the teacher must intervene because silence signals tacit approval. This is perhaps the most dynamic and challenging part of teachers' jobs, the heart of the profession.

Curriculum Planning for Social Development

Social curriculum happens everywhere in an early childhood program. Teaching social behavior usually occurs in response to spontaneous situations. And the acquisition of social skills can be enhanced in more formalized ways through planned curriculum activities (see Figure 14-13).

Setting The way the environment is arranged has a profound effect on social interaction among children. Most indoor activities are planned and set up to encourage participation by more than one child at a time. Arrange the space into learning centers with clear physical boundaries and ways to get around (see Chapter 9). Remember, the environment is one of the teachers.

- *The Arts.* At the art table, children share collage materials and paste that have been placed in the center of the table. When easels are placed side by side, conversation occurs spontaneously among children. A small table, placed between the easels, on which a tray of paint cups is placed, also encourages children's interactions. If there is only one of each color, the children have to negotiate with one another for the color they want to use.
- *Blocks/Manipulatives.* A large space for block cabinets gives children a visual cue that there is plenty of room for more than one child. Puzzle tables set with three or four puzzles also tell children that social interaction is expected. Many times, children talk, play, and plan with one another as they share a large bin full of Legos® or plastic building towers. A floor puzzle always requires a group: some to put the picture together, others to watch and make suggestions. As children build with blocks next to one another, they soon share comments about their work; many times this sharing leads to a mutual effort on a single building.
- *Discovery/Science.* Many science projects can be arranged to involve more than one child. A display of magnets with a tray of assorted objects can become the focus of several children as they decide which objects will be attracted to the magnets. Cooking together, weighing and measuring one another, and caring for classroom pets can be times when teachers reinforce social skills.
- *Dramatic Play.* This area more than any other seems to draw children into contact with one another.

Provide an assortment of family life accessories—dress-up clothes, kitchen equipment and utensils—and children have little trouble getting involved. A shoe needs to be tied or a dress zipped. Someone must come eat the delicious meal just cooked or put the baby to bed. A medical theme in this classroom area also enhances children's social skills. They learn to take each other's temperature, listen to heartbeats, and plan operations, all of which require more than one person. Sociodramatic play can provide curriculum integration in the primary grades as well.

- *Language/Library.* Children enjoy reading books and stories to one another, whether or not they know the words. Favorite books are often shared by two children who enjoy turning the pages and talking over the story together. Lotto games encourage children to become aware of one another, to look at each person's card in order to identify who has the picture to match. Name songs and games, especially early in the year, help children learn to call each other by name.
- *Music Movement.* Build in regular times for music and movement activities. The entire group can participate in familiar songs; a sense of community is built by everyone's participation. Activities during the free choice times usually involve smaller numbers, in which group members can challenge one another to new ways to dance with scarves or use the tumbling mat. Finally, one-to-one experiences encourage new friendships as the intimacy of a shared musical experience brings two children or a teacher and child together. Sharing music and dance from home is an ideal way to incorporate children's individual cultures into the classroom. Translate a simple song into another language; teach the children the song, working in the language that is "home base" for most of the children, then reteach it. Words and phrases made familiar by melody are remembered and made valuable.

Outdoors, children need a space to run, a place to yell, a place where adults are not hovering and directing each activity. The pretend play of boys, in particular, is usually richer than inside, and many of the rough-and-tumble activities prohibited indoors are safe here (see Figure 14-14). It may be more difficult to observe children, and directions are often harder to give with distance. The outdoor environment can be structured in ways to support group play:

- *Painting or Drawing.* Painting on murals or drawing chalk designs on the cement are art activities that promote social interaction.
- *Planning and Planting a Garden.* Planning and planting a garden is a long-range project that involves many children. Decisions must be made by the group about what to plant, where to locate the garden, how to prepare the soil, and what the shared responsibilities of caring for the garden will be.
- *Gross Motor Activities.* Most gross motor activities stimulate group interactions. Seesaws, jump ropes, and hide-and-seek require at least two people to participate. A-frames, boards, and boxes, as well as other movable equipment, need the cooperative effort of several children to be rearranged. Sand play, when accompanied by water, shovels, and other accessories, draws a number of children together to create rivers, dams, and floods. Ball games and relay races also encourage social relationships.

Daily Schedule Routines and transitions are often social experiences because they provide children with an opportunity for support and peer interaction. For instance, the routine of nap preparation can be structured with a "buddy" system so that older children are paired with the younger ones to set up the cots, choose a cuddly or books, and get tucked in. A clean-up time transition can be made fun and successful if children can wear a necklace to depict the job or area. Children with similar clean-up cards get a sense of teamwork when putting an activity area back in order.

As a directed learning experience, small group times afford an opportunity to focus on social skills in a more structured way. Small groups provide a setting for children and teachers to participate in more relaxed, uninterrupted dialogue. The intimacy of the small group sets the stage for many social interactions.

Group time discussions, such as circle time in preschool and class meetings for school-age children, can focus on problems that children can solve. Too many children crowding the water table, a child's fear of fire drills, or the noise level on a rainy day are subjects children talk about in small groups. The most relevant situations are ones that occur naturally in the course of a program. Another curriculum idea is to make "Situation Cards" of these and other common incidents. For instance, teachers can create illustrated cards that pose situations such as:

- You tell your friends to "stop it" when they take part of the toy you are using, but they do it again.
- You open your lunch and your mom or dad has packed your favorite foods.
- You come down the slide and your teacher calls "Hooray for you!"

A Curriculum of Cooperation

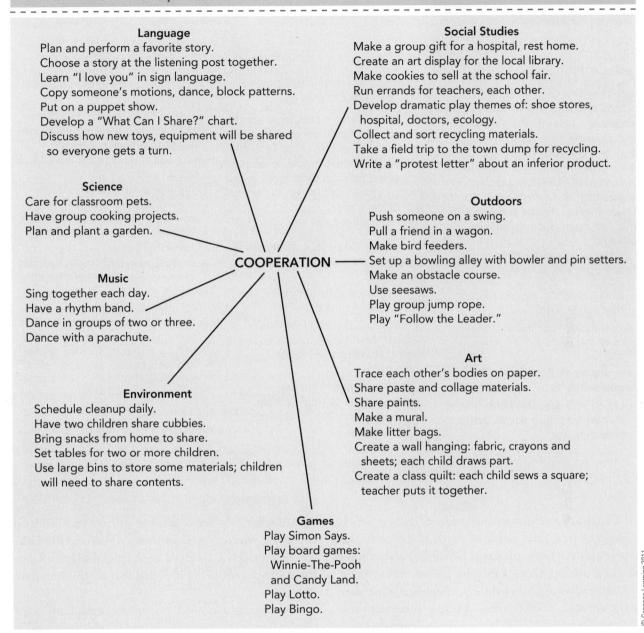

Language
Plan and perform a favorite story.
Choose a story at the listening post together.
Learn "I love you" in sign language.
Copy someone's motions, dance, block patterns.
Put on a puppet show.
Develop a "What Can I Share?" chart.
Discuss how new toys, equipment will be shared
 so everyone gets a turn.

Science
Care for classroom pets.
Have group cooking projects.
Plan and plant a garden.

Music
Sing together each day.
Have a rhythm band.
Dance in groups of two or three.
Dance with a parachute.

Environment
Schedule cleanup daily.
Have two children share cubbies.
Bring snacks from home to share.
Set tables for two or more children.
Use large bins to store some materials; children
 will need to share contents.

COOPERATION

Social Studies
Make a group gift for a hospital, rest home.
Create an art display for the local library.
Make cookies to sell at the school fair.
Run errands for teachers, each other.
Develop dramatic play themes of: shoe stores,
 hospital, doctors, ecology.
Collect and sort recycling materials.
Take a field trip to the town dump for recycling.
Write a "protest letter" about an inferior product.

Outdoors
Push someone on a swing.
Pull a friend in a wagon.
Make bird feeders.
Set up a bowling alley with bowler and pin setters.
Make an obstacle course.
Use seesaws.
Play group jump rope.
Play "Follow the Leader."

Art
Trace each other's bodies on paper.
Share paste and collage materials.
Share paints.
Make a mural.
Make litter bags.
Create a wall hanging: fabric, crayons and
 sheets; each child draws part.
Create a class quilt: each child sews a square;
 teacher puts it together.

Games
Play Simon Says.
Play board games:
 Winnie-The-Pooh
 and Candy Land.
Play Lotto.
Play Bingo.

© Cengage Learning 2011

FIGURE 14-14 The social skill of cooperation can be fostered throughout the curriculum.

● You promise your friend you will play with him at recess, but then someone else you like asks you to play with her.

The teacher then guides a discussion around the questions "How do you feel? What can you say? What can you do?" This activity can be simplified or elaborated depending on the individuals and group involved.

Focus on Skills Social development for the preschool child includes gaining an awareness of the larger community in which the child lives. The early childhood curriculum contains elements of what is often in the later grades called *social studies*. Community members such as police officers, mail carriers, restaurant workers, and dental staff may be available to visit a program. Try to invite men and women in nontraditional jobs to visit and talk about or demonstrate their work. Be sure to include skills that are important to each child's culture and family. Introducing children to a diverse range of creative adults—men and women from a variety of cultural backgrounds—helps children explore the world outside of their own experience.

Do I *Have* to Share?

Sharing involves using or enjoying something in common with others. Although sharing may seem simple to adults, it is not a skill that is learned overnight, nor is it easy to orchestrate in young children. When the dominant culture is one of individual competition, acquisition, and ownership, children get particular messages that can make teaching "sharing" difficult.

What does sharing mean to you? To a young child, it means:

- Giving up one's possessions more than taking turns;
- Holding onto a powerful position more than getting more power and fun;
- Losing the thread of the play more than adding to it;
- Losing what you have rather than dividing everything equally and getting more;

- Defining who I am rather than being a "me" who can give.

Thus, sharing makes more sense over time and with lots of guided experiences. As an adult, you know the advantages of sharing (the second half of the previous sentences), but young children still live on the left side of the phrase.
How can adults help?

- Understand that it is normal not to want to share and to have trouble doing so.
- Explain in simple terms what you want the child to do.
- Make sure that children "get back" what they have shared so that taking turns really works.
- Be an example of sharing because "Do as I do" is more powerful than "Do it because I told you to."

- Give children experience of there being enough.
- Let the children experience ownership, too, and the good feeling that an act of generosity brings.

Think About This

1. If grabbing what they want makes sense to toddlers and 2 year olds, how might you show them that sharing a toy or space isn't giving it up forever?
2. Because many preschoolers have had some experience "getting it back," what might be the reasons for still not wanting to share?
3. School-age children "know better" and still find ways to keep hold of items or privileges. What's a teacher to do about closed games, or "no room here?"

Cooperating is one primary social skill in which young children need plenty of practice. Toddlers and 2 year olds can begin to see the benefits of cooperation as they become more aware of others' feelings and wishes, and as teachers help all children get what they want through taking turns, dividing materials, and looking for another item when it is in demand. Three to 5 year olds become more cooperative as they learn more self-help skills (motor development) and can express themselves (language development) as well as remember guidelines and understand reasons for prosocial behavior (cognitive development). School-age children develop an emotional sense of psychosocial competence.

Being included is often a challenge. Young children get involved in a variety of interpersonal situations that are beyond their capacities to handle with grace. An overly aggressive child, one who withdraws or stays apart from social opportunities, someone who chronically interrupts or disrupts the play, and children

who deliberately leave another out all may end up becoming rejected by their peers. These socially awkward or troubled children need special help to learn the strategies for being included that all children have to learn.

Developing a conflict resolution curriculum helps all children learn the communication and coping skills necessary for being included. Children who learn good observation and body language skills can participate successfully in situations that require prosocial behaviors. In addition, children need guidance and practice in deciding how to include others whose appearance, interests, age, or behavior differs from their own. Research has shown long-term positive effects of such conflict resolution training. When elementary children were taught impulse control, how to get what they wanted without aggression, and how to recognize others' feelings, along with teacher training and family management skills, the children were in better mental health and had higher educational and economic achievement than a control group 15 years later (Hawkins et al., 2008).

Helping others is an area of social development that is sometimes not emphasized in an individualistic society. Developmentally appropriate programs emphasize cooperation and find that children spontaneously offer help and sympathy to those in need. Snack time is a natural setting for practicing helping others in both words ("Please pass the fruit"; "No, gracias") and deeds (handing someone the pitcher or a sponge). Remember to sit face-to-face, rather than hover behind. Teachers who stand behind often fall into the trap of withholding food while eliciting rote words, rather than genuine or spontaneous positive social interaction. Full-day programs can encourage children to help each other prepare and put away nap items. Curriculum can be developed from the classroom ("What can we do when someone's sad to say good-bye to Mom?") and the larger world ("Some children have noticed a lot of trash in the park next door") to enhance children's helping skills.

Themes A popular theme that lends itself to social growth is that of friendship (see Figure 14-15). Other themes can be generated from the children:

"Make It Fair"	Not enough raisins in the cereal, complained a kindergartner, sparking a class letter-writing campaign.
"The Girl No One Wanted to Play With"	Preschoolers rejecting another, so they wrote, made costumes for, and performed a play.
"Saving the World"	Third-graders put on a sale to buy rainforest acreage.

Helping: "I'll help clean up," is a spontaneous action of toddlers and 2 year olds that should be reinforced to become habit.

Curriculum for Creative Growth

It's OK to try something you don't know.
It's OK to make mistakes.
It's OK to take your time.
It's OK to find your own pace.
It's OK to bungle—so next time you are free to succeed.
It's OK to risk looking foolish.
It's OK to be original and different.
It's OK to wait until you are ready.
It's OK to experiment (safely).
It's OK to question "shoulds."
It is special to be you. You are unique.
It is necessary to make a mess (which you need to be willing to clean up!).

Permissions by Christina Lopez-Morgan (2002) opens our discussion of creativity, to give the tone for what creativity is and how it develops.

In this section, we discuss the development of creativity and creative skills, then look at the role of the teacher and creative curriculum.

The Development of Creativity

Creativity is the ability to have new ideas, to be original and imaginative, and to make new adaptations on old ideas. Inventors, composers, and designers are creative

Theme: Friendship

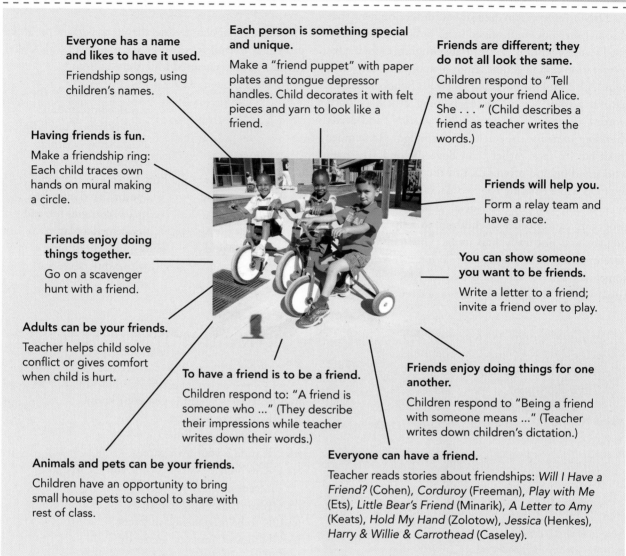

Everyone has a name and likes to have it used.

Friendship songs, using children's names.

Having friends is fun.

Make a friendship ring: Each child traces own hands on mural making a circle.

Friends enjoy doing things together.

Go on a scavenger hunt with a friend.

Adults can be your friends.

Teacher helps child solve conflict or gives comfort when child is hurt.

Each person is something special and unique.

Make a "friend puppet" with paper plates and tongue depressor handles. Child decorates it with felt pieces and yarn to look like a friend.

To have a friend is to be a friend.

Children respond to: "A friend is someone who ..." (They describe their impressions while teacher writes down their words.)

Animals and pets can be your friends.

Children have an opportunity to bring small house pets to school to share with rest of class.

Friends are different; they do not all look the same.

Children respond to "Tell me about your friend Alice. She . . . " (Child describes a friend as teacher writes the words.)

Friends will help you.

Form a relay team and have a race.

You can show someone you want to be friends.

Write a letter to a friend; invite a friend over to play.

Friends enjoy doing things for one another.

Children respond to "Being a friend with someone means ..." (Teacher writes down children's dictation.)

Everyone can have a friend.

Teacher reads stories about friendships: *Will I Have a Friend?* (Cohen), *Corduroy* (Freeman), *Play with Me* (Ets), *Little Bear's Friend* (Minarik), *A Letter to Amy* (Keats), *Hold My Hand* (Zolotow), *Jessica* (Henkes), *Harry & Willie & Carrothead* (Caseley).

FIGURE 14-15 A friendship unit can encourage children to express positive emotions while they use their cognitive, language, and motor skills to enhance their social development. (Photo © Cengage Learning)

people, as are those who paint and dance, write speeches, or create curriculum for children. Thinking in a different way and changing a way of learning or seeing something are all creative acts.

Definition and Steps

Creative thinking is a cognitive process, expressed by children in all developmental areas. Picture the two major ways of thinking as vertical and lateral. Vertical thinking involves learning more about something and tends to lead toward an answer. It is also known as **convergent thinking**, and it is used when asked, "What shape is this block?" Lateral thinking is a process used

to find the creative solution or unusual idea. Such **divergent thinking** tends to broaden the field of answers, as when responding to "how many different ways can you surprise your mother?"

Creativity engages certain parts of the brain. The left hemisphere controls the right side of the body and controls such operations as concrete thinking, systematic planning, language, and mathematical skills; what we might call the more rational and cognitive parts of thinking. It is the right brain that engages in more spontaneous ideas and thinks in nonverbal, intuitive ways. Of course, we need both sides to engage to develop, but clearly, the right side is the creative information processor.

The process of creating follows a predictable four-step pattern, although there are as many variations on the theme as there are children and art experiences.

1. *Preparation.* Gathering materials and ideas to begin.
2. *Incubation.* Letting ideas "cook" and develop.
3. *Illumination.* The "a-ha" moment when everything gels; the "light bulb turning on."
4. *Verification.* When exhilaration has passed, and only time will confirm the effort.

Expression Through the Arts

Whether the sweeping motion of a brush onto an easel, pounding the fist into clay, or rhythmic scissoring, art is a physical activity. Art may be an individual experience, but in the early childhood classroom, it is a social one as well. Children learn how to interact with others when sharing materials, taking turns, and exchanging ideas. Emotionally, children express their inner selves and work through feelings, both positive and negative, in their artwork. Indeed, art therapy has a long history in helping therapists understand children. Art reflects what the child knows; planning and organizing, revising and finishing are all cognitive tasks. Moreover, early childhood professionals can encourage children to talk about their processes, which makes creating art a language activity as well.

Rhoda Kellogg, in her seminal work on children's art (1969) described the developmental stages of art after having analyzed literally millions of piece of children's art from around the world over a 20-year period. Briefly, they are:

- *Placement stage:* Scribble, ages 2–3
- *Shape stage:* Vague shapes, ages 2–4; actual shapes, ages 3–5
- *Design stage:* Combined shapes, ages 3–5; mandalas and suns, ages 3–5
- *Pictorial stage:* People, ages 4–5; beginning recognizable art, ages 4–6; later recognizable art, ages 5–7

Children's artistic creations may be similar in its stages (see Figure 14-16) but are unique expressions of each child's creativity.

The roots of creativity reach into infancy because it is every individual's unique and creative process to explore and understand the world.

- Infants' creativity is seen in their efforts to touch and move.
- Toddlers begin to scribble, build, and move for the pure physical sensation of movement.

- Young preschoolers create as they try for more control, such as scribbling with purpose or bobbing and jumping to music.
- Older preschoolers enjoy their budding mastery. Their drawings and structures take on some basic forms, and they repeat movements deliberately while dancing or when pretend fighting.
- Five to 8 year olds have advanced motor control and hand–eye coordination, so their drawings are representational and pictorial, their dramatic play more cohesive.

Creativity is a process; as such, it is hard to define. As one becomes involved in creative activity, the process and the product merge. The young child is open to experience, exploring materials with curiosity and eagerness. It is delightful to watch confident children elaborate in their creative expression with increasing detail and using more complex forms.

Art Education

When Howard Gardner began his studies of intelligence (see Chapters 4 and 12), he became intrigued with artistic capacity. Project Zero is a program that has studied intelligence, the arts, and education for the past 30 years (Gardner, 1993) and has identified four key ideas about art education:

1. In the early childhood years, production of art ought to be central. Children need to work directly with the materials.
2. The visual arts ought to be introduced by someone who can think visually or spatially. An early childhood education team ought to be diverse enough to have someone with this intelligence on staff.
3. Whenever possible, artistic learning should be organized around meaningful projects. Both the project

When children have a chance to create, with permission to use an abundance of materials, the results are creative.

© Cengage Learning

Stages of Children's Art

1. Scribbling:

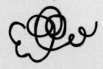

2. Drawing a single shape:

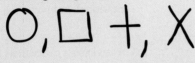

3. Combining single shapes into designs:

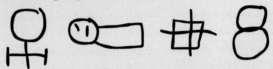

4. Drawing mandalas, mandaloids, and sun figures:

5. Drawing a human figure with limbs and torso:

FIGURE 14-16 Children's art follows a sequence of stages. (From Schirrmacher. *Art and Creative Development for Young Children*, 4e. Copyright © 2002 Cengage Learning, Inc. Reprinted by permission. www.cengage.com/permissions.)

approach and emergent curriculum address this (see Chapter 10).

4. Artistic learning must entail emotional reflection and personal discovery along with a set of skills. Integration of development is encouraged.

Taken together, these observations help teachers create developmentally appropriate art activities. If you work with infants or toddlers, be sure to help children explore materials and places with all their senses, and expect scribbling by 15 to 20 months. Young preschoolers work in manipulating tools and materials, discovering what can be done and needing lots of repetition. Do not expect much concern about the final product. By 4 to 6 years of age, children's art becomes more symbolic and planned; more detailed work with forms and shapes may be seen. Children become interested in what they are doing and how it turns out.

Giving art its place in early childhood curriculum requires space, time, and attention. An art center (Schirrmacher & Fox, 2009) is:

1. An artist's studio.
2. Conveniently located and easily accessible.

3. Well-stocked with developmentally appropriate materials.
4. Orderly and organized.
5. A place with rules and limits.

Basic categories of art materials should include tools for mark making; papers in a variety of shapes, sizes, and textures; modeling and molding materials, such as play dough and clay; items for cutting, fastening, and attaching, such as scissors and string; items for painting; and collage items (see Chapter 9 and Figure 14-17).

Merely labeling an activity as art is no guarantee that the activity has artistic merit. Some activities masquerade as creative and should be avoided. As Schirrmacher (2009) states:

> Crafts are often given as holiday gifts. Most parents would be delighted to receive a paperweight or pencil holder constructed by their child. Although it is important to please parents, it is equally important to meet the creative needs of children. Providing for child input, planning, decision making, and creative processing guarantees that each finished product will be as unique and individual as the child who produced it.

Taking the time to talk with families about children's art and creativity helps them appreciate the unique nature of children's creations.

Creative Skills

There are six characteristics common to creative people; fostering these skills encourages creativity.

Flexibility and Fluency

Flexibility and **fluency** are dual skills that allow for creative responses. Flexibility is the capacity to shift from one idea to another; fluency is the ability to produce many ideas. "How many ways can you move from one side of the room to another?" is a question likely to produce many different ideas, one example of fluency. Children are learning flexibility when they must think of another way to share the wagons when taking turns does not work.

Sensitivity

Creativity involves a high degree of sensitivity to one's self and one's mental images. Creative people, from an early age, seem to be aware of the world around them: how things smell, feel, and taste. They are sensitive to

---

Adapting Art for Children with Special Needs

___ **Visual:**

Verbally describe materials and how they might be used.

Provide a tray that outlines the visual boundaries.

Offer bright paint to contrast with paper.

Go slowly and encourage children to manipulate the items as you talk.

___ **Auditory:**

Model the process, facing the child and using gestures for emphasis.

Use sign language as needed.

___ **Physical:**

Make sure there is a clear path to the art center.

Provide adaptive art tools such as chunky crayons or large markers.

Provide double ambidextrous scissors so you can help, or a cutting wheel.

Velcro can be attached to marking instruments or paintbrushes.

Use contact paper for collage or glue sticks instead of bottles.

___ **Attention-deficit and/or behavioral:**

Provide children with their own materials and workspace, minimizing waiting and crowding.

Offer materials like play dough to express feelings and energy.

Limit children to few choices rather than overwhelming them with everything in the art center.

FIGURE 14-17 The value of art activities for children with special needs cannot be overemphasized.

mood, texture, and how they feel about someone or something. Creative people notice details; how a pine-cone is attached to the branch is a detail the creative person does not overlook.

A special aspect of this skill is sensitivity to beauty. Also known as **aesthetics**, this sensitivity to what is beautiful is emphasized in some programs (such as Reggio Emilia) and some cultures (such as tokonoma, an alcove dedicated to display, in Japanese homes). Teachers can ask the families of children in their care about special places, objects, and rituals that celebrate beauty and help children acquire an aesthetic interest in their environment.

Children have an awareness of and a value for their natural environment and what is aesthetically pleasing. Creative children take delight and satisfaction in making images come to life with their careful perspective and observations (see Figure 14-18). Their creative response is in the way they paint a picture, dance with streamers, or find a solution to a problem.

Imagination/Originality

Imagination is a natural part of the creative process. Children use their imagination to develop their creativity in several ways:

- *Role-Playing.* In taking on another role, children combine their knowledge of the real world with their internal images. The child becomes a new character and that role comes to life.
- *Image Making.* When children create a rainbow with a hose or with paints, they are adding something of their own to their understanding of that visual image. In dance, children use their imagination as they pretend to be objects or feelings, images brought to life.
- *Constructing.* In building and constructing activities, children seem to be re-creating an image they have about tall buildings, garages, or farms. In the process of construction, however, children do not intend that the end product resemble the building itself. Their imagination allows them to experiment with size, shape, and relationships.

A Willingness to Take Risks/Elaboration

People who are willing to break the ordinary mindset and push the boundaries in defining and using ordinary objects, materials, and ideas are creative people. They take risks. Openness to thinking differently or seeing things differently is essential to creativity.

When children create, they are revealing themselves. Art, for instance, is a form of cultural communication,

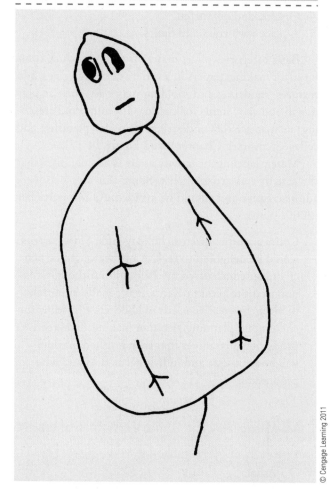

© Cengage Learning 2011

FIGURE 14-18 Sensitivity to one's own mental images, such as perceiving direction and movement, are part of creativity in the young child. A 5½-year-old sketched how a pet rat looked from below after picking it up often and watching it run on its exercise wheel.

one of the basic language skills children need to participate in a multicultural world. Increasing opportunities for creative expression allows for nonverbal response and success without directions. It encourages children (and families) to share themselves in enjoyable ways. It is, therefore, a good way to teach about cultures and learn about each other in a relaxed, accepting atmosphere.

Self-esteem is a factor in risk-taking because people who are tied to what others think of them are more likely to conform rather than follow their intuitive and creative impulses. People usually do not like to make mistakes or be ridiculed; therefore, they avoid taking risks. When a child is relaxed and not anxious about being judged by others, creativity is expressed.

Using Self as a Resource

Creative people who are aware of themselves and confident in their abilities draw on their perceptions, questions, and feelings. They know they are their richest source of inspiration. Those who excel in creative productivity have a great deal of respect for themselves, and they use the self as a resource.

Gathering Experience

Children need experience to gain skills in using materials creatively. They must learn how to hold a paintbrush before they can paint a picture; once they know *how* to paint, they can be creative in *what* they paint. Teachers of young children sometimes overlook the fact that children need competence with the tools to be creative with them. A sensitive, individual demonstration on proper use of a watercolor brush, sandpaper, or ink roller can expand a child's ability to create and eliminate needless frustration and disappointment that results in dashed-off work and giving up. The teachers of Reggio Emilia, for instance, demonstrate how to use the tools so that the children can then make outstanding creations. Anecdotes from highly accomplished people in creative endeavors (pianists, mathematicians, Olympic swimmers) highlight the value of long-term systematic instruction in a sort of apprenticeship with inspiring teachers as well as parents who are committed to assist. Vygotsky's scaffolding applies in the arts and can provide the initial palette of creative activities so that children can dabble and become experienced. When the skill of the medium is mastered, the child is ready to create.

Effective Approaches to Curriculum for Creative Growth

Considerations

To encourage creative development, follow these eight tips:

1. *Provide continuous availability, abundance, and variety of materials,* as is done in Reggio Emilia (see Chapter 10). Although you may not have a special art teacher (atelierista), you can create a studio-like area stocked with art materials and provide a more experienced adult that can help children excel in creating.

2. *Give children regular creative opportunities to experience and the skill necessary to be creative.* Children need frequent occasions to be creative to function in a highly creative manner.

3. *Encourage divergent thinking.* Do not interfere. Once you have presented the materials, try to forget how

Offer many materials to create an open-ended art center.

you intended them to be used. When there are no "right" or "wrong" answers, children are free to create. Avoid models, making things for children to copy. It insults children and can make them feel inadequate in the face of something you can do so much better.

4. *Help foster conversation on issues and seeking solutions to problems:*

Teacher: How do you think we could share the swings?

David: The kids who give me a turn can come to my birthday party.

Sabrina: No. We will have to make a waiting list.

Xenia: Only girls can use the swings. The boys can have all the cars.

Frederico: Buy a new swing set.

5. *Talk with young children about what they create.* Whether it is their artwork, table toy creations, or dramatic play sequences, talk helps creativity considerably. Rather than approach children's work with compliments, judgments, or even questions, Schirrmacher and Fox (2009) recommend that you:

- Allow children to go about their artistic discoveries without your comparing, correcting, or projecting yourself into their art.
- Shift from searching for representation in children's art to a focus on the abstract, design qualities.
- Use reflective dialogue.
- Smile, pause, and say nothing at first.

6. *Allow children to take the lead in their creative works from start to finish.* Adults do not need to take over at any point, particularly at the end with questions ("What is it?") or praise ("I like it!"). If a child seems to want more response, comment on the

color ("What a lot of blue you used"), texture ("I see wiggly lines all down one side"), or the child's efforts ("You really worked on this painting, huh?").

7. *Integrate creativity and learning in the classroom.* Early childhood theorists from Dewey and Piaget to Montessori and Malaguzzi (see Chapter 1) have advocated multisensory learning through experimentation and discovery.

8. *Teacher timing and attitudes stimulate creativity.* Do not delay; children want to see immediate results and act on their ideas now. Teacher timing and attitudes are important in stimulating creative development. Give plenty of time for a dramatic theme to develop, to pursue the props needed, or to find the players and audience.

Curriculum Planning for Creative Growth

An appropriate approach to creativity in the curriculum will emphasize children's self-expression in a number of ways.

Setting The setting provides an environment for creative endeavors—the center for activities, walls for displays, and areas for supplies. Children are motivated to try new ways to use materials when a project is flexible and challenging.

Indoors, every area has the potential for creativity:

- *The Arts.* A wide variety of materials and opportunities to choose how they are used is the basis of the creative process. An open table with a shelf of simple, familiar materials that can be combined in many ways leads to inventiveness. Two year olds like crayons, paste, and colored paper pieces; 3 to 5 year olds enjoy the addition of markers, string, hole punches and scissors, and tape. Older children can manage staplers, rulers, and protractors. Plenty of paper, such as recycled computer paper and cardboard, rounds out an open-ended, self-help art shelf. More organized art activities can also be offered, particularly for the preschool child, as long as the focus is on the child's process, rather than an end product or model. Avoid duplicated, photocopied, or mimeographed sheets, cut-and-paste activities, tracing patterns, coloring book pages, dot-to-dot books, and any art "project" that is based on a model for children to copy or imitate. As they approach the primary years, children become interested in what their creations look like and then are ready for practical help and advice on getting started.
- *Blocks/Manipulatives.* Children use their imagination when blocks become castles, tunnels, corrals,

The spirit of the children is allowed to bloom with time to contemplate and then create.

and swamps. These areas encourage creativity when children have enough materials of one kind to "really" make something; one long block is just not enough for a road. Also, creations have a sense of permanence when they are noted and kept. Sketching or photographing a block structure, attaching signs (including taking dictation) for the day, even rethinking clean up periodically shows how valuable these creations are.

- *Discovery/Science.* Building geoboards or making tangrams and cube art blend math and art. Art activities, such as color mixing, dissolving powder paint in water, and having water available with clay, can lead children to discover scientific principles. Natural materials can be used for rubbings, mobiles, and prints. Collecting materials during a "litter walk" makes interesting and informative collages.
- *Dramatic Play.* The dramatic arts offer opportunities for children to express themselves. Every "unit" in the dramatic play corner brings out children's interpretations of their world, whether it is a

house, shoe store, market, or a camp out, dinosaur cave, or space shuttle. Favorite books and stories can be acted out in the dramatic play area. Start with a simple nursery rhyme, and move to short stories with a few characters, simple plots, and manageable speaking lines.

- *Language/Library.* The book nook can be a place for teachers to ask open-ended questions for fun and pondering. "What if you were a twin? What would you wear or eat? Where would you live?" is a social creation; "If I were a hat, I would . . ." is a physical one.

Outdoors, creativity happens. Large, hollow blocks can become a stairway, and wagons and carts become fire engines, buses, doll carriages, moving vans, or trucks. Dancing with ribbons, making a banner for a parade, and rearranging equipment to make a tumbling or obstacle course all combine children's motor skills with music for creative growth. Sand, water, and mud provide a place for children to dig, haul, manipulate, and control in any number of ways.

Daily Schedule Teachers can apply their creativity to many routine situations. Children looking for a lost mitten organize a "hunt." Pretending to be vacuum cleaners, dump trucks, or robots gets the blocks picked up faster. Saying good-bye can be an exercise in creativity; the child can say, "See you later, alligator," and the adults can make up a silly response. Another day, the child and family member can reverse roles.

Creative "thinking games" can be part of any transition time. Because teachers are looking for unusual responses, children stay engaged and the game stays fresh over time:

- "What would happen if . . ." is the prompt; provide endings such as ". . . refrigerators ate food? . . . bath tubs could talk? . . . you could be invisible?"
- "Just Suppose" asks children to come up with endings to such short stories as "You found a magic flying carpet. Where would you go? What would happen?" or "You could be any animal."
- "Make It Better" uses a prop. The teacher brings a stuffed animal, race car, or other familiar toy. Pass it around carefully, and then ask, "How could we make it a better toy? What could we do to make it more fun to play with?"

Creativity does not respond well to the clock. Three issues—routines, transitions, and groups—must be handled so as not to interrupt children too often.

Children's creative expression in groups is enhanced through music (see Figure 14-19). Music is a universal language that develops every aspect of psychosocial development. It allows the expression of emotions and provides the opportunity to take roles as well as a delightful time to create with movement.

There is a kind of developmental sequence in the creative expression of music:

- The very young child is receptive to music, responding by listening, singing, and making noise with instruments.
- Preschoolers move to rhythmic music, often singing spontaneously in play and responding to repeated songs or repetitious phrasing. Their interest in musical instruments precedes their skill, and they often need instruments to be introduced and their proper use demonstrated.
- Older preschoolers and school-age children are more accurate in matching their pitch and tempo to the group or played music.

Music can set the tone at naptime, signal that a clean-up task is at hand, summon children to a group, and offer cultural experiences that are meaningful and enjoyable. For instance, New Year is often a noisy time; it can be celebrated by making ankle bells and doing a Sri Lankan dance or making a West Indian Conga line. In Waldorf schools, music is quite important. Children are engaged daily in eurhythmic exercises (developed by Steiner, see Chapter 1). Taught by a specialist, it is a kind of creative form that translates music and speech into movement. It is especially useful when teaching math (see TeachSource Video).

Focus on Skills The wide range of skills necessary for creative development can be supported throughout the early childhood program. The creative thinker is one who finds many ways to solve a problem, approach a situation, use materials, and interact with others. The teacher's role

---

TeachSource Video

Watch the TeachSource Video Case entitled "Learning Math through Music and Movement Activities in Early Childhood." After you study the video clip, view the artifacts, and read the teacher interviews and text, reflect on the following questions:

1. Music specialist Gwendolyn Jones states that music contains elements of math. What does she mean?

2. What kinds of art activities can support music?

3. How can teachers use the "fun" of music to teach math concepts?

Music and Movement: Stages and Activities

Stage of Musical Development	Appropriate Music/Movement Activity
2-year-olds	
Use their bodies in response to music	Bounce to music with different tempos
Can learn short, simple songs	Repetitive songs like "Itsy-Bitsy Spider" or "If You're Happy and You Know It"
Enjoy experimenting with sounds	Pound on milk cartons, oatmeal boxes
	Make shakers with gravel in shampoo bottles
3-year-olds	
Can recognize and sing parts of tunes	Select songs that include their names, such as "Do You Know the Muffin Man?"
Walk, run, jump to music	Use Ella Jenkin's recordings or try "Going on a Bear Hunt"
Make up their own songs	Start "Old MacDonald" and let them make their own additions; dance with scarves or use shakers to sing along with a child
4-year-olds	
Can grasp basic musical concepts like tempo, volume, pitch	Be a flying car, trees swaying in the wind, sing "Big, Bigger, Biggest" with variations
Love silly songs	Change "Where Is Thumbkin" to "Where Is Fi-fo" and improvise with their ideas
Prefer "active" listening	Accompany music with instruments, "Green Grass Grew All Around" with action
5- to 6-year olds	
Enjoy singing and moving with a group	Use a parachute to music
Enjoy call-and-response songs	Try "Did You Feed My Cow?"
Have fairly established musical preferences	Be sure to ask the group and use them in selecting music activities
7- and 8-year olds	
Are learning to read lyrics	Use large word charts
Enjoy musical duets with friends	Do partner games
	Children pick instruments in pairs

FIGURE 14-19 Creative experiences in music and movement engage the whole child and offer children integrated experiences throughout the curriculum (adapted from Schirrmacher & Fox, 2009).

is one of supporting imaginative use of equipment and using a multisensory approach to deepen learning.

Themes As teachers plan curriculum around a theme, they keep in mind what creative skills can be developed. Figure 14-20 charts the theme of "Green and Growing Things" and can bring out the child's creative nature as well as social responsibility by promoting ecological responsibility through the arts and nurturing an environmental and social ethic. Experiences in nature support creative learning in all developmental domains. They build community, offer multisensory experiences, and have been shown to reduce the severity of some symptoms of attention-deficit hyperactivity disorder (Wirth & Rosenour, 2012).

Creative themes can also revolve around other psychosocial issues.

- One teacher brought to her second grade class an activity from an acting workshop known as the "Emotion Map." After leading a discussion about imaginative maps (*The Hobbit, Harry Potter*), she listed their suggestions ("Slump Swamp," "Guilt Garage," "Boring Boulevard," "Bridge of Joy"). Rolling out a piece of paper on the floor, they began to sketch and talk. Once the map was made and elaborately decorated, the students used it to plot how they felt daily using a Post-it® they had drawn of themselves. New ideas cropped up: Children wanted "emotion maps" made into books for journaling and to plan for performances about different emotions.

- A preschool teaching team noticed the children's interest in shoes. They helped the children brainstorm what they knew about shoes and what they wanted to learn and do about them. The group built a shoe store; created a song and game called "Whose shoe are you?"; and made

Theme: Green and Growing Things

Outdoor Activities

1. Plant a garden in a corner of the yard, in an old barrel, or in a box flat on a table. Children learn through experimentation why some things grow and others don't. Make space for a compost heap.
2. Add wheelbarrows to the transportation toys.
3. Take a field trip to a farm, at planting time if possible, or a garden center.
4. Add gardening tools to the sand area. With proper supervision, children can see how trowels, hand claws, rakes, and shovels can be used to create new patterns in the sand and mud.
5. Plan group games that emphasize green and growing things. Older children could run wheelbarrow races, using one child as the wheelbarrow and another as a driver.
6. Play "musical vegetables" with large cards or chalk drawings. Dance with gourds, coconut instruments, sugar cane rhythm sticks.
7. Have children select a potted plant (have older children pick a partner), then have them draw, paint, or collage what they see. Let children look, talk and compare, then make another creation.

Indoor Activities

1. Leaf rubbings, printing with surplus apples, onions, carrots, potatoes, lemons, oranges, and celery, and painting with pine boughs are ways children can create art with green and growing things; make cornhusk dolls, avocado seed porcupines.
2. Book accessories might include blue felt forms for lakes, hay for corrals and barns.
3. In the manipulative area, match a photo of familiar plants with a sample of the plant. Add sorting trays with various kinds of seeds to count, feel, mix, and match. Match pictures of eggs, bacon, milk, and cheese with other animals from which they come.
4. In the science area, grow alfalfa sprouts and mung beans. Let children mix them in salads and feed to classroom pets. As the sprouts grow, children can chart the growth. This activity can lead to charting their own development, comparing it with when they were infants.
5. The dramatic play center can be transformed into a grocery store to emphasize the food we buy to eat, how it helps us, and why good nutrition is important. Other dramatic play units are a florist shop or nursery, stocked with garden gloves, seed packets, peat pots, and sun hats.
6. The language area can be stocked with books about how plants, baby animals, and children grow. In small groups, children can respond to "When I plant a seed . . . " or "When I was a baby I . . . Now I . . . " to stimulate creative expression.
7. Songs and fingerplays help focus on green and growing things, children's growth, and animals. "The Green Grass Grows All Around" can be sketched by a teacher so that children will have visual cues to each successive verse. A favorite fingerplay, "Way Up in the Apple Tree," can be adapted to a number of fruits and vegetables.

FIGURE 14-20 Creativity around the classroom. Creativity and problem solving may stem from the same source. Real-life experiences, such as planning and building a garden, expand to provide creative thinking and logic in the classroom.

elaborate "houses" out of old, donated adult shoes modeled after "I Know an Old Woman Who Lived in a Shoe." The project lasted nearly a month!

Curriculum for Spiritual Development

Spiritual development is rarely discussed in early childhood or developmental texts. In the United States, where the separation of church and state is mandated, the public classroom has avoided involvement in things spiritual or religious. Private schools are not under such legal restraints, and many (see Chapter 2) actively support or are sponsored by faith-based organizations. Still, the spiritual side of formal schooling is usually left to religious institutions and families.

Issues to Consider

Often adults tend to see children as not particularly spiritual. Without higher reasoning and abstract thinking skills, young children are seen as not able to have a spiritual life. Moreover, many think of spirituality solely in terms of religion; this narrow focus misses the mark

© Cengage Learning 2011

with children in the early years. By seeing children as faulty thinkers (because they cannot articulate or conceptualize like adults) or by focusing only on organized religion and its ways of explanation, we may overwhelm or overlook children's genuine spiritual experiences.

Some of the earliest contributors to the field have mentioned spiritual development. Froebel saw the child as having an innate spiritual capacity. Education was meant to build on the living core of the child's intrinsic spiritual capacity. Steiner developed the three spiritual dimensions of selfhood and felt that children of all levels of development were capable of spiritual experience. Montessori wrote (Wolf, 2000):

> If education recognizes the intrinsic value of the child's personality and provides an environment suited to spiritual growth, we have the revelation of an entirely new child whose astonishing characteristics can eventually contribute to the betterment of the world.

It would appear that "profound levels of spiritual reality are accessible even to the youngest human being.... These experiences typically involve unity, joy, mystery" (Dillon, 2000). Take, for instance, the children's awe as they see a banana slug inching its way up a redwood tree; or the wonder in their eyes at the many colors of autumn maple leaves; their gasp when they find a dead bird, or the sheer joy and outstretched arms (and tongues!) to catch snowflakes.

Saxton (2004) reminds us of the religious or spiritual influence on a child's cultural identity. Robert Coles (1990) conducted an inquiry of the spiritual life of children in the United States, Central and South America, Europe, the Middle East, and Africa. He concluded that children are "seekers, as young pilgrims well aware that life is a finite journey and as anxious to make sense of it as those of us who are farther along in the time allotted us." While Gardner did not commit to a spiritual intelligence per se, he did suggest an existential intelligence would be a useful construct in identifying the ability to perceive and consider issues and phenomena outside direct sensory experience (see Chapters 4, 10, and 12). Spiritual development in an early childhood program includes the child's deep experience with self and the world, with the mysterious and invisible, and with the joy and pain that real life offers (see DAP Box).

The Teacher's Role

Teachers are often unsure of their role in spiritual development. Juggling what is appropriate and lawful with what is respectful of diverse family values and affiliations is difficult. A teacher's identity and beliefs

DAP   Acknowledging the Spirit

As mentioned earlier, U.S. public education is mandated to keep issues of church and state separate, in order not to endorse a particular religion. At the same time, DAP encourages family traditions and priorities to have a place in early childhood education. And spiritual development is part of the psychosocial domain.

Early childhood programs address general spiritual development in these four ways:

1. *Teaching about right and wrong.* Caring adults contribute to children's moral education by encouraging integrity. Children need to learn issues of "right and wrong" in a caring setting, balancing their wishes with those of others. Erikson and Piaget both note the importance of these experiences for both cognitive and psychosocial domains. It is possible to educate children to respect self and others, to express generosity of spirit, and to develop compassion.

2. *Matters of death.* "For children . . . death has a powerful and continuing meaning" (Coles, 1990). Whether it be a class pet, an accident or injury to a classmate or family member, even a teacher's absence due to illness, children's curiosity about death is inevitable. For instance, a kindergarten pet rabbit died; the janitor had found it dead the night before. The group talked, asked questions, drew and painted pictures, made books and signs, and asked for stories and reassurance. The children were as interested in this experience as they were in anything else offered that week.

3. *Peace education.* Children need guidance (see Chapter 7) and a safe and peaceful place to solve problems nonviolently with their peers. At first, they require a great deal of adult support and input in negotiating their problems, and often, it is the adult who guides the discussion. A "Peace Table" is one tool used as part of the overarching approach to social interactions that encourages children to peacefully interact with each other. This method encourages children to accept diversity and to attempt to understand differing perspectives. This approach helps children to see all problems as solvable and scaffolds children in their attempts to "solve the problem." Within an environment where adults assist children to feel empowered to actively solve interpersonal problems, children quickly become peacemakers (Warford, 2011).

4. *Love of nature.* One way to connect with children spiritually is through a love of nature and appreciation of the environment. Give children the firsthand experiences of a seed sprouting a plant, a live animal to care for, a running stream to play in, and a sunset to watch, and they get closer to their spiritual side.

must be considered. Keep in mind the difference between nurturing spiritual growth and passing on a religion. As Elkind (1992) explains:

> Spirituality can be used in either a narrow sense or a broad one. In the narrow sense, spirituality is often used to indicate a particular set of religious beliefs. . . . Spirituality, however, can also be used in a much broader sense. Individuals who, in their everyday lives, exemplify the highest of human qualities such as love, forgiveness, and generosity might also be said to be spiritual. It is spirituality in the broad, nondenominational sense that I believe can be fostered by educational practice.

Families provide a vital ingredient in the development of children's spirituality. Working with families around spiritual issues is a delicate matter. Making clear your distinction between religion and spirituality helps parents see your priorities. Emphasize that you are thinking about the adults they may become and that you are trying to give them a framework to face the state of the world.

A child's spiritual growth can be measured in terms of his/her ability to trust, to give love willingly, and accept self and others. Families may disagree with the teaching of some of those concepts, but the dialogue is useful. In the end, teachers usually find that there is more agreement about these kinds of ideas than they expected. Once made clear, parents often have questions themselves about how to promote family spirituality.

Whether at home or in the classroom, spiritual nurturing does not happen according to schedule and does not entail a sense of teaching in the formal sense. "Spiritual nurturing can never be reduced to a set of techniques or a routine curriculum. It can only flow freely from the teacher's own inner essence and from his or her belief that each child is truly a spiritual being" (Wolf, 2000). Teachers and families have something to share—a way of setting the environment and the tone that opens up the process of self-knowledge, morality and relationship with others, and a reverence for life and spiritual experience.

Children as a Spiritual Resource

Children as a spiritual resource are active participants in their experience and learning. As the teacher plans, he or she must also be prepared to listen and sit back. "Interactions with children present us adults with the opportunity to regain a sense of connectedness, spontaneity, emotional sensitivity, philosophical wonder and mystery, and attentiveness to value that we have long since left behind"

(Dillon, 2000). Time to wonder, to be in awe, and to reflect need to happen and be in place in a program. A hurried or overscheduled program is unlikely to provide such times.

The basic curriculum of the early childhood program is to provide every child with repeated experiences of being loved, accepted, and understood, of finding people trustworthy and dependable, and of discovering the world to be a place that loves him/her and cares for him/her deeply. Spirituality is concerned with directly experiencing life via intuition and feeling. Early childhood educators can set the stage for these experiences in many ways (see Figure 14-21).

Special Topic: Nurturing Emotional Intelligence

Up until the early 1990s, intelligence, as defined by the IQ test, was considered the standard for success in school and in life. Whether this was determined by genetics or experience was the hot debate in psychological and educational circles. Then Daniel Goleman published *Emotional Intelligence* in 1995, which defined a new kind of intelligence and a new way of thinking about the ingredients for a successful life.

Emotional intelligence refers to "the capacity for recognizing our own feelings and those of others, for motivating ourselves, and for managing emotions well in ourselves and our relationships" (Goleman, 1995). His now-classic work proposed that the two different kinds of intelligence—intellectual and emotional—could express activities in different parts of the brain. Building on Gardner's theory of multiple intelligences (see Chapter 4), and the ideas of Saloney and Mayer (1990), Goleman fine-tuned these ideas.

Five basic emotional and social competencies define emotional intelligence (Goleman, 1995):

Self-awareness: Knowing what we are feeling in the moment and using those preferences to guide our decision-making; having a realistic assessment of our abilities and a well-grounded sense of self-confidence.

Self-regulation: Handling our emotions so that they facilitate rather than interfere with the task at hand; being conscientious and delaying gratification to pursue goals; recovering well from emotional distress.

Motivation: Using our deepest preferences to move and guide us toward our goals, to help us take initiative and strive to improve, and to persevere in the face of setbacks and frustrations.

Nurturing Spiritual Growth

Quiet Corner

Set aside a corner space or alcove, perhaps behind a shelf that holds the fish tank. Place a small table and chair where a child can sit alone, gaze at the water or out the window.

A Kindness Plant

Put a live plant next to a basket of artificial flowers. Each time a child receives a kindness, they put a flower in the plant.

The Peace Rose

Keep a lively silk rose in a vase within children's reach. Whenever two children have a quarrel, one of them, or a third child, collects the peace rose. Each child holds the rose while talking: Once they reach solution or simply get over it, together they put their hands on the stem of the rose and say, "We declare peace."

Guided Meditation

Have the children sit or lie down quietly and close their eyes. Lead them through a reflection, asking each child to think about his or her heart—the place where love lives.

The Garden

Plant seeds together, ask how things grow and how could a seed do that. Check as they sprout. Plant a button, a seed, and a penny—and see the power of the seed.

I Spy

Play the game of "I Spy" with the children you have observed helping others. "I spy someone who helped Danny clean up the paint he spilled."

The Universe Star

Make a star in your classroom. Taking turns, each child carries the star home, waits for a clear night, and goes outside at dark with a parent to look at the night sky. When the child brings back the star, take time as a class to talk about the wonder and size of the universe.

A Silence Game

At a time when the children are engaged and behaving well, give them a new challenge. Ask them to stop all talking and sit perfectly still for several minutes. Each time you initiate this activity, lengthen the time. When the time is up, children will report what they heard.

FIGURE 14-21 Curriculum ideas for nurturing the spirit (Wolf, 2000).

Empathy: Sensing what people are feeling, being able to take their perspective, and cultivating rapport and attunement with a broad diversity of people.

Social skills: Handling emotions in relationships well and accurately reading social situations and networks; interacting smoothly; using these skills to persuade and lead, negotiate and settle disputes, for cooperation and teamwork.

The ability to notice and label feelings in early childhood corresponds to Goleman's "self-awareness" dimension. Chapter 6 has suggestions for becoming a skillful observer. For instance, we can help young children produce a label for their feeling of anger or sadness by teaching them that they are having a feeling and that they can use a word to describe their angry feelings. We can ask them to "Use your words" only after we have helped them learn and find those specific words.

The appropriate expression of feelings is another skill children can learn in the first eight years if they have adults in their lives who can socialize effectively. Teachers who convey a simple, firm, consistent message assist in this learning. For example, acknowledging a child's right to feel anger while, at the same time, prohibiting expression of anger in destructive or hurtful ways shows

children that you know how to handle upsetting feelings or impulses and can teach them how to do it, too.

Conducting class meetings helps children deal with others' feelings (see Figure 14-11). Teachers guide children through a process that builds problem solving, compassion, and community. Helping children tolerate and appreciate how different people express their emotions leads to understanding and cooperation.

Perhaps the single most important intervention is you, the teacher, who is a confidant and a positive role model (see Chapter 5). Modeling how to deal with change, manage frustration and disappointment, and work to find agreement show children how to find and express emotional intelligence.

Since *Emotional Intelligence* was published, educators have embraced it. Early childhood programs have traditionally emphasized social and emotional learning (see Nursery Schools, Chapter 1); elementary and secondary schools began to develop character education, violence prevention, and antibullying programs worldwide. Analysis of 668 evaluations of students from preschool through high school who were enrolled in social emotional programs (Durlak & Weissber, 2005) showed improvement of 38 to 50 percent in achievement scores and grade-point averages. Additionally, misbehavior dropped, attendance rates rose, and more positive behavior occurred.

Goleman himself hopes that more programs expand their social and emotional programs and think of emotional intelligence as not just about an individual, but also about its influence on groups. "If EI were to become as widespread as IQ has become, and ingrained in society as a measure of human qualities, then, I believe, our families, schools, jobs, and communities would be all the more humane and nourishing" (Goleman, 2005). Early childhood education programs have already taken these steps.

Summary

LO 1 The psychosocial domain is the broadest developmental domain, encompassing affective elements of emotional, social, creative, and spiritual growth, emphasizing the development of a sense of self and identity. Psychosocial development is at the center of the early childhood curriculum. Planning for emotional, social, creative, and spiritual growth involves an understanding of how each develops in the young child and how they are interrelated. Curriculum development for psychosocial growth calls on teachers to play a supportive role, facilitating children's involvement with the materials and each other. Only then can children discover themselves, explore their relationships, develop the ability to use their imagination and resources, and explore deeper questions of self and spirit. Children learn many skills in these areas as they interact with each other, with adults, and in the environment.

LO 2 The central elements of children's emotional growth involve the development of emotions, the skills of dealing with feelings, handling change, exercising judgment, enjoyment of power, and resilience and effective approaches to curriculum that teach these skills.

LO 3 The central elements of children's social growth involve the development of social competence and peer relationships and the social skills of social intelligence and those learned with adults and children, both with peers and as an individual, and effective approaches for curriculum that teach these skills.

LO 4 The central elements of children's creative growth involve the development of creativity and its expression through the arts, as well as the creative skills of flexibility and fluency, sensitivity, imagination/originality, risk-taking, using self as a resource, and gathering experiences and effective approaches for curriculum that teach these skills.

LO5 The central elements of children's spiritual growth issues are the separation of church and state, matters of right/wrong, life/death, peace education, and nature as well as how children are spiritual resources themselves.

LO 6 Emotional intelligence is a special topic of psychosocial curriculum. Daniel Goleman published *Emotional Intelligence* in 1995, which defined a new kind of intelligence as the capacity for recognizing feelings of self and others and for managing emotions well within the self and in relationship to other people. Five basic competencies within emotional intelligence are self-awareness, self-regulation, motivation, empathy, and social skills.

Key Terms

psychosocial domain
affective
four "I"s
emotional intelligence
basic emotions
complex emotions
empathy
antipathy
positive stress
self-regulation

superhero
imaginary companions
resilience
social referencing
socialization
social competence
sociocentric
peer interactions
undifferentiated
unilateral

reciprocal
social skills
social cognition
social action
convergent thinking
divergent thinking
flexibility
fluency
aesthetics

Review Questions

1. Define the psychosocial domain and name the areas within it.
2. How can teachers help children articulate their feelings?
3. List some of the social skills that are learned in the major areas of the early childhood setting.
4. Write three examples of a child's divergent thinking and how teachers can encourage this type of creativity.
5. How can teachers nurture the spirit in nonsectarian environments?

Observe and Apply

1. How does your center promote positive self-concept? What else could be done?
2. Make behavioral definitions of emotions you think you will see in the children you teach. Observe the children; then check the accuracy of your definitions.
3. Taking turns and sharing equipment and materials are difficult for young children. Cite three examples you have seen in which children used their social skills to negotiate a turn. Was teacher intervention necessary?
4. Name five people you consider creative. Match their skills with those we have identified in early childhood. How are they similar? Different?
5. How do teachers in your setting plan for creativity? What place does such expression take in the priority of the school philosophy?
6. If spirituality includes the embodiment of the highest human qualities, name three and offer an idea of how to put this into the curriculum.

Helpful Websites

Collaborative for Academic, Social and Emotional Learning   **www.casel.org**

Creative Curriculum   **www.teachingstrategies.com**

Cultural Survival   **www.culturalsurvival.org**

Educators for Social Responsibility
www.esrnational.org

M.U.S.I.C.   **learningfromlyrics.org**

Youth Peace Literacy/Atrium Society
www.atriumsoc.org

Society for Myth and Tradition   **www.parabola.org**

Southern Poverty Law Center
www.teachingtolerance.org

The Education CourseMate website for this text offers many helpful resources and interactive study tools. Go to CengageBrain.com to access the TeachSource Videos, flashcards, tutorial quizzes, direct links to all of the websites mentioned in the chapter, downloadable forms, and more.

References

General

Berger, K. S. (2009). *The developing person through childhood and adolescence* (8th Ed). New York: Worth Publishers.

Berk, L. E. (2011). *Infants, children and adolescents* (7th Ed). Boston: Allyn & Bacon.

Booth-LaForce, C., et al. (2006). Attachment, self-worth, and peer-group functioning in middle childhood. *Attachment & Human Development*, 8(4), pp. 309–325.

Salmivalli, C., Ojanen, T., Haanpaa, J., & Peets, K. (2005). "I'm OK & you're not" and other peer-related schemas: Explaining individual differences in children's social goals. *Developmental Psychology*, 21(2), pp. 363–375.

York, S. (2003). *Roots and wings: Affirming culture in early childhood programs* (2nd Ed). St. Paul, MN: Redleaf Press.

Emotional Growth

Chua, A. (2011). *Battle hymn of the tiger mother.* New York: Penguin Books.

Cooper, R. M. (1992, November). The impact of child care on the socialization on African American children. Paper presented at the NAEYC Annual Conference, New Orleans, LA.

Dulak, J. A., & Weissber, R. P. (2005). A major meta-analysis of positive youth development programs. Presentation at annual meeting of American Psychological Association, Washington, D.C.

Dweck, C. (2006). *Mindset.* New York: Ballantine Books.

Galinsky, E. (2010). *Mind in the making: The seven essential life skills every child needs.* New York: HarperCollins Books.

Goleman, D. (1995). *Emotional intelligence.* New York: Bantam Books.

Goleman, D. (2005). Introduction to the tenth anniversary edition. In *Emotional Intelligence.* New York: Bantam Books.

Hoffman, E. (2004). *Magic capes, amazing powers: Transforming superhero play in the classroom.* St. Paul, MN: Redleaf Press.

Mayr, T., & Ulrich, M. (2009). Social-emotional well-being and resilience of children in early childhood settings. *Early Years: Journal of International Research and Development*, 29(1), pp. 45–57.

Pawlina, S., & Stanford, C. (2011, September). Preschoolers grow their brain: Shifting mindsets for greater resiliency and better problem solving. *Young Children*, 66(5), pp. 30–35.

Rothbart, M. K., & Rueda, M. R. (2005). The development of effortful control. In *Developing individuality in the human brain: A tribute to Michael Posner.* Washington, D.C.: American Psychological Association.

Social Growth

Browne, K. W., & Gordon, A. M. (2009). *To teach well.* Upper Saddle River, NJ: Pearson.

Copple, C., & Bredekamp, S. (Eds.). (2009). *Developmentally appropriate practice in early childhood programs serving children from birth through age 8* (3rd Ed.). Washington, D.C.: NAEYC.

Derman-Sparks, L., & Olsen Edwards, J. (2010). Anti-bias education for young children and ourselves. Washington, D.C.: NAEYC.

Gordon, A. M., & Browne, K. W. (1996). *Guiding young children in a diverse society.* Boston, MA: Allyn and Bacon.

Hawkins, J. D., Kosterman, R., Catalano, R. F., Hill, K. G., & Abbott, R. D. (2008). Effects of social development intervention in childhood 15 years later. *Archives of Pediatrics and Adolescent Medicine*, 162(12), pp. 1133–1141.

Kostelnik, M. J., Whiren, A. P., Soderman, A. K., Stein, L. C., & Gregory, K. (2008). *Guiding children's social development and learning* (6th Ed.).Clifton Park, NY: Delmar Cengage.

Paley, V. G. (1992). *You can't say you can't play.* Cambridge, MA: Harvard University Press.

Porro, B. (1996). *Talk it out: Conflict resolution in the elementary classroom.* Alexandria, VA: Association for Supervision and Curriculum Development.

Rushton, S. (2011, February). Neuroscience, early childhood education and play: We are doing it right! *Early Childhood Education Journal*, 39, pp. 89–94.

Rushton, S., Juola-Rushton, A., & Larkin, E. (2010, November). Neuroscience, play and early childhood education: Connections, implications and assessment. *Early Childhood Education Journal*, 37, pp. 351–361.

Thompson, R. (2001, Spring-Summer). Development in the first years of life. *The Future of Children*, 11(1), pp. 20–33.

Creative Growth

Kellogg, R. (1969). *Analyzing children's art.* Palo Alto, CA: Mayfield Publishing.

Lopez-Morgan, C. (2002). *Creative arts for the young child.* Cupertino, CA: De Anza College.

Schirrmacher, R., & Fox, J. (2009). *Art and creative development for young children* (6th Ed). Clifton Park, NY: Thomson Delmar Learning.

Wirth, S., & Rosenow, N. (2012, January). Supporting whole-child learning in nature-filled outdoor classrooms. *Young Children*, 76(1), pp. 42–48.

Spiritual Growth

Coles, R. (1990). *The spiritual life of children*. Boston, MA: Houghton-Mifflin.

Dillon, J. J. (2000, Winter). The spiritual child: Appreciating children's transformative effects on adults. *Encounter: Education for Meaning and Social Justice*, 13(4).

Elkind, D. (1992, Spring). Spirituality in Education. *Holistic Education Review.*

Fitzpatrick, J. G. (1991). *Something more: Nurturing your child's spiritual growth*. New York: Viking Press.

Saxton, R. R. (2004). A place for faith. In A. Gordon and K. W. Browne (Eds.), *Beginnings and beyond* (6th Ed). Clifton Park, NY: Thomson Delmar Learning.

Saxton, R. R., & McMurrain, M. K. (2002). *Spiritual diversity in the classroom*. Atlanta, GA: Georgia State University Research Project.

Wolf, A. D. (2000, January). How to nurture the spirit in nonsectarian environments. *Young Children*, 55(1).

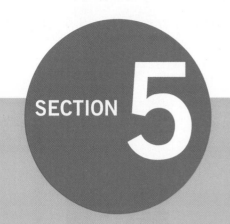

SECTION **5**

How Do We Teach for Tomorrow?

© Cengage Learning

© Cengage Learning

15

Issues and Trends in Early Childhood Education: Four Themes

Learning Objectives

LO1 Recognize and understand how changes in education are historically linked to social reforms.

LO2 Describe the importance of childhood and what factors diminish children's lives in today's society.

LO3 Articulate how the values of family and school are translated in today's world.

LO4 Examine how professionalism is expressed through standards for children, teacher preparation, and advocacy.

naeyc Standards For Professional Development

The following NAEYC Standards for Initial and Advanced Early Childhood Professional Preparation are addressed in this chapter:

Standard 1 Promoting Child Development and Learning

Standard 2 Building Family and Community Relationships

Standard 4 Using Developmentally Effective Approaches to Connect with Children and Families

Standard 5 Using Content Knowledge to Build Meaningful Curriculum

Standard 6 Becoming a Professional

Field Experience

naeyc Code of Ethical Conduct

These are the sections of the NAEYC Code of Ethical Conduct that apply to the topics in this chapter:

I-1.1   To be familiar with the knowledge base of early childhood care and education and to stay informed through continuing education and training.

P-1.8   We shall be familiar with the risk factors for and symptoms of child abuse and neglect, including physical, sexual, verbal and emotional abuse, and physical, emotional, educational, and medical neglect. We shall know and follow state laws and community procedures that protect children against abuse and neglect.

P-1.9   When we have reasonable cause to suspect child abuse or neglect, we shall report it to the appropriate community agency and follow up to ensure that appropriate action has been taken. When appropriate, parents or guardians will be informed that the referral will be or has been made.

I-2.2   To develop relationships of mutual trust and create partnerships with the families we serve.

I-2.3   To respect the dignity and preferences of each family and to make an effort to learn about its structure, culture, language, customs, and beliefs to ensure a culturally consistent environment for all children and families.

I-4.3   To work through education, research, and advocacy, toward an environmentally safe world in which all children receive health care, food, and shelter, are nurtured; and live free from violence in their home and their communities.

1-4.6   To promote knowledge and understanding of young children and their needs. To work toward greater social acknowledgement of children's rights and greater social acceptance of responsibility for the well-being of all children.

Introduction: Four Themes Revisited

Early childhood education has undergone remarkable changes in the past 50 years, evolving from being an option for middle class preschool children to a necessity for millions of families with children from infancy through the primary years. Such a transformation is a reflection of the economic, social, and political climate of the times, as well as research in child development and early education. Issues of today and trends for tomorrow grow out of the problems and solutions of the past. In the 1960s, social action and the War on Poverty resulted in the creation of Head Start programs and brought national attention to early childhood education. In the 1970s, families were affected by the job market, the end of the Vietnam War, an energy crisis, inflation, rising divorce rates, and the feminist movement. All of these factors led more women into the workplace rather than remaining in the home. The 1980s meant further budget cuts and reduced services for children and families, and many children were now in group care for most of their waking hours. Child abuse became a national cause for alarm. As the century ended, charter schools and homeschooling gained popularity, the result of failed educational reform. The quality and cost of programs for young children over the years has become a national issue.

To date, many of these issues are unresolved. Due to lack of funding, Head Start and Early Start can enroll only a small percentage of the children who need the programs. Government-mandated standards and testing are pressuring programs to put more emphasis on academics. Professionalism is making its way into early childhood certification. All these issues are making inroads into early childhood programs at every level.

It seems appropriate to discuss current issues in light of the history of the early childhood profession because they influence practices and policies of today. Look back at Chapter 1: The events and circumstances of the times described in that chapter reflected the issues and trends of the times, as they do today. Figure 15-1 highlights some of those influences.

For all its diverse and varied past, early childhood education has had a consistent commitment to four major themes:

- *Ethic of social reform:* the quality of child care and national education reform.

Who are the children of tomorrow, and how do we meet their needs?

- *Importance of childhood:* children's health and welfare and the changes in family life.
- *Transmission of values:* challenges presented by the media culture, violence, disaster, and diversity.
- *Professionalism:* standards for children's programs, teacher preparation, ethics, and advocacy in the early childhood field.

Ethic of Social Reform

The first theme suggests that schooling for young children leads to social change and improvement. Maria Montessori, the McMillan sisters, Patty Smith Hill, and Abigail Eliot were pioneers in improving children's lives through a comprehensive approach to education. Today, Marion Wright Edelman, creator of the Children's Defense Fund, is continuing the efforts started nearly 100 years ago. Louise Derman-Sparks and colleagues

A Web of Influences

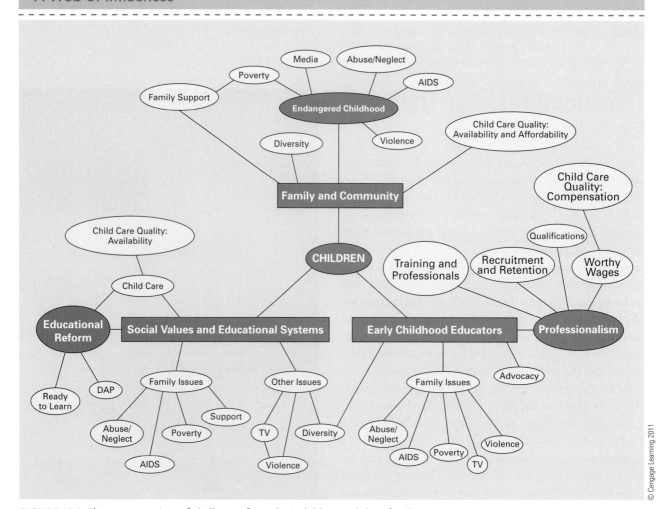

FIGURE 15-1 There are a variety of challenges for today's children and their families.

enlarged the issue when they published the *Anti-Bias Curriculum* and challenged our thinking about bias as a social issue for young children.

Today the ethic of **social reform** refers to an expectation that education has the potential for significant social change and improvement. This is demonstrated in the following discussions on child care, national education legislation, and developmentally appropriate practice (DAP).

Child Care

- For almost 20 years, more than 60 percent of women with young children have been in the labor force (Children's Defense Fund, 2010).
- Only 3 percent of the infants eligible are enrolled in Early Head Start, and 50 to 67 percent of those eligible for Head Start are enrolled (Children's Defense Fund, 2008).

- In 2005, 58 percent of 3 to 5 year olds were enrolled in a center-based, out-of-home child care program. In 2009, the number rose to 63.5 percent (U.S. Census Bureau, 2010).

The significant increase in enrollment in child care centers over the past 40 years, underscored by the demographic facts, firmly establishes the need for child care. Program quality, costs, and an unstable workforce continue to be the primary issues that negatively affect child care throughout the country. (See Chapter 2 for more discussion on child care.)

Program Quality

The key word is *quality*—the terms *good quality* and *high quality* identify specific features in early childhood programs as described in Chapter 2. In that chapter, three broad-based studies that examined quality are the High/Scope Perry Preschool Project, the Abecedarian Project, and the Chicago Child-Parent Centers study. All three

Pay Now or Pay Later?

Early intervention programs, such as the Perry Preschool Project, the Abecedarian Project, and the Chicago Child-Parent Centers, have been shown to have significant lasting effects for children at risk. These programs provided positive learning experiences and growth-promoting environments at a crucial time when the brain's circuits were being built. As a result, a strong foundation was created and served to support more complex brain structures rather than leave the children with a weak architectural foundation that would not support healthy brain growth (Shonkoff, 2002). Positive outcomes for the children of these three programs varied, but they included higher levels of education, socioeconomic status, better earning prospects, less teen parenthood, lower drop-out rates and grade retention, less incarceration, and less reliance on welfare.

The impact to society was noted by a number of economists who understand the dollars-and-cents benefits of investing in early childhood education now instead of funding remedial programs later in the child's life. Some of the most impressive arguments for early childhood intervention services come from one of the most highly regarded economists of our time, Nobel Laureate James Heckman. To support the assertion that the longer society waits to intervene in the lives of at-risk children, the greater the cost in the future, Heckman (2007) noted:

1. There is a "growing underclass" of youth who neither go to school nor work;
2. Seventy-five percent of youth who apply for military service are rejected because of inadequate cognitive abilities, criminal records, or obesity; and
3. Twenty percent of the American workforce is illiterate.

From an economic viewpoint alone, early intervention more than pays for itself by influencing children's academic achievement and fostering a skilled and knowledgeable workforce.

One noteworthy point made by Heckman (in Zigler et al., 2011) is that early intervention programs have a much higher rate of economic return than other strategies used later in life such as lower student–teacher ratios, public job training programs, adult literacy programs, and convict rehabilitation services. The early childhood field can be grateful that what we have known for a long time is being acknowledged on the national stage.

Questions

1. Why do you think Heckman and others economists are looking at the successful results of early childhood intervention programs? What effect will this have on your role as an early childhood professional?
2. What does neuroscientist Shonkoff mean when he says, "It's better to get it right for the first time than to try to fix it later." Do you agree or disagree with that statement?

The quality of a child care program is directly related to the experience and training of the teachers.

provide evidence that quality care can have far-reaching benefits for children. There is a dollar-and-cents benefit as well, given the fact that at-risk preschoolers who attend high-quality early childhood programs are more successful in school and likely to be employed, have less drug abuse cases, and fewer arrests.

These studies, among others throughout the years, also indicate that quality is a function of trained teachers and caregivers, group size, low teacher–child ratios, parent involvement, and more comprehensive services to children and their families.

The NACCRRA study of parental concerns, also cited in Chapter 2, found that parents *assumed* caregivers were trained to work with young children and that most child care programs were regularly inspected (National Association of Child Care Resources and Referral Agencies, 2008). However, in 2008, less than 10 percent of all child care centers and less than 1 percent of family child care homes were accredited and therefore were not being inspected on a regular basis (Children's Defense Fund, 2008).

Program Costs

The cost of quality is directly related to the needs of the families served by the specific program, the added costs of helping families connect with the right resources and providing the necessary comprehensive services, and fee reductions and financial aid for low-income families. The average cost of full time child care at a center for an infant is $4,500 to $18,700. The average cost for a 4 year old in a family child care home is $3,700 to $11,400 and the average cost for a school-age child in a center part time is $2,100 to $10,000 (NACCRRA, 2010). In 36 states, the annual cost of center-based care for a 4 year old exceeds that of the annual in-state tuition at a public four-year college (Children's Defense Fund, 2010). Families who live at or near the poverty line and middle income families are hard-pressed to afford these fees.

Cost and quality are significantly related to staff: how many adults there are compared with the number of children in a class; whether the salaries and benefits provide incentive for teachers to be retained for a number of years; and the level of staff education and training and their years of experience. In 2008, less than 10 percent of all child care centers and less than 1 percent of all family child care homes were accredited (Children's Defense Fund, 2010). Twenty percent of center teachers and 43 percent of assistant teachers had a high school diploma or less (NACCRRA, 2011). The difficulties of recruiting and retaining qualified staff for good early childhood programs profoundly affects program quality and costs and continues to be a serious issue facing the early childhood field.

The employee turnover rate for child care centers has hovered around 30 percent for a number of years. Centers often find it difficult to recruit and hire qualified replacement staff for those who leave. This is understandable when most centers do not provide health insurance or a living wage for their employees. The mean hourly wage for child care workers in 2009 was $9.88; for preschool teachers it was $16.61 per hour, and for kindergarten teachers, $34.24 per hour. Elementary school teachers earn $37.02 per hour (American Federation of Teachers, 2011).

The lack of quality child care that is affordable and accessible, that provides wages and benefits worthy of the early childhood profession, and that attracts an experienced and educated workforce has created a national crisis that still needs to be resolved.

Education Reform

One of the primary functions of the public school system in the United States is to prepare students for productive roles in society—to produce skilled workers who will enter the job market and contribute to a healthy, competitive economy worldwide. To achieve that goal, a number of reforms have emerged on the national agenda.

No Child Left Behind

In 2002, the Elementary and Secondary Education Act of 1965 was reauthorized to close the achievement gap between disadvantaged and minority students and their peers. By 2005, this act, known as the No Child Left Behind Act (NCLB), has reshaped American's public school culture for the past decade.

NCLB has been controversial because of its attempts to create new accountability measures and bring all children to grade level in math and reading by 2014. Critics stated concerns that the narrow focus on reading, literacy, and math creates an imbalanced curriculum that loses focus on the whole child. Critics also question whether teachers will be forced to "teach to the test" in order for a school to avoid sanctions, which seem to disproportionately impact the most seriously disadvantaged schools. Overall, there is the threat of facing sanctions without adequate resources or support to meet the requirements that are imposed by this plan. As of this writing, the Obama administration is developing ways to be more flexible in meeting the deadline of 2014 by allowing the states to design their own accountability and improvement programs (U.S. Department of Education, 2012). NCLB's legacy to narrow achievement gaps will likely remain for the foreseeable future, and we still have a culture of assessment, overtesting, and unfunded mandates. Perhaps initiatives like the following will become more common.

Race to the Top

In 2009, the Obama administration created a competitive grant program to states that create and adopt common academic standards for kindergarten to twelfth grade. Race to the Top was created to spur systemic reform by recognizing innovative approaches to teaching and learning. Through Race to the Top's Early Learning Challenge, nine states were awarded funds to increase the number of children at risk in high quality early childhood programs, design and implement high quality learning programs and services, and ensure that assessment procedures meet the National Research Council's early childhood standards. The challenge for the states is to close the school readiness gap, build a statewide system of high quality early learning programs, raise academic standards, and turn around low-performing schools (U.S. Department of Education, 2012).

Common Core State Standards

Under the aegis of the National Governors Association and the Council of Chief State School Officers, common standards for English language arts and mathematics have been developed for kindergarten to twelfth grade. Nearly all fifty states have adopted the Common Core State Standards (CCSS) to help students learn the knowledge and skills they need for college and work. The standards are clearly defined so that students know what is expected of them, and

How does education reform enhance the joy of learning?

parents and teachers can help them achieve success in school. Early childhood educators should monitor assessment and measuring procedures so that all of children's developmental domains are included in the curriculum.

School Readiness

Children need to start school ready to learn. They need to be physically, socially, emotionally, and cognitively ready and motivated to meet the challenges of kindergarten and beyond. Yet millions of children enter school without the background, support, and resources that foster their ability to learn. These children come from low-income families and from minority racial backgrounds and start kindergarten lagging behind their peers (Rouse et al., 2005).

The disparity among African American and Latino children and their white classmates is referred to as an achievement gap. At least one half of the achievement gap exists when children enter kindergarten. The larger the gap, the more difficult it is to achieve equality of learning for the children who enter school ill-prepared for the challenges (Shonkoff & Phillips, 2002). Poverty is the primary contributor to the achievement gap (Lee & Burkam, 2002) and is discussed further in this chapter.

Universal Preschool

Another example of the link between social and education reforms is the **universal preschool** movement. Early learning opportunities are unavailable to many children who could benefit from a quality early childhood program. This is especially true for low-income working families who would benefit the most from quality child care and are unable to afford it. There is a gap between the need and demand for quality child care and the government's willingness to fund it.

Universal preschool, called *preschool for all* in some areas, is an effort in many states to address this inequality. If successful, it would mean that there would be universal access to publicly funded, high quality preschool education for one or two years before kindergarten. More children who are at risk would have the early education to help them begin school ready to learn. Multiple studies by the National Institute for Early Education Research of state preschool programs found positive gains in children's math, language, and literacy learning (Barnett, 2010).

Forty states provided prekindergarten programs, primarily for 4 year olds, in 2010. In 2002, only 14 percent of American's 4 year olds were enrolled in state preschools. That number rose to 27 percent in 2010. The recession has put the growth of these schools in a holding pattern until more funding becomes available and created lower funding levels that affect the quality of the existing programs (Barnett et al., 2010).

Controversy about universal preschools centers on providing preschools for people who can afford it rather than just for low-income families; the high cost of providing quality programs; and the fear of imposing taxes to pay for the programs. Advocates cite the research that shows positive outcomes for children and families at risk; the potential for closing the achievement gap; and society's role in supporting all children's optimal learning opportunities.

Charter Schools

Reform efforts in the 1980s led to the creation of charter schools, which are public schools that have a specific mandate and that are governed by a group (often parents) or organization. The group operates under a legislative contract ("charter") with the state. Some charter schools focus on particular curriculum areas, such as arts or math; others may target low-income families; and others might follow an educational philosophy, such as the Waldorf Schools. The reviews of student performance in charter schools versus students in other public schools are mixed; some report higher gains for charter schools while others report little or no gains.

There are approximately 5,600 public charter schools. More than 50 percent of them serve children at the elementary school level. More than 500 new public charter schools opened in the 2011–2012 school year (National Center for Education Statistics, 2011). In New Orleans, more than 50 percent of the public schools students are enrolled in charter schools following a state take-over of education in the aftermath of Hurricane Katrina (National Center for Education Statistics, 2011).

Reform Strategies

To meet the needs of working parents and ensure that children are ready to learn, reform strategies need to:

1. Embrace the range of all early childhood programs with no distinction between child care and early childhood education;
2. Establish continuity between early childhood programs and the early elementary years;
3. *Create closer* relationships with early elementary grades for greater alignment so that curriculum, standards, and tests compliment and balance one another;
4. Address children's nonacademic needs so that they come to school physically, socially, and cognitively ready to learn;
5. Base programs on learning that is developmentally appropriate;
6. Initiate programs and policies that strengthen the family; and
7. Develop partnerships with the community and with businesses. Collaborate with other community agencies that service young children and their families to make better use of public funds and improve the quality of all programs.

Look back at the various reform initiatives and see how many of them address these issues.

Every child has the right to a full and wondrous childhood.

The Importance of Childhood

The second theme of early childhood is the importance and uniqueness of childhood. The notion rests on the concept of the child as a special part of human existence and, therefore, a valuable part of the human life cycle. When a society values its children, it takes the responsibility for providing a quality of life for them.

The impact of social changes in the past 40 years has been hardest felt by the children. The increase in the divorce rate; poverty and homelessness; and the dangerous effects of the media culture, drugs, and worldwide violence have thrust children into adult situations with adult troubles. Dual-parent careers and single working parents, together with the lack of extended families, have meant that children's behavior is not as closely monitored as it once was.

Childhood Stress

Experiences that produce stress in young children are often family related. Divorce, remarriage, a move to a new home, prolonged visits from a relative, and a new sibling are classic stress situations for children. Stress may also occur in families in which both parents pursue high-powered careers and children feel the need to live up to exceptional standards in academic achievement or sports proficiency. Apathetic parents, parents who ignore their children or have no time for them, and parents who push children into frantic schedules of activity also cause stress in their children.

Children respond to stress in many ways. Signs of stress include sleeping problems (such as nightmares or sleepwalking), depression, regression to the behavior of an earlier stage, aches and pains, acting out, eating problems, and overreactions, as well as medical problems (such as headaches, upset stomach, and bleeding ulcers).

Brazelton and Greenspan (2000), in response to the overwhelmed, stressed-out life of children and parents today, defined seven irreducible needs of children:

1. The need for ongoing nurturing relationships
2. The need for physical protection, safety, and regulation
3. The need for experiences tailored to individual differences

Teaching With INTENTION

Helping Children Cope with Stress

Strategies for coping with the various stages of stress include observing children, making time to talk with them individually, and working with them to find solutions.

Stage	Behavior	The Teacher Helps
Alarm	Feels arousal, fear, confusion Has swift mood changes	Notices when child is stressed Listens Offers words for child's feelings Is accepting of unpredictable behavior Reassures child of constant availability Alerts parents and other of child's state Takes preventative actions to lessen other stressful events
Appraisal	Attempts to understand the problem	Listens Offers age-appropriate explanations Helps child see situation more positively May make a simple list of problem Reassures that the problem will be solved Alerts other adults to the importance of the child's work
Search	Looks for coping strategy Selects from what is at hand	Listens Asks for the child's ideas Helps child list possible solutions Tells parents and others of child's solutions Demonstrates self-control and coping skills Encourages and enhances child's self-esteem
Implementation	Tries out a coping strategy; applies a solution to the problem	Listens Observes child's implementing a solution Gives support and feedback about relative success or failure of the plan Help child refine or revise strategy as needed Encourages child's efforts

When the teacher serves as a comforting resource to a child who is experiencing stress, the situation becomes more manageable. The teacher becomes an intentional role model for dealing with stress.

Think About This
1. How do you deal with stress?
2. Do you think these suggestions apply to you? Would you use them?

4. The need for developmentally appropriate experiences
5. The need for limit setting, structure, and expectations
6. The need for stable, supportive communities and cultural continuity
7. Protecting the future (on behalf of the world's children)

Stress is a natural part of life and is a factor in every child's development. It needs to be identified and addressed by the families, teachers, and other adults who care for them. Childhood stress is also discussed in Chapter 14. See the above "Teaching With Intention" Box for suggestions on dealing with childhood stress.

Child Abuse and Neglect

Every day, more than 2,000 children experience **child abuse** and child neglect. Infants are most likely to be abused. One third of all victims are younger than 4 (Children's Defense Fund, 2010). One third of abused and neglected children eventually victimize

How do we help children cope with stress?

their own children, perpetuating the cycle (Childhelp, 2012). These horrendous statistics tell us that child abuse and neglect are significant problems in this country.

A neglected child may be one whose waking hours are mostly unsupervised by adults, in front of the television or simply unconnected with—and unnoticed by—parents or an important caregiver. **Child neglect** takes other, more hazardous, forms, however. When the basic needs of adequate food, clothing, shelter, and health are unmet, parents are being neglectful. Failure to exercise the care that children need shows an inattention to and lack of concern for children. More than 70 percent of the reported child abuse in the United States is for neglect, 16 percent is physical abuse, and more than 9 percent is sexual abuse (Children's Defense Fund, 2010).

Signs of various forms of child abuse often indicate one or more types of abuse. According to Childhelp (2012), the most obvious signs are:

- *Signs of neglect:* unsuitable clothing for weather, dirty or unbathed, extreme hunger, and an apparent lack of supervision
- *Signs of physical abuse:* unexplained burns, cuts, bruises, or welts in the shape of an object; bite marks, antisocial behavior, problems in school, fear of adults
- *Signs of emotional abuse:* apathy, depression, hostility or stress, lack of concentration, eating disorders

- *Signs of sexual abuse:* inappropriate interest or knowledge of sexual acts, nightmares and bed-wetting, drastic changes in appetite, overcompliance or excessive aggression, fear of a particular person or family member

The residual effects of child abuse, which occurs at every socioeconomic, ethnic, cultural, religious, and educational level, are equally dramatic. Children who have been sexually abused are two-and-one-half times more likely to abuse alcohol and nearly four times more likely to become addicted to drugs than nonvictims. Children who experience abuse and neglect have a 59 percent chance of being arrested as a juvenile and are 25 percent more likely to become pregnant as a teenager (Childhelp, 2012).

Potential Solutions

A national call to action to increase public awareness and understanding of child abuse is under way. Standardized licensing procedures, upgrading of the certification of child care workers, and national **accreditation** of all preschools are some of the most frequently mentioned solutions to the problem. Helping parents identify what qualities to look for when placing their children in someone else's care is another way to prevent child abuse in centers. In 1996, NAEYC adopted a *Position Statement on the Prevention of Child Abuse in Early Childhood Programs and the Responsibilities of Early Childhood Professionals to Prevent Child Abuse.* The statement urges that early childhood programs in homes, centers, and schools adopt a set of policies based on guidelines such as:

- Employing adequate staff and adequate supervision of staff
- Environments that reduce the possibility of hidden places
- Orientation and training on child abuse detection, prevention, and reporting
- Defined and articulated policies for a safe environment
- Avoidance of creating "no-touch" policies by the caregivers and staff

In regard to staff recruitment, NAEYC recommends that early childhood programs in the home, center, or school initiate policies that require personal interviews, verification of references and education background and qualifications, criminal record checks, and disclosure of previous convictions. New employees should serve a probationary period, and programs should have policies that provide for the removal of anyone whose performance is unacceptable. Procedures must also be in place for responding to an accusation of child abuse and provide due process for the accused (NAEYC, 1997).

All those involved in early childhood care and education are well advised to secure a copy of the statement and use it to reflect on the effectiveness of their own program's policies and procedures.

The Adult's Responsibilities

Reporting suspected child abuse is mandated by law in all states. Educators must assume the responsibility to inform the proper authorities if they suspect that a child in their care is being abused by anyone.

The mandate to report suspected child abuse applies to teachers, principals, counselors, school nurses, and staff members of child care centers and summer camps. Certain knowledge that abuse took place is not required; reports are legally required if there is reasonable cause to suspect a child has been mistreated. For the protection of anyone reporting abuse or neglect, the person filing the report is held immune from civil or criminal liability if the report was made in good faith. Figure 15-2 discusses the steps to take if child abuse is suspected.

Families Under Stress

Families encounter many challenges today. American families have suffered the impact of social upheaval and changes in the past three decades. Family structures vary greatly, but the task remains the same: to provide safe and stable environments in which children are raised. The main sources of stress are divorce, work, and poverty.

Divorce

Perhaps no one single change has affected children as much as the divorce rate. Children rate divorce second only to the death of a parent as the most stressful event in their lives (DelCampo & DelCampo, 2006). The effects of divorce are felt for years. Getting over divorce and on with a productive life is critical for both child and parent; teachers can help.

The effects of divorce are felt by children well before the event itself. Children exhibit "pre-divorce family stress" by increased impulsive or aggressive behavior, and parents show the stress with headaches, fatigue, mood swings, or depression. Children's initial reaction to their parents' separation is traumatic—shock and distress (the *Stage 1* responses to stress as described in Chapter 14). Even if parents are not in violent conflict with each other, no child is happy about divorce. After divorce, many parents become overworked and overwhelmed. Children are often neglected or left with less than what both parents could provide, including emotional and financial support.

> Among employed adults, unmarried women who support families have the greatest risk of living in poverty. . . . Moreover, unmarried mothers often have time constraints that can affect their ability to supervise their children, offer emotional support, take an active part in their education, and arrange other activities for them. When children live with one parent, it is still most often the mother. (Casey Foundation, 2008)

Adjustment to divorce is difficult, and the psychological effects of divorce on children are often felt well into adulthood. "Divorce is a cumulative experience for the child. Its impact increases over time," writes Wallerstein (2002), reporting on a 25-year research project. For instance, of the people who were 2½ to 6 years old when their parents divorced one-third did

---

Helping an Abused or Neglected Child

- Be a calm and reassuring presence. Keep your emotions under control.
- Give unconditional support. Reassure the child that he/she did nothing wrong and were right to tell you.
- Let the child explain in his/her own words what happened. Do not interrogate the child or ask leading questions, but let him/her know that you are taking this seriously and that you believe what he/she is telling you.
- Report the alleged abuse to your supervisor/director/principal and follow the school's policies for reporting abuse and notifying the parents.
- Discuss with the supervisor/director/principal what is appropriate for staff members to do to support the child and the family during this time. Maintain the child and family's privacy.
- Work with the appropriate agencies, as necessary, during the investigation, and continue to support and be sensitive to the chid.

FIGURE 15-2 Reporting child abuse is mandated in every state. Become familiar with the policies your program has about reporting suspected child abuse (Helpguide, 2012). Retrieved from www.helpguide.org/mental/child-abuse on February 19, 2012.

not pursue any education beyond high school, although 40 percent of those who attended college did graduate.

Growing up in a divorced home does not mean children cannot live happy lives. Fortunately, children are amazingly resilient. The age and gender of the children involved seem to have some bearing on their adjustment. Very young children recover more easily than older ones, and boys react more intensely than girls to the loss of their fathers from the home. The parents' ability to be caring and available makes a difference, as does the parents' relationship with each other and the quality of the children's relationship with both parents.

Teachers of children whose parents are going through a divorce can help in several ways, including:

1. Researching the effects of divorce
2. Helping the family get help through support groups
3. Finding ways to help children talk about their feelings especially through books about children going through similar stress.
4. Keeping communications open with both parents and including both parents in all school events and communications.

Working Parents

More than two-thirds of all preschool children younger than age 6 have mothers in the workforce (Children's Defense Fund, 2010), and the percentage rises when considering school-aged children as well. The implications for families are considerable. For women, the double roles of job or career and family nurturer can be overwhelming, creating great conflict and the stress of chronic fatigue. Men are looking at their role in a different light; many are learning about greater involvement in child rearing and how to adjust to a new financial provider role. Yet there are vast differences among the various cultural groups and individuals parents about the value of and care for children. For all parents, three issues loom large:

The concern for quality child care, which is often unavailable and/or unaffordable;

The struggle to provide *quality time* with children as a family unit; and

The financial burden. Without parental leave, parents are forced to return to work during the critical early months of infancy or lose income and even their job. Further, while many mothers go to work from welfare, there are still few gains in the family's broader economic well-being. Women report still needing to use local food banks and taking second and third jobs. Self-sufficiency without income supports is rarely achieved.

For educators, working families have special issues. As more parents are fully occupied with work during the school day, they are less available for direct participation in a classroom or on a constant basis. Teachers plan flexible opportunities for them to become involved in their children's education.

Public policy reflects the attitude and values a nation holds toward children and families, and the inequities are glaring. Most European countries fund public programs for children and support services for parents at a much higher rate than in the United States. We look toward a future trend of clearer and more supportive public policies.

When both parents work outside the home, new roles for fathers emerge.

© Cengage Learning

TeachSource Video

Watch the TeachSource Video entitled "Divorce and Children." After you study the video, reflect on the following questions:

1. What do you think of parents who have 50-50 joint custody of their young children?
2. Do you think that divorce always has to add to the stress level of young children? Explain your answer.

Poverty

There is a group of Americans who are more likely to experience limited participation in the social, political, and economic mainstream of national life. The children who are at risk for academic failure are likely to be: those who live in poverty, members of minority groups, children with various physical and mental disabilities, children with limited English proficiency, children from single-parent families, or children attending schools with a high concentration of students who live in poverty (Casey Foundation, 2008).

The Children's Defense Fund (2010) tells another story:

- In 2010, 22 percent of American children lived in poverty, an increase from the 18 percent in 2002.
- In 2010, 33 percent of children lived in families where no parent had full-time, year-round employment.
- A record high of nearly 40 million people—one-half of them children—received food stamps.

At the same time, the average income of the top 1 percent of households grew 280 percent, whereas the income for the bottom 90 percent increased only 8 percent over the past three decades.

Black and Hispanic children are three times as likely to be born poor as are white, non-Hispanic children.

The number of homeless children in public schools increased 41 percent between the 2006–2007 and 2008–2009 school year, due to the impact of the recession.

There is a striking correlation between poverty and school failure. Children who start out at a disadvantage fall farther behind in academic achievement throughout their school years. Too many of them reach adulthood unhealthy, illiterate, and unemployable, with limited participation in the social, political, and economic mainstream of national life.

The changing school population suggests that these problems will only increase as the proportion of minority groups expands (because they are over-represented among the poor), as a larger and larger percentage of children fall below the poverty line, and as traditional patterns of child rearing and marriage change so that fewer children have the emotional and educational advantages of a two-parent family.

Transmitting Values

The third recurring theme in our educational heritage is that of transmitting values. Values—whether social, cultural, moral, or religious—have been the essence of education for centuries. Rousseau and Froebel valued childhood, so they created special places for children to express their innate goodness and uniqueness. Puritan fathers valued biblical theology; therefore, schools of their time taught children to read so that they might learn the Bible. Today, the anti-bias movement reflects a value of personal respect and appreciation of culture. Many sources shape children's values and behavior, notably the media culture, violence and disaster, and social diversity.

The Media Culture

Technology and media are solidly established in the daily life of children as they and their families engage in a variety of devices. In many homes, the television set and DVD's have replaced adult supervision. Ninety-nine percent of American households contain at least one television, with more than two-thirds containing two or more sets (Nielsen Media Research, 2008). Television and, for school-age children, the Internet and other technology media represent an influential force in the lives of children.

Television

Data from a Common Sense Media Research Study (2011) informs us that:

- >Each day, 47 percent of babies and toddlers watch TV or DVDs for an average of nearly 2 hours; nearly one in three has a TV in their bedroom.
- Seventy-three percent of 2 to 4 year olds watch TV every day, and 72 percent of 5 to 8 year olds watch TV every day.
- Thirty-nine percent of children from birth to age 8 live in a home where the TV set is on most of the time, even when no one is watching.
- Between birth and age 8, children spend an average of 1 hour and 45 minutes watching TV or videos compared to less than one-half hour reading or listening to music.

Television and the lessons it teaches are and will be a part of children's lives. "Perhaps if parents [and teachers] could accept the inevitable, that television is not only here to stay but viewing choices are expanding almost daily, then society could move past this dichotomy of thinking of television as simply good or bad. Television viewing could be thought of as an active endeavor rather than a passive one" (DelCampo & DelCampo, 2006).

Adults can modify the negative effects of TV watching with these strategies suggested by the American Academy of Child and Adolescent Psychiatry (2011):

1. Pay attention to what children are watching and join them to view what they see.

© Cengage Learning

Antidote to television.

2. Set limits on the amount of time they can watch TV.
3. Remove the TV from the child's bedroom. Turn off any television that is not being watched.
4. Help children understand that the violence they see portrayed on TV is not real, but in reality, similar behavior could cause pain or death.
5. Refuse to let children see programs that are violent, have offensive dialogue and story lines, and are racially or sexually stereotyping people. Turn the TV off if this occurs when children are watching such a program. Explain your reasons why you think it is wrong to watch the show.
6. Make your disapproval known at the time to let children know why the action is not a healthy way to solve problems.
7. Join with other parents to offset peer pressure and agree to enforce similar rules regarding the use of TV.

Although TV dominates children's media choice, the use of other digital media, including computers,

handheld and console video game players, cell phones, video iPods and iPads, is common:

- Among 0 to 8 year olds, 27 percent of all screen time is with digital media.
- Twenty-nine percent of parents have downloaded "apps" to a digital device, which 10 percent of babies use, 39 percent of 2 to 4 year olds use, and 52 percent of 5 to 8 year olds use.
- More than half of all children up to age 8 have played console video games. Seventeen percent of 5 to 8 year olds play them at least once a day.
- Half of all children have access to one of the newer mobile devices at home (Common Sense Media, 2011).

There are four basic concerns that parents and teachers express about children's viewing of media:

1. Media violence can lead to aggression and desensitization to violence.
2. Media viewing promotes passivity, slowing intellectual development and stifling imagination.
3. Media promote racist and sexist attitudes.
4. Television promotes materialistic consumerism.

Common Sense Media and the National Institutes of Health (NIH) analyzed 173 studies about the effect of media consumption on children, finding a strong correlation between greater exposure and adverse health outcomes. "Couch potato does, unfortunately, sum it up pretty well," says Ezekiel J. Emanuel, chair of bioethics department at NIH. "The research is clear that exposure to media has a variety of negative health impacts on children and teens. . . . We found very few studies that had any positive association for children's health" (Common Sense Media, 2008). This research highlights the significant effects on children of the models they see, whether they be of children, adults or fantasy characters (see Bandura, Chapter 4).

The media saturated environment that children live in today presents many challenges for the early childhood educator. Technology and media can be effective learning tools when used intentionally and appropriately. Home-school relationships can be strengthened through new ways of communicating and sharing interests and concerns. Vast resources available through technology enhance professional development and support teachers' ongoing education and learning.

We look forward to further research that will help us understand and evaluate the impact of children's use of technology and interactive media as new methods for learning in early childhood programs.

Violence and Disaster

The trend of children's increasing exposure to violence is alarming. Families feel unable to limit or influence their children's behavior due to the kinds of media and toys that are available. Teachers notice changes in children's play, commenting that the weapon and war play in classrooms is so single purpose and intense that it is difficult to redirect; rule setting and controlling overzealous play take an inordinate amount of teachers' energy.

When a catastrophe happens, whether personal or societal, children need help making sense of the calamity and then support in recovery. Shock, confusion, fear, anxiety, grief, anger, guilt, and helplessness are all common emotional responses to trauma. Such reactions generate changes in behavior, both in adults and in the children we care for.

Chapter 14 discusses children's reactions to stress and the role of the teacher in helping children process and cope with trauma. Figure 15-3 gives suggestions for how to help children in case of a disaster. Organizations such as Adults and Children Together (ACT) Against Violence, the Educators for Social Responsibility, and the National Association for Mediation Educators serve as both clearinghouses for information and material and as training institutes for teachers.

Children act out what they see in the media in their play. Should teachers allow unchecked aggressive pretend play or with limits and some kind of adult intervention? Or should this type of play be banned, contained, or otherwise redirected and altered? This dilemma illustrates children's play from two different viewpoints, a developmental one and a sociopolitical one.

The *developmental* viewpoint states that play, including war play, is the primary vehicle through which children work on developmental issues. Because children need to develop a sense of how the world works, of fantasy and reality, of good and bad, war play is an extension of superhero play (see Chapter 14), and is, therefore, a necessary part of children's play.

The *sociopolitical* view assumes that children learn basic social and political behavior at an early age and, therefore, learn militaristic concepts and values through war play. This viewpoint contends that children learn about conflict and resolution, the use of fighting, and the meaning of friends and enemies in their play, and that allowing war play endorses the use of force (Carlsson-Paige & Levin, 2005).

These two ideas give teachers the basic building blocks for how to deal with the issue of developing shared values and for engaging in a dialogue with fellow teachers and parents. Whatever your viewpoint, remember that exposure to violence is harmful, particularly when children are victims.

When disaster strikes, what children need most is reassurance, to know they are safe and that caring adults will still take care of them. Constancy and predictability, in the form of consistent routines and continued habits of behavior and tradition, help children feel anchored in their lives. Listening carefully, answering children's questions in simple ways, and asking questions to elicit their thoughts all encourage communication and a dialogue about their feelings. Figure 15-3 outlines ways to help children who experience a disaster.

Teachers help children find peaceful resolutions to their everyday conflicts, ensuring that, in their daily school life, war does not break out and take over (see Chapters 7 and 14 for suggestions):

- A family child care provider of infants and toddlers may spend extra time giving hugs and helping children share toys.
- A class of preschoolers may choose a cross-town child care center to exchange drawings and visits with, to increase their knowledge of their city neighbor.
- A first grade class might write letters to the President. ("I don't like it when you make war. My big sister says to use words when I have a problem and you should too.")

On an adult scale, teachers can:

- Talk about and decide on your viewpoint and values with parents and the school board.
- Develop guidelines that address your values and the needs of the children.
- Talk with parents about toys and the role of the media in the development of children's interests and the role of parents in helping children decide and choose what and how to play.
- Investigate peace education and building peaceable classrooms that have conflict resolution teaching as part of the curriculum (see Chapters 7 and 14).

Take care of yourselves as professionals; teachers need someone to talk to and may need to adjust the curriculum to give everyone more breathing room.

Social Diversity

America as a "melting pot," into which all racial and cultural differences are smoothly mixed into one single blend, is a myth. Much of America's history can be characterized as **racist, classist, sexist,** and **ethnocentric** by one group or another. The discrepancy between

When a Child Experiences Disaster

Infants/Toddlers

*Resume normal routines & favorite rituals.

*Give limited exposure to media & adult conversations about crisis.

*Give special time at nap & bed time.

Preschoolers

*Reassure verbally that they will be OK.

*Make sure they know where you are at all times.

*Give opportunities to write/dictate stories and draw about their experiences.

With All Children

*Spend time with child, being observant of their behavior.

*Give reassurance and physical comfort.

*Provide consistent, predictable structure during the day.

*Adapt curriculum to include relaxing, therapeutic activities such as sand, water, clay, and play dough.

*Spend more time in physical activity for emotional release.

*Connect with families frequently; share observations and ideas.

School-Age Children

*Ask what is on their minds, and answer their questions honestly.

*Share emergency plans so children know safety measures for the future.

*Provide guided exposure to media; watch/listen with them.

*Offer ways to take action, such as helping them organize relief efforts.

© Cengage Learning 2011

FIGURE 15-3 A catastrophe such as an earthquake, hurricane, or fire or a disaster such as war or an act of terrorism is frightening to both adults and children.

our ideals of equal opportunity and freedom and the daily reality can be altered only if we recognize the problems and then set specific goals for change.

Today's **demographics** point to a trend of an increasingly diverse society (see Chapter 3), but attitudes do not yet parallel reality. American schools are becoming increasingly segregated as 73 percent of black students and 78 percent of Hispanic students go to schools that are predominantly attended by minorities. Teachers in high-poverty schools have less experience, less training, and fewer advanced degrees than teachers who are in low-poverty schools (Children's Defense Fund, 2010).

We know that children exhibit an awareness of racial and gender differences by age 3 (Derman-Sparks & Edwards, 2010) and are formulating rudimentary

concepts about the meaning of those differences in the preschool years. It is logical to conclude that, by the end of the early childhood years, children have consolidated their attitudes about race, ethnicity, gender, and (dis)ability, and are far along the path of **attitude crystallization**. Unless the social environment changes, children re-create the prejudices of the current adult society. Teachers and families need to look with sensitivity to the meaning of diversity (see Figure 15-5).

Multicultural Education

Multicultural education is the system of teaching and learning that includes the contributions of all ethnic and racial groups. In other words, it is a comprehensive educational approach that reflects more than just the

DIVERSITY

Dropout Factories

Researchers at Johns Hopkins University (2004) identified 2,000 American high schools that they call "dropout factories," because 60 percent or less of the students in the ninth grade graduate in four years. The schools are "overwhelmingly minority and overwhelmingly poor." Add to that other research that say that college graduates earn more than twice as much as those with only a high school diploma, and more than two and one-half times more than high school dropouts earn. The result is what Marion Wright Edelman of the Children's Defense Fund calls a "pipe-line to prison."

Research shows a strong relation-ship between education attainment and economic well-being. Children who are provided a comprehensive, high quality education are less likely to be poor and more likely to find employment and receive higher wages than their less educated peers. In addition, we find that children from low-income families are constantly outperformed by their wealthier peers across a broad range of academic measures. Poor children, therefore, often find themselves in a Catch-22 with their economic circumstances denying them access to the escape valve out of a life of poverty—a quality education (Children's Defense Fund, 2008).

Figure 15-4 illustrates this point.

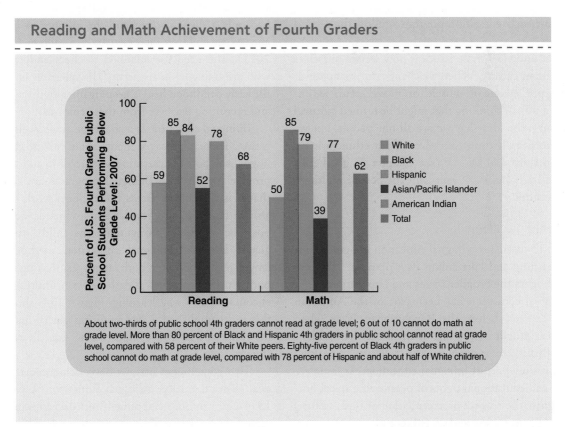

Reading and Math Achievement of Fourth Graders

About two-thirds of public school 4th graders cannot read at grade level; 6 out of 10 cannot do math at grade level. More than 80 percent of Black and Hispanic 4th graders in public school cannot read at grade level, compared with 58 percent of their White peers. Eighty-five percent of Black 4th graders in public school cannot do math at grade level, compared with 78 percent of Hispanic and about half of White children.

FIGURE 15-4 The disparate levels of education in America's diverse cultures confirm that school reforms have not yet met the needs of all children. (Reprinted with permission from Children's Defense Fund, 2010. Sources: U.S. Department of Education, National Assessment of Education Progress, The Nation's Report Card; calculations by Children's Defense Fund.)

dominant culture's perspective, providing all children with a fuller, more balanced truth about themselves and their history and culture. This means responsiveness to the child's origins, habits at home, and ways of self-expression.

At high levels of education there are contrasting views about how to deal with diversity. One viewpoint is a separatist education in which education is taught from a particular viewpoint—European, Afro-centrist, or the like. Many assert that most public schooling is a

Social Diversity and Teacher Attitudes

1. Recognize developmentally equivalent patterns. Before judging a child as difficult, assume s/he is normal and look again.
2. Do not value some ways of achieving developmental milestones more highly than others. Remember different is not deficient.
3. Start teaching in ways that are familiar to children. You may not be fluent in a child's language, but you can learn key words and phrases.
4. School learning is most likely to occur when family values reinforce family expectations. Partner up with parents so that the child is the big winner.
5. Deal with discrepancies between home and school directly. Instead of ignoring the differences, ask about them.

© Cengage Learning 2011

FIGURE 15-5 There are several guidelines teachers can follow regarding diversity.

European-dominant education. A second viewpoint is the more traditional pluralist approach in which education stresses the commonalities of varying peoples. Most early education programs follow the second approach.

What underlies these issues is how we see ourselves as a common culture. When we change the metaphor of "melting pot" to one of "mosaic" or "mixed salad," we encourage a way of thinking that might be termed **cultural pluralism**—the idea that we are all one people, but we do not necessarily divest ourselves of our ethnic origins. Based on DAP and DCAP (see Chapter 2), good early childhood programs can represent the best of multicultural education.

Bilingual Education

Chapter 13 discusses bilingual education in light of language learning and curriculum development. This section highlights the broader issues and implications.

Bilingual education has been part of the American experience since before the Revolutionary War, when school was taught in any one of the more than 18 languages that were spoken by the colonists. Speaking English is only part of bilingual education: At issue are the civil and educational rights of people who speak limited English, the respect or assimilation of their culture, and their participation and acceptance in society.

Changing populations and the influx of immigrants from Asia as well as from the Hispanic nations have brought new challenges to bilingual education. Bilingual programs serve primarily Spanish-speaking students. States that do not have bilingual programs still need to meet the needs of limited–English-proficient (LEP) students in schools through other means. Between 2000 and 2010, the Hispanic population grew by 43 percent, four times the nation's growth rate, primarily in the southern and midwestern United States (U.S. Census Bureau, 2011). Between 2000 and 2010, the number of white children declined by 4.3 million and black children had only a slight decline, and the number of Hispanic and Asian children increased by 5.5 million (Morello, 2011). The need for qualified teachers and caregivers who are bilingual is apparent. The question is whether the early childhood field is keeping up with these changes and recruiting teachers from these cultures.

Bilingual education is a challenge at all levels of education. There are disagreements about how to define bilingualism, how to determine who needs it, and who is to provide the services. Bilingual programs are so varied that it is difficult to assess them. Some work to mainstream children into regular classrooms as quickly as possible; others try to maintain the child's native language. The "dual/bilingual immersion" method blends language instruction in both languages. Putting together both English speakers and those with limited English encourages two-way learning. Figure 15-6 shows how this is accomplished. Laws requiring special instruction for children who lack competence in English vary from state to state.

Two government actions have influenced the bilingual issue: the 1968 Bilingual Education Act and the 1974 *Lau v. Nichols* Supreme Court decision that determined that a lack of instruction in one's first language is a violation of children's civil rights.

Since 1968, Title VII programs (The Elementary and Secondary Education Act, also known as the Bilingual Act) addressed the needs of students with limited proficiency in English. State bilingual education laws followed, requiring special instruction for children who lack competence in English. As a result, children are taught in public kindergarten and elementary schools by using both the primary language and English. Children

English Language Learning

Age of Children	How Taught	Noteworthy
0–5 years	Standard is "English-immersion": taught in English with little extra instruction, with some teacher use of home language vocabulary.	Can acquire native-like mastery of second language; risk for substantial erosion of home language and ability to communicate with family.
5+ years	Standard is "English immersion," but some subjects may be taught in home language to aid skill-building; school-aged children better at formal teaching of second language.	Children have complex social issues that may interfere; low competence in both languages may occur until mastery is achieved.

© Cengage Learning 2014

FIGURE 15-6 Bilingual programs vary and have mixed results.

may be taught to read in their primary language first; once they have learned to read in their own language, they are then taught to decode in English. Recently, the *dual* or *bilingual immersion* method attempts to blend language instruction by putting both English speakers and those with limited English into class together and teaching *two-way* bilingual education. Bringing both groups together for language instructions enhances the value of knowing both languages and demonstrates a true multicultural tool for desegregation. However, without consensus on the effectiveness and goals of bilingual education, we must press for continuing research and clarity.

Immigrant Issues

Another serious challenge for schools is posed by the educational and socioeconomic needs of immigrant children. Attempting to immerse new children into an *American* style of learning and to teach basic skills needed to succeed in the new country have been central functions of schools throughout history (see Chapter 1). School enrollment of Hispanic and Asian students increased more than 5 million students since the 1990s (USDE, 2012).

The language barrier is the most immediate problem, followed by that of acceptance of the immigrants' native

cultures. Further, many newcomers arrive from countries wracked with war, violence, and poverty. These children and families are under tremendous pressures and need help coping with the overwhelming stress and dislocation. Many young children in immigrant families do not have access to health and education services. Key issues are (Takanishi, 2006):

- Children's skills in kindergarten and their achievement at the end of third grade are important predictors of their future life prospects.
- Although well-designed early education and after-school programs hold promise to reduce ethnic group–related inequalities in children's cognitive skills and social competence, children in immigrant families are less likely to participate in these programs than are children in native-born families.
- Availability and access are important factors: When prekindergarten programs are offered in public schools, Hispanic and Asian American children are more likely to participate.
- Family literacy programs are a promising strategy for improving language skills of children in immigrant families, as well as their parents. The way schools place and monitor immigrant children—both their educational progress and their general well-being—challenges educators and all American citizens to clarify the responsibilities our society has toward its newcomers. Chapter 8 describes the needs of immigrant families.

Equal Play and Gender

Gender issues are part of the educational landscape. There is ample research to confirm the widespread occurrence of gender segregation in childhood (Grossman & Grossman, 1994). Sex differences are less apparent in early childhood than is gender-based behavior (see

Lawrence/fours/fives/IMG # 3559/© Cengage Learning 2011

Preserving his language is preserving his culture.

Chapter 4). Although adults may not always directly contribute to biased development, teachers and parents are indirectly responsible for the inequity between the sexes in their children.

Look at unstructured play situations. Free play is the backbone of early education programs and most at-home play, in which children choose playmates and play situations that are comfortable to them. They do not, typically, choose those activities with which they have had little or no experience, nor do they ordinarily choose cross-sex playmates (particularly as peer pressure increases with age). Sexist treatment in the classroom encourages the formation of patterns of power and dominance that occurs very early.

Adults must take an assertive role in recognizing this sexist bias and in replacing it with more equitable experiences for all children. Summaries of wide-ranging research indicate that both our homes and schools are "gendered environments" that spell different expectations and conduct for children on the basis of their gender (Grossman & Grossman, 1994). If we are committed to an anti-bias education and environment (see Chapters 9 to 14), we must attempt to reduce gender-stereotypical behavior. The following guidelines can help you make changes:

- *Begin where you are.* Start with self-awareness and reflection on your behavior, responses, and attitudes.
- *What you say and do can make a difference.* Acknowledge positive behaviors and milestones by describing what you see and avoiding using gender designations (such as "all boys get your jackets" or "all girls go to the snack tables").
- *Watch your language.* Avoid descriptions of children such as "pretty/handsome," and treat the class as a group ("friends" rather than "boys and girls"); be careful of word choices that reflect gender bias (such as "He is confident/She is full of herself").
- *Establish rules and conduct for cooperation and gender equity.* Everybody may play everywhere with any materials; blocks are not just for boys, and the house corner is not for girls only; no child may be kept from playing because of something she or he cannot change—skin color, disability, or gender.
- *Be ready to intervene and support.* If you hear a "No boys allowed" or "Girls can't do that," be ready to intervene in a supportive way, finding out why children think that, and what you think or what the class rule is.
- *Think about how to cope with superheroes and Barbie dolls.* Develop strategies for all children, including providing activities that all children may use, that are sex fair and sex affirmative in content. Use techniques such as teacher proximity and structured playtime to involve children in activities they may otherwise avoid.

Expanding children's learning styles is helpful. Girls need more experiences with spatial exploration and gross motor coordination as well as quality attention from—without dependence on—adults. Boys in particular need experiences in flexibility, nurturance, and learning from modeling.

Encourage cross-gender interaction, and use cooperative learning activities. Whereas there is little research about the long-term effects of these strategies, a combination of these techniques has been found effective to increase mixed-gender interactions, helping behavior and friendships. Help make and keep connections among children, so they do not get locked into narrow constraints.

Sexuality

One of the most complicated issues that touches the lives of early childhood educators is sexuality. Although human sexuality is not likely to be among typical early childhood curriculum topics, teachers are increasingly more likely to encounter issues of homosexuality in the following ways: working with gay or lesbian families or coworkers, dealing with aspects of femininity and masculinity in children's sex role identity, and having multicultural children's books about gay families.

If teachers are relinquishing stereotypes about ethnicity, ability, and gender, they must also consider avoiding the rejection of a family for its choice of lifestyle or the criticism of a child on the basis of some notion of "femininity" or "masculinity." Researchers have failed to find evidence that parental characteristics determine sexual orientation (Berger, 2007). The homophobia at the root of such biased behavior, either subtle on the part of teachers or overt by other children, can be hurtful and harassing. We deal with this type of bias just as we do with other forms of prejudice because children should never be made to feel ashamed about their family, their teachers, or themselves.

TeachSource Video

Watch the TeachSource Video entitled "0-2 Years: Gender in Infants and Toddlers." After you study the video clip, reflect on the following questions:

1. How did the mothers in the video reinforce stereotypes? Do you agree with them?
2. How did you feel about the mothers' perceptions of the baby girls and baby boys?
3. What would you say to those mothers about gender equity?

Professionalism

Every day, early childhood professionals open their doors to young children by the millions. As they do, they are influencing the course of our history in the 21st century. Consider this: A child born in 2010 will be a voting adult in 2028 and may live until the end of the century. We are teaching the children of the future!

If you are thinking about working with young children as a career, you may be wondering if early childhood education is a profession worthy of a lifetime commitment. Can you look forward to a challenging, intellectually stimulating, and rewarding future? To find those answers in today's world, we look at three issues: standards for children's programs, standards for teacher preparation and advocacy.

Standards for Children's Programs

In Chapter 2, you read about the rich array of programs offered for children in group care from infancy through age 8. Because they are so diverse, it is often difficult to define and assess the standard of care and education with one set of guidelines. Consider these statistics:

- In 11 states, providers in family child care homes do not need any training before being licensed (NACCRRA, 2010).
- Thirty-two states do not require prior training to teach in child care centers, and 39 and the District of Columbia do not require training of family child care providers (Children's Defense Fund, 2010).
- In 2009, more than 10,000 programs were accredited by NAEYC's National Academy of Early Childhood Programs. By 2012, that number dropped to more than 7,000 (NAEYC, 2012).

The most comprehensive set of standards for quality education and care in early childhood has evolved from DAP and are outlined in the NAEYC publication *Developmentally Appropriate Practice in Early Childhood Programs Serving Children from Birth through Age 8* (NAEYC, 2009).

Standards for Professional Preparation

In Chapter 5, you read about the multiple roles of teachers and the discrepancy regarding the quality of program, availability for families, and compensation for professionals. The challenge is before all of us—the child care professionals, the parents, the leaders of business and industry, and the legislators on the local, state, and national scene.

The quality of care in child development programs is linked to the training and education of the staff. Consequently, it is imperative that we attract and recruit to the field of early childhood education individuals who not only are dedicated to working with young children but also are skilled and competent. Many states are working on developing a career lattice and professional development plan for early childhood staff. Consideration must be given to developing a coordinated system that 1) welcomes people into the field from a variety of points; 2) offers clear career pathways with articulated training and credentialing systems; and 3) provides a variety of incentives to stay in the field.

Further, teacher preparation institutions are embarking on a cycle of self-study and articulation of coursework and experience that is offered at both the community college and four-year institutions in the United States. National efforts include the NAEYC Standards for Early Childhood Preparation as well as research efforts of groups such as the National Child Care Information and Technical Assistance Center (Sakai & Whitebook, 2004). Refer to the seven Standards for Professional Preparation on the back inside cover of this text as you read this book. The standards appropriate to each chapter are highlighted. See also Chapter 5 for a description of teacher preparation in the early childhood field.

Advocacy

The teacher who works to ensure high quality programs and services for children and their families also increases the likelihood of achieving the improved working conditions, professional opportunities, and public recognition that the field of early childhood education so richly deserves.

A program that responds to diversity is one that invites acceptance and respect.

How do adults become advocates to ensure a fulfilling life for children in the 21st century?

With the issues of diversity, distribution of resources, money, and educational reform of such immediate concern, we need to understand the forces that affect children and educate ourselves about the political process. We need to know the rules and regulations regarding public funding sources. It is important to know how monies are allocated and with whom to work to affect the decisions regarding education. By becoming acquainted with legislation, the teaching profession can rally support for bills that help children, families, and schools.

Every teacher can become an advocate. Figure 15-7 shows many forms of advocacy you may adopt. Find your voice and keep focused, and express your commitment to making changes. How can you take these steps?

1. Make a personal commitment.
2. Keep informed.
3. Know the process.
4. Express your views.
5. Let others know.
6. Be visible.
7. Show appreciation.
8. Watch the implementation.
9. Build rapport and trust.
10. Educate your legislators.

Different Kinds of Child Advocacy

Personal advocacy: Sharing personal views and philosophies with others.
   Example: "Maria was concerned about the safety of the neighborhood playground. While pushing her toddler on the swing, she mentioned to the mother next to her that she was frustrated by the litter in the park including broken glass in the sandbox. The two women agreed to ask other parents and neighbors to come back the next day with trash bags and gloves to pick up litter while taking turns playing with the children" (Robinson & Stark, 2002).

Public policy advocacy: Influencing public policies and practices so that they are more responsive to children.
   Example: Frustrated with changes the state legislature was considering, the local child care planning council sent a letter to state legislators and the chair of the funding committee. They also attended a hearing to offer testimony about how the allocation of preschool funds would affect everyone.

Private-sector advocacy: Changing private policies to better support children, families, and teachers.
   Example: A group of teachers approached its local school board about the lack of technology in the schools. They talked to local businesses and the parents of the community, identified a collaborative committee of all three groups, and began volunteering their expertise about children and learning. Within 2 years, the school had a list of needs and priorities, has received donations of time and technical assistance from parents, and received a grant for computers in the classrooms.

FIGURE 15-7 Early childhood advocacy takes many forms.

(DAP) Professional Reflections

Our profession is constantly growing, branching out, and ready to meet emerging challenges in flexible and innovative ways. We have professional organizations to guide us. The National Association for the Education of Young Children (NAEYC) is the largest professional organization. Association for Childhood Education International (ACEI) includes both preschool and elementary school. Children's Defense Fund (CDF), is the lobbying organization that advocates for all children. These efforts have resulted in significant improvements in the status of children, and they have begun to outline standards and practices for the people who call themselves early childhood professionals. The early childhood field is a worthwhile profession. Reflect on how you relate to the following aspects of being an early childhood professional.

- *Sense of identity.* Early childhood professionals see themselves as caregivers who strive to educate the whole child, taking into consideration the body, the mind, and the heart and soul (see Chapter 1).

- *Purpose to engage in developmentally appropriate practices (DAP).* Quality care and education calls for blending child development and learning the strengths, interests, and needs of each child, and the social and cultural contexts in which children live (see Chapter 2).

- *Commitment to ethical teaching and to child advocacy.* Being a professional means behaving with a child's best interests in mind, keeping confidentiality when discussing issues in the classroom and about families, upholding a code of ethics, and taking themselves and their work seriously (see Chapter 5 and Appendix A).

- *Participation in the work as a legitimate livelihood.* The people who provide care and education to young children deserve wages and working conditions that are worthy of their efforts (Chapters 5 and 15).

Summary

LO 1 The ethic of social reform is a recurring theme throughout the history of early childhood education. Progress in program quality and costs for child care emerged from the social issue of women in the workplace in greater numbers than before. Education reform is taking place through national and state initiatives such as No Child Left Behind, Race to the Top, Common Core State Standards, school readiness programs, the universal preschool movement, and the growth of charter schools.

LO 2 The importance of childhood, a second theme, is tainted with reports of childhood stress and child abuse and neglect. Families and children are living in stress with the impact of divorce; work-related issues; and, in some cases, intense poverty.

LO 3 We transmit values to our children through many channels. Media is one of the most prevalent and problematic. Children from a very early age spend hours watching TV, much of it age-inappropriate and too violent for any child. Disaster and violence of any nature further shakes the stable foundation that children need to grown and learn. Social diversity in America is manifested in multicultural education, bilingual education, immigration, and gender and sexuality issues, providing us with a rich opportunity to help children learn a worldview and live in a colorful world of diverse people.

LO 4 Professionalism is defined in many ways throughout this text. In this chapter the focus is on the standards for children's programs and the standards for the professional preparation of teachers and how they enlarge our view of the teaching profession. An important aspect of teaching is serving as an advocate for both children and their families and for greater influence and status of the early childhood field.

Key Terms

social reform
ethic of social reform
importance of childhood
universal preschool
professionalism

child abuse
child neglect
traumatic
racist
classist

sexist
ethnocentric
demographics
attitude crystallization
cultural pluralism

Review Questions

1. Describe how societal issues influence social reforms.
2. What are the major detriments to the importance of childhood in today's world?
3. How does today's culture translate its values to young children?

4. How do standards for teacher preparation and for children's programs support professionalism of the early childhood field?

Observe and Apply

1. Interview teachers from a child care center, nursery school, and kindergarten about their salary scales and health benefits. How do they compare with one another? What conclusions can you draw from their information?
2. In addressing social diversity in early childhood education programs, interview at least two professionals and then describe how you would address the following issues:
   a. A group of children says "No boys (girls) allowed."
   b. Children in your center have several different home languages, and the class is typically taught by English-dominant staff.

   c. The board of your program has decided to fully include children with special needs this year.
3. Reflect on your use of TV and how you have been influenced by some of the values that are transmitted across the screen. Would you change your TV watching habits now? Will you alter your children's viewing habits? Why? Why not?
4. How can you advocate for improving the working conditions for the early care and education workforce? Make a list of several concrete actions you can take in your community.

Helpful Websites

American Red Cross
   www.redcross.org/disaster/masters/

Center for the Child Care Workforce   **www.ccw.org/**

Child Maltreatment   **www.acf.hhs.gov**

Child Welfare League of America   **www.cwla.org**

Children's Defense Fund   **www.childrensdefense.org**

Common Sense Media   **www.commonsensemedia.org**

Coping with Disaster   **www.counselingforloss.com**

Educators for Social Responsibility
   www.esrnational.org

Child Welfare Information Gateway
   www.childwelfare.gov

National Indian Child Welfare Association
   www.nicwa.org

Prevent Child Abuse America   **www.childabuse.org**

Stand for Children   **www.stand.org**

🔘 The Education CourseMate website for this text offers many helpful resources and interactive study tools. Go to CengageBrain.com to access the TeachSource Videos, flashcards, tutorial quizzes, direct links to all of the websites mentioned in the chapter, and more.

References

Ethic of Social Reform

Child Care

American Federation of Teachers. (2011). Wage data for early childhood educators. http://www.aft.org. Accessed September 2011.

Children's Defense Fund. (2008, 2010). *The state of America's Children.* Washington, D.C.: Children's Defense Fund.

National Association of Child Care Resource and Referral Agencies (NACCRRA). (2008). *Child care in America: 2008 Fact Sheet.* http://www.naccrra. org. Accessed March 2009.

National Association of Child Care Resource and Referral Agencies (NACCRRA). (2010). Parents and the high cost of child care: 2010 update. http://www.naccrra.org. Accessed July 2010.

National Association of Child Care Resources and Referral Agencies (NACCRRA). (2010). Child care in America: 2010 fact sheet. http://www.naccrra.org. Accessed June 2010.

U.S. Census Bureau. (2010). Current population survey, October 1980 through 2009. Washington, DC: Author.

Education Reform

Barnett, W. S., Epstein, D. J., Carolan, M., Fitzgerald, J., Ackerman, D. J., & Friedman, A. H. (2011). *The state of preschool 2011: State preschool yearbook.* Brunswick, NJ: National Institute for Early Education Research.

Lee, V., & Burkham, D. (2002). *Inequality at the starting gate: Social background differences in achievement as children begin school.* Washington, D.C.: Economic Policy Institute.

National Center for Education Statistics. (2011). *The Condition of Education 2011 (NCES 2011-033): Indicator 3.* U.S. Department of Education.

Rouse, C., Brooks-Gunn, J., & McLanahan, S. (Eds). (2005). *School readiness: Closing the racial and ethnic gaps.* The Future of Children, Vol. 15, No. 1, Spring 2005. Princeton University/Brookings Institute.

Shonkoff, J., & Phillips, D. (Eds.). (2002). *From neurons to neighborhoods: the science of early childhood development.* Washington D.C.: National Academies Press.

U.S. Department of Education. (2009) Department releases state reports profiling first-year progress under Race to the Top. http://www.ed.gov. Accessed January 2012.

U.S. Department of Education (2011, September). Obama administration sets high bar for flexibility from NCLB in order to advance equity and support reform. http://www.ed.gov. Accessed January 2012.

The Importance of Childhood

Childhood Stress

Brazelton, T. B., & Greenspan, S. D. (2000, March). The irreducible needs of children. *Young Children,* pp. 6–13.

Child Abuse and Neglect

Childhelp. (2012). *Signs of child abuse, 2006.* http://www.childhelp.org/resources. Accessed January 2012.

Childhelp. (2012). *Child abuse in America, 2006.* http://www.childhelp.org/resources. Accessed January 2012.

Children's Defense Fund. (2008). *The state of America's children.* Washington, D.C.: Author.

National Association for the Education of Young Children. (1997, March). *Position statement on the prevention of child abuse in early childhood programs and the responsibilities of early childhood professionals to prevent child abuse (42–46).* Washington, D.C.: Author.

U.S. Department of Health and Human Services. (1998). *Child sexual abuse prevention—Tips to parents.* Washington, DC: Author.

Poverty

Balfanz, R., & Legters, N. (2004). *Locating the dropout crisis: Which high schools produce the nation's dropouts? Where are they located? Who attends them?* Johns Hopkins University, Center for Research on the Education of Students Placed at Risk (CRESPAR). Retrieved March, 2012 from www.csos.jhu.edu/crespar/reports.htm.

Casey Foundation. (2008). *Kids Count data book.* Baltimore: Annie E. Casey Foundation.

Children's Defense Fund. (2010). *The state of America's children.* Washington, D.C.: Author.

Families Under Stress

Children's Defense Fund. (2010). *The state of America's children.* Washington, D.C.: Author.

DelCampo, D., & DelCampo, R. (2006). *Taking sides: Clashing views in childhood and society* (6th Ed). Dubuque, IA: McGraw-Hill. (See Issue 7: Does Divorce Create Long-Term Negative Effects for Children?)

Wallerstein, J. (2002). *The unexpected legacy of divorce.* New York: Hyperion.

Transmitting Values

Media Culture

American Academy of Child and Adolescent Psychiatry. (2011). *Facts for Families: Children and TV Violence.* www.aacap.org/cs/root/facts_for _families. Accessed January 2011.

Common Sense Media and Department of Clinical Bioethics, National Institutes of Health. (2008, December). *Media + child and adolescent health: A systematic review.* http://www.commonsense media.org

Common Sense Media Research Study. (2011). *Zero to Eight: Children's media use in America.* http://www.commonsensem edia.org/zero-eight-children-media.

DelCampo, D. S., & DelCampo, R. L. (2006). *Taking sides: Clashing views in childhood and society* (6th Ed). Dubuque, IA: McGraw-Hill. (See Issue 8: Is Television Violence Viewing Harmful for Children?)

Nielsen Media Research. (2008). *Nielsen Report on television.* New York: Nielsen Media Research.

Violence and Disaster

Carlsson-Paige, N., & Levin, D. (2005). *The war play dilemma* (2nd Ed). New York: Teachers College.

Social Diversity

Children's Defense Fund. (2008, 2010). *The state of America's children.* Washington, D.C.: Author.

Derman-Sparks, L., & Edwards, J. O. (2010). *Anti-bias education for young children and ourselves.* Washington, D.C.: NAEYC.

Takanishi, R. (2006). *Leveling the playing field: Supporting immigrant children from birth to 8. The future of children.* Princeton, NJ: Brookings Institute.

United States Bureau of Census (2011). Newsroom: 2010 Census shows nation's Hispanic population grew four times faster than total U. S. population. *http://www.census.gov/newsroom/releases/archives* 2010.

Gender and Sexuality

Grossman, H., & Grossman, S. H. (1994). *Gender issues in education.* Boston: Allyn & Bacon.

Professionalism

Children's Defense Fund. (2010). *The state of America's children.* Washington, D.C.: Author.

National Association of Child Care Resources and Referral Agencies. (NACCRRA). (2010, June). Child care in America fact sheet. http://www.naccrra.org.

National Association for the Education of Young Children. (2009, 2012). Accreditation programs for young children. http://www.naeyc.org.

Robinson, A., & Stark, D. R. (2002). *Advocates in Action: Making a Difference for Young Children.* Washington, D.C.: NAEYC.

Sakai, L., & Whitebook, M. (2004). *By a thread: How child care centers hold on to teachers, how teachers build lasting careers.* Kalamazoo, MI: WE Upjohn Institute of Employment Research.

Code of Ethical Conduct and Statement of Commitment

A position statement of the *National Association for the Education of Young Children*

Revised April 2005. Reaffirmed and Updated May 2011.

Preamble

NAEYC recognizes that those who work with young children face many daily decisions that have moral and ethical implications. The NAEYC Code of Ethical Conduct offers guidelines for responsible behavior and sets forth a common basis for resolving the principal ethical dilemmas encountered in early childhood care and education. The Statement of Commitment is not part of the Code but is a personal acknowledgement of an individual's willingness to embrace the distinctive values and moral obligations of the field of early childhood care and education.

The primary focus of the Code is on daily practice with children and their families in programs for children from birth through 8 years of age, such as infant/toddler programs, preschool and prekindergarten programs, child care centers, hospital and child life settings, family child care homes, kindergartens, and primary classrooms. When the issues involve young children, then these provisions also apply to specialists who do not work directly with children, including program administrators, parent educators, early childhood adult educators, and officials with responsibility for program monitoring and licensing. (Note: See also the "Code of Ethical Conduct: Supplement for Early Childhood Adult Educators," online at www.naeyc.org/about/positions/pdf/ethics04.pdf and the "Code of Ethical Conduct: Supplement for Early Childhood Program Administrators," online at http://www.naeyc.org/files/naeyc/file/positions/PSETH05_supp.pdf.)

Core Values

Standards of ethical behavior in early childhood care and education are based on commitment to the following core values that are deeply rooted in the history of the field of early childhood care and education. We have made a commitment to

- Appreciate childhood as a unique and valuable stage of the human life cycle.
- Base our work on knowledge of how children develop and learn.
- Appreciate and support the bond between the child and family.
- Recognize that children are best understood and supported in the context of family, culture,* community, and society.
- Respect the dignity, worth, and uniqueness of each individual (child, family member, and colleague).
- Respect diversity in children, families, and colleagues.
- Recognize that children and adults achieve their full potential in the context of relationships that are based on trust and respect.

Conceptual Framework

The Code sets forth a framework of professional responsibilities in four sections. Each section addresses an area of professional relationships: (1) with chil-

*The term *culture* includes ethnicity, racial identity, economic level, family structure, language, and religious and political beliefs, which profoundly influence each child's development and relationship to the world.

dren, (2) with families, (3) among colleagues, and (4) with the community and society. Each section includes an introduction to the primary responsibilities of the early childhood practitioner in that context. The introduction is followed by a set of ideals (I) that reflect exemplary professional practice and by a set of principles (P) describing practices that are required, prohibited, or permitted.

The **ideals** reflect the aspirations of practitioners. The **principles** guide conduct and assist practitioners in resolving ethical dilemmas.† Both ideals and principles are intended to direct practitioners to those questions which, when responsibly answered, can provide the basis for conscientious decision making. While the Code provides specific direction for addressing some ethical dilemmas, many others will require the practitioner to combine the guidance of the Code with professional judgment.

The ideals and principles in this Code present a shared framework of professional responsibility that affirms our commitment to the core values of our field. The Code publicly acknowledges the responsibilities that we in the field have assumed, and in so doing supports ethical behavior in our work. Practitioners who face situations with ethical dimensions are urged to seek guidance in the applicable parts of this Code and in the spirit that informs the whole.

Often "the right answer"—the best ethical course of action to take—is not obvious. There may be no readily apparent, positive way to handle a situation. When one important value contradicts another, we face an ethical dilemma. When we face a dilemma, it is our professional responsibility to consult the Code and all relevant parties to find the most ethical resolution.

Section I: Ethical Responsibilities to Children

Childhood is a unique and valuable stage in the human life cycle. Our paramount responsibility is to provide care and education in settings that are safe, healthy, nurturing, and responsive for each child. We are committed to supporting children's development and learning; respecting individual differences; and helping children learn to live, play, and work cooperatively. We are also committed to promoting children's self-awareness, competence, self-worth, resiliency, and physical well-being.

Ideals

I-1.1—To be familiar with the knowledge base of early childhood care and education and to stay informed through continuing education and training.

I-1.2—To base program practices upon current knowledge and research in the field of early childhood education, child development, and related disciplines, as well as on particular knowledge of each child.

I-1.3—To recognize and respect the unique qualities, abilities, and potential of each child.

I-1.4—To appreciate the vulnerability of children and their dependence on adults.

I-1.5—To create and maintain safe and healthy settings that foster children's social, emotional, cognitive, and physical development and that respect their dignity and their contributions.

I-1.6—To use assessment instruments and strategies that are appropriate for the children to be assessed, that are used only for the purposes for which they were designed, and that have the potential to benefit children.

I-1.7—To use assessment information to understand and support children's development and learning, to support instruction, and to identify children who may need additional services.

I-1.8—To support the right of each child to play and learn in an inclusive environment that meets the needs of children with and without disabilities.

I-1.9—To advocate for and ensure that all children, including those with special needs, have access to the support services needed to be successful.

I-1.10—To ensure that each child's culture, language, ethnicity, and family structure are recognized and valued in the program.

I-1.11—To provide all children with experiences in a language that they know, as well as support children in maintaining the use of their home language and in learning English.

---

†There is not necessarily a corresponding principle for each ideal.

I-1.12—To work with families to provide a safe and smooth transition as children and families move from one program to the next.

Principles

P-1.1—**Above all, we shall not harm children. We shall not participate in practices that are emotionally damaging, physically harmful, disrespectful, degrading, dangerous, exploitative, or intimidating to children.** *This principle has precedence over all others in this Code.*

P-1.2—We shall care for and educate children in positive emotional and social environments that are cognitively stimulating and that support each child's culture, language, ethnicity, and family structure.

P-1.3—We shall not participate in practices that discriminate against children by denying benefits, giving special advantages, or excluding them from programs or activities on the basis of their sex, race, national origin, immigration status, preferred home language, religious beliefs, medical condition, disability, or the marital status/family structure, sexual orientation, or religious beliefs or other affiliations of their families. (Aspects of this principle do not apply in programs that have a lawful mandate to provide services to a particular population of children.)

P-1.4—We shall use two-way communications to involve all those with relevant knowledge (including families and staff) in decisions concerning a child, as appropriate, ensuring confidentiality of sensitive information. (See also P-2.4.)

P-1.5—We shall use appropriate assessment systems, which include multiple sources of information, to provide information on children's learning and development.

P-1.6—We shall strive to ensure that decisions such as those related to enrollment, retention, or assignment to special education services, will be based on multiple sources of information and will never be based on a single assessment, such as a test score or a single observation.

P-1.7—We shall strive to build individual relationships with each child; make individualized adaptations in teaching strategies, learning environments, and curricula; and consult with the family so that each child benefits from the program. If after such efforts have been exhausted, the current placement does not meet a child's needs, or the child is seriously jeopardizing the ability of other children to benefit from the program, we shall collaborate with the child's family and appropriate specialists to determine the additional services needed and/or the placement option(s) most likely to ensure the child's success. (Aspects of this principle may not apply in programs that have a lawful mandate to provide services to a particular population of children.)

P-1.8—We shall be familiar with the risk factors for and symptoms of child abuse and neglect, including physical, sexual, verbal, and emotional abuse and physical, emotional, educational, and medical neglect. We shall know and follow state laws and community procedures that protect children against abuse and neglect.

P-1.9—When we have reasonable cause to suspect child abuse or neglect, we shall report it to the appropriate community agency and follow up to ensure that appropriate action has been taken. When appropriate, parents or guardians will be informed that the referral will be or has been made.

P-1.10—When another person tells us of his or her suspicion that a child is being abused or neglected, we shall assist that person in taking appropriate action in order to protect the child.

P-1.11—When we become aware of a practice or situation that endangers the health, safety, or well-being of children, we have an ethical responsibility to protect children or inform parents and/or others who can.

Section II: Ethical Responsibilities to Families

Families* are of primary importance in children's development. Because the family and the early childhood practitioner have a common interest in the child's

---

*The term *family* may include those adults, besides parents, with the responsibility of being involved in educating, nurturing, and advocating for the child.

wellbeing, we acknowledge a primary responsibility to bring about communication, cooperation, and collaboration between the home and early childhood program in ways that enhance the child's development.

Ideals

I-2.1—To be familiar with the knowledge base related to working effectively with families and to stay informed through continuing education and training.

I-2.2—To develop relationships of mutual trust and create partnerships with the families we serve.

I-2.3—To welcome all family members and encourage them to participate in the program, including involvement in shared decision making.

I-2.4—To listen to families, acknowledge and build upon their strengths and competencies, and learn from families as we support them in their task of nurturing children.

I-2.5—To respect the dignity and preferences of each family and to make an effort to learn about its structure, culture, language, customs, and beliefs to ensure a culturally consistent environment for all children and families.

I-2.6—To acknowledge families' childrearing values and their right to make decisions for their children.

I-2.7—To share information about each child's education and development with families and to help them understand and appreciate the current knowledge base of the early childhood profession.

I-2.8—To help family members enhance their understanding of their children, as staff are enhancing their understanding of each child through communications with families, and support family members in the continuing development of their skills as parents.

I-2.9—To foster families' efforts to build support networks and, when needed, participate in building networks for families by providing them with opportunities to interact with program staff, other families, community resources, and professional services.

Principles

P-2.1—We shall not deny family members access to their child's classroom or program setting unless access is denied by court order or other legal restriction.

P-2.2—We shall inform families of program philosophy, policies, curriculum, assessment system, cultural practices, and personnel qualifications, and explain why we teach as we do—which should be in accordance with our ethical responsibilities to children (see Section I).

P-2.3—We shall inform families of and, when appropriate, involve them in policy decisions. (See also I-2.3.)

P-2.4—We shall ensure that the family is involved in significant decisions affecting their child. (See also P-1.4.)

P-2.5—We shall make every effort to communicate effectively with all families in a language that they understand. We shall use community resources for translation and interpretation when we do not have sufficient resources in our own programs.

P-2.6—As families share information with us about their children and families, we shall ensure that families' input is an important contribution to the planning and implementation of the program.

P-2.7—We shall inform families about the nature and purpose of the program's child assessments and how data about their child will be used.

P-2.8—We shall treat child assessment information confidentially and share this information only when there is a legitimate need for it.

P-2.9—We shall inform the family of injuries and incidents involving their child, of risks such as exposures to communicable diseases that might result in infection, and of occurrences that might result in emotional stress.

P-2.10—Families shall be fully informed of any proposed research projects involving their children and shall have the opportunity to give or withhold consent without penalty. We shall not permit or participate in research that could in any way hinder the education, development, or wellbeing of children.

P-2.11—We shall not engage in or support exploitation of families. We shall not use our relationship with a family for private advantage or personal gain, or enter into relationships with family members that might impair our effectiveness working with their children.

P-2.12—We shall develop written policies for the protection of confidentiality and the disclosure of children's records. These policy documents shall be made available to all program personnel and families. Disclosure of children's records beyond family members, program personnel, and consultants having an obligation of confidentiality shall require familial consent (except in cases of abuse or neglect).

P-2.13—We shall maintain confidentiality and shall respect the family's right to privacy, refraining from disclosure of confidential information and intrusion into family life. However, when we have reason to believe that a child's welfare is at risk, it is permissible to share confidential information with agencies, as well as with individuals who have legal responsibility for intervening in the child's interest.

P-2.14—In cases where family members are in conflict with one another, we shall work openly, sharing our observations of the child, to help all parties involved make informed decisions. We shall refrain from becoming an advocate for one party.

P-2.15—We shall be familiar with and appropriately refer families to community resources and professional support services. After a referral has been made, we shall follow up to ensure that services have been appropriately provided.

Section III: Ethical Responsibilities to Colleagues

In a caring, cooperative workplace, human dignity is respected, professional satisfaction is promoted, and positive relationships are developed and sustained. Based upon our core values, our primary responsibility to colleagues is to establish and maintain settings and relationships that support productive work and meet professional needs. The same ideals that apply to children also apply as we interact with adults in the workplace. (Note: Section III includes responsibilities to co-workers and to employers. See the "Code of Ethical Conduct: Supplement for Early Childhood Program Administrators" for responsibilities to personnel (*employees* in the original 2005 Code revision), online at http://www.naeyc.org/files/naeyc/file/positions/PSETH05_supp.pdf).

A—Responsibilities to co-workers

Ideals

I-3A.1—To establish and maintain relationships of respect, trust, confidentiality, collaboration, and cooperation with co-workers.

I-3A.2—To share resources with co-workers, collaborating to ensure that the best possible early childhood care and education program is provided.

I-3A.3—To support co-workers in meeting their professional needs and in their professional development.

I-3A.4—To accord co-workers due recognition of professional achievement.

Principles

P-3A.1—We shall recognize the contributions of colleagues to our program and not participate in practices that diminish their reputations or impair their effectiveness in working with children and families.

P-3A.2—When we have concerns about the professional behavior of a co-worker, we shall first let that person know of our concern in a way that shows respect for personal dignity and for the diversity to be found among staff members, and then attempt to resolve the matter collegially and in a confidential manner.

P-3A.3—We shall exercise care in expressing views regarding the personal attributes or professional conduct of co-workers. Statements should be based on firsthand knowledge, not hearsay, and relevant to the interests of children and programs.

P-3A.4—We shall not participate in practices that discriminate against a co-worker because of sex, race, national origin, religious beliefs or other affiliations, age, marital status/family structure, disability, or sexual orientation.

B—Responsibilities to employers

Ideals

I-3B.1—To assist the program in providing the highest quality of service.

I-3B.2—To do nothing that diminishes the reputation of the program in which we work unless it is violating laws and regulations designed to protect children or is violating the provisions of this Code.

Principles

P-3B.1—We shall follow all program policies. When we do not agree with program policies, we shall attempt to effect change through constructive action within the organization.

P-3B.2—We shall speak or act on behalf of an organization only when authorized. We shall take care to acknowledge when we are speaking for the organization and when we are expressing a personal judgment.

P-3B.3—We shall not violate laws or regulations designed to protect children and shall take appropriate action consistent with this Code when aware of such violations.

P-3B.4—If we have concerns about a colleague's behavior, and children's well-being is not at risk, we may address the concern with that individual. If children are at risk or the situation does not improve after it has been brought to the colleague's attention, we shall report the colleague's unethical or incompetent behavior to an appropriate authority.

P-3B.5—When we have a concern about circumstances or conditions that impact the quality of care and education within the program, we shall inform the program's administration or, when necessary, other appropriate authorities.

Section IV: Ethical Responsibilities to Community and Society

Early childhood programs operate within the context of their immediate community made up of families and other institutions concerned with children's welfare. Our responsibilities to the community are to provide programs that meet the diverse needs of families, to cooperate with agencies and professions that share the responsibility for children, to assist families in gaining access to those agencies and allied professionals, and to assist in the development of community programs that are needed but not currently available.

As individuals, we acknowledge our responsibility to provide the best possible programs of care and education for children and to conduct ourselves with honesty and integrity. Because of our specialized expertise in early childhood development and education and because the larger society shares responsibility for the welfare and protection of young children, we acknowledge a collective obligation to advocate for the best interests of children within early childhood programs and in the larger community and to serve as a voice for young children everywhere.

The ideals and principles in this section are presented to distinguish between those that pertain to the work of the individual early childhood educator and those that more typically are engaged in collectively on behalf of the best interests of children—with the understanding that individual early childhood educators have a shared responsibility for addressing the ideals and principles that are identified as "collective."

Ideal (Individual)

I-4.1—To provide the community with high-quality early childhood care and education programs and services.

Ideals (Collective)

I-4.2—To promote cooperation among professionals and agencies and interdisciplinary collaboration among professions concerned with addressing issues in the health, education, and well-being of young children, their families, and their early childhood educators.

I-4.3—To work through education, research, and advocacy toward an environmentally safe world in which all children receive health care, food, and shelter; are nurtured; and live free from violence in their home and their communities.

I-4.4—To work through education, research, and advocacy toward a society in which all young children have access to high-quality early care and education programs.

I-4.5—To work to ensure that appropriate assessment systems, which include multiple sources of information, are used for purposes that benefit children.

I-4.6—To promote knowledge and understanding of young children and their needs. To work toward greater societal acknowledgment of children's rights and greater social acceptance of responsibility for the well-being of all children.

I-4.7—To support policies and laws that promote the well-being of children and families, and to work to change those that impair their well-being. To participate in developing policies and laws that are needed, and to cooperate with families and other individuals and groups in these efforts.

I-4.8—To further the professional development of the field of early childhood care and education and to strengthen its commitment to realizing its core values as reflected in this Code.

Principles (Individual)

P-4.1—We shall communicate openly and truthfully about the nature and extent of services that we provide.

P-4.2—We shall apply for, accept, and work in positions for which we are personally well-suited and professionally qualified. We shall not offer services that we do not have the competence, qualifications, or resources to provide.

P-4.3—We shall carefully check references and shall not hire or recommend for employment any person whose competence, qualifications, or character makes him or her unsuited for the position.

P-4.4—We shall be objective and accurate in reporting the knowledge upon which we base our program practices.

P-4.5—We shall be knowledgeable about the appropriate use of assessment strategies and instruments and interpret results accurately to families.

P-4.6—We shall be familiar with laws and regulations that serve to protect the children in our programs and be vigilant in ensuring that these laws and regulations are followed.

P-4.7—When we become aware of a practice or situation that endangers the health, safety, or well-being of children, we have an ethical responsibility to protect children or inform parents and/or others who can.

P-4.8—We shall not participate in practices that are in violation of laws and regulations that protect the children in our programs.

P-4.9—When we have evidence that an early childhood program is violating laws or regulations protecting children, we shall report the violation to appropriate authorities who can be expected to remedy the situation.

P-4.10—When a program violates or requires its employees to violate this Code, it is permissible, after fair assessment of the evidence, to disclose the identity of that program.

Principles (Collective)

P-4.11—When policies are enacted for purposes that do not benefit children, we have a collective responsibility to work to change these policies.

P-4.12—When we have evidence that an agency that provides services intended to ensure children's wellbeing is failing to meet its obligations, we acknowledge a collective ethical responsibility to report the problem to appropriate authorities or to the public. We shall be vigilant in our follow-up until the situation is resolved.

P-4.13—When a child protection agency fails to provide adequate protection for abused or neglected children, we acknowledge a collective ethical responsibility to work toward the improvement of these services.

Statement of Commitment*

As an individual who works with young children, I commit myself to furthering the values of early childhood education as they are reflected in the ideals and principles of the NAEYC Code of Ethical Conduct. To the best of my ability I will

- Never harm children.
- Ensure that programs for young children are based on current knowledge and research of child development and early childhood education.
- Respect and support families in their task of nurturing children.
- Respect colleagues in early childhood care and education and support them in maintaining the NAEYC Code of Ethical Conduct.

---

*This Statement of Commitment is not part of the Code but is a personal acknowledgment of the individual's willingness to embrace the distinctive values and moral obligations of the field of early childhood care and education. It is recognition of the moral obligations that lead to an individual becoming part of the profession.

- Serve as an advocate for children, their families, and their teachers in community and society.
- Stay informed of and maintain high standards of professional conduct.
- Engage in an ongoing process of self-reflection, realizing that personal characteristics, biases, and beliefs have an impact on children and families.
- Be open to new ideas and be willing to learn from the suggestions of others.

- Continue to learn, grow, and contribute as a professional.
- Honor the ideals and principles of the NAEYC Code of Ethical Conduct.

Reprinted by permission of the National Association for the Education of Young Children. Copyright © 2011 by the National Association for the Education of Young Children.

Glossary

Accommodation. A concept in Piaget's cognitive theory defined as one of two processes people use to learn and incorporate new information; the person adjusts what is already known to "accommodate" new learning. Children usually change their way of thinking into a "schema" once they see that their usual ways do not take new information into account; then they add new thought patterns to handle the new knowledge.

Accommodations. Changes or modifications made in the environment, schedule, or materials to assist children with special needs to have successful educational experiences and meet their individualized education plan.

Accountability. The quality or state of being answerable to someone or of being responsible for explaining exact conditions; schools often must give specific account of their actions to a funding agency to assure the group that the funds and operation of the school are being handled properly.

Accreditation. A system of voluntary evaluation for early childhood centers. The goal is to improve the quality of care and education provided for young children. Accreditation is administered by the National Academy, a branch of the National Association for the Education of Young Children.

Active Listening. A child guidance technique of reflecting back to the speaker what the listener thinks has been said.

Activity Centers. Similar to learning centers and interest areas; areas in a classroom or yard that are designed and arranged for various activities to take place. An early childhood setting offers several centers, or stations, that are based on both children's interests and what the staff hopes for them to learn in class.

Adult-Child Ratio. The proportion of adults for the group of children. Calculated so that children can be educated and cared for appropriately, the ratio changes depending on the age range of the children.

Advocate. One who maintains, defends, or pleads the cause of another; in early childhood terms, an advocate is someone who furthers the principles and issues of the field by speaking to others about such issues.

Aesthetics. Sensitivity to what is beautiful; the study of beauty.

Affective. Of, caused by, or expressing emotion or feeling; emotional.

After-School Care. Programs designed to care for children after the regular academic school day.

Age-Level Characteristics. Those features of children's development and behavior that are most common among a given age group.

Alignment. The act of matching the subject matter of the curriculum with the desired outcomes required by the learning standards.

Anti-bias. A phrase describing the development of curriculum that emphasizes an inclusive look at people and problems, extending the tenets of multicultural education and pluralism.

Antipathy. A strong dislike or ill will, aversion or avoidance.

App. GLDEF abbreviation of "application," a small specialized program downloaded onto mobile devices.

Articulation. The manner in which sounds and words are actually spoken.

Assessment. An evaluation or determination of importance, disposition, or state of something or someone, such as in evaluating a child's skills, a teacher's effectiveness, or a classroom environment.

Assimilation. A concept in Piaget's cognitive theory defined as one of two processes people use to learn and incorporate new information; the person takes new information and puts it together with what is already known to "assimilate" the new information intellectually, such as when a toddler shakes a toy magnet first, as with all other toys, to get to know this new object. Children usually first try to put new experiences into the "schema," or categories, they already know and use.

Atelierista. A person trained in the arts who acts as a resource and teaches techniques and skills to children in the schools of Reggio Emilia, Italy.

Attachment/Attachment Behaviors. The relational bond that connects a child to another important person; feelings and behaviors of devotion or positive connection.

Attention-Deficit/Hyperactivity Disorder (ADHD). A condition affecting children and adults, making them prone to restlessness, anxiety, short attention spans, and impulsiveness.

Attitude Crystallization. To assume a definite, concrete form in one's attitudes; refers to the formation of a firm set of attitudes and behaviors about others' race, ethnicity, gender, and ability that may be prejudicial and difficult to change.

Auditory Learners. Those who prefer to listen to others and discuss what they learn.

Authentic Assessment. The quantitative and qualitative study of a child's work, activity, and interactions that focuses on the whole child within the context of family, school, and community. Such assessment occurs in a child's natural settings in which the child is performing real tasks. Viewed as a process rather than an end, authentic assessment includes collecting and organizing information over time, from multiple sources, and using a variety of methods.

Autism Spectrum Disorder. A broad definition of the neurological condition known as autism where the disabilities have common characteristics related to communication and social skills.

Autonomy. The state of being able to exist and operate independently, of being self-sufficient rather than dependent on others.

Basal Reader. An elementary school textbook that teaches reading by combining stories with practice exercises, such as the Dick & Jane series.

Baseline. A picture of the status of a child, teacher, or environment that serves as the basis for evaluation and later comparison.

Basic Emotions. Those emotions that are present and observable in the newborn or within the first few months of life; they include happiness, interest, surprise, disgust, distress, fear, anger, and sadness.

Basic Needs. Conditions, described by Abraham Maslow and other humanists, that are necessary for growth; these needs, such as physiologic conditions and safety and security, are critical for a person's survival.

Behavior Model. A guidance and behavior technique that uses adults' actions and behavior as examples to follow.

Behaviorist Theory. A psychological theory developed in the United States in the 20th century, which states that all important aspects of behavior and people are learned and can be modified or changed by varying external conditions.

Bias. A tendency that prevents unprejudiced consideration of a question, person, or action; a prejudice or favoritism that can affect one's thinking or behavior.

Bicognitive Development. A set of experiences and environments that promote children's ability to use more than one mode of thinking or linguistic

system. Each of us grows up with a preferred cognitive style, such as global or analytic, field dependent or field independent, seeing the parts versus seeing the whole, as well as a linguistic style. For true cultural democracy to take place, we need to develop a flexibility to switch learning styles or cognitive modes (i.e., develop bicognitive abilities) and have an awareness of and respect for differing cognitive styles.

Bilingualism. The acquisition of two languages during the first years of life; using or being able to use two languages.

Biracial. Having parents of two different races.

Bloom's Taxonomy. A scheme for ordering and classifying learning domains, first developed by Bloom and other colleges in the 1950s as a way to name categories of educational activities (cognitive, affective, and psychomotor).

Brainstorming. The process of thinking that involves bringing up as many ideas as possible about a subject, person, event, and so on.

Building Block Years. The phrase refers to the foundation years of early childhood; namely, the first eight years of life in which the basic skills of life and future learning are set, such as locomotor skills of walking and manipulating; cognitive skills of language/literacy and thinking; and affective skills of social interaction, personal identity, and self-expression.

Charter School. A public school operated independently of the local school board, often with a curriculum and educational philosophy different from the other schools in the system.

Checklist. A modified child study technique that uses a list of items for comparison, such as a "yes/no" checklist for the demonstration of a task.

Child Abuse. Violence in the form of physical maltreatment, abusive language, and sexual harassment or misuse of children.

Child Care Center. A place for care of children for a large portion of their waking day; includes basic caretaking activities of eating, dressing, resting, toileting, as well as playing and learning time.

Child-Centered Approach. The manner of establishing educational

experiences that takes into consideration children's ways of perceiving and learning; manner of organizing a classroom, schedule, and teaching methods with an eye toward the child's viewpoint.

Child Neglect. The act or situation of parents' or other adults' inattention to a child's basic needs of adequate food, clothing, shelter, and health care; child neglect may also include not noticing a child or not paying enough attention in general.

Classical Conditioning. The most common and basic category of learning in behaviorist theory, involving an association between a stimulus and a response so that a reflex response (eye-blinking, salivating, etc.) occurs whenever a neutral and new stimulus is activated (a bell for a light, food, etc.); conditioned-response experiments conforming to the pattern of Pavlov's experiment, sometimes known as "stimulus substitution."

Classification. The ability to group like objects in sets by a specific characteristic.

Classist. A biased or discriminating attitude based on distinctions made between social or economic classes.

Clinical Method. An information-gathering technique, derived from therapy and counseling fields, in which the adult observes and then interacts with the client (in this case, children) by asking questions and posing ideas to the person or group being observed.

Cognition. The act or process of knowing, thinking, and perceiving. Cognition involves perceptual, intellectual, and emotional skills that begin as a child makes connections among objects and people and later extends to formulating mental representations.

Cognitive Theory. The psychological theory developed by Jean Piaget and others; the theory focuses on thought processes and how they change with age and experience; this point of view contrasts with the stimulus-response aspects of behaviorist theory.

Competency-Based Assessment. Evaluation in which a teacher is judged or rated in comparison with a predetermined set of skills, or competencies, related to the job.

Complex Emotions. Those emotions that emerge in the child after infancy;

these include shame, guilt, envy, and pride.

Comprehensive. Inclusive, covering completely, such as a program for children that focuses on the physical, intellectual, social, emotional, creative, and health needs of the children.

Concrete. Concerning the immediate experience of actual things or events; specific and particular rather than general or symbolic.

Connected Knowledge. That kind of knowledge and information that is connected to the child in ways that are real and relevant to that individual; also known as meaningful knowledge in Piagetian terms, it is elaborated by Gilligan (see Chapter 4) and others.

Constructivism. A theory of learning, developed from the principles of children's thinking by Piaget and implemented in programs such as those in Reggio Emilia, Italy, which states that individuals learn through adaptation. The "constructivist" model of learning posits that children are not passive receptacles into which knowledge is poured but rather are active at making meaning, testing out theories, and trying to make sense of the world and themselves. Knowledge is subjective as each person creates personal meaning out of experiences and integrates new ideas into existing knowledge structures.

Context. The framework or circumstances and conditions that affect or influence a person or situation.

Continuing Education. The commitment of teachers to learning new approaches and ideas and to continuing to challenge themselves to higher levels of learning and competence.

Continuum. Something that is continuous; an uninterrupted, ordered sequence.

Convergent Thinking. Thinking that brings together information focused on solving a problem (especially solving problems that have a single correct solution).

Core Values. The basic purposes or issues a professional group acknowledges as common concerns to all its members.

Cortisol. Hormone released when the brain perceives a threat or stress.

Cultural Pluralism. A state or society in which members of diverse ethnic,

racial, or cultural groups maintain participation in and development of their traditional culture within the common society.

Culturally Appropriate Curriculum. Curriculum that helps children understand the way individual histories, families of origins, and ethnic family cultures make us similar to and yet different from others.

Curriculum. A framework in which teachers define the content, the process, and the context for what is being taught and what children learn.

Custodial. Those tasks relating to guardianship of a child's basic needs for food, clothing, and shelter; they include providing for eating, dressing, toileting, resting, and appropriate protection from physical hardships such as weather, danger, and so forth.

Daily Schedule. A plan or procedure that outlines the sequence and time periods for a child's day.

Decoding. Converting from code into ordinary language; in terms of language development, decoding is the process of making sense out of printed letters or words.

Deficiency Needs. see basic needs

Demographics. The statistical graphics of a population, especially showing average age, income, and so on.

Dendrites. Branches of brain cells that reach out to make connections with other cells.

Developmental Domains. The social-emotional, physical, language, and cognitive areas of growth that work together to make up the "whole child."

Developmentally Appropriate Practice (DAP). That which is suitable or fitting to the development of the child; refers to those teaching practices that are based on the observation and responsiveness to children as learners with developing abilities who differ from one another by rate of growth and individual differences, rather than of differing amounts of abilities. It also refers to learning experiences that are relevant to and respectful of the social and cultural aspects of the children and their families.

Dialect. A variation of a language, sufficiently different from the original to become a separate entity but not different enough to be considered as a separate language.

Diary Descriptions. A form of observation technique that involves making a comprehensive narrative record of behavior, in diary form.

Direct Guidance. Actions that involve a child or group of children in a straightforward way, such as setting a limit or giving choices to alter their behavior.

Disability. A measurable impairment or incapacity that may be moderate to severe. The Individuals with Disabilities Act defines 13 categories that identify specific limitations or challenges, such as hearing, speech, visual, or orthopedic impairments. Individuals who are classified with one or more impairments may be eligible for early intervention and special education classes.

Discipline. Ability to follow an example or to follow rules; the development of self-control or control in general, such as by imposing order on a group. In early childhood terms, discipline means everything adults do and say to influence children's behavior.

Discrimination. To make a distinction in or between, such as being able to note or distinguish as different two or more objects, processes, persons, or actions.

Divergent Thinking. The processes of thought and perception that involve taking a line of thought or action different from what is the norm or common; finding ideas that branch out rather than converge and center on one answer.

Documentation. Keeping written records of events, progress, correspondence, and so forth.

Down Syndrome. A genetic abnormality that results in mongolism, one of the most common and easily identified forms of mental retardation.

Dramatic Play. Also known as imaginative play, this is a common form of spontaneous play in which children use their imagination and fantasy as part of the setting and activity.

Dual Language Learners. Young children who are learning a second language while still acquiring their first.

Dynamic. Having energy or effective action; a basic skill is one with consequences that motivates the child, affecting development or stability.

Early Childhood Education. Education in the early years of life; the field of study that deals mainly with the learning and experiences of children from infancy through the primary years (up to approximately 8 years of age).

Early Learning Standards. Statements that describe expectations for the learning and development of young children across the domains of: health and physical well-being; social and emotional well-being; approaches to learning; language development and symbol systems; and general knowledge about the world around them (CCSSO, 2005).

Ebonics. Term used to describe "black English" and the center of a controversy in the late 1990s over whether such language is a dialect of standard English or a separate language.

Eclectic. Choosing what appears to be best in various doctrines, methods, styles; comprising elements drawn from various sources.

Educaring. A concept of teaching as both educating and care giving; coined by Magda Gerber in referring to people working with infants and toddlers.

Egocentric. Self-centered; regarding the self as the center of all things; in Piaget's theory, young children think using themselves as the center of the universe or as the entire universe.

Elaboration. The act of expanding language; developing language by building complex structures from simple ones and adding details.

Emergent Curriculum. A process for curriculum planning that draws on teachers' observations and children's interests. Plans emerge from daily life interests and issues. This approach takes advantage of children's spontaneity and teachers' planning.

Emergent/Early Literacy. The process of building on pre-reading skills in a child-centered fashion, so the ability to read evolves from children's direct experiences.

Emergent Writing. The early skills that help children learn to write, such as scribbling and invented spelling.

Emotional Framework. The basic "feeling" structure of a classroom that determines the tone and underlying sensibilities that affect how people feel and behave while in class.

Emotional Intelligence. An understanding of how to feel, interpret, and express emotions.

Empathy. A deep and positive understanding, affinity or appreciation of another's feelings or problems.

Entry Level. The level of development or behavior that a child shows on beginning a program or group experience; usually an observation-based informal assessment after the first few weeks of school.

Environment. All those conditions that affect children's surroundings and the people in them; the physical, interpersonal, and temporal aspects of an early childhood setting.

Environmental Adaptation. Forces that are not innate or hereditary aspects of development; in early childhood terms, environmental aspects of growth are all those influences of physical conditions, interpersonal relationships, and world experiences that interact with a person to change the way he or she behaves, feels, and lives.

Equilibration. To balance equally; in Piaget's theory, the thinking process by which a person "makes sense" and puts into balance new information with what is already known.

Ethic of Social Reform. The quality of programs and services needed for children younger than 8 years and the education reforms that provide it.

Ethics. A theory or system of stated principles and standards; what is "right and wrong"; one's values; the principles of conduct governing both an individual teacher and the teaching profession.

Ethnocentric. Having one's race as a central interest, or regarding one's race or cultural group as superior to others.

Evaluation. A study to determine or set significance or quality.

Event Sampling. An observation technique that involves defining the event to be observed and coding the event to record what is important to remember about it.

Exceptionalities. The preferred expression for the term *disabilities*, which are measurable impairments or incapacities that may be moderate to severe.

Experimental Procedure. An observation technique that gathers information by establishing a hypothesis, controlling the variables that might influence behavior, and testing the hypothesis.

Expressive. Those aspects of language development and skill that deal with expression: pronunciation, vocabulary, and grammar, as well as speaking and articulation.

Extended Discourse. Denoting written or spoken communication that goes on for longer than most; in the case of language development, this is meant to be a conversation between child and adult that serves to extend the child's expressive language skills.

Extrinsic. Originating from or on the outside; external, not derived from one's essential nature.

Family-Centered Approach. An attitude that supports parent involvement in their child's learning, parent education, and parent support to ensure a healthy beginning in school. Families and teachers work in partnership to collaborate on what is best for the child.

Family Child Care. Care for children in a small, homelike setting; usually six or less children in a family residence.

Feedback Loop. In terms of evaluation, feedback loop is used to describe the process whereby an evaluator gives information to a teacher, who in turn uses this information to improve teaching skills.

Fine Motor. Having to do with the smaller muscles of the body and the extremities, such as those in the fingers, toes, and face.

Flexibility. Capable of modification or change; willing or easily moved from one idea to another.

Fluency. The ability to produce many ideas; an easy and ready flow of ideas.

Formal Assessments. Evaluation instruments that are administered in a conventional, "test-like" atmosphere that have standardized measures and have statistics that are compared to data on other children and are usually described as standards or percentiles. They may or may not be developed commercially.

Four "I"s. The four components (I, Initiative, Independence, and Interaction) of early childhood curriculum for building self-esteem.

Full Inclusion. Providing the "least restrictive environment" for children with physical limitations.

Gender Differences. A distinction of characteristics, behaviors, or attitudes typically associated as being either male or female such that the differences are attributed to the sex that a person identifies with.

Gender Identity. The characteristics determining who or what a person is; in this case, those social and cultural differences defined as being male and female.

Gender Role. The function or part played by a person according to the social and cultural expectations of being male and female.

Genes. The biological elements that transmit hereditary characteristics.

Gifted and Talented Children. Children who have unusually high intelligence, as characterized by: learning to read spontaneously; being able to solve problems and communicate at a level far advanced from their chronological age; excellent memory; extensive vocabulary; and unusual approaches to ideas, tasks, people.

Gross Motor. Having to do with the entire body or the large muscles of the body, such as the legs, arms, and trunk.

Group Size. The number of children in a group care program. Optimal sizes change depending on the age range of the children, and the number of knowledgeable adults on the floor with the group.

Group Times. Those parts of the program in which the whole class or group is together during one activity, such as music, movement, finger plays, or stories.

Growth Needs. Conditions, as described by Abraham Maslow and other humanists, that are important to a person's well-being; these needs, such as love and belonging, self-esteem and respect for others, playfulness, truth, beauty, and so on, while not critical to a person's survival, are necessary for growth.

Guidance. The ongoing system by which adults help children learn to express and manage their feelings, solve their problems, and learn the difference between acceptable and unacceptable behavior.

Holistic. A viewpoint that takes into account several conceptions of a child or situation to form a wider, more rounded description; in early childhood terms, this view includes a child's history, present status, relationships with others, and the interrelationships of development to arrive at a picture of the child; in medicine, this view includes dealing with a person's mental and emotional state,

relationships, and so forth, as well as physical symptoms.

Humanist Theory. The psychological theory of Abraham Maslow and others; it involves principles of motivation and wellness, centering on people's needs, goals, and successes.

Hypothesis. A tentative theory or assumption made to draw inferences or test conclusions; an interpretation of a practical situation that is then taken as the ground for action.

Identity Crisis. A period of uncertainty or confusion in which a person's sense of self becomes insecure.

Imaginary Companions. Also known as imaginary friends, these are pretend characters often created by children.

Importance of Childhood. Children's health and welfare and the changes in family life.

Inclusion. When a child with a disability is a full-time member of a regular classroom with children who are developing normally.

Inclusive Curriculum. Those aspects of a program that reflect awareness of and sensitivity to a person's culture, home language, religion, gender, and abilities.

Indirect Guidance. Actions that do not involve children that a teacher uses to set up the environment and daily schedule so that they have a positive influence on children's behavior.

Individualized Curriculum. A course of study developed and tailored to meet the needs and interests of an individual, rather than those of a group.

Individualized Education Program (IEP). A federally mandated annual plan for children from ages 3 to 21 who have a disability and receive early intervention services. A team of specialists and teachers create long- and short-term goals that are approved by the child's parents.

Individualized Family Service Plan (IFSP). A federally mandated annual plan for children from birth to 3 years of age that describes early intervention services for both the child and the family.

Inductive Guidance. A guidance process in which children are held accountable for their actions and are called on to think about the impact of their behavior on others. Reasoning and problem-solving skills are stressed.

Inference. A conclusion reached by reasoning from evidence or after gathering information, whether direct or indirect.

Informal assessments. Observations and evaluations that are done in a simple, everyday, and sometimes spontaneous manner.

Inquiry. A process that uses questions to seek or request information, knowledge, or truth.

Integrated Curriculum. A set of courses designed to form a whole; coordination of the various areas of study, making for continuous and harmonious learning.

Integrated Day. A school schedule with no prescribed time periods for subject matter, but rather an environment organized around various interest centers among which children choose in organizing their learning experiences.

Intentional Teaching. Being clear about what is being taught, knowing its purpose, and articulating decisions to help children achieve certain goals.

Intelligence. The cluster of capabilities that involves thinking (see Chapter 12 for details).

Interactive Media. Digital and analog materials, including software programs, applications (apps), broadcast and streaming media, children's television programming (some), e-books, the Internet, and other forms of content designed to facilitate use by children's and social engagement.

Interdependence. Dependence on one another, as in the relationship between teachers' experience in the areas of discipline and their competence at knowing and using appropriate language for discipline.

Interest Areas. Similar to learning centers and activity areas; one way to design physical space in a classroom or yard, dividing the space into separate centers among which children move about, rather than assigning them desks.

Interpersonal. Relating to, or involving relationships with, other people; those parts of the environment in a school setting that have to do with the people.

Interracial. Relating to, involving, or representing different races.

Intervention. An action taken to change a child's behavior or group pattern; may be environmental, temporal, or interpersonal in nature, such as if teachers enter into children's interactions when behavior calls for some action on the part of an adult; may include families, community resources, or others that might affect a child's development or well-being.

Intrinsic. Belonging to the essential nature of or originating from within a person or body, such as intrinsic motivation, whereby one needs no external reward to do something.

Invented Spelling. Children's first attempts at spelling words the way they sound to them, based on their current knowledge of letters and sounds. Far from "correct" ("scnd" for second, "grrn" for green, or "relly" for really), invented spelling becomes more conventional over time.

Kindergarten (Children's Garden). A school or class for children 4 to 6 years old; in the United States, kindergarten is either the first year of formal, public school or the year of schooling before first grade.

Kindergarteners. 1) A modern term to describe the children who are attending kindergarten programs; 2) a term used in 19th-century America to describe early childhood practitioners who worked in kindergartens patterned after Froebelian models.

Learning Centers. Similar to interest areas and activity areas; hubs or areas in a classroom designed to promote learning; the classroom is arranged in discrete areas for activity, and children move from one area to another rather than stay at an assigned desk or seat.

Learning Styles. A child's preferred method of integrating knowledge and experiences.

Least Restrictive Environment (LRE). Under the Individuals with Disabilities Education Act (IDEA), a child with identified special needs is entitled to a placement into an environment that is most like that of other children in which the child can succeed; this refers to the physical location of the child's learning and how the child is taught, so the preference is that the child is included in regular education activities as much as possible.

Licensing. The process of fulfilling legal requirements, standards, and regulations for operating child care facilities.

Limits. The boundaries of acceptable behavior beyond which actions are considered misbehavior and unacceptable conduct; the absolute controls an adult puts on children's behavior.

Linchpin. Something that serves to hold together the elements of a situation.

Log/Journal. A form of observation technique that involves making a page of notes about children's behavior in a cumulative journal.

Logical Mathematical Knowledge. One of three types of knowledge in Piagetian theory; the component of intelligence that uses thinking derived from logic.

Looping. The practice of keeping a teacher and a group of children in a class together for two or more years.

Magnet Schools. A public school offering a specialized curriculum, often with high academic standards, to a student body representing a cross-section of the community.

Mainstreaming. The process of integrating handicapped children into classrooms with the nonhandicapped.

Maturation. The process of growth whereby a body matures regardless of, and relatively independent of, intervention such as exercise, experience, or environment.

Maturation Theory. A set of ideas based on the notion that the sequence of behavior and the emergence of personal characteristics develop more through predetermined growth processes than through learning and interaction with the environment; the theory of growth and development proposed and supported by Dr. Arnold Gesell and associates.

Meaningful Knowledge. The form of knowing that is learned within the context of what is already known; that knowledge that has meaning because it has particular significance or value to an individual.

Methode Clinique. A kind of information-gathering technique, first used extensively by Jean Piaget, that involves observing children and asking questions as the situation unfolds. The purpose of this technique is to elicit information about how children are thinking as they behave naturally.

Misbehavior. Improper behavior or conduct.

Mixed-Age Grouping. The practice of placing children of several levels, generally one year apart, into the same classroom. Also referred to as family grouping, heterogeneous grouping, multiage grouping, vertical grouping, and ungraded classes.

Modeling. A part of behavior theory, modeling is a way of learning social behavior that involves observing a model (either real, filmed, or animated) and mimicking its behavior, thus acquiring new behavior.

Multiple Intelligences (See also Frames of Mind). A theory of intelligence, proposed by Howard Gardner, that outlines several different kinds of intelligence, rather than the notion of intelligence as measured by standardized testing, such as the IQ.

Myelination. The forming of the myelin sheath, the material in the membrane of certain cells in the brain; the development of the myelination of the brain seems to parallel Piagetian stages of cognitive development.

Narratives. A major observation technique that involves attempting to record nearly everything that happens, in as much detail as possible, as it happens. Narratives include several subtypes such as baby biographies, specimen descriptions, diary descriptions, and logs or journals.

Naturalistic Assessments. Methods of appraisal or child evaluations done in the usual, natural surroundings.

Nature/Nurture Controversy. The argument regarding human development that centers around two opposing viewpoints; nature refers to the belief that it is a person's genetic, inherent character that determines development; nurture applies to the notion that it is the sum total of experiences and the environment that determine development.

Negative Reinforcement. Response to a behavior that decreases the likelihood that the behavior recurs; for instance, a teacher's glare might stop a child from whispering at group time, and from then on, the anticipation of such an angry look reinforces not whispering in the future.

Non-interactive Media. Includes certain television programs, DVD's, and streaming that are not included in the definition and description of effective and appropriate use and that lead to passive viewing and overexposure to screen time for young children.

Norm. An average or general standard of development or achievement, usually derived from the average or median of a large group; a pattern or trait taken to be typical of the behavior, skills, or interests of a group.

Norm-Referenced Tests. Standardized tests that compare the child's performance to a large sample of similar children (the norm sample) that represents the general population. There are strict procedures to be followed when administering the test.

Objectivity. The quality or state of being able to see what is real and realistic, as distinguished from subjective and personal opinion or bias.

Observational Learning. Any acquired skills or knowledge having to do with interacting with others; in Bandura's social learning theory, observational learning occurs when children watch other people directly or in film, and imitate what they have seen in the model.

Open-ended. Activities or statements that allow a variety of responses, as opposed to those that allow only one response; anything organized to allow for variation.

Open School. A style of education, developed in progressive American schools and in the British infant schools, that is organized to encourage freedom of choice and that does not use predetermined roles and structure as the basis of education; an educational setting whose ultimate goal and basis for curriculum is the development of the individual child, rather than of programmed academic experiences.

Operant Conditioning. A category of learning in behavior theory that involves a relation between a stimulus and a response. The response is learned, rather than reflexive, and is gradually and carefully developed through reinforcement of the desired behavior as it occurs in response to the stimulus; behavior leading to a reward.

Organic Reading. A system of learning to read, popularized by Sylvia Ashton-Warner, that lets children build their vocabulary with the words they choose.

Parent Cooperative Schools. An educational setting organized by parents for their young children, often with parental control and/or support in the operation of the program itself.

Pedagogista. A person trained in early childhood education who meets weekly with the teachers in the schools of Reggio Emilia, Italy.

Peer Interactions. Associations with people of the same age group or with those one considers equals.

Perceptual-Motor Development. The growth of a person's ability to move (motor) and perceive (perceptual) together; perceptual-motor activity involves the body and the mind working together to coordinate movement.

Phobia. A strong, exaggerated, and illogical fear of an object or class of things, people, and so forth; one of several reactions children often have to divorce.

Phonemes. Language sounds; the smallest units of meaningful speech; two examples of phonemes are /a/ (as in hat) and /p/ (as in sip).

Phonemic Awareness. Having knowledge or perception of the distinct units of sounds that distinguish one word from another; in English this includes buh [b], puh [p], and sss [s].

Physical Environment. Having to do with equipment and material, room arrangement, the outdoor space, and facilities available.

Physical Knowledge. One of three types of knowledge in Piagetian theory; physical knowledge is learned through external, sensory experiences.

Portfolio. An intentional compilation of materials and resources, collected over a period of time that provides evidence for others to review; for instance, a child portfolio will include observations, evaluations, work samples, and photos/sketches.

Positive Reinforcement. A response to a behavior that increases the likelihood that the behavior is repeated or increased; for instance, if a child gets attention and praise for crawling, it is likely that the crawling increases—thus, the attention and praise were positive reinforcement for crawling.

Positive Stress. Refers to an amount of strain or tension that encourages a person to be active and challenged rather than overwhelmed or discouraged.

Precedent. Something done or said that serves as an example or rule to authorize or justify other acts of the same or similar kind; an earlier occurrence of something similar.

Precursor. What precedes and indicates the approach of another; predecessor or forerunner.

Prejudices. Ideas and attitudes that are already formed about other people, situations, and ideas, before hearing or experiencing full or sufficient information; in teaching terms, those attitudes or biases that may be based less on mature thought and reasoning than on incomplete or nonexistent personal experiences.

Prepared Environment. The physical and interpersonal surroundings of an educational setting that are planned and arranged in advance with the group of children in mind.

Prerequisite. Something necessary or essential to carrying out an objective or performing an activity; when early childhood teachers determine what skills children need to successfully engage in an activity, they are clarifying the prerequisites for that activity.

Private (Inner) Speech. The language children use for self-guidance and self-direction, as well as for helping them think about their behavior and plan for action; once known as "egocentric speech," it is used for self-regulation.

Professional. One engaged and participating in a profession and accepting the technical and ethical standards of that profession; in early childhood terms, one who has accumulated methods, course work, and teaching experience with young children along with attitudes of competency, flexibility, and continual learning.

Professional Confidentiality. Spoken, written, or acted on in strict privacy, such as keeping the names of children or schools in confidence when discussing observations.

Professional Organizations. Those associations developed for the purpose of extending knowledge and teaching/learning opportunities in the field of education.

Professional Standards. The level of requirement, excellence, or attainment mandated by a professional group, organization, or association for its membership.

Professionalism. The competence or skill expected of a professional; in early childhood education, this includes a sense of identity, purpose to engage in developmentally appropriate practices, a commitment to ethical teaching and to child advocacy, and participation in the work as a legitimate livelihood.

Project Approach. An in-depth study of a particular subject or theme by one or more children. Exploration of themes and topics over a period of days or weeks. Working in small groups, children are able to accommodate various levels of complexity and understanding to meet the needs of all the children working on the project.

Prosocial. Behaviors that are considered positive and social in nature, such as sharing, inviting, including, and offering help or friendship.

Psychodynamic Theory. The psychological theory of Dr. Sigmund Freud and others; it asserts that the individual develops a basic personality core in childhood and that responses stem from personality organization and emotional problems as a result of environmental experiences.

Psychosocial. Those psychological issues that deal with how people relate to others and the problems that arise on a social level; a modification by Erikson of the psychodynamic theories of Freud with attention to social and environmental problems of life.

Psychosocial Domain. The area of development that includes the development of emotions, temperament, social skills, creativity, and spiritual development.

Public Law 94-142. The Education for All Handicapped Children Act. This so-called Bill of Rights for the Handicapped guarantees free public education to disabled persons from three to 21 years of age "in the least restrictive" environment. In 1990 Congress reauthorized PL 94-142 and renamed it the Individuals with Disabilities Education Act (IDEA). Two new categories, autism and traumatic brain injury, were included, and children from birth to age five years were now eligible to receive services.

Public Law 99-457. The Education of the Handicapped Amendments Act of 1986. Sections of this law provide funding for children who were not included in the previous law: infants, toddlers, and three-to-five year olds. This law also allows for the inclusion of "developmentally delayed" youngsters and

leaves local agencies the opportunity to include the "at-risk" child in that definition.

Punishment. The act of inflicting a penalty for an offense or behavior.

Racist. Attitudes, behavior, or policies that imply either a hatred or intolerance of other race(s) or involving the idea that one's race is superior and has the right to rule or dominate others.

Rating Scale. A modified child study technique similar to a checklist that classifies behavior according to grade or rank, such as using the descriptors "always, sometimes, never" to describe the frequency of a certain behavior.

Readiness. The condition of being ready, such as being in the state or stage of development so that the child has the capacity to understand, be taught, or engage in a particular activity.

Receptive Those aspects of language development and skill that deal with the ability to receive messages: listening, understanding, and responding.

Reciprocal. The stage of children's friendship in which friendship is given or felt by each toward the other; a kind of give-and-take or two-way relationship, this is the stage most often seen in the latter part of the early childhood years.

Reflective Teaching. Taking time to think more deeply about how learning and teaching interact and what this means as a teacher.

Reinforcement. A procedure, such as reward or punishment, that changes a response to a stimulus; the act of encouraging a behavior to increase its frequency.

Reinforcers. Rewards in response to a specific behavior, thus increasing the likelihood that behavior recurs; reinforcers may be either social (praise) or nonsocial (food) in nature and may or may not be deliberately controlled.

Resilience. the characteristic of adaptability to changing circumstances and an adaptability to flex with the demands and vagaries of one's environment.

Rote Knowledge. A form of knowing that is learned by routine or habit and without thought of the meaning.

Roughhousing. Rough and disorderly, but playful, behavior.

Routines. Regular procedures; habitual, repeated or regular parts of the school

day; in early childhood programs, routines are those parts of the program schedule that remain constant, such as indoor time followed by clean up and snack, regardless of what activities are being offered within those time slots.

Rubric. A formula that establishes the specifications or a blueprint to assessment or explanation.

Running Record. The narrative form of recording behavior; this kind of descriptive record of one's observations involves writing down all behavior as it occurs.

Scaffolding. A useful structure to support a child in learning. A child who gets advice or hints to help master an activity is said to have scaffolding learning, a term Vygotsky used.

Schema. A plan, scheme, or framework that helps make an organizational pattern from which to operate; in Piaget's theory, cognitive schemas are used for thinking.

School Readiness. The ability of children to be ready to learn by having appropriate skills and knowledge to participate in a more formal school setting.

Screening. Evaluations to determine a child's readiness for a particular class, grade, or experience.

Screen Time. The total amount of time spent in front of any and all types of screens, including computers, tablets, smartphones, handheld gaming devices, portable video players, digital cameras, video recorders, and televisions.

Self-Actualization. The set of principles set forth by Abraham Maslow for a person's wellness or ability to be the most that a person can be; the state of being that results from having met all the basic and growth needs.

Self-Awareness. An awareness of one's personality or individuality; in teaching terms, an ability to understand one's self and assess personal strengths and weaknesses.

Self-Care (See also Latchkey Children). A current description for latchkey children.

Self-Concept. A person's view and opinion of self; in young children, the concept of self develops as they interact with the environment (objects, people, etc.); self-concept can be inferred in how children carry themselves, approach situations, and use expressive materials such as art.

Self-Correcting. Materials or experiences that are built or arranged so that the person using them can automatically correct errors, without needing another person to check or point out mistakes.

Self-Efficacy. The feelings or thoughts about how competent a person perceives him/herself to be.

Self-Esteem. The value we place on ourselves; how much we like or dislike who we are; self-respect.

Self-Help. The act of helping or providing for oneself without dependence on others; in early childhood terms, activities that a child can do alone, without adult assistance.

Self-Regulation. The term used to describe a child's capacity to plan and guide the self. A disposition or part of the personality (rather than a skill or behavior such as self-control), self-regulation is a way of monitoring one's activity flexibly over changing circumstances.

Sensorimotor. Relating to or functioning in both sensory and motor aspects of body activity.

Sensory. Having to do with the senses or sensation, as in an awareness of the world as it looks, sounds, feels, smells, and tastes.

Separation Process. The act and procedure that occur when parents leave a child at school.

Seriation. The process of sequencing from beginning to end or in a particular series or succession.

Sex Differences. The biological differences between males and females.

Sex-Role Stereotyping. A standardized mental picture or set of attitudes that represents an oversimplified opinion of people's abilities or behavior according to their sex; overgeneralizing a person's skills or behavior on the basis of an inequitable standard of sex differences.

Sexist. Attitudes or behavior based on the traditional stereotype of sexual roles that includes a devaluation or discrimination based on a person's sex.

Shadow Study. A modified child study technique that profiles an individual at a given moment in time; similar to diary description, the shadow study is a narrative recorded as the behavior happens.

Simultaneous Acquisition. One of the major ways a child acquires fluency in a second language, occurring if a child is exposed to two languages from birth.

Social Action. Individual or group behavior that involves interaction with other individuals or groups, especially organized action toward social reform.

Social Cognition. The application of thinking to personal and social behavior; giving meaning to social experience.

Social Competence. The ability to successfully deal with social interactions and problems; the skills and personal knowledge to deal with others.

Social Knowledge. One of three types of knowledge in Piagetian theory; knowledge that is learned about and from people, such as family and ethnic culture, group behavior, and social mores.

Social Learning Theory. A psychological theory developed in the 20th century by Albert Bandura of Stanford University, which states that learning often takes place by observing and modeling others.

Social Referencing. The process used to gauge one's response to a situation by relying on another person's emotional reaction, such as a child who looks to a teacher after falling down before crying or getting up.

Social Reform. The ethic of social reform is a major theme in early childhood education and history, and it refers to the idea that schooling for young children leads to social change and improvement.

Social Skills. Strategies children learn to enable them to respond appropriately in many environments.

Socialization. The process of learning the skills, appropriate behaviors, and expectations of being part of a group, particularly society at large.

Sociocentric. Oriented toward or focused on one's social group rather than on oneself.

Sociocultural. Aspects of theory or development that refer to the social and cultural issues; key descriptor of Vygotsky's theory of development.

Sociodramatic Play. At least two children participating in dramatic play or play that involves two basic elements: imitation and make-believe.

Software. The programs used to direct the operation of a computer, as opposed to the physical device on which they are run (known as "hardware").

Spatial. Having to do with the nature of space, as in the awareness of the space around a person's body.

Special-Needs Children. Children whose development and/or behavior require help or intervention beyond the scope of the ordinary classroom or adult interactions.

Specimen Description. A form of narrative observations technique that involves taking on-the-spot notes about a child (the "specimen") to describe behavior.

Spontaneous Play. The unplanned, self-selected activity in which a child freely participates.

Standardized Testing. Formal assessment techniques whose results have been tabulated for many children and thus have predetermined standards, or norms, for evaluating the child being tested.

Standards. The degree or level of requirement, excellence, or attainment that is mandated by local or national government agencies that describe the learning outcomes for various age groups.

Stimulus–Response. The kind of psychological learning, first characterized in behavior theory, that makes a connection between a response and a stimulus; that is, the kind of learning that takes place when pairing something that rouses or incites an activity with the activity itself in such a way that the stimulus (such as a bell) triggers a response (such as salivating).

Stress. The physical and emotional reactions and behaviors that come from having to cope with difficult situations beyond one's capabilities.

Successive Acquisition. One of the two major ways second-language learning occurs, as a child with a single home language begins to learn another language with exposure from school or other experiences.

Superhero. Those characters who embody a higher nature and powers beyond ordinary human abilities, such as Superman, Wonder Woman, and so on.

Support System. A network of people who support each other in their work and advancement.

Synapses. The junction area in the brain that transmit information between neurons.

Tabula Rasa. A mind not affected yet by experiences, sensations, and the like. In John Locke's theory, a child was born with this "clean slate" upon which all experiences were written.

Tactile. Perceptible or able to be learned through the sense of touch.

Tactile Learners. Those who are full, active-body learners and learn by hands-on activities.

Team Teaching. Group-based manner of teaching, where a group composed of people with varying skills, experience, and training teach jointly.

Temporal. Having to do with time and time sequence; in the early childhood setting, refers to scheduling and how time is sequenced and spent, both at home and in school.

Theory. A group of general principles, ideas, or proposed explanations for explaining some kind of phenomenon; in this case, child development.

Time Sampling. A form of observational technique that involves observing certain behavior and settings within a prescribed time frame.

Traditional Nursery School. The core of early childhood educational theory and practice; program designed for children aged 2½ to 5 years of age, which may be a part- or an all-day program.

Transactional Model. A model of education that describes the interaction of an individual with one or more persons, especially as influenced by their assumed roles. This model implies that the role of parent, child, or teacher has an effect on what and how information is taught and learned.

Transcurricular. Able to be used or applied in a variety of situations or activities.

Transformative Curriculum. The process of viewing events and situations from diverse perspectives to gain new insights and ways of thinking in order to create more culturally appropriate curriculum.

Transitions. Changes from one state or activity to another; in early childhood terms, transitions are those times of change in the daily schedule (whether planned or not), such as from being with a parent to being alone in school, from playing with one toy to choosing another, from being outside to being inside, and so on.

Transmission Model. A model of education describing the transference of information directly from one person to another, such as in the sense of passing on knowledge directly from teacher to child.

Transmitting Values. A major theme in early childhood education and history, helping children learn and accept basic values of the family and community has been one of the reasons for education for centuries.

Trauma. A deeply distressing or disturbing experience.

Unconscious. Not conscious, without awareness, occurring below the level of conscious thought.

Undifferentiated. The stage of children's friendships in which children do not distinguish between "friend" and "person I'm playing with," considered the first stage, usually from infancy into the preschool years.

Unilateral. The stage of children's friendships in which children think of friendship as involving one side only; that is, a one-way situation in that a "friend" is "someone who does what I want him to do," usually spanning the preschool years and into early primary.

Universal Infection Control Precautions. These are procedures to be followed by all teaching staff who are caring for an injured or ill child who might be harboring a highly contagious, dangerous pathogen that is transmitted in blood, blood products, and other body fluids. Universal precautions were described in directives and guidelines issued by the Centers for Disease Control and Prevention in the late 1980s.

Universal Preschool. An international movement to make preschool education available for all families. It is sometimes called "preschool for all."

Vertical Groupings. See Mixed-Age Grouping.

Visual Learners. Those who prefer to learn through pictures, photos, charts, and graphs and represent their learning through reading, writing, and drawing.

Webbing. A process through which teachers create a diagram based on a topic or theme. It is a planning tool for curriculum and includes as many resources as teachers can name.

Whole Language. The area of graphic language development that refers to a particular way in which language, particularly reading and writing, is learned; whole language refers to that movement within primary education that emphasizes an integrated and literary-based approach rather than a phonics, decoding-skills approach.

Word Pictures. Descriptions of children that depict norms of development in words; in this text, these are age-level charts that describe common behaviors and characteristics, particularly those that have implications for teaching children (in groups, for curriculum planning, with discipline and guidance).

Working Portfolio. A type of child portfolio that is used and added onto regularly, that documents a child's skills and behavior over time. Rather than one that collects only a child's exemplary work or everything a child has done, this type of portfolio attempts to capture key documentation to demonstrate a child's growth.

Zone of Proximal Development. The term in Vygotsky's sociocultural theory that defines what children can learn. Interpersonal and dynamic, the zone refers to the area a child can master (skill, information, etc.) with the assistance of another skilled person; below that, children can learn on their own; above the limit are areas beyond the child's capacity to learn, even with help.

Subject Index

Name Index